RULE OF LAW IN THE EU

This book looks into the evolution and current state of the rule of law in the European Union (EU). The thirtieth anniversary of the fall of the Berlin Wall is chosen as a natural moment of stocktaking; assessing the progress made since the beginning of the democratic reforms in Central and Eastern Europe (CEE), but also critically analysing recent tendencies of rule of law backsliding and open revolt against liberal-democratic values in individual EU Member States. The volume is partly retrospective in that it reflects on the challenges of the post-communist transition and the process of Eastward Enlargement of the Union. Yet it is also prospective, in so far as it reviews the variety of novel mechanisms for strengthening rule of law enforcement in the EU and gauges their potential for bringing sustainable, positive change in this regard. All chapters are written by experienced scholars and practitioners in the field of EU law and policy.

Rule of Law in the EU

30 Years After the Fall of the Berlin Wall

Swedish Studies in European Law
Volume 15

Edited by
Antonina Bakardjieva Engelbrekt
Andreas Moberg
and
Joakim Nergelius

•HART•
OXFORD • LONDON • NEW YORK • NEW DELHI • SYDNEY

HART PUBLISHING

Bloomsbury Publishing Plc

Kemp House, Chawley Park, Cumnor Hill, Oxford, OX2 9PH, UK

1385 Broadway, New York, NY 10018, USA

29 Earlsfort Terrace, Dublin 2, Ireland

HART PUBLISHING, the Hart/Stag logo, BLOOMSBURY and the Diana logo are trademarks of Bloomsbury Publishing Plc

First published in Great Britain 2021

A catalogue record for this book is available from the British Library.

Library of Congress Cataloging-in-Publication data

Names: Bakardjieva Engelbrekt, Antonina, 1963- editor. | Moberg, Andreas, editor. | Nergelius, Joakim, editor.

Title: Rule of law in the EU : 30 years after the fall of the Berlin Wall / edited by Antonina Bakardjieva Engelbrekt, Andreas Moberg, and Joakim Nergelius.

Description: Oxford , UK ; New York, NY : Hart Publishing, an imprint of Bloomsbury Publishing, 2021. | Includes bibliographical references and index.

Identifiers: LCCN 2021041873 (print) | LCCN 2021041874 (ebook) | ISBN 9781509941599 (hardback) | ISBN 9781509954650 (paperback) | ISBN 9781509941612 (pdf) | ISBN 9781509941605 (Epub)

Subjects: LCSH: Rule of law—European Union countries. | Berlin Wall, Berlin, Germany, 1961–1989.

Classification: LCC KJE5037 .R85 2021 (print) | LCC KJE5037 (ebook) | DDC 341.242/2011—dc23

LC record available at https://lccn.loc.gov/2021041873

LC ebook record available at https://lccn.loc.gov/2021041874

ISBN: HB: 978-1-50994-159-9
ePDF: 978-1-50994-161-2
ePub: 978-1-50994-160-5

Typeset by Compuscript Ltd, Shannon

Preface

THIS BOOK HAS its beginnings in a conference held in Stockholm on 14–15 November 2019, almost exactly thirty years after the fall of the Berlin Wall and the seminal events of 1989 that gradually led to the transformation of the European continent. The conference was conceived and organised within the auspices of the Swedish Network for European Legal Studies. Like the present book, the conference focused on the state of the rule of law in the European Union. This focus was, of course, not accidental. While the demise of the Berlin Wall is celebrated as the symbolic moment in history when democracy, rule of law and respect for human rights were recognized as fundamental values in the countries of Central and Eastern Europe (CEE), the 2010s and the beginning of the 2020s witnessed, at least in some of the CEE countries, a powerful reverse movement causing the rule of law to backslide, accompanied by frequent attacks on judicial independence and media freedom, and the calling into question of liberal democracy. Although it is generally acknowledged that building sustainable institutions that uphold the rule of law is a slow and difficult process, the overt rejection of the rule of law as a constitutional value and policy goal, especially in countries that were at the forefront of the post-communist democratic transformation, is a recent and disturbing development. The conference therefore sought to link the past to the present and to critically examine the state of the rule of law in the European Union thirty years after the beginning of democratic reforms in CEE.

The 2019 conference brought together distinguished scholars and practitioners – both lawyers and political scientists – working on problems of European integration, the rule of law and Central and Eastern Europe. We are happy that many of the speakers are also contributors to the present book. At the same time, we would like to thank also those conference speakers who could not be part of this book project, but helped make the conference a memorable event, namely professors Anneli Albi, Antoaneta Dimitrova, Jan Komárek, Ulrich Sedelmeier and Laurent Pech. Special thanks go to the Swedish Minister of European Affairs Hans Dahlgren for his inspiring opening address. These thought-provoking interventions added new perspectives and nuances to the debate that are reflected in several chapters of the book.

Only months after the conference took place in Stockholm, the world was hit by a global pandemic interrupting with force the normal course of life and causing much human suffering. This inevitably slowed down the publication process. Still, the topic of the book did not lose relevance and importance. Regrettably, the illiberal turn in countries such as Hungary and Poland, which partly prompted the concern for the state of the rule of law in the Union, was not reversed. Quite to the contrary, the ruptures between authoritarian-leaning governments in these countries and EU institutions have only deepened and become more disquieting. A particularly prominent example of this development is the decision of the Polish Constitutional Court of 14 July 2021, effectively questioning the primacy of EU law in Poland and setting the country on a path toward open confrontation with the EU Court of Justice and other EU institutions. Furthermore, the covid-19 pandemic placed the problems of the rule of law into sharp relief. In the face of the pandemic and the global health crisis, the authoritarian instinct of illiberal governments prompted them to suppress civil liberties, reduce transparency and accountability of public institutions and decision-making and further curtail media freedom.

The two years between the conference and the publication of the book, have also seen an unprecedented activism in the area of rule of law on the part of EU institutions. The European Commission, the European Parliament and the Court of Justice of the European Union have, each within the sphere of its competence, engaged with the questions of the rule of law and judicial independence in the EU and its Member States. The list of normative acts, soft law instruments and judicial decisions has grown exponentially. While it has been our ambition that the book captures this dynamic development, it has not been possible to fully include the events of the spring and summer of 2021. Unless something else is explicitly indicated in individual chapters, the book reflects the state of law as of April 2021.

As members of the steering group of the Swedish Network for European Legal Studies (SNELS), we would like to acknowledge the role of SNELS as a platform for spurring initiated debate on fundamental issues of European law and European integration inside Sweden and beyond. Without the support of SNELS this book would not have been possible. We are also grateful to the publishing team at Bloomsbury Professional/Hart Publishing, Sinead Moloney, Sasha Jawed and Tom Adams for efficient and professional steering of the book project.

Finally, we would like to thank Marie Kagrell, PhD Candidate at Stockholm University, and Helena Eriksson, who have both worked at different times as SNELS coordinators; Marie Kagrell for her excellent support during the conference and Helena Eriksson for her help preparing the manuscript for publication. Dino Amorelli Federico has also provided valuable technical assistance.

Antonina Bakardjieva Engelbrekt
Stockholm

Andreas Moberg
Gothenburg

Joakim Nergelius
Örebro

Contents

List of Contributors

Antonina Bakardjieva Engelbrekt is Professor of European Law at the Faculty of Law of Stockholm University and Chair of the Swedish Network for European Legal Studies.

Leonard F.M. Besselink is Professor of Constitutional Law at the University of Amsterdam and also teaches at the School of Law and the School of Government of LUISS, Rome.

Graham Butler is Associate Professor of Law, Aarhus University, Denmark.

Iain Cameron is Professor in Public International Law at Uppsala University. His research interests lie in human rights/ civil liberties, international criminal law and police/security issues. Since 2005, he has been one of the two Swedish members of the Commission on Democracy through Law (Venice Commission).

Valentina Colcelli (PhD) is Researcher at the National Research Council (Italy), Co-chair of the Working Group on Regulatory, Ethics & GDPR, in European, Middle Eastern & African Society for Bio-preservation and Biobanking (ESBB) and External professor at the University of Perugia, Department of Medicine.

Xavier Groussot is Professor of European Law at the Faculty of Law, Lund University.

Gábor Halmai is Professor and Chair of Comparative Constitutional Law at the Law Department of the European University Institute, Florence. His primary research interests are comparative and European constitutional law.

Katalin (Capannini-)Kelemen is Associate Professor in Law at Örebro University in Sweden, where she teaches comparative law, comparative constitutional law and EU constitutional law. She graduated in law from Eötvös Loránd University in Budapest, Hungary, and obtaind her PhD in Comparative Law from Università degli Studi di Firenze in Italy.

Zdeněk Kühn is Professor of Jurisprudence at Charles University Law School and Judge at the Supreme Administrative Court of the Czech Republic.

María José Martínez Iglesias is Director-General for Security and Safety in the European Parliament, formerly Director for Legislative Affairs in the Legal Service of the European Parliament (2014–2020).

Andreas Moberg is Associate Professor of International Law, University of Gothenburg, Sweden.

Joakim Nergelius is Professor of Constitutional Law at the University of Örebro and Associate Professor of European and Comparative Law at Turku Academy since 2003. He has previously worked as EU Civil Servant at the Court of Justice and Committee of Regions.

Anna Perego has worked for 5 years in the Rule of Law Unit of the European Commission (DG Justice) and has since May 2021 moved to the EU Delegation to Bangladesh working on rule of law in the framework of the EU development policy. She has previously worked as Academic Assistant in the Law Department of the College of Europe, as well as in the Fundamental Rights Unit of the European Commission (DG Justice).

Linda Stefani is Member of the Legal Service of the European Parliament.

Daniel Tarschys is Professor Emeritus in political science at Stockholm University and a senior advisor at the Swedish Institute for European Policy Studies (SIEPS). He was Secretary General of the Council of Europe in 1994–1999.

Anna Zemskova is a PhD Candidate at the Faculty of Law, Lund University.

Introduction

1

Rule of Law in the EU 30 Years After the Fall of the Berlin Wall: Taking Stock and Looking Ahead

ANTONINA BAKARDJIEVA ENGELBREKT,
ANDREAS MOBERG AND JOAKIM NERGELIUS

I. INTRODUCTION

THE DEMISE OF the Berlin Wall in the Fall of 1989, amidst a series of breath-taking revolutions in Central and Eastern Europe (CEE),[1] was by many seen as the ultimate triumph of Western liberal values; of democracy, the rule of law and free markets. Commentators were quick to proclaim the end of ideological confrontation and even, famously, the of history.[2]

This perception was further strengthened by the firmly declared political will of the countries from CEE to join the European Union (EU). The subsequent process of preparing the candidate states for EU membership constituted probably the most ambitious operation of political and legal transformation in modern history. Despite its many challenges, the process resulted in 11 CEE countries joining the Union in the period between 2004 and 2013, and it was largely celebrated as a success.[3] At the end of this process, after the accession of Croatia in 2013, the Union could boast being the world's largest economic and political bloc; a zone of freedom, security and justice, encompassing 28 countries with a territory of approximately 4.5 million km^2 and a population of approximately 507 million people.[4]

[1] The abbreviation CEE is used in the following as a substantive to signify Central and Eastern Europe as a region, or alternatively as an adjective, eg Central and East European countries.

[2] F Fukuyama, 'The End of History?' (1989) 16 *The National Interest* 3; F Fukuyama, *The End of History and the Last Man* (New York, Free Press, 1992).

[3] These are the Czech Republic, Estonia, Hungary, Latvia, Lithuania, Poland, Slovakia and Slovenia (2005); Bulgaria and Romania (2007); and Croatia (2013).

[4] After the accession of Croatia in 2013 the Union was estimated to include more exactly a territory of 4,510,831 sq km and a population of 506,777,111 people. The numbers are obviously before the United Kingdom's withdrawal from the EU on 31 January 2020.

The Eastward Enlargement of the Union was obviously expected to bring considerable benefits for the accession countries in terms of economic prosperity and political prestige, and importantly in raising the standards of democracy, the rule of law and protection of fundamental rights. It was expected to help embed the still novel and fragile democratic institutions in the CEE countries and even contribute to making democratisation there irreversible.[5]

But Enlargement was seen by many as also bringing democracy and rule of law dividends for the Union itself. The prospect of Enlargement prompted a serious reflection on the fundamental values and institutional principles underpinning the European project, and led to a much-needed – and widely acclaimed – restatement of these values and principles in the Union Treaties and in the EU Charter of Fundamental Rights, solemnly proclaimed on 7 December 2000.[6] Although the ambitious project of a Constitution for Europe eventually did not garner the required support of the Member States, many of the ideas and formulas agreed during the European Convention found their way into the Lisbon Treaty.[7] And while the Charter of Fundamental Rights had a few years of unsettled legal existence, it was in 2009 recognised as having the same legal value as the Treaties, thus opening a new chapter in the constitutional history of the Union.[8]

Thirty years later, the situation is dramatically different. There is little left of the euphoria of the 1990s and the consensus about fundamental values is seriously shaken. In a number of EU Member States – both new and old – the values of liberal democracy and the rule of law are openly called into question.[9] What is particularly striking is that considerable rule of law backsliding is registered in some of the countries that were the pioneers of democratic transition in CEE and frontrunners in the process of EU accession.[10] Poland and Hungary, which together with the Czech Republic and Slovakia form the

[5] According to Sadurski, one of the main factors for the widespread support for EU accession in the CEE countries was the perception that it would 'serve to entrench and strengthen the process of democratisation after the fall of Communism': W Sadurski, 'Accession Democracy Dividend: The Impact of the EU Enlargement upon Democracy in the New Member States of Central and Eastern Europe' (2004) 10 *European Law Journal* 371, 371.

[6] ibid; G de Búrca, 'Beyond the Charter: How Enlargement Has Enlarged the Human Rights Policy of the European Union' (2003) 27 *Fordham International Law Journal* 679. On the more general constitutional impact of Enlargement in the Union, see B De Witte, 'The Impact of Enlargement on the Constitution of the European Union' in M Cremona (ed), *The Enlargement of the European Union* (Oxford, Hart Publishing, 2003) 209.

[7] See Laeken Declaration on the Future of the European Union, Annex I to the European Council conclusions, 14 and 15 December 2001, Council document 300/01 (ADD 1).

[8] See Art 6(1) Treaty on the European Union (TEU).

[9] M Claes, 'Editorial Note: How Common are the Values of the European Union?' (2019) 15 *Croatian Yearbook of European Law and Policy* vii, ix–x.

[10] The term 'backsliding' is by now well established in the legal and political science literature, although it has been criticised on a number of counts. Rule of law backsliding has been defined as 'the process through which elected public authorities deliberately implement governmental blueprints which aim to systematically weaken, annihilate or capture internal checks on power with the view of dismantling the liberal democratic state and entrenching the long-term rule of the dominant party': L Pech and K Scheppele, 'Illiberalism Within: Rule of Law Backsliding in the EU'

once exemplary Visegrád four, are now ruled by self-defined 'illiberal' governments and are steadily on a course of confrontation with EU institutions.[11] Disturbingly, they are no longer recognised as consolidated democracies by major democracy-screening institutes and non-governmental organisations (NGOs). In 2020, for the first time, Freedom House qualified Hungary as a transitional and hybrid regime, while Poland slipped back into the group of semi-consolidated democracies.[12] There is compelling evidence that the independence of the media and of the judiciary in these countries is seriously compromised, a development that undermines the very foundation of the Union, namely, mutual trust.[13] Even if other CEE Member States are not showing the same open disrespect for institutional checks and balances and for international commitments, there seems to be broad agreement among initiated observers that the quality of democracy and the rule of law in the region is deteriorating.[14]

This book aims at taking stock of the state of the rule of law in the EU 30 years after the fall of the Berlin Wall. It pays special attention to the challenges that the EU Member States from CEE and their citizens have been facing in the transition to democracy and the rule of law, and in the process of EU accession. But the book also inquires, more broadly, after the causes for what appears to be a more general weakening, if not an outright crisis, of the rule of law in the Union. Furthermore, the book reflects on the way forward, weighing alternative approaches for curbing instances of democratic backsliding in individual EU Member States and ensuring robust and sustainable rule of law

(2017) 19 *Cambridge Yearbook of European Legal Studies* 3, 10. Some have pointed out that while the term implies a regression from a previous state of consolidated democracy, for many countries in CEE the truth rather has been that they were not truly consolidated democracies at the time of accession in the first place. Moreover, the backsliding paradigm suggests a linear movement from autocracy to democracy and backwards, thus missing more complex, non-linear patterns of democratic development. See L Cianetti and S Hanley, 'The end of the backsliding paradigm' (2021) 31 *Journal of Democracy* 66, 67–68, with reference to the critique of the transition paradigm by T Carothers, 'The End of the Transition Paradigm' (2002) 13 *Journal of Democracy* 5. On the debate about different measurements of democracy and rule of law, see W Merkel, 'Measuring the Quality of Rule of Law. Virtues, Perils, Results' in M Zürn, A Nollkaemper and R Peerenboom (eds), *Rule of Law Dynamics. In an Era of International and Transnational Governance* (Cambridge, Cambridge University Press, 2013) 21.

[11] The illiberal turn is well documented in a number of scholarly publications. Instead of many, see Pech and Scheppele (n 10). See also the contributions in this volume, and in particular ch 3 and ch 4 by Halmai and Nergelius, respectively. A prominent instance of confrontation with European institutions is the decision of the Polish Constitutional Court of 14 July 2021, rejecting Poland's obligation to give precedence to EU law in cases of conflict with Polish constitutional law. See Trybunał Konstytucyjny, decision P7/20 of 14 July 2021. The decision was delivered in anticipation of the judgment of the EU Court of Justice in the Case C-791/19, European Commission v Republic of Poland, ECLI:EU:C:2021:596, finding the setting up and activity of the Disciplinary Chamber of the Polish Supreme Court to be in violation of EU law.

[12] See the democracy index put together by Freedom House at https://freedomhouse.org/ and the scores for Hungary at https://freedomhouse.org/country/hungary/nations-transit/2020. See also D Kelemen's analysis of what he calls the EU's autocratic equilibrium in RD Kelemen, 'The European Union's authoritarian equilibrium' (2020) 27 *Journal of European Public Policy* 481.

[13] On the principle of mutual trust, see CJEU, Opinion 2/13 of 18 December 2014, ECLI:EU:C:2014:2454.

[14] See the introduction by Cianetti et al to the special issue of *East European Politics* on 'democratic backsliding' in CEE: L Cianetti, J Dawson and S Hanley, 'Rethinking "democratic backsliding" in

in the Union. Crucially, the book addresses the question: What is and what should be the role of EU institutions in upholding the rule of law in the Union and its Member States?

II. THE RULE OF LAW IN THE EU AND THE DEMISE OF COMMUNISM: A COMPLEX RELATIONSHIP

Linking the state of the rule of law in the EU and the demise of communism, which quite symbolically culminated in the tearing down of the Berlin Wall in November 1989, can be seen as fully logical, even self-evident, but it can also be perceived as controversial. If we look at why the link appears logical, we can start by stating the obvious: although the fall of the Wall is not directly related to the EU, or to EU law, there is hardly any other historical event in the past half a century that has affected European law and politics more palpably. The fall of the Wall marked the end of the Cold War and of the ideological divide between the East and the West and signalled the start of the democratic transformation of CEE. Not least, it opened the way for the transition societies of CEE to gradually join the two most prominent European organisations – first the Council of Europe and then, after a long and extensive preparation process, the EU, leading to a previously unimaginable expansion and overhaul of these organisations.

A. CEE as a Source of Rule of Law Dividends and Losses for the EU

A link between the post-communist transformation of CEE and the current state of the rule of law in the EU can be discerned more specifically on at least three levels.

First, the ascent of the rule of law as a central element of EU law and policy occurred shortly after the 'velvet' revolutions swept across CEE, and was intimately connected to the process of Eastward Enlargement of the Union. As is well known, the Copenhagen European Council, which set out the conditions for membership of the countries from CEE in the Union, highlighted the rule of law and stable democracy as important political conditions for accession.[15] Acceptance of the principle of the rule of law was also a requirement for membership in the Council of Europe, following Article 3 of the Council's Statute.[16]

Central and Eastern Europe – looking beyond Hungary and Poland' (2018) 34 *East European Politics* 243. Cf also contributions by Dawson and Dimitrova, in the same special issue.

[15] Conclusions of the Copenhagen European Council, which established as political conditions for membership 'stability of institutions guaranteeing democracy, the rule of law, human rights and respect for and protection of minorities'. Conclusions of the Presidency, European Council in Copenhagen, 21–22 June 1993.

[16] See Art 3, 'Every member of the Council of Europe must accept the principles of the rule of law and of the enjoyment by all persons within its jurisdiction of human rights and fundamental

Given the fact that accession to these European organisations was an almost uncontested political priority in the new aspiring democracies from CEE, demonstrating stability of institutions guaranteeing democracy and the rule of law became a matter of urgency for the governments in the CEE countries. The process of accession to the Council of Europe and the EU thus turned into a major driving force for the constitutional and institutional transformation taking place in CEE. In this process, European institutions, such as the Council of Europe's Parliamentary Assembly, the Venice Commission and notably the EU Commission, were able to exert considerable leverage on shaping the legal framework of the rule of law and the institutions entrusted with rule of law supervision and enforcement in the applicant countries. Scholars speak of an external dimension of constitutionalisation in CEE and governance by conditionality.[17]

Second, the process of Eastward Enlargement was not only a laboratory for transforming the candidate countries. It was likewise – albeit less obviously – transforming the Union as well. Interestingly, an EU concept of the rule of law was largely non-existent prior to Enlargement. In the course of preparation of the candidate countries for EU membership, however, the Commission was gradually compelled to elaborate such a concept in order to be able to assess the degree of each candidate country's compliance with the Copenhagen criteria. The Commission documented its evaluations and conclusions in numerous annual country reports and progress reports, continuously testing and calibrating its approach, as well as the scope and direction of related technical assistance. So, with all its imperfections and incongruences, an EU rule of law concept was literally born in the process of Enlargement.[18]

What is more, in the course of Enlargement, the EU developed more consciously and clearly its fundamental values and constitutional principles, awarding them a prominent place in the Treaties. Regarding fundamental rights, there was initially a clear 'division of labour' between the EU and the Council of Europe, the latter having the main responsibility in this domain on the basis of the European Convention of Human Rights. The Union was, however, gradually nudged towards developing a human rights system of its own, culminating in the adoption of the EU Charter of Fundamental Rights.[19] These developments

freedoms, and collaborate sincerely and effectively in the realisation of the aim of the Council as specified in Chapter I.'

[17] See P Blokker, *New Democracies in Crisis? A Comparative Constitutional Study of the Czech Republic, Hungary, Poland, Romania and Slovakia* (Abingdon-on-Thames, Routledge, 2013) 5; Sadurski (n 5); A Sajó, 'Accession's Impact on Constitutionalism in the New Member States' in G Bermann and K Pistor (eds), *Law and Governance in an Enlarged European Union* (Oxford, Hart Publishing, 2004) 415.

[18] For a critical appraisal of this process, see the doctoral dissertation of Erik Wennerström, currently Sweden's judge in the European Court of Human Rights: E Wennerström, *The Rule of Law and the European Union* (Uppsala, Iustus förlag, 2007). In the book the author also discusses the role the rule of law came to play in the EU's external relations policy: ibid 224–85. See also the contribution by Bakardjieva Engelbrekt in ch 9 of this volume.

[19] de Búrca (n 6).

were partly an effect of the need to close the perceived gap between external and internal standards or, as Sadurski put it at the time, a consequence of 'the logic of liberal legalism'.[20] Against the background of pervasive monitoring and scrutinising of the respect for the rule of law and fundamental rights in the candidate countries, the absence of expressly formulated corresponding obligations for the Union and its Member States was becoming increasingly untenable.[21] The other, and more pragmatic, reason for the focus on fundamental values was of course the uncertainty as to the candidate countries' democratic credentials and the tenacity of their commitment to the rule of law and fundamental rights. A clearer statement of the common values and shared constitutional principles of the Union was consequently perceived as a necessary insurance against future political backlash.

Viewed in this light, the spelling out of the Union's fundamental values in Article 2 TEU, the inclusion of the explicit albeit imperfect mechanism for Member State sanctioning in the event of serious breaches of those values in Article 7 TEU, as well as the adoption of the EU Charter of Fundamental Rights in 2000, can all be conceived in important respects as products of EU Enlargement.[22] This was acknowledged in Commission documents and pointed out by political and academic commentators.[23] In the words of De Witte, Enlargement had assumed the role of a 'constitutional agenda-setter for the Union'.[24]

Admittedly, this constitutional awakening took place largely in anticipation of the problems that could arise when the still immature democracies in

[20] W Sadurski, 'Charter and Enlargement' (2002) 8 *European Law Journal* 340, 344. On the discrepancy between internal and external standards, concerning in particular respect and protection of minorities, see Ch Hillion, 'Enlargement of the European Union – The Discrepancy between Membership Obligations and Accession Conditions as Regards the Protection of Minorities' (2004) 27 *Fordham International Law Journal* 715. While protection of minorities figured prominently in EU accession conditionality, there were no adequate means for monitoring it internally. Hillion highlighted the paradoxical situation that the pressure on CEE countries to protect minorities would be less tangible once they became EU members than in the period of accession.

[21] On the problem of double standards as a driver for the internal development of rule of law standards for the EU, see De Witte (n 6) 233ff; with a focus on the discrepancy in the field of human rights, see Ph Alston and J Weiler, 'An "Ever Closer Union" in Need of a Human Rights Policy: The European Union and Human Rights' (1998) 9 *European Journal of International Law* 658; A Williams, 'Enlargement of the Union and Human Rights Conditionality: A Policy of Distinction?' (2000) 25 *EL Rev* 601.

[22] This is not to say that internal developments were not playing an important role. In particular, the experience from the so called 'Haider affair', with a largely unconvincing attempt by the Union to react to the formation of a coalition government including the rightist populist FPÖ (led by Jörg Haider) in Austria, had a notable influence on the shaping of Art 7 TEU.

[23] See references in Sadurski (n 20) 340ff, esp at 345, to Commission Communication on the Charter of Fundamental Rights of the EU, COM(2000) 559, 13 September 2000, para 12; de Búrca (n 6).

[24] De Witte (n 6) 209. In this contribution De Witte analyses in detail not only the role of Enlargement for the development of the Treaties in respect of a clear statement of fundamental values, but also in elaborating different constitutional safeguards for the continued effectiveness of the decision-making process within the Union, including new voting rules and, importantly, the introduction of various mechanisms for differentiation such as enhanced cooperation, etc.

CEE were to join the Union. However, the transformation was also undertaken in a spirit of optimism, and was praised as generally strengthening the Union's commitment to democracy, the rule of law and human rights.[25] Constitutional scholars were even arguing that the CEE countries, through their very condensed experience of post-communist constitution building, were bringing important insights to the table in the elaboration of the Constitution for Europe and more generally to European constitutionalism.[26]

Third, and less optimistically, the link between the end of communism and the current state of the rule of law in the EU becomes hard to overlook in the face of the deplorable regression in the respect for the rule of law and fundamental freedoms, observed with all clarity in some of the new EU Member States, with Hungary and Poland being the prime examples.[27] What initially appeared to be isolated incidents of weakening of democratic institutions in these Member States has increasingly taken the shape of systematic and deliberate – in some instances one might even say arrogant – disregard of the fundamental principles of the rule of law, that is separation of powers, independence of the media and the judiciary, and respect for fundamental rights. Appreciating the proper significance of the change has been complicated by the fact that there has been no single discrete event marking a shift to authoritarianism, but rather a gradual hollowing out of democratic institutions.[28]

At the EU level, the Commission, the Parliament and the Court have all weighed in on the issue of rule of law backsliding in Hungary and Poland, either in response to individual breaches or with regard more generally to the rule of law situation in these countries. Events have been unfolding at such a speed that it has been difficult to keep track of all the twists and turns in this seemingly endless saga.[29] And while the efforts to turn around the 'illiberal' trend are multiplying, so are the points of conflict, generating tension and gloomy predictions.[30] The almost incredible fact that these problems originate in the countries that were considered leaders of the democratic transition in CEE

[25] de Búrca (n 6) and DeWitte (n 6); Sadurski (n 20).

[26] Sadurski (n 20); see also R Arnold, 'Constitutional Courts in Central and Eastern European Countries as a Dynamic Source of New Legal Ideas' (2003) 18 *Tulane European & Civil Forum* 99, with a focus on the new constitutional courts in CEE.

[27] The process has been documented abundantly and discussed intensely in the academic literature. Instead of many, see Pech and Scheppele (n 10).

[28] ibid. According to Ganev, 'what we have been seeing in the region are shifts that are incremental and partial – tinkering with legal frameworks, but not their destruction': V Ganev, '"Soft decisionism" in Bulgaria' (2018) 29 *Journal of Democracy* 91.

[29] For a chronology of events in Hungary, see A Jakab, 'Institutional Alcoholism in Post-socialist Countries and the Cultural Elements of the Rule of Law: The Example of Hungary' in A Bakardjieva Engelbrekt and X Groussot (eds), *The Future of Europe: Political and Legal Integration Beyond Brexit*, SSEL vol XIII (Oxford, Hart Publishing, 2018) 209, as well as Halmai's contribution in ch 3 of this volume. For a similar mapping of events in Poland, see W Sadurski, 'Constitutional Design: Lessons from Poland's Democratic Backsliding' (2020) 6 *Constitutional Studies* 59.

[30] See H von den Burhard, 'Hungary and Poland escalate budget fight over rule of law: Orbán and Morawiecki warn that tying cash to democratic standards risks the "breakup" of the bloc' *Politico* (26 November 2020).

seems to suggest – at least prima facie – that the legal and institutional reforms introduced after the fall of the Berlin Wall and in the years of EU accession have not taken sufficiently deep root and that democratic institutions need more time to mature. As argued by András Jakab, amongst others, changes in formal rules alone can hardly bring about sustainable rule of law reform when actual practice is shaped by cultural patterns still linked to an authoritarian communist past.[31] Therefore, looking at these legacies, as well as at the early evolution of rule of law institutions in the CEE countries, can arguably give us important keys for understanding the current rule of law setbacks in the Union.

B. CEE as a *Sui Generis* Object of Study

And yet, as much as the topic of the book appears given and obvious, it can also be perceived as controversial. For one thing, it might be asked whether today, 30 years after the end of communism and more than a decade after the Eastward Enlargement of the Union was successfully completed, we can still treat the CEE countries as a separate object of study, as *sui generis*, to use the words of lawyer and political scientist Venelin Ganev.[32] Should we not accept that once the 11 states of CEE have joined the Union, having passed rigorous screening and evaluation, they should be considered fully-fledged members of 'the club', and not be subject to special attention and scrutiny? Such views are expressed, in various contexts, often by scholars and policy makers seeing developments from the perspective of the CEE countries, and there is of course merit in such arguments.[33]

As editors, we have sought to find some middle ground on this issue. While not seeing rule of law problems in the EU as problems exclusively of the new Member States and as a direct consequence of the Eastward Enlargement, we acknowledge that there are still sufficiently many elements *sui generis* that justify paying special attention to the challenges that the societies of CEE have been (and are still) facing on their journey to stable democratic institutions. In particular, we believe we should try to better understand the impact of past legacies, including the years of state socialism and the first decades of post-communist transition, on current legal and political institutions and practices. The transformation of the CEE societies, triggered by the velvet revolutions

[31] See Jakab (n 29); On the institutional legacies of communism and in particular on the legacy of dysfunctional institutions, see H Grabbe, *The EU's Transformative Power. Europeanization Through Conditionality in Central and Eastern Europe* (Basingstoke, Palgrave Macmillan, 2006) 102 and 105.

[32] V Ganev, 'The Rule of Law as an Institutionalized Wager: Constitutions, Courts and Transformative Social Dynamics in Eastern Europe' (2009) 1 *Hague Journal on the Rule of Law* 263, 264.

[33] See the already mentioned reflections of Sadurski on the logic of 'liberal legalism' in Sadurski (n 20) 344; see also Ch Hillion, *EU Enlargement: A Legal Approach* (Oxford, Hart Publishing, 2004).

of 1989, has been aptly described as 'rebuilding the ship at sea'.[34] The almost total collapse of the old societal order, and the absence of well-prepared actors and institutions ready to step in and steer towards the much-desired transformation, represented a challenge of previously unseen complexity, putting an excessive strain on the societies in these countries. One of the most distinctive characteristics of this transition has been the simultaneity of the required transformation (sometimes referred to as 'triple transformation').[35] Indeed, in contrast to other transitions, like the post-war reconstruction of West Germany or the post-authoritarian transitions in Latin America, the transformation in CEE required concurrent market, nation and civil society building, making the task truly daunting.[36]

Moreover, as already mentioned, the state of the rule of law in these countries and the shaping of the institutions that were tasked with safeguarding the rule of law have been uniquely influenced by the process of EU accession. Although the Union had experienced previous waves of enlargement, where in particular the accession of Greece, Portugal and Spain in the 1970s and 1980s had been in a similar manner conditioned on overcoming legacies of past authoritarian regimes, the way the Union stepped in and engaged in the transformation of CEE has been quite unprecedented. The strictness of the conditionality and the rigour of the screening exercise preceding accession have no counterparts in previous accessions.[37] As to the technical assistance in the form of twinning projects and infrastructural aid, it has in size been compared to the Marshall Plan following the Second World War, in complexity of administration probably surpassing this plan.[38]

While the engagement of the EU institutions has undoubtedly speeded up democratic reforms in the candidate countries, the governance of the accession process has been far from unproblematic. Regarding in particular the rule of law as a condition for accession, legal scholars and political scientists have been highly critical of the vagueness of this criterion, as well as the inconsistency and seeming arbitrariness of the assessment carried out by the European

[34] The authors described the quasi-impossible task as 'the constructive challenge of rebuilding the damaged boat essentially through the efforts of its passengers and in the "open sea"': see J Elster, C Offe and U Preuss, *Institutional Design in Post-communist Societies. Rebuilding the Ship at Sea* (Cambridge, Cambridge University Press, 1998) 28.

[35] Often also referred to as 'triple transformation'. See A Dimitrova, 'The uncertain road to sustainable democracy: elite coalitions, citizens protests and the prospects of democracy in Central and Eastern Europe' (2018) 34 *East European Politics* 257.

[36] Elster et al (n 34).

[37] See Hillion (n 33).

[38] See Jacques Santer's speech on 17 September 1997, presenting Agenda 2000, available at https://ec.europa.eu/commission/presscorner/detail/en/SPEECH_97_184: 'Included in the Agenda 2000 package is no less than 75 billion ECU to be spent on integrating the new Member States into the EU and the pre-accession package I mentioned above. I have called this an enlargement Marshall Plan. It is no less than that.' See, however, for scathing criticism of such comparisons, M Ivanova, 'Why There Was No "Marshall Plan" for Eastern Europe and Why This Still Matters' (2007) 15 *Journal of*

institutions, especially the Commission.[39] In an extensive analysis, Nicolaïdis and Kleinfeld have described the Commission's approach as institutions-focused, state-centred and means-based, dubbing the approach 'anatomical'.[40] In their view, in its analyses, the Commission was paying disproportionate attention to formal legal and institutional indicators, while turning a blind eye to 'law in action' and deeper layers of legal and political culture. In its Enlargement policy, the Commission was interacting mainly with state actors, failing to harness the potential of civil society in rule of law reforms. The emphasis of reform efforts was laid on the means rather than on the long-term ends of ensuring the sustainability of rule of law reforms. These failures have arguably negatively affected the still fragile rule of law institutions in the candidate countries.[41]

Given these and other distinguishing features of the CEE experience, on balance we agree with Ganev that there are still good reasons to 'continue the conversation about what is *sui generis* about post-communist polities', seeking to identify the more enduring legacies, both of the communist period as well as of the decades of transition.[42] Likewise, we find it meaningful to continue to study the process of EU accession and the first decade of EU membership, trying to gauge their effect on the quality of the rule of law in the CEE Member States.

C. The Limits of Treating CEE as a Separate Category

At the same time, we acknowledge that there are limits to treating CEE as a separate and special category. First, there are important variations across both new and old Member States, which makes treating the countries from any region as a homogeneous group precarious. Thus, in respect of CEE, more fine-grained empirical and comparative studies suggest that it would be too hasty to see developments in Hungary and Poland as representative of the whole region.[43] A more accurate picture for many CEE countries appears to be the one of 'democratic malaise', or 'low quality democracy' with relatively stable electoral regimes but a number of illiberal characteristics.[44]

Contemporary European Studies 345. Cf L Bruszt and J Langbein, 'Varieties of dis-embedded liberalism. EU integration strategies in the Eastern peripheries of Europe' (2017) 24 *Journal of European Public Policy* 297, 305.

[39] D Smilov, 'EU Enlargement and the Constitutional Principle of Judicial Independence' in W Sadurski, A Czarnota and M Kryiger (eds), *Spreading Democracy and the Rule of Law? The Impact of EU Enlargement on the Rule of Law, Democracy and Constitutionalism in Post-Communist Legal Orders* (Dordrecht, Springer, 2006) 313.

[40] K Nicolaïdis and R Kleinfeld, 'Rethinking Europe's "Rule of Law" and Enlargement Agenda: The Fundamental Dilemma' *Jean Monnet Working Paper Series* (NYU School of Law, 2012) available at www.JeanMonnetProgram.org.

[41] ibid. See also the contribution by Bakardjieva Engelbrekt in ch 9 of this volume.

[42] Ganev (n 32).

[43] Cianetti et al (n 14).

[44] ibid 246, with reference to Dimitrova's contribution to the same special issue.

Furthermore, it is quite clear that the current rule of law crisis in the Union can hardly be reduced to backsliding and failures only in the new CEE Member States. A surge of populism and mobilisation of anti-liberal forces may be noted in many established democracies in Europe: from the *Front national* of Marine Le Pen in France and Matteo Salvini's *Lega* in Italy, to the Swedish Democrats in Sweden and *Alternative für Deutschland* in Germany. While none of these political movements has managed to take a long-term grip on political power, the risk of this happening cannot be excluded, especially in the wake of consecutive financial and economic crises and an ongoing global pandemic.[45] After all, while the EU is occasionally and deservedly celebrated as the greatest peace project of our time,[46] we do not need to look too far back in the past to unearth 'darker legacies' of Europe, and of law in Europe in particular.[47] The memories of these legacies should keep us wary and cognisant about the fragility of the rule of law and of democratic institutions, and about the need for constant nurturing of these institutions.

Finally, the world around us is changing, and what initially appeared as a phenomenon characteristic primarily of former socialist countries in CEE could increasingly be viewed as part of a global trend. The international community has during the last few years come to experience the undermining of international commitments and of global institutions under US President Trump; a largely erratic Brexit process; as well as other incidents of rule of law violations, or in any event rule of law 'stretching', in countries that have long been perceived as beacons of liberal democratic values.[48] Constitutional scholars discern a global turn away from constitutional democracy toward autocracy, something supported by influential democracy and rule of law NGOs.[49] In its annual report 'Freedom in the World 2020', Freedom House found 2019 to be the 14th consecutive year of decline in global freedom, and arrived at the sombre conclusion that democracy and pluralism were under assault. In 2019, the same organisation noted that 'the reversal has spanned a variety of countries, from long-standing democracies like the United States to consolidated authoritarian regimes like China and Russia'.[50] This development appears also to speak against treating the situation in CEE as special and *sui generis*.

[45] A Bakardjieva Engelbrekt et al (eds), *The European Union and the Return of the Nation State* (London, Palgrave, 2020).

[46] See the prize motivation of the Nobel Peace Prize Committee in 2012 available at www.nobelprize.org/prizes/peace/2012/eu/facts/: 'Prize motivation: for over six decades contributed to the advancement of peace and reconciliation, democracy and human rights in Europe.'

[47] Ch Joerges and N S Ghaleigh (eds), *Darker Legacies of Law in Europe* (Oxford, Hart Publishing, 2003).

[48] See J Havercroft et al, 'Donald Trump as Global Constitutional Breaching Experiment (2018) 7 *Global Constitutionalism* 1.

[49] See the special issue 'Constitutional Decline, Constitutional Design and Lawyerly Hubris' (2020) 6 *Constitutional Studies*. See in particular A Jakab, 'What Can Constitutional Law Do against the Erosion of Democracy and the Rule of Law? On the Interconnectedness of the Protection of Democracy and the Rule of Law' (2020) 6 *Constitutional Studies* 5.

[50] See Freedom House, Freedom in the World 2020, available at: https://freedomhouse.org/sites/default/files/2020-02/FIW_2020_REPORT_BOOKLET_Final.pdf.

To account for these wider European and global trends, in the volume we have invited scholars to reflect more generally on the meaning of democracy and the rule of law as fundamental constitutional concepts, on their mutual relationship, as well as on their position as common values for the Union. Furthermore, the volume also includes contributions looking specifically at real or potential rule of law problems in older and more experienced democracies in the EU.[51]

III. THE DEEPER CAUSES OF RULE OF LAW BACKSLIDING: LOOKING BEYOND LAW

Another, probably more fundamental, objection to paying special attention to rule of law backsliding in the CEE countries in what is essentially a legal monograph, is related to the following question: Even if we acknowledge that such backsliding, or democratic deterioration, is taking place more visibly in the CEE countries, can we – and should we – discuss this predominantly as a problem of law? To be sure, constitutional lawyers tend to see the causes for the crisis in Hungary and Poland in the failure of these states to follow the agreed legal rules and commitments, and in the inadequacy of the legal response on the part of EU institutions. According to one of the vocal critics of rule of law backsliding in Poland and Hungary:

> Scholars have been clear on what the key causes of the [rule of law problems in Hungary and Poland] are: the lack of a clear will by the Member States and the inability of the EU institutions to utilise the full potential of the available legal instruments available [*sic*] to match the gravity of the problem.[52]

Yet such an answer only raises the question: And how can we explain the sudden absence of political will to follow commitments? After all, until only recently, the countries from CEE, or at least their governments and large numbers of their citizenry, were among the most enthusiastic supporters of European integration. Moreover, the early record of EU law compliance in these countries post accession was overall positive, even beyond expectation.[53] On the brink of EU Enlargement, Sadurski's optimistic prediction was that EU accession would suppress the nationalistic and populist forces in the new Member States and be instrumental in sustaining the liberal-democratic reforms. In his words, 'Accession will reconfigure political and discursive assets and incentives in ways that help the liberal-democratic and hinder the authoritarian political forces in new Member States.'[54]

[51] See the contributions of Valentina Colcelli on Italy and of Graham Butler on the Scandinavian countries in ch 10 and ch 11 of this volume, respectively.

[52] D Kochenov, 'Elephants in the Room: The European Commission's 2019 Communication on the Rule of Law' (2019) 11 *Hague Journal on the Rule of Law* 423.

[53] U Sedelmeier, 'After Conditionality: Post-accession Compliance with EU Law in East Central Europe' (2008) 15 *Journal of European Public Policy* 806.

[54] Sadurski (n 5) 401.

As is well known, 15 years later, sadly, the author of these hopeful words, Professor Sadurski, had to experience first hand the harsh methods of an increasingly authoritarian regime in his country of origin. In 2019 he faced an array of charges and lawsuits in Poland for his outspoken criticism of the governing party, PiS.[55] Apart from provoking justified indignation in the professional community, this appalling incident of harassment is yet further evidence of post-accession rule of law backsliding, raising the broader questions: What happened in the years that followed, and how could Sadurski's prediction turn out to be so wrong? Where should we look for explanations for the striking revolt against liberal values that we are currently observing across the region, or in any case in some of the CEE Member States?

A. Rule of Law Backsliding as a Function of Reduced External Incentives

An influential group of scholars in political science who closely studied the Europeanisation of the CEE countries in the course of accession, analysed this process through a rational-choice model of international relations, placing emphasis on candidate states' incentives for compliance with EU requirements (notably the EU *acquis*).[56] The main factors influencing incentives in their analysis were: (i) the determinacy of EU requirements; (ii) the expected reward for compliance or the cost of non-compliance, respectively; (iii) the credibility of the reward or the cost; and, finally, (iv) the domestic costs of effecting the required legal change, including political costs. The first three factors are external, dependent on the EU, while the fourth is internal. On the basis of a broad comparative study of a number of candidate countries and across different policy domains, the authors concluded that the success of EU conditionality[57] in terms of effected legal change and compliance, could best be explained by the credibility of the ultimate reward of EU membership. Therefore, the model was dubbed the 'External Incentives Model', or EIM.

The same scholars have recently sought to explain rule of law backsliding in some of the new Member States through a slightly adapted EIM.[58] They identify

[55] For details, also on the international mobilisation of legal academics in support of Professor Sadurski, see G de Búrca and J Morijn, 'Open Letter in Support of Professor Wojciech Sadurski', *VerfBlog*, 5 June 2019, available at https://verfassungsblog.de/open-letter-in-support-of-professor-wojciech-sadurski/.

[56] F Schimmelfennig and U Sedelmeier (eds), *The Europeanization of Central and Eastern Europe* (Ithaca, NY, Cornell University Press, 2005) 210; F Schimmelfennig and U Sedelmeier, 'Theorising EU enlargement: research focus, hypotheses, and the state of research' (2002) 9 *Journal of European Public Policy* 500.

[57] EU conditionality is defined as the 'EU's insistence that candidate countries apply the *acquis communautaire* as a prerequisite to membership', see M Pollack, 'Rational Choice and EU Politics' in KE Joergensen, M Pollack and B Rosemund (eds), *Handbook of European Union Politics* (London, Sage, 2007) 31, 42.

[58] See F Schimmelfennig and U Sedelmeier, 'The Europeanization of Eastern Europe: the external incentives model revisited' (2020) 27 *Journal of Public* Policy 814.

a number of factors that lower incentives for compliance post-accession, namely: the vagueness of the EU rule of law requirements; the high internal costs of compliance given the political salience of rule of law issues; and, most importantly, the sharp decrease in the reward for compliance post accession, and the lack of credible sanctions for infringement given that accession is already a fact. Seen through this analytical prism, rule of law backsliding in the new CEE Member States appears as a logical consequence of the changed incentives structure that follows with full Union membership.[59]

B. From Rationalist Accounts to Search for Deeper Explanations

Such rationalist accounts have the advantage of offering a clear and robust analytical framework with reasonable predictive power. However, not unlike the prevailing approach in legal scholarship, the proponents of this theoretical strand tend to focus all too much on formal rule compliance. Their analysis does not explain, and does not seek to explain, the more profound reasons for rule of law backsliding and the complex dynamics causing and reinforcing the illiberal turn. It is therefore not surprising that political scientists are in search for novel ways for studying and understanding the democratic deterioration in the region. In a special issue of *East European Politics* published in 2018, the conveners[60] observed a 'pull away from understanding (de-)democratisation in terms of a political science-based agenda of institutional design and institutional (de-)consolidation'.[61] Instead, the answers are increasingly sought at deeper levels of political economy, political sociology or even political psychology, trying to explain the ways in which social, cultural and economic practices shape legal and political institutions.

In a similar manner, legal scholars increasingly acknowledge the limitations of legal rules and institutions. In an attempt to explain the democratic regression in Poland, Sadurski concludes that 'formal institutions must be underwritten by norms which are by-and-large shared, and by common understandings about what counts as a norm violation, even if formal legal rules are silent about it'.[62] In a somewhat sober and even defeatist mood he contends:

> So ultimately it is a matter of culture and ethics: when they are missing, even the best-designed institutions are rendered hollow; in contrast, when they are strongly ingrained in professionals staffing institutions, they are likely to prevail over determined populists.[63]

[59] ibid.
[60] Cianetti et al (n 14).
[61] ibid.
[62] Sadurski (n 29).
[63] ibid; see also Jakab (n 29).

In truth, the interest in these deeper layers of cultural practices and institutional legacies is nothing novel. Such interest has driven some of the most insightful analyses of the early post-communist transition and of the meandering road of democratisation in CEE.[64] In a monograph that appeared in 1998, Elster, Offe and Preuss highlighted the limits of what could be achieved by way of legislation and formal institutions. Instead, they stressed the importance of informal institutions, and of cultural and institutional legacies, but also the power of deeply entrenched economic interests:

> [T]ransformation and systemic change is something that is only to a limited extent a matter of law making. Cultural patterns, identities and legacies, associative practices that help or hinder the solution of collective goods problems, and the vigor with which entrepreneurial and other economic interests are pursued are among those determinants of change that cannot easily be legislated into – or out of – being.[65]

The authors described succinctly the paradox of the post-communist transformation. While 1989 could in their view be conceived as a 'tabula rasa' in institutional terms, with no legitimate constituent authority surviving the old regime and no civil society to fill in the gap, the 'habits' of the old regime were unrelentingly entrenched and permeated every sphere of social activity.[66] From this starting premise, the book traced how post-communist societies in four CEE countries – Bulgaria, Czech Republic, Hungary and Slovakia – evolved from the post-1989 state of 'tabula rasa' to reasonably stable and consolidated institutions in the sphere of the economy, of constitution building, democratic politics and of social policy. The authors offered a useful model for assessing democratic consolidation along a vertical and a horizontal dimension. The vertical dimension relates to the 'vertical authority of self-imposed rules', that is actors' propensity to make decisions and act in accordance with higher-order decision-making rules without engaging opportunistically in questioning the validity of these 'second order' rules.[67] The horizontal dimension relates to the 'degree of insulation of institutional spheres from each other and the limited convertability of status attributes from one sphere to the other'.[68] Applying this analytical

[64] For an insightful legal theoretical approach that offers a way for analysing such deeper levels and acknowledging their importance for a coherent legal system, see K Tuori, *Critical Legal Positivism* (Abingdon, Routledge, 2002).

[65] Elster et al (n 34) 18.

[66] ibid 19. See, however, Heather Grabbe's analysis of Enlargement, where she questions the 'tabula rasa' conception of post-communist transition and demonstrates that in many domains institutions from the old regime continued to exist, albeit in an adapted form and with changing functions: Grabbe (n 31) 102ff.

[67] Indeed, students of post-communist legal and constitutional developments in CEE stress the importance of achieving an embeddedness of democratic norms and of a culture of self-restraint. According to Daniel Smilov, the most important factor for a mature democracy ensuring respect for the rule of law is the acceptance of those in power to not use it against political opponents despite formal legal possibilities to do so. D Smilov, 'Can populism coexist with constitutional principles?', FLJS webinar series, 22 June 2020, available at www.fljs.org/content/constitutional-expert-asks-can-populism-coexist-constitutional-principles-fljs-webinar.

[68] Elster et al (n 34) 30ff.

prism to the selected CEE countries, the authors reached a more positive evaluation of the state of democratisation in the first decade of transition than suggested by their initial assumptions. However, they warned against too-hasty optimism, and saw an imminent risk that popular toleration of the hardships of the reforms could wane in the event of economic and financial downturn, potentially giving way to a populist backlash.[69] These predictions ring particularly true today, when we are trying to make sense of developments in Hungary and Poland.[70]

C. Socio-economic Inequality and Suppressed Agency in the Post-communist Transition

Looking more closely at the socio-economic context in CEE, manifold analyses link the current backsliding to the gross economic and social inequality that followed in the aftermath of the post-communist transition, and the perceptions among wide groups of the population of being left behind and not being able to benefit from the open society the reforms purported to install. In an early analysis of East European backsliding, Ivan Krastev sought explanations in what he called the 'anti-egalitarian consensus' of the post-communist transition. In his view:

> The 'original sin' of the postcommunist democracies is that they came into being not as an outcome of the triumph of egalitarianism but as a victory of an anti-egalitarian consensus uniting the communist elite and the anticommunist counter-elite. Ex-communists were anti-egalitarian because of their interests. Liberals were anti-egalitarian because of their ideology.[71]

Arguably, such perceptions of socio-economic frustration were only exacerbated by the financial and economic crises of the late 2000s, and formed fertile soil for the surge of populist movements.[72]

A slightly different perspective on the first years of post-communist transformation in Poland is offered by Maurice Glasman in his book *Unnecessary Suffering*.[73] Building on the seminal work of Karl Polanyi,[74] the author delivers a forceful critique of the big-bang 'shock therapy' strategy followed in the Polish transition from state-controlled economy to free market, pursuant to the

[69] ibid 305ff.

[70] It should be noted that for Elster et al, it was countries like Bulgaria and Slovakia that were more likely candidates for regression into a populist-authoritarian rule, while Hungary was in a middle category, having achieved a higher degree of democratic consolidation than Bulgaria and Slovakia, but lower in comparison with the Czech Republic. See the Conclusion in Elster et al, ibid, 304-05.

[71] I Krastev, 'Is East-Central Europe Backsliding? The Strange Death of the Liberal Consensus' (2007) 18 *Journal of Democracy* 56, 60.

[72] See D Bohle and B Greskovits, 'East-Central Europe's Quandary' (2009) 20 *Journal of Democracy* 50.

[73] M Glasman, *Unnecessary Suffering. Managing Market Utopia* (London, Verso, 1996).

[74] K Polanyi, *The Great Transformation. The Political and Economic Origins of Our Time* (New York, Farrar & Rinehart, 1944).

(in)famous 'Balzerowicz plan'.[75] Like other students of the post-communist transition, Glasman's attention is drawn to the gross injustices of the transition and to the fact that the burdens of transformation were borne 'disproportionally by the working poor'.[76]

However, the gist of Glasman's critique lies elsewhere and is directed at the, in his view, suppressed agency in the post-communist transformation. Whereas Elster et al decry the absence of actors capable of shouldering the required triple transformation, Glasman contends that, at least in the Polish case, such actors were available but their ideas and aspirations were largely not allowed to sprout into a viable alternative to the dominant neo-liberal consensus. The Solidarity trade union (*Solidarność*) that had emerged as a spontaneous force during the last decade of the communist regime, and which played a critical role in the latter's collapse, had evolved into a vibrant social movement. According to Glasman, 'Solidarity defined a good society as one which provided the "conditions of a life free of poverty, exploitation, fear and deception, in a society that is democratically and lawfully organised".'[77]

Nevertheless, at least if we trust Glasman's account, these visions for social justice were not in line with the ideas of unfettered markets behind the Balcerowicz plan. Consequently, *Solidarność* had to surrender its role in the Polish economy in order to give way to the largely neo-liberal plans for economic restructuring backed at the time by all major international economic institutions, such as the IMF, World Bank and the EU.

Quite originally, Glasman draws a comparison with the post-war transformation of West Germany following the defeat of Nazism. He describes an intricate process of moulding of the very distinctive institutions of the German *Sozialstaat*, including the recognition of self-organised apprenticeship and insurance systems, co-determination in industry, and strong city and regional government. In his account, and contrary to conventional wisdom, these institutions were not so much reflecting ordo-liberal ideas, but rather were a product of the ideological congruence between the social theory and ethics of the Catholic Church and of the trade unions or, as Glasman puts it, 'of social Catholicism and social democracy'.[78] The resulting model secured a considerable measure of solidarity in the market, relying on broad-based societal institutions, while avoiding state authoritarianism.[79] That these ideas were allowed to permeate

[75] After Leszec Balcerowizc, leading Polish economist, Minister of Finance and Deputy Prime Minister in the first Polish Government after 1989.

[76] In Poland, a drastic decline in real wages had led to the doubling of those living below the poverty line. See Glasman (n 73) 126.

[77] ibid 92, with reference to Solidarity, 'Programme adopted by the First National Congress' in P Raina (ed), *Poland 1981: Towards Social Renewal* (London, 1981) 326.

[78] Glasman (n 73) 33.

[79] ibid 32–33. 'These two traditions formed the identity of the country's two main political parties, and provided the moral and intellectual ideals and organisations that underpinned what became known as the social market economy. … Social and Christian Democrats defined the dominant problem of modern society as a reconciliation of the market with a form of solidarity that did not descend into state authoritarianism'.

the German welfare state, despite the largely free-market prescriptions of the US occupying forces, was due to political contingency rather than deliberate political design.[80] Nonetheless, eventually, a model well embedded in the social texture of German society emerged, which resonated with the aspirations of wider layers of the West German polity. Returning to the comparison with the Polish transition, somewhat provocatively, Glasman concludes 'Although Germany was militarily defeated and occupied it had a greater degree of autonomy in its choice of institutions than Poland in 1989.'[81]

One can of course raise a number of objections to Glasman's account and question the cogency of the comparison with the German transformation. The author himself notes a few important differences, notably 'the level of technological productiveness and innovation of Nazi Germany (compared to Gierek's inefficient economy and obsolete technology in Poland)'.[82] Furthermore, his analysis focuses on the first years of transition, when the positive economic effects of the 'shock therapy' were arguably not yet fully realised. In addition, the role of responsible politicians, such as Konrad Adenauer and Ludwig Erhard in West Germany, for making the right choices at the right time is probably not sufficiently acknowledged. Yet the theme of suppressed agency, or lack of ownership in the reform of economic and political institutions, is powerful and has been echoed in other influential analyses of the post-communist transition.[83]

D. A Turn to Political Psychology? The Logic of the 'Imitation Imperative'

More recently, a variation on the theme of suppressed agency has been made a central point in an ambitious analysis of the general failure of the post-Cold War liberal consensus by two of the most initiated observers of democratisation of CEE, political analyst Ivan Krastev and constitutional law scholar Stephen Holmes. In an attempt to explain the turn to populism and illiberal authoritarianism in CEE and elsewhere, the authors advance a theory grounded in what could be described as political psychology. In their monograph *The Light that Failed*, the authors draw attention to what they call 'the Imitation Imperative'

[80] Glasman attributes this 'hands off' approach to the joint governance model established by the Allies, and the largely divergent and incongruent views of the US American and British occupying forces on a number of policy issues. This vacuum opened up room for more organic local solutions to institutionalise. Glasman speaks of 'competition and confusion' between the two states, which 'opened up the possibility for German society to develop its own distinctive institutions'. Cf ibid 59.

[81] ibid 132.

[82] ibid 131.

[83] See, for instance, political sociologist Paul Blokker's analysis, arguing that an often overlooked dimension of the current process of backsliding is the lack of social embeddedness of the post-1989 liberal-constitutional process: Blokker (n 17). Cf also J Komárek, 'The Struggle for Legal Reform after Communism', *LSE Legal Studies Working Paper No 10/2014* (10 February 2014) 17, available at https://ssrn.com/abstract=2388783.

of the post-communist transformation.[84] What they mean by that is the largely unquestioned dominance of the Western liberal ideal as the guiding light of the post-1989 transition. Reformists in the West, as well as in the East, were in agreement over the lack of viable alternatives to the Western liberal capitalist model as the only way for successful advancement of society. All that was required by the CEE countries in order to accomplish the desired 'return to Europe' was to emulate the example of the West; the authors speak of 'modernization by imitation' and 'integration by assimilation'.[85] In respect to EU accession more specifically, Krastev had already earlier argued that the EU, while playing a key role in empowering liberal institutions such as the courts and improving the quality of institutional performance, had contributed to the perception of the transition regimes as 'democracies without choices', which can at least partly be seen to be fuelling the current backlash against the liberal consensus.[86]

The tale of 'democracies without choices' and the 'imitation imperative' is certainly intellectually provocative and intuitively convincing. In its extreme version, however, it appears exaggerated, if only due to the broad variety of socio-economic models that have emerged in CEE in the wake of the post-communist transformation.[87] Still, the thesis receives some support in the legal literature on the EU Enlargement. Even celebratory accounts at the time of accession would openly refer to the main arguments in support of EU membership as 'civilizational', and would express a certain sadness that the citizens from the region could not trust their own states to achieve modernisation but needed to rely on external sources (the EU).[88] Sadurski pointed to the impoverishing effects of the mechanical law making induced by EU accession:

> The reduction in the parliament's power was sharpened by the fact that the EU presented the acquis as a non-negotiable package: implementation was portrayed as an administrative rather than political task. This obviously eroded the room for constructive deliberation at the parliamentary level, as the only available options were 'take it' or 'leave it'.[89]

To be sure, transposing multiple volumes of Community *acquis* is a common and unwaivable requirement for every country willing to join the Community/Union. What made this exercise more burdensome in the case of CEE, arguably negatively affecting the democratic process in these countries, was the fact that in many policy areas there was no prior national legislation or established local

[84] I Krastev and S Holmes, 'Imitation and its Discontents' in *The Light that Failed* (London, Penguin Books, 2019) 8.

[85] ibid.

[86] Krastev (n 71).

[87] See Cianetti et al (n 14); see also D Lane and M Myant (eds), *Varieties of Capitalism in Post-Communist Countries* (London, Palgrave Macmillan, 2007).

[88] Sadurski (n 5).

[89] ibid.

practice in the candidate countries. The *acquis* was thus having, to a much greater extent, the role of a blueprint, which was often uncritically accepted by still fragile and unexperienced decision-making institutions with no meaningful democratic deliberation.[90]

Following the theorising advanced by Krastev and Holmes, it would appear that in an ironic act of historical vengeance, the uncritical embracing of the unipolar imitation imperative has brewed resentment, ultimately leading to calls for authenticity and a return to (sometimes imagined) local and national traditions. Indeed, in a recent analysis of the ascent to power of Orbán's political movement in Hungary, Greskovits finds explanation for this success not so much in the discontent of the working poor, but rather in harnessing the sentiments of a conservative middle class through populist and nationalist narratives.[91]

E. A Panoply of Explanatory Approaches

To be sure, in this introduction we can only briefly touch upon some of the theoretical explanations for rule of law backsliding advanced in the social sciences. As demonstrated, the suggested approaches range from rationalist accounts seeking explanation in reduced external incentives for rule of law compliance following EU accession, to explanations grounded in political economy, institutional theory and even political psychology. These deeper levels of analysis are both theoretically important and intellectually fascinating. They remain, however, beyond the scope of this volume, mostly because of the predominantly legal affiliation of the contributing authors. This notwithstanding, the book is conceived in full awareness of the importance of penetrating these deeper layers for understanding the origins of the current problems, and for seeking meaningful and sustainable law and policy responses. Insights from political, economic and sociological enquiries thus inform the volume and – explicitly or implicitly – inspire many of the chapters.

IV. THE RULE OF LAW IN THE EU: WHOSE RESPONSIBILITY?

Finally, both the question about the *sui generis* nature of CEE as an object of study and the one about the deeper causes of rule of law backsliding in these countries come to bear when we discuss the probably most challenging and

[90] For a similar critique, see Schimmelfennig and Sedelmeier (2002) (n 56) 676; See also H Grabbe, 'How does Europeanization affect CEE governance? Conditionality, diffusion and diversity' (2001) 8 *Journal of European Public Policy* 1013; W Jacoby, *The Enlargement of the European Union and NATO* (Cambridge, Cambridge University Press, 2005) 70ff.

[91] See B Greskovits, 'Rebuilding the Hungarian Right through Conquering Civil Society: The Civic Circles Movement' (2020) 36 *East European Politics* 247.

controversial topic in this volume, namely: What should be done about rule of law backsliding, and who should carry the responsibility for defining and sustaining the rule of law in the EU and its Member States? Whereas there is a broad consensus that the problems with the rule of law in the EU are serious, and that decisive action is required, opinions differ widely when it comes to the more detailed task of designing effective institutional responses. The uncertainties abound. Should monitoring and enforcement instruments be designed to address the situation in only the most problematic (CEE) countries? Or should such instruments be conceived as universally applicable? How much should be left to the Member States and their domestic political and legal institutions? And when and how should European institutions intervene? What is the appropriate role of each of the EU institutions, and what should a reasonable division of labour between the EU and the Council of Europe look like? As is well known, there is a vibrant scholarly debate, where opinions differ on each of the issues outlined above.

Concerning the action required, an influential group of legal scholars has argued vehemently for rigorous application of the Treaties and stepping up the enforcement of the Union values and constitutional principles against recalcitrant Member States.[92] Scholars in this line of theorising see the rule of law standard in the EU as sufficiently clear and consistent across time, countries and policy domains to allow robust legal monitoring and, most importantly, strict enforcement and sanctioning.[93] Despite the deficit, at least until recently, of specific EU legislative instruments fleshing out the constituent facets of the EU rule of law concept, it is argued that the national constitutional traditions of the Member States provide sufficient common ground and legitimacy for such an exercise.[94] In addition, it is contended that the standards and requirements elaborated by the Commission in the process of Enlargement, despite certain incongruities, contain a coherent core of legal and institutional elements that can be legitimately required by Member States in order to show compliance with rule of law values under Article 2 TEU.[95]

Concerning the design of the enforcement tool, given the heavy mechanism of Article 7 TEU, some legal scholars advocate for a formal, vigorous legal enforcement mechanism by the Commission, based directly on Article 2 TEU, and channelled through proceedings before the CJEU. Such an understanding

[92] Pech and Scheppele (n 10).

[93] It could be added that the legal scholars in this strand of research, while advocating for strong sanctions, do not engage in the more empirical question of whether such sanctions have the capacity to actually bring about a positive change.

[94] L Pech and J Grogan, 'Unity and Diversity in National Understandings of the Rule of Law in the EU', RECONNECT, WP 1 D, April 2020, available at https://reconnect-europe.eu/wp-content/uploads/2020/05/D7.1-1.pdf;see also L Pech and J Grogan, 'Meaning and Scope of the EU Rule of Law', Reconnect, WP 7 D2, available at https://reconnect-europe.eu/wp-content/uploads/2020/05/D7.2-1.pdf.

[95] R Janse, 'Is the European Commission a credible guardian of the values? A revisionist account of the Copenhagen political criteria during the Big Bang Enlargement' (2019) 17 *I.CON* 43.

of Article 2 TEU as a fully 'operational' provision also feeds into the view that there are good reasons and sufficient legal basis for instituting proceedings against individual countries where the rule of law is being violated in a systematic and open manner, amounting to what Kochenov and others, with reference in particular to the developments in Hungary, call 'constitutional capture'.[96] Indeed, there is much persuasive force in the argument that the efficacy of generalised monitoring and reporting instruments, as advanced by the Commission, can be seriously doubted when rule of law infringements are the result not of misinterpretation or mistake, but of 'a calculated policy choice'.[97]

Other lawyers put their trust into the EU Court of Justice and see as the more promising approach the more piecemeal, case-by-case, careful monitoring and bringing before the Court of cases of specific infringements of EU law with rule of law repercussions.[98] As is well known, the CJEU has delivered a series of decisions concerning, in particular, judicial reform in Poland, prompting some commentators to observe that the Court, 'armed with Article 19 TEU', has 'emerged as the most robust critical interlocutor of the autocrats in Poland and Hungary'.[99]

Finally, the link between the rule of law and structural funds, also known as rule of law conditionality, advanced by Justice Commissioner Jurova in 2017 and more recently approved in a modified version after vigorous debates in the EU political process,[100] has gained both acclaim and criticism in the scholarly literature. Blauberger and Hüllen describe a trade-off between 'rule-based credibility and political flexibility'.[101] On the legal side, the authors consider the clarity and determinacy of the rule of law condition as wanting. Despite a more straightforward definition set out in the Commission Rule of Law framework launched in 2018 and in the Draft Regulation, other conditions such as 'systemic violations'

[96] See Pech and Scheppele (n 10) 39ff; cf Kochenov (n 52) 431.

[97] Kochenov (n 52) 430.

[98] ibid. On the role of the Court in ensuring the rule of law in the EU, see the reflections of the President of the Court, K Lenaerts, 'New Horizons for the Rule of Law Within the EU' (2020) 21 *German Law Journal* 29.

[99] Kochenov (n 52) 429. On this development, see the contribution by Perego in ch 13 of this volume.

[100] See Commission Communication on Strengthening the Rule of Law within the Union. A Blueprint for Action, COM(2019) Brussels, 17 July 2019; Commission Proposal for a Regulation of the European Parliament and of the Council on the Protection of the Union's Budget in case of Generalised Deficiencies as Regards the Rule of Law in the Member States, COM(2018) 324 Final, Brussels, 2 May 2018; European Parliament Legislative Resolution of 4 April 2019 on the Proposal for a Regulation of the European Parliament and of the Council on the Protection of the Union's Budget in case of Generalised Deficiencies as Regards the Rule of Law in the Member States, P8_TA-PROV(2019)0349, Brussels, 4 April 2019; European Court of Auditors, Opinion No 1/2018 Concerning the Proposal of 2 May 2018 for a Regulation of the European Parliament and of the Council on the Protection of the Union's Budget in case of Generalised Deficiencies as Regards the Rule of Law in the Member States [2020] OJ C291/1.

[101] M Blauberger and V van Hüllen, 'Conditionality of EU Funds: an instrument to enforce EU fundamental values?' (2021) 43 *Journal of European Integration* 1, 10.

or 'generalised deficiencies' have, in their view, remained underdeveloped.[102] Furthermore, as pointed out by the European Court of Auditors, there is a 'need to develop criteria that allow for a critical appreciation of the consistency in applying the provisions in view of ensuring equal treatment of Member States in cases of generalised deficiencies as regards rule of law, which puts sound financial management at risk'. Nevertheless, many commentators agree that at present this seems to be the most promising track, guaranteeing a combination of selective intervention in instances of clear breaches of the rule of law and credible sanctions.

At the same time, both political scientists and legal sociologists have pointed to the limitations of a purely legal and formalistic approach to the problem. The difficulty of enforcing the rule of law through formal legal procedures from outside becomes evident when we acknowledge that democratic backsliding is seldom reduced to infringement of constitutional rules or faulty institutional design, which can be rectified or repaired. As Sadurski describes the Polish case, 'Institutions and procedures remain the same, but their substance is radically changed by practice; they are "hollowed out".'[103]

In turn, many analysts draw attention to limitations of more political character. For one thing, the prospect of actively invoking the mechanism of Article 7 TEU appears bleak, to say the least, due to the raw reality of party politics and Member States' apparent unwillingness to use this ('nuclear') option due to general concerns about national sovereignty.[104] In addition, scholars stress the limited effectiveness of material sanctions against illiberal governments. Such governments' survival depends on maintaining their illiberal practices, and it is highly unlikely that they would yield to external pressure if they thereby risk losing their grip on power. What is worse, material sanctions may have the counterproductive effect of 'rallying around the flag' when populist leaders energise their supporters' nationalist loyalties in the face of external pressure.[105] Instead, more trust is placed in approaches that build on social pressure, such as the Commission Rule of Law framework.[106] However, for such 'soft' mechanisms to have any notable effects, the need for consistent application, formal and transparent process, and impartiality is highlighted.[107] Furthermore, measures taken must appear meaningful. Refusals to shake hands or take photos with ministers from certain countries, as during the Haider affair, are not likely to succeed.

[102] ibid 9. It should be noted that following an agreement between Council and the European Parliament in November 2020, the term 'generalised deficiencies' has been deleted from the title and from the final text of the Regulation. See Regulation (EU, Euratom) 2020/2092 of the European Parliament and of the Council of 16 December 2020 on a general regime of conditionality for the protection of the Union budget [2020] OJ L433I/1.

[103] Sadurski (n 29).

[104] U Sedelmeier, 'Political Safeguards against Democratic Backsliding in the EU: the limits of material sanctions and the scope of social pressure' (2017) 24 *Journal of European Public Policy* 337.

[105] ibid. Cf also the calls for setting up a Copenhagen Commission in J-W Müller, 'Should the EU Protect Democracy and the Rule of Law inside Member States?' (2015) 21 *European Law Journal* 141.

[106] Sedelmeier (n 104).

[107] ibid.

Misgivings of a different type are expressed with reference to the deeper causes for illiberal and populist trends, briefly touched upon in section III.B. Thus, scholars question the democratic legitimacy of enforcement of the rule of law that relies on formal legal frameworks but disregards deeply embedded elements of political and legal culture.[108] Acknowledging such limitations, alternative proposals for more deliberative, dialogical schemes, relying on monitoring and exchange of best practices and seeking to empower local civil society and democratic forces, are discussed both by EU institutions and academic commentators.[109]

Still, while a lasting change no doubt depends principally on internal political processes and on the empowering of democratic forces and civil society inside recalcitrant Member States, it is also true that the EU constitutes an exceptionally close-knit political community. As the EU Court of Justice has reminded us, it builds on mutual trust between its Member States to a much greater extent than other international organisations.[110] Or, to use the words of de Búrca, 'the conduct of any one State [in the Union] is of greater concern to all others than is generally true of the international community of States'. She also rightly points out that 'national sovereignty concerns over external intervention [should be] less stark and less compelling within the EU'.[111]

These alternative solutions, as well as the choice between – or the simultaneous use of – judicial and political instruments, are discussed in the volume by scholars and representatives of the European institutions. Obviously, these contributions will not be the last word on enforcement of the rule of law in the EU. However, we are convinced that it is essential that we lead an open debate about Europe's values and Europe's future, and that we do not shy away from controversial topics and difficult choices.

V. THE RULE OF LAW IN THE EU 30 YEARS AFTER THE FALL OF THE BERLIN WALL: FUNDAMENTALS, PROBLEMS AND PROSPECTS

Against the multifaceted background already sketched out, this volume seeks to take a holistic approach to the highly topical and contested theme of the

[108] P Blokker, 'Response to "Public law and populism"' (2019) 20 *German Law Journal* 284; see also P Blokker, 'Varieties of Populist Constitutionalism: The transnational dimension' (2019) 20 *German Law Journal* 332.

[109] See the parts on promotion of the rule of law in the Commission Rule of Law Framework of 2018 and Andreas Moberg's contribution in ch 15 of this volume.

[110] See CJEU, Opinion 2/13 of 18 December 2014, ECLI:EU:C:2014:2454, para 168: 'This legal structure is based on the fundamental premiss that each Member State shares with all the other Member States, and recognises that they share with it, a set of common values on which the EU is founded, as stated in Article 2 TEU. That premiss implies and justifies the existence of mutual trust between the Member States that those values will be recognised and, therefore, that the law of the EU that implements them will be respected.' Cf in this sense D Halberstam, '"It's the Autonomy, Stupid!" A Modest Defense of Opinion 2/13 on EU Accession to the ECHR, and the Way Forward' (2015) 16(1) *German Law Journal* 105, 131.

[111] de Búrca (n 6) 683.

state of the rule of law in the EU. The volume covers a broad ground: from general constitutional fundamentals, through the particularities of rule of law developments in the CEE Member States of the Union, including the legacies of the communist past and the impact of Europeanisation, to actual and potential rule of law limitations and flaws in other Member States, and finally to the mechanisms of rule of law monitoring and enforcement in the Union and its Member States. The volume presents a rich collection of contributions authored by legal scholars with diverse personal and professional backgrounds, but also by international civil servants working with rule of law issues in the European institutions. The chapters represent different theoretical and methodological perspectives, including constitutional theory, historical, comparative and interdisciplinary approaches. The volume is structured in the following four parts.

A. Part One – The Rule of Law in the European Union: Constitutional Fundamentals

The first part of the book sets out the theoretical foundations of the debate on the rule of law in the EU. The contributions in this part discuss the meaning of the fundamental constitutional law concepts comprising the rule of law, democracy and fundamental rights. These concepts are analysed individually and in their mutual relationship. The controversial notion of 'illiberal democracy' is also critically approached, establishing a link between the theoretical debate and the acute political reality of rule of law backsliding in some of the EU Member States from CEE, notably Hungary and Poland.

In chapter 2, Leonard Besselink sets himself the challenging task of disentangling the complex relationship between democracy and the rule of law. The author starts off by sharing a very personal memory from the events in East Germany in November 1989, when he incidentally became witness to the massive demonstrations in East Berlin, ultimately leading to *die Wende*, the turn to democracy. At the time of these dramatic events, somewhat worn out constitutional law concepts such as 'free elections', 'separation of powers' and 'free media' acquired very concrete and powerful political meaning, something that resonates with recent developments, where the same concepts have gained renewed relevance. Whereas legal scholars typically show greater interest in the more legalistic concept of the rule of law, the thrust of Besselink's contribution is to provoke stronger engagement of lawyers with the concept of democracy, despite the more political connotations of the latter term. The author argues convincingly that on many counts – such as separation of powers, fundamental rights, social and political rights, minority protection and the position of courts – legal scholars should critically reflect on the implications of the rule of law for contemporary democracy. Likewise, Besselink sees a need to constantly recalibrate our understanding of the two concepts and strive for a balance between them. Besselink concludes with a call addressed to legal scholars to dare to go beyond the safe confines of strictly legal analysis of rule of law issues into the more precarious normative questions of ethics and political morality, which are often missing in legal doctrine.

The subsequent chapter by Gábor Halmai (chapter 3) continues this challenging journey in the theoretical foundations of the constitutional concepts of the rule of law and democracy. In particular, Halmai grapples with the concept of 'illiberal democracy', as advanced by leading politicians and elaborated by legal and political science scholars in East Central Europe, and notably in Hungary and Poland. He tries to get to the core of the term, analysing it ideologically, philosophically, legally and politically. Here, arguments used by defenders of 'illiberal democracy' and/or 'illiberal constitutionalism', notably in Hungary and Poland, are given a thorough, critical and highly thought-provoking review.

Halmai demonstrates how court ideologists of populist autocrats misuse well-established political and constitutional theories, such as Max Weber's theory on leader democracy or Richard Bellamy's and others' ideas of political constitutionalism, to legitimise 'illiberal constitutionalism' in general and unchecked governance, the dismantling of constitutional review and non-compliance with European values, in particular. References to majoritarian (Westminster) system of governance and to national political identity are abusively invoked by these ideologists to the same end. Halmai's meticulous analysis lays bare the inconsistencies in such arguments and claims, showing ultimately that these attempts to legitimate 'illiberal constitutionalism' are best understood as attempts at hiding the authoritarian pursuits of rogue governments.

In the concluding chapter in this first part of the book (chapter 4), Joakim Nergelius, much in line with Halmai's analysis, contests the very idea that democracy within the area of the EU may ever be 'illiberal', thus partly answering Besselink's call for normative analysis of rule of law issues. Furthermore, Nergelius strongly regrets the lack of sanctions against EU Member States, within CEE or elsewhere, that do not respect the rule of law.

B. Part Two – The Rule of Law in CEE: Communist Legacies and the Road to EU Accession

The second part of the book directs the attention of the reader to legal and institutional legacies that can be identified as specific to the EU Member States from CEE, and that could be assumed to continue to influence the state of the rule of law in these countries after their accession to the EU and the Council of Europe. Given the central role of courts in upholding the rule of law, there is a focus on the judiciary in CEE, including judicial style and legal reasoning, the role of constitutional courts and the issue of judicial independence. Some of the contributions in this part tackle the question whether there are distinctive 'habits of the heart' and 'frames of mind' that characterise the Central and East

European judiciary, and which are at least partly shaped by the decades-long period of administration of justice under socialism.[112] The other theme in this part of the book is the role that the European institutions – Council of Europe, Venice Commission and the European Union – have played in shaping the legal framework of the rule of law in these countries and the domestic institutions tasked with enforcing the rule of law.

The first contribution in this part of the book (chapter 5) is by Zdenek Kühn, professor of Jurisprudence, but also judge at the Supreme Administrative Court of the Czech Republic. Building on his previous extensive work on the judiciary in CEE, he approaches the legacies of socialist constitutionalism and the equivocal role of courts in upholding the rule of law in the new EU Member States. Kühn argues that despite the differences in legal and institutional legacies between the CEE countries, one can discern a common authoritarian model of judicial process, which seems to prevail in the region. This model is characterised by viewing parties largely as passive objects in litigation, in contrast to their role as an important engine in applying law in Western Europe. Another common trait of an authoritarian model of judicial process is the practice of abstract interpretational statements issued by the collegium of supreme court judges, typically addressing incongruities in interpretation between different judicial chambers on important issues of law. This practice originates from the judicial system in the Soviet Union and is still common in many of the former countries of the CEE. Kühn describes the institute of abstract interpretation statements as 'legislating from the bench' without any real-life case pending before the courts. Despite all the comprehensive refurbishment of the judicial system of CEE countries in the period of transition and EU accession, these traits have retained a remarkable tenacity, which in Kühn's view impacts the self-perception of the judiciary and its capacity to step forward as an effective institution in the enforcement of the rule of law.

The other theme in Kühn's contribution is the gradual transformation of constitutional courts in the region. While these courts were the 'jewel in the crown' of post-communist democratic institution building, initially showing remarkable audacity in tackling constitutional conflicts on both the internal and the external planes, the gradual rule of law backsliding has led to a decline in judicial activism of constitutional courts in the region and, in Kühn's interpretation, to the return to the old tradition of a self-restrained judiciary.

In the next chapter (chapter 6), Katalin Kelemen addresses the question of whether there is a style of legal reasoning that is distinctive of the judiciary in CEE and that can still be identified today, taking a historical perspective. The author offers a thoughtful account of the different approaches to this rather controversial question in the legal and legal-sociological literature, showing the complexity of the issues and the importance of solid knowledge about deep

[112] On the phrase 'habits of the heart', see Elster et al (n 34) 18.

historical legacies and cross-country differences. While she elicits, with reference to historical and comparative legal scholarship, common traits of the judiciary formed in the early Stalinist and post-Stalinist periods of the communist regimes, she contends that these similarities do not have such long-lasting impact on CEE judicial style and reasoning. On the basis of a comprehensive review of the literature on the CEE judiciary, Kelemen takes the view that generalisations work poorly and are often ideologically motivated. Instead, the author calls for more empirically grounded comparative research, supported by solid data on judicial practice.

In the third chapter of this part of the book (chapter 7), Daniel Tarschys reflects on the role of the Council of Europe in the democratic transitions of the CEE countries and as an antechamber to the European Union. Concerning the rule of law in particular, Tarschys identifies six distinctive 'propagation' functions of the three 'great' international organisations, as he calls them – the Council of Europe, the OSCE and the EU – namely a "Cerberus" function, a deliberative function, a judicial function, imposing self-reporting obligations, a monitoring function and providing ad hoc support for reforms. Tarschys was Secretary General of the Council of Europe between 1994 and 1999, the time of the Big Bang expansion of the Council. His contribution should therefore be read as a personal testimony to the pioneering spirit of the 1990s and the efforts for building mutual trust between the East and West parts of a previously divided Continent on the basis of the values of democracy, the rule of law and human rights.

In the next chapter (chapter 8) Iain Cameron analyses the role of the Venice Commission, one of the signature institutions of the Council of Europe, in strengthening the rule of law in the CEE Member States of the EU. Being an expert member of the Commission himself, Cameron provides an initiated account of the operational principles of the Venice Commission and the procedural safeguards for the impartiality and high-quality expertise of its work. He also traces the Venice Commission's involvement in a number of high-profile cases where the opinion of the Commission was proffered on sensitive rule of law issues, notably in the two most prominent backsliding Member States Hungary and Poland, either at the request of these States, or at the request of the European institutions.

The chapter discusses critically the impact of the Commission's opinion and generally the situation of the rule of law, and in particular of the judiciary, in these countries. In conclusion, Cameron addresses the question of the alternative ways that are available for the EU in ensuring compliance with its fundamental values. He opines that while the Union must do what it can to defend its own democratic legitimacy, including exploring all avenues for combining dialogue with economic pressure, ultimately, the remedy for rule of law backsliding lies with the electorates of recalcitrant states. Therefore, he sees the way forward in continued dialogue, in which the Venice Commission has an important role.

In the fifth and final chapter in this part (chapter 9), Antonina Bakardjieva Engelbrekt revisits the link between the Eastward Enlargement and rule of law policy of the EU. She looks back at the process of rule of law assessment of the candidate countries as part of pre-accession conditionality. The chapter describes the precarious position of the Commission in a domain where previously there had been hardly any legislatively set requirements in the EU, making the Commission approach inevitably one of 'learning by doing'.

On the positive side, accession conditionality has spurred the candidate states to take rapid steps in the required direction of reinforcing the institutional framework of the rule of law. On the negative side, the vague and indeterminate content of the rule of law concept and its sometimes-inconsistent interpretation and application vis-à-vis individual candidate states may have contributed to wearing away the already weak respect for the rule of law in the region. The outcome, in particular in the sphere of judicial independence, has often been more visible in setting up formal institutions, such as Judicial Councils, but less palpable at the level of true reform and changes of institutionalised practice and mindset. The potential implications of the 'unfinished business' of judicial reform and of governance by conditionality for the current backsliding and rule of law deterioration in the region are critically discussed. Importantly, however, Enlargement has speeded up the Union's own advancement in this area, working as a driving force and testbed of EU's rule of law policy.

C. Part Three – The Rule of Law in an Enlarged Europe

The third part of the book takes a broader approach and looks at rule of law challenges in other Member States and regions of the Union. The contributions in this part provide on the one hand some examples of potentially volatile rule of law conflicts in Member States with longer legacies of democratic institutions, but where populist movements have gained access to political power. On the other hand, and more hypothetically, they discuss rule of law vulnerabilities and 'soft spots' in countries that are generally perceived as having robust rule of law traditions and an impeccable record of rule of law compliance. While Italy, with a number of alarming examples of rule of law-related problems or even violations, as discussed in the thought-provoking contribution of Valentina Colcelli, belongs to the former category, the Nordic countries that are the subject of Graham Butler's contribution belong to the latter.

In her chapter (chapter 10), Colcelli tells a troublesome story about recurrent attempts by populist political forces that had temporarily become part of the ruling coalition in Italy, to use the administrative structures of the state and local government for limiting free speech close to political elections. Such attempts were successfully curbed by the courts in the course of ensuing judicial proceedings, and the populist party, the Lega, subsequently lost its political influence. Nevertheless, these incidents demonstrate the propensity of populist regimes to seek to perpetuate their grip on political power. Colcelli reflects on the lessons that can be drawn from such developments, including for the relationship between the Member States and the Union, especially in the context of a global pandemic crisis. She sees the only way forward to be in strengthening the political role of the Union and its authority in setting common standards for democracy and the rule of law also in the Member States.

In his contribution (chapter 11), Graham Butler addresses the Nordic states that are typically regarded as unproblematic, and even exemplary, in their adherence to rule of law standards. However, Butler raises a warning flag in his contribution, providing a number of illustrations of potential deficiencies and vulnerabilities in respect of the rule of law and the protection of fundamental rights, in particular concerning the principles of the separation of powers, protection of individual rights and the role of the courts. While these examples, alarming as they may sound, still constitute only potential concerns, some examples from 2020 pointing in the same direction could actually be given in the context of coping with the Covid-19 crisis, during which fundamental rights were in fact limited surprisingly easily in some of the Nordic countries. The chapter seeks to demonstrate that rule of law challenges can occur anywhere – the Nordic states included – which prompts the author to conclude, on a similar note to Colcelli, that EU law will play a vital role in ensuring that the rule of law is maintained well into the future.

D. Part Four – Enforcing the Rule of Law in the EU: Current Mechanisms and Prospects

Finally, the fourth part of the book focuses on the very timely concern of finding the appropriate tools for enforcing the rule of law in the EU and its Member States. Although more than four decades of European Community cooperation passed before the EU found itself in want of an appropriate mechanism to handle a threat to its fundamental founding values,[113] the ensuing two decades, and the last of these in particular, have highlighted the need for effective protective mechanisms.

The four chapters that make up this part of the book describe and discuss a number of avenues available to the EU institutions in their effort to promote, preserve and enforce the rule of law. Some of these measures are based on age-old

[113] The so-called Haider affair caused the 14 EU Member State governments to react strongly in unison, outside of the legal framework of the EU Treaty, to the formation of a coalition government in Austria following the general elections in 1999. The Conservative Party (ÖVP) formed a government with the right-wing populist Freedom Party (FPÖ), which by general consensus was considered xenophobic and by some even anti-democratic. Cf P Cramér and P Wrange, 'The Haider Affair, Law and European Integration' [2001] *ERT* 1, 46. See also W Sadurski, 'Adding Bite to a Bark. The Story of Article 7, the EU and the Haider Affair' (2010) 16 *Columbia Journal of European Law* 385.

legal principles, while others are new-born mechanisms created for the specific purpose of enhancing respect for the rule of law. Some of the measures covered are not yet adopted and others are almost forgotten.

In the first chapter of the final part of the book (chapter 12), Xavier Groussot and Anna Zemskova revisit the procedural rule of law through the concepts of *effet utile*, effectiveness and effective judicial protection. Highlighted in recent years by the Court of Justice through an emphasis on Article 19 TEU and Article 47 of the Charter of Fundamental Rights of the European Union, the procedural rule of law has become one of the most effective mechanisms to counter rule of law backsliding. Groussot and Zemskova trace the historical foundations of the procedural rule of law and highlight the inherent normative contradiction that may erupt whenever an aspect of the EU procedural rule of law comes into conflict with national standards of legal review. However, even though the procedural rule of law is an effective measure to counter rule of law backsliding, judicial review of national measures remains a hot topic amongst the Member States, a fact exemplified by the infamous *Weiss* case from the German Federal Constitutional Court.

In the second chapter of this part of the volume (chapter 13), Anna Perego gives an overview of how the Commission works with the measures available to safeguard the rule of law in the EU. The chapter gives a thorough account of how recent events in several EU Member States have meant that the principle of the rule of law has become one of the central principles guiding the Commission's work. Perego combines the historical context with an account of how the ideological aspect of the principle has been developed, first and foremost through the interpretations advanced in the case law of the Court of Justice, but several other examples of how the principle of the rule of law has developed over the years are provided in the chapter. The two contexts form an important backdrop as Perego describes and discusses the Commission's current, and future, rule of law policy.

In the next chapter (chapter 14), Linda Stefani and María José Martínez Iglesias follow Perego's chapter, focused on the Commission's perspective, with a contribution devoted to the European Parliament's role in the safeguarding of the rule of law. The chapter starts with an analysis of the European Parliament's conception of the principle of the rule of law, based on the EU treaties and the Parliament's own interpretation. This section is followed by an analysis of how the Parliament has implemented its perception of rule of law protection through its actions and initiatives, as well as how its actions have contributed to the formation of the Parliament's rule of law policy. The chapter then concludes with a comprehensive account of how the Parliament has made use of its mandate, experience and normative power in the Article 7 TEU procedure initiated against Hungary.

Finally, in the last chapter of the volume (chapter 15), Andreas Moberg makes the argument that while a lot is expected from the EU in terms of results, the design of the tools available for enforcing the rule of law is under-theorised.

Thus, the expectations of what the EU may achieve in terms of rule of law protection may in fact be unrealistic, notwithstanding the fact that the EU's ambitions in the field may be very high indeed. Moberg uses compliance theory to discuss and analyse the measures available to the Commission, as described in the Commission's own 'Blueprint for Action'.[114] The chapter concludes that several of the measures available may well be effective against rule of law backsliding, while the only feasible option to deal with rejection of the rule of law is Article 258 TFEU.

***

This volume was inspired by a desire to commemorate a seminal anniversary from one of the most important instances (or probably the most important instance) of historical change in the lifetime of the editors and of many of the contributors to the book. The Fall of the Berlin Wall in November 1989 came suddenly and was predicted by few. Although it was induced and followed by what became known as 'velvet' revolutions across the CEE countries, it is also widely acknowledged that these revolutions were not the decisive factor for the demise of the communist regime. The old order collapsed largely by 'self-liquidation',[115] under the weight of its own dysfunctionality. The ease and the bloodlessness of this collapse was naturally a source of relief and a reason for celebration. However, at least for some of the citizens of the former Soviet bloc, there remained an awkward lingering feeling. If the harsh and seemingly invincible communist regimes fell apart so painlessly, could the change have come about earlier? And was at least part of the repressive regime's prolonged existence to be ascribed to sheer complacency?

On 9 November 2019, 30 years after the collapse of communism and the end of the East–West divide, fireworks filled the sky over Berlin. The heads of state of Germany, Hungary, Poland, the Czech Republic and Slovakia symbolically laid flowers at the remains of the Wall, paying respect to the victims of totalitarianism and celebrating the new era of democracy, unity, economic prosperity, and respect for the rule of law and fundamental rights following the events of 1989. Sadly, however, the solemnity of the moment could not hide the cracks that had appeared in the common vision for Europe made possible by 1989. The celebratory tone of the anniversary ceremony has been eclipsed by a common awareness that in some of the countries once at the forefront of democratic transition in CEE, illiberal values are in vogue, while respect for the rule of law and other shared European commitments is in decline.

[114] Communication from the Commission to the European Parliament, the European Council, the Council, the European Economic and Social Committee and the Committee of the Regions on Strengthening the rule of law within the Union. A Blueprint for Action, COM(2019) 343, 17 July 2019.

[115] Elster et al (n 34).

To be sure, there is no easy way for the EU to address such developments and to intervene in political choices made by sovereign national governments. At the same time, the mutual trust on which the Union builds cannot function as a foundation for the common European project unless each Member State of the Union can depend on other Members' respect for commonly agreed commitments and values. In the area of the Internal Market, it is succinctly observed that the principle of mutual recognition rests not on blind but on binding trust, which requires common standards, monitoring and engagement in one another's affairs.[116] It is high time for Member State governments to accept that weaving such binding trust is also imperative in the more sensitive political domain of democracy and the rule of law. As this volume demonstrates, the mechanisms for enforcing common standards and for organising mutual engagement in the area of rule of law can take many different shapes. What is important, however, is not to allow complacency to creep in and settle, once more, in the CEE, as well as in the other EU Member States.

[116] K Nicolaïdis, 'Trusting the Poles? Constructing Europe through Mutual Recognition' (2007) 14 *Journal of European Public Policy* 682.

Part One

The Rule of Law in the European Union: Theoretical Foundations and Political Reality

2

Rule of Law Problems as Problems of Democracy

LEONARD BESSELINK

WHEN TALKING ABOUT principles, constitutional lawyers usually hover somewhere between stating the obvious and being apodictic. So do I in this chapter. I feel somewhat consoled with the memory of the placards carried during that great demonstration in East Berlin on Saturday, 4 November 1989, which I feel privileged to have witnessed in person. It was after an academic conference organised by the constitutional law section of the University of Amsterdam together with the then Karl-Marx-Universität in Leipzig, under the title *Menschenrechte in unserer Zeit* (Human Rights in our Time), which took place in Leipzig in the very last week of October.[1] The title had already been suggested by Amsterdam in 1988, when it could not be guessed how appropriate and timely it would be a year later. We stayed over with three Amsterdam colleagues for the weekend in East Berlin. The impressive and massive procession of people passed our hotel, inviting us to walk with them, with many placards, among which:

Freie Presse! Free Press!

Gewaltenteilung! Separation of Powers!

Freie Wahlen! Free Elections!

These and other traditional constitutional concepts, which were by then in the West considered somewhat shallow and worn-out concepts that stood in need of replacement with others, were used to justify *die Wende*, the turn towards democracy. It gave pause for reflection on the merits such classic notions evidently seemed to have in such revolutionary circumstances.

[1] The papers were published as an edited volume, K Bönninger, I Wagner and G van Wissen (eds), *Menschenrechte in unserer Zeit* (Arnhem, Gouda Quint; Deventer, Kluwer, 1990). On the cover, there is also a series title: Wissenschaftliche Serie Universität von Amsterdam juristische Fakultät, Karl-Marx-Universität Leipzig Sektion Rechtswissenschaft. The volume contains contributions to the 17th Leipziger Rechtstheorie-Konferenzen, under the theme 'Menschenrechte (Grundrechte) und subjektives Recht in unserer Zeit' (Leipzig, 1989).

When we discuss the rule of law 30 years after the Fall of the Wall, we do so in light of developments we witness in Member States of the European Union (EU) like Hungary and Poland. The EU approach to these has been framed in terms of 'the rule of law'. In this short essay, I start from the premise that the rule of law as a frame of reference is too limited.[2] European lawyers, no less than other lawyers, tend to have a strong affinity with the legal approach that is implicit in the notion of the rule of law. The strong legal drive of European integration may explain why the rule of law has been picked out from the various founding principles of the Union (Article 2 TEU). Democracy is easily considered a thing for political scientists. However, in my view, staying in the comfort zone of the rule of law only fails to grasp the kind of problem we are facing. Law is not going to stop the facts. Law is not going to prevent revolutions, nor are constitutions going to prevent 'constitutional backsliding' or 'constitutional capture'. What we must fear these days in Europe is that law is no longer democratically legitimate in the way it was sought for in those days in November in Berlin. I emphasise that it is not only developments in Poland and Hungary, nor only in the Central and East European Member States, that cause concern, but also those in the older Member States that have not yet gone as far down the road to authoritarianism as others. There is a need to focus on what such developments mean for *democracy* in states under the rule of law. Democracy may be more difficult to grasp for us lawyers, but avoiding it risks remaining irrelevant.

I. OXYMORON OR PLEONASM?

When speaking of democracy and the rule of law, the classic question arises whether expressions that combine the two, such as *demokratisk rättsstat*, *demokratischer Rechtsstaat*, *État de droit démocratique*, *demokratikus jogállamiság* and *demokratycznego państwo prawa*, form a pleonasm or an oxymoron. We should not take this question for granted. My starting-point on this, and I return to it in the conclusion, is that if it is a pleonasm, democracy would seem to be redundant; and that if it is an oxymoron, democracy and the rule of law would seem to be antagonistic and basically incompatible. Both are undesirable states of affairs.

So how do the terms relate? In order to assess this, I briefly go through some minimum characteristics of the rule of law and try to relate them to democracy. I take four of those minimum characteristics to do so: the principle of legality; fundamental rights; the separation of powers; and judicial protection.

[2] For an earlier discussion, see L Besselink, 'Talking about European Democracy' (2017) 13 *European Constitutional Law Review* 207.

II. LEGALITY

Legality, in the traditional French Revolutionary interpretation dominant on the Continent, protects citizens' liberty:[3] citizens are free to do what they prefer unless the law prohibits it; but public authorities are not free to act, they do not have the power to act unless that power has a basis in parliamentary legislation or the constitution. This requirement for a legislative basis in principle ensures a democratic anchoring of legislation that affects citizens, in as much as the legislature that empowers public authorities is composed of representatives of the people. Legislation empowers public authorities to act in the general interest and is supported by legislative majorities. Viewed thus, legality may be the least problematic of the rule of law requirements. The rule of law and democracy coincide in a felicitous manner.

But this is the case only when the representative claim is made plausibly. This claim can formally be considered valid as long as the legislation we are talking about is parliamentary legislation. However, we see today that the executive – which in parliamentary systems derives its constitutional legitimacy from either not being censored or being actively supported by parliamentary majorities – also claims a mandate from the people in a more direct manner. The 'government of the day' now appeals to the people also, or particularly, when this is in the context of fluctuating parliamentary majorities in fragmented parliaments. Governmental leaders occasionally claim power even when it is not granted by a parliamentary majority, and justify it as the caretaker and even true representative of the people – it is the silence of the people that in the 1970s' political jargon was turned into 'the silent majority'. The Coronavirus emergency and similar moments framed as 'crises' that ask for 'critical' decision making, provide examples in various Member States.

In the EU itself, legality is ensured under the principle of conferral (Article 5 TEU). This principle, as transpires from the language of Article 5, is embedded in a federal notion of division of competences rather than the democratic notion of legality. Nevertheless, since the European Parliament has been elected directly, and nearly all EU legislation needs its cooperation, the representational claim of the Parliament is constitutionally similar to that of national parliaments in the EU. The main difference is in the curious semi-parliamentary structure of governance in the EU, which can be said to be parliamentary in relation to the Commission but not in relation to the Council (and European Council). This makes the Union constitutionally an in-between zone between a democracy and demoï-cracy,[4] in which competing claims as to democratic legitimacy are further

[3] The Revolutionaries and Napoleon never crossed the Channel, and one of the consequences is that the British and common law understanding of the principle of legality is rather different from that on the Continent.

[4] Critical about such an in-between zone, see K Nicolaïdis and R Howse, 'This is my EU-topia: narrative as power' (2002) 40 *Journal of Common Market Studies* 767; also K Nicolaïdis, 'The new constitution as European "demoi-cracy?"' (2004) 7 *Critical Review of International Social*

complicated by the overall relatively low turnout at European Parliament elections. This provides ample scope for the Council and European Council, and their members taken together, to claim to represent the citizens in the EU decision making.

Another shift towards the executive is the change in substance of parliamentary legislation. In modern welfare states, legislation has turned into a set of framework acts, initiated by the executive itself, that have gained parliamentary approval but which delegate the setting of the actual concrete rules to the executive. In that way the executive has to both enact and apply the rules in practice. Delegation of legislative power is one thing, granting discretion another. This discretion is not only discretion to execute in the literal sense but also to legislate, thus turning the executive into an actual legislature itself. So-called 'Henry VIII clauses', under which the executive can override, withdraw or disapply parliamentary legislation, keep popping up in many different contexts, usually – but not only – in complex legal and legislative situations such as Brexit, and more generally in the implementation of international and European decisions.[5] We see such things happening also in various other contexts, and again crisis situations are a case in point. The climate crisis is one of them. The European Parliament has declared 'a climate and environment emergency', piously hypothesising that 'no emergency should ever be used to erode democratic institutions or to undermine fundamental rights [and] all measures will always be adopted through a democratic process'.[6] Many crises and emergencies, when not prepared for and (potentially) severely and negatively affecting large parts of the population, may indeed provide a temporary justification for measures that would not ordinarily be taken in that fashion; this at any rate is the assumption: the people as such is unable to act, parliaments are undecisive and uninformed talk shops, executives are the ones that have the expertise or can hire it effectively, act upon it, take decisions and enforce them – just what is needed in an emergency. But unfortunately, most emergencies lead to at least some measures that well outlast the duration of the actual emergency. It is unlikely that this will be any different in the climate and Coronavirus emergencies from, let us say, the 9/11 counter-terrorism or the banking and Euro crises.

In short, legality operates in function of democracy as long as the locus of democratic legitimacy is clear not only constitutionally, but also in institutional practice. And in a variety of circumstances this becomes obfuscated and legality becomes more tenuously related to democracy.

and Political Philosophy 76, 83. See also the work of Bellamy in its latest version in R Bellamy, *A Republican Europe of States: Cosmopolitanism, Intergovernmentalism and Democracy in the EU* (Cambridge, Cambridge University Press, 2019).

[5] On the UK, where the expression 'Henry VIII clause' originates, see N Barber and A Young, 'The rise of prospective Henry VIII clauses and their implications for sovereignty' [2003] *Public Law* 112. On the British case law's partial acceptance, see, amongst others, C Forsyth and E Kong, 'The Constitution and Prospective Henry VIII Clauses' (2004) 9 *Judicial Review* 17.

[6] European Parliament resolution of 28 November 2019 on the climate and environment emergency (2019/2930(RSP)). The pious hypothesis is under point C of the preamble.

III. FUNDAMENTAL RIGHTS

In the 'long nineteenth century' in Europe, constitutional law was mainly about government and democracy. In the latter half of the twentieth century it shifted towards constitutional rights understood as individual rights. Clearly, a number of individual fundamental rights are in the service of democracy, such as the freedoms of expression and association. But rights have more and more become understood as purely individual rights and freedoms. Such rights, for example the right to privacy, stand in no other relation to the democratic political order than in terms of a zero-sum calculus between individual rights and the general interest. In Europe, even the freedom of religion – historically mainly understood as a matter of group rights and hence politically highly significant – is now conceived of in such terms.

The focus on the individual has driven minority rights to the margin of the fundamental rights discourse. Its relation to democracy has been tenuous. Democracy is often viewed as a corrective mechanism, in the sense that it should be premised on the possibility of political change: today's majority may be tomorrow's minority, and today's minority may be tomorrow's majority.

The virtue of this view is that it basically requires a dynamic openness. This is in a sense a requirement of an ethical openness, but with a political edge. Everyone needs to be able to participate on equal basis, and engage – in principle – on the basis of whatever political views.

More problematic about viewing democracy and democratic rights in terms of shifting majorities is the fact that permanent minorities exist, that is, certain groups that are unlikely ever to become a majority. We might typically think of cultural minorities, or minorities that define themselves territorially. These also need rights guarantees, including of their democratic rights. This may force us to think of representation not merely in terms of arithmetic equality. Democracy in the situation of diversity in representation may need to be approached in a way that moderates arithmetic proportionality. In the EU context, we might think of digressive proportionality in the composition of the European Parliament for the sake of ensuring politically diverse representation of smaller Member States.

Without necessarily thinking of such moderations or modifications of arithmetic representation, in Member States we may need also to think of minorities other than the cultural groups we mentioned, and need to take more seriously into consideration the fact that what were the poor masses in nineteenth-century industrialising economies, are now indeed minorities of often quasi-permanently economically, financially and socially disadvantaged persons. It is by now generally received knowledge that such economic marginalisation has, for instance, pernicious consequences for the health of these marginalised groups. This has led to the formulation of a set of Ten Tips for Better Health by the British Chief Medical Officer, as shown in Table 2.1 alongside the Alternative Tips of the Townsend Centre for

International Poverty Research at Bristol University.[7] The first of the Alternative Tips is 'Don't be poor. If you are poor, try not to be poor for too long'; the second might very well have been 'Don't have poor parents', because that will surely extend the time you are poor. The American dream may no longer apply in America, but it does not really apply in Europe either; 'born as a dime that never becomes a dollar' still exists. Transgenerational poverty and social marginalisation may have been more entrenched than is recognised, precisely because we are no longer dealing with the poor masses but with what are now relative minorities.

In the fundamental rights discourse, social rights are often not taken for what they are intended to be. Lawyers especially still systematically discuss them in terms of issues of justiciability, most often reducing their meaning to those of individual rights. By doing so, social rights have effectively become understood

Table 2.1 Ten Alternative Tips for Better Health

	The Chief Medical Officer's Ten Tips for Better Health	**Alternative Tips**
1	Don't smoke. If you can, stop. If you can't, cut down.	Don't be poor. If you are poor, try not to be poor for too long.
2	Follow a balanced diet with plenty of fruit and vegetables.	Don't live in a deprived area. If you do, move.
3	Keep physically active.	Don't be disabled or have a disabled child.
4	Manage stress by, for example, talking things through and making time to relax.	Don't work in a stressful low-paid manual job.
5	If you drink alcohol, do so in moderation.	Don't live in damp, low quality housing or be homeless.
6	Cover up in the sun, and protect children from sunburn.	Be able to afford to pay for social activities and annual holidays.
7	Practise safer sex.	Don't be a lone parent.
8	Take up cancer screening opportunities.	Claim all benefits to which you are entitled.
9	Be safe on the roads: follow the Highway Code.	Be able to afford to own a car.
10	Learn the First Aid ABC: airways, breathing and circulation.	Use education as an opportunity to improve your socio-economic position.
	Source: DoH (1999) Saving Lives: Our Healthier Nation. London: The Stationery Office	*Source*: Townsend Centre for International Poverty Research, University of Bristol

[7] Available at www.bristol.ac.uk/poverty/healthinequalities.html.

as non-discrimination rights, or have become reduced to other individual rights, such as the right to health morphing into the right to life, and the right to work or to adequate social subsistence rights becoming the right to property. In this manner, lawyers have contributed to eventually depriving social rights of their very nature as *social* rights.

This fitted neatly into what now goes under the general label of 'neo-liberalism', the legacy of Margaret Thatcher to Continental Europe, whose political programme was initially despised but gradually embraced, crucially also by social-democratic and Christian-democratic parties.

Human rights discourse in Europe has in the main overlooked that social rights are in function of and crucial to achieving social goods. Social rights essentially concern distributive justice. That requires democratic decision making, as it is liable to contestation in circumstances of scarcity. If legal discourse is to have an impact on the current populist wave we witness in all Member States, it will have to take social rights seriously, not as individual rights but as social rights. And it is far from obvious why that would detract from their character as legal rights, that is, not 'legal' in the British sense of 'law' as identical to 'enforceable in a court of law', but as legally binding duties on the part of public authorities to realise and respect the social goods they aim at within the polity.

IV. THE SEPARATION OF POWERS

The idea of the separation of powers seems perhaps the most difficult principle to reconcile with ideas of democracy, which after all unavoidably hinge on decision making by majority. When the ultimate legislative power is supposed to reside in the people or its elected representatives, the inference is that the legislature should hold primacy over the other powers that exercise authority within the state.

Let us here concentrate on the political powers of the legislature and the executive. These have become more merged than separated in parliamentary systems of government, precisely because the executive's mandate is democratically legitimated through parliament.[8] The mechanics of democratic legitimation from the people to the actual wielders of power, whether one views this metaphorically as the chain-belt or as the plumbing of democratic legitimacy, seem to be in order. In this respect, parliaments and executives are no longer the mutually countervailing powers they were viewed to be in the nineteenth century. They are the very expression of the dominance of democracy.

[8] When, as in France, the other head of the executive, the President, who has ways of interfering with the government that is under control of the parliament, does so because he has a direct mandate from the electorate.

In practice, of course, we have a not-so-mechanical reality in which one has to concede that executives in all the Member States dominate the legislatures, if not formally then materially – that at least is the case in situations where the executive enjoys actual majority support. In a situation of more and more fragmented parliaments, there are situations in which ideologically coherent executives can get things done their way precisely because parliament is fragmented. But the opposite also occurs: the executive cannot have things their way because they fail to acquire support for a certain course of action. Brexit in the parliament under Theresa May provided many examples of the latter. Interestingly, the British electorate did not like the spectacle and, after a number of 'hung' or 'nearly hung parliaments', finally managed to elect a parliament with a clear majority. Many found the situation under May not a good thing for democratic government. Even if not necessarily sharing the political views of the Johnson Government, many found that, whoever has the majority, majoritarian government leads to better functioning of democratic government.

The desirability of majoritarian arrangements or of systems with a more broadly spread form of representation remains the object of distinct differences between Member States, as is reflected in the variety of their electoral systems. The EU's institutions reflect a penchant for broad representation. The European Parliament has an electoral system of modified proportional representation, which is enhanced in order to guarantee the ability of the smallest Member States to be represented too ('degressive proportionality', Article 14(2) TEU). The Council has a voting system of in principle broad representation, modified in order to enhance the ability to act (the ordinary majority voting rule requiring 15 out of 27 Member States (55 per cent), but also 65 per cent of the population, with the aim of increasing the weighting of the vote by size of Member State (Article 16(4) TEU)). There is, moreover, still a practice of voting by consensus[9] whenever practicable, although there is some evidence of more majority voting.[10] So broad representation, giving a say to as many participants as possible, is institutionally the norm – with the corollary that often decisions cannot actually be made or made easily.

So what, then, is the rationale for spreading the exercise of power, for dividing powers and institutionally translating that also into separating them over different actors or institutions? For that purpose, we must turn to the origins of its introduction into European constitutional thought.

[9] Contrary to what is sometimes thought, nowadays a vote is always taken in the Council, even in cases of consensus (see the Comments on the Council's Rules of Procedure, available at www.consilium.europa.eu/en/documents-publications/publications/council-rules-procedure-comments/#, March 2016, at 53), though a vote only takes place when there is the certainty that it will pass (there are no cases of a proposal's being rejected in the Council).

[10] See L Besselink, K Swider and B Michel, 'The impact of the UK's withdrawal on the institutional set-up and political dynamics within the EU' (2019), Research paper requested by the European Parliament's Policy Department for Citizens' Rights and Constitutional Affairs at the request of the AFCO Committee, 16–18.

The idea of separating the exercise of powers over various public authorities, though not novel, took hold in eighteenth-century writings with the rationale of avoiding despotism. It was canonised in the French Revolution, forming part of such documents as the *Déclaration des droits de l'homme et du citoyen.*[11] Around that time, the archetype of the despot was the fearsome Easterly, Persian, in particular Ottoman or Turkish, prince, probably enhanced by the experience and memory of the Second Siege of Vienna of 1683. The problem with the despots was that they considered everything their property, to dispose of at their discretion. Their power is δεσποτεία, despotism, the power over persons and things they regard as theirs. Separation of powers was thought of as an antidote against such an accumulation of power, against δεσποτεία, which was viewed as the cause of maladministration of the polity.[12] In the eighteenth century this was taken to imply that to protect civil liberty, a division of powers was necessary.

This in fact is still prevailing as the very notion of liberty in a democracy under the rule of law. It is hardly a coincidence that those leaders who have difficulty with having to share the exercise of public powers, with division and separation of powers over various actors and institutions, are the same leaders who have a problem with things liberal. Is it a coincidence that in its extreme form they claim to strive for an 'illiberal democracy'? Is it a coincidence that these are the same leaders who do away with division of power in the traditional understanding? Is it a coincidence that they happen to have as their ultimate programme to accrue as much power as possible in few or even one pair of hands, considering 'countervailing powers' as a diminution of their elective title? Despotism is a threat to liberty. It is a threat to democracy as well, by pushing out and stymieing other voices. It undermines the openness required for democracy under the rule of law, and required for attaining the common good.

V. JUDICIAL PROTECTION

Concerns about the rule of law focus strongly on the position of the judiciary in some of the EU Member States – the judiciary, which in parliamentary systems is the most separate branch of government in the classic understanding of the *trias politica*. Despots dislike courts' and judges' independence. They actually dislike any independence in the judicial system, including independence of the public prosecution. That is why they like to have a firm grip over who is prosecutor general and other prosecutors and investigators. We have seen moves in

[11] Art 16, 'Toute Société dans laquelle la garantie des Droits n'est pas assurée, ni la séparation des Pouvoirs déterminée, n'a point de Constitution.'

[12] A classic place is the third book of Plato's *The Laws*, where it is said of the Persian Empire that 'its present evil administration is due to excess of slavery and of despotism' (Plato, *The Laws*, 698a) (the number refers to the so-called Stephanus pages, which has been the standard reference in all critical editions since the end of the 16th century).

that direction in the USA recently[13] and in Ukraine with every change of regime over the last decades,[14] and unfortunately it is also an issue in some of the EU Member States.

The annoyance with the independence of the judicial machinery that frustrates power-seeking elected despots, logically tempts them into 'normalising' the courts, filling them with politically friendly judges in order to make them work in function of the power holders' claim to have authority because the people wants them to have that authority.[15]

Having said that, we cannot be naive enough to deny that indeed the judiciary is a branch of government, one of the powers of the *trias politica*. It is indeed exercising public authority, in the classical sense of *political* authority. This requires us to assess the democratic nature of the judiciary's role and activity, a calibration of its democratic role in a state under the rule of law.

The democratic legitimacy of courts is determined by the democratic nature of their mandate. That mandate is substantively determined by the democratic nature of the law that grants them their powers: constitutional law, parliamentary acts, and possibly delegated acts and rules established by judicial self-government. Also substantively, the democratic nature of their mandate is determined by the democratic nature of the law that they have to interpret and apply.

Functionally, judges tend, to a very large extent, to understand their role and *habitus* to be to provide judicial protection of citizens against other citizens and, in relevant cases, against public authorities. This typically turns them into a counter-majoritarian institution. I would argue that in a non-pathological, that is an overall well-ordered and reasonably well-functioning, democratic state

[13] Beginning with Donald J Trump's complaint on 2 November 2017 (less than a year in office) about the independence of the Justice Department: 'The saddest thing is that because I'm the President of the United States I'm not supposed to be involved with the Justice Department, I'm not supposed to be involved with the FBI, I'm not supposed to be doing the kinds of things I would love to be doing and I'm very frustrated by it. I look at what's happening with the Justice Department, why aren't they going after Hillary Clinton with her emails and with the dossier and the kind of money … ?' Larry O'Connor Radio show, transcripts at http://edition.cnn.com/TRANSCRIPTS/1711/05/ip.01.html; for further context of his tweets along the same lines, see at www.redstate.com/streiff/2017/11/03/donald-trump-not-happy-justice-department-neither/. President Trump turned the somewhat convoluted constitutional doctrine of a strongly unitary executive (see, eg, L Lessig and CR Sunstein, 'The President and the Administration' (1994) 94 *Columbia Law Review* 1), into a diatribe for easy consumption, which asserts 'I have an Article II [of the Constitution] where I have the right to do whatever I want as a President'; for a compilation of him making these assertions in the context of investigative powers of the Justice Department and the public prosecution, see at https://youtu.be/sl_gO3uOds8. In the context of his powers over State governors, the claim is that '[w]hen somebody is president of the United States, the authority is total' (13 April 2020), see at www.youtube.com/watch?v=r3QXrQDTDYo.

[14] See T Kuzio, 'Ukraine: Democratization, Corruption, and the New Russian Imperialism' (2015) 53(5) *Praeger Security International* 327 *et passim*.

[15] At the time of writing we saw the totally politicised effects of that claim in the wrangling over the succession of Justice Ruth Bader Ginsburg, where the appointment had even become an electoral campaign issue of prime importance. Political appointments to the judiciary have a long history in the USA that goes back to the early decades of the skirmishes after President Adams, the Federalist, was defeated in the presidential elections and appointed the 'midnight judges' during the last weeks

under the rule of law, this makes it necessary to respect limits to judicial activism, for the sake of retaining the democratic character of the state.

In this context, I would argue there is a difference between a counter-majoritarian court and a (quasi-)legislative court. I am fully aware of the nuances in practice, and of the various pros and cons; but still there is merit in the distinction between a court that disapplies legislation ('negative legislation') because of its (more or less evident) conflict with a superior norm, and a court that issues injunctions telling the legislature what to do ('positive legislation'). The latter occurs not only when courts formally exercise the power to give injunctions ordering certain legislation to be passed; it also can occur when a court engages in 'consistent interpretation', that is an interpretation of legislation, whether a constitutional one or an EU or international norm, in such a manner that the legislation becomes in accordance with the superior norm. This may end up in courts' determining the manner in which the legislation that is being reviewed has to be applied in practice, which may be an application of the norm that was not evidently the one intended by the legislature.[16]

If we look at the case law of constitutional courts in the EU Member States, it would appear that in most instances they operate in a manner that respects and even legitimises the constitutional nature of the legislation, in so far as these courts – as far as I am aware – mostly reject claims of unconstitutionality. Hence, to the extent that that legislation has been democratically adopted, that case law legitimates and reinforces the democratic quality of the legislation. Also, there are constitutional court judgments that actually favour and reinforce the role of parliaments as against the powers of executives. Probably something similar could be traced in at least some of the case law of the Court of Justice of the EU – although here the difficulty must be acknowledged that there exist competing claims of the respective democratic credentials of EU acts and certain Member State acts.[17]

of his term before Jefferson, the Republican, could take up office. Clearly, this was an attempt to keep Federalist control over the federal courts after the defeat of the Federalists by the Republicans. Its legacy is *Madison v Marbury*, 5 US 137 (1803), but it acquired fame for reasons unconnected to the power grab over the judiciary.

[16] This plays out differently in different legal orders. In the 1980s, the *Hoge Raad* (Supreme Court) of the Netherlands found the system of parental authority in the Civil Code of 1972 to be in contravention of the right to family life under Art 8 ECHR. Instead of declaring relevant domestic legislation inapplicable (a power granted to courts in Art 94 of the Netherlands Constitution), it proceeded to develop a new system of parental authority under the guise of ECHR-consistent interpretation. In the UK, the matter is elaborately discussed in the context of s 3 of the Human Rights Act 1998, which instructs courts that '[s]o far as it is possible to do so, primary legislation and subordinate legislation must be read and given effect in a way which is compatible with the Convention rights'; this in contradistinction to the declaration of incompatibility under s 4 of the 1998 Act. The literature is large, and instead of many, I here mention P Sales and R Ekins, 'Rights-consistent interpretation and the Human Rights Act 1998' (2011) 127 *Law Quarterly Review* 217, who discuss the division of powers core explicitly in relation to democracy and the rule of law.

[17] The initial lack of Court of Justice case law striking down secondary legislation, prior to data protection and anti-terrorism cases, may be a case in point, where the Court legitimates the political institutions' decisions. But the Court's initial reticence to strike down secondary legislation

I see problems when courts are dealing with general interest litigation. I am strongly inclined to think that courts and judges are not better able to assess what the general interest requires than the other political organs, and at any rate are not the best placed to make choices when various general interests clash. They are not well situated to take into account competing arguments about costs and benefits, particularly those that do not easily translate into law and legal considerations. Are courts the best situated, for instance, to balance the economic and political cost of the climate crisis and the public health crisis in situations of scarce financial means, when they are asked to order measures in this or that respect? I would think that in such situations, deference is judicial wisdom.

VI. CONCLUSION

The rule of law is in most of its essential elements a pre-twentieth-century concept. We need to rethink constitutional fundamentals in the light of what they mean for democracy as we have come to understand it since the early twentieth century in the context of twenty-first-century circumstances. We need to balance democracy and the rule of law. We want to prevent turning the concept of a democratic state under the rule of law, *demokratische Rechtsstaat*, *demokratisk rättsstat*, *État de droit démocratique*, *demokratikus jogállamiság*, *demokratycznego państwo prawa*, into an oxymoron. Such expressions should rather be turned from oxymorons into pleonasms, the one element implying the other. To do so requires us to have recourse to constitutional principles beyond the rules as they stand; a reliance on the underlying values that may once upon a time have seemed self-evident but are no longer so. This also implies going beyond too lawyerly concepts of the rule of law and daring to move towards notions of political normativity, of political morals and ethics. That is not what we lawyers are necessarily good at. But it is one of those challenges that have to be faced nevertheless.

could also be viewed in the context of the EU versus the Member States. This is different for the case law favouring the institutional rights of the European Parliament, like Case 294/83 *Les Verts*, ECLI:EU:C:1986:166, Judgment of 23 April 1986, and Case C-70/88 *European Parliament v Council*, ECLI:EU:C:1990:217, Judgment of 22 May 1990, on the capacity of the European Parliament to bring an action for annulment of decisions interfering with its prerogatives.

3

Illiberal Constitutionalism in East-Central Europe

GÁBOR HALMAI

IN SECTION I of this chapter I try to answer the question whether there is a genuine constitutional theory of 'illiberal constitutionalism', recently advocated in some East-Central European Member States of the European Union (EU), especially in Hungary and Poland. Section II focuses on some attempts in legal and political scholarship to legitimise 'illiberal constitutionalism' in general, and unchecked governance, the dismantling of constitutional review and the non-compliance with European values in particular.

I. IS THERE SUCH A THING AS 'ILLIBERAL OR NON-LIBERAL CONSTITUTIONALISM'?

A. Populist Autocrats against Liberal Democracy and Constitutionalism

In a speech delivered on 26 July 2014, before an ethnic Hungarian audience in the neighbouring Romania, Prime Minister Viktor Orbán proclaimed his intention to turn Hungary into a state that 'will undertake the odium of expressing that in character it is not of liberal nature'. Citing as models he added:

> We have abandoned liberal methods and principles of organizing society, as well as the liberal way to look at the world ... Today, the stars of international analyses are Singapore, China, India, Turkey, Russia ... and if we think back on what we did in the last four years, and what we are going to do in the following four years, then it really can be interpreted from this angle. We are ... parting ways with Western European dogmas, making ourselves independent from them ... If we look at civil organizations in Hungary ... we have to deal with paid political activists here ... [T]hey would like to exercise influence ... on Hungarian public life. It is vital, therefore, that if we would like to reorganise our nation state instead of it being a liberal state, that we should make it clear, that these are not civilians ... opposing us, but political activists attempting to promote foreign interests ... This is about the ongoing reorganization

> of the Hungarian state. Contrary to the liberal state organization logic of the past twenty years, this is a state organization originating in national interests.[1]

Four years later at the same venue Orbán again expressed his support for illiberal democracy, adding that he considers Christian democracy as illiberal as well:

> There is an alternative to liberal democracy: it is called Christian democracy … Let us confidently declare that Christian democracy is not liberal. Liberal democracy is liberal, while Christian democracy is, by definition, not liberal: it is, if you like, illiberal.[2]

In June 2019, after Fidesz was suspended from the centre-right party family, the European People's Party set up a special committee to examine the Fidesz party's adherence to democratic standards. One of the questions the members of the committee, comprising former Austrian Chancellor Wolfgang Schüssel, former European Council President Herman Van Rompuy and former European Parliament President Hans-Gert Pöttering, addressed to Viktor Orbán was 'Please explain what you mean by the expression "illiberal state".' Here is the response of the Fidesz chairman and Hungarian Prime Minister:

> We are Christian democrats and we are differing nowadays at least in three aspects from the liberals: The first one is the conviction that family is fundamental, and family is based on one man and one woman. We believe that this needs to be protected, which the liberals deny. Secondly, while the cultural life of every country is diverse, a Leitculture, a cultural tradition is present everywhere. In Hungary this is Christian culture. We respect other cultures, but our own has a prominent role for us, and it is our responsibility to preserve it. Liberals refuse this concept. The third aspect is that liberal democrats are everywhere pro-immigration while we are against immigration. So, whether one admits it or not: Christian democrats are illiberal by definition.[3]

In a conversation with the French philosopher Bernard-Henry Lévy, Orbán identified liberalism with totalitarianism, and illiberalism with true democracy:

> Liberalism gave rise to political correctness – that is, to a form of totalitarianism, which is the opposite of democracy. That's why I believe that illiberalism restores true freedom, true democracy.[4]

[1] See Viktor Orbán, Speech at Băile Tuşnad (Tusnádfürdő) of 26 July 2014, *Budapest Beacon* (29 July 2014) available at http://budapestbeacon.com/public-policy/full-text-of-viktor-orbans-speech-at-baile-tusnad-tusnadfurdo-of-26-july-2014/.

[2] See Prime Minister Viktor Orbán's Speech at the 28th Bálványos Summer Open University and Student Camp, *Tusnádfürdő (Băile Tuşnad)*, 28 July 2018, available at www.miniszterelnok.hu/prime-minister-viktor-orbans-speech-at-the-29th-balvanyos-summer-open-university-and-student-camp/.

[3] The leaked letter has been published by Politico at www.politico.eu/article/viktor-orban-rejects-epp-concerns-rule-of-law/.

[4] B-H Lévy, 'How an Anti-totalitarian Militant Discovered Ultranationalism. After 30 years, I spoke with Viktor Orbán again' *The Atlantic* (13 May 2019).

In July 2019, in the yearly Băile Tuşnad/Tusnádfürdő Free University, Orbán admitted that 'illiberalism' carries a negative connotation, and therefore he changed the terminology, calling illiberalism 'Christian liberty', which according to him is 'a genuine model of a theory of state, a unique Christian democratic state'. He made it clear, however, that 'Christian liberty does not mean individual liberty, because individual freedoms can never encroach on the interests of the community. There is indeed a majority that must be respected, that is the foundation of democracy.'[5]

In a speech delivered in mid-September 2019 at the 12th Congress of the Association of Christian Intelligentsia, Orbán said that 'Christian liberty' is superior to the individual liberty – defined by John Stuart Mill in his 'On Liberty' – which can only be infringed upon if the exercise of one's liberty harms others. Christian liberty, by contrast, holds that we ought to treat others as we want to be treated.[6] The teachings of 'Christian liberty' – he added – maintain that the world is divided into nations. As opposed to liberal liberty, which is based on individual accomplishments, the followers of 'Christian liberty' acknowledge only those accomplishments that also serve the common good. While liberals are convinced that liberal democracies will eventually join together to form a world government à la Immanuel Kant in the name of liberal internationalism, Christian liberty by contrast considers 'nations to be as free and sovereign as individuals are, and therefore they cannot be forced under the laws of global governance'.[7]

In the system 'Christian liberty', Hungary has a special place:

> We shouldn't be afraid to declare that Hungary is a city built on a hill, which, as is well known, cannot be hidden. Let's embrace this mission, let's create for ourselves and show to the world what a true, deep, and superior life can be built on the ideal of Christian liberty. Perhaps this lifeline will be the one toward which the confused, lost, and misguided Europe will stretch its hand. Perhaps they will also see the beauty of man's work serving his own good, the good of his country, and the glory of God.[8]

[5] See at www.miniszterelnok.hu/yes-to-democracy-no-to-liberalism/. As Yale law and history professor Samuel Moyn pointed out, President Trump has also begun to nudge the political culture to the same direction. He quoted Sohrab Ahmari, a conservative journalist, who approvingly explained Trump's policy as re-ordering the common good and ultimately the 'Highest Good', that is, the Christian God – Moyn argues. See S Moyn, 'We Are in an Anti-Liberal Moment. Liberals Need Better Answers' *The Washington Post* (21 June 2019).

[6] See at www.miniszterelnok.hu/orban-viktor-beszede-a-kereszteny-ertelmisegiek-szovetsegenek-kesz-xii-kongresszusan/. This time the webpage of the Prime Minister, besides the original Hungarian text of the speech, contains no English but only a German-language translation, available at www.miniszterelnok.hu/viktor-orbans-rede-auf-dem-kongress-des-verbandes-der-christlichen-intellektuellen-kereszteny-ertelmisegiek-szovetsege-kesz/.

[7] ibid.

[8] ibid. As Éva S Balogh points out, this passage is taken from the Gospel of Matthew (5:13–15), without identifying it. See ÉS Balogh, 'Orbán, the New Jesus Delivers His Sermon on the Mount' *Hungarian Spectrum* (15 September 2019) available at https://hungarianspectrum.org/2019/09/15/orban-the-new-jesus-delivers-his-sermon-on-the-mount/.

Another new element of the speech is that Orbán puts 'Christian liberty' at the centre of the 'Christian democratic state', 'a new and authentic model of state and political theory', which has been reached in the last 30 years by the taking of two big steps. The first has been the liberal democratic transition in 1989, while the second, more important one is the national or Christian regime change in 2010.

Regarding the new constitutional order, introduced by the 2011 Fundamental Law of Hungary, Orbán admitted that his party did not aim to produce a liberal constitution. He said:

> In Europe the trend is for every constitution to be liberal, this is not one. Liberal constitutions are based on the freedom of the individual and subdue welfare and the interest of the community to this goal. When we created the constitution, we posed questions to the people. The first question was the following: what would you like; should the constitution regulate the rights of the individual and create other rules in accordance with this principle or should it create a balance between the rights and duties of the individual. According to my recollection more than 80% of the people responded by saying that they wanted to live in a world, where freedom existed, but where welfare and the interest of the community could not be neglected and that these need to be balanced in the constitution. I received an order and mandate for this. For this reason, the Hungarian constitution is a constitution of balance, and not a side-leaning constitution, which is the fashion in Europe, as there are plenty of problems there.[9]

Orbán also refused the separation of powers, checks and balances as concepts alien to his illiberal constitutional system, saying 'Checks and balances is a US invention that for some reason of intellectual mediocrity Europe decided to adopt and use in European politics.'[10] The ideological foundation of Orbán's illiberalism can be found in the works of his two court ideologues, the sociologist and former liberal MP Gyula Tellér, and András Lánczi, a political scientist. It is easy to prove that Orbán, in his 2014 speech on 'illiberal democracy', recited a study by Tellér published earlier on that year, which Orbán assigned as compulsory reading for all his ministers.[11] Tellér claims that the 'system of regime-change' has failed because the liberal constitution did not commit the Government to protecting national interests, therefore the new 'national system' has to strengthen national sovereignty, and with it the freedom of degree of government activity. This, Tellér argues, is necessary to counter the moral

[9] 'A Tavares jelentés egy baloldali akció' ('The Tavares report is a leftist action'), Interview with PM Viktor Orbán on Hungarian Public Radio, Kossuth Rádió, 5 July 2013.

[10] Interview with *Bloomberg News*, 14 December 2014. Similarly, Tünde Handó, head of the National Judicial Office, a close ally of Orbán, said '[t]he rule of law over the State, like, for example, in the United States, is not the right way'. See at https://nepszava.hu/3029940_hando-nem-kell-a-birosagoknak-szembehelyezkedniuk-az-allammal.

[11] See G Tellér,' Született-e Orbán-rendszer 2010 és 2014 között?' [Was an Orbán System Born between 2010 and 2014?], NAGYVILÁG, March 2014.

command of the liberal rule of law regime, according to which 'everything is allowed that does not harm others' liberty'.

Lánczi's anti-liberal concept can be found in his book *Political Realism and Wisdom*, which was published in English in 2015, as well as in an article published in 2018, after Fidesz' third consecutive electoral victory.[12] Lánczi's critique is an outright rejection of liberalism as a utopian ideology, which is – similar to communism – incompatible with democracy.

Like Orbán, the then Prime Minister Beata Szydło (with Kaczyński, ruling from behind the scenes as he holds no official post) described the actions of the PiS Government in dismantling the independence of the Constitutional Tribunal and the ordinary courts as a blitz to install an illiberal state. In mid-September 2016, at a conference in the Polish town of Krynica, Orbán and Kaczyński proclaimed a 'cultural counter-revolution' aimed at turning the EU into an illiberal project. A week later at the Bratislava EU summit, the prime ministers of the Visegrád Four countries demanded a structural change of the EU in favour of the nation states.[13] Witold Waszczykowski, Poland's Minister of Foreign Affairs, expressing his own and his governing PiS Party's anti-liberalism, went as far as to mock liberalism as 'a world made up of cyclists and vegetarians, who only use renewable energy and fight all forms of religion'.[14]

Ryszard Legutko, the main ideologue and MEP of PiS, similarly to his Hungarian counterpart, Lánczi, also likens liberal democracy with communism, both being fuelled by ideas of modernisation and progress, arguing that liberalism – in its 'sterility' – has little if anything to say about substantive, human moral questions; indeed liberalism is 'comparably simplistic and equally impoverishing as communist thought was'.[15] Another critique of liberalism expressed by Legutko is its inauthenticity, 'being more and more remote from reality'.[16] As Paul Blokker observes, Lánczi makes a similar point in his *Political Realism and Wisdom*, that liberalism fails to engage with reality.[17] According to Legutko, a further problem with liberalism is that it drives egalitarianism, which renders 'all social hierarchies as immediately problematic because they were obviously, not natural'.[18] In his communitarian reading, human rights become 'arbitrary claims, ideologically motivated, made by various political groups in

[12] See A Lánczi, 'The Renewed Social Contract – Hungary's Elections' (2018) 9 *Hungarian Review* at www.hungarianreview.com/article/20180525_the_renewed_social_contract_hungary_s_elections_2018. For a detailed analysis of Lánczi's arguments, see KL Scheppele, 'The Opportunism of Populists and the Defense of Constitutional Liberalism' (2019) 3 *German Law Journal* 314.

[13] S Sierakowski even speaks about an 'illiberal international'. See S Sierakowski, 'The Polish Threat to Europe' *Project Syndicate* (19 January 2016).

[14] See at www.bild.de/politik/ausland/polen/hat-die-regierung-einen-vogel-44003034.bild.html.

[15] See R Legutko, *The Demon in Democracy: Totalitarian Temptations in Free Societies* (New York, Encounter Books, 2016) 118.

[16] ibid 13.

[17] P Blokker, 'Populist Counter-Constitutionalism, Conservatism, and Legal Fundamentalism' (2019) 15 *European Constitutional Law Review* 519, fn 18.

[18] See Legutko (n 15) 132.

blatant disregard of the common good, generously distributed by the legislatures and the courts, often contrary to common sense and usually detrimental to public and personal morality'.[19]

In Poland, besides Legutko, Marek Cichocki, Marcin Król, Dariusz Gawin, Zdzislaw Krasnodebski and Lech Morawski are recognised as prominent illiberal intellectuals.[20] The late Lech Morawski, who was one of PiS's illegally appointed judges of the Constitutional Tribunal, harshly criticised the 'liberal state, in which the political system is based on the individualistic concept of rights as trump card against community (R Dworkin)'.[21]

Both Lánczi and Legutko assert, together with other anti-liberals, with one voice, that liberalism and communism, or for that matter its ideology, Marxism, are secretly allied and share a common ancestry in that they are two offshoots of an Enlightenment tradition. Legutko also accuses liberalism of a tendency to root out all forms of inequality, and asserts that human rights – as legal norms that promote equality – become 'arbitrary claims, ideologically motivated, made by various political groups in blatant disregard of the common good'.[22]

This anti-liberal political theory is present outside East-Central Europe as well. For instance, Patrick Deneen's book[23] is directed at the left in the US, targeting both contemporary progressivism and the 'classical liberalism' of conservatives. The Israeli political theorist Yoram Hazony in his book[24] also criticises those conservatives who defend liberal democracy. The common goal of all these thinkers is to conflate liberal democracy with contemporary progressivism, and thus to suggest that conservatives should have no interest in supporting or defending liberal democracy.[25]

This critique of liberalism goes back to the concept of *Volksgemeinschaft* (national community), or *völkisches Recht*, one of the core principles of National Socialist law, which can be characterised negatively by rejection of the individualistic, normative concept of the people (*Volk*) as the sum of nationals of the state, as presented in the 1918 Weimar Constitution.[26] *Volksgemeinschaft* together with the *Führerprinzip*, the other main principle

[19] ibid 140.

[20] See B Trencsényi, M Kopecek, LL Gabrielcic, M Falina and M Baár, *A History of Modern Political Thought in East Central Europe*, vol II: *Negotiating Modernity in the 'Short Twentieth Century and Beyond* (Oxford, Oxford University Press, 2018).

[21] L Morawski, Contribution to Symposium 'The Polish Constitutional Crisis and Institutional Self-defense', Trinity College, University of Oxford (9 May 2017).

[22] Legutko (n 15) 135. In a recent article, Paul Blokker characterises both Legutko and Lánczi as conservative intellectuals who have provided ideas for the conservative populist project, and an important contribution to rethinking/re-imagining constitutional democracy in the contemporary European context. See Blokker (n 17) fn 18.

[23] P Deneen, *Why Liberalism Failed* (New Haven, CT, Yale University Press, 2018).

[24] Y Hazony, *The Virtue of Nationalism* (New York, Basic Books, 2018).

[25] See M Plattner, 'Illiberal Democary and the Struggle on the Right' (2019) 30 *Journal of Democracy* 5, 16–17.

[26] About the role of Volksgemeinschaft in National Socialist law, see O Lepsius 'The Problem of Perceptions of National Socialist Law or: Was There A Constitutional Theory of National Socialism?' in C Joerges and N Singh Ghaleigh (eds), *Darker Legacies of Law in Europe.*

of National Socialist *Weltanschauung*, aim to overcome individualism, hence meaning strong anti-liberalism. Given Carl Schmitt's well-known flirtation with National Socialism, it is not surprising that the critical stance of the new illiberals towards liberal constitutionalism is also related to a Schmittian understanding of the constitution, and to his critique of liberal constitutionalism and its conception of the rule of law.[27] The constitution in Schmitt's view is an expression of 'the substantial homogeneity of the identity and the will of the people', and a guarantee of the state's existence, and ultimately any constitutional arrangement is grounded in, or originates from, an arbitrary act of political power. The absolute authority of the political will of the people overrides all constitutional requirements, which according to Schmitt are signs of depoliticisation tendencies caused by liberal democracies. This is the reason that he elaborated 'The concept of the Political'[28] (*das Politisches*), based on the distinction between friend and enemy, which is precisely the opposite of liberal neutrality.[29]

In other words, in Schmitt's view, the basis of the constitution is 'a political decision concerning the type and form of its own being', made by the people as a 'political unity', based on their own free will. This political will 'remains alongside and above the constitution'.[30] Schmitt also portrays the people as an existential reality as opposed to the mere liberal representation of voters in parliament, holding, therefore, that Mussolini was a genuine incarnation of democracy. Schmitt goes so far as to claim the incompatibility of liberalism and democracy, and argues that plebiscitary democracy based on the homogeneity of the nation is the only true form of democracy. But Schmitt is talking about these intermittent plebiscites as a tool to tap the resource of consent by the governed within a 'qualitative' and strong totalitarian state, the authority of which rests on the military and the bureaucracy, and which cannot accept the existence of political opposition.[31] In other words, the strong state cannot be liberal.[32]

The Shadow of National Socialism and Fascism over Europe and its Legal Traditions (Oxford, Hart Publishing, 2003) 19–41.

[27] As Heiner Bielefeld demostrates, Carl Schmitt systematically undermines the liberal principle of the rule of law. See H Bielefeld, 'Deconstruction of the Rule of Law. Carl Schmitt's Philosophy of the Policial' (1996) 82 *Archiv für Rechts- und Sozialphilosophy* 379, 396.

[28] C Schmitt, *The Concept of the Political* (Chicago, IL, University of Chicago Press, 2007).

[29] See H Bielefeld, 'Carl Schmitt's Critique of Liberalism: Systematic Reconstruction and Countercriticism' (1997) X *Canadian Journal of Law and Jurisprudence* 67.

[30] See C Schmitt, *Constitutional Theory* (Durham, NC, Duke University Press, 2008). This idea is also shared by a part of the French constitutional doctrine, influenced by Rousseau's general will. This is the reason why the representatives of this doctrine hold that during a constitutional transition, a referendum is sufficient to legitimate a new constitution. See the French Constitutional Council's approval of De Gaulle's 1962 amendment to the 1958 Constitution, ignoring the Constitution's amendment provisions.

[31] See C Schmitt, '*Legalität and Legitimität*' in *Verfassungsrechtliche Aufsätze* (Berlin, Duncker & Humblot, 1958) 93–94. Quoted by A Somek, 'Authoritarian Constitutionalism: Austrian Constitutional Doctrine 1933–1938 and Its Legacy' in Joerges and Singh Ghaleigh (eds) (n 26) 375.

[32] Regarding the revival of Carl Schmitt in the Hungarian political and constitutional theory, see A Antal, 'The Rebirth of the Political – A Schmittian Moment in Hungary', transcript of the lecture given at the Constitutional Systems in Middle Europe, the cycle of meetings about political ideas of

As Mattias Kumm argues, Carl Schmitt's interpretation of democracy, inspired by Rousseau and used by authoritarian populist nationalists like Viktor Orbán as 'illiberal democracy', becomes an anti-constitutional topos.[33] The Hungarian political scientist, András Körösényi, implementing the Weberian concept, calls the Orbán regime a 'plebiscitary leader democracy', where the activity of the leader (or Führer? – GH) is posteriorly approved by the people; but since this approval can be withdrawn, this is still a democratic system.[34] In contrast, Wojciech Sadurski, using Guillermon O'Donnell's 'delegative democracy' concept, characterises the Polish system after 2015 as 'plebiscitary autocracy', in which the electorate approves of governmental disregard of the constitution.[35] In Hungary, even the electoral approval is manipulated, hence the formal democratic character of the regime can also be questioned. This leads Larry Diamond to call the Hungarian system 'pseudo-democracy'.[36]

Tadeusz Mazowiecki organised by Polska Fundacja im. Roberta Schumanaon, 6 November 2017, Warsaw, available at www.academia.edu/35061692/The_Rebirth_of_the_Political__A_Schmittian_Moment_in_Hungary_Transcript_of_Lecture?email_work_card=thumbnail. Also Z Balázs, 'Political Theory in Hungary After the Regime Change' (2014) 7 *International Political Anthropology* 5. On Schmitt's influence on the Polish constitutional discourse, see D Bunikowski, 'The Crisis in Poland, Schmittian Questions, and Kaczyński's Political and Legal Philosophy', available at www.academia.edu/31450497/The_crisis_in_Poland_and_Schmittian_questions_in_the_rule_of_law_debate.

[33] M Kumm, 'Demokratie als verfassungsfeindlicher Topos' *Verfassungsblog*, 6 September 2017, at https://verfassungsblog.de/demokratie-als-verfassungsfeindlicher-topos/.

[34] See A Körösényi, 'Weber és az Orbán-rezsim: plebiszciter vezéremokrácia Magyarországon' [Weber and the Orbán-regime: Plebisciter Leader Democracy in Hungary], *Politikatudományi Szemle*, 2017/4, 7–28. In a more recent interview, however, Körösényi admitted that for the withdrawal of approval, currently a miracle is needed. See *Csak a csoda segít* [Only a Miracle Helps], hvg, 20 June 2019.

[35] See W Sadurski, *Poland's Constitutional Breakdown* (Oxford, Oxford University Press, 2019) 242–43. Similarly, Juan José Linz, to avoid confusion, proposes the addition of adjectives to 'authoritarianism' rather than to 'democracy' for such regimes, eg 'electoral authoritarianism'. See JJ Linz, *Totalitarian and Authoritarian Regimes* (Boulder, CO, Lynne Rienner, 2000) 34. Also, Larry Diamond refers to 'electoral authoritarianism' in hybrid regimes. See L Diamond, 'Thinking About Hybrid Regimes' (2002) 13 *Journal of Democracy* 21, 24.

[36] 'The test of a democracy is not whether the economy is growing, employment is rising, or more couples are marrying, but whether people can choose and replace their leaders in free and fair elections. This is the test that Hungary's political system now fails. When Viktor Orbán and his Fidesz party returned to power in 2010 with a parliamentary supermajority, they set about destroying the constitutional pillars of liberal democracy … By the 2014 elections, Orbán had rigged the system. Yes, multiparty elections continued, but his systematic degradation of constitutional checks and balances so tilted the playing field that he was able to renew his two-thirds majority in parliament with less than a majority of the popular vote (and did so again in 2018) … Orbán has transformed Hungary into not an illiberal democracy but a pseudo-democracy.' See L Diamond, 'How Democratic Is Hungary?', *Foreign Affairs*, September/October 2019. Similarly, Steven Levitsky and Lucan Way recently argued, 'Clearly, Hungary is not a democracy. But understanding why requires a nuanced understanding of the line between democracy and autocracy … Orbán's Hungary is a prime example of a competitive autocracy with an uneven playing field': S Levitsky and L Way, 'How autocrats can rig the game and damage democracy' *The Washington Post* (4 January 2019). See also A Bozóki and D Hegedűs, 'An externally constrained hybrid regime: Hungary in the European Union' (2018) 25 *Democratization* 1173.

B. Authoritarian Populism as a Rhetoric

The illiberal regimes in Central and Eastern Europe manifest themselves as populist, using anti-representation and pro-direct democracy arguments. But in reality this is only rhetoric, which does not necessarily correspond with these populists' practice. For instance, Viktor Orbán's Fidesz party tried to undermine the legitimacy of representation after losing the 2002 parliamentary elections.[37] He refused to concede defeat, declaring that 'the nation cannot be in opposition, only the government can be in opposition against its own people'. After the 2010 electoral victory, he claimed that through the 'revolution at the voting booths', the majority has delegated its power to the Government representing it. This means that the populist Government tried to interpret the result of the elections as the will of the people, viewed as a homogeneous unit. Also, the Orbán Government, after overthrowing its predecessor as a result of a popular referendum in 2010, made it more difficult to initiate a valid referendum for its own opposition. While the previous law required only 25 per cent of the voters to cast a vote, the new law required at least 50 per cent of those eligible to vote to take part, otherwise the referendum would be invalid.[38] The ambivalence of authoritarian populists towards representation and referenda in government and in opposition applies to their attitude regarding established institutions. While they readily attack the 'establishment' while in opposition, they very much protect their own governmental institutions once in power.

The situation is different with transnational institutions, like the EU, which are also attacked by these autocratic populist governments as threats to their countries' sovereignty.[39] A good example is again the Hungarian Parliament's reaction to the European Parliament's critical report from July 2013 on the constitutional situation in Hungary. The Hungarian parliamentary resolution on equal treatment reads:

> We, Hungarians, do not want a Europe any longer where freedom is limited and not widened. We do not want a Europe any longer where the Greater abuses his power, where national sovereignty is violated and where the Smaller has to respect the Greater. We have had enough of dictatorship after 40 years behind the iron curtain.

[37] Regarding the use of populist rhetoric by Viktor Orbán and his Government, see a more detailed description in my article G Halmai, 'Populism, Authoritarianism and Constitutionalism' (2019) 20 *German Law Journal* 296, 313.

[38] It is the irony of fate that due to these more stringent conditions, the only referendum that the Orbán Government initiated – one against the EU's migration policy – failed exactly because of the new validity requirement.

[39] Andrea Pin, in the parallel special issue, argues that supranational courts are partially also responsible for the rise of populism by judicialisation of political choices and replacing national debates and rules. In my view this critique does not apply in the case of Member States of the EU, such as Hungary and Poland, where the democratic process is not operating satisfactorily and the political institutions of the EU seem to be unable or unwilling to act. Here the CJEU, or the ECtHR for that matter, despite its otherwise problematic de-politicised language, can be the last resort to enforce compliance with European values. See A Pin, 'The Transnational Drivers of Populist Backlash in Europe: The Role of the Courts' (2019) 20 *German Law Journal* 225, 244.

These words very much reflect the Orbán Government's view of 'national freedom', the liberty of the state (or the nation) to determine its own laws: 'This is why we are writing our own constitution … And we don't want any unconsolidated help from strangers who are keen to guide us … Hungary must turn on its own axis.'[40]

Orbán repeated the same populist, nationalist mantra at the plenary debate of the European Parliament on 11 September 2018, when defying the Sargentini Report, on the basis of which the Parliament launched Article 7 TEU proceedings against Hungary:

> [Y]ou are not about to denounce a government, but a country and a people. You will denounce the Hungary which has been a member of the family of Europe's Christian peoples for a thousand years; the Hungary which has contributed to the history of our great continent of Europe with its work and, when needed, with its blood. You will denounce the Hungary which rose and took up arms against the world's largest army, against the Soviets, which made the highest sacrifice for freedom and democracy, and, when it was needed, opened its borders to its East German brothers and sisters in distress. Hungary has fought for its freedom and democracy. I stand here now and I see that Hungary is being arraigned by people who inherited democracy, not needing to assume any personal risk for the pursuit of freedom. … [T]he report before you is an affront to the honour of Hungary and the Hungarian people. Hungary's decisions are made by the voters in parliamentary elections. What you are claiming is no less than saying that the Hungarian people are not sufficiently capable of being trusted to judge what is in their own interests. You think that you know the needs of the Hungarian people better than the Hungarian people themselves.[41]

Hence, I claim that autocrats' populism is 'false',[42] and they may use populist rhetoric but their decisive characteristic is authoritarianism. What makes them distinct from non-populist autocrats are the democratic elections through which they come to power, even though being in government they often change the electoral law to keep their power.

The Hungarian Government of Viktor Orbán proved this spectacularly by introducing their Enabling Act[43] on 30 March 2020, similar to Hitler's

[40] The English-language translation of excerpts from Orbán's speech was made available by Hungarian officials, see eg *Financial Times*: Brussels Blog, 16 March 2012.

[41] See at www.kormany.hu/en/the-prime-minister/the-prime-minister-s-speeches/address-by-prime-minister-viktor-orban-in-the-debate-on-the-so-called-sargentini-report.

[42] The term 'false' populism was used by Isaiah Berlin, defining 'the employment of populist ideas for undemocratic ends'. See *To Define Populism*, The Isaiah Berlin Virtual Library, Isaiah Berlin 1968, The Isaiah Berlin Literary Trust 2013, posted 14 October 2013, available at http://berlin.wolf.ox.ac.uk/lists/bibliography/bib111bLSE.pdf.

[43] See the translation of the draft law, which was enacted by the Hungarian Parliament in its last session before the emergency power entered into force without any change. The Government rejected all the proposed amendments submitted by opposition parties, including one that aimed at imposing a 90-day time limit on governmental actions, and the President of the Republic, a founder of Orbán's Fidesz party, signed the bill within two hours. See at https://hungarianspectrum.org/2020/03/21/translation-of-draft-law-on-protecting-against-the-coronavirus/.

Ermächtigungsgesetz of 1933. The Act grants dictatorial powers under cover of declaring a state of emergency to fight COVID-19. The Act was needed, because on 11 March the Government by its decree declared a 'state of danger', a special state of emergency regulated by the Fundamental Law in order to get exceptional competences to combat the Coronavirus. According to the Fundamental Law, the Parliament is required to authorise the extension beyond 15 days. But the Act violates Fidesz' own constitution, the Fundamental Law of Hungary enacted in 2011 with the exclusive support of the governing party, and not just because the 15-day deadline had already expired when the law was enacted. Article 53 of the Fundamental Law mentions only natural disasters and industrial accidents, not pandemics. This last cause of a state of danger is only covered by Act 128 of 2011 concerning the management of natural disasters. In other words, there was no constitutional authorisation either for the decree, or for the Enabling Act.

The Act, enacted exclusively with the votes of the governing majority, enables the Government to take any measure by executive decree for an indefinite period of time. These measures, which are not tailored to fight the Coronavirus, can include suspending or overriding any laws, or simply departing from them, and suspending by-elections and referenda as well as the functioning of ordinary courts. The Constitutional Court, which could be the only body to check the Government, is allowed to continue to exercise its review power, but it has been packed by judges loyal to the Government since 2013. The Enabling Act has inserted two new crimes into the Criminal Code, which will not go away when the emergency is over. Anyone who 'claim[s] or spread[s] a distorted truth in relation to the emergency in a way that is suitable for alarming or agitating a large group of people' can be punished for a term of up to five years in prison. Also, anyone who interferes with the operation of measures that the Government takes to fight the pandemic could also face a jail sentence of up to five years. These clearly unconstitutionally disproportionate threats to freedom of expression can silence the remaining free media and independent civil society organisations. Besides the law, governmental decrees enacted after 11 March also contain unconstitutional provisions, the validity of which has now been extended by the Enabling Act. One of those allowed for the army to commandeer around 140 state-owned and private strategic factories. In this case neither the Fundamental Law, nor even the law on the management of natural disasters, mentioned above, gives power to the Government to make extraordinary rules concerning the army.

The blanket authorisation of uncontrolled executive power will last as long as the 'state of danger' persists, which will be determined by the Government itself. There are legitimate worries about the end of the current emergency power, because the special 'state of emergency caused by mass migration' introduced in 2015 is still in force without there being any refugees in the country.

C. Is there Such a Thing as Authoritarian Constitutionalism?

Constitutionalism is often defined as 'limited government'. For instance, Giovanni Sartori defines constitutionalism as 'a fundamental law, or a fundamental set of principles, and a correlative institutional arrangement, which would restrict arbitrary power and ensure "limited government"'.[44] András Sajó and Renáta Uitz also describe constitutionalism as a liberal political philosophy that is concerned with limiting government.[45] The main aim of limiting government is to guarantee individual rights. In other words, modern constitutionalism is by definition liberal.[46] This does not mean, however, that constitutions cannot be illiberal or authoritarian. Therefore, it is legitimate to talk about constitutions in authoritarian regimes, as Tom Ginsburg and Alberto Simpler do in their book,[47] but I do not agree with the use of the terms 'authoritarian constitutionalism'[48] or 'constitutional authoritarianism'.[49]

Mark Tushnet, for instance tries, generally to pluralise the normative understanding of non-liberal constitutionalism, differentiating between an absolutist, a mere rule of law and an authoritarian form of constitutionalism, Singapore being the main example of the last of these.[50] Tushnet defines authoritarian constitutionalism as an intermediate normative model between liberal

[44] See G Sartori, 'Constitutionalism: A Preliminary Discussion' (1962) 56 *The American Political Science Review* 855.

[45] A Sajó and R Uitz, *The Constitution of Freedom: An Introduction to Legal Constitutionalism* (Oxford, Oxford University Press, 2017) 13.

[46] In contrast, others also pay regard to other models of constitutionalism, in which the government, although committed to acting under a constitution, is not committed to pursuing liberal democratic values. See, eg, M Tushnet, 'Varieties of Constitutionalism' (2016) 14 *International Journal of Constitutional Law* issue 1, editorial 1. On 11 October 2019, Tushnet posted the following message on his Facebook page: 'My lecture today was on "Varieties of Constitutionalism," and argued that a thin version of constitutionalism requires only (1) that there be some entrenched provisions, (2) that there be some mechanism for resolving disputes about what the law is that is oriented solely to making decision according to law, and (3) that the regime receive popular consent to the regime as a whole measured over some reasonable period of time. (Lots of complexities elided here.) The first subtext, which almost surfaced in the discussion afterwards, is that the Chinese leadership doesn't really have to fear constitutionalism as such (as it seems to do), if the very thin version I outlined counts as constitutionalism (which I think it does). The second subtext is that, if the idea of thin constitutionalism were accepted the way would be open for discussions about whether thin constitutionalism should be thickened (discussions that are harder to have if the idea of constitutionalism is ruled off the table from the outset.)' Similarly, Gila Stopler defines the state of the current Israeli constitutional system as 'semi-liberal constitutionalism': cf G Stopler, *Constitutional Capture in Israel*, ICONNECT, 21 August 2017.

[47] T Ginsburg and A Simpser, *Constitutions in Authoritarian Regimes* (Cambridge, Cambridge University Press, 2014).

[48] See, eg, Somek (n 31); T Isiksel, 'Between Text and Context: Turkey's Tradition of Authoritarian Constitutionalism' (2013) 11 *International Journal of Constitutional Law* 702.

[49] S Levitsky and LA Way, 'The Rise of Competitive Authoritarianism' (2002) 13 *Journal of Democracy* 51.

[50] M Tushnet, 'Authoritarian Constitutionalism' (2015) 100 *Cornell Law Review* 391.

constitutionalism and authoritarianism[51] that has moderately strong normative commitments to constitutionalism in nations with specific social and political problems, such as a high degree of persistent ethnic conflict.[52] In other words, he refers to a distinct type of regime, wherein there are faulty practices and a constitution with an authoritarian content.

In contrast to Tushnet's understanding of authoritarian constitutionalism, which can also be considered as an empirical work about hybrid regimes, Roberto Niembro Ortega provides a more conceptual approach that refers to a very sophisticated way in which ruling elites with an authoritarian mentality exercise power in not fully democratic states.[53] Here the regimes do have a liberal democratic constitution, but instead of limiting the power of the state, the constitution is used for practical and authoritarian ideological functions to mask the idea of constitutionalism. But, as pointed out earlier, if the constitution does not limit the government's power, it cannot fulfil the requirements of constitutionalism, and can only be considered as a sham constitution[54] and as a rhetorical tool, just as populism is in the hands of autocrats.

Most of the chapters in a recently published book[55] – as the editors' preface states – 'challenge the notion of a single "proper sense" of constitutionalism that is coextensive with and exhausted by the discrete elements of the liberal paradigm'. In the introductory chapter, Günter Frankenberg argues that 'liberal orthodoxy treats authoritarian constitutionalism not just as a contested concept, but as a mere travesty or deceitful rendition of the rules and principles, values and institutions of what is innocently referred to as "Western constitutionalism"'.[56]

Referring to Roberto Gargarella's book on Latin American constitutionalism,[57] Frankenberg claims that the orthodoxy pays 'obsessive attention to issues of rights', especially enforceable civil and political rights, at the expense of

[51] Tushnet provides the following rough definition of authoritarianism (ibid 448): all decisions can potentially be made by a single decision maker (which might be a collective body), whose decisions are both formally and practically unregulated by law.

[52] In the case of Singapore, Tushnet argues that the Government needs to preserve ethnic and religious harmony, without indicating why this goal can only be achieved with authoritarian tools. He mentions Malaysia, Mexico before 2000, Egypt under Mubarak, and Taiwan between 1955 and the late 1980s, and South Korea between 1948 and 1987, as candidates for authoritarian constitutionalism. See ibid 393.

[53] See R Niembro Ortega, 'Conceptualizing Authoritarian Constitutionalism' (2016) 49 *Verfassung und Recht in Übersee* 339.

[54] Regarding the concept of sham constitution, see DS Law and M Versteeg, 'Sham Constitutions' (2013) 101 *California Law Review* 863.

[55] H Alviar Garcia and G Frankenberg (eds), *Authoritarian Constitutionalism: Comparative Analysis and Critique* (Cambridge, Cambridge University Press, 2019).

[56] See G Frankenberg, 'Authoritarian Constitutionalism: Coming to Terms with Modernity's Nightmares' in Alviar Garcia and Frankenberg (eds) (n 55) 1.

[57] CFR Gargarella, *Latin American Constitutionalism 1810–2010: The Engine Room of the Constitution* (Oxford, Oxford University Press, 2013).

redistributive policies or social entitlements, free and fair elections, separation of powers and judicial review. He introduces authoritarian constitutionalism as 'one of modernity's narratives alloying rule and law' by using Machiavellian constitutional opportunistic technology, like Chinese head of state Xi Jinping's observing an established constitutional amendment procedure while stripping himself of the existing term limit, or more Hobbesian claims to defend the public good and people's interest, like that of Hungarian Prime Minister Viktor Orbán, referring to European Christian values while denouncing the human rights of refugees.[58]

As Helena Alviar Garcia and Michael Wilkinson demonstrate in their contributions to the same book, political authoritarianism entertains an affinity with economic neoliberalism.[59] This can be proved to perfection by the neoliberal economic policy of the current authoritarian regime in Viktor Orbán's Hungary. One of the most tragic historical examples of this relationship is the politics of the van Papen Government in the last period of the Weimar Republic, as clearly seen already by Hermann Heller in 1933.[60] Heller claims that Papen wanted the state and the economy to be 'strictly' separated, one from the other. Legitimising this policy, Carl Schmitt in November 1932 lectured on 'the state and economy', arguing that the total state makes an attempt to order the economy in an authoritarian way, drawing a sharp line of separation vis-à-vis the economy, although ruling on the other hand with the strongest military means and means of mass manipulation (radio broadcasting, cinema).[61] Besides retreating from economic and social policy, this authoritarian state is also supposed to retreat from socio-cultural policy. Heller concludes that this 'authoritarian liberalism', which is characterised by the retreat of the authoritarian state from social policy, liberalisation of the economy and dictatorial control by the state of politico-intellectual functions, cannot be ruled in democratic forms, proving the claim made earlier here that not only does democracy presupposes liberalism, but there is also no liberalism without democracy. Together with Juan José Linz we can also be sceptical regarding the efforts to distinguish between an ostensibly benevolent 'authoritarian, antidemocratic political solution' and totalitarianism in the 1930s.[62] Based on the experiences of the current authoritarian regimes, for instance in Russia,[63] I would add the same doubts about the benevolence of 'authoritarian constitutionalism' altogether.

[58] See Frankenberg (n 56).

[59] See H Alviar Garcia, 'Neoliberalism As a Form of Auhoritarian Constitutionalism' in Alviar Garcia and Frankenberg (eds) (n 55) 37; and MA Wilkinson, 'Authoritarian Liberalism As Authoritarian Constitutionalism' in Alviar Garcia and Frankenberg (eds) (n 55) 317.

[60] Cf Heller's paper on 'Authoritarian Liberalism?', which originally appeared in (1933) 44 *Die Neue Rundschau* 289–98. See the English translated version in (2015) 21 *European Law Journal* 295.

[61] ibid 299.

[62] See Linz (n 35) 51.

[63] Among the Machiavellian technologies, Frankenberg mentions the Putin-Medvedev tandemocracy: Frankenberg (n 56).

Besides the constitutions in the communist countries, both current theocratic and communitarian constitutions are considered illiberal.[64] Theocratic constitutions, in contrast to modern constitutionalism, reject secular authority.[65] In communitarian constitutions, like the ones in South Korea, Singapore and Taiwan, the well-being of the nation, the community and society receives utilitarian priority rather than individual freedom, which is the principle of liberalism. But in these illiberal polities, there is no constitutionalism; their constitutions – using Pablo Castillo-Ortiz's term – are 'de-normativised'.[66] In other words, in my view, 'illiberal constitutionalism' is an oxymoron.

D. Can 'Non-liberal Constitutionalism' Really be Constitutionalist?

Besides illiberal constitutionalism, there are also attempts to legitimate 'non-liberal constitutionalism' as a subtype of constitutionalism. Graham Walker uses the term for constitutionalist structures, 'wherever people value some aspects of communal identity more than autonomy of individual choice'.[67] Walker's main example for the non-liberal, rather local than universal values is the multicultural grant of group rights to native peoples and the distinct society of Québec, but he also mentions the state of Israel, which fails its non-citizen residents in many regrettable ways, as well as the tribal life of the Native American nations in the US. The common characteristic of all these approaches is 'to indict the notion of individual autonomy rights as a form of naïve and homogenizing universalism, and to unmask the ethnic and moral "neutrality" of the liberal state as a covert form of coercion'.[68] Walker builds up his concept using Charles Howard McIlwain's understanding of constitutionalism in his 1940 book.[69] According to McIlwain, the limitation of government by law is not necessarily liberal, because the rights of individuals are not centralised, and there is no need for a public authority to be a neutral arbiter among competing value systems. Among the more contemporary thinkers, Walker relies on Stanley Fish's scepticism about individual rights of all kinds. In his notorious articles from 1987[70] and 1992[71]

[64] L-A Thio, 'Constitutionalism in Illiberal Polities' in M Rosenfeld and A Sajó (eds), *Oxford Handbook of Comparative Constitutional Law* (Oxford, Oxford University Press, 2012). Contrary to my understanding, Thio also talks about 'constitutionalism' in illiberal polities.

[65] There are two subcategories distinguished here: the Iranian subcategory, where Islam is granted an authoritative central role within the bounds of a constitution; and the Saudi Arabian subcategory, where Islam is present, without the formal authority of modern constitutionalism.

[66] See P Castillo-Ortiz, 'The Illiberal Abuse of Constitutional Courts in Europe' (2019) 15 *European Constitutional Law Review* 48, 67.

[67] G Walker, 'The Idea of Nonliberal Constitutionalism' (1997) 39 *Nomos* 154, 155.

[68] ibid 157.

[69] CH McIlwain, *Constitutionalism, Ancient and Modern* (Ithaca, NY, Cornell University Press, 1940).

[70] S Fish, 'Liberalism Doesn't Exist' (1987) 6 *Duke Law Journal* 997.

[71] S Fish, 'There's No Such Thing as Free Speech and It's a Good Thing, Too' (1992) 17 *Boston Review* 3.

respectively, Fish argues that because liberalism conceives its rational principles precisely as supranational and non-partisan, 'one can only conclude, and conclude nonparadoxically, that liberalism doesn't exist'. According to Walker, non-liberal constitutionalism historically was anticipated in some features of Republican Rome or of medieval Europe, or in the millet system of the Ottoman Empire, and in more recent history in Canada before the 1982 Charter of Rights and Freedoms. He also considers the evolving multiculturalist/tolerationist American university campus practices as an embryonic version of non-liberal constitutionalism, and 'politically correct' thinkers who promote such policies as hostile to the notion of 'individual rights'.

The problem with Walker's concept is that he conflates constitutionalism with the constitution. While the latter indeed pre-dates the Enlightenment, the former, together with liberalism, does not.[72] The 'constitution', as the configuration of public order defined by Aristotle or Cicero, did not require the notion of individual rights, while modern constitutionalism does.[73] For instance, Montesquieu in *The Spirit of Laws* argues that the constitutional system based on the separation of powers is necessary for securing political liberty and preventing the emergence of 'tyrannical laws' and 'execution of laws in a tyrannical manner'.[74] This means that 'fettered power', which, according to Walker, is the essence of constitutionalism, presupposes guaranteed individual rights. In other words, not only the anti- or illiberal version of constitutionalism discussed earlier, but also the non-liberal one is oxymoronic.

II. ATTEMPTS TO LEGITIMISE 'ILLIBERAL CONSTITUTIONALISM'

A. Majoritarian (Westminster) System

Proponents of the Fidesz illiberal constitution, such as Béla Pokol, professor of law and member of the packed Hungarian Constitutional Court, argue that

[72] 'Classic liberalism' in its 19th-century European sense means individual liberty and a free market. See A Sajó and R Uitz, *The Constitution of Freedom: An Introduction to Legal Constitutionalism* (Oxford, Oxford University Press, 2017) 13.

[73] Carl J Friedrich, one of the authors to whom Walker refers, in the later editions of his famous text on *Constitutional Government and Democracy* emphasises that the single function of constitutionalism is safeguarding each person in the exercise of 'individual rights'. See CJ Friedrich, *Constitutional Governance and Democracy: Theory and Practice in Europe and America*, 4th edn (Waltham, Blaisdell Publishing, 1968) 24, 7. Walter Murphy, another author quoted by Walker after the democratic transition in Eastern Europe, has also talked about 'protecting individual liberty' as the ultimate civic purpose of constitutionalism. Cf WF Murphy, 'Constitutions, Constitutionalism and Democracy' in D Greenberg, SN Katz, MB Oliviero and SD Wheatley (eds), *Constitutionalism and Democracy: Transitions in the Contemporary World* (Oxford, Oxford University Press, 1993).

[74] Montesquieu, *The Spirit of the Laws*, eds AM Cohler, BC Miller and HS Stone (Cambridge, Cambridge University Press, 1999) bk XI, ch 6, 157 (quoted by GA Tóth, 'Constitutional Markers of Authoritarianism' (2018) *Hague Journal on the Rule of Law* 1).

the post-2012 constitutional system envisages the Westminster-type of parliamentary system, in which the 'winner takes all' and where the principle of the unity of power prevails.[75] But the Hungarian, or for that matter Polish, constitutional system cannot be considered as a monistic democracy, which simply gives priority to democratic decision making over fundamental rights.[76] In fact, the new Hungarian constitution and the Polish constitutional practice do not comply with any model of government based on the concept of the separation of powers. The more traditional models of government forms are based on the relationship between the legislature and the executive. For instance, Arendt Lijphart differentiates between the majoritarian (Westminster) and consensual models of democracy, the prototype of the first being the British model, the second being the Continental European parliamentary model, as well as the US presidential system.[77] Giovanni Sartori speaks about presidentialism and semi-presidentialism, as well as about two forms of parliamentarism, namely, the premiership system in the UK, or *Kanzlerdemokratie* in Germany, and the assembly government model in Italy.[78] Bruce Ackerman uses, besides the Westminster and the US separation of powers systems, the constrained parliamentarism model as a new form of separation of powers, which has emerged against the export of the American system in favour of the models in Germany, Italy, Japan, India, Canada, South Africa and other nations, where both popular referendums and constitutional courts constrain parliamentary power.[79]

Hungary and Poland, from 1990 until 2010, and 2015 respectively, belonged to the consensual and constrained parliamentary systems, close to the German *Kanzlerdemokratie*, in Poland with a more substantive role for the President of the Republic. But in Hungary, the 2011 Fundamental Law abolished almost all possibility of institutional consensus and constraints on governmental power. In Poland, in spite of the fact that the governmental majority is not able to change the Constitution, due to the legislative efforts of the PiS Government, the 1997 Constitution has become a sham document. In both countries, the system has moved towards an absolute parliamentary sovereignty model, without the cultural constraints of the Westminster form of government. Not to mention the fact that in the last decades, the traditional British model of constitutionalism has also been changed drastically with the introduction of

[75] B Pokol, 'Elismerés és kritika' ['Recognition and Criticism'] *Magyar Nemzet* (24 March 2011).

[76] Bruce Ackerman distinguishes between three models of democracy: monistic; rights fundamentalism, in which fundamental rights are morally prior to democratic decision making and impose limits; and dualist, which finds the middle ground between these two extremes, and subjects majoritarian decision making to constitutional guarantees. See B Ackerman, *We the People* (Cambridge, MA, Harvard University Press, 1992) vol 1, 6–16.

[77] A Lijphart, *Patterns of Democracy. Government Forms and Performance in Thirty-Six Countries* (New Haven, CT, Yale University Press, 1999).

[78] G Sartori, *Comparative Constitutional Engineering*, 2nd edn (New York, New York University Press, 1997).

[79] B Ackerman, 'The New Separation of Powers' (2000) 113 *Harvard Law Review* 633.

bills of rights by left-of-centre governments – and opposed by right-of-centre opposition parties – in Canada (1982), New Zealand (1990), the United Kingdom (1998), the Australian Capital Territory (2004) and the State of Victoria (2006). Contrary to the traditional Commonwealth model of constitutionalism, in the new Commonwealth model the codified bills of rights became limits on the legislation, but the final word remained in the hands of the politically accountable branch of government. In this respect, this new Commonwealth model is different from the judicial supremacy approach of the US separation of powers model, as well as from the European constrained parliamentary model. The biggest change occurred in the UK, and some even talk about the 'demise of the Westminster model'.[80] The greatest deviation from the system of unlimited parliamentary sovereignty was the introduction of judicial review. In just over two decades, the number of applications for judicial review nearly quadrupled, to over 3,400 in 2000, when the Human Rights Act 1998 came into effect in England and Wales.[81] The Human Rights Act has a general requirement that all legislation should be compatible with the European Convention on Human Rights. This does not allow UK courts to strike down, or 'disapply', legislation, or to make new law; instead, where legislation is deemed to be incompatible with Convention rights, superior courts may make a declaration of incompatibility under section 4(2) of the Act. The Government and Parliament then decide how to proceed. In this sense, the legislative sovereignty of the UK Parliament is preserved. Some academics argue that although, as a matter of constitutional legality, Parliament may well be sovereign, as a matter of constitutional practice it has transferred significant power to the judiciary.[82]

Others go even further and argue that although the Human Rights Act 1998 is purported to reconcile the protection of human rights with the sovereignty of Parliament, it represents an unprecedented transfer of political power from the executive and legislature to the judiciary.[83]

Besides the aforementioned Commonwealth countries, a similarly new model has emerged in Israel, where the Basic Law on occupation, re-enacted in 1994, contains a 'notwithstanding' provision, similar to the Canadian one. The new model of Commonwealth constitutionalism is based on a dialogue between the judiciary and the parliament. In contrast to these new trends, in the Hungarian and Polish constitutional systems the parliamentary majority not only decides every single issue without any dialogue, but in practice there is no partner for such a dialogue, due to the fact that the independence of both the ordinary judiciary and the constitutional courts has been eliminated.

[80] Cf P Norton, 'Governing Alone' (2003) 56(4) *Parliamentary Affairs* 543, 544.

[81] See D Judge, 'Whatever Happened to Parliamentary Democracy in the United Kingdom' (2004) 57(3) *Parliamentary Affairs* 682, 691.

[82] Cf KD Ewing, 'The Human Rights Act and Parliamentary Democracy' (1999) 62 *MLR* 79.

[83] See M Flinders, 'Shifting the Balance? Parliament, the Executive and the British Constitution' (2002) 50(1) *Political Studies* 23.

B. Political Constitutionalism

It is striking, and of significance, how the illiberal authoritarians in Central and Eastern Europe attempt to legitimise their actions by referring to political constitutionalism as their approach to constitutional change. The main argument of Central and Eastern European illiberals to defend their constitutional projects is grounded in a claim to political constitutionalism, which favours parliamentary rule and weak judicial review. To be clear, despite some academics' efforts to apply the concept of political constitutionalism in defence of illiberalism, I do not consider political constitutionalism, based on republican philosophy, or all of the concepts rejecting strong judicial review, or judicial review altogether, as populist.[84] Some scholars and constitutional court justices, both in Hungary and Poland, have attempted to interpret the new constitutional system as a change from legal to political constitutionalism. In my view, these interpretations are simply efforts to legitimise the silencing of judicial review.

One of the 'fake judges' of the Polish Constitutional Tribunal, the late Lech Morawski, emphasised the republican traditions, present in both Hungary and Poland, mentioning the names of Michael Sandel, Philip Pettit and Quentin Skinner.[85] Also, constitutional law professor Adam Czarnota explained the necessity for the changes, with the argument that 'legal constitutionalism alienated the constitution from citizens … The place of excluded citizens was taken by lawyers.'[86] He proudly acknowledges that the governing party, PiS, has appointed judges that represent its worldview, which according to Czarnota is based 'on the principle of supremacy of the Parliament in relation to constitutional review and acceptance of a role of judicial restraint not judicial activism which was earlier the norm'.[87] Czarnota interprets the present constitutional crisis in Poland and in some other countries in Central-Eastern Europe as 'an attempt to take the constitution seriously and return it to the citizens'[88] – what he considers the fulfilment of political constitutionalism.

In Hungary, István Stumpf, constitutional judge, nominated without any consultation with opposition parties by Fidesz right after the new Government took over in 2010, and elected exclusively with the votes of the governing parties, argued in his book for a strong state and claimed the expansion of political constitutionalism regarding the changes.[89] It is remarkable that two other members of the current packed Constitutional Court also argue against legal

[84] See for the opposite view L Corso, 'What Does Populism Have to Do with Constitutional Law? Discussing Populist Constitutionalism and Its Assumptions' (2014) III(2) *Rivista di Filosofia del Diritto* 443.

[85] L Morawski, 'A Critical Response', *Verfassungsblog*, 3 June 2017.

[86] A Czarnota, 'The Constitutional Tribunal', Verfassungsblog, 3 June 2017.

[87] ibid.

[88] ibid.

[89] See I Stumpf, *Erös állam – alkotmányos korlátok* [*Strong State – Constitutional Limits*] (Budapest, Századvég, 2014) 244–49.

constitutionalism, decrying it as 'judicial dictatorship'[90] or 'juristocratic'.[91] In the scholarly literature, Attila Vincze argued that the decision of the Constitutional Court accepting the Fourth Amendment to the Fundamental Law – which among other things also invalidated the entire case law of the Court prior to the new Constitution – was a sign of political constitutionalism's prevailing over legal constitutionalism.[92] Even those, like Kálmán Pócza, Gábor Dobos and Attila Gyulai, who acknowledge that the Court has not been confrontational as regards the current legislature and the Government, characterise this behaviour as a special approach within the system of the separation of powers, best described as a partnership in a constitutional dialogue.[93]

Political constitutionalists like Richard Bellamy, Jeremy Waldron, Akhil Amar, Sandy Levinson and Mark Tushnet, who themselves differ from one another significantly, emphasise the role of elected bodies instead of courts in implementing and protecting the constitution, but none of them rejects the main principles of constitutional democracy, as 'illiberal' populist constitutionalists do. Even Richard D Parker, who announced a 'constitutional populist manifesto', wanted only to challenge the basic idea, central to constitutional law, 'that constitutional constraints on public power in a democracy are meant to contain or tame the exertion of popular political energy rather than to nurture, galvanise, and release it'.[94] Similarly, those who describe a new model of constitutionalism based on deliberation between courts and the legislator, with the latter retaining the final word, have nothing to do with illiberal constitutionalism.[95] Those scholars realise that parliamentary sovereignty tends to be increasingly restrained,

[90] See AZ Varga, *From Ideal to Idol? The Concept of the Rule of Law* (Budapest, Dialóg Campus, 2019) 16.

[91] B Pokol, *The Juristocratic State: Its Victory and the Possibility of Taming* (Budapest, Dialóg Campus, 2017).

[92] A Vincze, 'Az Alkotmánybíróság határozata az Alaptörvény negyedik módosításáról: az alkotmánymódosítás alkotmánybírósági kontrollja' ['The Decision of the Constitutional Court on the Fourth Amendment to the Fundamental Law: The Constitutional Review of Constitutional Amendments)'] (2013) 3 *Jogesetek Magyarázata* 12.

[93] See K Pócza, G Dobos and A Gyulai, 'The Hungarian Constitutional Court: A constructive partner in constitutional dialogue' in K Pócza (ed), *Constitutional Politics and the Judiciary. Decision-Making in Central and Eastern Europe* (Abingdon, Routledge, 2018) ch 5.

[94] Analysing T Mann's novel *Mario and the Magician*, written in 1929, Parker draws the conclusion for today that 'the point is to get out and take part in politics ourselves, not looking down from a "higher" pedestal, but on the same level with all of the other ordinary people': RD Parker, 'Here, the People Rule: A Constitutional Populist Manifesto' (1993) 27 *Valparaiso University Law Review* 531–84, 583.

[95] Regarding the new model, see S Gardbaum, *The New Commonwealth Model of Constitutionalism* (Cambridge, Cambridge University Press, 2013). This model has also come to be known by several other names: 'weak-form of judicial review' (M Tushnet, 'Alternative Forms of Judicial Review' (2003) 101 *Michigan Law Review* 2781); 'weak judicial review' (J Waldron, The Core of the Case Against Judicial Review' (2006) 115 *Yale Law Journal* 1348); 'the parliamentary bill of rights model' (J Hiebert, 'Parliamentary Bill of Rights. An Alternative Model?' (2006) 69 *MLR* 7); 'the model of democratic dialogue' (AL Young, *Parliamentary Sovereignty and the Human Rights Act* (Oxford, Hart Publishing, 2006)); 'dialogic judicial review' (K Roach, 'Dialogic Judicial Review and its Critics' (2004) 23 *Supreme Court Law Review* 49);

either legally or politically, and that the last decades have witnessed less and less scope for the exercise of traditional *pouvoir constituant*, conceived as the unrestrained 'will of the people', even in cases of regime change or the establishment of substantially and formally new constitutional arrangements.[96] The remnants of both Hungarian and Polish constitutional review have nothing to do with any types of political constitutionalism or a weak judicial review approach, which all represent a different model of the separation of powers. In the authoritarian Hungarian and in the Polish sham systems of constitutionalism, there is no place for any kind of separation of powers.

Following Tamás Györfi's theory, there are three different forms of weak judicial review: each of them is lacking one of the defining features of strong constitutional review, but all of them want to strike a balance between democracy and the protection of human rights that differs from the balance struck by the 'new constitutionalism' of strong judicial review.[97] First, judicial review is limited if the constitution lacks a bill of rights, as is the case in Australia. Second, judicial review is deferential if courts usually defer to the views of the elected branches, as in the Scandinavian constitutional systems, or are even constitutionally obliged to do so, as in Sweden and Finland. Finally, and probably most importantly, there is the Commonwealth model of judicial review, where courts are authorised to review legislation, but the legislature has the possibility to override or disregard judicial decisions.[98]

In my view, neither the Polish nor the Hungarian model fits any of these approaches to weak judicial review, as their aim is neither to balance democracy nor the protection of fundamental rights. The weakening of the power of constitutional courts started in Hungary right after the landslide victory of the centre-right Fidesz party in the 2010 parliamentary elections. What happened in Hungary resonated with some less successful, similar attempts to weaken constitutional review in other East-Central European countries that took place roughly around the same time. In the Summer of 2012, there was a constitutional crisis in Romania too, where the ruling socialists tried to dismantle both the Constitutional Court and the President, but the EU was able to exert a stronger influence over events there.[99] From 2014, there has also been a constitutional

'collaborative constitution' (A Kavanaugh, 'Participation and Judicial Review: A Reply to Jeremy Waldron' (2003) 22 *Law and Philosophy* 451); or 'democratic constitutionalism' (R Post and R Siegel, 'Democratic Constitutionalism', White Paper, available at https://constitutioncenter.org/interactive-constitution/white-pages/democratic-constitutionalism).

[96] C Fusaro and D Oliver, 'Towards a Theory of Constitutional Change' in D Oliver and C Fusaro (eds), *How Constitutions Change – A Comparative Study* (Oxford, Hart Publishing, 2011).

[97] See T Györfi, *Against the New Constitutionalism* (Cheltenham, Edward Elgar Publishing, 2016).

[98] See Gardbaum (n 95).

[99] Regarding the Romanian crisis, see V Perju, 'The Romanian Double Executive and the 2012 Constitutional Crisis' (2015) 13 *International Journal of Constitutional Law* 246–78; B Iancu, 'Separation of Powers and the Rule of Law in Romania: The Crisis in Concepts and Contexts' in A von Bogdandy and P Sonnevend (eds), *Constitutional Crisis in the European Constitutional Area* (Oxford, Hart Publishing, 2015) 153.

crisis in progress in Slovakia, where the Constitutional Court has also worked short of two – and from February 2016 three – judges, because the President of the Republic refused to fill the vacancies.[100] But the most successful follower of the Hungarian playbook on how to dismantle constitutional review has been Jaroslaw Kaczynski's governing party (PiS) and its Government in Poland. After the 2015 parliamentary election in Poland, the Law and Justice Party (PiS) also followed the playbook of Viktor Orbán, and started by first capturing the Constitutional Tribunal.[101] But these efforts have nothing to do with political constitutionalism, partly because they do not question the capacity of constitutional courts to invalidate legislation passed by parliaments, partly because they are not based on the mechanism of political accountability and checks on power.[102] Also, political constitutionalism emphasises the importance of legislatures over courts, and not the direct role of citizens, as Czarnota argues. This dismantlement of constitutional review cannot be considered as a par-excellence majoritarian project either.[103]

C. Constitutional Identity

From the very beginning, the Government of Viktor Orbán has justified non-compliance with the principles of liberal democratic constitutionalism also enshrined in Article 2 of the Treaty of the European Union (TEU) by referring to national sovereignty. Lately, as an immediate reaction to the EU's efforts to resolve the refugee crisis, the Government has advanced the argument that the country's constitutional identity, being Christian, and thus conflicting with the acceptance of Muslim refugees, is guaranteed in Article 4(2) TEU.

After some draconian legislative measures were adopted, the Government started a campaign against the EU's plan to relocate refugees. The first step was a referendum initiated by the Government. On 2 October 2016, Hungarian voters went to the polls to answer one referendum question: 'Do you want to allow the European Union to mandate the relocation of non-Hungarian citizens to Hungary without the approval of the National Assembly?' Although 92 per cent of those who cast votes and 98 per cent of all the valid votes agreed with the Government, answering 'No' (6 per cent were spoiled ballots), the referendum was invalid because the turnout was only around 40 per cent, instead of the required 50 per cent.

[100] T Lálik, 'Constitutional Crisis in Slovakia: Still Far from Resolution', ICONNECT, 5 August 2016, available at www.iconnectblog.com/2016/08/constitutional-court-crisis-in-slovakia-still-far-away-from-resolution/.

[101] The same playbook was also used outside the region, in Turkey by Erdoğan and in Venezuela by Chavez.

[102] See these requirements of political constitutionalism in Castillo-Ortiz (n 65) 64.

[103] As Wojciech Sadurski rightly points out, the Polish governing party, PiS, obtained 18% of the votes of all eligible voters. See Sadurski (n 34) 1.

As a next attempt, Prime Minister Orbán introduced the Seventh Amendment, which would have made it 'the responsibility of every state institution to defend Hungary's constitutional identity'. The most important provision of the draft amendment reads 'No foreign population can settle in Hungary.' Since the governing coalition lost its two-thirds majority, even though all of its MPs voted in favour of the proposed amendment, it fell two votes short of the required majority. After this second failure, the Constitutional Court, loyal to the Government, came to the rescue of Orbán's constitutional identity defence of its policies on migration. The Court revived a petition of the also loyal Commissioner for Fundamental Rights, filed a year earlier, before the referendum was initiated. In his motion, the Commissioner asked the Court to deliver an abstract interpretation of the Fundamental Law in connection with Council Decision 2015/1601 of 22 September 2015.

The Constitutional Court in its decision held that 'the constitutional self-identity of Hungary is a fundamental value not created by the Fundamental Law – it is merely acknowledged by the Fundamental Law, consequently constitutional identity cannot be waived by way of an international treaty'.[104] Therefore, the Court argued, 'the protection of the constitutional identity shall remain the duty of the Constitutional Court as long as Hungary is a sovereign State'.[105] This abuse of constitutional identity aimed at not taking part in the joint European solution to the refugee crisis is an exercise of national constitutional parochialism,[106] which attempts to abandon the common European liberal democratic constitutional whole.

The Constitutional Court in its Decision 3/2019. (III. 7.) AB also ruled on the constitutionality of certain elements of the 'Stop Soros' legislative package, and found that the criminalisation of 'facilitating illegal immigration' does not violate the Fundamental Law. The Court again referred to the constitutional requirement to protect Hungary's sovereignty and constitutional identity, to justify this clear violation of the freedom of association and freedom of expression, hiding behind the alleged obligation to protect the Schengen borders against 'masses entering [the EU] uncontrollably and illegitimately'.[107] Besides infringing the rights of the non-governmental organisations, the Decision deprives all asylum seekers of the protection of all fundamental rights by stating that

> the fundamental rights protection … clearly does not cover the persons arrived in the territory of Hungary through any country where he or she had not been persecuted

[104] Decision 22/2016 AB of the Constitutional Court of Hungary [67]. See, for a detailed analysis of the Decision, G Halmai, 'Abuse of Constitutional Identity. The Hungarian Constitutional Court on Interpretation of Article E) (2) of the Fundamental Law' (2018) 43 *Review of Central and East European Law* 23.

[105] Decision 22/2016 AB of the Constitutional Court of Hungary [67].

[106] See the term used by M Kumm, 'Rethinking Constitutional Authority: On Structure and Limits of Constitutional Pluralism' in M Avbelj and J Komárek, *Constitutional Pluralism in the European Union and Beyond* (Oxford, Hart Publishing, 2012) 51.

[107] 3/2019. (III. 7.) AB [43].

> or directly threatened with persecution. Therefore, the requirements set forth by Article I Paragraph (3) of the Fundamental Law regarding the restriction of fundamental rights shall not be applied to the regulation of the above listed cases.[108]

With this the Court denies the core of human dignity: the right to have rights.

III. CONCLUSION

In the chapter I have tried to demonstrate that court ideologists of populist autocrats use Carl Schmitt's concept of political sovereignty and the collective identity of the people, or misuse Max Weber's leader democracy or Richard Bellamy's or others' political constitutionalism ideas, to legitimise 'illiberal constitutionalism' in general, and unchecked governance, the dismantling of constitutional review and the non-compliance with European values in particular. The dismantlement of checks on the government is based on references to the majoritarian (Westminster) system of governance. The silencing of the once very powerful and activist Hungarian and Polish Constitutional Courts, which happened through the shrinking of their jurisdiction and packing them with judges loyal to the Government, has been explained by misuse of the concept of political constitutionalism. The abuse of national constitutional identity by the Governments, the packed Constitutional Courts and academics serves to legitimise the non-compliance of Hungary and Poland as Member States with the EU's constitutional identity.

I have argued that the constitutional concept, which rejects liberalism as a constitutive precondition of democracy, cannot be in compliance with the traditional idea of liberal democratic constitutionalism. All these attempts to legitimate 'illiberal constitutionalism', I have argued, are rather pretexts to hide the authoritarian pursuits of these rogue governments with the help of their court ideologists.

[108] ibid [49].

4

Why the Rule of Law Can Never be Part of an 'Illiberal' Democracy

JOAKIM NERGELIUS

I. BACKGROUND AND INTRODUCTION

THIS CHAPTER WILL focus on the issue of which specific concept of democracy the European Union (EU) adheres to today and will be pursuing in the future. As we shall see, there are a few to choose from. The analysis is made against the somewhat sinister background of what the Hungarian Prime Minister Viktor Orbán in 2014 advocated as being an 'illiberal democracy', that would in his view respond to contemporary challenges such as migration and terrorism in a better way than the traditional, liberal and pluralist democracy.[1] A very important part of the background is of course also the deep conflict of values that has, at least for the last five years, characterised the whole western world.

This crisis or clash of values probably started in Hungary in 2010, with the great or even landslide electoral victory of the Fidesz party in Hungary, which won a two-thirds majority in the Parliament and immediately began to use that huge majority in order to appoint new judges and chief executives to various public bodies. Without any doubt, Orbán's ideas have inspired authoritarian, populist right-wing leaders in other parts of the world. My view, presented below, however, is that after the introduction into the EU Treaty, gradually since 1993, of ideals such as human rights, democracy and the rule of law, the EU is bound – or has in fact bound itself – to a liberal, *material* model of democracy, based in particular on the rule of law and human rights. While Orbán's so-called illiberal model is based on nothing else – and respects nothing else – than the will of the alleged sovereign 'people', which is here given an almost mythical status, the liberal model of democracy currently prevailing in the EU requires that values such as human rights and the rule of law are respected if democracy is to be said to exist at all.

[1] The full text of Orbán's speech, given at Tusnafürdö in Romania on 26 July 2014, is available at https://budapestbeacon.com.

While the former 'vision', emphasising no other traditional democratic value than popular sovereignty itself, may with some good will be called a formal view of democracy, the view enshrined in Articles 2, 6 and 7 of the Treaty on European Union (TEU) is definitely a material one. This clash of values within the EU itself is likely to lead to a huge, maybe even dramatic, conflict between the majority of EU Member States and the more authoritarian ones, the outcome of which is hard to predict. The low-intensity battle between the two colliding views at the EU summit in July 2020 was probably just a first glimpse of what may be expected in the future. Here in this chapter, however, some solutions will eventually be suggested, based on the assumption that in the long run, it will be better for the EU to cling or stick to its basic idea(l)s of democracy, the rule of law and human rights than to yield to populist temptations and allow Member States a wide discretion in such crucial matters.

II. THE CURRENT LEGAL FRAMEWORK

One clear aspect of the value crisis that distinguishes it from other current crises, in connection not least with the refugee crisis, is that it is of a highly legal nature, which means that some legal issues need to be clarified here. For instance, when Hungary announced in 2015 that it refused to take part in a common asylum policy, and then brought a case to the Court of Justice of the EU (CJEU) together with Slovakia, followed by a legally doubtful referendum on the reception of refugees in October 2016, the mixture between legal and political measures in this area became clearer than ever, since this must be seen to amount to a basic challenge against the supremacy of EU law and against the principle of solidarity and loyalty that follows from Article 4(3) TEU. How can we today, some five years later, analyse the consequences of this unpredicted, unforeseen and deeply problematic situation?

The rule of law took its place in the EU Treaty for the first time in 1993, when the three European Communities were changed into one 'European Union'. On the entry into force of the Amsterdam Treaty, on 1 May 1999, the former Article F was changed into two new articles (Articles 6 and 7 TEU) and the rule of law was made a principle upon which the Union was founded. The rule of law was, above all, instrumental in the context of the Eastward Enlargement of the Union, since it was a pillar of the Copenhagen criteria, adopted in 1993 as the basic preconditions for states wanting to become EU members.

Since the entry into force of the Lisbon Treaty in 2009, the founding principles have been moved from Article 6 TEU to Article 2 TEU. Article 7 TEU contains the procedure envisaged for the protection of the values in Article 2 TEU, which means that the two articles together form the EU's main mechanism for the protection of the rule of law in the Member States.

It may be noted that a widespread discussion on the application of Article 7 TEU (which was by then Article 6) took place as early as 2000, when a majority of the Member States appeared to be willing to introduce some very mild and, in reality, informal sanctions against Austria, due to the fact that the right-wing populist party FPÖ had joined the Austrian Government. For a number of reasons, though (the most important being that Austria had in fact not violated any of the said values), the rather bizarre measures initiated at the time, such as refusals from other Member State governments to shake the hands of Austrian Ministers or let them join common photo sessions, quickly ended.[2]

Still, for some time, all the other Member States refused to cooperate with the Austrian Government because it included members of FPÖ, though Austria had not (yet) violated any of the principles in Article 6(1) TEU. This lack of legal clarity was addressed in the following treaty revision in 2000 (the Nice Treaty), when Article 7 TEU was changed to include the possibility of determining the existence of both *a breach* and *a clear risk of a serious breach*. This is, in other words, the current legal point of departure.

III. THE CONFLICT OF VALUES WITHIN THE EU (AND THE WESTERN WORLD)

If we view the situation in a somewhat wider context, it is obvious that what in this chapter is called the 'refugee crisis' is in fact a part of a much wider crisis, which here may be referred to as a crisis of values, characterised by fundamental conflicts of values between different EU Member States and, even more, between different ideologies and ideological camps in the EU and the whole Western world. In this wider conflict, a general distrust of the EU and its institutions clearly features, a distrust that many actors may believe to be in their interest and which they therefore promote further.

This rather deep conflict of values, which is at the core of this chapter, is centred on but not limited to Eastern Europe. The urgent refugee crisis that started in 2015 has increased it, and has also led to a clear division between the Northern and Western EU Member States, on the one hand, and most of the Eastern ones, on the other, who simply refuse to accept or host refugees from Africa and the Middle East. As mentioned, Hungary and Slovakia even brought a case to the CJEU in 2015, questioning an EU decision on redistribution or repartition of refugee quotas (a case, or rather joined cases (C-643/15 and C-647/15) they eventually lost, through a judgment in September 2017).[3] In the period while the outcome of that case was pending, but also afterwards,

[2] This was partly also due to a report from three so-called 'wise men', former Finnish President Ahtisaari, former Spanish Foreign Minister Oreja and German law professor Jochen Frowein, published in September 2000: Report by Martti Ahtisaari, Jochen Frowein and Marelino Oreja, adopted in Paris on 8 September 2000 [92], available at www.virtual-institute.de/en/BerichtEU/index.

[3] Case C-643/15 *Slovakia v Council*, ECLI:EU:C:2017:631.

the EU unfortunately was and continues to be unable to advance significantly in this area.

Nevertheless, what seems to amount to a majority of Member States, as well as the EU Commission and Parliament (that voted on this as recently as 19 October 2017), do still advocate receiving refugees within the EU, provided that adequate mechanisms for redistribution of them may be found. In September 2018, the Parliament also voted on a report on Hungary from MEP Judith Sargentini, which was adopted by an absolute majority of MEPs (with 448 votes in favour and 197 against),[4] and again on 16 January 2020.[5]

This majority of Member States, led by Germany, is also critical of the authoritarian tendencies in countries such as Hungary and Poland. A crucial question for the future, then, is whether they should use the existing mechanisms of the EU treaties, such as qualified majority voting (QMV) in the Council and increased control of Member States who seem to ignore the rule of law, to enforce more liberal values on reluctant states who seem to prefer an authoritarian model of society.[6] How is that goal best achieved? And may authoritarian states even remain members of the EU under the current treaties?

Thus, the question is this: What possibilities do the EU treaties offer for a qualified majority of Member States (or rather, Member States who hold a qualified majority in the Council) to 'curb' a minority of reluctant Member States, who seem to question and openly challenge the basic democratic ideals of the Union?

Once again, the event that in my view marked the beginning of the above-described crisis or clash of values within the EU, was the landslide electoral victory in 2010 of the Fidesz party in Hungary, which won a two-thirds majority in the Parliament. The initial moves of the Fidesz Government to appoint new judges and chief executives to various public bodies were then followed by a new media law, as well as a new Constitution in 2011, and then also by a decision to force all judges of the age of 62 or over to retire. The media law strengthened the Government's control over all state media, and the new Constitution displays remarkably nationalistic language and approach, while also curtailing the independence of the judicial system and huge parts of the public administration.[7]

[4] LIBE – Committee meeting (4 December 2018); Judith Sargentini – LIBE rapporteur 10:07/10:30 (4 December 2018). After this, Hungary has brought a case against the Parliament to CJEU (Case C-650/18, pending).

[5] European Parliament resolution of 16 January 2020 on ongoing hearings under Article 7(1) of the TEU regarding Poland and Hungary, P9_TA(2020)0014.

[6] In Art 238(2)–(3) TFEU, a qualified majority is defined as 72% of the Member States, representing at least 65% of the Union's population or, when not all the Member States are participating, 55% of the Member States representing at least 65% of the Union's population.

[7] For an overview, see J Nergelius, 'The Hungarian Constitution of 2012 and Its Protection of Fundamental Rights' (2012) 3 *European Policy Analysis* 1. A more general perspective on the development, from 2010 until 2014, in Hungary and Romania is provided in A von Bogdandy and P Sonnavend, *Constitutional Crisis in the European Constitutional Area – Theory, Law and Politics in Hungary and Romania* (Oxford, Hart Publishing, 2015).

In many respects, that is where the global right-wing populist movement, which has since then shocked the Western world with such force, must be said to have started.

These and other assaults on the rule of law and other crucial values set out in Articles 6 and 7 TEU did of course cause a number of reactions from the EU. Among the actions initiated by the EU, it may be noted that the EU Commission brought a case to the CJEU against Hungary concerning the forced retirement of judges older than 62 years. The Court found in 2012 that this amounted to unlawful discrimination on grounds of age (Case C-286/12). We may also point to the Opinion of Advocate General Sharpston from October 2019, criticising Hungary, Poland and the Czech Republic for refusing to comply with the provisional mechanism for mandatory relocation of asylum seekers, and the CJEU's judgment against these states of 2 April 2020.[8] As recently as June 2020, the CJEU found that Hungary had violated EU law by striking down on the financing of non-governmental organisations and other civil organisations.[9]

As already noted, the CJEU found in 2012, when the EU Commission brought a case against Hungary concerning the forced retirement of judges older than 62 years, that this amounted to unlawful discrimination on grounds of age.[10] Here, however, it seems that the Commission deliberately chose that quite technical approach, with claims of an alleged treaty violation according to Article 258 of the Treaty on the Functioning of the EU (TFEU), rather than claiming that the basic, fundamental principle of the rule of law was actually violated. In fact, the EU until very recently refrained from invoking Articles 6 and 7 TEU, according to which a Member State that does not respect the rule of law and/or other key values of European integration (such as democracy, human rights, human dignity, freedom, equality, by reference to Article 2 TEU) may temporarily lose some of its rights as a member, including the right to vote in the EU Council. Such a harsh measure against a Member State, which has to be decided upon by all the others, would of course be controversial for a number of reasons, but may in the long run be hard to avoid should one or a number of Member States repeatedly and almost provocatively – as has been the case in recent years – show that they do not want, and have in fact no wish whatsoever, to respect those basic values.

IV. LEGAL OBSTACLES FOR ACTIONS AGAINST FAILING MEMBER STATES

Now, at least, some recent developments, which are dealt with in the next section, have to some extent changed the legal situation described in the preceding

[8] Joined Cases C-715/17, 718/17 and 719/17 *Commission v Poland*, Opinion of AG Sharpston of 31 October 2019 and Judgment of 2 April 2020, ECLI:EU:C:2020:257.

[9] Case C-78/18 *Commission v Hungary*, ECLI:EU:C:2020:476.

[10] Case C-286/12 *Commission v Hungary*, ECLI:EU:C:2012:687.

sections. Thus, the need to initiate procedures in the area of the rule of law itself can probably no longer be avoided if the issue of rule of law violations is going to be addressed in a serious way, though it may yet not be necessary to invoke Article 2 TEU.

Sadly enough, in the discussions that have occurred since 2010 concerning the situation in Hungary, but at times also in, for example, Romania and, since early 2016, not least in relation to Poland, governments have expressed profound doubts concerning the very *validity* of key European values such as the rule of law and human rights.[11] GOOD This is something new and unforeseen in the history of the EU. It is thus no wonder that, since 2010, Hungary has been the focus of this whole conflict, which has been escalating since 2011, at least from a political point of view.[12] From the legal point of view, anyhow, it seems very clear that Hungary has not complied with the key values of European integration (see Article 2 TEU).

Ever since 2011, it has been discussed when the threshold, in this respect, will be passed in relation to Hungary – or rather when Article 7 must be activated if it is to have any real significance at all. Since 2015, the resistance from Hungary and a few other Member States to the existing or proposed EU policy on refugees has also added fuel to the fire, while the development in Poland, with its new conservative Government, seems to be almost mirroring what happened in Hungary a few years before.

An eventual decision of the EU to react against a Member State that is allegedly failing in this respect would, according to Article 7 TEU, have to be carried out in two steps. First, the Council must establish, with a majority of four-fifths of the other Member States, that a clear risk exists that a Member State really does violate the basic values set out in Article 2 TEU. After that, the Council may unanimously (the failing state in question again not participating) declare that the state thus identified does in fact, in a serious and persistent manner, ignore these values.

In hindsight, the EU certainly took its time before reacting sharply to what happened in Hungary. Concerning Poland, on the other hand, the Commission initiated a dialogue with the then new Polish Government as early as January 2016.

Since March 2014, the EU Commission has had at its disposal a new instrument for this and other current dialogues of the same kind with the

[11] The most well-known statement with such significance was probably the one made by the Hungarian Prime Minister, Viktor Orbán, in a speech given in 2014. See n 1.

[12] At the same time, there has been intense legal discussion on the accession of the EU to the European Convention on Human Rights, particularly after the Opinion of the CJEU in December 2014 stating that such an accession would not be legally possible (Opinion 2/13). Still, the question of when the majority of the EU Member States may wish to act against one or a few Member States who do, in fact, violate fundamental rights is, in fact, wider and more dramatic and, probably, also more urgent.

Member States, namely, the so-called Rule of Law Framework.[13] The main purpose of this instrument seems to be to make it possible for the EU Commission to start a dialogue with a Member State, based on critical observations of developments in the country in question, without immediately having to resort to the controversial and politically difficult procedure envisaged in Article 7 TEU. (In fact, the actual use of the procedure in Article 7(2) and (3), whereby a Member State might lose its vote in the Council, does now seem more remote than ever, since Hungary has promised to use its veto in the event of a vote on Poland and Poland has made a similar declaration concerning Hungary.)

It is hard to say whether the rather imminent use of this mechanism in relation to Poland, as opposed to the quite passive attitude initially shown towards Hungary, was due to the simple fact that the Commission thought that the Polish Government would be more inclined towards constructive dialogue than the Hungarian Government. There may also be other reasons, such as the fact that Hungary adopted a new Constitution in 2011, after which Hungary did not violate its own national rules as evidently as Poland has done since 2016. Nevertheless, the difference in the (strength of) reaction from the EU against the two countries is striking. And regardless of the Commission's reasons for its somewhat different approach to the two countries, it should also be noted that the Polish Government has during the entire 'dialogue' refused to provide the Commission with sufficient answers and full information. Throughout this time, Poland has treated the Commission quite arrogantly, stating that it acts in accordance with its own Constitution (or rather the Government's own interpretation thereof), and sometimes even responding to the Commission in Polish. In fact, when the Commission decided finally to present a reasoned proposal to the Council on 20 December 2017,[14] its decision was based partly on the failure of the Polish authorities to engage 'in a constructive dialogue in the context of

[13] European Commission, 'A new EU Framework to strengthen the rule of law' COM(2014) 158.

[14] Commission Recommendation (EU) 2018/103 of 20 December 2017 regarding the rule of law in Poland complementary to Recommendations (EU) 2016/1374, (EU) 2017/146 and (EU) 2017/1520, COM(2017) 835 final, Reasoned Proposal in accordance with Article 7(1) of the Treaty on European Union regarding the rule of law in Poland, 20 December 2017. On the same day, the Commission also referred an infringement case against Poland to the CJEU, Case C-192/18 *European Commission v Republic of Poland*, Judgment of 5 November 2019, ECLI:EU:C:2019:924, where the Commission contended that Poland had failed to fulfil its obligations under the treaties on two accounts. It thus held that Poland had breached its obligations under Art 157 TFEU and Arts 5(a) and 9(1)(f) of Directive 2006/54/EC of the EU Parliament and Council of 5 July 2006 relative to the implementation of the principle of equal opportunities and equal treatment between men and women in matters of employment and work, by introducing retirement ages of 60 for women and 65 for men for judges of the ordinary courts, public prosecutors and judges of the Supreme Court; and, second, that Poland had 'failed to fulfil its obligations under the combined provisions of the second subparagraph of Art 19(1) TEU and Art 47 of the Charter of Fundamental Rights of the European Union, by lowering, in Art 13(1) of the Amending Law of July 2017, the retirement age of judges of the ordinary courts, while at the same time vesting the Minister of Justice with the discretion to prolong the period of active service of individual ordinary court judges under Art 1(26)(b) and (c) of the same law'. The CJEU agreed with this view.

the Rule of Law Framework'.[15] This somewhat arrogant attitude of the Polish Government may actually also have made the Commission more eager to bring cases against Poland before the CJEU.[16] Furthermore, we might note that in April 2020, the Commission wrote a letter to the Polish Government, strongly criticising the highly controversial judicial law of 2020 that is said to be 'silencing' judges. Here, the Commission clearly declared that unless changes to the law were made within two months, a new case would be brought before the CJEU.[17]

V. ALTERNATIVE ROUTES FOR ENFORCEMENT OF EU VALUES

As mentioned in section IV, until very recently the EU refrained from invoking Article 7 TEU against Hungary or Poland, according to which a Member State that does not respect the rule of law and/or other key values of European integration may temporarily lose some of its rights as a member, including the right to vote in the EU Council. The same was true for Articles 2 and 6 TEU. Here, however, we have seen a clear change in recent years, when arguments based on those values have been invoked against those two countries in a number of cases, notably by the EU Commission. Apart from Case C-619/18, concerning the law on the Polish Supreme Court,[18] and the similar Case C-192/18,[19] we might here also point to the judgment against Hungary, Poland and the Czech Republic for refusing to comply with the provisional mechanism for mandatory relocation of asylum seekers of 2 April 2020.[20] And on the current agenda we find not

[15] See European Commission, Press Release, 'Rule of Law: European Commission acts to defend judicial independence in Poland', 20 December 2017, IP/17/5367.

[16] Apart from Case C-192/18 *European Commission v Republic of Poland*, Judgment of 5 November 2019, ECLI:EU:C:2019:924 (n 14), we might here also point to Case C-619/18, concerning the law on the Polish Supreme Court, Judgment of 24 June 2019, ECLI:EU:C:2019:531, and the similar Case C-192/18, Judgment of 5 December 2019, ECLI:EU:C:2019:924. Here too, Poland was found to have violated Art 19(1) TEU on grounds similar to those in the previous case. Finally, we should mention Case C-216/18 PPU *Minister for Justice and Equality*, EU:C:2018:586, where the Irish High Court was in doubt whether an alleged criminal could be extradited to Poland according to the European Arrest Warrant (EAW), given the risk that he would not receive a fair trial within the Polish legal system. The CJEU basically stated that such decisions by courts in other Member States will need to be based on the circumstances in the individual case; in other words, the general, unconditional obligation for national authorities to obey the EAW seems to have been suspended in relation to Poland.

[17] EU Commission, Press Release, 'Rule of Law: European Commission launches infringement procedure to safeguard the independence of judges in Poland', 29 April 2020, IP/20/772. The law was originally adopted in December 2019 but entered into force in February 2020. See also in this regard the interim decision of 8 April 2020 in Case C-791/19, pending.

[18] Case C-619/18 *Commission v Poland*, Judgment of 24 June 2019, E CLI:EU:C:2019:531.

[19] Case C-192/18 *Commission v Poland*, Judgment of 5 December 2019, ECLI:EU:C:2019:924.

[20] See Joined Cases C-715/17, 718/17 and 719/17 *Commission v Poland*, Opinion of AG Sharpston of 31 October 2019 and Judgment of 2 April 2020, ECLI:EU:C:2020:257.

only the very critical letter from the Commission to the Polish Government of April 2020, questioning the highly controversial judicial law of 2020 said to be 'silencing' judges, clearly declaring that unless changes in the law were made within two months, a new case would be brought to CJEU,[21] but also the even more controversial Hungarian law of 2020, giving the Government more or less unlimited powers in the wake of the Coronavirus crisis – but without time limits – which gave rise to heated debates within the EU,[22] though the Commission did choose on this occasion to await further developments before taking action. Nevertheless, an eventual legal action before the CJEU was also likely here, though in the event, this particular piece of legislation was repealed in June 2020.[23]

Thus, the EU institutions are now clearly less hesitant than just a few years ago to invoke the values enshrined in Article 2 TEU and to apply them in specific, concrete legal cases against EU Member States who fail to respect them. This is also highly logical, given that Article 2, as well as Articles 6 and 7 TEU, is based on the idea of a *liberal* democracy, with clear emphasis on the rule of law and human rights. We may thus say that the EU, or at least its leading institutions such as the Commission, Parliament and CJEU, is now returning to, or rather for the first time trying to live up to, the standard it set for itself and all its activities in the treaties. It is also important to underline that from the perspective of human rights and the rule of law, the situation in Hungary and Poland today is far worse than – and actually totally different from – that in Austria 20 years ago. From the viewpoint of Europe's authoritarian populists, what happened in Austria in 2000, when FPÖ temporarily joined the Government without causing any real harm to the rule of law or human rights, was just an appetiser, a 'warm-up' for what is now happening in Hungary and Poland (and may happen in other countries as well). Once again, it is highly regrettable that the EU did not react more quickly against the authoritarian development in Hungary that was already clearly visible in 2011. But as always, better late than never.

The most recent occasion on which a majority of the Member States of the EU, including in practice all of its economic 'net contributors', tried to impose new conditions on notorious 'rule of law violators', such as Hungary and Poland, was at the Special Meeting of the European Council in Brussels in July 2020 – the so-called 'corona summit'. In the conclusions from this summit,[24]

[21] European Commission, Press Release, 29 April 2020 (n 17).

[22] For example, the heated debates in the EU Parliament in April and May 2020, that have now led the Parliament to ask for economic sanctions against Hungary. See European Parliament, Press Release, 'Hungary's emergency measures: MEPs ask EU to impose sanctions and stop payments', 14 May 2020.

[23] However, the law repealing it seems to allow the Government to impose similar measures in the future. Thus, the Commission and Parliament are likely to keep their eyes open here.

[24] European Council, 'Special meeting of the European Council (17, 18, 19, 20 and 21 July 2020) – Conclusions' EUCO 10/20, CO EUR 8, CONCL 4, 21 July 2020.

a connection was finally made between the right to receive financial support from the EU and the obligation to respect the rule of law. The two relevant paragraphs read as follows:

> 22. The Union's financial interests shall be protected in accordance with the general principles embedded in the Union Treaties, in particular the values of Article 2 TEU. The European Council underlines the importance of the protection of the Union's financial interests.
>
> The European Council underlines the importance of the respect of the rule of law.
>
> 23. Based on this background, a regime of conditionality to protect the budget and Next Generation EU will be introduced. In this context, the Commission will propose measures in case of breaches for adoption by the Council by qualified majority.
>
> The European Council will revert rapidly to the matter.

After the summit, these provisions were criticised for being too vague. A previous version of the text is supposed to have been somewhat more precise, but this is not entirely clear. What may be a problem here, however, is the idea to create a link between EU funding and respect for the rule of law. The Commission argues that respect for the rule of law is an essential precondition for sound financial management and effective EU funding, and therefore has for a long time argued for 'a new mechanism to protect the EU budget from financial risks linked to generalised deficiencies as regards the rule of law'.[25] The idea, then, is that if such deficiencies impair or threaten to impair sound financial management or the protection of the financial interests of the Union, EU funding may be stopped. Such a decision is to be proposed by the Commission and then adopted by the Council through QMV. This new procedure may be seen as quite radical in itself, but at the same time, less is said than before about the possibility to stop support to a Member State due to violations of human rights or the rule of law as such, for their own sake, so to speak. It may be noted that the possible negative economic effects of rule of law violations are perhaps sometimes hard to prove. Certainly, a relationship between the rule of law and economic development and prosperity does exist, as clearly proved by many leading economic scholars such as Coase and others,[26] but nevertheless, the 'conditionality criterion' should perhaps be upheld for its own sake rather than be seen as a part of or as a complement to 'the Union's financial interest'.

Regrettably, the agreement finally reached in December 2020 was not much clearer and has already led to heated discussions, not least among EU lawyers. However, that very interesting issue has to be left to one side here.

[25] ibid.

[26] See, eg, RH Coase, 'The Problem of Social Cost' (1960) 3 *Journal of Law and Economics* 1; or D North, *The Rise of the Western World: A New Economic History* (Cambridge, Cambridge University Press, 1973).

VI. CONCLUSIONS

To sum up, then. At least as long as a clear majority of the EU Member States do still believe in the basic values enshrined in Article 2 TEU, it is, in my view, in an ever more turbulent world a good idea for the EU to protect and promote them, in spite of the short-term costs involved. In the long run, a steady and consistent stand in those value conflicts is likely to pay off and lead not only to greater respect worldwide, but also to the EU's finding itself – its own soul, so to speak – which will then make it easier for the Union to deal with future conflicts of the same kind.

The EU will quite simply be stronger and enjoy more 'soft power' throughout the world if it does not lose sight of its core values. Such a stand is also likely to promote the unity between those Member States who will now refuse to back down in this crucial conflict.

Finally, I would like to conclude with a personal view. Having been active as a scholar within Swedish and European constitutional law since the 1990s, it is impossible – or at least difficult – not to acquire a certain historical perspective on various developments that have taken place during this time. And from that perspective, it is particularly striking that when advocating for stronger judicial review and more separation of powers in Sweden or other Nordic countries in the 1990s, on the brink of EU membership, most of the critical reactions came from the left, from strong socialist or social democratic parties, who were used to governing with more or less unlimited powers (at least in Sweden) and whose only constitutional ideal was popular sovereignty.[27] Today, when the same kind of arguments in favour of the rule of law are put forward in a European context, almost all the criticism comes from ever more aggressive conservative or authoritarian movements. Certainly, that tells us something about how Europe has changed in the last 25 or 30 years, but sometimes it is not easy to discern the causes and direction of this change.

[27] For an overview of this debate in English, see M Scheinin (ed), *The Welfare State and Constitutionalism in the Nordic Countries* (Copenhagen, Nordic Council of Ministers, 2001) Nord 2001:5; or J Nergelius (ed), *Nordic and Other European Constitutional Traditions* (Leiden, Brill, 2006).

Part Two

The Rule of Law in CEE: Communist Legacies and the Road to EU Accession

5

Legacies of Socialist Constitutionalism: The Eastern European Judiciary

ZDENĚK KÜHN

THE OLD SOCIALIST legal cultures of Central Eastern Europe are long dead. The legal systems of the countries in the region were replaced by new laws that enabled the re-emergence of capitalism. The laws of the old communist system would have been dysfunctional facing the conditions of the market economy. Moreover, in the 1990s the basis of new constitutional systems was founded. They were openly inspired by the political ideology of liberal constitutionalism, which dominated the discourse of the 1990s. In the 2010s, however, this political consensus has disappeared. The political systems in many countries of the region changed course again, and their legal systems followed the path.

In this chapter, I will first show the rise of constitutional liberalism and the Western-inspired rule of law in the 1990s. I will then explain the reasons why some socialist and pre-socialist concepts of law are quite alive and well in the new legal systems. First, I am going to deal with the authoritarian model of judicial process, which seems to prevail in Central and Eastern Europe. While the activity of parties and their close collaboration in discussing issues of law with their judges is an important engine in applying law in Western Europe, in the post-communist litigation the parties continue to be viewed as passive objects. Subsequently I am going to explain a specific socialist novelty, the concept of supreme courts' interpretational statements, legislating from the bench without any real-life case pending before those courts. Last but not least, I will show the gradual decline of the activist role of constitutional courts in the region and the return to the old tradition of a self-restrained judiciary.

I. OVERTURE: THE RISE OF CONSTITUTIONAL LIBERALISM IN THE 1990s

At first glance, the fall of the existing socialism in the late 1980s in Central and Eastern Europe meant total eradication of the old legal and constitutional values. New constitutions and laws were adopted, the old textbooks replaced.

Moreover, the collapse of communism in 1989/1990 was accompanied by the rise of the judicial branch in general and the creation of new constitutional courts in particular, in virtually all the countries in Central and Eastern Europe. The 1990s in post-communist Europe saw a shift towards judicialisation and the creation of a conflict society. The judiciary saw its old competences restored, including the power of judicial review of administrative acts.

Most importantly, however, constitutional courts were established in all post-communist states. Even in those few countries (Poland and the former Yugoslavia) where constitutional courts existed before the fall of socialism, their role expanded after 1990. The actual functions of those constitutional courts faced limitations prior to 1990, imposed on them by their authoritarian governments, so that they did not gain any major political influence until the fall of the authoritarian regimes. It was only after the collapse of socialist dictatorships that the constitutional courts in Poland and the successor states of the former Yugoslavia started to act as a genuine check on their governments.[1]

In practice, judicial review has become even more important after 1990, given the relative immaturity of the parliamentary structures and party organisation in the transition countries, which resulted in poorly developed systems of parliamentary oversight. A lack of party cohesion, as well as public scepticism towards the institutions of government, further undermined the 'horizontal' accountability exercised by the legislature over the executive. Unlike in Western Europe, where legislative oversight has declined over time relative to the role of other public- and private-sector agencies, the Central and Eastern European countries generally failed to develop strong systems of parliamentary control and stable political parties from the outset. Hence the significance of constitutional courts.[2]

The post-communist constitutional courts were designed as powerful institutions capable of protecting the rule of law and fundamental rights against the will of the parliamentary majority. Their most important powers include the review of the constitutionality of legislation and, in some nations (the successor countries of the former Yugoslavia, the Czech Republic, Slovakia, recently Hungary[3]), the review of the constitutionality of decisions of state authorities, including courts.

[1] The Federal Constitutional Court of Yugoslavia, together with the state constitutional courts of the republics, was established in 1963. See, for an early socialist description of those courts, D Kulic, 'The Constitutional Court of Yugoslavia in the Protection of Basic Human Rights' (1973) 11 *Osgoode Hall Law Journal* 275. The Federal Constitutional Court of Yugoslavia disappeared with the disintegration of Yugoslavia and the subsequent violent civil war of the 1990s. In Poland, the Constitutional Tribunal was created by the law of 1982; the Tribunal started to operate in 1986. For a description of the Polish Constitutional Tribunal prior to 1990, see W Sadurski, *Rights before Courts: A Study of Constitutional Courts in Postcommunist States of Central and Eastern Europe*, 2nd edn (New York, Springer, 2014) 4–13.

[2] Cf Z Kühn, 'The Judicialization of European Politics' in E Jones, P Heywood, U Sedelmeier and M Rhodes (eds), *Developments in European Politics* (London, Macmillan/Palgrave, 2006) 216.

[3] In Hungary, the power of the Court over constitutional complaints was created as late as in 2012, in the new Constitution enacted at the beginning of the Orbán era. See the Constitution of Hungary

Initially, the post-socialist constitutional courts were viewed as successful examples of those institutions that were bringing in new conceptions of the rule of law, the separation of powers and notions of liberal democracy. The original practice of constitutional review of the 1990s and the early 2000s was linked to judicial activism, unrestrained and seemingly unopposed judge-made law. The constitutional courts of Eastern Europe acted as the agents of social change of their respective national legal systems towards liberal capitalism.[4] Moreover, in some systems they attempted to transform the entire concept of law, Westernise the post-communist application of law, and teach the new and proper methods of how to approach the application of law. They did so by mentoring ordinary judges and criticising them for not taking constitutional and human rights seriously enough. Effectively, the constitutional courts often replaced the legal academia in this task.[5]

When analysing the early phase of the post-communist constitutional courts one should not forget the consensus of liberal constitutionalism prevailing among the elites of post-communist transition. The constitutional courts emphasised the primacy of an individual over the state.[6] There was a vast consensus that new democratic constitutions should restrain the parliamentary majority and executive branch, and ensure adherence to the state's basic law through its counter-majoritarian functions.[7] Law and its application were believed to be non-political and able to restrain crude politics.

The idea of 'taking rights seriously' was accepted by the framers of the New Constitutionalism in Central Eastern Europe. The constitutional courts emphasised that ideologically they were not neutral because they stood on the side of liberal democracy. Perhaps the best example of those early cases is the following judgment of the Czech Constitutional Court:

> Our new Constitution is not founded on value neutrality, it is not simply a mere demarcation of institutions and processes, rather it incorporates into its text also certain governing ideas, expressing the fundamental, inviolable values of a democratic

of 2011, available at www.kormany.hu/en/news/the-new-fundamental-law-of-hungary. In Slovakia, constitutional complaints were introduced in 2001, following the successful Czech example. On Slovakia, see R Procházka, *Mission Accomplished. On Founding Constitutional Adjudication in Central Europe* (Budapest, New York, Central European University Press, 2002) 189ff.

[4] For some early jubilant views, see eg G Halmai (ed), *A Megtalált Alkotmány? A Magyar Alapjojagi Bíráskodás Elsö Kilenc Éve/The Constitution Found? The First Nine Years of Hungarian Constitutional Review on Fundamental Rights* (Budapest, INDOK, 2000); Procházka (n 3); W Sadurski (ed), *Constitutional Justice, East and West. Democratic Legitimacy and Constitutional Courts in Post-Communist Europe in a Comparative Perspective* (Alphen aan den Rijn, Kluwer Law International, 2002).

[5] I tried to show this transformative potential of some constitutional courts in Z Kühn, *The Judiciary in Central and Eastern Europe: Mechanical Jurisprudence in Transformation?* (Leiden, Brill, 2011) ch 5.

[6] eg judgment of the Czech Constitutional Court of 18 October 1995, no Pl ÚS 26/94.

[7] Cf, on the counter-majoritarian function of constitutional review, M Troper, 'The logic of justification of judicial review' (2003) 1 *International Journal of Constitutional Law* 99.

> society. The Czech Constitution accepts and respects the principle of legality as a part of the overall basic outline of the rule of law; positive law does not, however, bind it merely to formal legality, rather the interpretation and application of legal norms are subordinated to their substantive purpose, law is qualified by respect for the basic enacted values of a democratic society and also measures the application of legal norms by these values. This means that even while there is continuity of 'old laws' there is a discontinuity in values from the 'old regime'. … Whatever the laws of a state are, in a state which is designated as democratic and which proclaims the principle of the sovereignty of the people, no regime other than a democratic regime may be considered as legitimate. Any sort of monopoly on power, in and of itself, rules out the possibility of democratic legitimacy.[8]

The constitutional liberalism of the 1990s was linked to the 'The End of History' thesis, that is, the ultimate triumph of liberal capitalism, often presented through its neoliberal array and a plethora of free market policies.[9] No one dared to question 'the only possible' road to the future. In their neoliberal zealotry, the new constitutional courts' case law was often one-sided, especially in comparison with the application of similar principles in the Western jurisprudence.[10]

Moreover, the political elites of the 1990s often seemed quite unaware of the enormous political power of courts exercising constitutional review. The concept of law was understood in a non-political way; law was viewed as a logical set of rules and principles destined for the use of endowed professionals capable of using the law's logic. Constitutional courts initially faced little external criticism or opposition to their decision making, which resulted in the situation described by some scholars as the 'liberal government of judges'. Mainstream legal ideology threw a protective veil over the constitutional courts' activities, even against the most radical examples of judicial law making.[11] Although criticism of judicial activism appeared among the ranks of the local legal academia and majority of ordinary judges, it was relatively easy to downplay that sort of criticism as the reaction of the conservative scholarship and judiciary associated with the old regime.[12]

Those circumstances often shaped the environment for the unbound judicial activism of constitutional courts. The President of the Hungarian Constitutional Court of the 1990s, Sólyom, once (in)famously remarked that a genuine

[8] The case of the Law on the Lawlessness of the Communist Regime, no Pl ÚS 19/93 of 21 December 1993. English translation available at www.usoud.cz/en/decisions/19931221-pl-us-1993-lawlessness-1/.

[9] A Sulikowski, 'Government of Judges and Neoliberal Ideology' in R Mańko, C Cercel and A Sulikowski (eds), *Law and Critique in Central Europe: Questioning the Past, Resisting the Present* (Oxford, Counterpress, 2016) 16.

[10] Cf, for analysis of the Hungarian Court, C Dupré, *Importing the Law in Post-Communist Transitions: The Hungarian Constitutional Court and the Right to Human Dignity* (Oxford, Hart Publishing, 2003) 126–27.

[11] Sulikowski (n 9).

[12] See Kühn (n 5) 229 (and the sources quoted ibid fn 143).

purpose of the Court was to read '*the invisible constitution*'.[13] Although other constitutional courts were less open about their judicial legislating, judicial activism became a common phenomenon of the 1990s and 2000s.

The constitutional courts often styled themselves the sole and indispensable guardians of the new constitutions, entering the scene like a *deus ex machina* to settle issues that could not be decided by other bodies. As a consequence, one of the most fundamental problems that emerged after 1989 was the 'over-centralisation' of constitutional review. By this I mean that the continuing guarantee of the existence of the rule of law was entirely centralised in the constitutional court, while the powers of the ordinary judiciary, respectively, were limited.[14] If the constitutional court were to come under the control of one political faction, as happened in Orban's Hungary after 2010 and in Poland after 2015, the gates for systemic change would be open while the guardians of the constitution would effectively be missing.

II. THE REVIVAL OF ILLIBERAL JUDICIARIES

The successes of the legal transitions of the 1990s were dubious. Although as a result of the Enlargement, much of the 'other Europe' became part of the European Union (EU), it would be too simplistic to assume that the region had become part of Western European political and legal landscape with the fall of the Berlin Wall. Alas, the region disappeared from the attention of comparative scholarship. The old 'Socialist Legal Family', which most comparative law treatises had posited, had seemingly been replaced by a legal black hole.[15]

Although the books of the old era were discarded, laws repealed and new institutions created, we should not underestimate the continuing strength of the

[13] See Sólyom's Concurring Opinion in the Death Penalty Case, Decision 23/1990 of 31 October 1990 (translated in L Sólyom and G Brunner, *Constitutional Judiciary in a New Democracy: The Hungarian Constitutional Court* (Ann Arbor, MI, The University of Michigan Press, 2000) 126. This conception has been criticised for blatant activism (What is the 'invisible constitution', are judges above the lawmakers and are they the only legitimate power to read it?) and neither the Court nor its President has used this expression again. Cf A Sajó, 'Reading the Invisible Constitution: Judicial Review in Hungary' (1995) 15 *OJLS* 253. Cf also GA Tóth, 'Joint Symposium on "Towering Judges": László Sólyom's Constitutional Symphony for the Republic of Hungary' *I.CONnect*, 3 April 2019, available at www.iconnectblog.com/2019/04/joint-symposium-on-"towering-judges":-laszlo-solyom's-constitutional-symphony-for-the-republic-of-hungary.

[14] Cf Z Kühn, 'Making Constitutionalism Horizontal: Three Different Central European Strategies' in A Sajó and R Uitz (eds), *The Constitution in Private Relations: Expanding Constitutionalism* (Utrecht, Eleven International Publishing, 2005) 217.

[15] Cf R Mańko, 'The Culture of Private Law in Central Europe after Enlargement: A Polish Perspective' (2005) 11 *European Law Journal* 527, 547–48, discussing the fact that the most recent edition of Zweigert and Kötz's treatise on comparative law simply discarded the Socialist Legal Family, 'without writing anything in their place'. For most recent elaboration by the same author, see R Mańko, 'Survival of the Socialist Legal Tradition? A Polish perspective' (2014) 4 *Comparative Law Review* 1, available at www.comparativelawreview.unipg.it/index.php/comparative/article/view/14/11.

old values, principles and legal thought in general. After all, the authors of those discarded books remained in the academia (with a specific exception of East Germany, which was 'taken over' by its bigger Western brother), despite the fact that they started to produce, virtually overnight, new material, defending new values and principles. Alongside the academics, the entire legal personnel of the old era survived the systemic change, which contributed to the persistence of the spirit of the old legal culture.

That is why the philosophies of the old socialist legal system were able not only to survive, but also to govern a substantial portion of the post-socialist legal and judicial discourse. The deepest layers of the old legal culture were and are by their very nature resistant to sudden changes. They seldom had a direct connection to the former official political ideology, but they were often clothed in the new legal vocabulary.[16] Furthermore, the most persistent features of socialist legal culture were often those linked to the region's illiberal pre-socialist past, although substantively modified during the era of socialism.

To give some examples, it is easy to see that many lawyers and the public in general tend to overemphasise the importance legislative enactments have in the legal process, underestimating the significance of their subsequent application by courts and public authorities. In the view of many scholars, legislation is everything and precedent (case law) nothing. Ironically, this trend has been reinforced by the processes of European integration, with its overproduction of directives and regulations.

However, what is even more important is the specific authoritarian conception of the judicial process that dominates legal discourse in the region, as I am going to explain in the next section.

III. AUTHORITARIAN UNDERSTANDING OF THE JUDICIAL PROCESS

In practice, socialist regimes, like any other sort of dictatorship, by necessity generated an authoritarian understanding of law. As explained by Professor Siniša Rodin:

> Instead of rational discourse that shaped legal and institutional landscape of Europe's West, the predominant discourse in Central and Eastern Europe was authoritarian. The main characteristic of such authoritarian discourse is the proclamation and imposition of one truth as universal and final. Such discourse was authoritarian since it purported to have a social monopoly over determining the meaning of legal and political language at the top of political hierarchy and communicating it downward. It was, nevertheless, a discourse, since communication of meaning defined in

[16] Cf, for the socialist legal culture and its impact, Kelemen's 'Legal Reasoning in Central and Eastern Europe from a Historical Perspective' in ch 6 of this volume.

> authoritarian way was indispensable to support the claim of universal acceptance, the maintenance of which is a condition of the system's integrity.[17]

Authoritarian judicial discourse must be distinguished from authoritative judicial discourse. The judicial discourse of *any* legal system is inherently authoritative. This is a result of the facts (i) that by definition courts must decide as *if there were* one correct answer to the questions presented to the court (the judicial 'one right answer' thesis); and (ii) that judicial decisions are final because of their authority within the judicial and legal system.[18] Authoritative judicial discourse does not preclude but on the contrary presupposes a pluralism of opinions and the participation of all competent persons in the legal decision-making process. Plurality of opinion and the fact that the court takes all relevant opinions seriously give the decision-maker of last resort the legitimacy to provide the 'right' answer, which is a necessary condition for the discourse to remain authoritative.[19]

In contrast, authoritarian discourse means something very different. Here, the pluralism of opinions is absent. The 'right' answer is achieved through a 'one-way' process and is backed entirely by an institutional power. Those to whom decisions are addressed cannot participate on finding the 'right' answers; instead of being subjects, they are rather objects of authoritarian decision making. Authoritarian discourse implies that legal meanings are produced from above and that the existence of any dispute, questioning, legitimate disagreement, or construction of the law from the bottom up is unthinkable.[20]

Such authoritarian discourse is combined with the maxim *iura novit curia*, the idealistic principle of Continental law that the 'judge knows the law' and must apply the appropriate legal rule regardless of whether either party cited it to the court.[21] This principle, taken too seriously and too literally, deeply influences the self-perception of the post-socialist judiciary.

One of the effects of the principle *iura novit curia* is that while the parties before a Continental court have the duty to raise issues of fact, they are not obliged to raise issues of law, because the court is itself obliged to do that even without the litigants' assistance. As a consequence, pleadings to trial courts in

[17] S Rodin, 'Discourse, Authority in European and Post-Communist Legal Culture' (2005) 1 *Croatian Yearbook of European Law and Policy* 1, 7–8 (footnotes omitted).

[18] See chapters in N MacCormick and RS Summers (eds), *Interpreting Statutes: A Comparative Study* (London, Dartmouth Publishing, 1991) (although the degree of the discursive nature of judicial decisions differs, at one pole standing the common law system and at the other the French civil system, all courts work on the assumption that their decisions are objectively 'right').

[19] I think this argument is best made by the US Supreme Court Associate Justice Robert Jackson. When evaluating judges of (any) supreme court, he famously declared 'We are not final because we are infallible, but we are infallible only because we are final.' See *Brown v Allen*, 344 US 443, 540 (1953), Justice Jackson concurring.

[20] I take my inspiration from J Vining, *The Authoritative and the Authoritarian* (Chicago, IL, The University of Chicago Press, 1986).

[21] Cf on this, eg, JA Jolowicz, 'Da mihi factum dabo tibi jus: a problem of demarcation in English and French law' in P Feuerstein and C Parry (eds), *Multum non Multa: Festschrift für Kurt Lipstein* (Heidelberg, CF Müller, 1980) 79, 84.

most Continental countries are quite brief, without major excursus into legal issues; after all, it is the judge who is supposed to supply the relevant rule. In contrast, in the systems of the common law culture (which is typically more pragmatic), the judges have a more passive role, and greater responsibility is placed on parties not only to provide issues of fact, but also to argue the issues of law. This is so because in constructing their opinions, Anglo-American judges draw heavily upon the parties' competing arguments as to what the 'correct' statement of the law is.[22]

In Western Europe, however, the principle that the judge knows the law is not taken literally. Appeals in Western Europe tend to be longer and more elaborate when issues of law are controversial. That is so because the basic, and often the only, reason for an appeal, and accordingly the main focus of the appellant's brief, is to persuade the higher court that the appellant's interpretation of the law is correct and their opponent's (or the lower court's) interpretation is incorrect. In contemporary Continental culture, the judges technically 'know' the law, but they often need parties' attorneys to help them find the relevant provision and to determine its best reading.

In Central and Eastern Europe, the maxim *iura novit curia* is taken more seriously than in Western Europe. During the socialist era, idealistic readings of this principle drove the legal arguments out of parties' pleadings. According to the leading Czechoslovak commentary on civil procedure in the 1970s and 1980s, law cannot be subject to judicial recognition during the proceedings before the court; it must be known to the court in advance of the dispute's arising. 'The knowledge of law must be produced by the [judicial] body itself; it is possible to say *prior to* the [civil] proceedings and *beyond* these proceedings.'[23] No cooperation on law finding was necessary. Even more, such cooperation was considered harmful, as the parties would interfere in the court's exclusive domain. An additional reason why, during the entire communist era, no help was sought from the parties in constructing the law, was the fact that few parties were represented by a lawyer.[24] Moreover, scant attention was paid to the attorneys' arguments; something that fitted well within the vision of the socialist application of law, because socialist legal systems claimed that no party should gain an advantage from having a better lawyer.[25]

This approach mirrored the communist *authoritarian* approach to the law, which is in fundamental contradiction to the discursive authoritative approach

[22] For the reasons behind this, cf MR Damaška, *The Faces of Justice and State Authority. A Comparative Approach to the Legal Process* (New Haven, CT, Yale, 1986) 139.

[23] J Rubeš et al, *Občanský soudní řád. Komentář* [*Code of Civil Procedure. Commentary*] (Prague, Orbis, 1970) 447 (emphasis added).

[24] ibid 455, where a communist scholar does not seem even to expect that it was also possible for a party to be represented by a competent lawyer who might provide a qualified legal opinion to the court.

[25] *Sbírka rozhodnutí československých soudů* [*Collection of Decisions of the Czechoslovak Courts*] (1949) 1.

to law that meanwhile prevailed in Europe. Let us recall that by an authoritarian approach, I mean the approach whereby legal answers can be constructed solely from the top of the system, the top holding 'a social monopoly over determining the meaning of legal and political language' and 'communicating it downward'.[26]

The authoritarian approach to law, combined with formalist textual positivism and the ideology of bound judicial application of law, accords to the judge the exclusive role in constructing the meaning of the law. It is so because (i) the application of law is conceptually viewed as the resolution of easy cases by the court, which does not, in that process, require the assistance of either party (formalist aspect);[27] and (ii) the construction of the law is the result of a top-down process, where parties are the addressees of the result of construction rather than direct or indirect participants in that construction (authoritarian aspect).

It is clear that the authoritarian approach to law still governs post-communist legal discourse (at least in the Czech and Slovak legal systems). The principle *iura novit curia* appears to function as a barrier separating the parties before the court from their judges. An intriguing vicious circle is at work here. The legal arguments made by parties' attorneys in their briefs rarely exceed a few paragraphs, and almost never include proper cites to the literature and case law, thus providing the judge with little useful information. Perhaps because the legal arguments made by the parties are worthless, the judge will often ignore even those rare arguments that are valuable and might help him or her to find the relevant case law, useful comparative materials from abroad, etc. Instead, the judge will only elaborate the court's own legal theories.[28] Thus, when taken too seriously, the principle *iura novit curia* becomes self-fulfilling, discouraging parties from contributing to the court's legal reasoning and judges from drawing upon the attorneys' expertise.

IV. SUPREME COURTS' INTERPRETATIONAL STATEMENTS AND GUIDELINES: THEIR EMERGENCE AND PERSISTENCE IN CENTRAL EASTERN EUROPE

In the 1950s, one phenomenon almost unknown in the Western world appeared in the then socialist states of Central Europe. As with many other inventions of the early socialist era, it had Soviet origins. Following the Soviet model of

[26] Rodin (n 17) 7.

[27] Rubeš (n 23) 455 (claiming that 'as legal professionals, judges must know their legal order, and no one can claim that it would be impossible to know all the laws').

[28] This approach is often criticised by the Czech Constitutional Court, which has repeatedly insisted that ordinary courts have to address every legal argument made by either party. Cf the Decision of 26 September 1996, III. ÚS 176/96.

guiding explanations issued by the plenum of the supreme court,[29] in all Central European countries during communist rule the supreme courts had the power to issue guidelines and interpretative statements dealing with important legal questions. Those statements were enacted *in abstracto*, without any real-life case pending before the court. In some states such directives were formally binding on the lower courts. Many of the directives were long treatises analysing the correct and incorrect applications of the specific law by lower courts within some period of time, without taking into account the particulars of the case at hand.[30]

The socialist supreme courts prepared these documents as evaluations and appraisals of case law to react promptly to the Communist Party Congresses; at the beginning of these evaluations, they often emphasised the Party politics of the respective time. In these official documents, the anti-formalism of the socialist judiciary always won out, at least rhetorically, against 'capitalist' positivism and dogmatism. For instance, 'The Report of the Chief Justice of the Czechoslovak Supreme Court on the Significance of Ideology in the Judiciary' instructed the judiciary to be a reliable tool to strengthen state authority and the authority of state bodies, and also to be an effective 'instrument' in the enforcement of socialist ideology.[31]

In the Czech Republic, those interpretative statements would be encountered in 1953 for the very first time in our legal history. Then they were called 'guidelines for the proper interpretation of legislation and other laws' (*směrnice pro správný výklad zákonů a jiných právních předpisů*).[32] Since the late 1960s the term 'statements ensuring unified interpretation of law' (*stanoviska k zajištění jednotného výkladu zákona*) has been used instead.[33] The statements and guidelines, faithful to the spirit of the time of their creation at the peak of Czechoslovak Stalinism, were linked to a strong emphasis on centralised interpretation of the law, distrusting the decentralised law-making powers of lower courts. Moreover, lacking proper interaction between legal scholarship and the

[29] On Soviet interpretative statements, see AK Saidov, *Comparative Law*, tr WE Butler (London, Wildy, Simmonds and Hill, 2003; Russian original 2000) 206.

[30] In Hungary, see a critical evaluation from the point of sources of law in P Schmidt, 'Konstitucionno-pravovye voprosy sistemi istochnikov prava VNR' ['Constitutional Problems of the Hungarian System of Sources of Law'] (1985) 27 *Acta Juridica Academiae Scientiarum Hungaricae* 133, 146–48. In Poland, see A Rzepliński, *Die Justiz in der Volksrepublik Polen*, tr M Jansen (Frankfurt am Main, Vottorio Klostermann, 1996) 163ff.

[31] 'Zpráva předsedy Nejvyššího soudu Československé socialistické republiky o významu ideologické práce v justici' ['The Report of the Chief Justice of the Supreme Court of the Czechoslovak Socialist Republic on the Significance of Ideology in the Judiciary'], *Collection of Decisions 1974*, 432, 439.

[32] § 26 para 1 of Law no 66/1952 of Collection of laws (hereinafter 'Coll'), on the organisation of courts.

[33] See Law no 156/1969 Coll, amending Law no 36/1964 Coll, on the organisation of courts and election of judges.

judiciary, these statements in a sense served as a substitute for it, linked to a strong, and of course, centralised and formal authority of the Supreme Court.

One of the rare occasions when the judges in socialist Central Eastern Europe could speak freely (the 1968 Prague Spring, a short-lived attempt to liberalise the Czechoslovak socialist regime) revealed that just this power of the supreme courts was considered to be a danger to judicial independence.[34] And it was soon after the Soviet invasion of 21 August 1968 when the communist apparatchiks started to criticise the weakening role of these interpretational statements as one of the typical products of the 1968 'reactionary' movement.[35] Because the communist regime deeply distrusted the ability of its judges to apply law by their own reasoning and best judgment, it was necessary for the 'socialist application of socialist law' to guide judges and direct them through the directives of the high courts.[36]

The situation did not change much after 1989 in this respect. Forty years on, interpretational statements have become firmly internalised by the domestic legal cultures. Surprisingly enough, old-fashioned traditional ideas about precedents still dominate judicial and legal discourse.[37] Instead of precedent, most Central Eastern European legal systems continue to use interpretational statements and various guidelines prepared by the high courts, specific instruments of unbound judicial law making *par excellence*. The statements are still issued by supreme courts on certain legal issues, in order to unify the conflicting case law without any real-life case pending before the supreme court.

Unlike the situation in some states prior to 1990, at present such statements are usually not formally binding, though they naturally possess a high degree of force throughout the judicial system. The statements do not have a direct impact on any individual case, because they are decided *in abstracto*, on the proposal of the Supreme Court, Minister of Justice or similar authorities, when those bodies opine that the interest of uniform case law so demands.[38] In Hungary, the only system with a pre-communist tradition of this sort of abstract judicial law

[34] A Bajcura, 'Výsledky ankety o postavení sudcov' ['The Results of the Poll on the Status of Judges'] (1968) 51 *Právný obzor* 834, 835.

[35] J Němec, 'XIV. sjezd KSČ a úkoly justice' ['XIV. Congress of the Communist Party of Czechoslovakia and the Task of the Judiciary'] (1971) 19 *Socialistická zákonnost* 385, 390.

[36] O Rolenc and V Rolenc, 'K ústavní zásadě nezávislosti soudců' ['On the constitutional principle of the independence of judges'] (1971) 19 *Socialistická zákonnost* 391, 396 and 401.

[37] F Emmert, 'The Independence of Judges – A Concept Often Misunderstood in Central and Eastern Europe' (2002) 3 *European Journal of Law Reform* 405. In more detail, see Kühn (n 5) 207ff.

[38] In the Czech Republic, the competence to request such a statement is vested, inter alia, in the Minister of Justice, see Art 123(3) and Art 14(3) of the Act on the Judiciary of 30 November 2001, no 6/2002 Coll. Similarly in Slovakia, see Art 21(3) and Art 23 of the Act on the Judiciary of 9 December 2004, no 757/2004 Z.z. [Official Gazette]. In Poland, the Supreme Court's resolutions are requested, inter alia, by the Spokesman for Citizens' Rights, the Public Prosecutor General or, within his/her competence, by the Spokesman for the Insured. See Art 60(2) of the Act on the Supreme Court of 23 November 2002, Dz.U. Nr 101 of 2002, item 924.

making, these so-called 'uniformity decisions' are even formally binding, so that the lower courts must follow interpretative directions found therein.[39]

German judges react to this socialist institution with a mixture of surprise and embarrassment,[40] because they view it as being in conflict with their ideal that the judiciary makes law only through deciding cases 'interstitially',[41] not through making law *in abstracto*. Thus, it is possible to argue that the continuing adherence to this institution confirms what the post-communist systems understand by the notion of judicial law making, and demonstrates why they have difficulties in understanding proper judicial law making.

In the Czech Republic, both supreme courts have the power to enact the interpretative statements. The actual practice differs, however. The Supreme Court, the final court for civil, commercial and criminal cases, uses this power very often. In practice, the statements seem to be the most important tool for the unification of case law and judicial law making. The Supreme Court rarely uses its grand chambers for this purpose.

In contrast, the Supreme Administrative Court, a new court established in 2003, has used this power only twice, in the first two years of its existence. Since 2005 it has never used the power to enact statements. The prevailing mood at this court is that statements are an improper way of judicial decision making, a sort of unrestrained legislating from the bench, being in conflict with the separation of powers. Unlike the Supreme Court, the Supreme Administrative Court uses its grand chamber to unify conflicting case law of its small chambers.[42]

I claim that one important reason not only for the survival but also for the well-being of the imported (from the Soviet Union) concept of plenary interpretational statements, is the continuing supremacy of the authoritarian conception of law and legal discourse. Authoritarian discourse might face serious difficulties with internalising judicial law making via precedent proper, based on interactions between private parties and judges, both those in the lower echelons and those of the high courts who possess the final authority to say what the law is in an individual case. That is why authoritarian discourse openly prefers

[39] Cf Á Erdei, 'Law of Criminal Procedure' in A Harmathy (ed), *Introduction to Hungarian Law* (The Hague/London/Boston, Wolters Kluwer, 1998) 211.

[40] As did the German judges in their reports on the Czech judiciary of 2003. All of them actually criticised this institution, which is, according to them, a waste of the Supreme Court's energy. Moreover, they noted that it resolves a question *in abstracto*, without proper judicial testing at the lower levels. 'Souhrn návrhů pro českou justici v oblasti organizace soudnictví, civilního a trestního řízení' ['A Set of Proposals for the Czech Judiciary the Area of organization of the Judiciary and Civil and Criminal Procedure'], Twinning Project CZ 01/IB/JH/01 Judicial Reform and Court Management Czech Republic – Germany – United Kingdom (not published, on file with the author).

[41] As Justice Holmes once famously noted in *Southern Pacific Co v Jensen*, 244 US 205, 221 (1917) (Holmes J dissenting), 'I recognize without hesitation that judges must and do legislate, but they do so only interstitially; they are confined from molar to molecular motions.'

[42] I should point out that I am a judge of the Supreme Administrative Court.

centralised judicial law making by supreme courts without listening to anyone else, including the lower courts.

Politically, interpretational statements might be a welcome tool for politicians to model their laws via abstract judicial statements. The ministerial power to request such statements might be easily misused, to intervene in politically sensitive cases pending in lower courts. The politicians are doing this by inviting judges to decide on some particular problem, sometimes punishing those who do not follow the rules of the game. To name one example, the former Chief Justice of the Czech Supreme Court was infamously dismissed in February 2006 by the President Václav Klaus. One of the crucial reasons for his dismissal was the fact that the Chief Justice did not ensure 'unification of law' via judicial interpretational statements. The President's dismissal of him was annulled by the Constitutional Court, which rejected all the President's arguments.[43]

The single most important added value of such statements is their speediness and clarification of the law, without the need to wait until the case arrives at the supreme court in the regular way, through appellate proceedings or cassation. On the other hand, these statements and guidelines tend to turn supreme courts into weird quasi-academic institutions, debating legal issues detached from the colourful circumstances of real-life cases. The legitimacy of judicial law making is vested in the judicial duty to address the facts of a pending case, not to address any issue the judge considers worthy of his or her attention, disregarding the fact that no case bringing this issue before the bench has yet emerged.

The very procedure of issuing statements gives rise to yet another concern. As a rule, it is the entire court that issues them. However, the judicial deliberation is and must be different from parliamentary debates. The difference between judicial deliberations and political discussions is qualitative rather than quantitative. The debate in the legislature brings a number of speakers from various political groups, plus tens of more-or-less disinterested listeners, who would later follow the opinion of their political club on a particular issue.

In contrast, judicial deliberation is effected through the actual participation of all the judges involved. Even though no one knows exactly the maximum number of people who could deliberate in a meaningful way, it is certain that dozens of judges could hardly take part in rational judicial deliberation. The supreme courts in the common law systems deciding as a whole have never comprised more than nine judges. In the civil law world, various grand chambers of supreme courts have never been composed of more than 20 judges. The same also applies to the constitutional courts. Otherwise there would be no time for all the judges to speak, and it would be close to impossible to have a rational legal debate in this way. Last but not least, it is not likely that dozens of judges

[43] The judgment of the Constitutional Court of 11 July 2006, Pl US 18/06. For the best description of this case in English, see M Bobek, 'The Fortress of Judicial Independence and the Mental Transitions of the Central European Judiciaries' (2008) 14 *European Public Law* 99.

involved in issuing statements could prepare well enough to debate complex issues of law. In the end, if some judges were not properly prepared to debate the issue, this would not be obvious in an assembly comprising dozens of people, most of whom would have to remain silent for the sake of time management. At the end of the day, the entire 'judicial' deliberation would move towards a sort of parliamentary debate, with a lot of silent listeners, who would then follow in their voting the opinions of the leaders they trust most.

When debating the issue of interpretational statements, we must be always aware that judges are the final *authoritative* interpreters not because they are omniscient and infallible, but because of their function and status within the legal system. The authority of the judge to decide the case 'correctly' must ultimately be tested by real-life cases. The judges are not free riders, picking up the legal questions they want to consider depending on their immediate will and changing mood. If understood from this perspective, abstract judicial interpretational statements are not only against the very core of authoritative legal discourse, they are also in conflict with the basic tenets of the separation of powers.[44]

V. THE REVIVAL OF THE CONCEPT OF DEFENSIVE LEGALISM

Liberal democracy and the rule of law were taken for granted, being the only political model for the region in the early 1990s. Two decades later, the situation changed considerably. The political systems of many countries found an alternative ideology in illiberalism, and populist democracies have been gaining ground in the region. Many constitutional courts in the region failed to act as a powerful check on the will of political beasts (Hungary); in some countries, the constitutional courts were even utilised to play a part in creating a new model of illiberal populist democracy (Poland).

The imported notion of judicial activism seems to be slowly dying away in the region. As I mentioned at the start, the region's conception of constitutional courts during socialism, if they existed at all (Poland, Hungary), was that of self-restrained constitutional courts, with crude politics being supreme over the so-called socialist legality. This was the conception of the general judiciary under socialism as well. Textualism and strict adherence to the letter of

[44] This issue is debated in many other legal systems in the region. Cf, from a Croatian critical perspective, M Bratković, 'Roots of the Resistance to the Change in the Supreme Court's Role' in A Uzelac and C van Rhee (eds), *Transformation of Civil Justice. Ius Gentium: Comparative Perspectives on Law and Justice*, vol 70 (New York, Springer, 2018). For a critical debate in Ukraine, see TA Tsuvina, 'Спеціальні механізми забезпечення єдності судової практики в цивільному судочинстві: Досвід зарубіжних держав' ['Special mechanisms for ensuring the unity of judicial practice in civil proceedings: The experience of foreign countries'] *Право і Суспільство* [*Law and Society*] no 1/2020, 170ff (cf especially the text at 173–75).

the law insulated socialist judges from daily politics and gave them a limited area of autonomy. This idea of defensive legalism is slowly advancing again in the region. The revival of activist constitutional courts in the 1990s could be viewed as a short-term deviation from the established rule of self-restrained and semi-dependent judiciaries.

The regimes in the region prefer (generally more legitimate) control over their constitutional courts by the process of appointing or electing judges. Exceptionally, however, we can see also open disrespect for the judgments of the constitutional courts.

The degrees of political interference with the process of appointment or election to the constitutional bench have differed in the region. Interestingly, no system has proved to be immune from malfunctions and judicial vacancies. In some countries the appointment procedures failed, which resulted in empty benches and the courts' inability to perform their tasks (Hungary already in the late 1990s, the Czech Republic in the early 2000s, Slovakia in 2019). In some countries the courts are indirectly but effectively controlled by the political forces that control all branches of the government (Russia, Hungary after 2010). In some other countries the constitutional courts faced hostile takeovers by the ruling political forces (the Polish Constitutional Tribunal's crisis in 2015–16).

Open disrespect for the rulings of constitutional courts is rare, although one does see this in the region as well. In Poland, the Constitutional Tribunal's decisions were openly disrespected, and the Tribunal was afterwards taken over by the Government through questionable judicial appointments and open violation of the electoral procedure (Polish Constitutional Tribunal Crisis of 2015–16). This took place because the Polish illiberal ruling Law and Justice Party (PiS) won a simple majority of the parliamentary seats but was far from achieving a constitutional majority, so it was necessary to control the body that could assess the constitutionality of the ruling party's new legislation. Attempts at political control of the general judiciary then followed.[45]

In yet other countries, the constitutional courts have fallen under the control of illiberal majorities peacefully, due to the long-term dominance of one political party in the parliament, quite often combined with packing of the court, that is, expanding the number of judges and appointing friendly ones to the bench (Russia since the mid-1990s, Hungary after 2010[46]).

Be it one way or the other, the common feature is that the region's constitutional courts have become much more self-restrained when compared with the 1990s. Even in those countries where constitutional courts still operate autonomously and are not influenced by the executive branch, the level of judicial

[45] For detailed analysis of the Polish development after 2015, see C Davies, 'Hostile Takeover: How Law and Justice Captured Poland's Courts' (Freedom House, May 2018) available at https://freedomhouse.org/sites/default/files/poland%20brief%20final.pdf.

[46] Sadurski (n 1) 10–13.

activism is not comparable to what it used to be in the first two decades after the fall of the Iron Curtain (an example might be the Czech Republic).

In some countries, such as Poland, a captured court could become a welcome tool for the politicians in power to dismantle constitutional guarantees and structures. When the Polish Constitutional Tribunal came under the full control of the PiS in December 2016 (by very questionable means, most likely in direct conflict with the Constitution and the law on the Constitutional Tribunal), the Tribunal immediately started to side with the ruling party. Judges elected by the previous parliamentary majority were not allowed to take part in deciding important cases by a new Chief Justice who controls the assignment of cases. Interestingly, the PiS deputies challenged several laws for their unconstitutionality (despite the fact that they could easily annul those laws on their own, taking into account the majority they enjoyed in the parliament) and the Tribunal swiftly provided the answer the PiS needed.[47]

In contrast, the Hungarian ruling party (Fidesz) does not need this sort of justification or legitimacy, because since 2010 it has enjoyed a qualified majority in the parliament, necessary for making a new constitution, as well as electing the personnel of all-important political institutions. The real practice of the Hungarian Constitutional Court, after becoming fully dominated by people close to the ruling Fidesz Party, is its self-restraint with respect to the legislature. As Sadurski has mentioned, this was nicely indicated in a decision of the Constitutional Court, before the Court was completely taken over by the new ruling elite. One of the early Fidesz appointees, Justice Béla Pokol, argued in his Dissenting Opinion that the protection of basic rights, as adjudicated earlier, should be lessened, if necessary to protect societal interests.[48] This nicely indicates a deviation from earlier judicial philosophies, which emphasised the primacy of the individual over a state, not vice versa.[49]

In yet another role, constitutional courts could also protect national constitutional values and principles against encroachment by supranational courts. After all, it is of course much more stylish if the verdicts of the Strasbourg Court are rejected by the national constitutional court, defending the national constitutional identity, than if the same is done by an autocratic domestic government.[50]

[47] See W Sadurski, 'Polish Constitutional Tribunal Under PiS: From an Activist Court, to a Paralysed Tribunal, to a Governmental Enabler' (2018) 11(2) *Hague Journal on the Rule of Law* 1 (explaining how the Tribunal started to protect the Government from the laws enacted long before PiS took power). In more detail, see W Sadurski, *Poland's Constitutional Breakdown* (Oxford, Oxford University Press, 2019).

[48] Sadurski (n 1) 12.

[49] See also B Pokol, 'The Juristocratic Form of Government and its Structural Issues' (2016) 9 *Pázmány Law Working Papers*.

[50] A Trochev, 'The Russian Constitutional Court and the Strasbourg Court: Judicial Pragmatism in a Dual State' in L Mälksoo and W Benedek (eds), *Russia and the European Court of Human Rights: The Strasbourg Effect* (Cambridge, Cambridge University Press, 2017) 125.

To sum up: it is not likely that the Central and Eastern European constitutional courts will be abolished altogether in the foreseeable future. The effects of the global rise of constitutional adjudication still control the mainstream political rhetoric. Even authoritarian regimes do not want to be viewed in a bad light, as belonging to a company of autocrats running wild, unrestrained by any checks and balances. But the actual importance of constitutional courts is withering away. It is very likely that in many countries of the region, the actual political importance and the real independence of the constitutional courts will come to resemble the situation prior to 1990. They would appear as politically loyal constitutional tribunals as they operated in those few countries that practised constitutional review under socialism.

6

Legal Reasoning in Central and Eastern Europe from a Historical Perspective

KATALIN KELEMEN

I. WHAT LEGAL REASONING IS AND WHY IT MATTERS

THIS CHAPTER BUILDS on a talk that I delivered at the conference in Stockholm that inspired the present volume. The talk bore the title 'Legal argumentation and interpretation in Central and Eastern Europe', a title suggested to me by the conference organisers. When conceiving the present chapter, however, I decided to change the title by replacing 'legal argumentation and interpretation' with 'legal reasoning'. This gives me the opportunity to reflect on terminology choices. In legal science, terminology usually does matter a lot. In this case, however, it seems that the choice between these terms is a matter of taste rather than of substance.

Legal reasoning, a popular expression in legal research in recent times, encapsulates both argumentation and interpretation, which constitute its essential elements. Legal reasoning is a process. Every lawyer performs legal reasoning in his or her work, and its clearest manifestation can be found in written legal documents, primarily in pleadings and decisions. While we may distinguish between motivating reasons and justificatory reasons,[1] legal documents typically contain the latter. Thus, legal reasoning as manifested in legal documents consists of justifying one's elected course of action. The term 'argumentation' is often used as synonymous with reasoning.[2] Argumentation in law usually aims to interpret a normative text, or to establish its applicability.[3]

[1] The motivating reasons are the motives and mental processes that lead a decision-maker to choose a particular course of action, while the justificatory reasons consist of the justifications that the decision-maker adduces publicly for that course of action. See A Jakab, A Dyevre and G Izcovitch, 'Introduction' in A Jakab, A Dyevre and G Izcovitch (eds), *Comparative Constitutional Reasoning* (Cambridge, Cambridge University Press, 2017) 1, 10–11.

[2] A Jakab, 'Judicial Reasoning in Constitutional Courts: A European Perspective' (2013) 14 *German Law Journal* 1215, 1219.

[3] Jakab considers the latter type of arguments to be preliminary questions of interpretation. See ibid 1222.

Interpretation, on the other hand, consists of determining the content of a normative text.[4]

But why does all this matter? And why should we talk about legal reasoning in a given region from a historical perspective? Moreover, since legal reasoning encapsulates a variety of activities performed by the members of different legal professions, which type of legal reasoning should we focus on? First, there is a common understanding among comparative law scholars that legal reasoning, and in particular judicial reasoning, demonstrates the prevalent conception of law and the self-perceptions of lawyers, and as such it is contained in the deepest level of legal culture.[5] This also means that legal reasoning is the most resistant to change. Second, the self-perception and the legitimacy of the judiciary have obvious consequences for the societies in which it operates.[6] Therefore, my chapter will mostly focus on judicial reasoning as a specific type of legal reasoning performed by judges.[7] However, rather than presenting the results of a specific research project, I will sum up the research that has been done (mostly by others) so far. My goal is to present and critically assess old and new research, possibly identifying new directions for future investigations.

When examining legal reasoning in Central and Eastern Europe, it is easy to see how it has resisted change. As Uzelac observed, no matter how much the Soviet doctrine insisted on adding socialist attributes to existing legal notions,[8] the real functions of the law and the legal institutions were more affected by the features that could exist independently from the ideological labels that had been accepted by the ruling elites.[9] Similarly, the breakdown of socialism did not automatically bring about a change in how lawyers and judges reason. Several scholars have included judicial reasoning among the surviving traces of old legal cultures. They use different labels when describing these traces, but all point in the same direction: judges in Central and Eastern Europe are more formalist in their reasoning than their Western colleagues.[10] Thus, we first need to define and examine judicial formalism.

[4] This determination of content can be argued for or against with the help of arguments. See ibid 1219–20.

[5] Z Kühn, *The Judiciary in Central and Eastern Europe: Mechanical Jurisprudence in Transformation?* (Leiden, Brill, 2011) xvii. See also Zdenek Kühn's contribution in ch 5 of this volume.

[6] P Cserne, 'Discourses on Judicial Formalism in Central and Eastern Europe: Symptom of an Inferiority Complex?' (2020) *European Review* 1, 3–4.

[7] Another popular term in legal research is 'judicial ideology', which would determine and prescribe the proper method of the judicial interpretation of the law as well as the ideal role that a judge should have in society. See Kühn (n 5) 67. Uzelac claims that the ruling ideologies of society have a natural impact on the specific ideology of jurists, but this particular ideology can still be different, and sometimes even significantly different. See A Uzelac, 'Survival of the Third Legal Tradition?' (2010) 49 *Supreme Court Law Review* 377, 380.

[8] Thereby creating idioms such as 'socialist legality', 'socialist law', or 'socialist justice'. See Uzelac (n 7).

[9] ibid.

[10] This formalism has been described as 'mechanical jurisprudence' by Zdenek Kühn (who borrows this expression from Roscoe Pound), and as hyper-positivism or textualism by Rafael Mańko. See

II. JUDICIAL FORMALISM AND HYPERPOSITIVISM IN CENTRAL AND EASTERN EUROPE

In general, judicial formalism usually means that judges see their role as applying, rather than creating, the law, and it is associated with a positivist approach to legal sources. Thus, formalist judges focus on enacted law rather than on a broader range of normative principles.[11] A formalist approach also relies heavily on literal interpretation. In comparative law, English judges are usually considered to have a more formalist approach than American (US) judges, who are more substantive-orientated (ie value-laden) in their argumentation.[12] Thus formalism is in fact a catch-all term for a wide range of features.

Primarily, judicial formalism may refer to methodological formalism,[13] textual positivism being its principal methodology. Textual positivism in practice consists of the literal rule of interpretation (or 'plain meaning rule' in the American terminology). Judges claim to apply the literal meaning of a normative text and present their analysis as a sort of inevitable logical deduction from this text. They do not acknowledge that rules are vague, uncertain and conflicting.[14] 'Hyper-positivism' is, instead, the term used by Rafael Mańko when describing the mode of legal thought in the socialist legal tradition. This notion also insists on preferences for linguistic and logical interpretation, with other methods treated as subsidiary ones.[15] A consequence of methodological formalism is that more sophisticated methods of legal reasoning, such as reasoning by balancing of interests or by reference to underlying policies, are unknown.[16] Moreover, it also entails a high level of purely procedural formalism, whereby courts tend to dismiss cases on formal grounds in order to avoid analysing them on the merits.[17] Finally, formalist reasoning can be also described in more general terms as 'a purely mechanical mental operation', performed by the judge regardless the complexity of the case.[18]

Kühn (n 5) 208; and R Mańko, 'Survival of the Socialist Legal Tradition? A Polish Perspective' (2013) 4(2) *Comparative Law Review* 1.

[11] See Cserne (n 6) 2.

[12] See K Kelemen, *Judicial Dissent in European Constitutional Courts: A Comparative and Legal Perspective* (Abingdon, Routledge, 2018) 77. In the US, substantive reasoning arose as a reaction to legal formalism during the Lochner era. See Note, 'Plurality Decisions and Judicial Decisionmaking' (1981) 94 *Harvard Law Review* 1127, 1140–41.

[13] See Kühn (n 5) 75.

[14] ibid.

[15] Mańko (n 10) 6.

[16] See R Mańko, 'The Culture of Private Law in Central Europe' (2005) 11 *European Law Journal* 527, 534.

[17] Mańko (n 10) 6.

[18] Formalist argumentation has adopted the justification of 'easy cases' as its paradigm. For anti-formalists, instead, any case is at least potentially a hard one. See Kühn (n 5) 76. As Matczak, Bencze and Kühn put it, 'all judges are bound by rules, but the formalist judge overstates this bindingness, while the anti-formalist judge downplays it'. See M Matczak, M Bencze and Z Kühn, 'Constitutions, EU Law and Judicial Strategies in the Czech Republic, Hungary, and Poland' (2010) 30 *Journal of Public Policy* 81, 87.

Judicial formalism, however defined, is certainly not a Central and Eastern European phenomenon. It might be a common feature of Central and Eastern European legal systems, but it is not unique to them. Judicial formalism, both its methodological and its procedural facets, may be found in other judiciaries as well. Thus it is worth considering whether Central and Eastern European legal systems are special in any way compared to other legal systems.

A. Are the Legal Systems of Central and Eastern Europe Special?

Is there a distinct Central and Eastern European style of legal reasoning? The classification of Central and Eastern European legal systems has always been a challenge for comparatists. The rise and demise of socialism in the region complicated the picture even more. These developments have largely contributed to the profound crisis that the traditional conceptual framework of legal families faced during the 1990s.[19] It is no longer possible to homogenise the region, relying upon a uniform political system such as government. Codes and constitutions now differ considerably and follow different models, sometimes even non-European models.[20]

The experience of socialism definitely facilitated the work of the comparatists, creating as it did a seemingly homogeneous area classifiable as a 'socialist legal family'. So a new comparative discipline was born in the West, called Sovietology,[21] which focused on the study of the Soviet Union (due to its prominent position in international relations) and dealt with the satellite countries only marginally. The majority of comparatists joined the separatist thesis, which applied a tripartite classification of the Western legal tradition, dividing it into civil law/common law/socialist law.[22] Certain comparatists of the socialist world tried to make a distinction between Soviet law and the legal systems of the satellite states of the Soviet Union, mostly on historical and economic grounds.[23] So, scholars of the 'other side' were also aware of the existing differences within the socialist legal family.[24]

[19] K Kelemen and B Fekete, 'How Should the Legal Systems of Eastern Europe be Classified Today?' in A Badó, DW Belling, J Bóka and P Mezei (eds), *International Conference for the 10th Anniversary of the Institute of Comparative Law, Lectiones Iuridicae 11* (Göttingen, Universitätsverlag, 2014) 197.

[20] ibid 199.

[21] The most eminent scholars of this discipline were John Hazard, Ferdinand JM Feldbrugge and Harold J Berman.

[22] There were, however, also some other scholars who continued to consider the legal systems of socialist countries as a subgroup of the civil law family. See F Ferreri, 'Quale posto spetta al diritto dei paesi ex-socialisti?' (1992/3) *Sociologia del diritto* 77; and J Quigley, 'Socialist Law and the Civil Law Tradition' (1989) 37 *American Journal of Comparative Law* 781.

[23] See, eg, Z Péteri, 'Reception of Soviet Law in Eastern Europe: Similarities and Differences between Soviet and East-European Law' (1986–1987) 61 *Tulane Law Review* 1397; and Gy Eörsi, *Comparative Civil Law* (Akadémia Kiadó 1979) 203.

[24] Kelemen and Fekete (n 19) 199–200.

With the collapse of the Soviet Union and the end of the socialist regimes, the picture has obviously become even more complex.[25] Tomasz Giaro, like many others, claims that the ongoing difference between legal life in the East and West is a matter of legal culture and of juristic style rather than of substantive law.[26] Indeed, legal reasoning, and in particular judicial reasoning, as established in section I, is contained in the deepest level of legal culture; it is one of its essential aspects. Therefore, if we detect a special Central and Eastern European style of legal reasoning, it may possibly justify the existence of a distinct legal family.

As discussed before, some scholars – such as Mańko – claim that a hyperpositivist working legal thought is dominant in the region.[27] He wonders whether this amounts to a barrier to functional interoperability. The criterion of functional interoperability was proposed by the well-known French scholar René David, who claimed that in order to establish whether two legal systems belong to the same legal family, we have to consider if their lawyers can fairly easily understand each other's working method.[28] The assumption is that lawyers cannot easily grasp the functioning of the law within a jurisdiction from outside their family. It seems that Kühn would argue for such interoperability between Central and Eastern European systems, as he claims that when lawyers and academics from post-communist countries meet, they always find that they are all beset by a common set of problems.[29]

But can we also say that Central and Eastern European lawyers cannot easily grasp how their Western European colleagues think about law? This is more difficult to assert. In Mańko's view, while in the post-war period the Western European legal systems fundamentally restructured the legal discourses, acknowledging the law-making power of courts, in the East 'Soviet domination mummified legal development, insulating the evolution of legal cultures for four decades'.[30] But does this mean a lack of interoperability? Still according to Mańko, this 'mummification' of legal development has led to problems in the European integration process. In particular, these problems are best evidenced by situations such as when the new Central and Eastern European Member States of the European Union (EU) understand the implementation of EU law in a hyperpositivist reductionist manner as merely the enactment of statutes, while treating the judicial and administrative practice as irrelevant.[31] This would suggest that we do have problems with interoperability in Europe between West and East. However, this interoperability problem can be understood and described in different ways.

[25] Cf ch 5 by Zdenek Kühn in this volume.

[26] T Giaro, 'Legal Tradition of Eastern Europe. Its Rise and Demise' (2011) 2 *Comparative Law Review* 1, 21, referring to Mańko (n 16).

[27] Mańko (n 10) 24–26.

[28] R David and JEC Brierley, *Major Legal Systems in the World Today: An Introduction to the Comparative Study of Law* (London, Stevens, 1968) 12.

[29] Kühn (n 5) 293.

[30] Mańko (n 10) 26.

[31] ibid. See also section IV in this chapter.

B. Narratives on Judicial Formalism in Central and Eastern Europe

Péter Cserne, in his meta-study on discourses on judicial formalism in Central and Eastern Europe, claims that formalism is not a distinctive feature of Central and Eastern Europe, as it can be observed in most modern legal systems.[32] He claims that what is symptomatic of Central and Eastern European political cultures is that the debate on judicial formalism has been conducted in simplified and misguided terms. There have been two ideological narratives about the formalist heritage of CEE judiciary, and – Cserne argues – both have been based on a misguided common assumption: the distinctiveness of formalism.[33] He explains that the distinctiveness-of-formalism discourse is a symptom or a symbolic battleground, which reflects patterns of thought and unresolved problems of collective (political) identity in the region.[34] Long-lived ideological tensions are inherent in the intellectual life of Central and Eastern European countries, and the rivalry of the two narratives would be a product of these tensions.[35] Cserne partly builds his meta-study on István Bibó's idea that national political discourses of the region are dominated by two stereotypical views about the relation of these nations to the West or to empires more generally: 'false realism' (a kind of pragmatism); and 'national self-sufficiency' (essentialist nationalism).[36]

The narratives examined by Cserne are ideological in the sense that they combine historical and normative jurisprudential claims in the service of practical political or legal goals. As such, they are mutually exclusive but not jointly exhaustive.[37] The first narrative interprets formalism in Central and Eastern European judiciary as the persistent heritage of socialist legal thought and practice. It sees a historical link with the ideology of socialist normativism, characterised by a rigid statist conception of law and formalism theory of adjudication.[38] Thus, this narrative is based on the historical-sociological claim that there is continuity between the past and post-socialist present. Another essential element of this narrative is that it views formalism negatively, as a sign of a limited mind, blind conservativism, incompetence or lack of transparency.[39] Cserne calls this the 'formalism-as-bad-heritage narrative', which he claims

[32] Cserne (n 6) 2.

[33] ibid 4.

[34] ibid.

[35] ibid 9.

[36] ibid. István Bibó was a Hungarian political theorist. See I Bibó, *The Art of Peacemaking. Selected Political Essays*, tr P Pásztor, ed IZ Dénes (New Haven, CT, Yale University Press, 2015).

[37] Cserne (n 6) 5.

[38] ibid. Sophisticated versions of this narrative acknowledge the different phases of Marxist theory, for instance that in the post-revolutionary period in the Soviet Union and for a short period after the communist takeover in the satellite states, certain anti-formalist ideas about the judiciary had some currency. Cserne here refers to authors such as Zdenek Kühn and Gianmaria Ajani.

[39] ibid.

would usually be combined with a positive appreciation of the educative or transformative effect of EU law and national constitutional/supreme courts on the judiciary. This narrative has gained a *de facto* dominance in the discourse and led to a reformist agenda.[40]

The second narrative is, instead, generally motivated by the perception of EU law (or other supranational entities) as threatening the national legal system. In some of its versions, it interprets judicial formalism as an embodiment of the courts' commitment to the rule of law.[41] The historical claim can be either that formalism is congruent and continuous with socialist judicial ideology, or that judges learned to resist anti-formalism arguments in the Stalinist period of socialism. Cserne calls this the 'formalism-as-noble-heritage narrative'.[42] He also observes that arguably, with recent changes in the fate of the rule of law in Poland and Hungary, this dichotomy has become more complex and is going to change further.[43]

III. HISTORY OF LEGAL REASONING IN CENTRAL AND EASTERN EUROPE

Most of the literature on judicial reasoning in Central and Eastern Europe focuses on relatively recent periods, not looking at eras preceding the nineteenth century. It may be in part explained by the fact that prior to the socialist era, the Central and Eastern European region was influenced by different legal traditions, so it is more difficult to apply a regional perspective. However, there had been some common traits, such as the lack of a formal reception of Roman law in the Middle Ages.[44] It was not until the nineteenth century that the entire region was subject to legal transfers from the Continental European legal systems. This reception then led to the erasure of traces of earlier local cultures to a large extent.[45] Moreover, an even stronger factor bringing the Central and Eastern European legal systems together was the impact of socialism.[46]

A. The Historical Roots

Can we define Central and Eastern Europe as a truly autonomous area, or is it merely a contemporary construct of Western discourse? Numerous scholars, within and outside legal science, have debated this question. Many claim

[40] ibid. Other authors Cserne refers to as representing this narrative are Anders Fogelklou and Marcin Matczak, together with Mátyás Bencze and Zdenek Kühn.
[41] Cserne (n 6) 6.
[42] ibid.
[43] ibid.
[44] Giaro (n 26) 4.
[45] Mańko (n 10) 25.
[46] ibid.

that the idea of 'Eastern Europe' was born during the Enlightenment and perpetuated during the Cold War of 1945–1989.[47] An important distinguishing feature of Eastern Europe in the field of legal history on which there seems to be a large scholarly consensus is the non-reception of Roman law during the era of the *ius commune*. Before codifications, there were only isolated cases of Romanist influence in the East.[48]

Legal historians teach us that given the absence of urbanisation and the weak position of the middle class, the late medieval Eastern Europe did not require legal Romanisation.[49] The international circulation of legal models remained limited in the East to Catholic canon law and German town laws. Western law and legal doctrine were transferred wholesale to the East only during the nineteenth century.[50] The universities on the Eastern periphery, although founded at a relatively early date,[51] did not participate in the development of jurisprudence. Although they had taught Roman law since the Middle Ages, these institutions reached a level comparable to Western law faculties only during the nineteenth and twentieth centuries due to the imitation of German Pandectist science.[52] The Eastern universities also functioned with considerable intermissions, leaving their chairs of Roman law vacant for long periods.[53] Moreover, there were no universities throughout South-Eastern Europe and Russia until the nineteenth century.[54]

A further difficulty in discussing legal development in Central and Eastern Europe is represented by the region's internal heterogeneity. In legal literature it is common to make a distinction between Central or East-Central Europe, on the one hand, and Eastern Europe in the strict sense, on the other hand.[55] From the beginning of the modern era, the legal culture of Central Europe was shaped by the Habsburg Empire.[56] From the seventeenth century, the absolutist

[47] Giaro (n 26) 4.

[48] As Giaro explains, even the West never experienced a direct transfer of legal rules from Antiquity to the Middle Ages, but merely a process of intellectualization of local legal orders. The Byzantine world, instead, offers quite the opposite, a static picture. Since the reception bearer was here the Orthodox Church, the secular Roman-Byzantine law was received in one package with the canon law of Byzantium. See ibid 4.

[49] ibid 6.

[50] ibid.

[51] Prague in 1348, Cracow in 1364 and Pécs in 1367.

[52] At the same time, courses in national law were already established in Poland and Hungary during the first half of the 17th century, considerably earlier than in Western Europe: Giaro (n 26) 15.

[53] The modest level of the 'Eastern' universities is also confirmed by the mass peregrinations of Czechs, Poles and Hungarians to Western universities until the 19th century. See Giaro (n 26) 6, referring to V Vanecek, 'La penetrazione del diritto romano e canonico nel territorio dell'odierna Cecoslovacchia' in *Atti del Convegno di Studi Accursiani III* (1968) 1282.

[54] With the exception of Moscow University, founded in 1755.

[55] K Kelemen, 'I sistemi giuridici dell'Europa orientale' in V Varano and V Barsotti, *La tradizione giuridica occidentale*, 6th edn (Torino, Giappichelli, 2018) 182.

[56] Kühn (n 5) 1. The Empire originated in 1526. Until the 18th century, the Empire was a personal union of more or less autonomous parts. The law of the Empire consisted mostly of local medieval customary law supplemented by some royal ordinances. See ibid 2.

rule opened the door to a cultural Germanisation and juristic Romanisation.[57] Still, Eastern European tradition was characterised by the longer persistence of traditional customary law, strongly differentiated according to feudal estates.[58] The local gentry firmly condemned and rejected Roman law as an agency of over-strong government. Moreover, the administration of justice in the realm of land law was reposed completely in the hands of lay judges, whereas the learned judge of the German type remained completely unknown.[59] It was not until the nineteenth century that the legal localism characteristic of feudalism was replaced in all countries – with the exception of Hungary – by a unified legal culture.[60]

During the nineteenth century, the Central European countries took pride in enlightened codification projects, while other Eastern European countries, such as Russia under Catherine the Great, at least developed a clear consciousness of the need to reform their national law.[61] Giaro, indeed, claims that 'Eastern European history, which excludes the West, remains an intellectual impossibility'.[62] Of equal importance is the second part of his claim, arguing that, on the other hand, 'it is possible to conceive a legal history of Western Europe without the East'.[63]

B. The Period Preceding the Socialist Era

From a comparative perspective, Central and Eastern European legal systems have experienced more interruptions in their legal development than their Western European counterparts. Western legal development, at least in the field of private law, has been more continuous in nature. There, codification constituted the 'organic crowning' of legal development,[64] whereas in the East codes were either imposed or borrowed.[65] Giaro claims that, in consequence, contemporary legal culture of Eastern Europe hardly contains any national elements that go back to times earlier than the nineteenth century.[66] Moreover, the successor states of the Austro-Hungarian Empire inherited from the bureaucratic Habsburg state deep confidence in positive law.[67]

[57] Giaro (n 26) 14.
[58] ibid.
[59] ibid 15.
[60] Kühn (n 5) 2.
[61] Prior to this time, no learned law, no juristic literature and no juristic profession were known throughout Russia and South-Eastern Europe. See Giaro (n 26) 16–17.
[62] ibid 8.
[63] ibid 7.
[64] ibid 17.
[65] Kelemen (n 55).
[66] Giaro (n 26) 17.
[67] Kühn claims that Hungary 'used to have one of the most unique legal cultures in Europe'. See Kühn (n 5) 4.

Hungary, however, represented an exception in some respects.[68] Until the late 1950s it was an uncodified civil law system. Civil law was based on customary law. Hungarian jurists considered Roman law to be a tool of the Austrian emperors to assault the autonomy of the Hungarian Kingdom.[69] Roman law started to influence and reshape Hungarian law in the seventeenth and eighteenth centuries, but Hungarian law remained independent.[70] The spirit of Hungarian customary private law required the judiciary to play an important role in the law-making process. The Supreme Court's decisions were proclaimed formally binding. However, Hungarian judicial decisions generalised the tendencies of former judicial practice in a vague way, and not by tracing back the judgments to specific precedents.[71]

After the dissolution of the big empires in Europe and the end of the First World War, new sovereign states were born. After the Trianon Peace Treaty of 1920, Hungarian inter-war politics was in a permanent state of crisis.[72] A new Polish state, reborn in 1918, was a curious mix of five distinct legal systems.[73] In subsequent developments, German legal influence prevailed in the area of public law, while French legal culture dominated in general private law.[74] In Czechoslovakia, the old Austrian legal tradition was continued in the Czech lands, and Hungarian legal culture was followed in the Slovakian part.[75] Despite all attempts at legislative unification, Czechoslovak law remained separated into two distinct legal systems until early in the communist era. In contrast, Polish efforts at unification were much more successful, with the exception of the field of civil law.[76]

During this period, the tradition of an independent judiciary was firm and solid. However, the judiciaries had been damaged on other fronts by the First World War and its aftermath, including an economic crisis.[77] Democracy entered a crisis in Central Europe in the late 1930s, while judges across the

[68] ibid.

[69] J Zlinszky, 'Two Questions About the Adaptation of Juridical Models: The XII Tables and Hungarian Reception' (1991) 33 *Acta Juridica Hungarica* 39, 52.

[70] Kühn (n 5) 5.

[71] 'It is a thesis of law that …', the court held. See Gy Eörsi, *Fundamental Problems of Socialist Civil Law* (Budapest, Akadémiai Kiadó, 1970) 31.

[72] Kühn (n 5) 6.

[73] In the southern part of Poland, formerly the Austrian province of Galicia, Austrian law was applicable. German law was valid in the formerly Prussian western province of Posen. Russian law was applied in the Russian provinces in the East. Further, in the former Polish Grand Duchy of Warsaw, the Napoleonic Civil Code prevailed. Finally, in certain small areas, the Hungarian legal system was applied. See WJ Wagner (ed), *Polish Law Throughout the Ages* (Stanford, CA, Hoover Institution Press, 1970).

[74] Kühn (n 5) 7.

[75] As Kühn explains, the Czech legal culture was, however, dominant in Czechoslovakia, because most Hungarian experts had left Slovakia for the rump Hungary and had been replaced by Czech judges, who were educated in Austrian law and did not speak Hungarian: ibid.

[76] ibid.

[77] Also, judges' salaries declined drastically. See Kühn (n 5) 9.

region were among its most devoted advocates.[78] Consequently, the judiciary became weaker, even though its independence remained unchallenged.[79] The Second World War and Nazi occupation just further increased this weakness, as it changed the landscape and ethnic composition of Central Europe drastically, and reduced the strength of pre-war intelligentsia.[80] However, Jan Komárek claims that a serious study of how the Nazi occupation affected legal culture in Czechoslovakia (or more widely, Central Europe) is still missing.[81]

C. Legal Reasoning During the Socialist Era

Legal historians identify three phases in the evolution of the socialist legal tradition: the initial Bolshevik period (1920s), dominated by Lenin's views on the withering away of state and law; the anti-formalist Stalinist period (1930s–1950s); and the formalist post-Stalinist period (from the 1950s).[82] The Stalinist phase was characterised by an internal tension between anti-formalism and formalism. While on the one hand, in the atmosphere of the building of socialism, the judicial application of law was clearly activist and anti-formalist, on the other hand the Stalinist theory of law developed clear textualist, positivist and formalist features.[83] In this phase, the leading legal scholar of the Soviet Union, Andrei Vyshinsky, refused the thesis that law was supposed to disappear in socialism. Law, instead, was seen as essential to preserve order and communist power.[84] The post-Stalinist phase saw, instead, the opposite trend: the retreat from activism and the rise of formalism.[85] The following sections will briefly discuss these three phases.

i. Transition to Socialist Law in Central and Eastern Europe

Only following the Second World War was Soviet socialism able to aim at reversing the effects of the antecedent westernisation of law in the whole of Eastern Europe. However, as Giaro observes, the legal instruments of Sovietisation had previously been westernised by Russian legal scholarship during the

[78] In sharp contrast to their German counterparts, as Kühn observes, ibid 13–14.
[79] ibid 14.
[80] ibid 20, referring to WI Hitchcock, *The Struggle for Europe: The Turbulent History of a Divided Continent 1945–2002* (New York, Random House, 2003). Jan Komárek criticises Kühn for exonerating the 'democrats' of the post-war era, whose contribution to the decline of Central Europe was not negligible. See J Komárek, 'The Struggle for Legal Reform after Communism', *LSE Legal Studies Working Paper No 10/2014* (10 February 2014) 17, available at https://ssrn.com/abstract=2388783 (accessed 11 June 2021).
[81] Komárek (n 80) 11.
[82] Mańko (n 10) 5.
[83] Kühn (n 5) 94.
[84] ibid 93. In short, Stalinist socialism produced a simplified 'command theory of law': ibid 94.
[85] Komárek (n 80) 6.

pre-revolutionary period.[86] Soviet civil law was undoubtedly part and parcel of the Continental legal family[87] or a chapter of Western legal history.[88] There were evident elements of continuity between the pre-revolutionary era and the Soviet period.[89] As regards private law, some old civil codes survived, particularly in Eastern Germany and in Romania.[90] Moreover, some formally new civil codes of socialist countries, in particular those enacted by Hungary in 1959 and by Poland in 1964, substantially shadowed the German Pandectist tradition.[91] The other satellite states followed socialist innovations with more faith and hope.[92]

Most of the importation of the Soviet model into the rest of Central and Eastern Europe occurred before 1955. The totalitarian power of the Communist Party and the politicisation of the legal academia attacked the intellectual independence of the law faculties and destroyed pre-Second World War legal culture.[93] All social sciences, and especially legal science, were severely purged, as they were considered the centre of the previous 'bourgeois' regime.[94] Legal scholarship was forcibly subjugated to the ideology of Marxism-Leninism.[95] The quality of legal argumentation deteriorated rapidly in the first decade of communist rule, as law had to become 'popular' and easily accessible to all.[96] Moreover, the political trials of the 1950s caused general distrust towards judges among a wide public.[97]

Despite being relatively short, the Stalinist era left a strong mark on the Central and Eastern European socialist regimes until the very last moment of their existence.[98] While the era of Stalinism was overwhelmingly uniform, subsequent developments from the 1960s varied in different parts of the region.

[86] Giaro (n 26) 20.

[87] J Quigley, 'The Romanist Character of Soviet Law' in FJM Feldbrugge (ed), *The Emancipation of Soviet Law* (Leiden, Brill, 1992) 27.

[88] AJ Schmidt, 'Soviet Civil Law as Legal History' in D Barry, G Ginsburgs and W Simons (eds), *The Revival of Private Law in Central and Eastern Europe, Essays in honor of FJM Feldbrugge* (Leiden, Brill, 1996) 46.

[89] Even in Russian public law, in both constitutional and administrative law. In fact, Russian constitutional theory knew the German concept of *Rechtsstaat* already during the 1880s. See GP van den Berg, 'Elements of Continuity in Soviet Constitutional Law' in WE Butler (ed), *Russian Law* (Leiden, AW Sijthoff, 1977) 215. In administrative law, the organisational structure of the Government and ministries was taken over from the tsarist times. See Giaro (n 26) 21.

[90] The BGB of 1896 was in force in Eastern Germany until 1976, while the Romanian *codul civil* of 1864 was not abrogated until the fall of communism. See ibid 21.

[91] ibid.

[92] See also Z Kühn, 'Development of Comparative Law in Central and Eastern Europe' in N Reimann and R Zimmermann (eds), *The Oxford Handbook of Comparative Law* (Oxford, Oxford University Press, 2006) 223.

[93] Kühn (n 5) 22. Poland, however, represented an exception. There pre-war professors survived in their chairs throughout the Stalinist era. See ibid 25.

[94] ibid 22.

[95] ibid 23.

[96] ibid 25.

[97] See K Kulcsár, 'Position of Lawyers and their Role in the Last Four Decades of Hungary' (1987) 29 *Acta Juridica Hungarica* 303, 316.

[98] Kühn (n 5) 28.

Polish and Hungarian legal doctrine was able to develop to some extent along independent lines. However, these regimes were more the exception than the rule in Central and Eastern Europe.[99] In post-Stalinist Czechoslovakia, an era of gradual liberalisation in the 1960s was followed by two decades of intellectual stagnation and the closure of society.[100]

ii. The Heritage of the Civil Law Tradition in the Socialist Civil Codes

While official socialist doctrine, in particular Stalinist theoreticians, emphasised that law should be as simple and easily comprehensible as possible,[101] this kind of simplified normativism was not taken equally seriously by all socialist regimes.[102] The Hungarian and Polish Civil Codes are two of the socialist codes that remained true to the Continental legal culture. In contrast, the 1964 Czechoslovak Civil Code annihilated that legal tradition.[103] The Czechoslovak Civil Code was, in fact, the only 'truly revolutionary' civil code in Central Europe.[104] In contrast, in the Hungarian and Polish Civil Codes, enacted in 1959 and 1964 respectively, the only major structural deviation was the exclusion of family law from the field of civil law.[105] Moreover, Poland never formally repealed its Commercial Code during the Socialist era, even though it was not applied in practice.[106]

Ultimately, as some scholars observe, the core of the Soviet conception of law was, in fact, a set of formalistic doctrines resembling classical Continental positivism. Thus, many typical Germanic features appeared in Czechoslovak civil law, although they had been introduced through the indirect route of Soviet law transplants. The first socialist civil code of Czechoslovakia, enacted in 1950, included a General Part, unknown in Czechoslovak-Austrian legal heritage until then.[107]

[99] ibid 29.

[100] As it is well known, this gradual liberalisation erupted in the Prague Spring, suppressed by the Soviet army in 1968. See ibid 30.

[101] As the Hungarian legal scholar Gyula Eörsi wrote in 1979, 'Socialist codification avoids casuistic but does not rest content with framing skeleton rules. Socialist civil codes so far enacted do not contain more than 800 rather short sections.' Gy Eörsi, *Comparative Civil (Private) Law. Law Types, Law Groups, the Roads of Legal Development* (Budapest, Akadémiai Kiadó, 1979) 549.

[102] Kühn (n 5) 32 and 63.

[103] ibid 32. The Code introduced a completely new terminology. The traditional Romanist Book on Obligations was abolished, replaced by new categories, such as 'services', 'civic aid', 'personal use', etc. See AW Rudziński, 'New Communist Civil Codes of Czechoslovakia and Poland: A General Appraisal' (1965) 41 *Indiana Law Journal* 33.

[104] Kühn (n 5) 33.

[105] ibid. Thus, family law was not regulated in the Code but in a special law. See also A Harmathy, 'A Survey of the History of Civil and Commercial Law' in A Harmathy (ed), *Introduction to Hungarian Law* (Alphen aan den Rijn, Wolters Kluwer, 1998) 11.

[106] Kühn (n 5) 34. Indeed, the Hungarian Civil Code enacted in 1959 did not require major revisions after the fall of the socialist regimes, and it remained in force until 2014. The new Civil Code was enacted by Act no V of 2013 and entered into force on 15 March 2014.

[107] Kühn (n 5) 63.

iii. The Reflection of the Socialist Ideals in Court Proceedings

A few words have to be said about socialist procedural law as well, as the way court proceedings are handled has an important effect on the judges' socialisation. Consequently, it left long-lasting marks on the legal profession and, indirectly, on legal reasoning. Socialist civil proceedings were more estranged from the Continental model than were criminal proceedings.[108] There are at least four features of socialist civil procedure to be pointed out: the role of laymen; the limited competences of courts; the ideal of objective truth; and state interference in court proceedings through prosecutorial intervention.

Laymen were involved in socialist court proceedings both in the quality of judges or prosecutors and as lay assessors.[109] They decided both questions of law and fact in any lawsuit.[110] And while several pre-socialist legal systems in Central and Eastern Europe provided for trial by jury,[111] one of the first acts of the socialist regime was to abolish the 'bourgeois' jury system.[112] Especially during the first years of the regime, these lay assessors were used as a tool of control by the regime over the old judges.[113] Later, however, the lay assessors lost this purpose and became only a decorative part of the socialist civil and criminal procedure.[114]

A second feature to mention is that the competences of state courts were substantially limited in the socialist era. Litigation between nationalised enterprises was not brought before courts but was, rather, decided by state arbitration tribunals,[115] as these cases were not considered to be legal disputes. The issues at dispute concerned the planned economy and were supposed to be of a technical rather than legal character, and judges allegedly did not have sufficient knowledge to decide these issues.[116] Moreover, even in cases that reached the courts, the judge was expected to emphasise the priority of extrajudicial settlement over judicial decision making. Kühn explains this with the socialist ideals

[108] ibid 41.

[109] It was sufficient to attend a course at a law faculty to be appointed as a judge or prosecutor, so not all judges and prosecutors completed the full legal education. See ibid 34.

[110] ibid 35.

[111] For example, Polish pre-socialist law. See Mańko (n 10) 20.

[112] Kühn (n 5) 35.

[113] See K Kulcsár, *People's Assessors in the Courts. A Study on Sociology of Law* (Budapest, Akadémiai Kiadó, 1982) 37.

[114] Kühn (n 5) 36. As a rule, a panel of the district court was composed of one professional judge and two lay assessors, making decisions by majority vote. The higher courts usually comprised a majority of professional lawyers.

[115] With the exception of Hungary, where state arbitration was abolished in 1973. See V Knapp, 'State Arbitration in Socialist Countries' in K Zweigert and U Drobnig (eds), *International Encyclopedia of Comparative Law*, vol XVI (Martinus Nijhoff, 1982) ch 13. In Poland, in 1988, state arbitration decided 87,209 disputes while the judiciary disposed of 177,690 civil cases. A Rzepliński, 'Principles and Practice of Socialist Justice in Poland' in G Bender and U Falk (eds), *Recht im Sozialismus, Analysen zur Normdurchsetzung in osteuropäischen Nachkriegsgesellschaften (1944/45–1989)*, vol 3: *Sozialistische Gesetzlichkeit* (Frankfurt, Vittorio Klostermann, 1999) 8.

[116] Kühn (n 5) 37.

of consensus and societal harmony.[117] In addition, many labour disputes were settled extra-judicially, through the authority of special arbitration bodies and lay tribunals. Similarly, various administrative controversies were judged by administrative agencies instead of courts. These limitations on court competence obviously substantially eased the judiciary's docket.[118]

Third, pursuing ideals of objective truth, the purpose of the socialist trial was to find the truth. Judges were free to decide for themselves what evidence should be admitted at trial.[119] Correct fact-finding was the principal task of the court.[120] In other words, idealistic readings of the principle *iura novit curia* drove the argument of law out of parties' pleadings, based on the claim that no party should gain an advantage from having a better lawyer.[121] Kühn defines this approach to law as authoritarian, which 'accords to the judge the exclusive role in constructing the meaning of the law'.[122]

Finally, the right of prosecutors to intervene in court proceedings in civil matters also represented an attempt to achieve just socialist litigation, which would require an aid for the weaker party.[123] The side-effect was that it contributed to totalitarianism, as the state had influence over any potential dispute.[124] General supervision over socialist legality was also entrusted to the prosecutors. Individual citizens could lodge petitions with the prosecutors if their rights had been breached by actions of administrative bodies of the state.[125] Prosecutors were the loyal servants of the socialist state more than judges. In fact, almost all prosecutors were members of the Communist Party, while the same was not true of judges.[126]

[117] ibid 42. Interestingly, these ideals are not included among the features of the Rule of Political Law – where socialist legal systems undoubtedly belong – in the taxonomy proposed by Ugo Mattei, who instead considered the high value placed on harmony in society to be an aspect common to legal systems where the hegemonic pattern of law is the Rule of Traditional Law. See U Mattei, 'Three Patterns of Law: Taxonomy and Change in the World's Legal Systems' (1997) 45 *American Journal of Comparative Law* 5, 39.

[118] Kühn (n 5) 38.

[119] ibid 41. Therefore, a judge was subject to reproach for uncritically adhering to the conforming assertions of opposing parties. See ibid 42. Cf M Damaška, *The Faces of Justice and State Authority. A Comparative Approach to the Legal Process* (New Haven, CT, Yale University Press, 1986) 195.

[120] As Uzelac puts it, 'if the parties failed to submit relevant evidence, it was not the end, but the beginning, of the judicial quest'. See Uzelac (n 7) 384.

[121] Kühn (n 5) 290. Obligatory representation by an attorney was abolished, and judges were required to instruct ignorant persons about their procedural and substantive rights and duties. See ibid 43.

[122] ibid 291. See also Kühn's contribution in ch 5 of this volume.

[123] ibid 43–44.

[124] Even more so in criminal proceedings, where prosecutors were made the undisputed masters of the pre-trial procedure. See Damaška (n 119) 195.

[125] Prosecutors could also supervise compliance with socialist legality on their own initiative. See Kühn (n 5) 44.

[126] ibid. Moreover, it was the prosecutors, not the judges, who held the key posts in the administration of justice.

iv. The Role of Law in Socialist Society

In the totalitarian socialist regime, the omnipresent ruling ideology penetrated the whole of society, and reduced the role of law.[127] An important fact contributing to the lack of litigation in the socialist era was that a number of the real transactions were going on in the grey zone of unlawful but in fact tolerated dealings.[128] Consequently, the number of civil actions brought to the courts declined dramatically during the socialist era, while criminal adjudication flourished as some specific socialist crimes were introduced.[129] A useful comparison can be made between the two parts of Germany. Data show that civil litigation rates in the GDR were clearly lower than in West Germany.[130] The only field of law in which East Germans were almost as likely as West Germans to go to court was family law.[131]

It is not just that socialist judges had fewer cases to decide than their Western colleagues; these cases were also typically simpler. The most complex legal controversies left the courtroom to be decided by different bodies, or simply did not exist in the socialist state.[132] The fact that legal relationships were either simplified or pushed outside the legal sphere explains the reduced need for lawyers during socialism. Consequently, access to law faculties was restricted[133] and nepotism flourished.[134] This inevitably lowered the quality of legal education.

In this period, an 'instrumentalist approach' to law prevailed,[135] which saw the law as 'a flexible instrument of social engineering'.[136] According to Uzelac, this approach was, in itself, ideologically neutral, and therefore also capable of surviving after the demise of Soviet Marxism.[137] The instrumentalist approach,

[127] ibid 45.

[128] For example, trading with foreign currency. See ibid 46. On the 'second economy' of the Socialist regimes see I Markovits, 'Law and Order – Constitutionalism and Legality in Eastern Europe' (1982) 34 *Stanford Lew Review* 513, 597–600.

[129] Such as parasitism. See Kühn (n 5) 47. Parasitism, similarly to hooliganism (see Arts 206 and 209 of the Soviet Criminal Code enacted on 26 May 1961), was deliberately vaguely defined, offering a ground for politically motivated persecutions. See S Pomorski, 'Communists and Their Criminal Law: Reflections on Igor Andrejew's "Outline of the Criminal Law of Socialist States"' (1981) 7 *Review of Socialist Law* 7, 13.

[130] Even adjusting for differences in population, the number of civil law cases brought before West German courts was still almost nine times higher than cases brought before East German courts. See I Markovits, 'Pursuing One's Right under Socialism' (1986) 38 *Stanford Law Review* 689, 719.

[131] See ibid 720. In Hungary too, around half of the first-instance civil suits were family-related issues. See Kühn (n 5) 49, referring to K Kulcsár, 'Social Aspects of Litigation in Civil Courts' in M Cain and K Kulcsár (eds), *Disputes and the Law* (Budapest, Akadémiai Kiadó 1983) 85, 89–90.

[132] Kühn (n 5) 48.

[133] ibid 49.

[134] ibid 51.

[135] To use Uzelac's words (n 7) 379.

[136] JN Hazard, *Communists and Their Law. A Search for the Common Core of the Legal Systems of the Marxian Socialist States* (Chicago, IL, University of Chicago Press 1969) 69, cited by Kühn (n 5) 53.

[137] Uzelac (n 7) 380.

coupled with the ideal of accessibility and the fact that many matters were not regulated by law but rather by means of state planning and party directives, called for simplicity of legal argumentation. Consequently, the need for highly educated professionals diminished considerably. This offers a further explanation for the restricted access to legal education and the lower number of law students during socialism.

v. Judicial Careers and Judicial Methodology During Socialism

In the circumstances mentioned in section III.C.iv, the profession of judge was no longer attractive for lawyers. The socialist model of judicial selection represented a mix between the professional and political models that Kühn describes as being close, in practice, to the West German professional model.[138] The socialist judge was a career judge rather than a recognition judge,[139] and therefore in this respect there was continuity with the pre-socialist tradition to a certain extent. The political element in the judicial selection process was represented by the use of popular vote (for trial judges) or political bodies.[140] Still, most socialist judges started their career at a young age, after graduation from law school, and they worked their way up to the higher levels of the judiciary.[141]

The politicised selection process and the fact that judges were poorly paid invited corruption and reduced judges' resistance to the demands of 'telephone justice'.[142] Thus, in the socialist regimes, although the principle of judicial independence was enshrined in all socialist constitutions, genuine judicial independence could not be found.[143] According to Kühn's account, however, we can see a difference in the judges' attitude between the Stalinist and the post-Stalinist period, so before and after 1953.[144] While Stalinist judges were radical activists

[138] Save the specifics of the early Stalinist era. See Kühn (n 5) 59.

[139] On the distinction between career and recognition judges, see, among others, NL Georgakopoulos, 'Discretion in the Career and Recognition Judiciary' (2000) 7 *University of Chicago Law School Roundtable* 205; and N Garoupa and T Ginsburg, 'Hybrid Judicial Career Structures: Reputation versus Legal Tradition' (2011) 3 *Journal of Legal Analysis* 411.

[140] In Czechoslovakia, for example, after 1957, the law provided that trial judges and lay assessors be elected for a term of four years. These elections were not free. The voter had no choice but to vote for a candidate selected by the political bodies. The regional national councils elected judges of the regional court, while supreme court judges were elected by the Parliament upon proposal by the National Front. Moreover, the body that elected judges also had the power to recall them. See Kühn (n 5) 60.

[141] ibid 59.

[142] ibid 53. 'Telephone justice' means that party instructions were passed on by telephone calls, which would leave no trace. See I Markovits, 'Children of a Lesser God: GDR Lawyers in Post-Socialist Germany' (1996) 94 *Michigan Law Review* 2270, 2288. Membership of judges in the Communist Party in East-Central Europe was welcome, although unlike in the Soviet Union it was not necessary. However, it was a necessary pre-condition of their career promotion. See Kühn (n 5) 56.

[143] Kühn (n 5) 58 and 62.

[144] ibid 66.

and anti-formalists, servants of the dominant ideology and the needs of the ruling Party,[145] after the death of Stalin, 'Socialist legal scholarship produced a strange amalgam of old-fashioned pre-Socialist positivism and Stalinist (and post-Stalinist) legal doctrine'.[146] In general, the notion of 'law' in the socialist legal tradition was reduced to cover only abstract and general enactments of state authorities, to the exclusion of judge-made law, general principles of law or customary law.[147] The classical hierarchy of legal sources, the very paradigm of Continental European legal thinking, in fact largely disappeared. The decisive role of the statute, which had characterised Eastern Europe before the socialist era, was abandoned, as the most important questions were regulated in sub-legislative acts, such as ministerial decrees and government regulations. In most socialist countries, the acts of parliament came to consist more of abstract principles and policies than of rules.[148]

Strong positivism was also part of the heritage of the German legal culture, which has traditionally exercised a major influence on Central European legal systems,[149] including the highly formalist nineteenth-century *Begriffsjurisprudenz* ('conceptual jurisprudence'), and some influence in the whole of Eastern Europe.[150] Thus, as Mańko explains, formalism was not strange or foreign, nor were the substantive features of the socialist legal tradition, such as the use of abstract notions and concepts.[151] This means that a hyperpositivist approach was already a faithful reflection of the everyday experience of lawyers. According to the 'formalism-as-noble-heritage narrative' already discussed,[152] in these circumstances formalism also proved to be a useful tool, because it enabled judges to avoid difficult cases by dismissing them on formal grounds or postponing their decision.[153] In this way lawyers in general, not only judges, could insulate themselves from politics by claiming that they were performing a technical activity.[154]

[145] Stalinist judges' radical activism could be seen in the open use of political and ideological arguments and judicial creation of new legal rules. For example, in the guise of the 'principles of social intercourse', a new general clause was introduced in Polish private law in 1950. See Mańko (n 10) 8.

[146] Kühn (n 5) 66.

[147] Mańko refers to this understanding of law as 'the concept of limited law'. It also implied a very sharp distinction between binding and non-binding sources. The latter were considered to be irrelevant for deciding a legal controversy. See Mańko (n 10) 6–7; and Kühn (n 5) 209.

[148] In Hungary, after 1950, two or three statutes were enacted each year (disregarding acts on the state budget and national planning). See Kühn (n 5) 39–40.

[149] See S Wood, *Germany and East-Central Europe* (Aldershot, Ashgate, 2004), and Mańko (n 16) 531.

[150] See W Sadurski, 'Marxism and Legal Positivism: A case study on the impact of ideology upon legal theory' in DJ Galligan (ed), *Essays in Legal Theory* (Melbourne, Melbourne University Press 1984) 187, 203.

[151] Mańko (n 10) 9.

[152] See section II.B, text to nn 41–43.

[153] Mańko even calls it a 'survival strategy'. See Mańko (n 10) 9. See also D Piana, 'The Power Knocks at the Courts' Back Door: Two Waves of Postcommunist Judicial Reforms' (2009) 42 *Comparative Political Studies* 816, 820, and Uzelac (n 7) 383–84.

[154] Mańko (n 10) 9.

This does not mean, however, that judges would have been independent during socialism. Even though in the post-Stalinist period to a more limited extent, there was political interference in court adjudication in concrete cases. As Cserne observes, it is not clear whether the relatively low level of politicisation of the judiciary can be seen as an effect of formalism.[155] There are other possible explanations. First, it may rather be the case that most legal controversies were too unimportant politically, while many others, which were sufficiently important, were not regulated by law. Second, the lack of direct political influence could rather be the outcome of prudential considerations of those in power. Third, case assignment could be easily manipulated for political reasons. Thus, politically important cases could be assigned to the politically most reliable judges.[156] These explanations may be seen as cumulative rather than alternative. Probably all four played a role in limiting political interference in everyday judicial decision making. Still, this limiting effect was not enough to find the socialist judiciary genuinely independent.[157]

On a final note, it is also important to remark that, during the socialist era, the official reporter of judicial decisions covered only a small percentage of judicial decisions, including only those carefully selected by the editors. Thus most case law remained unknown.[158] This represents an important challenge for students of judicial reasoning in Central and Eastern Europe. As Komárek rightly argues, it is difficult to convincingly portray the mentality of the whole judiciary and its transformation in the region.[159] It seems that two opposite phenomena characterised the socialist judiciary. On the one hand, a 'Stalinisation' of the judiciary was going on; on the other hand, there was opposition to it by older judges educated in the previous legal system, who could stay on the bench even after the Communist Party had taken power. We do not know, however, the proportions of these two phenomena, as empirical research is lacking, partly due to the difficulty caused by selective case reporting.[160]

D. The Post-socialist Era: Continuity and Discontinuity

Giaro claims that what remains the nearly exclusive historical common feature of Eastern European countries is the legacy of their 'peripheral or semi-peripheral

[155] Cserne (n 6) 8.
[156] ibid.
[157] As a Czechoslovak judge quoted by Kühn put it, even if in about 90% of the court's agenda there was no interference, this does not warrant the conclusion that 'some sort of ninety percent judicial independence and integrity' existed. Also, because of the awareness that interference could happen at any time, this conditioned all adjudication: Kühn (n 5) 62.
[158] In contrast to pre-socialist practice, when private or semi-private reporters took care of the reporting of judicial decisions: ibid 128.
[159] Komárek (n 80) 12.
[160] ibid.

nature' and 'tendency to gravitate around a Western centre'.[161] Central and Eastern European legal systems are, however, not the only ones in the world of a 'peripheral or semi-peripheral nature'. So even though 'special' in Europe, we might still wonder whether these legal systems own any unique distinguishing feature from a broader comparative perspective. Their peripheral nature, even though not unique, is an undoubtedly significant distinguishing feature of Central and Eastern Europe. Even the opposition between the two ideological narratives on judicial formalism, which reveals conflicting views of how peripheral nations should cope with the challenges of modernisation, is not limited to this region, Cserne claims.[162]

Since the fall of the Berlin Wall, no comparatist has attempted to place every single Central and Eastern European country in a suggested new taxonomy, but all have limited themselves to citing some examples. This is, on the one hand, due to the region's fragmented nature and to the linguistic difficulties that in all likelihood discourage scholars from a comprehensive study of the region.[163] On the other hand, it may also be attributable to the general crisis of the mainstream classifications of legal families.[164]

As part of the process of transition from socialism to capitalism and democracy, the Central and Eastern European countries incorporated many Western legal institutions into their legal systems during a relatively brief period.[165] Certain key components of this legal transition were, for instance, constitutional courts providing constitutional review of legislation,[166] human rights as international and constitutional standards,[167] and ombudspersons and equality bodies devoted to anti-discrimination issues.[168] These institutions further flourished in the region due to aspirations to European integration and various legal assistance activities of the 1990s.[169] Thus, Western legal thinking comprehensively shaped the Central and Eastern European legal systems, whereby many new institutions and instruments arrived from the West.[170]

[161] Giaro (n 26) 22–23.
[162] Cserne (n 6) 9.
[163] Kelemen and Fekete (n 19) 207.
[164] See also section II.A.
[165] See G Ajani, 'By Chance and Prestige: Legal Transplants in Russia and Eastern Europe' (1995) 43 *American Journal of Comparative Law* 93.
[166] K Lach and W Sadurski, 'Constitutional Courts of Central and Eastern Europe: Between Adolescence and Maturity' (2008) 3 *Journal of Comparative Law* 212.
[167] A Sajó, 'Rights in Post-Communism' in A Sajó (ed), *Western Rights? Post-Communist Application* (Alphen aan den Rijn, Kluwer Law International, 1996) 139.
[168] G Moon, 'Enforcement Bodies' in D Schiek et al (eds), *Cases, Materials, and Text on National, Supranational and International Non-Discrimination Law* (Oxford, Hart, Publishing 2007) 871.
[169] For instance, Ajani argues that birth and modernisation of the antitrust law in the region occurred under the strong influence of the EC antitrust model. G Ajani, 'Law and Economic Reform in Eastern Europe. The Transition from Plan Market during the Formative Years of 1989–1994' in *International Encyclopedia of Comparative Law*, vol XVII/3 (The Hague, Martinus Nijhoff, 2006) 14.
[170] Kelemen and Fekete (n 19) 209–10.

However, this importation process also had its natural limits. Both the historical setting of the region and its macro-sociological features were able to hinder the functioning of these Western institutions in the same way as in their countries of origin, since after the transfer they became parts of a different socio-historical background.[171] The Central and Eastern European legal systems have formed such regional peculiarities as could even impede their real reception, thereby compromising not only the legal reconstruction of the region but also the entire transition process.[172] As regards legal, and in particular judicial, reasoning, the inability to engage in creative judicial decision making seems to have been a problem common to post-communist countries.[173] Kühn claimed, however, already two decades after the end of socialism, there was a gradual erosion of the post-communist conception of limited law.[174]

There is no doubt that a certain degree of continuity existed between socialist and post-socialist law. It was both inevitable and required by the rule of law.[175] Mańko presents three perspectives on continuity with the socialist legal tradition: an institutional perspective; a methodological perspective; and a normative perspective.[176] All three types of continuity affect the judiciary and judicial decision making. Institutional continuity,[177] at least in some Central Eastern European countries, he claims, was remarkable. In Poland, for example, the transition did not entail any revolutionary change in the structure or staffing of courts or the bar,[178] save for three exceptions: a re-staffing of the Supreme Court, even though many of the old judges got reappointed; re-appointment of prosecutors; and the transformation of the state arbitration tribunals into economic courts.[179] A first lustration act concerning judges was adopted only in 1997, and it covered only those judges who had collaborated with the Secret Service before 1990.[180] A similar tendency was observed in most post-socialist countries.[181] Institutional continuity is also secured by the way in which judicial

[171] B Fekete, 'Rule of Law in a 'Post-Communist' Legal Pluralism – On the Social Conditions of the Rule of Law from an East-Central European Perspective' (26 October 2012), available at https://ssrn.com/abstract=2167227 (accessed 11 June 2021).

[172] Kelemen and Fekete (n 19) 210.

[173] Kühn (n 5) 207–08, relying also on A Sajó, 'The Judiciary in Contemporary Society: Hungary' (1993) 25 *Case Western Reserve Journal of International Law* 293, 300.

[174] This was in his view demonstrated by the increasing length of judicial decisions. See Kühn (n 5) 208.

[175] See R Teitel, 'Transitional Jurisprudence: The Role of Law in Political Transformation' (1997) 106 *Yale Law Journal* 2009, 2028.

[176] Mańko (n 10) 2.

[177] The term 'institution' is used by Mańko in the legal sense, not in a sociological one. By institutions, he means legal institutions such as courts, the prosecution service or bar associations. See ibid 10.

[178] ibid.

[179] ibid 11. On state arbitration tribunals see also section III.C.iii.

[180] See M Safjan, 'Transitional Justice: The Polish Example, the Case of Lustration' (2007) 1 *European Journal of Legal Studies* 1.

[181] The exception is East Germany. See Mańko (n 10) 11 and 27–28; and Kühn (n 5) 163 and 188.

appointments are made. The progress of a judicial career depends not so much on qualitative factors but on quantitative ones, namely, the speed of deciding cases and the number of reversals on appeal.[182]

One could also see methodological continuity in the (ordinary) judiciary.[183] The concept of law continued to be narrow, and preference for linguistic interpretation strong. Judicial precedent, as Mańko argued in 2013, is still understood in a superficial way, although increasingly accepted as a source of law. Judicial proceedings in post-socialist countries are conducted in a strictly formalist manner, and courts strive to dismiss cases on formal grounds in order to avoid entering into the merits.[184]

Last but not least, normative continuity is reflected in concrete legal norms that survived the regime change. Mańko offers some striking examples from Polish law. For instance, despite numerous amendments to the Code of Civil Procedure, the prosecutor's general *locus standi* remained unaffected. The 'extraordinary revision', a special form of appeal against a final judicial decision with the force of *res judicata*,[185] also survived until 1998.[186] The Guidelines of the Supreme Court, which contained abstractly formulated interpretations of statutory rules, although officially abolished in 1989, are still frequently cited and relied on by judges.[187] Finally, lay assessors still hear civil cases concerning crucial matters of labour law and family law, as well as criminal cases with felony charges.[188] In Polish substantive private law, certain prominent socialist general clauses survived and remained in place in the Civil Code even after the reforms. Mańko mentions the 'principles of social intercourse' (*współżycia społecznego* in Polish) and the 'socio-economic purpose' (*społeczno-gospodarczym przeznaczeniem*) as the two most prominent legal concepts inherited from the socialist legal tradition.[189] A deeper continuity with socialist law is ensured by Polish

[182] Mańko (n 10) 11–12.

[183] Actually not only in the judiciary, but in the legislature and the academia as well. See ibid 12–16. Constitutional courts, on the other hand, were completely new bodies (with the exception of the short-lived Czechoslovak Constitutional Court of the 1920s), which built up their processes and jurisprudence from scratch.

[184] ibid 13. See also Uzelac (n 7) 383–85.

[185] This 'extraordinary revision', known to all socialist systems, was available to certain high public officials but not to the parties. See Mańko (n 10) 17.

[186] However, in 2000 a functionally similar form of appeal (with a different name) was re-introduced: ibid 19.

[187] ibid. See also Zdenek Kühn's contribution in ch 5 of this volume, where he discusses supreme courts' interpretational statements and guidelines. Kühn explains that in the Czech Republic, the two Supreme Courts still have the power to enact interpretative statements today, even though the Supreme Administrative Court used this power on only two occasions.

[188] Mańko (n 10) 20.

[189] ibid. See Art 5 of the Polish Civil Code. For a deeper discussion, see R Mańko, 'Quality of Legislation Following a Transition from Really Existing Socialism to Capitalism: a Case Study of General Clauses in Polish Private Law' in *The Quality of Legal Acts and Its Importance in Contemporary Legal Space* (University of Latvia Press, 2012) 540, available at https://ssrn.com/abstract=2159271 (accessed 11 June 2021).

court practice, which still relies on socialist case law applying these clauses.[190] In property law, we can find socialist *iura in re aliena*, such as the proprietary right to an apartment in a cooperative and the right of perpetual usufruct.[191] In contract law, two types of nominate contracts of socialist creation survived: the supply contract and the cultivation contract.[192] After 1990, these contracts were kept but adapted to the new economic conditions. Both are still used in practice.[193]

Together with the gradual decline of the socialist traces in the region's legal systems, Central and Eastern Europe is now facing a populist or even authoritarian backlash, following the period of 'democracy fatigue' that characterised the region when it joined the EU.[194] As Komárek explains, simplistic accounts ascribe this phenomenon to the backwardness of post-socialist countries, which would continue to look back to nineteenth-century nation building rather than – as in Western Europe – forward to twenty-first-century transnational integration.[195] However, he continues, a different consciousness has emerged in Central and Eastern Europe: that its 1989 revolutions were somehow taken away from the people, who never gained control over their lives. Liberal democracy, coupled with market economy, was presented to them as the only alternative.[196] Komárek's sound conclusion is that, in this light,

> the present 'populist backlash' can be seen as a reaction to the suppression of many social conflicts, which were contained in the name of the Return to Europe. To really understand the present problems of post-communist Europe requires more open engagement with their communist past, which rejects the simple triumphalism of the early post-1989 period.[197]

IV. THE IMPACT OF EUROPEAN INTEGRATION

If we want to discuss the historical development of legal reasoning in Central and Eastern Europe, the impact of the European integration process, in which

[190] Mańko (n 10) 21.
[191] ibid 21–22.
[192] The former involves a supplier who undertakes to produce generic goods and deliver them in parts or periodically to another 'unit of socialised economy' (using the Marxist terminology) in exchange for the price, while by the latter a farmer undertakes to produce and sell a certain quantity of agricultural produce to an entity of the socialised economy in exchange for a fixed price. The social function of the cultivation contract was the integration of the mainly privately held Polish agricultural sector with the socialised economy. See ibid 22.
[193] The requirement that a unit of socialised economy be party to the contract was removed: ibid.
[194] There is an extensive literature discussing this development. See, eg, J Rupnik, 'Is East-Central Europe Backsliding? From Democracy Fatigue to Populist Backlash' (2002) 7 *Journal of Democracy* 17, and the other articles in the same issue; and the more recent special issue, 'Rethinking "democratic backsliding" in Central and Eastern Europe' (2018) 34:3 *East European Politics*.
[195] Komárek (n 80) 10.
[196] ibid.
[197] ibid 10–11.

all countries of the region participated to at least some extent, must not be neglected. Of course, the impact is especially strong in those countries that became members of the EU over the last two decades, but even the other countries, including Russia, have been seriously affected by the EU's policies and decisions. Moreover, all Central and Eastern European countries, with the sole exception of Belarus, are members of the Council of Europe and signatories to the European Convention on Human Rights (ECHR).

However, the impact of the EU legal culture is a factor that today sharply divides the former socialist legal family into two distinct groups: one composed of the post-socialist EU Member States; and one that has retained many more features of the Soviet regime and has been less exposed to Europeanisation.[198] Therefore, the reflections presented in this section will be limited to the first group of countries.

The impact of European integration has not been a one-sided process. There are two sides to be taken into consideration. In this section, I first discuss the impact of EU law and the ECHR on national courts of the region, then I briefly consider the impact of the arrival of new judges from Central and Eastern European on the European courts.

A. The Impact of European Law on Judicial Reasoning in National Courts

Accession to the EU and to the Council of Europe gave new tools to national courts, even in purely domestic cases.[199] Especially those scholars who embrace the 'judicial-formalism-as-bad-heritage narrative' see this as an empowerment of the judiciary and a sort of treatment for many problems.[200] It is, for example, clear that the jurisprudence of the Court of Justice of the EU (CJEU) and the European Court of Human Rights (ECtHR) empowers ordinary judges in ways that undermine, or could potentially undermine, the centrality of constitutional tribunals when it comes to reviewing national legislation.[201] It is impossible to do justice to the richness of existing research on this specific matter, and I will limit myself to a few observations.

Kühn claims that EU law has had 'a clearly disruptive effect on national legal orders, questioning old values of legal science and calling for novel answers to old problems'.[202] There were several challenges that Central and Eastern Europeans countries faced within a relatively short period. Transition to democracy in

[198] Mańko (n 10) 27.
[199] Kühn (n 5) 294.
[200] See section II.B.
[201] V Ferreres Comella, *Constitutional Courts and Democratic Values* (New Haven, CT, Yale University Press, 2009) 122.
[202] Kühn (n 5) 267.

practice overlapped with the beginning of their participation in the European integration process. The aforementioned institutional continuity[203] implied that national courts were not fully equipped with the necessary knowledge to face these challenges. Poland might have been an exception, as its judges had experience with the application of international law. But this was not the case for the other Central and Eastern European judges, as the socialist constitutions were typically silent on the status of international law in their legal orders.[204]

In this new context, several factors defied judicial formalism. The new institutional conditions, in particular EU law and the new national constitutions, have provided strong incentives for judges to resort more frequently to non-formalistic argumentation in judicial reasoning. General principles became compelling and applicable in concrete cases.[205] At the same time, other factors contributed to the persistence of judicial formalism. The period of transition was characterised by legislative optimism, which produced an atmosphere in which ordinary judges and lawyers generally overemphasised the impact of European legal transplants made by the legislature, while they understated the judicial role in that process.[206] The persisting hyperpositivist approach that ignores non-binding sources and persuasive arguments posed a serious challenge to the harmonisation process.[207]

We cannot, however, treat all national courts on equal terms. There are significant differences between constitutional courts and other, ordinary or special, courts. The problem of ordinary courts seems to have been rather a lack of knowledge and ability than that of open defiance or a flouting of their new duties. Obvious problems are presented by their hyperpositivist approach, including an excessive reliance on literal interpretation and limited recourse to teleological arguments, and their inability to apply abstract legal principles.[208] The constitutional courts, on the other hand, have been more keen to use policy arguments and to consider the non-legal context of the case in their reasoning from the outset, which may be attributable to their very nature and the scope of their jurisdiction. Interpreting a constitution does not substantially differ from statutory interpretation,[209] but the difference lies in the frequency with which certain types of arguments are used. More precisely, teleological interpretation is more common in constitutional reasoning than in statutory interpretation,

[203] See section III.D.
[204] Kühn (n 5) 268.
[205] Matczak et al (n 18) 82.
[206] Kühn (n 5) 271–72.
[207] ibid 272. A typical example is the doctrine of indirect effect of European directives. Central European judges are not likely candidates to use such doctrines. See ibid 286–87.
[208] ibid 281.
[209] As András Jakab puts it, 'constitutional interpretation is just a specific case of statutory interpretation'. See Jakab (n 2) 1224.

and not only in Central and Eastern Europe, for a number of reasons. First, constitutions are more difficult to amend, therefore judges have to be more creative to adjust them to new challenges.[210] Second, the degree of generality of constitutional provisions is on average higher, which also calls for more creativity. Third, constitutional courts in particular are most often composed of recognition judges, most of whom do not come from the ordinary judiciary but rather from academia or other public institutions.[211]

As regards the relationship of constitutional courts with EU law, the picture that emerges is different from that of ordinary courts. Here it is more difficult to find commonalities among the Central and Eastern European constitutional courts, which all chose their own way of handling their relationship with the European courts and possible conflicts between their national constitution and European law. They have been, for example, more reluctant to make preliminary references to the CJEU than ordinary courts.[212] Moreover, the tension between the CJEU and national constitutional courts regarding the supremacy of EU law over national constitutions involved Central and Eastern European constitutional courts as well, which, however, chose different approaches. Most of them, just as in Western Europe, made reservations to the absolute primacy of EU law in the name of the same constitutional values: fundamental rights,[213] state sovereignty[214] and constitutional identity.[215] The Estonian Supreme Court's Constitutional Chamber and the Latvian Constitutional Court are the only ones that have adopted the full primacy of EU law.[216] Some other constitutional courts of the region have still not developed a clear-cut view on these questions.[217] Therefore, it seems that as regards the impact of EU law on constitutional reasoning, we cannot talk about a special Central and Eastern European style or approach, as these countries' constitutional courts show just as much variation as their Western European counterparts.

[210] ibid 1225.

[211] ibid.

[212] Some of them have not perceived themselves as a court or tribunal in the sense of Art 267 of the Treaty on the Functioning of the European Union. The first preliminary reference from the region came from the Lithuanian Constitutional Court in 2007. See D Piqani, 'Relation of Constitutional Courts/Supreme Courts to EU Courts' (2018) *Max Planck Encyclopedia of Comparative Constitutional Law*, para 9.

[213] See, eg, the Polish Constitutional Tribunal's decision on the European Arrest Warrant, Decision P 1/05 (2005).

[214] Following the German Federal Constitutional Court's ultra vires doctrine. See, eg, the Czech Constitutional Court's *Sugar Quotas* decision (Pl ÚS 50/04) of 2006.

[215] Again, following the lead of the German Federal Constitutional Court. See, eg, the Hungarian Constitutional Court's Decision no 22/2016 (XII. 5.) AB. See K Kelemen, 'The Hungarian Constitutional Court and the concept of national constitutional identity' (2017) 15–16 *Ianus* 23, available at www.rivistaianus.it/numero_15-16_2017/02_Kelemen_23-33.pdf (accessed 11 June 2021).

[216] See Piqani (n 212) para 45.

[217] These are the Bulgarian, Croatian and Romanian Constitutional Courts. See ibid para 49.

B. Eastern European Judges on the European Courts

Even if it is not directly relevant to the reasoning of Central and Eastern European national courts, the other side of the coin is also worth mentioning. That is how Central and Eastern European judges have affected the work of the European courts. This may in any case also teach us something about how Central and Eastern European judges reason, albeit in an international environment. We know little to nothing about the behaviour of Central and Eastern European judges on the CJEU, as the Court's deliberations are entirely confidential and separate opinions are not allowed.[218] The ECtHR, though, allows for the publication of concurring and dissenting opinions, so we can use these to explore differences in the behaviour and reasoning of the individual judges.

A quantitative analysis of the separate opinions in the Grand Chamber of the ECtHR delivered between 1998 and 2006 revealed that judges elected in respect of the new Member States of Central and Eastern Europe delivered significantly fewer separate opinions than judges elected in respect of the old Member States.[219] Bruinsma claims that due to a less developed independent legal profession in the new Member States, the non-diplomatic voice of human rights and justice in the case at hand is underrepresented in the ECtHR as a whole.[220] Judges from the new Member States were, moreover, on the whole younger than judges from the old Member States.[221] A third explanation offered by the authors was that when it comes to writing separate opinions, insufficient language skills in the working languages of the Court (English and French) also play their role.[222] However, all the factors pointed to as possible explanations for the lower dissent rate among Central and European Eastern judges are likely to change over time, and therefore research based on more recent cases might give different results. All in all, Bruinsma's explanation tells us little about the style of reasoning of Central and Eastern European lawyers, other than that they are (or at that time were) less acquainted with human rights arguments. Interestingly, he does not discuss the absence of the possibility to write separate opinions (and to dissent in a broader sense) in socialist legal systems as a feasible further explanation, neither does he discuss the hyperpositivist approach to law of Central and Eastern European lawyers.

[218] This is not unproblematic and has indeed been the object of criticism, especially in relation to specific decisions that were poorly reasoned. See K Kelemen, 'Opinion 2/13 of the CJEU: Whose opinion?' *Diritti Comparati* (4 June 2015), available at www.diritticomparati.it/opinion-213-of-the-cjeu-whose-opinion/ (accessed 11 June 2021).

[219] FJ Bruinsma, 'The Room at the Top: Separate Opinions in the Grand Chambers of the ECHR (1998–2006)' (2008) *Ancilla Juris* 32, available at www.anci.ch/articles/ancilla2008_32_bruinsma.pdf (accessed 11 June 2021).

[220] ibid 39.

[221] As of 2006, the median year of birth was 1942 for judges from old Member States, and 1950 for judges from new Member States: ibid 40, fn 35.

[222] ibid 40.

In another study conducted between 1998 and 2001, Arold concluded, instead, that there is a legal culture within the ECtHR that successfully overrides the (legal) differences between its Member States. The rich diversities that come to the Court create no obstacles to its work. The Court would thus be an example of convergence, as the permanent judges adapt to the Court's legal culture.[223] According to Arold, interviews with the judges and study of the Registry confirmed the hypothesis that the distinction between civil, common and former socialist legal systems at the Court does not impact decision making significantly.[224] It does not mean that there is no impact at all, though. While some interviewees found no impact, a majority of them found different legal traditions to impact on the specifics of a case.[225] It was also observed, however, that many of the judges from the former socialist states had been trained in Western Europe or in the United States. In addition, perhaps more significantly, there was a commitment to the Strasbourg case law.[226] This means that the ECtHR's judges would probably adopt a different approach if sitting on a national court.

V. EMPIRICAL RESEARCH ON JUDICIAL REASONING IN CENTRAL AND EASTERN EUROPE

While judicial reasoning and Separate Opinions on the ECtHR have been analysed with empirical methods, much of the literature concerning Central and Eastern European courts is 'theoretical', relying on intuitions and anecdotes rather than solid data.[227] Cserne warns that a thorough analysis of the discourse on judicial formalism would require detailed case studies, pursued perhaps with the methods and analytical tools of cultural anthropology, political and social psychology.[228] Actually, during the last decade, there have been a few very interesting comparative research projects on judicial reasoning that used empirical methods, although most (but not all) of them with a focus on constitutional cases. Indeed, a wider empirical shift is taking place within comparative constitutional scholarship. Even though most of these recent projects have not limited themselves to Central and Eastern Europe, they all involved at least a couple of courts from the region. Thus, we can certainly learn something about legal reasoning in Central and Eastern Europe from these projects.

[223] N-L Arold, *The Legal Culture of the European Court of Human Rights* (The Hague, Martinus Nijhoff, 2007) 160.

[224] ibid 75.

[225] 'The nationality matters in the detail; even the meaning of specific words can be quite different,' said one of the interviewees. See ibid 74.

[226] RCA White and I Boussiakou, 'Separate Opinions in the European Court of Human Rights' (2009) 9 *Human Rights Law Review* 37, 58.

[227] Cserne (n 6) 3.

[228] ibid 4.

A. The CONREASON Project: Constitutional Reasoning in a Comparative Perspective

The CONREASON project, housed in the Max Planck Institute for Comparative Public Law and International Law and the Hungarian Academy of Sciences, ran from 2011 to 2016.[229] The comparative analysis involved a thorough examination of the reason-giving practice of a total of 18 courts, including seven supreme courts, nine constitutional courts and the two European courts (the ECtHR and the CJEU).[230] From Central and Eastern Europe, the Czech and the Hungarian Constitutional Courts were included. The empirical analysis was carried out on the basis of 40 leading cases from each jurisdiction involved, chosen by the authors of the country reports after consulting five mainstream legal experts of the respective legal system designated by the authors themselves.[231]

An important achievement of the CONREASON project is that there is now empirical evidence demonstrating that the common law versus civil law divide does have relevance when it comes to judicial style and constitutional reasoning, even if the differences are not highly remarkable.[232] Also, mixed systems seem to be closer to the common law than to the civil law tradition in this respect.[233] They are actually '*not* the middle way between common law and civil law, but rather the extreme value', with the common law tradition being the middle ground between mixed systems and civil law. The authors qualify this finding as a true, unexpected 'discovery'.[234]

Since only two Eastern European countries were included in this project, it would be far-fetched to draw conclusions on constitutional reasoning in Central and Eastern Europe on the basis of its findings. However, it can still be interesting to look at the results concerning the Czech and Hungarian Constitutional Courts, and at what they have in common. Even so, we can only speculate whether these common features can be extended to the whole region. Actually,

[229] The findings and conclusions of the project were published in A Jakab, A Dyevre and G Itzcovich (eds), *Comparative Constitutional Reasoning* (Cambridge, Cambridge University Press, 2017).

[230] The complete dataset of the CONREASON Project is available on the website of the Hungarian Academy of Sciences at https://openarchive.tk.mta.hu/369/ (accessed 11 June 2021).

[231] On the methodology in more detail, see A Jakab, A Dyevre and G Itzcovich, 'CONREASON – The Comparative Constitutional Reasoning Project. Methodological Dilemmas and Project Design' (2015) *MTA Law Working Papers 2015/9*, available at http://real.mtak.hu/36806/1/2015_09_jakab.pdf (accessed 11 June 2021).

[232] Namely, common law judges make more frequent use of precedent-based arguments, their opinions have a more conversational and free-flowing style, and they show greater candour when it comes to acknowledging the influence of policy considerations and non-legal factors on the judicial process. A Jakab, A Dyevre and G Itzcovich, 'Conclusion' in Jakab, Dyevre and Itzcovich (eds) (n 230) 761, 768–72 and 781.

[233] Canada, Israel and South Africa were included in the CONREASON project. See ibid 779.

[234] ibid 797. For a longer comment on this work, see K Kelemen, 'Constitutional Reasoning: A flourishing field of research in comparative law' (2019) 17 *International Journal of Constitutional Law* 1336.

in relation to the Hungarian Constitutional Court (HCC) two samples were taken, examining separately the 40 leading cases of the period 1990–2010 and the 40 leading cases of the two-year period 2012–2013. This choice is justified by the important changes that occurred in Hungarian constitutional justice between 2010 and 2012, with the adoption of a new Fundamental Law and several substantial changes in the powers of the Court.[235]

Examining the findings of the CONREASON project can lead us to some interesting observations. As regards the argumentative and conceptual diversity in the Courts' leading judgments, the Czech and Hungarian Constitutional Courts are relatively close to each other, even though there are other courts that are closer to them.[236] Namely, the HCC in the first period displayed the same extent of diversity as the Spanish Constitutional Tribunal, while the Czech Constitutional Court's (CCC's) argumentative and conceptual diversity was closest to that of the UK Supreme Court. The second sample from the HCC (2012–2013) got closer to the CCC, as they displayed the same extent of argumentative diversity, while the HCC displayed a lesser degree of conceptual diversity. Still, the HCC in its second period was much closer to the US Supreme Court than to the CCC. In any case, neither the HCC nor the CCC was an outlier as concerns argumentative and conceptual diversity.[237] The project measured argumentative and conceptual diversity through the average number of argument types and key concepts used in landmark constitutional cases, and it found a general growing trend. According to the authors, this shows that judges have become more flexible in their argumentation, as they can avail themselves of a larger repertoire of arguments, thus having greater freedom to choose and justify the outcome they regard as optimal.[238]

In the cluster analysis of general opinion characteristics, the HCC (both samples) and the CCC fell into two different broad clusters. The purpose of such an analysis was to establish the degree of 'parentage' between the Courts.[239] According to the findings of the CONREASON project, as regards reasoning practice, the HCC and the CCC are only distant relatives. The HCC in the first period would be, again, a kind of sister to the Spanish Constitutional Tribunal, while the second period's argumentative practice is closest to the Austrian and Italian practices (which might be surprising). The CCC, on the other hand, would be a sister of the Brazilian Constitutional Court.

[235] A Jakab and J Fröhlich, 'The Constitutional Court of Hungary' in Jakab, Dyevre and Itzcovich (eds) (n 230) 394.

[236] Jakab, Dyevre and Itzcovich (n 232) 766. By conceptual and argumentative diversity the authors mean the repertoire of arguments and concepts the Courts draw on. Its calculation is based on the average number of arguments and key concepts used in the Courts' leading cases.

[237] The outliers were, instead, the French Constitutional Council, with a very low level of argumentative and conceptual diversity, and the German and South African Constitutional Courts, with an elevated level of diversity: ibid.

[238] Jakab, Dyevre and Itzcovich (n 232) 788.

[239] ibid 779.

Of course, it is difficult to generalise these findings either geographically to the entire region of Central and Eastern Europe, or to courts in general regardless of jurisdiction. What we can see from this research, however, is that the HCC and the CCC are not 'close relatives' in their style of reasoning. One may reasonably assume that region-focused research using the same empirical methods would reach a similar conclusion in relation to all constitutional courts of the region. That is to say that Central and Eastern European constitutional courts would show a considerable degree of diversity. But more research needs still to be done to confirm or reject this hypothesis, and to find possible Central and Eastern European patterns.

B. Research on the Use of Foreign Precedents by Constitutional Judges

A comparative project led by Tania Groppi and Marie-Claire Ponthoreau on the use of foreign precedents by constitutional judges also represents an important contribution to the field.[240] It examined the practice of 16 constitutional and supreme courts from all over the world with empirical methods. From among Central and Eastern European countries, Hungary and Romania were included in this project.[241]

The research found that the examined courts can be divided into two categories: courts in which citation of foreign precedents is common practice; and courts that are more reluctant to use foreign precedents in their reasoning.[242] These two categories actually seem to correspond to the legal traditions to which these courts belong: the first includes courts of the common law and mixed legal traditions, while the second belongs to the civil law tradition,[243] where law has traditionally been a 'national' matter.[244] Groppi and Ponthoreau claim that even though constitutional interpretation favours legal reasoning based on general principles, and thus is less formalistic, 'the force of the tradition seems to prevail over the special structural features of constitutional adjudication'.[245]

The Hungarian and Romanian Constitutional Courts, obviously, belong to the second category.[246] Since all other Central and Eastern European legal

[240] T Groppi and M Ponthoreau (eds), *The Use of Foreign Precedents by Constitutional Judges* (Oxford, Hart Publishing, 2013).

[241] See Z Szente, 'Chapter 10. Hungary: Unsystematic and Incoherent Borrowing of Law. The Use of Foreign Judicial Precedents in the Jurisprudence of the Constitutional Court, 1999–2010' in Groppi and Ponthoreau (eds) (n 240) 253; and ES Tanasescu and S Deaconu, 'Chapter 13. Romania: Analogical Reasoning as Dialectical Instrument' in Groppi and Ponthoreau (eds) (n 240) 321.

[242] T Groppi and M Ponthoreau, 'Conclusion: The Use of Foreign Precedents by Constitutional Judges: A Limited Practice, An Uncertain Future' in Groppi and Ponthoreau (eds) (n 240) 411, 412.

[243] With the notable exception of the US Supreme Court: ibid 413.

[244] ibid 414.

[245] ibid 413.

[246] The former cited foreign precedents in only 1.8% of the cases during the examined period (1999–2010); while in the latter, only 0.1% of the decisions contain a clear reference to a foreign case: ibid 412.

systems belong to the civil law tradition, we may speculate that we would find the same reluctance to refer to foreign precedents if we examined their case law. This research, however, does not offer such a broad comparison.

C. The JUDICON Project

The JUDICON project, carried out by political scientists and concluded in 2018, focused on six Central European states: the Czech Republic, Germany, Hungary, Poland, Romania and Slovakia. This is therefore the largest comparative study with a special focus on part of the region that used empirical methods. The JUDICON project examined the case law of constitutional courts between 1990 and 2015, with the aim of exploring empirically and systematically the practice of constitutional adjudication, with a special focus on the diversity of judicial decisions and the strength of the constraint they exercise on the legislatures.[247] Thus, while this project examined the relationship between constitutional courts and legislatures rather than looking into the reasoning style of constitutional judges, it still bears relevance for the reasoning practice of these courts, as it explores the different strategies employed by them. This research found that, surprisingly, it was the Slovakian Constitutional Court that made the most powerful rulings, rather than the Hungarian or the German ones.[248] The main value of this project is that it draws attention to the fact that the practice of constitutional adjudication in the Central and Eastern European region is more diverse than we expected based on the previous literature. The Courts are different not only in their composition and powers, but also in their use of a range of tools to position themselves within the system of the separation of powers.[249]

D. Measuring the Quality of Judicial Reasoning

Another recent comparative project, concluded in 2018, that is worth mentioning is the research led by Mátyás Bencze, a Hungarian legal scholar, investigating

[247] K Pócza, 'Introduction' in K Pócza (ed), *Constitutional Politics and the Judiciary. Decision-making in Central and Eastern Europe* (Abingdon, Routledge, 2019) 1, 3. Its starting point is the observation that refined practices of constitutional adjudication clearly exceed the upholding/strike-down dichotomy, therefore the project disaggregates all judicial decisions into rulings and maps their diversity: ibid 4–5. Using rulings instead of decisions as the unit of examination, the project encodes them according to their strength, taking into account not only the order (rejection, unconstitutionality by legislative omission, procedural unconstitutionality, constitutional requirement, substantive unconstitutionality, constitutional interpretation *in abstracto*) but also such factors as completeness, temporal effect and prescription: ibid 11.

[248] K Pócza, G Dobos and A Gyulai, 'Courts compared' in Pócza (ed) (n 247) 213, 214.

[249] E Bodnár, 'Review of 'Constitutional Politics and the Judiciary: Decision-Making in Central and Eastern Europe' (Kálmán Pócza ed)' *I-CONnect* (9 November 2019), available at www.iconnectblog.com/2019/11/book-review-eszter-bodnar-on-constitutional-politics-and-the-judiciary-decision-making-in-central-and-eastern-europe-kalman-pocza-ed/ (accessed 11 June 2021).

the measurability of the quality of judicial reasoning.[250] This project, unlike the others mentioned, did not focus specifically on constitutional justice or constitutional reasoning. The same two Central and Eastern European countries were involved in this research as in the CONREASON project: the Czech Republic and Hungary.[251]

This interesting project, focusing on the question of quality, shows us how difficult it is to define quality in the first place, and then to measure it, as it requires quantification.[252] Indicators and performance metrics that are applied to measure the courts' performance are often based on quantitative criteria, such as the number of cases decided in a given period.[253] They usually do not take the judges' reasoning into account. Even the evaluative projects of the Council of Europe and the EU focus mostly on efficiency issues, and not on the content of judicial decisions.[254]

The latter, however, recently developed a tool to measure the quality of the content of judicial decisions. In the 2019 EU Justice Scoreboard, for the first time, one of the four factors taken into account when examining quality is the use of quality standards.[255] They also offer a definition of 'high-quality judicial decision'. According to the European Commission, high-quality judicial decisions 'are clearly drafted, structured, and strike a proper balance between clear reasoning and conciseness, thus being easily understood and enforceable'.[256] Their evaluation of this factor relies on data collected by the Association of the Councils of State and Supreme Administrative Jurisdictions of the EU through a questionnaire answered by the national (ordinary and administrative) supreme courts. But even this questionnaire focuses on existing obligations and legal training of the judges, rather than on the actual content of the decisions.[257] All Central and Eastern European EU Member States, except for Romania, provided data. These data reveal, for example, that among the supreme courts

[250] M Bencze and GY Ng (eds), *How to Measure the Quality of Judicial Reasoning* (New York, Springer, 2018).

[251] This project also included both national and international courts.

[252] See M Bencze and GY Ng, 'Measuring the Unmeasurable?' in Bencze and Ng (eds) (n 250) 1.

[253] ibid 3.

[254] The Council of Europe set up a commission for the efficiency of justice, known by the French acronym CEPEJ, to analyse the results of judicial systems and provide assistance to Member States: see at www.coe.int/en/web/cepej (accessed 11 June 2021). The European Commission, on the other hand, established the EU Justice Scoreboard to provide 'comparable data on the independence, quality, and efficiency of national justice systems': see at https://ec.europa.eu/info/policies/justice-and-fundamental-rights/upholding-rule-law/eu-justice-scoreboard_en (accessed 11 June 2021).

[255] The four factors are: accessibility of justice; adequate resources; the existence of assessment tools; and the use of quality standards. European Commission Communication on the 2019 EU Justice Scoreboard, COM(2019) 198/2, 38 and 43.

[256] ibid 38.

[257] The indicators are (i) predetermined elements of reasoning or structure, (ii) obligation of conciseness, (iii) mechanism for clarifying judgments, (iv) obligation to use clear and simple language, (v) training, (vi) assessment of the quality of judgments: ibid 39.

of the region, only the Polish Administrative Supreme Court has an internal mechanism to assess the global quality of its own decisions.[258] In general, the data show that quality standards differ considerably among Member States, and in some Member States even between the ordinary and administrative supreme courts. However, most Member States provide some kind of professional training for judges on the structure, style of reasoning and drafting of judgments.[259] Finally, in most Member States, the structure and reasoning of decisions include predetermined elements, with the notable exception of the two common law jurisdictions, the UK and Ireland.[260] Concluding, it is difficult to detect any pattern that would be common and at the same time limited to the Central and Eastern European supreme courts.

Similarly, in the research led by Bencze there is no sign of unique Central and Eastern European features other than the legacy of socialism. However, as discussed earlier, formalism is not unique to socialist systems.[261] Today, two decades after the breakdown of the socialist regimes, this legacy, a 'formalistic style of legalistic argumentation', is limited to the civil and criminal courts, while administrative and constitutional judges tend to be anti-formalists.[262] At the same time, it should also be pointed out that this research project focused on the question of how to measure the quality of judicial reasoning, and the various possibilities and methods that can be employed to evaluate that quality. It discussed the style and methods of judicial reasoning only to a limited extent, as much as necessary to answer the main questions in focus.

E. Adjudication Strategies in Administrative Court Decisions 1999–2004

A further research study to be mentioned focused on administrative courts in three countries of the region: Hungary, Poland and the Czech Republic. In their article, Marcin Matczak, Mátyás Bencze and Zdenek Kühn examine whether adjudication strategies have adapted to the changes in the legal-institutional environment with empirical methods, through the analysis of 1,187 administrative court decisions passed between 1999 and 2004.[263] They examined the types of standards that judges invoked in their judgments, categorising them as

[258] Even in Western Europe, only a few supreme courts have such a mechanism, ie the Belgian and the Italian ordinary Courts of Cassation, and the French and Dutch Councils of State: ibid.

[259] With the notable exception of Luxembourg and Ireland: ibid 38 and 43.

[260] ibid.

[261] See section II.

[262] Z Kühn, 'The Quality of Justice and Judicial Reasoning in the Czech Republic' in Bencze and Ng (eds) (n 250) 173, 183–84.

[263] Matczak et al (n 18) 82, comprising 352 Czech cases, 335 Hungarian cases and 500 Polish cases concerning tax matters and other decisions relevant to business activities: ibid 88. The administrative judiciary was created in Central and Eastern Europe in the 1980s and 1990s, mainly as an antidote to the unrestricted powers of the administration: ibid 87.

follows: (1) standards internal to the law,[264] (2) standards external to the law,[265] (3) constitutional standards, and (4) EU law standards.[266] Judges relying heavily on standards internal to the law use a formalistic strategy, while the more references they make to the other three sets of standards, the more they use or move towards a non-formalistic adjudication model.[267]

The results show the predominance of references to internal law standards: between 70 to 87 per cent of all references in the judgments examined fell into this group. Within this group, judges mainly referred to a linguistic interpretation of legal texts. Frequent references were also made to compliance with earlier administrative court rulings, to the result of system interpretation and to the legal literature. References to standards external to the law rank second.[268]

This study also found that administrative judges continued to adopt the most-locally-applicable-rule approach and were reluctant to apply general principles of law. The analysis links these weak institutional effects to the role of constitutional courts, case overload and educational legacies.[269] Matczak, Bencze and Kühn go as far as stating that judges 'seem to have largely blocked change that could have been expected from the new institutional framework' introduced by the new constitutions and EU accession.[270] It still remains to be seen if a new study applying the same methods would reach similar conclusions today. As Kühn himself writes in a more recent study, the setting up of a Supreme Administrative Court in the Czech Republic in 2003 brought about a turn in the Czech administrative judges' reasoning. The ideal of reasoning of administrative courts now clearly follows the anti-formalist patterns developed in the 1990s by the Czech Constitutional Court.[271]

VI. CONCLUSION

Legal reasoning in Central and Eastern Europe is a complex matter for a number of reasons. Legal reasoning obviously has its dogmatic and theoretical foundations, but if we want to understand how it works in practice, an empirical approach is needed. The heterogeneity of the region then further complicates the picture. One might rightly ask whether it makes sense to talk about Central and Eastern Europe as a region at all more than 20 years after the fall of the

[264] Linguistic interpretation, systemic interpretation, rational lawmaker assumption (*argumentum ad absurdum*), consistency of the legal system and previous administrative court decisions: ibid 89.
[265] Compliance with the lawmaker's intentions and the social objectives and purposes of the law.
[266] ibid.
[267] ibid 90.
[268] ibid.
[269] ibid 93–96.
[270] ibid 96.
[271] Kühn (n 262) 184.

Berlin Wall. In order to give a satisfactory answer to this question, we would need more empirical and historical research.

In particular, a combination of quantitative and qualitative methods could be used to discover changes in the argumentative patterns of judges. We would need to look into cases from pre-socialist, socialist and post-socialist times to be able to draw conclusions on historical development and possible traces of previous legal cultures. A careful selection of cases that represent all types of courts would enable us to generalise. Almost all the aforementioned research projects focused on relatively new types of courts (constitutional and administrative) that did not exist for most of the socialist era. A historical analysis should focus on ordinary courts, for it is in civil and criminal cases that we may examine the development of judicial reasoning throughout a longer period of history.

Such a research project would certainly be a huge but worthwhile endeavour, which would need to include a large number of researchers from various Central and Eastern European countries and the analysis of a reasonably large number of cases. The researchers would probably have to face many methodological challenges, most importantly the problem of accessibility of the judgments and the question of representativeness of the reported cases, especially in the socialist period. Still, it would be the best possible way to find out if we can talk about a Central and Eastern European style of legal reasoning, or of a Central and Eastern European legal tradition for that matter. It would probably not resolve or end the tension between the two narratives on judicial formalism in the region, but it would certainly inform those debates and bring them to a higher level of sophistication.

7

The Council of Europe as an Antechamber to the European Union

DANIEL TARSCHYS

THE THREE GREAT European organisations – in chronological order of their establishment the Council of Europe (CoE), the Organisation for Security and Cooperation in Europe (OSCE) and the European Union (EU) – have each played a distinctive yet complementary role in promoting and defending the rule of law as a fundamental principle in European cooperation.

The differences start with the varying inclusiveness of their membership. The CoE was set up in 1949 by 10 founding states, and eventually extended first to all of Western Europe and then, after the *Wende* and the corrosion of the Iron Curtain, to the newly liberated states in Central and Eastern Europe (CEE) and to the post-Soviet states, with the exception of Belarus and those in Central Asia. The OSCE was set up in 1994 through the transformation of the looser grouping of states participating in what was first called the Geneva and then the Helsinki Process, or the Conference on Security and Cooperation in Europe (CSCE). This organisation covers the Northern hemisphere of the globe, beyond geographical Europe to include the United States and Canada. The EU, finally, dates from 1992 in its present form, but its core structures evolved in the 1950s in the guise of the European Coal and Steel Community (ECSC), the European Economic Community (EEC) and Euratom, which eventually merged into the European Communities (EC). The membership of the EU grew from a core of six states to 12, 15 and 28, with Brexit eventually reducing the number to 27 Member States.

As far as the rule of law is concerned, it might be useful to distinguish six separate propagation functions of these organisations:

1. A *Cerberus function*, by which they set up more or less demanding standards at the point of entry. With its essentially geographical criterion for membership, the CSCE-OSCE has never had this function, and the extension of the CoE was long relatively generous, but with the Eastern expansion in the 1990s it grew somewhat stricter. A very elaborate process of scrutiny has

been developed by the EU, including 38 chapters that are opened and closed in the course of the membership negotiations.

2. A *deliberative function*, by which they provided fora for discussing the evolving conditions in the different countries and exerting political pressure when transgressions were alleged to have occurred. The parliamentary bodies were not part of the original design in any of the organisations but emerged gradually as the more modest bodies foreseen in the respective statutes asserted themselves and became more vocal, without much support of the governments. The consultative assembly of the CoE established itself as a parliamentary assembly with gradually increasing powers; the CSCE created a parliamentary assembly in 1991; and the Common Assembly of the ECSC eventually came to serve all three communities and subsequently acquired the name 'European Parliament', a body that has been directly elected since 1979. Through its annual debates on around a dozen other international organisations, the Parliamentary Assembly of the CoE also provided an opportunity for parliamentary scrutiny of other forms of global cooperation.
3. A *wailing wall and judicial function*, by which complaints could be made to commissions or courts about alleged violations and binding sanctions could be imposed. Neither the European Commission of Human Rights nor the European Court of Human Rights was intended to become an influential body, but each gradually attained this status through its case law. The same happened in the EC and the EU, with the European Court of Justice successively rising to the role of a European supreme court in wide areas of law.
4. A *self-reporting obligation*, by which Member States were obliged to provide information on their implementation of the commitments they had undertaken. Such provisions were included in a great many conventions, normally enforced by independent expert bodies' giving feedback to the Member States about their transgressions or non-fulfilment of their obligations.
5. A *monitoring function*, by which the record of various countries was followed and examined. Specialised committees or commissioners for particular policy areas have been created in each of the organisations, often interacting with similar functions in the United Nations system.
6. *Ad hoc support* for reforms in special legal areas was very much in demand from the new democracies in CEE. Each of the organisations set up programmes for such assistance, often through study visits, consultancies or secondment of national experts. Of particular importance for the rule of law issues was the Venice Commission, responding to requests for analysis of moot constitutional provisions.

The clear primary ambition of the many states emerging out of the collapse of the Soviet Union and its sphere of dependent countries was to join the EU, but this door was not open in the 1990s. How difficult it was to gain membership of this exclusive club was made abundantly clear by the lengthy negotiations of Austria, Finland and Sweden. That political elites wishing to make this step were also compelled to engage in difficult negotiations with their own electorates was illustrated by Norway. The only former communist country that managed to slink into the EU by the back door was the German Democratic Republic. For all others, accession was many years ahead.

The obvious choice was then to aim for doors that seemed easier to pry open. The oldest of the three organisations, the CoE, had earned prestige in CEE, not least due to the hostility with which it had always been treated by Moscow. With good reason, it was seen as a reliable bulwark of resistance to communism, totalitarianism and dictatorial practices. Even Finland, with its limited dependence on the Soviet Union, had long been prevented from joining the Council as a full member, which did not prevent the Finns from taking part in all kinds of CoE activities. In 1988, Finland became the last West European country to join the CoE before the *Wende* and the great transition.

Preparing for this accession, the Finns made a thorough inventory of their own legislation, identifying potential sources of conflict that might necessitate legal reforms. This exercise became a paragon for later applications. But before the new or reformed states in CEE even arrived at the application stage, they entered into many forms of contacts with the CoE and its many specialised bodies.

The organisation was quite porous. Many conventions and partial agreements were open to participation by non-Member States. The Parliamentary Assembly created a committee for contacts with European non-Member States. Under the leadership of its Swiss president, Peter Sager, a veteran cold warrior turned crusader for contacts across the crumbling Iron Curtain, this committee invented the special guest status for CEE parliaments that in various ways had started their reorientation to pluralist democracy. Members of the guest delegations were given the right not only to attend but also to speak in the plenary, committees and the party groups. Disregarding a number of hesitant governments in the Committee of Ministers, the Parliamentary Assembly placed itself in the driver's seat and moved ahead, full throttle.

What ensued was a deeper mutual understanding. When the CEE states eventually submitted their applications for full membership, they were well aware of the basic principles of the organisation. They had heard the mantra 'democracy, the rule of law and the respect for human rights' so often that it had started penetrating their own speeches. To what extent it penetrated their political practice at home was a different story. Many teams of experts were despatched to the candidate countries to examine the progress made. Their assessments were often bleak, but mixed with some dose of optimism they nevertheless tended to hand in positive recommendations. Support was extended in many forms, and new mechanisms of monitoring were invented to lay the worst apprehensions to rest. A case in point was the Halonen procedure, named after the future

President of Finland. Through this and other innovations, the list of conditions for membership was split into two parts: one set of requirements that must have been fulfilled at the time of accession, and another set that everybody agreed was not yet accomplished but that remained on the observation list as specified obligations for future scrutiny.

Several requirements for membership of the CoE were more or less identical with those set by the EU, such as the ban on capital punishment. The CoE accession process was in many ways a dress rehearsal for the later, more rigid entrance examination in Brussels. But the CoE also provided many other inputs for this latter screening procedure by adding flesh to the doctrine of the rule of law. Through participation in the Congress of Local and Regional Government (CLRAE), this influence and learning process also extended to lower-level politicians.

A vast sphere of human rights, a democratic Europe from Iberia to Siberia – this was the vision of the 1990s. It did not quite turn out that way in the ensuing decades, but the many steps taken in this direction should not be underrated. When the CoE organised its second Summit meeting in Strasbourg on 10 October 1997, every single one of its 47 Member States and candidate states was represented by its prime minister or head of state. A beautiful end to the millennium!

8

The Role of the Venice Commission in Strengthening the Rule of Law

IAIN CAMERON*

I. INTRODUCTION

THE COMMISSION FOR Democracy through Law, popularly known as the Venice Commission (VC) is part of the Council of Europe (CoE) dealing with constitutional and other legal matters of importance for democratic and rule of law development. The present chapter will deal with the role of the VC in strengthening the rule of law in Europe. I begin with some background on the VC, how it works and how it influences states, before looking briefly at the phenomenon of 'rule of law backsliding'. I then give a brief overview of relevant VC opinions on Hungary, Poland and Romania, before looking at the ways in which the VC interacts with EU mechanisms for rule of law oversight, and how it might work in the future. I close with a number of concluding remarks.

II. THE VENICE COMMISSION

A. Mandate and Composition

The Venice Commission was created in 1990 by 'partial agreement', meaning that CoE states were free to join or not. It served an immediate purpose for the new democracies in East and Central Europe, which emerged from a period of Soviet control, and which wished to 'rejoin' Europe. The CoE was widely perceived as a 'waiting room' for EU membership, and extensive changes

* I would like to thank Kaarlo Tuori, Johan Hirschfeldt and Laurent Pech for helpful comments. The usual disclaimer applies. This contribution is written purely in a personal capacity, not on behalf of, or representing, the Venice Commission. It was completed in May 2020. At the proof stage, I have been able to make some updates, but I have not taken into account all developments since this date.

were necessary in these states' legal systems, systems of public administration and constitutional justice. All 47 CoE states are now members, the last CoE state that joined being Russia in 2003. With effect from 2003 the partial agreement was turned into an 'enlarged agreement',[1] which made it possible for non-European states to accede. The 60 member states now include states in North Africa and the Middle East (eg Morocco, Algeria, Tunisia, Israel), North and South America (eg Brazil, Chile, Mexico, Canada and the USA) and Asia (eg Kazakstan, South Korea). Two international organisations, the European Union (EU) and the Organization for Security and Cooperation in Europe (OSCE, the principal institution of which is the Office for Democratic Institutions and Human Rights (ODHIR)), are also parties to the enlarged agreement.

The VC's functions are set out in Article 1 of its Statute: strengthening the understanding of the legal systems of the participating states, notably with a view to bringing these systems closer; promoting the rule of law and democracy; examining the problems raised by the working of democratic institutions and their reinforcement and development; and responding to states' requests for advice on draft laws amending constitutions and related legal norms.

The VC consists of experts, appointed by state parties but serving in an individual capacity. Pursuant to the Statute of the VC, these experts are to 'have achieved eminence through their experience in democratic institutions or by their contribution to the enhancement of law and political science'.[2] Individual members' backgrounds vary. There are serving and past members of supreme and constitutional courts, former prime ministers and ministers of justice, ombudsmen, and, particularly, professors in constitutional and administrative law. Members are not remunerated. Their travel and accommodation costs when attending the four plenary sessions in Venice are paid by the government that appointed them. When a working group is formed (on which more later), a small per diem allowance is paid by the CoE, as well as any necessary travel and accommodation costs.

The Commission is funded in the same way as other parts of the CoE, in proportion to the member state's population size and per capita income. As international organisations go, the Venice Commission is ludicrously cheap: it costs about €4m per year. Most of the cost consists of salaries for the approximately 25 lawyers and administrative staff in the secretariat. The secretariat is recruited through the normal – fairly rigorous – CoE procedures. The secretariat has a Secretary-General and Deputy Secretary-General. It is governed by the President, assisted by three Vice-Presidents and steered by an eight-person Bureau

[1] Resolution (2002)3 Revised Statute of the European Commission for Democracy through Law (adopted by the Committee of Ministers on 21 February 2002).

[2] Statute, Art 2. See also CDL-AD(2018)018 Venice Commission Rules of Procedure, Art 3(1), 'Members shall act in a manner that is, and is seen to be, independent, impartial and objective with respect to any issue examined by the Commission.'

(the President, the Vice-Presidents and four other members). The incumbents of all of these posts are chosen for four-year periods from amongst the members. A larger body, the Enlarged Bureau, consists of the Bureau and the chairs of the various sub-commissions. The process of election of the President, the Vice-Presidents, the Bureau and the chairs of the sub-commissions is prepared by a group of wise-persons, usually drawn from the substitute members, who themselves are not eligible to be the President, Vice-Presidents or chairs.

B. The Work of the Venice Commission

The VC does three main things.[3] Most of its work consists of opinions that are responses to states requesting advice on draft laws amending constitutions and related legal norms. The great majority of these opinions have dealt with the post-socialist countries of East and Central Europe. The request forms the framework for the opinion, although the VC decides itself which issues are necessary to discuss to answer the request. This part of its work is rarely like major projects of constitutional engineering, occasionally engaged in by the United Nations (for failed states) or as academic exercises, where the goal is the production of a whole constitution.[4] Instead, it resembles more the type of abstract constitutional review of a legislative proposal that is made by a constitutional court. In many jurisdictions where abstract constitutional review exists it is binding, but this is not the case for opinions of the VC. A state typically asks the Commission to examine the compatibility of its own laws or legal proposals with European rule of law standards. Where an opinion is requested by a state on a matter that concerns another state, the Commission shall inform the state concerned and, unless the two states are in agreement, submit the issue to the Committee of Ministers.[5]

In international law, a state is usually seen as a monolithic entity, acting on the international level only through its government. In the consistent practice of the VC, however, the 'state' (Article 5 of the Statute) is interpreted widely: any state institution can request an opinion within its sphere of constitutional competence.[6]

[3] For another perspective on the work of the VC, see W Hoffmann-Riem, 'The Venice Commission of the Council of Europe – Standards and Impact' (2014) 25 *European Journal of International Law* 579.

[4] I say 'rarely' because in the 1990s (and in the 2000s, concerning Armenia and Tunisia), the VC was asked to assist in producing a totally new constitution.

[5] Statute, Art 3(2).

[6] For example, the Polish Senate, after the most recent elections, is not controlled by the Law and Justice Party (PiS). The Marshal (Speaker) of the Senate requested an opinion on a legislative proposal that involved a further undermining of the independence of the Polish courts: see CDL-PI(2020)002 Poland Joint Urgent Opinion of the Venice Commission and the Directorate General of Human Rights and Rule of Law (DGI) of the Council of Europe on Amendments to the Law on the Common Courts, the Law on The Supreme Court, and some other Laws.

The VC also prepares, on request, amicus curiae briefs for constitutional courts, usually when the court is faced with a novel issue. In such cases, the VC usually tries to provide guidance based on comparative constitutional law and European standards (on which more later). It will usually defer to whatever interpretations a constitutional court has made of national law, the court being the expert on the subject.

The second main thing the VC does is respond to requests for opinion from CoE institutions. These can be requests for general constitutional or international law studies in a particular area, but also requests regarding the law of specific CoE member states. Member states must thus tolerate that the VC may be asked to make an independent review of their national legislation or legislative proposals in a particular area. The Committee of Ministers, an Assembly (PACE), the Congress of Local and Regional Authorities of Europe, and the Secretary-General can all ask for opinions, but most requests for opinions come from PACE, in particular from the Committee on Legal Affairs and Human Rights and the Monitoring Committee. The Political Affairs Committee also sometimes requests opinions. Between five and 15 general studies or opinions (concerning the legislation of a particular country) adopted each year have their origins in requests from PACE.

The European Court of Human Rights (ECtHR) can request an amicus curiae brief, or the Venice Commission can request to submit such a brief. This occurs relatively often, and the ECtHR relatively often refers to VC studies in its judgments.

The EU is able to request an opinion regarding a matter within its competence. The EU Commission has done this twice so far, in 2012 concerning Bosnia-Herzegovina and in 2015 concerning the Former Yugoslav Republic of Macedonia (now the Republic of North Macedonia). The EU Special Representative for Kosovo requested an opinion in 2014. The European Parliament requested an opinion on emergency law during the Covid-19 pandemic.

The third main thing that the VC does is to undertake, of its own motion, constitutional studies in particular areas. Such studies are to be general, not of specific states, although specific states' legislation can and does form a part of the general study. The general studies of the VC can be in the form of 'check-lists' or guidelines in different areas (eg electoral systems, the rule of law, financing of political parties, freedom of assembly), based on its earlier opinions and comparative law. In some such studies the VC has worked together with OSCE-ODIHR.

C. Working Practices and Standards Applied

The VC is widely considered to be a success.[7] One key to understanding this success is the Commission's flexibility. It has a semi-autonomous status within

[7] Measuring 'success' in this area is not without difficulties. States and PACE committees, the main consumers, continue to request opinions, which would indicate that, at least, they see some

the CoE, which facilitates the speedy response to political crises. When a report is requested, the secretariat quickly assembles a working group. The composition of the working group depends on a variety of different factors. The individual members have different areas of expertise, and they have differing language skills and knowledge of legal cultures. The members should preferably represent different constitutional traditions. The availability of the members in question at short notice is also important: most are still employed in different capacities in their home states.

When it comes to opinions on a particular country, the working group usually visits the country in question, albeit for only a short time (normally two days). While a government department often takes the lead in arranging the practicalities of the visit (often the Foreign Ministry), to have a chance to really change anything in the country's legal order in a positive way it is necessary to communicate with the 'factory floor'. Thus, the VC working group tries to meet not only senior civil servants involved with the preparation of a legal reform (usually in the Ministries of Justice and the Interior), but also a wide range of groups representing different interests. Who these groups are will depend upon the proposal in question (the political leaders, the political opposition, non-governmental organisations (NGOs), associations of judges and prosecutors, etc). In my experience, even when dealing with governments that are not enthusiastic about a Venice Commission visit, there almost always is a large degree of professionalism in how one is treated. There may be great differences in the substantive values being discussed, but there is still a common 'language' that professionals can speak to each other.

The VC is not a 'fact-finding' body: it is largely dependent on the factual information made available to it (on which more later). Having said this, over the years, the VC secretariat has built up good contacts with political groups and civil society in the states that are the main 'customers' of the VC. Local contacts and locally produced material is often very useful, although the Commission strives not to become a chip in an internal political game. After the information-gathering phase, the working group compiles a draft opinion. This draft must be distributed to the individual members and the government concerned at least two weeks before the plenary session. The day before the plenary session, which takes place in Venice,[8] the opinion is usually discussed at a preparatory meeting (there are several different thematic sub-commissions). At this meeting, members may make suggestions for additions and amendments, which are often adopted. The draft is then presented at the plenary session. The government has usually

value in this. In terms of 'output', results, I would argue that one would need to evaluate the actual impact, in the short term but also in the long term, the VC has on constitutional reforms in states specifically concerned by an opinion and VC member states as a whole (eg influenced by VC general standard setting), but also other actors (such as EU institutions). I deal with some of the factors affecting impact later.

[8] During the Coronavirus crisis, a written procedure of discussion and adoption has been applied.

filed written comments in advance of the plenary session. It has a further opportunity to make oral comments at the plenary session. The VC listens particularly carefully to any criticism from the government that it has failed to understand some element of the state's laws or institutions under consideration. If it finds this criticism justified, it will modify the opinion accordingly. It happens occasionally that governments express considerable dissatisfaction with the views expressed in the opinion, without being able to point to any inaccuracies (simply that the government does not like the result). The VC is not scared to express very critical views, even if these, as is fitting for an international organisation dealing with sovereign states, tend to be expressed in diplomatic terms.

There are four plenary sessions per year, so the above process is not particularly slow. Mainly because of the expertise of the individual members and the secretariat, an opinion can be produced, from beginning to end, in a few months. This is remarkably fast, bearing in mind that the legislative process in a state, particularly in constitutional matters, is supposed to be slow, to allow for a many-sided debate. However, states can also request an accelerated VC procedure. There is a Protocol on the Preparation of Urgent Opinions, allowing a preliminary opinion to be issued pending endorsement by the plenary session.[9] During the Covid-19 pandemic, there has been a relatively large number of requests for urgent opinions.

As regards the 'law', the standards that it applies, the CoE works in three broad fields: human rights; the rule of law; and democracy. The 'hard' law of the CoE is easiest to find, namely the provisions of treaties when these bind the state in question. The International Covenant on Civil and Political Rights and the European Convention on Human Rights (ECHR) are particularly important, and one of the qualities it is helpful for individual members to have is a good knowledge of the case law of the ECtHR. The ECtHR jurisprudence is regarded as a minimum standard.[10] The Venice Commission aims for 'best practices', and may accordingly set the criteria higher than the ECtHR. It has done so on several occasions (eg as regards political parties, or democratic control of security agencies). The rule of law can be partly concretised by the ECtHR's case law,[11] but also by distilling 'best practices' from comparative constitutional law. The third element, democracy, comes in as many variations as there are democratic states, and it has accordingly been more difficult to concretise standards. Electoral systems vary, with greater or lesser weight being put on different values, particularly the balance to be drawn between producing an effective government and producing a legislature that accurately reflects

[9] CDL-AD(2018)019. For example, the opinion requested by the Polish senate, CDL-PI(2020)002 (n 6) was adopted under the accelerated procedure, and subsequently endorsed by the plenary.

[10] Art 53 ECHR.

[11] See, eg, F Steiner, 'The Rule of Law in the Jurisprudence of the European Court of Human Rights' in W Schroeder (ed), *Strengthening the Rule of Law in Europe* (London, Bloomsbury, 2016) 135.

the popular vote. Nonetheless, standards for the fairness of elections have been developed by the VC and other actors, and the VC has produced best practices for other aspects of democracy, particularly for the role of the opposition in a democracy.[12]

The VC is thus not simply a 'consumer' of soft law, but also a producer of soft law, particularly as regards the rule of law.[13] However, an important qualification should be made here. The VC does not try to harmonise its member states' legislation on constitutional issues (notwithstanding the wording of Article 1 of its Statute). There are such variations in constitutional systems among members of the Council of Europe that it is not possible to talk about a single 'European best practice'. Instead, the VC almost always suggests several alternative solutions, outlining their advantages and disadvantages, and the factors that should be taken into account for each.[14] This increases the acceptability of its opinions: the sovereign right of the state to choose its own solutions is explicitly recognised. It is also important for practical reasons connected to working methods, as it makes it easier for members of the working group to agree. In my experience, members almost invariably have an open and professional way of approaching the review work, and usually agree relatively quickly on what the technical and other shortcomings are of the specific law or bill they are discussing. On the other hand, the discussions would run the risk of being endless if the working group was obliged to propose only one solution in the area in question, a 'minimum European standard'.

D. The Authority of the Venice Commission

The Commission works through 'soft power', rational persuasion. As Kaarlo Tuori has noted, the prerequisites for the successful functioning of a body of constitutional consulting, such as the VC, include *expertise*, *experience*, *independence* and *authority*. Authority is a consequence of expertise, experience and independence. No institution can gain authority by the simple fact of its establishment: authority must be earned.[15] The Commission has been working now for 30 years. During this time it has built up considerable experience in constitutional assessment and consulting. This experience is stored not only in Commission documents, but also in institutional memory, borne by long-time members of both the Commission and its highly qualified secretariat of

[12] See, in particular, CDL-AD(2019)015 Parameters on the Relationship Between the Parliamentary Majority and the Opposition in a Democracy: A Checklist.

[13] See in particular CDL-AD(2016)007 Rule of Law Checklist. These 'soft law' standards can become 'hard' law, eg where the ECtHR adopts, in a concrete case, a solution suggested by the VC.

[14] Although, having said this, it has had a tendency to prefer certain types of institutional solution. See section III.

[15] K Tuori, 'From Copenhagen to Venice' in C Closa and D Kochenov (eds), *Reinforcing Rule of Law Oversight in the European Union* (Cambridge, Cambridge University Press, 2016) 225.

lawyers, which assists working groups in preparing opinions and reports.[16] As already noted, members are appointed by the governments of their states, which means that how 'independent' they actually are will vary. However, for reasons explained further later, those members who take instructions, or otherwise let themselves be strongly influenced by their governments, have had only a limited influence on the work of the Commission.

As already noted, the Commission's chances of exerting an influence on a state in a constitutional or legal question are at their greatest when the government genuinely wants input on the issue, and has requested this input well before the proposal is implemented, instead of asking for a 'last-minute blessing', or even a 'blessing after the fact'. A government's willingness to entertain different solutions can increase the more 'technocratic' or 'long-term' the issue is perceived as being, and decrease the more the issue is perceived as having immediate political significance. One of the ideas behind constitutionalism is a separation of 'ordinary' politics from 'the rules of the game'.[17] However, even if the ambition is that such rules of the game be framed in neutral terms, they can obviously favour a political party or grouping, an obvious example being different rules on electoral representation, such as the choice between different methods of proportional representation, or between such methods and a 'first-past-the-post' system. It is asking a lot of a political party in power to agree to changes in the rules of the game that will exercise an immediate negative effect on its hold on power. No hard-and-fast line between 'technocratic' and non-technocratic rules can be drawn. It will depend entirely on the context in the state in question. One might think that all states have an interest in a better functioning, neutral system of public administration, and any improvements in this are likely to be welcomed. However, this is unlikely to be the case for a political system with a 'spoils system' or a large element of 'clientelism'. Having said this, in many states there are coalition governments, or power is split between a president and a prime minister, and one element may be in favour of one of the alternative solutions proposed by the VC. Moreover, minority governments may be more susceptible to taking heed of a critical report. There may be a similar situation where there are two chambers of parliament and the party of government dominates only one chamber. Even in a state with a stable majority government, where the state is relatively democratic, a critical report may strengthen the political opposition's voice on the issue in question, especially if the political opposition is acting in tandem with civil society and the media.

Pressure to take account of the opinion may also come from outside the country. The main responsibility for 'follow up' of reports a CoE body has

[16] ibid.

[17] For a brief discussion on constitutionalism generally, see, eg, A Godden and J Morison, 'Constitutionalism', *Max Planck Encyclopedia of Comparative Constitutional Law* (2017). For the distinction, see, eg, G Brennan, and JM Buchanan, *The Reason of Rules: Constitutional political economy* (Cambridge, Cambridge University Press, 1985).

requested lies with the body itself, usually the PACE legal affairs and monitoring committees. Pressure can also in some cases come from other influential international players, such as foreign governments (especially those helping the state in question with public administration, etc aid projects) and the International Monetary Fund. The most important such actor is the EU, to which I now turn.

The EU Commission is a significant international actor in aid projects for third states, particularly states in the EU neighbourhood. The CoE and the EU signed a Memorandum of Understanding in 2007 that set out the general basis for cooperation.[18] The Joint Programmes (JPs) framework, started in 1993, consists of capacity-building projects.[19] The EU acts as a donor, providing the vast majority of funding, while the CoE assumes the role of an implementing partner, working on the ground through its offices and missions in countries. The VC fits seamlessly into this system. A VC report can identify a deficiency in a state's system of constitutional justice or public administration, and the European Commission can then offer the state in question funding to fix the deficiency. Where the European Commission has already been giving aid, and the issue is whether the deficiency has been fixed, it may suggest that the state request an opinion from the VC. As the VC, by EU terms, is operating on a shoestring, the EU often gives it special project funding to perform such an analysis. The economic muscle of the European Commission melds very well with the authority of the VC. This is obviously something that can work particularly well with countries that have, or wish to have, an association agreement with the EU, and particularly with EU candidate countries, such as Serbia. An overarching goal in the foreign policy of a number of non-EU states in Europe is to become an EU member. For such states, this means a corresponding increase in the influence of the VC.[20]

This link between the VC and the convergence criteria used by the European Commission already applied for the candidate states from Central and Eastern Europe (CEE) (now members of the EU) in the process of Eastern Enlargement. One can certainly take the view that in the last wave of EU accessions, the European Council let several states with weak rule of law cultures too easily into

[18] Available at https://rm.coe.int/16804e437b.

[19] For a short discussion, see J Jaraczewski, 'Old friends, new friends? Prospects for EU's cooperation with intergovernmental organisations in promotion of the rule of law', 13 November 2019, available at https://verfassungsblog.de/old-friends-new-friends-prospects-for-eus-cooperation-with-intergovernmental-organisations-in-promotion-of-the-rule-of-law/.

[20] The importance of the link to EU economic muscle cuts both ways. There has been discussion of the potential for the VC to develop into a global actor, see, eg. M de Visser, 'A Critical Assessment of the Role of the Venice Commission in Processes of Domestic Constitutional Reform' (2015) 63 *American Journal of Comparative Law* 963–1008. Many of the standards the VC develops and applies indeed have universal application; however, I think the conditions for these having an actual impact on non-CoE member-states are less favourable where these states are not strongly linked to the EU in some way (candidate countries, countries with association agreements, etc). Thus, I do not think the VC can serve quite the same purposes on the global level as it has in the European 'neighbourhood'.

the EU. As is well known, special monitoring procedures (the cooperation and verification mechanisms, CVM) were put in place for only two of the new EU Member States, Bulgaria and Romania, which were admitted as EU Members in 2007.[21] The European Commission, for its part, has usually taken rule of law issues relatively seriously in monitoring fulfilment of the convergence criteria, and it refers extensively to VC reports in this respect.[22] It remains to be seen if the European Commission will continue to place such emphasis on rule of law issues in the future.[23]

The problem, as many have noted, is that once a state has become a Member of the EU, there is no longer a strong financial/economic incentive to comply with the 'soft' values of EU membership. Why have these values not been 'self-supporting'? Before dealing with the role the VC has played as regards existing EU Members, and the possible roles it can play in the future, something should be said about the 'malaise' – or to put it another way, why the constitutional situation in certain EU Member States has raised such concern that the VC has been asked to look into it.

III. SOMETHING ON THE BACKGROUND TO, AND REASONS FOR, RULE OF LAW BACKSLIDING

When I first became a member of the VC in late 2005, the EU Fundamental Rights Agency (FRA) had just been established, and the general opinion in the first plenary session I attended seemed to be that, as far as EU states were concerned, the work of the VC was more or less over.[24] Romania and Bulgaria continued to have problems, but it was expected, naively as it turned out, that these would disappear by themselves, given time.

In 2010, Victor Orban's Fidesz Party won the elections in Hungary. The 'bonus' the Hungarian electoral system gives the winning party meant that it obtained the necessary two-thirds majority to make constitutional reforms. The process of what has since been called 'rule of law backsliding' began.

[21] There are many examples of the mutual support between VC and the Commission in the CVM. See, eg, Recommendation no 1 of the European Commission CVM Report of 15 November 2017, which reiterated the recommendation put forward by the European Commission in previous CVM reports to Romania, to 'put in place a robust and independent system of appointing top prosecutors, based on clear and transparent criteria, drawing on the support of the Venice Commission'.

[22] A non-exhaustive list of such references can be found at www.venice.coe.int/WebForms/pages/?p=02_references&lang=EN#EU.

[23] In the von der Leyens Commission, the new Commissioner in charge of the enlargement process is from Hungary, something that has drawn criticism from commenters; see P Bard, 'The von der Leyen Commission and the Future of the Rule of Law', available at www.verfassungsblog.de/the-von-der-leyen-commission-and-the-future-of-the-rule-of-law/ (accessed 11 March 2020).

[24] Although, for those who would see, one can say that there were worrying indications at the time, which was during the 'war on terror', that certain EU states were prepared to let their territories be used for the purposes of secret detention.

A good working definition of this phenomenon is that suggested by Scheppele and Pech, namely, the process through which elected public authorities deliberately implement governmental blueprints which aim to systematically weaken, annihilate or capture internal checks on power with the view of dismantling the liberal democratic state and entrenching the long-term rule of the dominant party'.[25] A related term, more common in political science, is 'democratic backsliding'.[26] The two terms overlap if one has a material definition of democracy, that is as requiring not simply periodic elections, but also the enjoyment of certain freedoms (in particular, those of expression, association, assembly and information).[27] In this section and that following, I concentrate upon three states, Poland, Hungary and Romania, because these have been the EU states at which the Venice Commission has primarily been asked to look. However, it should be stressed that these are not the only EU states that have experienced serious rule of law problems in recent years.[28]

In the 2015 Polish elections, Jaroslav Kaczyński's Law and Justice Party (PiS) won a majority and set about removing what it saw as institutional obstacles blocking its hold on power. The situations in Poland and Hungary display certain similarities. Both Victor Orban's Fidesz Party and Jaroslav Kaczyński's PiS obtained power democratically, and, importantly, their hold on governmental power was confirmed in the next general elections (respectively, in 2014 and 2018, and in 2019). There are also, undoubtedly, similarities in how these two governing parties have gone about concentrating executive power and removing checks and balances that existed before.[29] Common to both states was the

[25] See KL Scheppele and L Pech, ' Illiberalism Within: Rule of Law Backsliding in the EU' (2017) 19 *Cambridge Yearbook of European Legal Studies* 3.

[26] Meaning the state-led debilitation or elimination of the political institutions sustaining an existing democracy. See, eg, N Bermeo, 'On Democratic Backsliding' (2016) 27 *Journal of Democracy* 5. Landau refers to 'abusive constitutionalism': using the tools of constitutional amendment and replacement by would-be autocrats to undermine democracy with relative ease. D Landau, 'Abusive Constitutionalism' (2013) 47 *UC Davis Law Review* 189. A third term is that of 'constitutional capture'; see, eg, JW Müller, 'Rising to the challenge of constitutional capture: Protecting the rule of law within EU member states', 21 March 2014, available at https://www.eurozine.com/rising-to-the-challenge-of-constitutional-capture/ (accessed 3 June 2019). Although this last term is undoubtedly accurate for the case of Hungary, technically it is less apposite for Poland (see further section III).

[27] Cf Art 1:1 of the Swedish Instrument of Government, 'Swedish democracy is founded on the free formation of opinion'.

[28] At least one other state should be mentioned here, namely, Malta. In its Opinion CDL-AD(2018)028, the VC considered that the Prime Minister (PM) was at the centre of power while other actors – the President, (part-time) Parliament, Cabinet of Ministers, Judiciary, Ombudsman, etc – were too weak to provide sufficient checks and balances. The VC considered that the Judicial Appointments Committee, established in 2016, fell short of ensuring the independence of the judiciary. The Opinion was also critical of the double role of the Attorney-General as adviser to the Government and as prosecutor. The PM's wide powers of appointment make this institution too powerful, creating a serious risk for the rule of law; in particular, the PM's influence on judicial appointments resulted in the absence of crucial checks and balances. This problem was reinforced by the weakness of civil society and independent media.

[29] Laurent Pech and Kim Scheppele have argued that PiS has closely followed the 'play book' of Victor Orban's Fidesz Party: see Scheppele and Pech (n 25).

fact that the constitutional courts were strong, independent bodies that exercised considerable political power. Both Fidesz and PiS saw the constitutional courts as political actors that stood in the way of their political ambitions, and which therefore had to be 'captured' or neutralised. However, while the objects of attack – the judicial system and other institutional checks and balances – were the same, the national contexts are not. For example, the actors' underlying motivations may be different (economic-kleptocratic/political/mixed), and there may be differences as to why a significantly large part of the Hungarian or, respectively, Polish electorates have accepted their policies.

The situation in Romania is different again. Before a country can have rule of law backsliding, it needs to have achieved a reasonable level of respect for the rule of law from which it then 'backslides'. Romania (and, for that matter, Bulgaria) have had great difficulties in getting there in the first place. In Romania, the communist dictator Nicolae Ceauşescu was toppled from power in 1989, but, as it later transpired, by a coup rather than a revolution. Since this time, reformist political and legal movements in Romania have had an uphill struggle to establish a (reasonable) standard of compliance with the rule of law. Corruption has been endemic. Politics and political parties have been used as means to take over and maintain economic power. After the 2016 elections, the socialist (ex-communist) PSD formed a coalition government with a (supposedly) liberal party. The PSD leader, Liviu Dragnea, was unable to become Prime Minister because of ongoing judicial proceedings for electoral fraud and corruption. However, Dragnea steered through three different prime ministers between 2017 and 2019. The PSD also launched an assault on legal institutions, but opposition – inter alia, from Romania's elected President – has meant that the PSD's success has not been as complete as that of the ruling parties in Hungary or Poland. From the end of 2019, a fragile anti-PSD coalition has ruled in Romania.

The explanations for rule of law backsliding fall into two broad groups: those that stress primarily endogenous (internal) factors, such as longer-term historical and cultural considerations; and those that stress primarily exogenous factors, that is, reactions to 'external shocks'.

Cultures are complex matters, and difficult for both insiders and outsiders to understand. I am not a historian, political scientist or sociologist, and I would not presume to state definitively what endogenous factors are at work in Hungary, Romania and Poland. As regards exogenous factors, however, something, albeit brief, should be said. First, because it has been claimed that externally imposed technocratic solutions were the cause (or part of it) of rule of law backsliding in the first place.[30] Second, the solutions that are being discussed today at EU level to deal with rule of law backsliding would also be 'externally imposed'

[30] For example, Kosař et al describe the rule of law backsliding in Hungary and Poland as 'overreactions to overreactions': D Kosař, J Baroš and P Dufek, 'The Twin Challenges to Separation of Powers in Central Europe: Technocratic Governance and Populism' (2019) 15 *European Constitutional Law Review* 427.

technocratic solutions. In order to evaluate whether such proposed solutions will in fact help, in any way, it is necessary to know something about the exogenous factors at work.

It is undoubtedly the case that to become CoE and, later, EU members, eastern and central European states generally introduced major reforms of electoral systems, constitutional systems, the courts and the economy. As regards the introduction of a market-based economy, there were groups of the population who lost a lot compared to what they had during the Soviet period: job security, health care, accommodation, social care, etc. Universal social benefits became rights, and rights became something for the 'wide-awake'. The amount of suffering in each state has depended in part on how brutally, and how fast, the transition to a market economy was carried out. A population that has been told that an era of prosperity, at Western European levels, is just around the corner will have, understandably, high expectations. But economic development, when it came, naturally enough followed the logic of the market: certain sectors benefited and others did not. Nor was prosperity spread equally throughout the country. In some states, rural areas, or former industrial areas, were often left behind. In all eastern and central European states, even those not dominated by oligarchs, large disparities in wealth among the population emerged, and corruption thrived. So, one simple explanation for rule of law backsliding is that economic liberalism and constitutionalism have become intertwined in the minds of large sections of the public, and that disillusionment with the former has tainted the reputation of the latter.[31] One might add political instability to this mix. As Rupik has put it, the opposition to communism, the dissidents, failed in the 'next phase of institutionalizing pluralism – the creation of viable political parties'.[32] The economic downturn caused by the global financial crisis of 2008 did not help matters either. The ground was undoubtedly well prepared for populist politicians playing nationalist cards.[33] Of course, disillusionment with government and populist responses are global phenomena. What is different, compared to the communist period, is that the population can now vote the government out of office.

Even if the above remarks primarily concern the CEE states that became EU members, I should stress that I do not see a clear 'East-West' divide when it comes to 'rule of law backsliding'.[34] It is definitely not a purely 'Eastern' phenomenon. And I do not think it is a uniform phenomenon, even if there

[31] On these lines, but more nuanced and elegant, see J Rupnik, 'Explaining Eastern Europe: The Crisis of Liberalism (2018) 29 *Journal of Democracy* 24.

[32] ibid 32.

[33] I use Mudde's definition of populism, an ideology that considers society to be ultimately separated into two homogeneous and antagonistic groups – 'the pure people' and 'the corrupt elite' – and that argues that politics should be an expression of the general will of the people. C Mudde and CR Kaltwasser, *Populism: A Very Short Introduction* (Oxford, Oxford University Press, 2017).

[34] Cf J Grogan and L Pech 'Unity and Diversity in National Understandings of the Rule of Law in the EU', Reconnect WP 7.1 (June 2020), available at https://reconnect-europe.eu/blog/unity-and-diversity-in-national-understandings-of-the-rule-of-law-in-the-eu/.

are similarities in the developments between Poland and Hungary. Nor do I think that all future threats to the rule of law are likely to follow the same trajectory.[35]

I now turn to the question of whether the CoE caused, or contributed to causing, the backsliding problem. As already mentioned, the three areas of activity of the CoE are democracy, the rule of law and human rights. As regards democracy, the CoE, OSCE and the EU Commission, in its convergence criteria, encouraged different measures, such as the creation of independent electoral commissions and the transparent regulation of political parties. The actual choice of electoral system, and how this balances effective government with the degree of representativeness, is a sensitive question and there is less common ground between states in such issues. However, as regards human rights, there is a large measure of agreement in CoE (and EU) states that civil and political rights should be justiciable at national level, with a 'back-up' system in the ECtHR. As regards the rule of law, CEE states were encouraged to build up checks and balances, in particular, legal institutions such as independent courts (appointment and disciplinary procedures being safeguarded by the involvement of judicial councils, dominated by the judiciary),[36] constitutional courts and constitutional review, ombudsmen, autonomous or quasi-autonomous prosecutors, parliamentary controls over executive powers, and statutory or constitutional limitations on executive control over the civil service and the state-owned media. The VC, as an element of the CoE, has played its part in this process, it must be admitted. The CoE and OSCE-ODIHR also supported the growth of civil society and free media.

However, while such measures were encouraged as part of the process of joining the CoE, and later the EU, it is wrong to say that these measures were imposed. Nor were these measures uniform or unitary solutions ('one size fits all'), although it must be conceded that the VC has tended to prefer strong constitutional courts and judiciary-dominated judicial councils. Still, even the most superficial examination of the constitutions and relevant laws of the CEE states shows that there are considerable national variations in constitutional courts (standing, type of review, etc) and how judicial councils are composed, their functions, etc. Nonetheless, it is correct that all of the measures the CoE in general, and the VC in particular, encouraged fall under the broad title of 'constitutionalism' and were aimed at the diffusion of power, particularly executive power.

[35] See, eg, S Hanley and MA Vachudova, 'Understanding the illiberal turn: democratic backsliding in the Czech Republic' (2018) 34 *East European Politics* 276.

[36] See, eg, Recommendation CM/Rec(2010)12 of the Committee of Ministers to member states on judges: independence, efficiency and responsibilities, para 27, 'Not less than half the members of such councils should be judges chosen by their peers from all levels of the judiciary and with respect for pluralism inside the judiciary.'

If it were not a tautology, it would be better to call this model 'legal constitutionalism', because there is another broad European model of control of executive power, namely, 'political constitutionalism'.[37] This latter model, simply expressed, means putting a large part of your faith in the restraint and good sense of parliamentarians. This model has, generally speaking, worked well in states with mature political systems, such as the UK, the Netherlands and the Nordic states. All of these states have coped well without a constitutional court or judiciary-dominated judicial councils with disciplinary, etc functions. However, and this must be stressed, in these states, the ordinary courts may have a less upfront constitutional role than in states with a constitutional court, but they still have a constitutional role, and they are *independent*. Assuming there is a real consensus in society,[38] it is legitimate to move from a system of 'legal' to 'political' constitutionalism. However, if in so doing you undermine the independence of the courts, you are throwing the baby out with the bathwater. Similar points can be made regarding capturing the civil service and the publicly owned media, as well as attacking civil society and undermining academic freedom. A 'winner takes it all' mentality is not political constitutionalism.

Eastern and central European states had constitutions during the Soviet period, but these had meant little in practice to the citizen. The new idea was that the constitution should henceforth matter in practice, and this meant rights that could be invoked by individuals and enforced in courts. Moreover, the constitution was to contain the struggle for political power in states that had either not had a pluralistic (democratic) system for 40 years, or never had such a system. As already mentioned, one of the ideas behind constitutionalism, either 'legal' or 'political', is that there should be a difference between the 'rules of the game' (the constitution and institutions of the state) and day-to-day political struggles over power. The rules of the game should be respected, even if the struggles over political power may be bitter. Such an insight can grow over time among the political elites of a state. For example, in both England and Sweden during the middle of the seventeenth century, the conditions for the adherence to the rule of law were strong, in that it became obvious that no single grouping (the Crown, the nobles, the yeomanry, burghers, merchants and clergy) could be certain that it could retain absolute power for long. It therefore made sense to accept distribution of, and limits on, power. All of the mechanisms and institutions for diffusing political power make sense if you accept that there are dangers in concentration of power, and that even if you win political power in an election, there is no guarantee that you can keep this power very long. For example, one explanation for politicians' acceptance of strong courts

[37] See, eg, R Bellamy, *Political Constitutionalism: A Republican Defence of the Constitutionality of Democracy* (Cambridge, Cambridge University Press, 2009).

[38] Something I consider seems to be lacking, despite the electoral victories of Fidesz and PiS.

exercising, inter alia, a power of constitutional review, is that this can serve as a political 'insurance policy', limiting your political opponent, when he or she achieves political power, in 'rolling back' all the changes you made while in office.[39] Similar arguments apply to other mechanisms for dispersing political power. However, if you think that you can get *all* the power, and you think you can hang on to it for ever (or at least, a very long time) then you do not need the insurance policy. This, of course, means taking steps to concentrate state power, and ensure the continuation of your grip on that power.

IV. BRIEFLY ON THE VENICE COMMISSION OPINIONS SO FAR ON HUNGARY, ROMANIA AND POLAND

In 2010, there was no EU mechanism for monitoring rule of law backsliding. There was accordingly a sudden need for some authoritative body with competence in the area, and the VC stepped up, or rather was invited to step up.[40]

The sweeping changes made by Orban's Fidesz Party are well known and need not be summarised here.[41] Basically, a new constitution and cardinal laws (which enjoy special constitutional status) were adopted that, inter alia, curbed the powers of the – previously very powerful – Hungarian Constitutional Court. The number of justices was increased and the appointment procedure changed, allowing the Government to pack the court. The ordinary courts were emasculated quickly, by reducing the compulsory retirement age, forcing the retirement of many of the most senior judges, reducing the powers of the judicial council, and transferring control over judicial appointments and disciplinary matters to a newly created body staffed by Fidesz loyalists. The power of appointment meant that control was taken over various other state bodies designed to have a degree of independence, such as the State Audit Office, the National Media and Telecommunications Authority, and the National Electoral Commission.

Between 2011 and 2019, 17 opinions were delivered by the VC concerning Hungarian laws and draft laws. Most of these opinions were requested by CoE bodies. A number of these opinions found that the changes made, or being proposed, were not contrary to European standards. In what follows, I take up only a few of the more critical opinions.

The first VC opinion on the (then) draft constitution, adopted in March 2011, was requested by the Hungarian Government.[42] It was limited to three

[39] See, eg, T Ginsburg, 'Economic Analysis and the Design of Constitutional Courts' (2002) 3 *Theoretical Inquiries in Law* 20.

[40] For a useful brief overview, see R Clayton, 'The Venice Commission and the rule of law crisis' [2019] *Public Law* 450.

[41] See, eg, J Kornai, 'Hungary's U-Turn' (2015) 10(1) *Capitalism and Society* Art 2. Good short summaries of the steps taken in Hungary and Poland can be found in Kosař et al (n 30).

[42] CDL-AD(2011)001.

issues: whether to incorporate the EU Charter on Fundamental Freedoms, and whether it was compatible with good European practice standards to limit the *actio popularis* before the Constitutional Court and to restrict this Court's ex ante constitutional review of statutes. The VC advised against the first, because this would have the effect of concentrating rights review in the Constitutional Court, in potential violation of EU law, but it did not criticise either the second or third measures, considering these as being not contrary to good European practice. However, the VC did criticise the procedure of drafting, deliberating and adopting the new Constitution for its tight time limits, and for the limited possibilities for debate of the draft by political parties and within the media and civil society. The second VC opinion[43] was requested by the PACE monitoring committee. This was wider in scope. Again, the VC was balanced in its criticism. It expressed concern – it later turned out, with good cause – about the lack of detail in the Constitution about judicial independence, which was instead left to cardinal and other laws to elaborate upon. It warned against passing cardinal laws not expressing consensual political and moral values, as these would 'lock' discussion of these issues, making future changes of these dependent on a two-thirds majority in the parliament.

In its opinion on the court reform laws, requested by the Secretary-General of the CoE in 2012, the VC was very detailed, and very critical.[44] Basically, the reforms in question handed over control of all significant issues concerning the appointment, transfer and disciplining of judges to a single person, the President of the National Judicial Office (PNJO), appointed by the Government. The Hungarian arguments for the necessity of doing this, and of compulsorily retiring judges aged over 62, were analysed. These arguments were dismissed as totally inadequate.[45] The Commission concluded that the reforms 'not only contradict European standards for the organisation of the judiciary, especially its independence, but are also problematic as concerns the right to a fair trial under Article 6 ECHR'.[46]

[43] CDL-AD(2011)016.

[44] CDL-AD(2012)001.

[45] It is useful to quote this part of the opinion *in extenso*: '104. The Venice Commission examines this issue not from the special angle of age discrimination, but from its effect on judicial independence. From this point of view, the retroactive effect of the new regulation raises concern. A whole generation of judges, who were doing their jobs without obvious shortcomings and who were entitled – and expected – to continue to work as judges, have to retire. The Commission does not see a material justification for the forced retirement of judges (including many holders of senior court positions). The lack of convincing justifications may be one of the reasons for which questions related to the motives behind the new regulation were raised in public. 105. The sudden change of the upper-age limit creates the problem that a significant part of nearly 10% of the Hungarian judges will retire within a short period of time (between 225 and 270 out of 2900 judges in Hungary). The argument, which has been made, that a higher number of younger judges with "up-to-date qualifications" will increase the performance of the judiciary, since they are expected to be "more suitable to carry a higher workload" as well as "more ambitious and more flexible", must be dismissed as not being sufficiently proven.'

[46] At para 120.

In March 2013, the Hungarian Parliament enacted the Fourth Amendment to its Fundamental Law, and the Secretary-General of the CoE requested an opinion from the Commission.[47] The Commission was again very critical both of provisions in it, but also of how the new Constitution had come into being. The Constitution confirms the position and powers of the PNJO, which in effect removes any judicial independence. Why this was done was 'unclear', all the more so because there was no 'indication of the necessary limitations and the checks and balances to which it must be subject'.[48] Several new provisions of the Constitution have

> no constitutional character and should not be part of the Constitution (eg homelessness, criminal provisions on the communist past, financial support to students, financial control of universities). In addition to shielding these provisions from control by the Constitutional Court, this ensures that future governmental majorities in Parliament without a two-thirds majority cannot change these policies.[49]

The Commission criticised the instrumental and partisan use of constitutional amendments, noting that before the entry into force of the new Constitution, the previous Constitution had been amended 12 times after the elections of 2010. The amendments, which casually nullified Constitutional Court rulings, undermined the whole idea behind constitutional control. A constitution should be

> a stable act, not subject to easy change at the whim of the majority of the day. A constitution's permanence may not be based solely on arithmetical considerations stemming from the relationship between the numerical strength of the ruling and opposition parties in parliament. … [A] constitution should set neutral and generally accepted rules for the political process. For its adoption and amendment, a wide consensus needs to be sought.[50]

Another critical opinion was on the law introducing restrictions on foreign-funded NGOs.[51] The opinion analyses the government arguments for introducing wide-reaching restrictions and reporting requirements, and finds these to be unjustified. Similar criticisms are made on the so-called 'Stop Soros' Draft Legislative Package.[52] This package was aimed particularly at NGOs working in the fields of human rights and asylum. The VC noted that draft Article 353A criminalises organisational activities not directly related to illegal migration,

[47] CDL-AD(2013)012.
[48] ibid para 70.
[49] ibid para 136.
[50] ibid para 137.
[51] CDL-AD(2017)015. See the subsequent judgment of the CJEU in Case C-78/18, *Commission v Hungary (Transparency of associations)*, ECLI:EU:C:2020:476.
[52] CDL-AD(2018)013. See Case C-821/19, pending before the CJEU. I might also mention here that the VC issued an opinion on the Hungarian Government's targeting of the Central European University, CDL-AD(2017)022, a matter that was subsequently brought before the CJEU by the European Commission in Case C-66/18 *Commission v Hungary (Higher education)*, ECLI:EU:C:2020:792.

such as 'preparing or distributing informational materials', something restricting disproportionally the rights guaranteed under Article 11 ECHR. Moreover, the VC noted it criminalises advocacy and campaigning activities, something that is an illegitimate interference with Article 10 ECHR. People and organisations acting in good faith to fulfil the provisions of the international law on asylum would risk prosecution. The VC also stated that draft Article 353A lacked the required clarity to qualify as a 'legal basis' within the meaning of Article 11 ECHR.[53]

A number of interesting points can be made regarding the VC opinions on Hungary. The first is that the VC was not, and has never been, asked to give an overall assessment of all the Fidesz legal measures. With the benefit of hindsight, one can argue that Fidesz' intentions should have been obvious from the beginning. However, the VC is not in the business of identifying underlying 'intentions'. It is asked to look at specific proposals, albeit within a wider constitutional context. It can criticise the procedure (haste, lack of inclusiveness, etc) for making important changes in a legal system, but it has to begin its consideration of the substantive aspects of draft laws of a sovereign state from an objective perspective: Are adequate reasons advanced by the government for the need to make the reforms, and for constructing the reforms in the way it has? Are the reforms internally consistent? Are they likely to achieve their stated objectives? Is there a degree of proportion between the ends sought and the means used? Moreover, if one wishes to argue that a given legal measure is not only not in accordance with '*best* European practice' but violates some *minimum* European standard, there obviously has to *be* such a minimum standard. Here, a difficulty emerges because of the rich variation in how European states construct their systems of constitutional control. The Hungarian Government advanced arguments that this or that measure could be found in X or Y's laws, and so it could hardly be described as in violation of a minimum European standard.

The VC opinion on the Fourth Amendment to the Constitution is a good example of both analysing specific reforms from a wider perspective, and of dealing with the (mis)use of comparative constitutional law. The VC stated:

> In constitutional law, perhaps even more than in other legal fields, it is necessary to take into account not only the face value of a provision, but also to examine its constitutional context. The mere fact that a provision also exists in the constitution of another country does not mean that it also 'fits' into any other constitution. Each constitution is the result of balancing various powers. If a power is given to one state body, other powers need to be able to effectively control the exercise of this power. The more power an institution has, the tighter control mechanisms need to be constructed. Comparative constitutional law cannot be reduced to identifying the existence of a provision in the constitution of another country to justify its democratic credentials in the constitution of one's own country. Each constitution is

[53] CDL-AD(2018)013 (n 52), paras 101–103.

> a complex array of checks and balances and each provision needs to be examined in view of its merits for the balance of powers as a whole.[54]

Another example of the VC's ability to look at a reform in a wider context is the previously mentioned opinion on the court reform laws.[55] By contrast with the case brought before the Court of Justice of the EU (CJEU) by the Commission, which reduced the whole issue to age discrimination, the VC was able to focus on the heart of the issue: the effect of such measures on judicial independence.

A second interesting point regards what can be called the 'good faith' problem. It is difficult to show lack of good faith, something illustrated by high standards of proof set by the ECtHR case law on Article 18 ECHR.[56] If a draft law on its face provides for certain powers, backed by certain safeguards, some form of proof is needed before one can say that the powers will be used wrongly or that the safeguards will not work in practice. There is a link here to the first point, in that in many well-established *Rechtsstaaten* safeguards may have been internalised in legal culture. However, this leaves it open for authoritarian state A to argue that democratic *Rechtsstaat* B has a similar institution, or a similarly worded legal power. The difference between the two cases is that the institution or the legal power in state B is not used or is used with great restraint.

The VC does take account of legal cultural safeguards.[57] However, it is more difficult to criticise a law or legal institution that resembles, on its face, a law or legal institutions in a well-functioning democratic *Rechsstaat*. Mere allegations by NGOs and in newspaper reports that safeguards are not working, or that power is being abused, may not, in themselves, be sufficient proof. However, where government actions, or statements, themselves indicate how the law will be used in practice, there is more scope for criticism. The VC confronted this issue in its opinion on the law introducing restrictions on foreign-funded NGOs. The VC noted that

> while on paper certain provisions requiring transparency of foreign funding may appear to be in line with the [international] standards, the context surrounding the adoption of the relevant law and specifically a virulent campaign by some state authorities against civil society organisations receiving foreign funding, portraying them as acting against the interests of society, may render such provisions problematic.[58]

[54] CDL-AD(2013)012, para 139.

[55] Case C-286/12, *Commission v Hungary*, ECLI:EU:C:2012:687.

[56] *Merabishvili v Georgia* App no 72508/13 (GC, 28 November 2017).

[57] See, eg, CDL-AD(2012)01, para 8: 'When analysing a piece of legislation, the Venice Commission takes into account the manner of its implementation and factors, which determine this implementation and which depend on the context of the respective country, namely its legal and political culture. Every context requires provisions adapted to its specificities and demands. It is due to the decisive role of the concrete contexts, that an allegedly deficient regulation may result in a non-deficient outcome. Nevertheless, the aim of legal reform should be to provide an institutional and regulatory environment that is least likely to be misused.'

[58] CDL-AD(2017)015, para 65.

I will turn now to the opinions regarding Poland.[59] As PiS did not achieve a constitutional majority in the 2015 parliamentary elections, PiS, led by Kaczyński, used ordinary laws to, first, emasculate the Polish Constitutional Tribunal and then capture it, by securing the presidency for a PiS appointee, who then brought in three (unlawfully appointed) PiS judges, thus securing a majority for PiS appointees. This was an extended process. It resembled, in a way, repeated hacking into a computer system. Points of vulnerability were identified and then exploited. The procedure for selection of the National Council for the Judiciary (NCJ) was changed, and the parliamentary majority (mainly PiS) then appointed 21 of the 25 members. The NCJ has significant power over the assessment, promotion and disciplining of judges, the appointment of new judges and the selection of court presidents. Many lower-court presidents and vice-presidents were replaced. Thereafter the Polish Supreme Court was targeted. The compulsory retirement age for judges was reduced from 70 to 65 years, which applied to more than one-third of the Supreme Court judges, including the President. At the same time, the number of judges on the Supreme Court was increased from 81 to 120. Then the EU Commission brought an action, and the CJEU intervened issuing interim measures.[60] This had the effect of blocking the 'packing' of the Supreme Court. The Government thereafter responded by creating two special chambers in the Court, the composition of which it controlled, and granting one of these special disciplinary powers.[61]

Between 2016 and 2020, the VC delivered six opinions on legal reforms in Poland: two on the Constitutional Tribunal, two on the reorganisation of the courts system, one on police powers and one on the prosecutor. Five of these opinions were requested by CoE institutions (PACE or the Secretary-General), the sixth and final one by the Polish Senate. I will limit myself to taking up a few points in some of these opinions.

The Commission's first and second opinions on the Constitutional Tribunal were delivered during the period when PiS had not yet secured control over it. The VC was highly critical of the Government's undermining of the work of the Tribunal, inter alia by refusing to publish its judgments. It noted in the first opinion, amongst other things, that

> [c]rippling the Tribunal's effectiveness will undermine all three basic principles of the Council of Europe: democracy – because of an absence of a central part of checks and balances; human rights – because the access of individuals to the Constitutional Tribunal could be slowed down to a level resulting in the denial of justice; and the rule of law – because the Constitutional Tribunal, which is a central part of the Judiciary in Poland, would become ineffective. Making a constitutional court ineffective is inadmissible and this removes a crucial mechanism which ensures that potential

[59] A much more detailed analysis can be found in W Sadurski, *Poland's Constitutional Breakdown* (Oxford, Oxford University Press, 2019).

[60] Case C-619/18R *Commission v Poland*, ECLI:EU:C:2018:1021.

[61] See also Case-791/19 *Commission v Poland (Régime disciplinaire des juges)*, ECLI:EU:C:2020:277.

> conflicts with European and international norms and standards can be resolved at the national level without the need to have recourse to European or other subsidiary courts, which are overburdened and less close to the realities on the ground.[62]

In its opinion on the public prosecutor, the Commission noted that the merger of the offices of Minister of Justice and Prosecutor General

> falls short of international standards as to the appointment of the Prosecutor General and to his/her qualifications. Furthermore, the main problem concerns the attribution of extensive powers to the Prosecutor General-Minister of Justice by the 2016 Act, notably with regard to direct intervention in individual cases. This, in addition to the very broadly formulated power of the Public Prosecutor General of 'maintaining law and order' which appears as a sort of general supervisory power commonly found in 'prokuratura' type systems, creates a potential for misuse and political manipulation of the prosecutorial service, which is unacceptable in a state governed by the rule of law. The problems related to the merger of the positions of the Public Prosecutor General and of the Minister of Justice are exacerbated by the entry into force of the Act on the Organisation of Common Courts, which gives strong powers to the Minister of Justice in particular the right to dismiss and replace the court presidents.[63]

The Venice Commission's first opinion on the reorganisation of the courts is another detailed and very critical analysis of the Government's arguments for reform and the different measures taken. The VC noted in conclusion that the stated goal of the 2017 reform was to enhance the democratic accountability of the Polish judiciary. However, the VC concluded that, instead, this reform jeopardised judicial independence and 'enabled the legislative and executive powers to interfere in a severe and extensive manner in the administration of justice'.[64]

I will turn now to Romania. The VC delivered seven opinions concerning Romania between 2012 and 2019. I will content myself with quoting from three of them. The first of these concerned a constitutional crisis in 2012 between then President Traian Băsescu and Prime Minister Victor Ponta. The Constitutional Court, among other institutions, may be described as getting caught in the cross-fire. The opinion is interesting for several reasons, inter alia because it explicitly notes the limitations of the law in general, and the Constitution in particular, when the main problem is the lack of a mature political culture, where state office-holders pursue their own or their parties' interests, rather than the interests of the state as a whole. This, of course, is hardly a problem exclusive to Romania, but it is particularly severe there. The VC emphasised the need

[62] CDL-AD (2016)001 Opinion on Amendments to the Act of 25 June 2015 on the Constitutional Tribunal of Poland, para 138.

[63] CDL-AD (2017)028 Opinion on the Act on the Public Prosecutor's office, as amended, para 111.

[64] CDL-AD(2017)031, Opinion on the draft act amending the Act on the National Council of the Judiciary, on the draft act amending the Act on the Supreme Court, proposed by the President of Poland, and on the Act on the Organisation of Ordinary Courts, para 129.

for office-holders to comply with the principle of loyal cooperation between institutions.[65]

The second opinion was requested by the President of Romania in 2017, and concerns the then Government's attempts to exert increased political control over the prosecutors and the courts. The background to the issue was allegations that some prosecutors had been using elements in the intelligence services to obtain evidence of corruption. As before, in its opinion on the 2012 political crisis, the VC gives a detailed and objective analysis of the proposals made and the reasons given for them, trying to steer a path between different problematic alternatives.[66] The third opinion concerned an attempt by the then Government to undermine ongoing and future investigations and prosecutions into corruption, under cover of the need to make reforms of the criminal code and criminal procedure code.[67] Substantive criminal offences were modified to make it much more difficult to prove corruption. Procedural changes were made to put obstacles in the way of investigating alleged corruption. The VC makes a careful analysis of each of the reforms proposed. It concludes, with what I consider is admirable self-restraint:

> Some of the proposed amendments are in conflict with the international obligations of the country, especially regarding the fight against corruption, or go far beyond the requirements resulting from the case law of the Constitutional Court or the country's international obligations. The Commission is concerned that, taken separately, but especially in view of their cumulative effect, many amendments will seriously impair the effectiveness of the Romanian criminal justice system in the fight against various forms of crime, including corruption-related offences, violent crimes and organised criminality.[68]

More examples can be given, but these will suffice. The VC opinions have been objective and balanced analyses, produced after a fair procedure, in which the government concerned has had every opportunity to explain and justify its actions. The VC is not imposing a particular 'European' constitutional model without reference to national traditions, but has instead examined the measures taken, and the justifications given for these, on their own merits.

[65] CDL-AD(2012)026, see particularly paras 72–74.

[66] CDL-AD(2018)017-e, Opinion on draft amendments to Law No 303/2004 on the Statute of Judges and Prosecutors, Law No 304/2004 on Judicial Organisation, and Law No 317/2004 on the Superior Council for Magistracy. See the preliminary ruling pending before the CJEU concerning a number of issues relating to the appointment, etc of the Romanian prosecutors, Joined Cases C-83/19, C-127/19, C-195/19, *Asociația Forumul Judecătorilor din România and others*, ECLI:EU:C:2021:393.

[67] CDL-AD(2018)021-e, Opinion on draft amendments to the Criminal Code and the Criminal Procedure Code. The measures of the then Government included the dismissal of the head of the specialist anti-corruption prosecution body, a step later found by the ECtHR to be in violation of Arts 6 and 10 ECHR, in *Kövesi v Romania* App no 3594/19 (5 May 2020).

[68] CDL-AD(2018)021-e (n 66) para 184.

V. THE VENICE COMMISSION'S ROLE IN STRENGTHENING THE RULE OF LAW IN THE EU

The preceding discussion of developments in Hungary, Poland and Romania makes it abundantly clear that all is not well in a number of EU Member States. I will not go into the question of *whether* a reaction is called for by EU institutions and other EU Member States.[69] Of course one can argue that, with a free trade organisation, you do not need to like your neighbours, or have any values in common with them. So, if the EU retreated back to being only a free trade organisation, it might be justified to leave democracy, the rule of law and human rights to the European organisation that was the first to declare and commit to these values, namely, the CoE.

However, the EU is a lot more than a free trade organisation today. It is also more than an internal market. Even in an internal market, soft values (human rights, rule of law, democracy) tend to creep in whether one wants them there or not. To take an extreme example, if my neighbouring state has enslaved its population, it can sell its goods more cheaply to me. This will undermine the profitability of my production of the same goods. Moreover, its population will not have the money to buy any of the consumer goods I produce (although its government might want to buy weapons). Thus, my neighbour's respect for basic human rights becomes my concern. To take a less extreme example, if there is an internal market, with freedom of movement, I can expect an exodus of people from states where there is a lack of respect for basic human rights. This is happening already in the EU. The principle of mutual recognition is central in an internal market. The independence of the courts in my neighbour is thus of the utmost concern to me, because behind the principle of mutual recognition is an independent court. Why should I otherwise accept the certification made by the food standards authority in my neighbour's state?

Thus, even on the crass economic level, it is clear to me that it is not only legitimate but also absolutely necessary for EU institutions, and EU Member States, to be concerned with rule of law backsliding. But it goes beyond economic factors. As Scharpe, amongst others, has pointed out, the EU largely receives its democratic legitimacy through a two-stage mechanism, that is, through Member States' democratic procedures.[70] As a number of commentators have noted, this reason alone means that the EU institutions, or other Member States, cannot remain indifferent in the face of developments threatening democracy and the rule of law in individual Member States. At stake is democratic legitimacy not merely in the country concerned, but also in the EU as a whole.[71]

[69] See, amongst many good inputs on this issue, C Closa, 'Reinforcing EU Monitoring of the Rule of Law' in Closa and Kochenov (eds) (n 15); and JW Müller, 'Should the EU Protect Democracy and the Rule of Law inside Member States?' (2015) 21 *European Law Journal* 141.

[70] See, eg, FW Scharpf, *Reflections on Multilevel Legitimacy* (Cologne, Max Planck Institute for the Study of Societies, 2007), available at www.mpi-fg-koeln.mpg.de/pu/workpap/wp07-3.pdf (accessed 12 May 2020).

[71] Cf Tuori (n 15).

There has been criticism of the unwillingness and/or inability of Member State governments to activate the mechanism in the treaties supposedly designed for dealing with this problem, namely the 'nuclear option' in Article 7(2) of the Treaty on European Union (TEU).[72] This is hardly a surprise. The procedural requirements, unanimity minus one, are most unlikely to be fulfilled, even if simultaneous proceedings are brought against both Poland and Hungary. The governments of some states, for example Finland, Sweden and the Netherlands, may be prepared to grasp the nettle, but others are not. In the endless series of negotiation that is the EU, governments are understandably reluctant to burn their bridges with another government they will probably need on their side tomorrow. Moreover, there are plenty of other crises to take up time and energy, and that argue against rocking the boat too much, such as the Covid-19 emergency and its financial aftermath, climate change and filling the hole in the budget caused by Brexit. Member States of the EU have traditionally been content to provide the EU Commission with the evidence and let it start infringement proceedings, rather than bringing actions before the CJEU themselves. Thus, it is to the EU Parliament, the EU Commission and the CJEU to which we must look.

The VC has helped to strip away the Polish, Hungarian and Romanian Governments' attempts to maintain a veneer of respectability, a facade of constitutionality, when they have deliberately undermined the rule of law.[73] The VC opinions sketched out in section IV have had direct and indirect inputs in the efforts of these EU institutions to raise rule of law issues. In its activation of the Article 7(1) procedure as regards Hungary, and its resolutions on Hungary and Poland, the European Parliament has referred directly and indirectly to the VC opinions.[74] The European Commission referred repeatedly to the VC opinions in its reasoned proposal on Poland[75] and the infringement proceedings it has subsequently brought before the CJEU.[76] The Advocates General have referred to the VC in their Opinions in these Commission cases.[77] Specific VC opinions can provide an objective background for the Commission, for example that a particular measure is problematic, or that a government justification for introducing the measure is inadequate. However, the VC can also concretise

[72] Art 7(1) TEU provides for a preventive mechanism that can be activated in case of a 'clear risk of a serious breach' of the values set out in Art 2 TEU; and Art 7(2) TEU provides for a sanctioning mechanism only in the event of a 'serious and persistent breach by a Member State' of these values.

[73] Tuori refers to 'parasitical legitimacy' in K Tuori, *European Constitutionalism* (Cambridge, Cambridge University Press, 2015) 36.

[74] See eg EP resolution of 12 September 2019, [2019] OJ C433/09 (Hungary); EP resolution of 17 September 2020, P9_TA(2020)0225 (Poland).

[75] See Commission Reasoned Proposal in Accordance with Article 7(1) of the TEU Regarding the Rule of Law in Poland, Brussels, 20 December 2017, COM(2017) 835 final.

[76] See in particular Case C-619/18 *Commission v Poland*, ECLI:EU:C:2019:531; Case C-791/19, *Commission v Poland*, Order of 8 April 2020, ECLI:EU:C:2020:277 (interim measures).

[77] See, eg Opinion of AG Tanchev in Case C-619/18 *Commission v Poland*, ECLI: EU:C:2019:325; and Opinion of AG Campos Sánchez-Bordona in Case C-78/18, *Commission v Hungary*, ECLI:EU:C:2020:1.

the general standards in question, providing substance to the 'rule of law' obligations undertaken by EU Member States under Article 2 TEU.[78]

Moreover, the VC opinions can be, and have been, used by national courts in the course of the preliminary reference procedure. National courts, applying EU law, are a fundamental part of the EU legal order. As is well known, the CJEU provided in Case C-216/18 *PPU v Minister for Justice and Equality*[79] for a two-stage procedure by which a national court may suspend the application of the principle of mutual recognition (in this case, refuse to implement a European arrest warrant issued in another state). The first stage is to make a determination, on the basis of objective information, that there are general or systemic failures in the justice system of the other EU state.[80] In *PPU v Minister for Justice and Equality*, the CJEU stopped short of stating that VC opinions are themselves a sufficient basis for reaching such a determination. It expressed a preference for the European Commission performing a gate-keeper function, deciding in a reasoned opinion when and if the 'systemic' or 'generalised' threshold had been reached. Still, the CJEU did not rule out that a national court might reach its determination on the basis of other information, so long as this was objective, as the VC opinions are. Nor does the national court requesting a preliminary ruling from the CJEU have to be in another Member State. One of the referring Polish courts in Case C-585/18, C-624/18 and C-625/18 *AK v Krajowa Rada Sądownictwa, and CP and DO v Sąd Najwyższy*,[81] referred to the VC opinion on the Polish courts in its preliminary reference to the CJEU. The case concerned the alleged lack of independence of the newly established Supreme Court disciplinary chamber.[82] The CJEU criteria of independence track the concerns expressed earlier by the VC, even if the CJEU did not refer to the VC opinion directly.[83]

[78] The VC Rule of Law Checklist (n 13) is particularly valuable in this respect.

[79] ECLI:EU:C:2018:586.

[80] ibid para 61 (emphasis added), 'The executing judicial authority must, as a first step, assess, on the basis of material that is objective, reliable, specific and properly updated concerning the operation of the system of justice in the issuing Member State … whether there is a real risk, connected with a lack of independence of the courts of that Member State on account of systemic or generalised deficiencies there, of the fundamental right to a fair trial being breached. Information in a reasoned proposal recently addressed by the Commission to the Council on the basis of Article 7(1) TEU is *particularly relevant* for the purposes of that assessment.' See also the earlier Case C-64/16, *Associação Sindical dos Juízes Portugueses v Tribunal de Contas*, ECLI:EU:C:2018:117.

[81] ECLI:EU:C:2019:982.

[82] ibid para 171, 'Where the objective circumstances in which that court was formed, its characteristics and the means by which its members have been appointed are capable of giving rise to legitimate doubts, in the minds of subjects of the law, as to the imperviousness of that court to external factors, in particular, as to the direct or indirect influence of the legislature and the executive and its neutrality with respect to the interests before it and, thus, may lead to that court not being seen to be independent or impartial with the consequence of prejudicing the trust which justice in a democratic society must inspire in subjects of the law.'

[83] In CDL-AD(2017)031 (n 64) the VC sketches out a number of the structural problems involved in creating a chamber within the Supreme Court that has disciplinary powers over the rest of the Court, before noting in para 43 that 'it is of particular concern that the Draft Act seems to enable the President of the Republic to determine almost completely the composition of these two chambers and to ensure that they are wholly or mainly composed of newly appointed judges. This would

Before taking up a possible enhanced role for the VC in the future, this is a suitable place to discuss reservations against this. There are three reservations as I see it. The first concerns institutional dependency. The second, related reservation concerns the standards to be applied. The third concerns the vulnerability of the VC itself to 'capture'.

First, is it not better for the EU, a sui generis organisation, to be self-sufficient? If the EU has been shown to need an organisation like the VC, should it not have its own? Jan Werner-Müller proposed the creation of an EU 'Copenhagen Commission' on the lines of the VC.[84] One of his reasons for doing so is the fact that the CoE contains states with a poor record on the rule of law, democracy and human rights. Another is that the VC cannot be proactive, whereas a Copenhagen Commission could routinely monitor situations in Member States, and have resources to make deeper analyses.

It is true that the VC cannot be proactive, other than producing general (ie non-country-specific) studies. However, that has not been a problem so far, as when cause for concern has emerged, one or other CoE institution has decided, rather quickly, to refer the issue to the VC. The VC itself has shown itself able to produce detailed analyses in a very timely fashion.[85] Although I am not impartial in this matter, I find it difficult to see how a new body, starting from scratch, could match let alone surpass the expertise of the VC. As I have already noted, the institutional memory of the VC is deep, and it has, through its experienced membership and secretariat, a unique competence in comparative constitutional law. It may not have the resources to carry out extended field studies, but it has so far not needed to do so. Law is a practical science and the VC does not need to understand every aspect of the historical or sociological background behind a legal proposal. It analyses the proposal as such, and the justifications advanced for it. Moreover, as the excerpts from the Hungarian opinions previously discussed show, it is able to take a holistic approach to an issue, setting the legal reform in its proper context.

As regards the issue of its 'dubious' membership, it must be admitted that the membership of the VC includes authoritarian states, and even one state that cannot, by any stretch of the imagination, be called a democracy, namely, Azerbijan. However, this membership problem also exists for the other 'jewel in the CoE crown', the ECtHR. The EU institutions, especially the CJEU, have, however, been happy to refer to, and be influenced by, the case law of the CJEU, even if the CJEU is careful to regard it as a minimum standard.[86] This brings me to the second reservation, the standards to be applied.

mean that judges appointed by a NCJ dominated by the current political majority would decide on issues of particular importance …'

[84] See, eg, JW Müller, 'Safeguarding Democracy inside the EU: Brussels and the Future of Liberal Order' *Transatlantic Academy, 2012–2013 Paper Series, No 3* (February 2013).

[85] Indeed, bearing in mind the accelerated procedure, very quickly. As Tuori (n 15) has put it, the Commission has come to play the role of a constitutional fire brigade.

[86] This is in accordance with Art 53 of the Charter of Fundamental Rights of the EU. The CJEU signalled clearly in the – heavily criticised – ECHR accession opinion that it would not be compatible

Are the CoE standards too low? As is well known, the standards in the ECHR are a minimum standard. The CJEU has made it very clear that, in human rights, the EU can aim higher than the ECHR. However, as pointed out earlier, the VC itself uses 'best practices'. It too can go beyond ECtHR case law. Moreover, bearing in mind the rich variety of solutions European states have in the areas of democracy and the rule of law, all of them within a 'spectrum' of acceptability, it is difficult to see how a Copenhagen Commission could apply standards different from those used, and elaborated, by the VC.[87]

The third reservation relates to the potential for the VC itself to be 'captured': if this is a real risk then it obviously makes sense for the EU not to put its eggs into this particular basket. This opinion has been expressed by two of the commentators who have been most active in taking up the rule of law problems in Hungary and Poland, Pech and Kochenov.[88] However, I think this is based on a misunderstanding on how the VC actually works. The individual members are appointed by their governments. The VC has no power to object to a member proposed by a government, or make appointment subject to the approval of some sort of independent body.[89] There is, indeed, an argument that such a procedure should be introduced. The requirement that an individual member be 'independent' has not always been respected. There have been cases where still active political figures or senior officials in government departments have been appointed – something I think is not appropriate. The existing rules of procedure provide for removal of a serving individual member only in extreme cases, which has so far been interpreted only to cover personal wrong-doing (criminal offences, etc).[90] I think that some form of independent confirmatory body, and/or increased grounds for removal, should be discussed for the future – even if formulating the latter will be tricky.[91] However, the absence of such a procedure at the present time does not undermine the integrity of the VC as

with EU law for it to be bound by ECtHR judgments; see Opinion 2/13, ECHR, EU:C:2014:2454. See also the – again heavily criticised – judgment in Case C-399/11 *Melloni*, ECLI:EU:C:2013:107.

[87] Cf Tuori (n 15).

[88] L Pech and D Kochenov, 'Strengthening the Rule of Law within the European Union: Diagnoses, Recommendations, and What to Avoid' (13 June 2019) *RECONNECT Policy Brief No 1*, 2019 (Leuven); University of Groningen Faculty of Law, *Research Paper No 28/2019*, 12, 'The Venice Commission could be routinely asked to produce a report on relevant matters as soon as for instance, the Rule of Law Framework is activated – but this more systematic involvement should not be sought until the Venice Commission itself strictly enforces its current eligibility requirements so as to prevent the appointment of manifestly unsuitable members.'

[89] Cf Art 255 TFEU.

[90] Art 1.3.c of the Rules of Procedure provides that an individual member's mandate can be terminated 'the day the Commission notes, on the proposal of the Bureau, by a majority of two-thirds of its members that the member concerned is no longer able or qualified to exercise his or her functions'.

[91] A substantive ground such as 'repeatedly acting contrary to the values of the CoE' might be considered, but this leaves a very wide area of discretion, even if accompanied by procedural safeguards (eg a proposal by the Bureau, and a two-thirds majority vote in the plenary).

a whole. As described earlier, the main work of the VC is done by the working groups. Unlike the situation for cases before chambers of the ECtHR, a VC member from a state that is the subject of an opinion has no right to sit in the working group considering the law of that state. Indeed, no member can insist on being on any working group. The membership of working groups is determined by the President, on proposal by the secretariat, and backed up by the Bureau. Nor may a member vote after the plenary debate discussing the adoption of an opinion concerning his or her state. The same applies to anyone whom the President determines has a conflict of interest in the case.[92] Opinions are usually adopted by consensus, but any member is free to call for a vote and orally signal his or her lack of agreement with the opinion or parts of it. However, the VC is not a court, and there is no right to append written 'dissenting' views to opinions adopted.

The situation can admittedly arise where a member from authoritarian state A makes an objection on behalf of another member from authoritarian state B. However, in my experience, on those relatively rare occasions when an obviously political statement is made by a member, without objective merit, the atmosphere in the plenary can be described as embarrassment. Members know that they are appointed as independent experts, and a certain peer-group pressure to maintain this independence definitely applies. Thus, even in the event that a 'manifestly unsuitable' person is appointed by a state, this person will usually only have an indirect influence at best on the actual work of the VC.

I will devote the remainder of this section to discussing briefly what role the VC can have in a future EU rule of law mechanism. The Commission has recently introduced enhanced monitoring of compliance with the rule of law by Member States.[93] The report covers all Member States and includes a summary of the situation in Member States as regards the rule of law. The Commission also plans to bring more rule of law-related cases to the Court, improving the procedure used to decide on the existence of a breach of EU values under Article 7 TEU and modifying the 2014 Rule of Law Framework to involve other EU institutions in the process. As part of its 'improved toolbox', it announced that it plans to strengthen cooperation with the CoE, mentioning specifically the VC and the anti-corruption body GRECO.[94]

It is not clear yet what form such 'strengthened cooperation' can or will take. The Commission cannot, within the confines of EU law, 'outsource' to the VC the job of determining whether a systemic, or generalised, deficiency exists in an EU Member State. Nor can the VC, within the wording of its Statute, take

[92] CDL-AD(2018)018 Venice Commission Rules of Procedure, Art 3(4). Members are under a prior obligation to reveal any conflict of interest.

[93] Seeathttps://ec.europa.eu/info/publications/2020-rule-law-report-communication-and-country-chapters_en.

[94] EU Commission, Further strengthening the Rule of Law in the Union, 3 April 2019, COM(2019)163.

such a competence upon itself. Nor is it likely that it would want to do so, even if its Statute was changed by the CoE Committee of Ministers (which has the competence to do this). One interpretation is that 'strengthened cooperation' does not mean much more than the existing, already strong, cooperation. It is undoubtedly a strength for the Commission to be able to show that there is independent support for its view that the situation in X-land has got so bad as to be 'systemically deficient'; in other words, that other international judicial and legal bodies, the VC, Greco, the ECtHR, the UN Human Rights Committee, etc, share its concerns.[95] As the VC is reactive, if the Commission does not want to wait too long, it will need CoE bodies to continue referring issues of concern to the VC in a speedy fashion.

One difficulty relates to the EU *acquis*. While we now know that this includes independent courts, and independent data inspectorates, there is a host of other areas where Fidesz and PiS have taken control over, or undermined, checks and balances and where no *acquis* exists. How do you bring an infringement action to reverse the politicisation of the civil service, or the capture of the public media? States have different degrees of politicisation of their civil services and different types of safeguard designed to compensate for the risk of abuse of political power. There is no *acquis* here, beyond the 'arm's length'/independence requirements imposed on a small number of bodies, such as data protection inspectorates, which apply particular parts of EU law. As regards the media, there are EU anti-competition law rules on concentration of the media, but these will not necessarily help here. What *acquis* is there in areas where states have widely differing approaches to central government control? For example, when 'should' central government respect local government autonomy, or when should it act with restraint and avoid dictating to public universities exactly what to teach and publicly-funded research institutes exactly what to research?

Infringement actions would presumably be backed by (palpable?) economic sanctions. Other economic pressurising mechanisms include conditionality of, or even denial of, EU funds (eg structural funds), or suspension of the principle of mutual recognition. Bearing in mind the fact that Poland and Hungary are net recipients of EU funding, such proposals have a certain attraction, especially for people from states that are net contributors to the EU. There is something particularly galling in having to pay for people who are rude to you. However, the EU Member States compromised on the conditionality mechanism that was

[95] Cf A von Bogdandy, 'Principles and Challenges of a European Doctrine of Systemic Deficiencies', *Max Planck Institute for Comparative Public Law & International Law Research Paper No 2019–14*, 'a situation or measure is more likely to qualify as systemically deficient the more institutions of the various legal orders share this assessment'. *Contra*, R Kelemen, et al, 'The Perils of Passivity in the Rule of Law Crisis: A Response to von Bogdandy', *VerfBlog* (26 November 2019) available at https://verfassungsblog.de/the-perils-of-passivity-in-the-rule-of-law-crisis-a-response-to-von-bogdandy/.

finally introduced, severely limiting its usefulness.[96] I will not discuss this mechanism further, beyond noting two general problems well known from the area of international sanctions. The first is how to tailor sanctions so as to strike at the ruling elites and avoid the general population's being too disadvantaged. The second is how to avoid the 'rally around the flag' effect. An authoritarian government with a monopoly over, or substantial control over, the broadcast media can easily put a spin on sanctions as 'foreign interference' directed against the nation as such.

Whatever approach one takes to economic pressurising measures, it is not wrong to hold the view that the European Commission should show caution in bringing infringement procedures in such sensitive areas as democracy, the rule of law and human rights, and it is good to have 'strength in numbers'. However, the sensitivity of rule of law issues can be overplayed. I would also object if it was about imposing a uniform EU solution in an important institutional issue (eg 'every state has to have a constitutional court'), or a uniform conception of judicial independence ('every state must apply the principle of the lawful judge').[97] But it is not about this. The goal of European Commission infringement proceedings on judicial independence has been much more modest: it is about establishing that a given system, in given circumstances, is not satisfactory, not about designing and imposing a 'perfect' system or an obligatory standard.

As regards the idea of an annual rule of law review cycle, monitoring all EU states' performance in rule of law issues might seem outwardly appealing to some. It may be easier for the European Commission to defend bringing infringement proceedings against specific states, if it also can say it has a general 'even-handed' monitoring system. No state is being singled out. All states have something to learn. However, it can end up being a bureaucratic exercise, expensive, time-consuming and of little added value. There is already a mechanism for identifying which states have particular rule of law problems, namely, the possibility for CoE bodies to refer to the VC concerns related to specific issues concerning draft laws, laws and legal institutions. I think it naive to believe that the Governments of Hungary and Poland will be more receptive to criticism that has emerged out of a more general monitoring procedure.

[96] Regulation (EU, Euratom), 2020/2092 of the European Parliament and the Council of 16 December 2020 on a general regime of conditionality for the protection of the Union budget, [2020] OJ L433/1. For criticism, see Editorial Comment, 'Compromising (on) the general conditionality mechanism and the rule of law' (2021) 58 *CML Rev* 267.

[97] Meaning a system where cases are allocated to judges in strict rotation, with no discretionary powers for court presidents to take into account other factors. I feel the same way about CJEU case law that leaves insufficient room for national legislatures or courts to balance different rights against each other (employees wearing headscarves), or ruling out an investigatory measure (general retention of metadata for a limited period), however strong the safeguards on it that are provided, and applied, in national law.

VI. CONCLUDING REMARKS

I will not try to summarise the arguments I have made already. I will content myself with making a number of concluding remarks. I began writing this contribution in November 2019 and finished it in May 2020. In the meantime, the Covid-19 pandemic arrived. It remains to be seen what long-term effects this, and the financial crisis it has triggered, will have on the EU. East and West, North and South have even more reasons for drifting apart from each other. However, the idea of the EU is still strong. Indeed, one might argue that the pandemic should ultimately strengthen the feeling of mutual dependence, and that only together are the 27 EU states strong enough to protect and promote their interests in a more uncertain world. The question, however, is how strong the EU's commitment is to one of these interests, the rule of law, when the majority of the electorate in a state has shown itself more interested in other things.

The experiences of Hungary and Poland show that it is not possible for courts in a state to defend themselves against a sustained attack from their own government. It is understandable that lawyers are particularly offended by assaults on legal institutions, but my point here is that if the problem is in essence a failure of political culture then this cannot be simply corrected by strengthening legal institutions.[98] It is not for nothing that Alexander Hamilton called the courts the 'least dangerous branch' of government, in that they tended to operate only as a veto over the other branches of government, and lacked power over both the military and economic resources of the state.[99] The Hungarian Fidesz Party has a supermajority and could change its Constitutional Court as it chose, but even when such a majority is lacking, and a government has to work through ordinances and normal laws, a constitutional court has too many vulnerabilities to allow it to hold out for any length of time. As regards Poland, it was evident to the VC that, sooner or later, PiS would secure control over the Polish Constitutional Tribunal. The ordinary court system is bigger, and so more difficult to take clear control over. However, given enough time the ordinary judges will be sufficiently 'chilled' to say that judicial independence no longer exists. Courts and judicial councils cannot be entrenched so deep to be protected against any attack, at least if one wants to maintain the main principle of governance for an EU state, namely, democracy.

While the CJEU can, and should, come to the assistance of the beleaguered Polish judiciary (it is probably too late for the Hungarian judiciary),[100] the CJEU

[98] One can argue that the problem is not so much that Hungary and Poland have experienced a *failure* of political culture, but rather that Fidesz and PiS have carried out a sort of legal coup d'état, deliberately undermining democracy and the rule of law. Democracy no longer becomes 'self-regulating'. But even if such an approach is taken to the problem, strengthening legal institutions would provide only a partial solution.

[99] See further A Bickel, *The Least Dangerous Branch: The Supreme Court at the Bar of Politics* (New Haven, CT, Yale University Press, 1986).

[100] Although some Hungarian judges, at least, are still sufficiently independent to ask the CJEU about controversial issues. See Joined Cases C-924/19 *PPU* and C-925/19 *PPUFMS and Others*

cannot govern Poland by judgments. There are many ways in which CJEU judgments can be undermined and, as noted previously, the EU *acquis* does not cover everything that needs to be protected.

Lawyers are practical creatures, and the interesting question for them is what the EU institutions can and should do while we wait for the majority of the electorates in these states to see the long-term advantages in having a state with the separation of powers, the rule of law, independent courts, objective public media, etc. The former British diplomat, Robert Cooper, put it very succinctly when he stated that there were only three ways of influencing foreign countries: by military force; by money; and by talking to them and getting them, over time, to change their views.[101] As regards military force, Europe has been there, done that and everybody knows this is a very bad idea. No one wants to invade Hungary or Poland. The problem with money is that, once given, you cannot get it back. You can, however, withhold it. But this is not a basis for a long-term relationship based on mutual trust: the recipient will be inclined to try to trick you whenever it can. Long term, it is only the third method that works.

This is not to preach defeatism. As I noted before, the EU can and must do what it can to defend its own democratic legitimacy, and this includes exploring all avenues for combining dialogue with economic pressures. The fact that Fidesz and PiS have been democratically elected does not mean that their actions are legitimate, or acceptable in the European constitutional tradition.[102] As I have argued, the 'winner takes it all' approach shown by the governing parties in Hungary and Poland is not another variant of political constitutionalism. It is the opposite of it. Still, we should not lose sight of the fact that, ultimately, the remedy for rule of law backsliding lies with the electorates in these two states. As the VC has put it, 'The Rule of Law can only flourish in a country whose inhabitants feel collectively responsible for the implementation of the concept, making it an integral part of their own legal, political and social culture.'[103] In the meantime, we are obliged to keep talking, and the VC is an important part of that dialogue.

v Országos Idegenrendeszeti Főigazgatóság Dél-alföldi Regionális Igazgatóság and Országos Idegenrendeszeti Főigazgatóság, ECLI:EU:C:2020:367.

[101] R Cooper, *The Breaking of Nations: Order and Chaos in the Twenty-first Century* (London, Atlantic Books, 2003).

[102] And, of course, the 'democratically elected' argument loses its force the more the overall fairness of the elections can be called into question (eg when a government does not give fair airtime in publicly owned media to the political opposition, or when it has unreasonably changed the electoral rules in its own favour).

[103] CDL-AD(2016)007 (n 13) para 43.

9

The Eastward Enlargement as a Driving Force and Testbed for Rule of Law Policy in the EU

ANTONINA BAKARDJIEVA ENGELBREKT

I. INTRODUCTION

THE EUROPEAN UNION'S (EU's) advancement in the area of the rule of law and fundamental rights in the 1990s and 2000s is by many perceived as a natural step in the evolution of EU law and governance. However, initiated students of European integration are well aware of the intimate connection between this development and the Eastward Enlargement of the Union.[1] To be sure, the European Court of Justice (ECJ/CJEU, or 'the Court') had early on launched its doctrine on general principles of EC/EU law and recognised the rule of law and fundamental rights as such principles building on the common constitutional traditions of the Member States and their allegiance to the European Convention on Human Rights (ECHR). The Court had also in its jurisprudence affirmed the position of the European Community as a Community bound by law.

Yet much of this development was taking place in an incremental, one might say 'organic' fashion. Principles were stipulated and doctrines established on a

[1] See E Wennerström, *The Rule of Law and the European Union* (Uppsala, Iustus förlag, 2007); D Kochenov, *EU Enlargement and the Failure of Conditionality* (Alphen aan den Rijn, Kluwer Law International, 2008); G de Búrca, 'Beyond the Charter: How Enlargement Has Enlarged the Human Rights Policy of the European Union' (2003) 27(3) *Fordham International Law Journal* 679; W Sadurski, 'EU Enlargement and Democracy in New Member States' in W Sadurski, A Czarnota and M Kryiger (eds), *Spreading Democracy and the Rule of Law? The Impact of EU Enlargement on the Rule of Law, Democracy and Constitutionalism in Post-Communist Legal Orders* (Dordrecht, Springer, 2006) 27; W Sadurski, 'Charter and Enlargement' (2002) (8)(3) *European Law Journal* 340; W Sadurski, 'Accession Democracy Dividend: The Impact of the EU Enlargement upon Democracy in the New Member States of Central and Eastern Europe' (2004) 10 *European Law Journal* 371; C Hillion, 'The Copenhagen Criteria and their Progeny' in C Hillion (ed), *EU Enlargement: A Legal Approach* (Oxford, Hart Publishing, 2004) 1; C Hillion, 'Enlarging the European Union and Deepening its Fundamental Rights Protection' (2013) 11 *SIEPS European Policy Analysis*.

case-by-case basis without marked ambition for a comprehensive constitutional build-up. In fact, incrementalism and minimalism have from the outset been the signature approach of the Communities to the constitutional question in the whole European integration project. By avoiding any attempts at grand constitutional design, the European constitution was left to evolve gradually and only when and where the pragmatic needs of the Union made this necessary.[2]

So, it would be fair to say that it was only after the fall of the Berlin Wall, at the time when the Central and Eastern European countries (CEEC) embarked on the path to democracy and market economy and clearly stated their desire to join the EU, that the need became pressing to give unequivocal expression of the commitment of the EU and its Member States to the rule of law as a shared constitutional value. The incrementalism and minimalism previously characterising the status of the rule of law in EU law were obviously no longer tenable if the Union was to embrace at least 10 new Member States with dramatically different constitutional legacies and rule of law culture, or, as many feared, an absence of such.

In sharp contrast to the gradual and cautious approach of the earlier stages of European integration, the years of preparation of the 10 CEEC for their accession to the Union saw an unprecedent constitutional mobilisation towards building a legal framework for guaranteeing the rule of law and respect for fundamental rights in the EU. This occurred most conspicuously through several Treaty amendments and the adoption of the EU Charter of Fundamental Rights (EUCFR). Less visibly, in the process of Enlargement, a myriad of Council and Commission documents were produced fleshing out the conditions for accession to the Union, notably the requirements of democracy, the rule of law and fundamental rights under the Copenhagen criteria, and setting up the more specific benchmarks for measuring candidate countries' progress in meeting these requirements. Ambitious programmes of technical and legal assistance were rolled out, engaging EU institutions in an effort of reforming the legal and institutional frameworks of the candidate countries (CCs) and making them compatible with EU standards. In combination, the gradual formalisation and legalisation of the constitutional fundaments of the EU, and the massive deployment of resources in the direction of the rule of law and fundamental rights in the course of Enlargement, have brought about significant changes in the status of the rule of law in the Union.

In this chapter, I revisit the link between the Eastward Enlargement of the EU and the expansion of the Union's legal framework of, and institutional commitment to, the rule of law. I review some of the legal and political science literature on Enlargement analysing the process of preparation of the CCs for membership of the Union, and in particular the efforts of EU institutions to enhance

[2] See Weiler's 'do and hearken' metaphor in J Weiler, 'Does Europe Need a Constitution? Demos, Telos and the German Maastricht Decision' (1995) 1 *European Law Journal* 219, 220.

compliance with EU rule of law standards in these countries. The aim is to critically assess what was gained and what was lost in this massive operation of legal and institutional transformation steered by conditionality.

A closer look is given to EU's engagement in reforming the judiciary in the CCs as a central component of the rule of law. The chapter highlights the difficulty of formulating clear-cut and consistent criteria in an area where there is considerable diversity of approaches among the EU Member States, as well as limited competence and a poor track record of EU institutions. This uncertainty only exacerbates the already considerable challenge of achieving lasting and genuine change through external incentives. At the same time, the Enlargement runs parallel to processes of deepening and widening of European integration. The chapter therefore seeks to capture the constantly evolving character of accession requirements and the dynamic interplay between internal and external standards.

Importantly, the chapter outlines the self-generating logic of entering this politically sensitive field and the inevitable follow-up step of deeper involvement of the Union in the state of the rule of law in the Member States. This logic is dictated partly by the regrettable reality of rule of law backsliding in some of the new Member States post accession,[3] but also by the imperative of the principle of equality (or 'liberal legalism').[4] In conclusion, the chapter critically discusses the challenges that come with this new level of engagement of the Union in issues of the rule of law and judicial independence in the Member States.

II. ENLARGEMENT AS A DRIVING FORCE FOR THE RULE OF LAW IN THE EU

In recent academic debate, it is argued that there is a sufficiently firm common understanding of the meaning and scope of the principle of the rule of law in the EU. According to Pech, 'there is now a broad legal consensus in Europe on the core meaning of this principle, its minimum components, and how it relates to other key values such as democracy and respect for human rights'.[5]

While this statement may be correct as a reflection of the current state of affairs, at the time when the Eastward Enlargement first came into sight as a political option for the EU, the situation was quite different. As most commentators agree, there was at that juncture a relatively thin express normative basis

[3] L Pech and K Scheppele, 'Illiberalism Within: Rule of Law Backsliding in the EU' (2017) 19 *Cambridge Yearbook of European Legal Studies* 3–47; W Sadurski, 'Constitutional Design: Lessons from Poland's Democratic Backsliding' (2020) 6 *Constitutional Studies* 59.

[4] Sadurski, 'Charter and Enlargement' (n 1) 344.

[5] L Pech and J Grogan, 'Unity and Diversity in National Understandings of the Rule of Law in the EU', *Reconnect*, WP 1 D, April 2020, available at https://reconnect-europe.eu/wp-content/uploads/2020/05/D7.1-1.pdf, 6 (hereinafter 'Unity and Diversity'); see also L Pech and J Grogan, 'Meaning and Scope of the EU Rule of Law', *Reconnect*, WP 7 D2, April 2020, available at https://reconnect-europe.eu/wp-content/uploads/2020/05/D7.2-1.pdf (hereinafter 'Meaning and Scope').

for the rule of law as a condition for EU membership, and scarce detail as to the exact content of the rule of law as an EU law principle.[6]

A. The Rule of Law in the EU Legal Framework Prior to Enlargement

Indeed, if one tries to trace the evolution of the concept of the rule of law in Community/Union law, we must start by acknowledging that the four decades of legal history preceding the process of Eastward Enlargement testify to the relatively rare appearances of the concept in legislative documents, and its late and hesitant entrance into ECJ jurisprudence.

i. The Rule of Law in the Original Treaties

The original treaties of the European Communities contained no solemn declarations or formal commitment to the rule of law, democracy and fundamental rights.[7] There is no consensus in the literature as to the reasons for this conspicuous silence. Some seek the explanation in the fact that the United Kingdom (UK) was not among the founding Members of the European Communities. Since 'the rule of law' is a very central concept in UK law, it is seen as not surprising that the concept does not appear in the founding Treaties of the European Communities, while in contrast it occupies a prominent place in the Statute of the Council of Europe (CoE) and the ECHR.[8] At the same time, it is argued that by defining the function of the ECJ as being to guarantee 'that the law is observed', the legal system of the EU has from its inception been solidly based on the rule of law. Certainly, the very existence of the ECJ and the bold scope of its jurisdiction, including a mandate to review the legality of the acts of EU institutions, are in themselves robust evidence of the importance of the rule of law in the legal and institutional system of the EU.[9] However, this can hardly equate to a conscious and clear commitment to the rule of law, as was done, for example, in the relevant instruments of the CoE, and to an explicit requirement of respect for the rule of law vis-à-vis the Member States.

A more plausible explanation for the silence is in my view to be sought in the different approaches to European cooperation represented by the two major European organisations established in the aftermath of the Second World War.

[6] See Kochenov (n 1); Wennerström (n 1); Hillion, 'Enlarging the European Union' (n 1) 10.

[7] On the original provision of Art 31 ECSC Treaty and the controversies around the correct translation of the concept 'respect du droit' used therein, see L Pech, 'The Rule of Law in the EU: The Evolution of the Treaty Framework and Rule of Law Toolbox' (2020) *Reconnect*, WP 7, available at https://reconnect-europe.eu/wp-content/uploads/2020/03/RECONNECT-WP7-2.pdf, 7.

[8] See Art 3 Statute of the Council of Europe. As to the corresponding German and French concepts, namely *Rechtsstaat* and *état du droit*, the emphasis on statehood in these concepts is considered a plausible explanation for their avoidance in the founding Treaties and in subsequent ECJ jurisprudence. See Pech (n 7) 8–9.

[9] See Pech (n 7) 8 et seq; Wennerström (n 1).

Whereas the CoE was conceived as an intergovernmental organisation with the main mission of upholding human rights in its Member States, the European Coal and Steel Community and, later on, the European Economic Community (and Euratom) were set up as international organisations of a hybrid type, with a substantial degree of delegation of sovereignty to supranational institutions and centered around the idea of a Common Market. This approach, aptly referred to as 'functionalist', relies on achieving political unity through the logic of market integration.[10] It envisages pragmatic steps towards intertwining the economies of the Member States, while avoiding a debate over 'the political'.[11] If this view is accepted, the absence of a reference to the rule of law in the original Treaties was not an unfortunate omission but rather a conscious choice that followed logically from the model of European cooperation pursued by the Communities.

Undeniably, this minimalist approach was partly possible due to the lack of sharp incongruences in the original Member States' understanding of fundamental constitutional values.[12] The traumatic heritage of the Second World War, and the living example of the detriments caused by authoritarian rule in the European countries within the Soviet sphere, had the effect of limiting, if not eliminating, the basis for political movements questioning the values of democracy, the rule of law and human rights in Western Europe. Moreover, all founding Member States of the European Communities were Members of the CoE. One might say that the rule of law, understood as a fundamental limitation on the exercise of state power, had been taken for granted among existing Member States.[13]

ii. The Rule of Law in the ECJ's Jurisprudence

Given the absence of an explicit reference to the rule of law in the original Treaties, it famously fell to the ECJ to painstakingly educe the rule of law as a general principle and undergirding value of the EU legal order. Some scholars see the seminal judgments of *Costa v ENEL* and *Van Gend en Loos* as early recognition of a vision of the Communities as bound by law and constituting a

[10] See EB Haas, *Beyond the Nation-State: Functionalism and International Organization* (Stanford, CA, Stanford University Press, 1964).

[11] As succinctly put by Grabbe, 'This is the heart of the "Monnet method" of European integration: focus on practical economic integration and knit interests together so that people will stop paying so much attention to nationalist claims.' See H Grabbe, 'Six Lessons of Enlargement Ten Years on: The EU's Transformative Power in Retrospect and Prospect (2014) 52 (Annual Review) *Journal of Common Market Studies* 46.

[12] See I Damjanovski, C Hillion and D Preshova, 'Uniformity and Differentiation in the Fundamentals of EU Membership: The EU Rule of Law Acquis in the Pre- and Post-accession Contexts' (2020) *EU IDEA Research Papers No 4*, available at www.iai.it/sites/default/files/euidea_rp_4.pdf, 5.

[13] ibid.

separate legal order with a clear hierarchy of norms, where EU law prevails over conflicting rules of national law and citizens can derive individual rights directly from EU law and enjoy judicial protection of these rights.[14]

The Court also gradually developed other principles that constitute essential components of the rule of law, such as the principles of legality, legal certainty, separation of powers (or, in the EU context, of functions), prohibition of retroactivity, and judicial review of administrative acts.[15] Notably, in a line of creative jurisprudence, the ECJ recognised fundamental rights as constituting general principles, and thus an integral part, of EU law. In early cases such as *Stauder* and *Internationale Handelsgesellschaft*, the Court developed its sophisticated methodology of identifying individual fundamental rights in the common constitutional traditions of the Member States or in the ECHR, to which all Member States were signatories, and elevating them to general principles of EU law.[16] But it was in the seminal decision in '*Les Verts*' that the ECJ recognised most prominently the principle of the rule of law as a general principle of EU law.[17] The Court famously referred to a principle of legal community (*Rechtsgemeinschaft*), or a community under the rule of law.

No doubt, this jurisprudence contributed greatly to consolidating the self-perception and the international standing of the European Community as a Community of law, cherishing the principles of legality and the rule of law and guaranteeing respect for fundamental rights. Based on the analysis of individual Treaty provisions and most of all on the case law summarised above, scholars have argued that the concept of the rule of law was at the end of the 1980s considerably developed in Community law, in both its formal and its substantive dimensions, as a declaratory and a procedural concept.[18] However, it is also admitted that the case law has predominantly been spurred by concerns about safeguarding the supremacy of EU law, rather than by substantive ambition about raising the level of respect for the rule of law and human rights in the Community. As aptly formulated by de Búrca, the jurisprudence has been 'reactive', one might even say defensive, in character.[19] On the other hand, the Court has been rather cautious about acknowledging general Community competences in the field of human rights.[20] As a consequence, Member States have been subject to EU or ECJ jurisdiction in matters of the rule of law and fundamental rights only 'within a highly circumscribed context'.[21]

[14] See Wennerström (n 1) 117 et seq. Cf Case 6/64 *Costa v ENEL*, ECLI:EU:C:1964:66; Case C-26/62 *Van Gend & Loos*, ECLI:EU:C:1963:1.

[15] For a detailed account of the ECJ case law, see Wennerström (n 1) 117 et seq; see also Pech (n 7).

[16] Case C-29/69 *Stauder*, ECLI:EU:C:1969:57 and Case C-11/70 *Internationale Handelsgesellschaft*, ECLI:EU:C:1970:114. For the methodology, see de Búrca (n 1); and K Lenaerts, 'Interlocking Legal Orders in the European Union and Comparative Law' (2003) 52 *ICLQ* 873.

[17] Case C-294/83 *Parti écologiste 'Les Verts' v Parliament*, ECLI:EU:C:1988:94. See also Opinion 1/91 *EEA*, ECLI:EU:C:1991:490; cf Pech (n 7) 10.

[18] On the different dimensions of the rule of law, see Wennerström (n 1) 154–57.

[19] de Búrca (n 1) 686.

[20] See Opinion 2/94, ECLI:EU:C:1996:14, para 27.

[21] de Búrca (n 1) 686.

In sum, the approach of the Communities/Union to the constitutional question, including the rule of law and fundamental rights, has from the outset been one of minimalism and incrementalism. Whenever the rule of law and fundamental rights were pronounced as general principles, this was done indirectly, with reference to the common constitutional traditions of Member States or to the ECHR, and in a defensive manner. The tension has systematically stemmed from Member States' claiming higher levels of protection of constitutional principles and fundamental rights in the national constitutional legal order, and voicing concerns that the same high levels could not be guaranteed by the EC/EU. As we shall see in the following, exactly the reverse concern has become the driving force behind the next stage in the development of the rule of law in the Union, a development propelled largely by the prospect of Eastward Enlargement of the Union.

B. Reinforcement of the EU Rule of Law Framework in Anticipation of Enlargement

Against this background, it is fair to say that the principle of the rule of law made its true entry into the Treaties and EU constitutional law only after the collapse of communism in CEE and when the prospect of a closer relationship with the CEEC came within reach. Prior to that, the contours of the rule of law as a general principle were rather fuzzy. The situation changed quite dramatically in the decade following the fall of the Berlin Wall.

i. The Entry of the Rule of Law into the Treaties

The first mention of the rule of law in the Treaties was in the Treaty of Maastricht, where the principle was expressly acknowledged as an EU concept. Member States officially confirmed 'their attachment to the principles of liberty, democracy and respect for human rights and fundamental freedoms and of the rule of law'.[22] However, this was done only in the Preamble, in relatively vague or, to use Pech's word, 'symbolic', terms, and with no specific definition or obligations attached.[23] It is notable that in the Preamble, the clause on the rule of law came immediately after a clause recalling 'the historic importance of the ending of the division of the European continent'. Thus, the link between elevating the status of the rule of law in the Union and the end of the Cold War was openly acknowledged.

Surely, at the time of drafting of the Maastricht Treaty, the exact fate of the relationship between the former socialist states from CEE and the EU was still not conclusively decided. In a Commission Communication from August 1990,

[22] See Maastricht Treaty, Preamble, third indent.
[23] Pech (n 7) 12.

the Commission outlined the immediate way forward as being one of Association Agreements with the countries of CEE.[24] Still, the prospect of opening the EU to new members from CEE was already on the table, something confirmed by the fact that a special article on the procedure for accepting new members was included in the Treaty on European Union (TEU) (Article O Maastricht Treaty, now Article 49 TEU). More importantly, the context in which the Maastricht Treaty was drafted was starkly shaped by the dramatic events in CEE. It was exactly within this historical timespan that democracy, the rule of law and fundamental rights received world-wide attention and recognition as never before.[25]

Against this backdrop, it is surprising that while the Maastricht Treaty included a provision on accepting new Members, clearly in anticipation of such applications from the CEEC, it did not set out any specific criteria for membership and did not mention the rule of law as such a criterion. This only comes to confirm that the rule of law has been a concept in the making, the content and importance of which were evolving in parallel with the process of Eastward Enlargement.

ii. The Crucial Role of the Copenhagen Criteria

Only a year after the entry into force of the Maastricht Treaty, at the Copenhagen European Council of June 1993, the EU declared that 'the associated countries in Central and Eastern Europe that so desire shall become members of the European Union'. The Council also famously defined the economic and political conditions required for the associated countries to join the Union. These conditions or criteria are divided into three groups:

(a) Political conditions, requiring that 'the candidate country has achieved stability of institutions guaranteeing democracy, the rule of law, human rights and respect for and protection of minorities'.
(b) Economic conditions, requiring 'the existence of a functioning market economy as well as the capacity to cope with competitive pressure and market forces within the Union'.
(c) The *acquis* criterion, that is, 'the ability to take on the obligations of membership, including adherence to the aims of political, economic and monetary union'.[26]

[24] Communication from the Commission to the Council and the Parliament on Association agreements with the countries from Central and Eastern Europe: a general outline, COM(90) 398 final, 27 August 1990, Brussels.

[25] See Conclusions of the Dublin European Council of 20 April 1990. See also the Paris Charter signed in 1990 by the Heads of State or Government of the CSCE (Commission on Security and Cooperation in Europe) states, further committing themselves to democracy, the rule of law, and respect for human rights and fundamental freedoms.

[26] Copenhagen European Council, Presidency conclusions, 21–22 June 1993.

Importantly, the Madrid European Council in 1995 complemented the third criterion by stressing the necessity not only of formally transposing the *acquis*, but also of implementing it effectively through appropriate administrative and judicial structures. Some analysts treat this addition as a separate, fourth criterion requiring (d) institutional and administrative capacity to implement the *acquis*.[27] This is in my view a useful distinction, since the organisation of administrative and judicial structures had been, at least at the beginning of the accession process, a matter reserved to the Member States, with very few binding *acquis*.

Students of EU Enlargement have been adamant to point out that the Copenhagen criteria should not be regarded as a novelty but rather as a consolidation and codification of the experience and practice of previous enlargements.[28] At the same time, it is also acknowledged that among the criteria there are many new elements in both substantive and in institutional terms. For one, the political conditions for membership have been formulated in greater detail, extending to areas where the Union itself has limited competence (see section III.C). Second, they are set out in more straightforward, even 'command' terms.[29] Third, whereas in previous accessions, candidate states were expected to fulfil the EU admission conditions without much interference from the Union, in the conclusions from the Copenhagen European Council the EU declared its intention to engage actively in preparing the CCs for membership, steering and monitoring the process.[30] This design of the accession process had the effect of giving considerable leverage to the political and economic conditions for membership.

iii. Increased Formalisation of the Principle of the Rule of Law in the Treaties

The prominent place awarded to the rule of law in the Copenhagen criteria had notable political repercussions for the Union. Very soon, the principle found expression in the texture of the EU Treaties. The Amsterdam Treaty, which was signed in 1997, when the official negotiations on CEEC membership of the EU had already taken off, stipulated this time more clearly in the Treaty text that the Union is founded on the principles of liberty, democracy, respect for human rights and fundamental freedoms, and the *rule of law*, principles that are common to the Member States (Article F(1), now Article 2 TEU, considerably amended).

[27] See Wennerström (n 1) 64.

[28] See Hillion, 'The Copenhagen Criteria and their Progeny' (n 1) with reference to the Declaration on Democracy, Annex C, Copenhagen European Council, Final text, 20 April 1978, *EC Bulletin* 3-1978; cf Kochenov (n 1) 24. See also Pech and Grogan, 'Meaning and Scope' (n 5) 7.

[29] See Hillion, 'The Copenhagen Criteria and their Progeny' (n 1) 3, 10–11.

[30] Hillion, 'Enlarging the European Union' (n 1) 3; R Janse, 'Is the European Commission a Credible Guardian of the Values? A Revisionist Account of the Copenhagen Political Criteria during the Big Bang Enlargement' (2019) (17)(1) *I.CON* 43, 47.

The most obvious provision preparing for the future Eastward Enlargement was the amended Article O (now Article 49 TEU), which through reference to Article F(1) finally cemented the political conditions for membership as known from the Copenhagen criteria, namely democracy, the rule of law and fundamental rights (minus minority rights), elevating them into Treaty requirements. At this juncture, it was also considered important to introduce an insurance against possible future democratic and rule of law backlash in a Member State through the setting up of a sanctioning mechanism in case of serious and persistent breach of the values and principles laid down in Article F(1) TEU (see Article F.1, now Article 7 TEU).

As acknowledged by the Commission in subsequent accession documents, through the Treaty of Amsterdam 'the political criteria defined at Copenhagen were essentially enshrined as constitutional principles in the Treaty on European Union'.[31] Scholars speak of codification of the Copenhagen criteria.[32]

C. Effect of Enlargement on Fundamental Rights Protection in the Union

Similar and even more revolutionary development can be traced in the closely related domain of human rights and fundamental freedoms. The Eastward Enlargement of the EU can also in this area be seen as providing a powerful impetus for the advancement of a genuine human rights agenda for the Union. Developments followed a parallel trajectory to the one regarding the rule of law, with successive anchoring of the commitment to fundamental rights in the Treaties as a general principle of EU law through Article F Maastricht Treaty (now Article 6 TEU), codifying in this way the doctrine developed by the ECJ, and on the other hand as a condition for membership through the Amsterdam Treaty. These changes were clearly intended to 'signal to the candidate countries that membership comes out of the question before it is certain that they have legislation which protects and guarantees citizens' rights'.[33]

Decisively, the Union's commitment to human rights and fundamental freedoms received solemn recognition and reinforcement through the EUCFR signed in 2000. This move was undertaken on the one hand as a safeguard and insurance against unwanted backlash in the CEE candidate countries post accession. Less conspicuously, it was prompted by the criticism that had started to mount against EU institutions for applying double standards in the ongoing Enlargement process, setting stricter requirements in respect of the CCs than

[31] See eg Regular Report Bulgaria (2002), at 18, note 3.

[32] de Búrca (n 1) 696; cf Hillion, 'Enlarging the European Union' (n 1) 3.

[33] See speech by Sweden's Minister of Justice Laila Freivalds, 'Rule of Law in an Enlarged European Union' (1998) *Europarättslig tidskrift* 15; in a similar sense, Sadurski, 'Accession Democracy Dividend' (n 1).

the Union could demand from its own Member States.[34] The Charter can thus be conceived as a step towards strengthening the integrity and trustworthiness of the Union's fundamental rights policy, closing the gap between external and internal standards (see section V.A.i).[35]

Still, despite the bold step that the Charter undoubtedly constitutes in the direction of bolstering fundamental rights in the EU, it did not fully succeed in placing internal and external standards on the same level. As is well known, the scope and impact of the Charter are limited in several respects, notably through the horizontal clauses confining the application of the Charter to the European institutions and to Member States only when they apply and implement EU law, and assuring that it does not accord new powers to the Union.[36]

III. THE RULE OF LAW AS PART OF THE PRE-ACCESSION SCREENING OF THE CANDIDATE COUNTRIES

As seen in section II, the Eastward Enlargement worked as a powerful force, raising the status and visibility of the rule of law in the constitutional framework of the EU. The question to be discussed in this section is how the Union approached the rule of law in its pre-accession policy. To be able to analyse this question, it is important to look not only at the specific rule of law requirements that were spelled out vis-à-vis the countries aspiring for EU membership, but also at the overall approach of EU institutions to the process of accession, centered around conditionality.

A. General Approach: The Rise of Rule of Law Conditionality

In the legal and political science literature on EU Enlargement, the concept 'conditionality' has acquired almost canonical status.[37] Interpreted narrowly, conditionality implies that the CEEC are allowed to become Members only after certain political and legal conditions are fulfilled. Conceived more broadly, conditionality represents the key component of EU institutions' approach to

[34] For the academic critique, see J Weiler and P Alston, 'An "Ever Closer Union" in Need of a Human Rights Policy' (1998) 9 *EJIL* 658; A Williams, 'Enlargement of the Union and Human Rights Conditionality: A Policy of Distinction?' (2000) 25 *EL Rev* 601; cf de Búrca (n 1).

[35] See Sadurski, 'Charter and Enlargement' (n 1). In de Búrca's words, 'The EU ... has been hoisted on its own petard.' See de Búrca (n 1) 680.

[36] According to de Búrca, a number of Member States met the prospect of having a full-fledged Union human rights policy with anxiety, and sought to limit the application of the Charter: de Búrca (n 1) 702.

[37] On accession conditionality, see F Schimmelfennig and U Sedelmeier, 'Governance by Conditionality: EU rule transfer to the candidate countries of Central and Eastern Europe' (2004) 11 *Journal of European Public Policy* 661; F Schimmelfennig and U Sedelmeier (eds), *The Europeanization of Central and Eastern Europe* (Ithaca, NY, Cornell University Press, 2005) 210–28.

accession, seeking to engender change in the laws and institutions of the CCs by applying continuous pressure on them through a system of specific targets and tangible rewards, with the aim of bringing the countries closer to EU standards and requirements. The concept captures well the asymmetric relationship between the parties involved – the EU (the Commission) setting the conditions for entry 'into the club' and the CCs striving to meet those conditions.[38]

The term 'conditionality' first entered the enlargement discourse with the conclusions of the Copenhagen European Council of 1993 and the stipulation of the Copenhagen criteria. The years before that, that is the initial phase in the relations between the CEEC and the EU, had the character of a traditional diplomatic exchange. The emphasis had been on 'meetings of an advisory nature' and the tone was one of 'co-operation and assistance'.[39] Once the conditions for membership were set out in unambiguous and non-negotiable terms, the approach changed palpably, and the relationship became increasingly skewed and formalised.

Still, the true rise of conditionality is associated not with the Copenhagen criteria, but rather with the Commission Communication 'Agenda 2000' from 1997. In this document, the Commission presented a comprehensive vision for a reinforced pre-accession strategy.[40] The main tenet of the strategy was advancing conditionality by setting specific priorities and intermediate targets adapted to each CC's particular problems and challenges, and enhancing the scrutiny of CCs' progress towards meeting the Copenhagen criteria. The European Council had earlier emphasised that the Union would proceed with accession only after an in-depth and ongoing scrutiny of the political conditions for membership had been carried out.[41] Thus, positive evaluation by the Commission became decisive for the start, and thereafter the progress, of accession negotiations. Most analysts therefore consider Agenda 2000 to be the point when rule of law conditionality 'acquired teeth' or real 'bite'.[42] While the enhanced strategy comprised a myriad of documents and policy instruments, two of the instruments stand out as particularly important: individual country assessments and Accession Partnerships.[43]

[38] On asymmetry in EU accession policy, see K Engelbrekt, 'Multiple Asymmetries: The European Union's Neo-Byzantine Approach to Eastern Enlargement' (2002) 39 *International Politics* 37.

[39] Williams (n 34).

[40] See European Commission, 'Part II: The Challenge of Enlargement' and 'Enhanced Pre-accession Strategy' in Agenda 2000, Volume I – Communication: For a stronger and wider Union, COM(97) 2000 final, Brussels, 15 July 1997.

[41] Conclusions of the Madrid European Council, Bulletin of the European Communities, No 12/1995. See also Williams (n 34) 608.

[42] Williams (n 34) 608; see also Sadurski, 'Accession Democracy Dividend' (n 1) 375.

[43] For the different types of documents that made the Copenhagen principle workable, see Kochenov (n 1) 76–77.

i. Individual Country Assessments

Throughout the pre-accession process, the Commission kept producing regular and individualised assessments of the level of compliance of the CCs with the criteria for membership. The first round of such assessments comprised the so-called Country Opinions attached to Agenda 2000, giving an initial appraisal of the situation in the applicant countries, also in respect of the political conditions for accession. These initial opinions were then followed up by annual country reports (so called Regular Reports (RRs)) measuring the applicant countries' progress toward meeting the conditions for membership. The RRs were drawn up and published simultaneously for all CCs, introducing in this way a strong comparative and competitive element in the procedure and amplifying the level of scrutiny and pressure on the applicants.

ii. Accession Partnerships and Conditionality of Technical and Financial Assistance

The second instrument in the 'toolbox' of conditionality was the so-called Accession Partnership (AP). Such partnerships, between the Council, on the one hand, and each of the CCs, on the other, were signed following a proposal from the Commission, and were thereafter regularly revised and updated. The instrument allowed the Commission to break down the otherwise daunting task of preparing the CCs for membership into more specific short-term and intermediate objectives, and to adapt its assessments and recommendations to the situation and performance of each applicant.

The most important dimension of the instrument was, however, that it offered a framework for enforcing 'strict conditionality' in allocating technical and financial assistance to the CCs.[44] Throughout the pre-accession process, the CEEC had been able to benefit from considerable financial and structural aid, notably through the PHARE programme, but also through twinning programmes and access to Community programmes such as SAPARD.[45] With the introduction of APs this much-needed assistance was made conditional upon compliance with the objectives and commitments specified in the APs. Failure to respect these conditions and commitments could lead to a decision by the Council to suspend financial assistance.[46] Thus, the instrument gave EU institutions, and the Commission in particular, powerful leverage in micro-steering reforms in the

[44] See Agenda 2000 (n 40) 53.

[45] The assistance was in Commission statements compared to the Marshall Plan. For a critical view on this proposition, see M Ivanova, 'Why There Was No "Marshall Plan" for Eastern Europe and Why This Still Matters' (2007) 15(3) *Journal of Contemporary European Studies* 345.

[46] See Art 4, Council Regulation (EC) No 622/98 on assistance to the applicant States in the framework of the pre-accession strategy, and on the establishment of Accession Partnerships.

CCs and enforcing accession conditionality. According to Kochenov, the APs laid the ground 'for a fully-fledged conditionality of sticks and carrots'.[47]

A less-observed aspect of the AP instrument is that it was conceived, as the name indicates, as a partnership, that is, as a framework of common engagement, with priorities and precise objectives set up in collaboration between the EU and the CCs. While conditionality is usually analysed as building on one-sidedness and asymmetry, the active engagement of EU institutions in preparing the CCs contributed to gradually transforming Enlargement into a common project in which both the CCs and the Union institutions had a shared interest and stakes.[48]

B. Methodology of Assessment

In Agenda 2000, the Commission described the methodology applied for the individual country assessments as going beyond formal indicators and seeking to establish how democracy and the rule of law 'actually work in practice'.[49] At the same time, when looking at the sources of information on which the Commission relied, it appears that the assessment has been 'largely paper based'.[50] Central place among the sources was awarded to a questionnaire that was sent out to each of the applicant countries. According to commentators who have looked closely into the process, the questionnaire was composed of numerous but often rather scattered and arbitrary questions, which were then left to the self-assessment of the candidate states' governments.[51] Other sources that are named explicitly are assessments by the Union Member States, European Parliament reports and resolutions, and more broadly 'the work of various international organisations, non-governmental organisations and other bodies'.[52]

The questionnaire method was complemented by bilateral meetings held with each of the applicant countries. The information gathered through those meetings is apparently processed in an informal manner, without employing any quantitative or qualitative methods established in social sciences.[53]

[47] Kochenov (n 1) 74. The Commission admits that such linking of individual countries' progress with the degree of financial assistance is quite unprecedented; however, it defends this approach by citing the enormous task involved in preparing the CCs for membership. See Agenda 2000 (n 40) 89.

[48] The perception of Enlargement as a joint project is visible in other Commission documents as well. See eg European Commission, 'Making a Success of Enlargement', Strategy Paper and a Report, COM(2001) 700 final, Brussels, 13 November 2001, 5. See also S Grimm, 'Democracy promotion in EU enlargement negotiations: more interaction, less hierarchy' (2019) 26 *Democratization* 851, who argues that the process of accession is more interactive and less one-sided than usually believed.

[49] See Agenda 2000 (n 40) vo. 1, 42.

[50] See Williams (n 34) 609. See also Wennerström (n 1) 179 et seq.

[51] See Janse (n 30) 54–55.

[52] Agenda 2000 (n 40) 39; cf Williams (n 34) 609.

[53] For criticism on this point, see the analysis by K Nicolaïdis and R Kleinfeld, 'Rethinking Europe's "Rule of Law" and Enlargement Agenda: The Fundamental Dilemma' (2012) *NYU School of Law, Jean Monnet Working Paper Series*, available at www.JeanMonnetProgram.org.

C. The Rule of Law Standard as a Moving Target

The preceding admittedly cursory review of the EU's pre-accession strategy and the methodology for assessment provides an insight in the modalities of the Commission's rule of law screening and assessment exercise. However, the most important variable in this assessment is the very benchmarks against which the performance of the CCs was measured. Following the Copenhagen European Council, it was clear that commitment to the rule of law was one of the political conditions for membership of the Union. Yet, the precise meaning and contents of this condition remained vague. According to one of the early critics of EU enlargement policy and rule of law conditionality, the concepts of the rule of law and democracy were undetermined in the EU legal framework and thus open to interpretation and contestation. They were 'almost impossible to measure' – something making their use as conditions for membership precarious.[54]

Given this indeterminacy, the role of EU institutions, and notably the Commission, for defining the standards, establishing compliance thresholds and assessing individual CCs' performance looms large. The Commission was well aware of the exceptional character of its mission. In Agenda 2000, it described its task not merely as difficult, but as unprecedented. The two main challenges as the Commission saw it were (i) that the broadly defined political criteria went far beyond the *acquis communautaire* and (ii) that the *acquis* had expanded since previous enlargements, including, among others, the area of justice and home affairs (JHA).[55] Both concerns were highly relevant for the rule of law component of political conditionality.

Concerning the first point in particular, at the beginning of the accession process there was little in terms of binding EU *acquis* in the area of the rule of law, as well as concerning administrative and judicial structures. Importantly, given competence limitations stemming from the principle of conferral, the Union had not been in a position to set out general requirements as to the regulation of these domains in the EU Member States.[56] Correspondingly, there were no tools for systematic monitoring and assessment of these fundamental features of Member States' constitutional orders. Hence, the Enlargement process inevitably had to be one of learning by doing, and the resulting methodology was vacillating and eclectic.

Probably the most fundamental challenge to the accession process was that the legal and administrative systems in the CCs were in a process of major rehaul as part of their post-communist transformation. This process ran parallel to EU accession, which made keeping track of relevant legislation and

[54] See Kochenov (n 1) 2.
[55] Agenda 2000 (n 40) 39.
[56] See de Bùrca (n 1); Kochnenov (n 1) 80–81.

practice difficult. The Commission thus found itself in the precarious position of having considerable leverage in shaping rule of law institutions and legislative frameworks in the CCs, while having no firm ground for offering advice and guidance.

The EU institutions approached the challenges in a pragmatic manner. The Commission proceeded to put more flesh on the bones of political conditionality through general policy documents, such as Agenda 2000, composite and strategy papers, as well as country-specific documents such as APs and RRs. The screening and assessment documents were typically structured following the Copenhagen criteria. Interestingly, the rule of law in the CCs was scrutinised not only as (i) a political condition for membership under the first Copenhagen criterion; requirements were also formulated under two additional heads or titles, namely, (ii) the fourth Copenhagen criterion, concerning administrative and judicial capacity, and (iii) as binding *acquis*, principally in the area of JHA. A dividing line between scrutiny under each of these criteria was not always clearly drawn and was, moreover, in flux.[57]

i. The Rule of Law as Part of the Political Conditions for Membership

Concerning the rule of law as a political criterion for membership, Agenda 2000 drew up three thematic fields to be examined under this point:

(a) democracy and the rule of law;
(b) human rights; and
(c) respect for minorities.

Within the rule of law field, on the basis of the RRs, scholars elicit five main areas that were part of the Commission's scrutiny: (i) supremacy of law, (ii) the separation of powers, (iii) judicial independence, (iv) fundamental rights and (v) the fight against corruption. It has been argued that these areas broadly correspond to the rule of law concept as it had evolved in the internal legal order of the Community/Union, probably with the exception of the fight against corruption, which was still a novel domain for the EU.[58] Yet it is also acknowledged that the Commission never ventured to offer an analytical definition of the rule of law. If anything, a definition could be derived from the individual elements and indicators included in the RRs, but there was no attempt to explain how these elements fit together into a coherent concept.[59]

In the individual country Opinions attached to Agenda 2000 and the subsequent RRs, the rule of law was mostly analysed through the main institutions representing the different branches of power, principally the executive and the

[57] See Wennerström (n 1) 179.
[58] ibid 213.
[59] ibid 180. On the EU's reluctance to conceptualise the rule of law, see Nicolaïdis and Kleinfeld (n 53) 16. See also Kochenov (n 1) 110.

judiciary in the respective state. The Opinions contained descriptive details about the organisation of public administration, the laws governing public service and the organisation of the judiciary. Particular attention was paid to the relevant institutional structures, such as constitutional courts, ombudsmen, supreme courts, the hierarchy of the court system, the position of the public prosecution, etc.

ii. The Rule of Law as Part of Administrative and Judicial Capacity

The second basis for the Commission's scrutiny of the rule of law in the CCs was the fourth Copenhagen criterion, putting emphasis on the capacity of administrative and judicial structures to apply the *acquis*. Scrutinising the rule of law under this criterion highlighted its importance not only as a political, but also as a highly pragmatic condition of vital importance for the functioning of all other Union policies, and notably for giving full effect to the Internal Market *acquis*.[60]

Throughout the Enlargement process, the 'capacity' criterion has been used as a basis for demanding substantial reform of the public administration and the judiciary in the CCs, with a view to making them independent, professional, accountable, and up to the task of applying the *acquis* and participating in processes of administrative and judicial cooperation.[61] Since the institutional structure of public administration and the judiciary, as well as enforcement, was at the time of Enlargement largely governed by the principle of national procedural and institutional autonomy, requirements under this point constituted another way of expanding the external mandate of the Commission vis-à-vis the CCs beyond the scope of its internal mandate in respect of the Member States.[62]

iii. From Political Condition to Binding Rule of Law Acquis

Finally, with the advancement of European integration, specific EU rules and standards relating to certain aspects of the rule of law (for instance concerning the judiciary, or the fight against corruption) were gradually enshrined in the Treaties, in the EUCFR or in legislative acts, thus becoming part of the increasing corpus of binding EU *acquis*. For instance, with the Amsterdam Treaty, the Union policy in the area of JHA moved from the third to the first pillar as defined by the Maastricht Treaty, opening for new legislative instruments and

[60] See European Commission, White Paper, COM(95)163 final, section 2.30.

[61] See eg A Dimitrova, 'Europeanisation and Civil Service Reform in Central and Eastern Europe' in F Schimmelfenninng and U Sedelmeier (eds), *The Europeanisation of Central and Eastern Europe* (Ithaca, NY, Cornell University Press, 2005) 84.

[62] See M Avbelj 'National procedural autonomy: concept, practice and theoretical queries' in A Lazowski and S Blockmans (eds), *Research Handbook in EU Institutional Law* (Cheltenham, Edward Elgar, 2016) 421.

requirements, and formally creating the Union's area of freedom, security and justice (AFSJ). Development in this policy area intensified with the Tampere and Haag programmes of 1999 and 2004.[63] This internal development translated almost immediately into changes in EU Enlargement policy, transforming certain issues from political conditions for membership into binding *acquis* forming novel chapters of the negotiation framework (see section IV.B.i).

iv. External Sources for Rule of Law Assessment

Over and beyond the three internal bases for the Commission's rule of law assessment of the CCs, and partly due to the rather limited and vague content of the requirements derived on this ground, the Commission has been working with various external sources of authority. The most natural such sources have emanated from the CoE's work in the field of the rule of law and fundamental rights. Although the CoE is only occasionally mentioned in EU pre-accession documents, at the time the Union embarked on its Eastward Enlargement, the CoE had just finalised, or was in the process of finalising, its own enlargement to the East, involving massive screening of applicant states and assessment of their eligibility for membership based on adherence to democracy, the rule of law and respect for fundamental rights.[64] The CoE could claim expertise and authority in the field, and could in many respects be considered the antechamber to the EU.[65] Importantly, the CoE had been quick to establish the Venice Commission on Democracy Through Law and a plethora of informal expert networks that provided valuable normative input regarding rule of law and fundamental rights standards, also in the course of EU Enlargement (see section IV.B.ii).[66]

Obviously, there were considerable synergies between the CoE and the EU in respect of their policies vis-à-vis the CEEC. The cooperation between the two organisations unfolded initially in a rather informal manner. With the progress of EU Enlargement, a step towards some structuring of the relationship was taken through a Joint Declaration on cooperation in the field of the rule of law, democracy and human rights. On this basis, Joint Programmes were launched, laying the ground for the exchange of legal expertise and information and offering legal advice in drafting law reforms, often in CEE recipient countries.[67]

[63] See HE Hartnell, 'EUstitia: Institutionalizing Justice in the European Union' (2002–2003) 23 *Northwestern Journal of International Law and Business* 65.

[64] On the screening procedure of the Parliamentary Assembly of the Council of Europe, see T Kleinsorge (ed), *Council of Europe* (Alphen aan den Rijn, Kluwer Law International, 2015) 85 et seq.

[65] See the Council of Europe's self-description at www.coe.int/en/web/yerevan/the-coe/about-coe/overview. See also the contribution by Daniel Tarschys in ch 7 of this volume.

[66] On the role of the Venice Commission, see the contribution by Iain Cameron in ch 8 of this volume.

[67] See Joint Declaration Council of Europe and the European Commission, 2001. Cf D Piana, *Judicial Accountabilities in New Europe: From Rule of Law to Quality of Justice* (Farnham, Ashgate, 2010) 62.

D. A Hammer without a Nail?

Summing up, the evolution of the EU's pre-accession rule of law policy suggests that the policy took shape somewhat hesitantly and intuitively, but gradually gained momentum and was equipped with increasingly powerful tools for inducing follow-up and compliance on the part of the CCs. The strong attraction of EU membership in combination with non-trivial financial and technical assistance coupled with short-term and medium-term targets, has given conditionality a powerful leverage in steering law and institution building in the CEEC.

At the same time, the content of the rule of law standard that the Union projected has remained poorly defined, relying on external sources for filling the gaps. Somewhat provocatively, one might say that the EU institutions had a hammer but they did not have a nail, given the fundamental uncertainty about the concrete measures required from the CCs to meet the rule of law condition for EU membership.

IV. A CLOSER LOOK AT THE JUDICIARY AS PART OF RULE OF LAW CONDITIONALITY

The judiciary is one of the three branches of power included in the EU assessment of political conditionality, emphasised in the pre-accession strategy as a central institution for guaranteeing the rule of law in the CCs. The importance of an independent and efficient judiciary for the success of democratic transition in the CEEC and for their membership of the EU had become apparent relatively early on in the Enlargement process.

As in many other respects, the challenge lay in the fact that EU accession ran parallel to a comprehensive transformation seeking to recast the post-communist judiciary in the CEE countries. The legacies from decades of monolithic authoritarian rule, with no conception of separation of powers whatsoever, had left a heavy mark on the judicial systems of these countries. The judiciary was typically perceived as part of the ruling elite, wanting in both competence and integrity,[68] making it ill-fit for the needs of a democratic society with an open market economy. Therefore, in all CCs, thorough institutional reforms of the judicial branch were rolled out after the collapse of the old regime. Importantly, the judiciary had to be placed on a new footing, with constitutional and institutional guarantees of independence and responsibility.

This dynamic made it challenging for the European institutions to actually assess progress. The task of steering judicial reform was further confounded by the fact that formal constitutional assurances often proved rather ephemeral, as courts were drawn into fierce battles for political control and ensuing attempts at tweaking the institutional design of the judiciary to suit the

[68] See Damjanovski et al (n 12) 5.

interests of changing governments. In these highly politicised struggles, European institutions often assumed the role of unwilling arbiters, expected to pronounce a verdict as to the compatibility of intended reforms with European standards.

A. Between Judicial Independence and Judicial Accountability

In terms of substance and guiding principles, initially, strong emphasis was put on judicial independence in the context both of post-communist transformation and of Enlargement.[69] This emphasis is not surprising. It is widely noted in the literature on democratic transition that reforms of the judiciary following periods of authoritarian rule almost exclusively focus on securing judges' independence from political influence in their substantive decisions. Security of tenure and insulation from the executive appear paramount from this perspective.

Yet the process has been convoluted to say the least. The obvious challenge was having to carry through a major rehaul of the judicial system with staff trained and socialised in the profession during the times of authoritarian rule, when direct intervention in the work of the judiciary was commonplace. In well-established democracies, judicial independence builds on hard-won trust in the competence, professional ethic and integrity of judges. It is often undergirded by long legacies of a judiciary that is cognizant of the enormous responsibility falling on its institutional shoulders. In the transition democracies of CEE, such professional ethic and integrity were in scarce supply. Therefore, as the reform process evolved, there was an increasing need to complement the guarantees for judicial independence with mechanisms for ensuring the efficiency and quality of the administration of justice.

B. The Challenge of Eliciting an EU Standard for Judicial Governance

The dilemma for EU institutions was that, in a way similar to that with the general rule of law criterion, there were, prior to the process of Eastward Enlargement, hardly any EU rules on the organisation of the judiciary in the Member States. Although the ECJ had started to develop doctrines of effectiveness and equivalence of national remedies and procedures for ensuring the *effet utile* of EU law, the principle of procedural and institutional autonomy of the Member States was still well acknowledged.[70] Thus, in the course of preparing the CEEC for EU accession, standards had to be formulated without a blueprint. At the same time, this domain was undergoing a dynamic evolution, partly through Treaty changes and partly through new and expanding EU law

[69] Piana (n 67) 54, calls judicial independence 'the most evaluated aspect of judicial systems'.
[70] See Avbelj (n 62).

and policy. Consequently, the area of judicial governance experienced the same, and probably even more visible, fluctuations as other rule of law domains.

i. Internal Bases

Somewhat simplified, one might say that EU institutions derived their mandate to scrutinise the judiciary in the CCs from the same three internal bases as the overall rule of law policy of Enlargement, namely: (i) as part of the political conditions for membership, (ii) as part of administrative and judicial capacity, and (iii) as binding *acquis*.[71]

First, the emphasis when scrutinising the judiciary under the first Copenhagen criterion was placed principally on providing institutional guarantees for judicial independence. Given the centrality of the separation of powers under the rule of law notion, ensuring the insulation of the judiciary from political influence, and mostly from the executive, has been treated as paramount. In the RRs, the Commission proceeded along two main tracks. The first track concerned the legislative foundations of the judiciary, that is, verifying that basic legislation on the organisation of the judiciary and administration of justice was in place. The second track related to the institutional framework for the judiciary, that is, making sure that institutional structures such as supreme courts, constitutional courts or judicial councils were set up and functioning.

Second, the emphasis under the fourth Copenhagen criterion, concerning applicant countries' institutional and administrative capacity, was on the efficiency and competence of the judiciary to apply the *acquis*. The importance of a functioning judiciary for the smooth operation of the Internal Market was underlined in Agenda 2000,[72] and especially in the White Paper of 1995, describing the consolidation of judicial reform as a basis for 'the mutual confidence between all participants on which the internal market depends'.[73] Establishing the link with the Internal Market arguably emboldened the Commission to spell out specific requirements concerning judicial training, the number and staffing of courts, the length and efficiency of judicial proceedings, and the resources devoted to the administration of justice.[74]

Finally, as the Union advanced its policy in the domain of JHA, and later on AFSJ, specific requirements concerning the national judiciary were gradually elaborated as binding *acquis*, albeit with greater autonomy for Member States to choose the mode of implementation. This development prompted adjustments in the accession negotiation framework. Following the Amsterdam

[71] Some authors speak of two bases: the first Copenhagen criterion and the *acquis* criterion. See D Bozhilova, 'Measuring Successes and Failures of Europeanization in the Eastern Enlargement: Judicial Reform in Bulgaria' (2007) 9 *European Journal of Law Reform* 285.

[72] European Commission, Agenda 2000 (n 40) 46.

[73] White Paper COM(95) 163 final, 2.12; Annex, White Paper COM(95) 163 final/2, 2.

[74] See European Commission, Agenda 2000 (n 40) 46.

Treaty, a new Chapter 24 on JHA was introduced, setting out requirements as to the role of the national judiciary in specific policy fields, such as border control, the fight against corruption, fraud and other criminal activity directed at the Internal Market, where the judiciary is treated as a policy actor and participant in European judicial cooperation.[75] Starting from the negotiations with Croatia, further differentiation has taken place, adding a separate chapter (Chapter 23) entitled 'Judiciary and fundamental rights', comprising more general requirements as to judicial independence. This shift indicates that some questions regarding the judiciary are now treated as part of the Union *acquis* under the third Copenhagen criterion, and not only as part of the political conditions for membership.[76]

In sum, an increasing corpus of binding *acquis* has been taking shape as the accession process progressed. Nevertheless, even after Chapter 23 was introduced in the negotiation framework of EU enlargement, there have not been many clear and unambiguous Union rules, or 'hard *acquis*' in respect of Member States' judiciaries.[77]

ii. External Sources

While the EU could offer very few normative inputs, or 'hard *acquis*' in the judicial field, the 1990s and 2000s saw a proliferation of soft-law instruments in this domain, elaborated mostly within the auspices of the CoE.[78] The CoE was ahead of the EU both in terms of time, having started a formal procedure of expansion to the East before the EU, and in terms of competence, having unquestioned authority on issues of the rule of law and fundamental rights, notably through the work of the Venice Commission.

In the area of judicial governance, the CoE has produced a number of authoritative soft-law instruments, most prominently Recommendation No R (94) 12 on the independence, efficiency and the role of judge adopted by the Committee of Ministers of the CoE in 1994,[79] the European Charter on the Statute for Judges, adopted in 1998,[80] and Recommendation 12(2010), replacing

[75] Piana (n 67) 74.

[76] Chapter 23 stresses the paramount importance of an independent and efficient judiciary, and defines judicial independence as a binding EU *acquis* and in more specific terms as including a commitment to eliminating external influences, ensuring adequate resources, providing legal guarantees for fair trial procedures, etc. Chapter 24 is renamed as 'Justice, freedom and security'. See Hillion, 'Enlarging the European Union' (n 1) 4. For a list of the chapters in the current negotiation framework for Enlargement, see https://ec.europa.eu/neighbourhood-enlargement/policy/conditions-membership/chapters-of-the-acquis_en.

[77] According to Nozar, 'Due to the limited amount of "hard acquis" in many of these areas, the requirements to be met are mainly to be found in general principles and European standards. This sometimes makes it difficult to determine exactly what the target to be reached is and how to measure progress.' W Nozar, 'The 100% Union: The Rise of Chapters 23 and 24' (2012) *Clingendael Paper*, available at www.clingendael.org/publication/100-union-rise-chapters-23-and-24, 2.

[78] Piana (n 67) 70.

[79] Recommendation No R (94) 12 on the independence, efficiency and the role of judge.

[80] European Charter on the Statute for Judges, July 1999, available at https://rm.coe.int/16807473ef.

and enhancing Recommendation R(94) 12.[81] While the Recommendations are formally adopted by the Committee of Ministers, they result from the work of several European judicial networks and associations either composed exclusively of judges, or in which judges have a decisive influence.

Indeed, the 1990s saw the rise of judicial networks under the auspices of the CoE, and later on the EU. A particularly influential network has been the Consultative Council of European Judges (CCJE), founded in 2000 and composed of judges from all (now 47) member states of the CoE, coming chiefly from the higher ranks of the judiciary in these states. The Charter is likewise an emanation from many years of work on the organisation of justice carried out in the CoE. With the advancement of Enlargement and of EU policy in the area of JHA, the EU has promoted its own web of judicial networks, such as the European Network of Judicial Councils (ENJC), which started in 2002,[82] and the Network of the Presidents of the Supreme Courts of the EU.[83] These networks have been instrumental in reforming the judiciaries of the CEEC. As we shall see, they have also been essential for EU pre-accession policy in respect of judicial governance.

C. Two Ways of Compensating for Uncertain Rules and Standards

The scarcity of common rules and binding EU standards as to judicial governance made eliciting clear benchmarks and formulating recommendations in this domain a precarious task. The Commission employed two main strategies for compensating for this deficiency: (i) to project, or emulate, a common European standard for the judiciary based mainly on external sources, an approach that may be described as vertical or 'top-down'; (ii) to engage the judiciary in the CEEC in various programmes and networks, working as platforms for socialisation, where standards and best practices were diffused through professional exchange, an approach that may be described as horizontal or 'bottom-up'.

i. Projecting Common European Standards for the CEEC

Within the first strategy, concerning in particular the institutional guarantees for judicial independence, the Commission gradually elicited a model of judicial governance, an alleged European standard, which served as a basis for its assessments and recommendations. Scholars who have studied closely EU influence on judicial governance in the CEEC identify two institutional components of this model: (i) a strong Judicial Council (JC) as the main institution for

[81] Recommendation CM/Rec(2010)12, Judges: Independence, efficiency and responsibility, and Explanatory Memorandum, available at https://rm.coe.int/16807096c1.
[82] Information on the network is available at https://www.encj.eu/; cf Piana (n 67) 170.
[83] Information on the network is available at https://network-presidents.eu/.

self-governance of the judiciary; and (ii) a centralised and specialised body or institute for the training of the judiciary.[84]

Concerning the first institutional component, the JC model promoted by the Commission comprises the following non-exhaustive list of features:

1. The JC as the main organ of judicial self-governance enjoying constitutional status.
2. The JC should be composed predominantly (more than 50 per cent) of judges nominated and elected by their peers.
3. The JC should have representative and administrative functions, and control all mechanisms for the recruitment, promotion and evaluation of judges.
4. The JC should be in charge of the budget for the judiciary.
5. The JC should be chaired by the President of the Supreme Courts or an independent Head of State.[85]

To be sure, this model was not announced openly and explicitly, but rather transpires when putting together the many bits and pieces of criticism, praise and recommendations of specific solutions in the CCs, scattered across various documents produced in the course of accession.[86] For instance, where a JC reform had not yet been undertaken, the RRs would recommend such a reform, or would praise the creation of a JC as the optimal institutional solution for guaranteeing judicial independence. In a similar vein, a high degree of judicial autonomy and self-governance received consistently positive Commission evaluations. Piana therefore speaks of an implicit view of judicial independence.[87]

The problem with promoting the JC model is that in actual fact it is far from being the only, and at the beginning of the accession process was not even the dominant, approach to judicial governance in Europe. Quite to the contrary: according to Piana, the coexisting models of judicial governance in Europe revealed a 'spectacular variety of institutional solutions'.[88] In an ambitious study on judicial self-governance, Kosar identifies as many as five models of court administration in Europe: (i) the 'Ministry of Justice' model, represented by Austria, the Czech Republic, Finland and Germany; (ii) the JC model,

[84] See Piana (n 67) 75, Table 2.10; M Bobek and D Kosar, 'Global solutions, local damages: A critical study in Judicial Councils in Central and Eastern Europe' (2014) 15 *German Law Journal* 1257–92, 1263.

[85] See Piana (n 67) 75; Bobek and Kosar (n 84) 1263; D Kosar, *Perils of Judicial Self-Governance in Transitional Societies* (Cambridge, Cambridge University Press, 2018) 128 et seq. The last feature is not mentioned explicitly by Piana.

[86] Bobek and Kosar (n 84) 1262; Kosar (n 85) 126.

[87] See Piana (n 67) 77; cf. Kosar (n 85) 126 et seq. The model is apparently actively promoted by the Commission in accession negotiations with the countries from the Western Balkans, especially after the introduction of Chapter 23; see Damjanovski et al (n 12) 6–7.

[88] D Piana, 'Beyond Judicial Independence: Rule of Law and Judicial Accountability in Assessing Democratic Quality' (2009) 9 *Comparative Sociology* 40.

nowadays followed by a majority of EU countries;[89] (iii) the courts service model, followed by the Nordic countries except Finland; (iv) hybrid models, including a mix of countries with idiosyncratic approaches; and, historically, (v) the socialist model.[90] Although the socialist model no longer exists in Europe, Kosar insists that discussing it is important, since its legacies of strict hierarchy and the excessive power of higher courts' presidents can still be traced in the organisation of the judiciary in CEE.[91]

Thus, as critically analysed in the literature on judicial governance, the JC model was not anchored in common or converging European legal traditions and solutions. Instead, the model was apparently influenced by the constantly increasing body of soft law produced within the auspices of the CoE and with the active involvement of the professional networks previously mentioned. Already the first Recommendation R (94)12 stressed the need for a special authority that is independent from the government and the administration, and which takes decisions on the selection and career of judges. It highlighted the importance of ensuring that the members of the authority are selected by the judiciary.[92] The follow-up Recommendation 12(2010) also builds on self-governance as the preferred way for organising the judiciary. This is also the vision advanced in the European Charter on the Statute for Judges.[93] The model has been further advocated in special reports and opinions of some of the CoE and EU judicial networks.[94]

The active promotion of the JC model in the EU's pre-accession strategy can probably at least partly be explained by the fact that it developed originally as a reaction to authoritarian regimes in Southern Europe, and Italy in particular, in an effort to provide safeguards against abuse of political power. Therefore, the model can be perceived as fitting the particular needs of the transition societies of CEE. Yet, as critically noted by Bobek and Kosar, this choice can at least partly also be explained by certain biases in the way in which the standard was elicited and diffused.[95] I will return to this issue in section V.A.ii.

[89] In his study from 2018, Kosar finds that the model exists with variations in Belgium, Bulgaria, France, Hungary (until Orbán's 2011 judicial reform), Italy, Lithuania, the Netherlands, Poland, Portugal, Romania, Slovakia, Slovenia and Spain. Kosar (n 85) 132.

[90] ibid 131–33.

[91] According to Kosar, the model is characterised by the dominance of three institutions: 'the Chief Prosecutor, the Supreme Court, and court presidents – which are then themselves controlled by the Communist Party'. See ibid 133.

[92] See Principle I Independence of the judiciary, sec 2, lit c, Recommendation No R (94)12 of the Committee of Ministers to Member States on the Independence, Efficiency and Role of Judges.

[93] See European Charter on the Statute for Judges (1998), paras 1.2, 1.3, 3.1, 4.1, 7.2. Piana (n 67) 75–76; Bobek and Kosar (n 84) 1263.

[94] See CCJE, Opinion no 10 (2007) to the attention of the Committee of Ministers of the Council of Europe on the Council for the Judiciary at the service of society (Strasbourg, 21–23 November 2007); European Network of Councils for the Judiciary, Councils for the Judiciary Report 2010–2011.

[95] Bobek and Kosar (n 84) 1270.

ii. Enhancing Judicial Accountability and Efficiency

Whereas the JC model was advocated as the European 'golden standard' for institutionally guaranteeing judicial independence, with time, the focus of the Commission was increasingly redirected to strengthening judicial accountability and efficiency in the CEEC. This shift of attention had been prompted by mounting evidence of poor performance of the judiciary in CEE, not only in terms of the excessive time it took for cases to be decided, but also in terms of the poor quality of administration of justice, widespread corruption and low public confidence. Much of the pre-accession activity in this domain took place under the fourth Copenhagen criterion on strengthening administrative and judicial capacity. The attention here has been not on the macro level but on the micro and meso levels, or on what Piana denotes as 'managerial accountability', requiring courts to comply with benchmarks for efficiency and effectiveness borrowed from other professions, such as public administration.[96]

The modes for communicating EU requirements have also been different, with a predominance of bottom-up or socialisation approaches.[97] One surreptitious avenue for influence has been the systematic monitoring and performance evaluation of the judicial systems in the CCs, which included massive data gathering, processing and reporting, on the basis of which benchmarks were elaborated and progress measured. Furthermore, much emphasis was placed on the financing of twinning projects promoting the transfer of know-how and expertise coming from the old Member States, for instance on the development of court management tools. In addition, judicial training has played a key role in the promotion of European standards for the judiciary.[98] Finally, judges from the CEEC were readily included in the judicial networks listed in section IV.B.ii, apparently with the aim of using these networks as platforms for promoting standards and best practices concerning the quality of justice. According to Piana, within these networks, judges 'developed stronger routines of interaction', with an expectation of reinforcing mutual trust among network members.[99]

V. A CRITICAL ASSESSMENT OF RULE OF LAW CONDITIONALITY

The pre-accession strategy outlined in the preceding two sections and its enforcement in the area of the rule of law and judicial governance in the CCs have been the subject of intense debate in legal and political science scholarship, provoking

[96] Piana (n 67) 5.

[97] See ibid 162. On social learning, see J Checkel, 'Why Comply? Social Learning and European Identity Change' (2001) 55 *International Organisation* 553.

[98] It has been described as a 'key leverage in the construction of the European legal space'. See Piana (n 67) 37.

[99] ibid 37.

both praise and criticism. In the limited space of this contribution, I can only touch upon some of the key points of controversy in this debate.[100]

A. Grey Zones and Legitimacy Deficits

A recurrent line of criticism levelled at EU institutions in their rule of law policy vis-à-vis the CCs has concerned the uncertain standards on which the requirements are built and the ensuing question about the legitimacy of EU Enlargement policy in this domain. Political scientists working in the area of Europeanisation measure legitimacy by the quality of EU rules, the quality of the rule-making process and the quality of the rule transfer.[101] Arguably, Enlargement rule of law policy, as a form of Europeanisation, exhibits problems on all three counts.

i. Unclear Rules and Double Standards

The lack of clarity over EU rule of law standards is an important factor negatively influencing the quality of the rules. As already discussed in section II, at the time when the pre-accession process was launched, the rule of law had not been elaborated in much detail in the Treaties, nor in secondary legislation.[102] Uncertainty was further added by the dynamics of constitutional developments in the EU, moving some of the relevant issues of the rule of law from the domain of political conditionality to the more specific chapters of binding *acquis*. Despite the many policy documents, EU institutions showed a reluctance to conceptualise the rule of law. The Commission never offered 'a general and authoritative conceptual document on the EU rule of law', opting for a 'description-based' rather than 'analytically-based' approach.[103] Even scholars who are generally positive of the Commission's work in the area, agree that the individual country evaluations had a relatively 'diverse and superficial nature'.[104]

This uncertainty is by many perceived as undercutting the overall success of EU rule of law policy in the CEEC. For one thing, it has inevitably given rise to information costs, since the CCs could not know what exactly was expected of them and what measures were required to satisfy the standard.[105] To put it in the provocative words of Kochenov, 'the candidate states were told to comply,

[100] To frame the discussion, in section V.A and section VII I use the title of my contribution from 2006, which analysed a similar dynamic in other areas of pre-accession policy, A Bakardjieva Engelbrekt, 'Grey Zones, Legitimacy Deficits and Boomerang Effects: On the Implications of Extending the Acquis to the Countries of CEE' in N Wahl and P Cramér (eds), *Swedish Studies in European Law*, vol. 1 (Oxford, Hart Publishing, 2006) 1.

[101] J Checkel, 'Sanctions, Social Learning and Institutions' (1999) 11 *Arena Working Papers*.

[102] See Kochenov (n 1) 109; Hillion, 'Enlarging the European Union' (n 1) 4.

[103] See Nicolaïdis and Kleinfeld (n 53) 16. In a similar sense, Kochenov (n 1) 110.

[104] Pech and Grogan, 'Meaning and Scope' (n 5) 11.

[105] See Sadurski, 'EU Enlargement and Democracy in New Member States' (n 1) 31; cf Nozar (n 77) 2.

but not told with what'.[106] As a result, the standards have been difficult to explain to local stakeholders and have formed an unstable ground for inducing compliance.

An even more important aspect of the quality of the rules, from the perspective of legitimacy, is the extent to which the rules are also binding internally for the EU Member States.[107] In areas where the EU has strong competences and European institutions have accumulated considerable practice, for instance in the area of competition law, the requirements spelled out in the accession process have enjoyed high authority and legitimacy.[108] In the field of the rule of law, the Union lacked corresponding authority and legitimacy. The Commission itself admitted that in many respects the screening of the CCs for rule of law and democracy compliance went far beyond any *acquis communautaire*, and hence beyond the requirements that could be directed internally to the Member States.[109]

A particularly conspicuous example of the gap between external and internal standards was the early requirement of respect for minority rights under the Copenhagen political criteria. At the time when the criteria were spelled out, none of the EU Member States were subject to a similar requirement.[110] But also in the area of the rule of law, the perception of double standards has plagued the Enlargement process on a number of issues. As the example of judicial governance shows, CCs were required to undertake changes in the organisation of their judicial systems while such requirements applied to EU Member States would have been impossible.[111] Hillion critically contends that the criteria applied to the CCs in the Enlargement process offer a distorted reflection of the EU's constitutional identity (*miroir déformant*).[112]

ii. Modes of Transfer

Turning to the quality of rule transfer, as illustrated by the case of judicial governance, one way used by the Commission to compensate for the lack of binding *acquis* in the field of rule of law policy, was to project an image of an alleged common European standard that the CCs were urged to adopt or

[106] Kochenov (n 1) 315.

[107] Or as succinctly formulated by Sadurski, the legitimacy and effectiveness of the standards are influenced by 'the seriousness and determination with which the EU has held its own member states to those standards', Sadurski, 'Accession Democracy Dividend' (n 1) 378.

[108] See Bakardjieva Engelbrekt (n 100).

[109] Agenda 2000 (n 40) vol 1, 42.

[110] C Hillion, 'Enlargement of the European Union – The Discrepancy between Membership Obligations and Accession Conditions as Regards the Protection of Minorities' (2004) 27 *Fordham International Law Journal* 715–40, 716. Sadurski, 'EU Enlargement and Democracy in New Member States' (n 1) 31.

[111] On double standards in the domain of human rights, see Williams (n 34), calling EU human rights policy in the process of Enlargement 'a policy of distinction'. In a similar sense, P Maier, 'Popular Democracy and EU Enlargement' (2003) 17 *East European Politics and Societies* 58, 63.

[112] Hillion, 'Enlarging the European Union (n 1) 1; see also Nicolaïdis and Kleinfeld (n 53) 52.

approximate. In a study on the impact of Enlargement on judicial governance, Smilov conceives of such common standards as 'myths', with the Commission emulating unity where there is none.[113]

In an insightful analysis of the spread of the JC model, Bobek and Kosar are highly critical of this approach, partly because of the procedure for eliciting the European standard. They point in particular to the lack of transparency as to patterns of participation and representation in the consultative networks and bodies engaged in setting the JC standard that was subsequently imposed with considerable rigour upon the CCs. In their view, the standards elaborated within these networks reflect to a great extent the preferences of the judicial profession, and even more narrowly of the higher tiers of the judiciary, often court presidents, who typically represent the profession in the networks. A bias in favour of the JC model arguably also resulted from the strong activism of Italy and Spain, as main proponents of the model, within both judicial networks and twinning projects with CEEC. Furthermore, once the model was adopted by some of the CEEC, a self-generating logic was set in motion, whereby the model could be advanced as predominant in Europe. The influence was further institutionalised with the setting up of a network of judicial councils.[114]

Certainly, the Commission was also advancing the JC model with the conviction of the model's superiority, especially for guarding the CEE judiciary from the legacies of the socialist past. The approach thus, at least partly, represents what Smilov dubs 'normative harmonization'. Under the notion of a common standard, the Commission promotes a desired normative model or solution.[115] However, and importantly for the quality of rule transfer, by insisting on one particular model of judicial governance without support in binding *acquis* or in a common European tradition, the Commission is narrowing the range of alternative institutional models for the CCs. The more serious danger of an approach building on 'myths' lies, according to Smilov, in the fact that such myths are inevitably unstable and provide shaky ground for building long-term relationships of trust. Once the lack of binding rules is discovered, the myth as a basis for mutual obligations collapses, and there is a risk of backlash and even regression into Euro-scepticism and nationalism.[116] This prediction is to a certain extent confirmed in the current open 'double standards' rhetoric of illiberal governments and their intellectual supporters.[117]

[113] D Smilov, 'Enlargement and EU Constitutionalism in the Balkan Periphery' in W Sadurski, J Ziller and K Zurek (eds), *Après Enlargement: Legal and Political Responses in Central and Eastern Europe* (Florence, Robert Schuman Centre, 2006) 161; D Smilov, 'EU Enlargement and the Constitutional Principle of Judicial Independence' in Sadurski, Czarnota and Kryiger (eds) (n 1) 313.

[114] Bobek and Kosar (n 84) 1270 et seq.

[115] Smilov, 'Enlargement and EU Constitutionalism' (n 113) 176 et seq.

[116] ibid. In a similar sense, Sadurski, 'EU Enlargement and Democracy in New Member States' (n 1) 33 with reference to formulas such as 'EU model' and 'part of common constitutional traditions'.

[117] On this rhetoric, see Pech and Grogan, 'Unity and Diversity' (n 5) 68 et seq.

iii. Lack of Consistency

Still concerning the quality of rule transfer, another line of criticism, partly related to the previous one, is the lack of consistency in the Commission's evaluations: between individual CCs, across policies and over time. Here only the first point will be addressed.[118]

One of the distinctive features of the Eastward Enlargement has been the high number of states with similar historical legacies that applied for membership at approximately the same time. As a consequence, applications had to be reviewed, and accession negotiations carried out, simultaneously. This parallel treatment brought a great deal of political prestige in the project and has in the literature been aptly dubbed a 'regatta' approach.[119] The EU institutions were well aware of this politically sensitive aspect of the Eastward Enlargement. In the individual Opinions attached to Agenda 2000, the Commission was adamant that while the analysis of each application was made on its merits, all applications were judged according to the same criteria.[120]

Yet despite this assurance of equal treatment, evidence from systematic review of individual country opinions and RRs suggests otherwise. While the areas of rule of law assessment were broadly the same, the specific components addressed under each area differed considerably between countries. Scholars note with amazement the inclusion of certain elements and requirements in some country reports and their absence in others – without, moreover, providing any justifications for the different treatment.[121]

Divergence is noted also in the rigour with which the Commission carries out its scrutiny of candidate states' compliance with prescriptions and recommendations. Whereas some applicants were held strictly to account on all points of rule of law conditionality, others could gloss over individual criteria with little or no assurances of conditions being actually met. Furthermore, measures that in some country reports were assessed as steps in the right direction, were in other country reports criticised or not mentioned at all.

The unequal treatment is well illustrated by the Commission's approach to the question of judicial governance. While the Commission has promoted the model of JC as the best guarantee of judicial independence in respect of most CCs, it has not been entirely consistent in its approach. Thus, it has been widely observed that the introduction of a JC was spelled out as an almost non-waivable condition for EU membership vis-à-vis Slovakia.[122] Judicial independence was identified as a serious problem in this country at an early stage. As pre-accession

[118] As to inconsistencies across policy documents, see Wennerström (n 1) 213; Kochenov (n 1) 30–31.

[119] On the 'regatta approach', see Engelbrekt (n 38).

[120] A common text was used in this sense in all country Opinions. See eg Commission Opinion on Bulgaria's Application for Membership of the EU, COM(97)2008 final, 2.

[121] See Nicolaïdis and Kleinfeld (n 53). In a similar sense, Janse (n 30) 54–55.

[122] See European Commission, Regular Report Slovakia, COM(1999) 511 final, 14.

conditionality tightened up, the Commission became increasingly assertive in advancing the JC model as a guarantee of judicial independence until a JC was ultimately introduced in 2001.[123] Similar pressure for setting up a JC was exerted towards Latvia, Estonia and Romania. In the case of Bulgaria, where a JC had been set up prior to the start of accession negotiations, the pressure was rather towards bringing the design of the JC, and its composition and functions, closer to the Euro-model previously outlined.[124]

Yet the attitude was markedly different in respect of the Czech Republic. This country opted to preserve its institutional framework for judicial governance with important functions for the Ministry of Justice and did not institute a JC. Surprisingly, this choice did not prompt objections on the part of the Commission. In the RRs it is only noted that while formally judges and prosecutors could be recalled by the Minister of Justice, this had not happened in practice.[125]

This divergence in approach is problematic on many counts.[126] First, it raises serious doubts as to the objectivity in the Commission's assessment and the credibility of the Commission's self-declared ambition to treat all applicant countries equally. Certainly, one could argue that a JC may be a desirable solution in one institutional and political context and not in another. However, in the case of the Czech Republic and Slovakia, there was much that spoke for identical treatment, given their common legal and institutional legacies. Moreover, the Commission did not provide any justifications for the difference in approach. Thus, the impression is formed that the countries had different leverage in the accession negotiations, and probably different self-confidence in their overall record as CCs, something giving the respective governments a different degree of audacity to defend national preferences and positions.[127]

Second, the ease with which the Commission was able to drop certain requirements in respect of some countries does not strengthen the credibility and authority of these requirements, and goes against the very claim of a common European standard.

Third, just as in the case of double standards, lack of consistency may lead to disillusionment among enlargement supporters and strengthen the positions

[123] In the RR of 2000, the Commission notes with dissatisfaction that a reform expected to shift the competence for judicial appointments to the JC has not yet been adopted. Regular Report Slovakia SEC(2001) 1754, 17. In the RR of 2000, the Commission expresses its approval of the legislative amendments setting up a JC, with broad administrative functions and competences regarding judicial appointments. At the same time, the pressure for further reforms in this direction is stepped up. See European Commission, Regular Report Slovakia (2000), 16.

[124] Particular problems have related to treating the investigation service as part of the judiciary, and thus being represented in the Supreme Judicial Council. The parliamentary quota is also seen as a concern. See Piana (n 67) 135; cf Bozhilova (n 71) 292.

[125] See European Commission, RR Czech Republic (1999), 13.

[126] For a critique of this differential approach, see Bobek and Kosar (n 84); Piana (n 67), Damjanovski et al (n 12).

[127] For similar dynamic in other policy areas, see Bakardjieva Engelbrekt (n 100) 30.

of anti-European and nationalist forces. Bozhilova considers the most dramatic flaw of this approach to be that it gives national 'veto players' leeway to contest the desired reforms by accusing the EU 'of subjectivity and favouritism, and an *a la carte* approach to accession'.[128]

iv. In Defence of the Commission

The criticism of the vague and inconsistent standards on which rule of law conditionality built is widely shared in Enlargement scholarship, but it has not remained uncontested. On the basis of a comprehensive review of Commission pre-accession documents, Janse has more recently argued that despite the many flaws in its work, the Commission has been consistent in articulating 'a clear vision on the core meaning of the political accession criteria'.[129] The documents produced by the Commission refer in his view to a set of elements that are adequately selected and indeed essential for securing democracy and the rule of law. Therefore, Janse contends that the Commission's work deserves more positive overall evaluation, with the important implication that it can also be entrusted with the task of monitoring rule of law compliance in the Member States beyond Enlargement. Janse's view is largely shared by Pech and Grogan, who, while admitting the many deficiencies in the Commission's approach, consider that the EU is not 'exporting' a vague or incoherent ideal' but instead seeks compliance with a set of specific sub-components of the rule of law.[130]

The work of Janse, and of Pech and Grogan, adds an important nuance to the debate on rule of law conditionality and the role of EU institutions. Given the unprecedented task the Commission was faced with, and the condensed timeframe it had to develop and apply its pre-accession strategy, it would indeed be unrealistic to measure the success of the approach against too rigid standards. It is also true that once we put together the different jigsaw pieces from all Commission pre-accession documents, a more coherent conception of democracy and the rule of law would emerge than what might appear at first sight. Yet the lack of coherence in the Commission's vision of democracy and the rule of law has been only one line of criticism in the academic literature. The more serious point has concerned the discrepancy between internal and external standards. Whether the rule of law conception advanced by the Commission is internally consistent has only limited bearing on the 'double-standards' critique.

[128] Bozhilova (n 71) 290; see also Smilov, 'EU Enlargement and Judicial Independence' (n 113).
[129] Janse (n 30) 46. The analysis builds on a review of general policy documents such as Agenda 2000, as well as country-specific documents such as RRs.
[130] Pech and Grogan, 'Meaning and Scope' (n 5) 11.

B. Focus on Formal Laws and Institutions

When explaining its methodology, the Commission, as already shown, has been adamant that it was basing its assessment not on formal compliance but on the actual operation of laws and institutions. Yet in an extensive analysis of rule of law conditionality in the process of Eastward Enlargement, Nicolaïdes and Kleinfeld have criticised the Commission's approach as being precisely formalistic. In their view, the Commission was paying disproportionate attention to formal legal and institutional indicators, while turning a blind eye to 'law in action' and deeper layers of legal and political culture.[131]

The focus on formal laws and discrete institutions is to a certain extent inevitable. It is partly predetermined by the compressed time-schedule of Enlargement and the enormous strain on scarce resources it exerted on both sides of the Union threshold. Another reason for this emphasis on institutional structures is what I have in a previous contribution called 'the joint interest of the "rational accession seeker" and the "rational accession-provider"'.[132] Whereas politicians and public officials of the CCs seek rapid accession and want to demonstrate visible progress, politicians and officials of EU institutions (notably the Commission) require palpable results that are easy to identify, measure and monitor. Seen in this light, the preference for discrete interventions in the form of enacting specific legislation and setting up institutions corresponding neatly to EU policy compartments and requirements is well understood. For the CCs, on the other hand, formal laws and institutions are attractive because they can point to their existence in progress reports and when criticised for insufficient administrative capacity.

This pre-accession dynamic and the strong legal-institutional focus have been identified systematically in analyses of Enlargement-induced reform of judicial governance.[133] The model promoted by the Commission has revolved around two institutions – the JC and the centralised body for judicial training. Over and beyond these two bodies, it was not unusual for CCs to point to ad hoc institutional solutions, in an apparent attempt to demonstrate progress. For instance, various special anti-corruption bodies, inspectorates and commissions were being invoked as evidence of the priority given to the fight against corruption. In addition, formal legislation, such as Acts on the Judiciary, but also policy documents such as Strategy on the Reform of the Judiciary, or National Anti-Corruption Strategy, typically receive the Commission's approval.[134]

[131] Nicolaïdis and Kleinfeld (n 53) 16; of a different opinion, Janse (n 57).

[132] A Bakardjieva Engelbrekt, 'An End to Fragmentation? The Unfair Commercial Practices Directive from the Perspective of the New Member States of CEE' in S Weatherill and U Bernitz (eds), *The Regulation of Unfair Commercial Practices under EC Directive 2005/29: New Rules and New Techniques* (Oxford, Hart Publishing, 2007) 47, 81 et seq.

[133] See Bobek and Kosar (n 84); Piana (n 67); Damjanovski et al (n 12) 5. For other areas of pre-accession policy, see Bakardjieva Engelbrekt (n 100).

[134] See Regular Report Bulgaria, 2003, 19–20;

An unfortunate consequence of such an approach is what Nicolaïdes and Kleinfeld call 'legal-institutional mimetism'. There is a proliferation of laws and institutions that are supposed to implement EU legislation, or legislation required by the EU, but which do not bring actual change in underlying social relations and practices. Moreover, such laws are often changed and institutions frequently refurbished. Paradoxically, a situation is created where pre-accession policy as applied by the Commission contributes to eroding legal certainty, the latter being a key goal of rule of law reform.[135]

C. Implications for Democracy in the Candidate Countries

The legitimacy of Enlargement cum Europeanisation can also be measured by its impact on the quality of the rule-making process in the applicant countries. In this regard, many critical analyses note the impoverishing effects 'external governance' has occasionally exerted on the legislative process, and ultimately on democracy and democratic institutions in the CCs. Such effects have been observed on several levels.

For one, the unquestionable priority of EU accession on the political agenda in the CEEC in combination with the detailed steering of rule of law reform through specific short-term and intermediate targets and strict monitoring, has implied excessive pressure on the legislative process in these countries. Comparative research on Enlargement's effects in CCs provides evidence of a legislative process plagued by fast-track procedures, lack of information and insight, and poor, if any, consultation with affected stakeholders and civil society, where the role of parliament is reduced to rubber-stamping.[136]

A related effect of the pre-accession strategy is the priority given to government and state actors, who are chief interlocutors in accession negotiations and typically have the mandate of communicating EU requirements to domestic stakeholders and institutions. Intergovernmental negotiations are as a rule based on 'informal contacts between negotiators on both sides, not easily subject to formal control'.[137] This limited insight exacerbates the power of government and public agencies at the expense of democratically elected parliaments, as well as of civil society participation. Thus, another paradox of accession conditionality is revealed: by giving priority to efficiency over legitimacy, the EU undermines its own efforts to promote democratic development in the CCs.[138]

Finally, as observed by Nicolaïdes and Kleinfeld, a more subtle distorting effect for democratic law making comes with long-term prioritisation of

[135] Nicolaïdis and Kleinfeld (n 53) 19.

[136] H Grabbe, 'How does Europeanisation affect CEE governance? Conditionality, diffusion and diversity' (2001) 8 *Journal of European Public Policy* 1013, 1016.

[137] Sadurski, 'EU Enlargement and Democracy in New Member States' (n 1) 383.

[138] Grabbe (n 136). For arguments in the same vein, see Maier (n 111) 63; Nicolaïdes and Kleinfeld (n 53) 26.

implementing EU *acquis* and requirements over systemic domestic demands. Such law making steered by external governance may to some extent deprive the polities in the candidate states from the feeling of ownership over important democratic and rule of law transformation in their societies. Sajó warns, somewhat prophetically, that democratic reforms carried out with 'an apparent lack of constitutional commitment and passion among the citizenry might become a problem in the event that a tyrannical or corrupt elite should ever attempt to govern'.[139]

D. Contested Outcomes

Probably the most important parameter when evaluating the EU's pre-accession policy is the long-term impact of this policy on the rule of law in the CCs. Have the required changes in legal rules and institutional structures been applied by the intended beneficiaries of the respective policies? Have these changes brought about a higher level of respect for the rule of law in those states? Obviously, this contribution cannot provide comprehensive answers to these questions. Instead, I will offer a glimpse of the aftermath of judicial reform in some of the new Member States, trying through selected examples to illustrate the limits and opportunities of EU-induced legal and institutional change.[140]

i. Judicial Independence through the European JC Model?

As demonstrated in section IV.C.i, the JC model has been vigorously promoted in the course of Enlargement as the best institutional solution for guaranteeing judicial independence in the applicant countries. A pertinent question in this regard is to what extent the institutional reforms undertaken in the context of accession have indeed improved the independence of the judiciary and the quality of justice. The question has received extensive treatment in the legal and political science literature on Enlargement, on which I build in the following review.

a. Judicial Reform in Slovakia

The first example is the reform of judicial organisation in Slovakia, where the Government, very much upon the insistence of the Commission, introduced a version of the JC model in 2001. The reform was carried through after repeated criticism in the Commission's RRs on Slovakia. However, as demonstrated through careful empirical evidence by Kosar in his comparative study on judicial

[139] A Sajó, 'Constitution without the constitutional moment: A view from the new member states' (2005) 3 *International Journal of Constitutional Law* 243, 249.
[140] The examples are deliberately chosen so as not to include the cases of Poland and Hungary, which are extensively discussed in other chapters of this volume.

governance in Slovakia and the Czech Republic, very simplified, the JC has not had the desired positive effect.[141] This disappointing result is, according to Kosar, to be explained chiefly by the fact that at the root of the problem of poor judicial governance in Slovakia, as in other CEEC with post-communist legacies, was the excessive power enjoyed by presidents of higher courts. This power was not curbed but rather enhanced by the institutional arrangement with a JC. Conversely, in the Czech Republic, where the Ministry of Justice retained considerable competences in the sphere of judicial governance, the power of High Court presidents was effectively constrained, and a better functioning system of judicial accountability was arguably put into effect.[142]

Kosar's study is of particular interest, since the comparison between Slovakia and the Czech Republic could be conducted almost as a natural experiment, with two polities having the same starting positions and institutional legacies but choosing different institutional solutions for judicial governance. The analysis shows convincingly that the JC model does not in itself constitute a guarantee of a higher level of independence or accountability in any judicial system. More mundane aspects of organisation of the judiciary, such as the position of the presidents of high courts, methods for court management and assignment of cases between judges, material conditions and division of labour, often prove to be of greater importance for the quality of administration of justice. Importantly for the purposes of this analysis, the study demonstrates the weakness of an accession policy that emphasises formal legal and institutional solutions without deeper insight into the institutional context and the actors involved.

b. Judicial Reform in Bulgaria

Another, even more traumatic example is the saga of judicial reform, or rather the failure of introducing such reform, in Bulgaria. The country has been plagued by poor governance at all levels of public institutions ever since the beginning of the post-communist transition, but the malaise has been particularly severe in the court system. From the very first Commission Opinion of 1997 through all the subsequent RRs in the pre-accession process and the post-accession Coordination and Verification Mechanism (CVM),[143] and up to the present day, the state of the country's judiciary has been a soaring problem. A Supreme Judicial Council (SJC) was introduced as the main institution for governing the judiciary even before the launch of the accession process.[144] Consequently, the

[141] Kosar (n 85).

[142] Kosar's analysis is of course much more sophisticated and is here presented in a simplified manner.

[143] On the CVM, see Commission Decision 2006/928/EC on CVM for Romania and Commission Decision 2006/929 on CVM for Bulgaria. See Hillion, 'Enlarging the European Union' (n 1) 10.

[144] The first Act on the Supreme Judicial Council dates from 1992.

bone of contention has not been the setting up of such a body, but rather the design, functions, and mostly the composition and the procedure for nomination and selection of the Council members.

Initially, a majority of the SJC members were nominated by Parliament, based on the structure of political representation in the legislative body. Following repeated recommendations from the European Commission, the model of nominations was amended, giving predominance to judges and prosecutors nominated and elected by their peers. The Chief Prosecutor and the Presidents of the Supreme Administrative Court and the Supreme Court of Cassation are members of the SJC *ex officio*, and the President of the Supreme Court of Cassation is Chair of the SJC. Nevertheless, in a way similar to that in Slovakia, these reforms have not produced convincing evidence of improved judicial governance. Both Kosar and Piana find patterns in Bulgaria of excessive power of High Court Presidents and of the Chief Prosecutor comparable to those in Slovakia, and poor guarantees of the independence of individual judges.[145] According to reports by the Commission and the Venice Commission, the performance of the Bulgarian judiciary remains sub-standard. The confidence of Bulgarian society towards the judiciary is still strikingly low, and has even been deteriorating.[146]

c. Judicial Independence as a Double-edged Sword

These examples seem to suggest that changes in formal laws and in the institutional design of the judiciary in the direction of the promoted European institutional model, often under the direct or indirect pressure of conditionality and under the close watch of the Commission, have only rarely translated into the intended long-lasting and sustainable improvement of judicial governance. They may have even caused 'unintended' negative effects. For instance, it is pointed out that the emphasis on judicial autonomy, or self-governance, does not necessarily strengthen judicial integrity and independence. According to Maria Popova, who has studied closely the protracted and largely unsuccessful judicial reform in Bulgaria, the high guarantees of the irremovability of magistrates, in combination with the lack of adequate mechanisms for judicial accountability,

[145] See Piana (n 67) 43–44; Kosar (n 85) 393. The reform of the Public Prosecution has been another hard nut to crack. The existing system of 'severe' hierarchy and almost unchecked discretionary powers still bears the mark of Soviet legacies. The model has proved highly dysfunctional but is protected by the Constitution of 1991, and any change is staunchly resisted by the incumbent actors. See Bozhilova (n 71) 296–97.

[146] See M Popova, 'The Postcommunist Judiciary: One Step Forward, Two Steps Backwards' in P Kostadinova and K Engelbrekt, *Bulgaria's Democratic Institutions at Thirty* (Lanham, MD, Rowman & Littlefield, 2020) 241, 249–51. The limited success of pre-accession policy in reforming judicial governance in the CCs is also confirmed by the very need to introduce post-accession mechanisms in the form of the CVM for Bulgaria and Romania. Damjanovski et al (n 12) 6.

have not helped but rather hindered the fight against corruption and eroded the quality of justice.[147]

Popova is not the only scholar who identifies the 'double-edged sword' effect of judicial independence in transition societies characterised by a weak state and serious corruption problems. In such an institutional context, strong guarantees of judicial independence may have the positive effect of shielding the judiciary from attempts at political or economic influence, but may likewise exacerbate corruption and shirking among magistrates, and may create fertile soil for collusion between politicians and judges.[148] Smilov speaks of 'judicial corporatism' in Bulgaria, whereas Bobek and Kosar describe outright the JC in Slovakia as a 'mafia-like' structure of intra-judicial oppression.[149] This line of research suggests that it may be naive to expect that any judicial reform that bolsters the judiciary's insulation from the other branches of power will automatically bring positive results.

The examples further indicate that accession-induced institutional reform of the judiciary in CEE has poor prospects of achieving lasting change if such change is against deeply ingrained institutional 'habits of the heart',[150] or against the interests of influential incumbent actors within and outside the judiciary. In the wake of judicial reform, old informal patterns of judicial governance linger on. Commentators also observe path dependence in the choices made in the early days of post-communist transition. Actors who have been empowered in the first round of judicial reform tend to preserve their power. The inputs from EU institutions are thus 'filtered' through the behaviour of such actors and their resistance to change in the status quo.[151] More disturbingly, there is evidence that networks of economic and political power find their channels for compromising judicial reform and, ultimately, the quality of justice.[152]

[147] She goes as far as claiming that 'Bulgaria's highly insulated magistrates seem to be more engaged in perpetrating corruption than in prosecuting it. In addition, judicial insulation reduces the incentives for the judiciary as a whole to strive for public support and legitimacy, which in turn undermines the possibility of strong self-policing of internal corruption.' M Popova, 'Why Doesn't the Bulgarian Judiciary Prosecute Corruption?' (2012) 59 *Problems of Post-Communism* 35, 46. About the links between politics and justice in Bulgaria, see Piana (n 67) 158.

[148] Popova (n 147); Bobek and Kosar (n 84) 1288. See in this sense Sadurski (n 3) 69.

[149] D Smilov, 'Populism, Courts and the Rule of Law: Eastern European Perspectives', 28 June 2007, *FLJS Policy Brief*, available at www.fljs.org/content/populism-courts-and-rule-law, 7.

[150] On the concept 'habits of the heart' in institutional theory, see J Elster, C Offe and U Preuss, *Institutional Design in Post-communist Societies. Rebuilding the Ship at Sea* (Cambridge, Cambridge University Press, 1998) 18.

[151] Piana (n 67) 163.

[152] On such networks as a factor obstructing the institutionalisation of EU-induced norms in CCs, see A Dimitrova, 'The New Member States of the EU in the Aftermath of Enlargement: Do New European Rules Remain Empty Shells?' (2010) 17 *Journal of European Public Policy* 137, also with reference to V Ganev, *Preying on the State: The Transformation of Bulgaria After 1989* (Ithaca, NY, Cornell University Press, 2007).

ii. Modes of Judicial Socialisation

A more optimistic story transpires in areas of judicial governance where EU standards and best practices have been diffused through non-hierarchical, horizontal modes of transfer based on coordination and inclusion, such as standard-setting, training, twinning programmes and networking. In her comprehensive study on judicial accountability in CEE, Piana finds these informal mechanisms of socialisation to be fairly successful in strengthening what she calls 'professional accountability'.[153] As particularly influential stand out mechanisms for standard-setting, that is, eliciting benchmarks for evaluating the performance of the judiciary.[154]

In the area of training, EU pre-accession strategy has allegedly helped create patterns of judicial cooperation through judicial schools and training facilities, including judges from old and applicant states or, later on, new Member States. Participation of magistrates from CEE in massive training programmes and socialisation through networks has arguably contributed to democratisation of the judiciary, raising competence in EU law and, importantly, socialising magistrates in legal values that are part of European constitutional principles.[155]

On a related track, twinning projects and other forms of cooperation have been instrumental in enhancing managerial accountability. Through the financial support under the twinning programme, know-how and expertise from old Member States has been used for introducing court management tools in CEE courts, ensuring greater transparency and efficiency in the administration of justice. Interestingly, Piana notes that mechanisms for managerial accountability and control occasionally come into conflict with strengthened judicial independence, which can lead to tensions and internal resistance to such mechanisms.[156]

In sum, the abundant research on the EU Enlargement policy in the area of the rule of law and judicial governance seems to suggest that EU influence has been more effectively diffused and internalised by relevant actors in the CEE candidate countries through mechanisms of 'socialization, international communication, imitation and policy transfer'.[157] These horizontal and bottom-up approaches have emerged as more influential forces than pressure to adopt formal laws and institutions under political conditionality. These findings should be highly interesting for the budding EU rule of law policy post accession.

[153] In her research, Piana considers twinning, training and standard-setting as 'true leverages of influence.' See Piana (n 67) 162.

[154] Such standards are typically developed through soft-law instruments of the transnational judicial networks mentioned in section IV.B.ii.

[155] On European systems of judicial training, see Piana (n 67) 176.

[156] See ibid 162.

[157] ibid 39.

VI. BOOMERANG EFFECTS: EU RULE OF LAW POLICY POST ENLARGEMENT

The first part of this chapter described how Enlargement prompted a major upheaval in EU rule of law policy, mostly in view of raising the standards for membership and precluding the possibility for entry into the Union of polities with low respect for the constitutional principles of democracy, the rule of law and fundamental rights. Although this development was taking place through amendments in EU Treaties and legislation, the effects were mostly outward-bound, intended for the post-communist candidate states from CEE. In the remainder of this chapter, I will look at the inward-bound effects of Eastward Enlargement, that is, its impact on the internal rule of law policy of the Union.

Clearly, after the fifth EU Enlargement has been successfully completed, problems of rule of law backsliding in recently acceded states can no longer be treated as external to the Union. With the illiberal turn in Hungary and Poland and the deteriorating quality of democracy in a number of other CEE Member States,[158] the misgivings that the new Member States might lapse into political practices going against the rule of law, with little or no possibilities for the EU to counteract such a development effectively, have indeed materialised. As shown in other chapters of this volume, the Union is constrained in its ability to curb such developments in at least two significant ways. First, the procedure for sanctioning Member States under Article 7 TEU is notoriously heavy-handed and has proved to be grossly inadequate to check illiberal developments in the Member States.[159] Second, and more problematic, the EU has limited and selective competences in the policy areas at the core of rule of law backsliding.[160] Rule of law conditionality in the process of accession included requirements that went beyond the scope of the EU *acquis*, and even beyond the limits of the principle of conferral in EU constitutional law.[161] Such stretching of competences is hardly practicable post accession.[162]

To overcome these constraints, all EU institutions are currently engaged in an attempt to find a blueprint for a coherent multi-layered and multi-institutional EU rule of law policy, a philosopher's stone of sorts.[163] In this process one can arguably observe how monitoring mechanisms, policies and standards developed in the course of Enlargement travel back to the Union and produce

[158] On the illiberal turn, see the contributions by Halmai and Nergelius in ch 3 and ch 4 of this volume respectively. See also U Sedelmeier, 'Anchoring Democracy from Above? The European Union and Democratic Backsliding in Hungary and Romania after Accession' (2014) 52 *Journal of Common Market Studies* 105. Concerning the deteriorating quality of democracy in the region, see L Cianetti, J Dawson and S Hanley, 'Rethinking "democratic backsliding" in Central and Eastern Europe – looking beyond Hungary and Poland' (2018) 34(3) *East European Politics* 243.

[159] For an analysis, see the contribution by Moberg in ch 15 of this volume.

[160] See section II.C on the limitations of the scope of the EUCFR.

[161] Hillion (n 110) 716.

[162] See Hillion, 'Enlarging the European Union' (n 1) 8.

[163] See European Commission, 'Strengthening the rule of law within the Union. A blueprint for action', COM(2019) 343 final, Brussels, 17 July 2019.

spill-over or boomerang effects. Such boomerang effects can be said to work along three tracks.[164] First, instruments for country-specific rule of law monitoring and assessment developed in the course of Enlargement are refined and extended horizontally to apply to all Member States, leading to increased proceduralisation of EU rule of law policy. Second, rule of law conceptualisations and systematisations precipitated in the course of Enlargement acquire increased sophistication and feed into new instruments of EU internal rule of law policy. Third, and probably most decisively, a process of enhanced judicialisation of EU rule of law policy is unfolding, whereby CJEU jurisprudence works as a bridge between pre-accession and post-accession rule of law standards. Each of these tracks is discussed further in the subsections that follow.

A. Proceduralisation of EU Rule of Law Policy

Along the first track, EU institutions seek to compensate for the limited competence and inadequate mechanisms for enforcing rule of law in the Member States, by developing instruments for monitoring, data gathering and periodic country-specific rule of law assessments, expecting this benchmarking exercise to promote best practices and expose deficiencies. Early such mechanisms include the EU Justice Scoreboard, by which the efficiency, quality and independence of Member States justice systems are reviewed, as part of the European Semester.[165] More recently, a full-blown Rule of Law Mechanism (RLM) was launched by the Commission.[166] The Commission describes the instrument as a process for an annual dialogue on the rule of law between the Commission, the Council and the European Parliament together with Member States as well as national parliaments, civil society and other stakeholders. The basis of this dialogue is the Rule of Law Review Cycle with the annual Rule of Law Report, consisting of a general report and 27 country chapters with Member State-specific assessments. The first Annual Rule of Law Report was published in September 2020.[167]

These instruments are apparently emulating those developed in the course of Enlargement and lead to increased proceduralisation of EU rule of law policy. When explaining the method for preparing the Annual Report, in particular,

[164] There is yet another track, namely the selective and time-limited post-accession conditionality associated with the CVM applied to Bulgaria and Romania. Since this mechanism is conceived as an exception, it will not be discussed here.

[165] Hillion, 'Enlarging the European Union' (n 1) 10. See European Commission, 'The EU Justice Scoreboard A tool to promote effective justice and growth', COM(2013) 160 final, Brussels, 27 March 2013.

[166] See European Commission, 'Rule of Law Mechanism. Further strengthening the Rule of Law within the Union', COM(2019) 163 final, Brussels, 3 June 2019.

[167] European Commission, 2020 Rule of Law Report, COM(2020) 580 final, Brussels, 30 September 2020. The 2021 Rule of Law Report was published in July 2021. See European Commission, 2021 Rule of Law Report, COM(2021) 700 final, Brussels, 20 July 2021.

the Commission describes a process very close to the one employed in its pre-accession strategy.[168] The methodology builds on questionnaires sent out to the Member States and on involvement of professional networks, civil society, other international organisations and expert bodies, etc. However, there are also notable differences. Importantly, the instrument includes all Member States, thus seeking to avoid criticism of double standards and unequal treatment. In contrast to the pre-accession approach, the Commission is now more transparent about the external actors involved and openly announces strengthened cooperation with CoE bodies.[169] Furthermore, the RLM aims not only, and even not predominantly, at elaborating and clarifying legal standards or imposing sanctions, but also at promoting rule of law culture. Thus it appears that some lessons are drawn from pre-accession monitoring. Yet despite its stated ambitions, the first Annual Report seems to repeat one major failure of the pre-accession strategy, namely, to be excessively focused on legal and institutional frameworks. The Report does not discuss major cases of corruption in the Member States and carefully avoids confronting the political causes of rule of law failures.[170] In this, the RLM seems to sustain EU's traditional legalistic approach, shying away from uneasy questions of abuse of political power.

Still, the RLM lacks the most important element of the pre-accession rule of law strategy, namely, conditionality. While it can undoubtedly work as an early warning system and a welcome preventive instrument, it is less apt as an instrument for sanctioning and deterrence. Higher expectations in this respect are therefore vested in the other novel mechanism proposed by the Commission and adopted by Council and Parliament at the end of 2020, namely, Regulation 2020/2092 on a general regime of conditionality for the protection of the Union budget.[171] The Regulation introduces rule of law conditionality in the EU budgetary framework and the possibility to impose sanctions in the form of intercepted access to EU funds in the case of established breaches of rule of law in a Member State that 'affect or seriously risk affecting the sound financial management of the Union budget or the protection of the financial interests of the Union in a sufficiently direct way'. The Regulation provides a detailed description of incidences that are considered indicative of breaches of the principles of rule of law.[172] It also contains a detailed list of breaches that can trigger the sanctioning procedure.

This mechanism is certainly reminiscent of the coupling of pre-accession financial and structural assistance with strict conditionality assessment,

[168] Piana (n 67) 4–5.

[169] Damjanovski (n 12) 16–17.

[170] For a critical appraisal, see A Mungiu-Pippidi, 'Unresolved Questions on the EU Rule of Law Report' (2020) *Carnegie Europe*, available at https://carnegieeurope.eu/2020/10/20/unresolved-questions-on-eu-rule-of-law-report-pub-82999, pointing also at methodological flaws.

[171] Regulation (EU, Euratom) 2020/2092 of the European Parliament and of the Council of 16 December 2020 on a general regime of conditionality for the protection of the Union budget [2020] OJ L 433I/1.

[172] ibid Art 4.

introduced with Agenda 2000 and the APs as part of the EU's pre-accession policy.[173] Damjanovski et al observe that the conditionality mechanism would 'allow the EU to supervise and influence the operation of state structures, in a way that resembles the pre-accession methodology'.[174] But here as well there are differences from pre-accession conditionality. For one, there is no asymmetry in the relationship, given that the modalities of the mechanism are defined jointly by, and apply equally to, all EU Member States. Furthermore, the intervention on the part of EU institutions is expected to occur *ex post*, in reaction to specified incidences of rule of law infringement. This would make prospective interventions targeted and concrete, in contrast to the often broad, *ex ante* requirements formulated in the course of Enlargement, directed at institutional design and steered by ambitions of normative harmonisation. However, as is well known, the Regulation has been controversial and has been challenged by Hungary and Poland before the CJEU.[175]

B. Enhanced Rule of Law Conceptualisation and Systematisation

Probably the most significant rule of law dividend of Enlargement is that it has triggered a reflection over the fundamental values of the Union and set in motion a process of conceptualisiation and systematisation of these values so that they fit into a coherent and sustainable constitutional framework. This 'spill-over' effect has been widely acknowledged in the area of judicial governance[176] and, more generally, in the domain of the rule of law.[177] Looking at the concept of the rule of law, it is hard to deny that the concept has matured and is now much more developed and settled in EU law and policy. In the array of documents produced by EU institutions – Commission, Council and Parliament[178] – in the course of Enlargement and post accession, gradually a consensual and increasingly sophisticated vision of the rule of law is transpiring. This vision also appears in the Commission's approach to particular incidents of rule of law violations in the Member States.[179] Remarkably, the recent Regulation now includes a legislative definition of the rule of law.[180] By including this definition in the Regulation, the Union's approach to the rule of law has reached a new level. The jigsaw

[173] For critical analysis of the earlier proposal of the Commission, see M Blauberger and V van Hüllen, 'Conditionality of EU funds: an instrument to enforce EU fundamental values?' (2021) 43 *Journal of European Integration* 1.
[174] Damjanovski et al (n 12) 16–17.
[175] See actions for annulment lodged by Hungary and Poland, Case C-156/21 *Hungary v Parliament and Council* and Case C-157/21 *Poland v Parliament and Council*.
[176] Piana (n 67) 4–5, seeing the process of rule of law promotion as a self-reflection.
[177] Hillion, 'Enlarging the European Union' (n 1), although with a critical edge, see section V.A.i.
[178] On this development, see the contributions by Perego and by Stefani and Martinéz Iglesías in ch 13 and ch 14 of this volume respectively.
[179] Pech and Grogan, 'Meaning and Scope' (n 5); Damjanovski et al (n 12).
[180] See Regulation 2020/2092, Art 2(a).

puzzle of rule of law bits and pieces that has been assembled in the course of Enlargement has ultimately resulted in a fairly coherent rule of law concept that now claims normative status, including vis-à-vis Union Member States.

Again, it appears that EU institutions have drawn some lessons from Enlargement policy. In the area of judicial governance in particular, EU institutions have developed a position that more successfully balances acceptance of institutional diversity in organising judicial governance and rigorous requirements for safeguarding judicial independence as a principle.[181] The reporting of reliance on external sources, for instance CoE instruments or position papers by the Venice Commission of Democracy Through Law, is more explicit and transparent.

C. Judicialisation as a Bridge Between Pre-accession and Post-accession EU Rule of Law Policy

Finally, and potentially most decisively, Member States' obligations to respect the rule of law, and in particular the principles of judicial independence and impartiality, have become subject to judicial oversight, following broader interpretation by the CJEU of its own mandate to exercise such oversight. A central role in this evolution is played by Article 19 TEU and Article 47 EUCFR. The Court interprets Article 19 TEU as giving expression to the fundamental EU value of the rule of law. According to the Court, Article 19(2) TEU vests the responsibility for providing effective judicial protection not only in the EU Court itself, but also in national courts and tribunals, and this not exclusively when these courts apply EU law *stricto sensu* but also more broadly when they exercise responsibilities 'in fields covered by EU law'.[182] The Court stresses the central role of national judiciaries in ensuring the effective application of EU law at the national level and for sustaining the mutual trust on which the EU legal order essentially builds. This is only possible if national judiciaries follow principles of the rule of law and judicial independence, and if they are 'not immune from EU oversight' for compliance with such principles.[183]

This reading of Article 19 TEU, in conjunction with Article 47 EUCFR, opens a way for the Court to set specific requirements vis-à-vis Member States courts as to their independence and impartiality, going beyond a narrow understanding of EU competences.[184] Importantly, it has allowed the CJEU to develop a coherent concept of judicial independence, outlining its internal and external

[181] See Damjanovski et al (n 12) 13, with reference to Commission Proposal for a Council Decision on the determination of a clear risk of a serious breach by the Republic of Poland of the rule of law COM(2017) 835 final, para 182.

[182] See Case C-64/16 *Associação Sindical dos Juízes Portugueses*, ECLI:EU:C:2018:117, para 29; see already earlier in Case C-506/04 *Wilson v Ordre des avocats du barreau de Luxembourg*, ECLI:EU:C:2006:587.

[183] Damjanovski et al (n 12) 14.

[184] See Case C-64/16 *Associação Sindical dos Juízes Portugueses* ECLI:EU:C:2018:117, para 32. Cf Damjanovski et al (n 12) 12.

aspects, with reference to the case law of the ECtHR.[185] In this novel jurisprudence, the CJEU walks a fine line between respecting the institutional autonomy of Member States and at the same time formulating constraints on the way this autonomy is exercised, notably in the field of judicial governance. Thus, in Joined Cases *AK and Others v Sąd Najwyższy*, the Court on the one hand reaffirms that where there are no EU rules governing the matter, 'it is for the domestic legal system of every Member State to designate the courts and tribunals having jurisdiction and to lay down the detailed procedural rules governing actions for safeguarding rights which individuals derive from EU law'.[186] However, the Court insists, with reference to the right to effective judicial protection in Article 47 EUCFR, that 'the Member States are … responsible for ensuring that those rights are effectively protected in every case'.[187]

In contrast to the Commission's approach in its pre-accession policy, the CJEU is careful not to allege the existence of a common standard or normative vision as to the institutional design of Member States' judiciaries. At the same time, the Court is more boldly relying on broad constitutional principles such as judicial independence, applying them in specific cases of encroachment on these principles in the Member States. This point of balance appears well found. While the Commission in its pre-accession strategy works mostly prospectively, *ex ante*, and addresses questions of judicial governance in general terms, the CJEU decides *ex post* on concrete incidences of questionable law and practice in the Member States, and can set these incidences in their context and assess them against overarching principles of the rule of law and judicial independence. This gives greater legitimacy to the Court's findings.

Commentators have observed that these judicial interpretations have quickly entered both the internal EU rule of law policy as well as the ongoing EU Enlargement policy, for instance when formulating accession requirements vis-à-vis the applicant countries from the Western Balkans.[188] Thus, in a dynamic process of cross-fertilisation, the standards and interpretations developed by the CJEU feed back into the work of EU institutions. In the course of handling of particular cases and situations, the Court refines and fleshes out the general principles of the rule of law and judicial independence, and thus contributes to sharpening the monitoring and benchmarking tools of European institutions, providing a bridge between internal and external EU rule of law policy.[189]

[185] See Joined Cases C-585/18, C-624/18 and C-625/18 *AK and Others v Sąd Najwyższy*, ECLI:EU:C:2019:982, paras 121–123.

[186] ibid para 115.

[187] ibid. For similar reasoning in the context of the Polish legislation on lowering the retirement age of Supreme Court judges, see Case C-619/18 *Commission v Poland*, ECLI:EU:C:2019:531, para 110; see also Case C-192/18 *Commission v Poland*, ECLI:EU:C:2019:924 on lowering the retirement age of judges of the ordinary Polish courts, para 118.

[188] See Damjanovski et al (n 12).

[189] See, for instance, para 2, European Commission, Reasoned proposal in accordance with Article 7(1) TEU regarding the Rule of Law in Poland, COM(2017) 835 final, Brussels, 20 December 2017. See in this sense and for a detailed analysis, Damjanovski et al (n 12), showing how the CJEU's case law is now explicitly integrated in the Commission's Enlargement strategy and documents.

VII. CONCLUDING REFLECTIONS

The purpose of this chapter has been to capture the intricate dynamic between the Eastward Enlargement of the EU and the evolving rule of law policy of the Union. As the first section of the chapter has demonstrated, the prospect of Eastward Enlargement that opened up immediately after the fall of the Berlin Wall has worked as a driving force for the advancement of the rule of law as a fundamental value and principle of EU law. The resulting development, through consecutive amendments of the Treaties and the enactment of the EUCFR, can be considered a remarkable step in the evolution of the Union's constitutional framework.

More ambiguous is the appraisal of EU's involvement in rule of law reform in the CEE candidate countries in the process of preparing these countries for membership of the Union. The chapter describes the conditionality approach adopted by EU institutions, building on strict monitoring and reporting procedures and coupling financial assistance with evidence of progress in bringing the laws and institutions of the applicant states closer to EU standards. The chapter highlights the precarious position of the Commission in a domain where previously there had been very few legislatively set requirements in respect of EU Member States.

On the positive side, the EU's involvement has spurred the CCs to take rapid steps in the required direction of reinforcing the institutional framework of the rule of law, emboldening constitutional courts and introducing institutional guarantees of judicial independence. Although the process has been decidedly imperfect, it would be myopic not to see significant improvements in many areas of law and governance in the CEEC. If measured by the standard of the 'best' EU Member States, the CEE countries still in many respects stand out as laggards. But if one tries to imagine what development would have occurred in the absence of EU assistance and monitoring, I believe one is bound to acknowledge that EU accession has been a positive force. On many counts – transparency, accountability, citizen participation and access to justice – the societies of the new CEE Member States of the EU have made considerable progress, especially bearing in mind their unenviable starting positions at the outset of the accession process. One should likewise not underestimate the arguably more important change taking place in the shadow of accession, which is not necessarily visible in Commission reports. The engagement of NGOs, expert and professional associations, CoE institutions, such as the Venice Commission, all have played their part in creating a local constituency of interlocutors in the CCs, who are ultimately those who can achieve long-lasting and sustainable change in the mindset and 'habits of the heart'.

On the negative side, the vague and indeterminate content of the rule of law concept and its sometimes inconsistent interpretation and application vis-à-vis individual CCs may have contributed to wearing away the already weak respect for the rule of law in the region. The outcome, in particular in the sphere of judicial independence, has often been more visible in setting up formal institutions, such as JCs and anti-corruption units, but less palpable at the level of true reform and the changing of informal practices. The implications and limits of governance by conditionality are arguably partly visible in the 'unfinished business' of judicial reform and the current rule of law crisis in some of the new Member States.

While this development has rightly caused wide-spread concern and sober predictions, even questioning the future of European integration, one can also observe an unusual mobilisation of EU institutions, supported by Member States and civil society, in the direction of defining, explicating and asserting the EU's authority in the rule of law domain. This mobilisation proceeds along multiple and intersecting tracks of proceduralisation, conceptualisation and judicialisation. Interestingly, in this process we can see how procedures and standards developed in the course of Enlargement serve as prototypes for new and bolder EU internal rule of law policy tools, but also how hard-learned lessons from EU pre-accession policy help avoid some of the missteps in this policy. It appears that in this respect the pre-accession strategy has worked as a 'testbed' for EU rule of law policy.

Finally, Enlargement has laid bare a more fundamental problem for EU rule of law policy, namely, that at the core of the rule of law are questions of power that EU institutions are reluctant to address. As pointed out by Nicolaïdes and Kleinfeld, the rule of law is most often flawed because political leaders, governments or powerful economic actors do not want it to exist. Impediments to rule of law reform are thus typically to be sought not primarily at the level of formal laws or faulty institutional design, but at the level of political power and political culture.[190] This analysis resonates with Smilov's overarching criticism of the formalistic legalism that has come to dominate the European integration project, including Enlargement, and the reluctance to embrace European constitutionalism as an imperative of political morality.[191] While avoiding the political by focusing on legal-technical issues has been at the very heart of Monnet's method of European integration, Grabbe reminds us of a fundamental downside to this approach – 'if the unsolved political question re-emerges, it can disrupt all the careful technical [and one might add legal] work'.[192]

This realisation leaves EU rule of law policy in an uneasy place. On the one hand, it requires audacity from EU institutions to confront political questions even when the latter are uncomfortable for those in power, and intervention may seem a delicate matter for Member State governments. Leaving such questions

[190] See Nicolaïdis and Klein (n 53) 28, with reference to T Carothers, 'The Rule of Law Revival' in T Carothers (ed), *Promoting the Rule of Law Abroad: In Search of Knowledge* (Washington, DC, Carnegie Endowment for International Peace Washington, 2006) 4.

[191] Smilov, 'Enlargement and EU Constitutionalism' (n 113) 176.

[192] Grabbe (n 11) 46.

outside the scope of rule of law assessment and EU internal rule of law scrutiny would be irresponsible and even 'foolhardy'.[193] On the other hand, it requires careful tailoring of EU interventions and humility, because sustainable change can only come from within.[194]

[193] Nicolaïdis and Kleinfeld (n 53) 36.

[194] As pointed out by Bugaric, 'ultimately democratic political parties and social movements with credible political ideas and programs offer the best hope for the survival of constitutional democracy'. B Bugaric, 'Central Europe's Descent into Autocracy' (2018) *CES Open Forum Series Harvard* 33.

Part Three

The Rule of Law in an Enlarged Europe

10

The Rule of Law in Italy under the Power of Populism, and its Impact on the Future of the EU: What the Pandemic Crisis Can Teach Us

Some Reflections on Populism, Europe, the Rule of Law and Fundamental Rights During the Time of Quarantine in Italy

VALENTINA COLCELLI

I. INTRODUCTION

THE CONTAINMENT OF the populist drift that can be observed in many countries in Europe today is strongly reflected at the European level in the values of the rule of law. This is precisely what is dealt with in this chapter. The chapter will discuss certain events that occurred in Italy in the second half of 2019 and that, although they were resolved positively by judicial decisions, at the time seemed capable of compromising some principles of the rule of law in that country. I will briefly describe the episodes to which I refer, with the intention of reflecting, descriptively and illustratively, on how populist parties – when they are in power – try to realise their simplifying vision of institutional reality, and the constitutional freedoms that this represents, contrary to the structure of the rule of law as we have known it since the end of the Second World War. Between 2018 and 2019, during the rallies of the then Interior Minister Matteo Salvini, some citizens exhibited banners the content of which expressed verbal disagreement with the Minister. This sparked a debate in Italy about the limits placed on the freedom to express critical opinions against political parties or views during the holding of electoral rallies.

These episodes gave rise to great concern, from the point of view of the guarantees of the right of criticism and freedom of expression protected by Article 21 of the Italian Constitution and Article 10 of the European Convention on Human Rights, in the face of acts of the executive power that could be considered arbitrary. Although at the judicial level they were resolved positively, their repetition seemed to assume an intimidating tone. This is one of the reasons why the prohibition on the executive power proceeding arbitrarily is one of the pillars of the rule of law: in all legal systems of the Member States, the intervention of public powers in the field of the private activity of each person, whether physical or legal, must be based on the law and justified by reasons provided by law. These regulations establish, although with different modalities, protection against arbitrary or disproportionate interventions. The need for this protection must be recognised as a general principle of European Union (EU) law.[1]

The topic of this contribution was considered in the autumn of 2019 in relation to the events mentioned above, and was presented at a conference entitled *30 Years After the Fall of the Berlin Wall: Rule of Law in the European Union*, held in Stockholm in November 2019. In Stockholm, there was a broad agreement that the EU legal framework for the rule of law is the only limit on possible populist movements in the Member States, which, when in power, can legislate to reduce the guarantees of the state and the constitution as they have been known since the Second World War. This chapter is now being written by the author while in quarantine, faced with a recent poll produced in Italy by Swg s.p.a[2] that shows that the approval of Italians for the work and the figure of Giuseppe Conte – the current Prime Minister – is rising, but their approval of the EU is collapsing. Italians feel that the EU is guiltily absent and not very supportive in this health and economic crisis that, after bringing Italy to its knees, is putting the whole Old Continent to the test. My conclusion remains that the only solution to address the populism of the governments of some Member States is to strengthen the EU, which is understood as a bulwark of the rule of law, but that there are problems with the current structure of the EU, which has moved too far away from its original intentions.

To defend the rule of law, the EU has finally to become a political union and to discover once again the reasons why it was first founded. Only by consolidating this function will there be a limit to the possible populist drifts in the Member States that can, once in power, legislate to reduce the guarantees of the rule of law as we know it.

[1] Joined Cases C-46/87 and C-227/88 *Hoechst AG v Commission of the European Communities*, ECLI:EU:C:1989:337.

[2] See at www.la7.it/aggiornamenti-sul-coronavirus/video/sondaggio-coronavirus-sale-la-fiducia-al-governo-scende-quella-allue-06-04-2020-318085 (accessed 21 April 2020).

II. CHRONICLE OF THE FACTS OF THE ITALIAN ELECTORAL SPRING OF 2019

In Italy in 2019, or more precisely from the inauguration in 2018 of the then Interior Minister Matteo Salvini until July 2019, but with particular intensification during the 2019 European election campaign (which on the Italian peninsula coincided with local elections), a phenomenon was observed that raised some concerns about the actions of the Division of General Investigations and Special Operations of the Police (DIGOS). DIGOS had paid special attention to protecting the Interior Minister during the electoral rallies in which he participated as secretary of the Lega Party. It should be noted that the Interior Minister has sole authority for public security and is the supreme political police chief.

One morning in mid-May 2019, a fire engine crane was used to remove a banner that addressed the Interior Minister with the words 'You are not welcome' and that was hanging on the facade of a building in a square in Brembate, near Bergamo. A few days earlier, in Salerno, the police had entered a private home to force the removal of another banner. These were just the latest episodes in a long series in which the police had shown great diligence in removing 'guilty' banners containing various political claims. Some of these seizures were not carried out during rallies. Sometimes the banners were located far from meeting places or from where the Minister was. Two banners were removed and seized from a bridge over the motorway at Gioia del Colle, and another from a railway bridge in the same city. One of these banners used a phrase from a song by the Neapolitan singer Pino Daniele: 'This League is a disgrace.' Another, on the other hand, used harsher tones and addressed the Lega Party using clichés typical of the language of this populist party: 'Better to be a lesbian and communist than Salvini and fascist.' A banner placed inside the stand of the UIL (Unione Italiana del Lavoro) in Piazza del Popolo in Rome, which was installed on the occasion of a joint demonstration by the CGIL (Confederazione Generale Italiana del Lavoro), CISL (Confederazione Italiana Sindacati Lavoratori) and UIL demanding the renewal of public administration contracts, was also seized. The huge picture represented the two Deputy Prime Ministers at the time, Matteo Salvini and Luigi Di Maio. Above their heads the words read 'Standing up to the union brings bad luck.' The Minister was not present at the demonstration and the banner was not displayed during any appearance by the Minister.

It is obvious that in the Italian legal system there are rules to punish those who prevent or disturb electoral meetings or rallies, and the reason for these rules is understandable. The Constitutional Court itself has said that 'disturbing the development of a political act is a very dangerous fact for public security and justifies that the code provides for severe penalties equivalent to those contemplated for obstruction'.[3]

[3] CortCost (*Bartelloni*) 1974, n 125, Gazz Uff n 126 of 15 May 1974.

The applicable legislation is abundant: Article 72 of Law 26 of 1948 and Article 99 of the Decree of the President of the Republic 361/1957 provide that 'anyone who by any means prevents or disturbs an electoral meeting, public or private, will be punished with imprisonment from one to three years and with a fine'. As for political acts, the rules are contained in Articles 660 and 654 of the Italian Penal Code, and refer to 'cases of obstruction and inappropriate shouting'. Law 212 of 1956 prohibits certain forms of party-political information in the 30 days prior to an election, but the aforementioned cases did not fall within these circumstances. We should add that the law expressly prohibits the display of banners or posters only when they contain phrases or images that incite violence, or are injurious or threatening (for example, Article 2 *bis* of Decree Law 8/2007 prevents and represses acts of violence during football matches or in connection therewith).Therefore, the hypothesis that could justify the intervention of the police force (which is what actually occurred) is that the police were seeking to prevent individuals who were participating in the electoral rally from uncivilly expressing their intolerance of the liberties of others and behaving in a violent manner. It is true that if a very boisterous protest occurs simultaneously with the holding of a legally authorised political meeting, in such a way that it impedes or strongly hinders its occurrence, this protest is unlawful and sanctions should be imposed. However, at the time the facts were checked, the problem was the tense political climate in Italy, poisoned by the tones that the Minister himself used on a daily basis. The banners were intended to express disgust at the Minister's immigration policy decisions.

In many of these episodes, when evaluating whether the banners were to be given back to their owners and allowed to be displayed in a public space, the prosecutors who had to pass judgment on these events ordered this to happen (ie the prosecutors ordered the banners to be returned to their owners and affirmed that they could be displayed in public, and registered a complaint against 'unknown persons'/'*Denuncia contro ignoti*' in accordance with Article 331 of the Italian Code of Criminal Procedure, to investigate whether any member of the police had abused his or her authority).

In the Italian legal system, the prosecutor is in charge of validating or not validating the seizure order according to Articles 321 and 335 of Code of Criminal Procedure. For example, the prosecutor of Gioia del Colle found that saying 'fascist' to a politician during a rally is not a crime but a 'normal political criticism, although it is manifested harshly', and established that displaying the banners did not constitute an offence but rather an expression of a person's own political conviction, which, as is known, in this context can be expressed abruptly and in lively language with much use of slang, calling into question the prestige of the public function and institution represented.[4] The prosecutor based his decision to require the filing of an investigation on various judgments of the

[4] Trib Catanzaro 2008, n 380.

Supreme Court and the Constitutional Court, and on the right to criticism and freedom of expression of thought protected by Article 21 of the Constitution and Article 10 of the European Convention on Human Rights.

The truth is that a crime is committed not through any expression of thought, but through behaviour that, in practice, prevents the normal continuation of a meeting.

> Therefore, although a manifestation of disagreement is admissible, as an expression of the right of criticism of the speaker's thought, it must be kept strictly within the limits of civility and moderation, without constituting a pretext to vent animosity and impede the regular development of the meeting.
>
> …
>
> The manifestation of a thought contrary to the political ideas of those who organised the electoral act cannot be considered illegal a priori, and this because of the constitutional value of the freedom of expression of thought regulated by article 21 of the fundamental Charter, but only when it manifests itself in a way that prevents or disturbs the meeting itself.[5]

It is evident, then, that the phrase 'You are not welcome' addressed to a political representative, or the other, more acute 'This League is a disgrace', cannot be considered disturbances in the sense of altering the regular performance of a political act.

III. WHAT IS THE RELATIONSHIP BETWEEN POPULISM AND MODERN CONSTITUTIONALISM?

The episodes mentioned raised concerns in some sectors of Italian society, as they clearly represented the populists' simplistic perception that, once a populist party has come to power, serious changes can be generated on the legal and institutional planes of a country. This populist simplification is equivalent to suppressing the constitutionally guaranteed freedoms, especially those based on freedom of expression, but also the collective freedoms of association and assembly, without which the exercise of the right to vote can be manipulated, transforming elections into rites whose purpose is merely the legitimation by plebiscite of the government that already exercises power. With these systems, governments that are not fully liberal, once established, tend to stabilise their position of power.

The ideology and actions of the populist parties coexist with modern constitutionalism because of the very nature of the latter. Modern constitutionalism, as well as the rule of law of the second half of the last century, combines the democratic legitimacy of political power with its legal limitation, in order to protect fundamental rights. Precisely in respect of fundamental rights, the claim

[5] CortCost (*Bartelloni*) 1974, n 125, Gazz Uff n 126 of 15 May 1974.

of a populist leader to manifest the popular will does not affect the system of controls and balances established by modern constitutionalism, given that this is based on a pluralistic vision of politics. Indeed, populists run for election without opposing the representative procedures, although populist ideologies and populist political styles show some nervousness about the rule of law.[6]

Populism is 'an ideology … that considers society, ultimately, as divided into two homogeneous and antagonistic camps, "the pure people" against "the corrupt elite" and maintains that politics should be the expression of the general will of the people'.[7] Populism is an intensely moralistic approach to politics that embodies a homogeneous 'we the people', frequently conceived in ethnic or national terms, in a leader who speaks and expresses the will of that undifferentiated community, against alleged 'corrupt' or 'elite' groups (hence the tendency to believe in conspiracy theories in this type of political reasoning) and against 'external' minorities of a different nature.[8]

According to the above-mentioned political definition, the constitutional rules bring into question the populist's narration that a populist leader – he and only he – embodies the powers of the people and is thus linked to the execution of the pure will of the people. The system of checks and balances provided by modern constitutionalism, since the latter is based on a pluralistic vision of politics, seems not to be affected by a populist leader's affirmation that he manifests the popular will. On the other hand, the checks and balances of the rule of law, by their very nature, create a risk of entering into conflict with the populist leader.[9]

Consequently, both constitutional rights and the institutions that protect them, especially the judiciary but also the media, are often the object of criticism and populist aggression. Institutions, even those that act as guarantees of the rule of law, such as the courts, are accused of usurping powers that in a democracy would correspond to the people. Once elected and in power, populist parties can jeopardise the institutional forms by which they were elected.

In ways called 'abusive constitutionalism' or 'discriminatory' or 'autocratic' legalism,[10] the law may be used to persecute minorities, or to punish dissent, and to disguise the discursively legitimised executive power by popular will. Populists assert themselves as a result of proposals and practices that represent a drastic simplification of the institutional structure and the framework of fundamental principles inherent in the rule of law. Continuing with the simplistic narration

[6] N Urbinati, *Democracy Disfigured: Opinion, Truth and the People* (Cambridge, MA, Harvard University Press, 2014) 13, 129, 153.

[7] C Mudde and C Rovira Kaltwasser, *Populism: A Very Short Introduction* (Oxford, Oxford University Press, 2017) 6.

[8] N Lacey, 'Populism and the Rule of Law' (2019) 15 *Annual Review of Law and Science* 9.

[9] Mudde and Rovira Kaltwasser (n 7) 18.

[10] ibid.

of the reality that they propose, once they are within the structures of government, they can change the rule of law that guaranteed them participation in free elections. The style of polarised and moralistic populism (friend/enemy, 'we the pure'/'corrupt others') tends to erode the common norms of civilisation and law from within,[11] that is, when it comes through democratic elections guaranteed by that same rule of law it calls into question.

IV. THE EUROPEAN UNION AS AN ULTIMATE GUARANTOR OF THE RULE OF LAW IS THE ONLY SOLUTION TO POPULISM

According to the Communication from the Commission to the European Parliament and the Council, 'A new EU framework to strengthen the rule of law':

> The rule of law is the backbone of any modern constitutional democracy. It is one of the founding principles stemming from the common constitutional traditions of all the Member States of the EU and, as such, one of the main values upon which the Union is based. This is recalled by Article 2 of the Treaty on European Union (TEU), as well as by the Preambles to the Treaty and to the Charter of Fundamental Rights of the EU. …[12]

The Communication defines the rule of law as a legal principle guaranteeing that all public powers act within the limits set by law, respecting the values of democracy and fundamental rights, under the control of an independent and impartial judiciary. It further stipulates that the specific content of the principles and norms emanating from the rule of law may vary at national level depending on the constitutional order of each Member State.

In any case, and guided by judgments of the European Court of Justice, the European Court of Human Rights, the work of the Council of Europe and the Venice Commission, the aforementioned Communication from the Commission presents a synthesis from which the following common elements can be extracted: (i) the principle of legality; (ii) legal certainty; (iii) a prohibition on the arbitrary exercise of executive power; (iv) independent and effective judicial control, also with respect to fundamental rights; (v) the right to a fair trial and the separation of powers; and (vi) equality before the law.

The formation of a common European law based on respect for the principles that traditionally constitute the rule of law is also being developed through the contribution of the system for the protection of fundamental human rights

[11] P Ostiguy and KM Roberts, 'Putting Trump in comparative perspective: populism and the politicisation of the sociocultural law' (2016) 23 The *Brown Journal of World Affairs* 43.

[12] Communication from the Commission to the European Parliament and the Council on a new EU framework to strengthen the rule of law, COM(2014)158 final, section I.

created in Europe through the European Convention for the Protection of Human Rights and Fundamental Freedoms (Rome, 1950),[13] and this becomes more and more true as the points of contact between the systems examined become more numerous. The Court of Justice and Article 6 TEU refer to the European Convention on Human Rights as the common legal basis of fundamental rights in the Union together with national constitutional traditions.[14] The cultural plurality of the national legal systems becomes an element of the identity of European legal culture that, in this way, also performs the task of integrating a set of different cultures in a process that can appreciate different identities and the common aspiration to certain values recognised as fundamental.

Thus, Europe resembles a 'garden of rights'.[15] There are rights of all kinds and natures: civil and political rights; economic, social and cultural rights; rights of all men; rights of citizens of nation states only; rights of citizens of the European Community only; foreigners' rights; women's rights; workers' rights; rights of the child and of the elderly; rights of the disabled; gay rights; the right to change sex; the right to life; the right to know; and the right to remain silent. Within this overpopulated panorama of rights, the principle of equality stands out. This is not only traditionally considered as a limit to the discretion of power, but, above all, it marks the difference, which we could say is ontological, between rights and privileges until it becomes synonymous with justice.

There is no doubt that there is a process of ever deeper integration in Europe through primary and secondary European law and the jurisprudence of the European Court of Justice. The greater presence of the Union in the lives of citizens is accompanied by the construction of mechanisms that are capable, directly or indirectly, of spreading the legal protection of each individual in recognised legal situations, both in relation to the state and to other individuals, in particular with regard to the guarantee of fundamental rights and the rule of law.

The great lessons of European civil and legal history must not be lost, but rather must be adapted and reinforced according to the most advanced requirements of modern life and of the European Continent, so that we can 'consider with a different spirit the role of political borders'[16] to reinforce them as they are overcome, especially in the critical moment through which we are living.

[13] P van Dijk and GJH Vanhoof, *Theory and Practice of European Convention on Human Rights* (Leiden, Brill, 1998).

[14] A Manzella, 'Dal mercato ai diritti' in A Manzella, P Melograni, E Paciotti and S Rodotà (eds), *Riscrivere i diritti in Europa* (Bologna, Il Mulino, 2000) 42ff.

[15] M Patrono, *I diritti dell'uomo nel paese d'Europa* (Padova, Cedam, 2000) 3ff.

[16] S Caprioli, 'Introduzione al Seminario di studi "I problemi dei contratti", San Marino, 8–9 September 1998', *Miscellanea dell'Istituto giuridico sammarinese*, 6, 2000, 10ff.

V. THE CRISIS OF THE PRINCIPLE OF SOLIDARITY AND TIME FOR A CLEAR CHANGE OF STEP BY THE EU: LESSONS FROM THE CORONAVIRUS EMERGENCY

The epidemiological crisis could represent a decisive factor in the political fate of the EU, sharpening the statement that either there will be real political union or we will face the end of the Ventotene project. The Coronavirus crisis could be a useful opportunity to fight populism, because at the national level the crisis has shown how science- and expert-led government seem to be the only voices to be trusted in such extreme circumstances.

According to a recent article in *The Guardian*:

> Populist leaders seem to have lost their voice, for now: the attempts to blame migrants, porous borders and the forces of globalisation for the coronavirus have received short shrift. Fear and deference have, momentarily at least, rendered citizens less inclined to question mainstream governments and turn to populism's snake oil vendors.[17]

The Guardian article continues:

> If Italy can be counted on to listen to the orders of a government that only a few weeks ago was viewed as accidental and temporary, perhaps the tide has turned on the populist Lega party leader Matteo Salvini.[18]

In a huge number of EU Member States – as well as in Italy – the health crisis is underlining the importance of a dialogue with the scientific community for the taking of public decisions involving technical-scientific evaluations for the purposes of the protection of the fundamental rights involved, such as, in particular, the right to health.[19] This approach is contributing to a weakening of the rhetoric that feeds populism.

In the EU scenario, anyway, the same article in *The Guardian* asks, if science- and expert-led government has 'turned on Salvini, why should it not have turned on all populists'?[20] To answer this question we need only recall that Victor Orbán, under the pretext of fighting the emergency, has since 20 March 2020 assumed unlimited rights of government and exceptional, renewable sweeping powers. Democracy, freedom of information, institutions and the values of the rule of law as defined by the European Treaties have been suspended in Hungary. During the pandemic crisis, and because of the absence of an EU-wide response,

[17] C Fieschi, 'Europe's Populists will Try to Exploit Coronavirus. We can Stop Them' *The Guardian* (London, 17 March 2020), available at www.theguardian.com/world/commentisfree/2020/mar/17/europe-populists-coronavirus-salvini?CMP=share_btn_fb (accessed 21 April 2020).

[18] ibid.

[19] L Del Corona, 'Le decisioni pubbliche ai tempi del coronavirus: tra fondatezza scientifica, principio di precauzione e tutela dei diritti Diritto, diritti ed emergenza ai tempi del Coronavirus' (2020) 2 *BioLaw Journal – Rivista di BioDiritto*, available at www.biodiritto.org/content/download/3789/45303/version/1/file/18+Del+Corona.pdf.

[20] Fieschi (n 17).

EU citizens lost one of the most extraordinary achievements of EU cooperation: the Schengen Area. A coordinated EU-wide response would make these border restrictions unnecessary. Border controls are inevitable when Member States lack any coordinated action plan for containment. Emergency measures, like emergency powers, are brought in daily by national governments, but, as seen in Hungary, there is a real risk that these measures may be used to corrode not only the rights of free movement, but also civil rights, and ultimately democracy.

The EU – as the ultimate guarantor of the rule of law – should not only monitor these numerous repressive measures but also prevent them from violating citizens' civil liberties and from weakening institutions under the auspices of addressing the crisis in the state. The EU has not done enough at this time to ward off populism, a force that can be reignited at a stroke in tumultuous times, even if populism is falling in the polls around Europe.[21] The Coronavirus crisis is a test of policy, of solidarity, but also of transparency for each political institution at every level. It is an opportunity to show that a new, widespread technocracy can benefit the greater good. A huge number of EU citizens look to the EU for protection and joint solutions, but the answer seems to be insufficient or unclear.

The poll mentioned at the outset of this chapter showed, among other things, that in Italy more than 25 per cent of the Italian people – at the same time as displaying growing trust in the national expert-led government – are losing confidence in the EU.[22] The absence of a coherent EU-wide response to the pandemic, and the lack of will for unitary management of the crisis, risks surrendering the floor to the populists just as they are losing their position. The cost of hesitation may be irreversible, the former President of the European Central Bank reminds us.[23]

Thus, although according to Article 5 TEU '[t]he Union shall act only within the limits of the powers conferred on it by the Treaties', and of course in the field of health the Union has only a supporting competence, if we adhere to what is set out in the Treaty of Lisbon, this ongoing health emergency is a rare chance to demonstrate that the EU not only matters, but also can protect us.

In the words of Mario Draghi again:

> Faced with unforeseen circumstances, a change of mindset is as necessary in this crisis as it would be in times of war. The shock we are facing is not cyclical. The loss of

[21] E Lauria, 'Crollo nei sondaggi, le destre populiste vittime della pandemia' *La Repubblica* (20 April 2020), available at https://rep.repubblica.it/pwa/generale/2020/04/20/news/crollo_nei_sondaggi_le_destre_populiste_vittime_della_pandemia-254556960/ (accessed 21 April 2020).

[22] To the question 'How much confidence do you have in the European Union?', today 27% of Italians – or at least of the sample interviewed – respond positively. Going backwards, confidence in the EU was 42% in 2019, 37% in 2018, 38% in 2017, 40% in 2016 and 30% in 2015.

[23] M Draghi, 'We Face a War against Coronavirus and Must Mobilise Accordingly' *Financial Times* (25 March 2020), available at www.ft.com/content/c6d2de3a-6ec5-11ea-89df-41bea055720b?shareType=nongift&fbclid=IwAR0t_8clg09a2UBhx6cYenHgLlIFn--siEkgygQp-iPf7ALM-C8D19gDa4RY (accessed 21 April 2020).

> income is not the fault of any of those who suffer from it. The cost of hesitation may be irreversible. The memory of the sufferings of Europeans in the 1920s is enough of a cautionary tale. The speed of the deterioration of private balance sheets – caused by an economic shutdown that is both inevitable and desirable – must be met by equal speed in deploying government balance sheets, mobilising banks and, as Europeans, supporting each other in the pursuit of what is evidently a common cause.[24]

Regardless of the tug-of-war on Eurobonds and the economic decisions that it will take, the EU has to take a step further. All the instruments that will be adopted will still be guaranteed on the basis of an agreement reached unanimously between the Member States to finance individual states. The first changes therefore have to be related to the decision-making mechanism. The mechanism that excludes the European Parliament from any decision or control over revenue cannot remain unchanged, because the deficit of supranational legitimacy in the current system cannot persist intact.

The economic logic that seems to drive all EU decisions condemns us to a perennial crisis, especially because there is no fiscal union. The European Parliament (without the mediation of the Member States), having been given new powers, for instance, has to have the direct power to tax the European economy and European citizens, as well as more power to draft general fiscal policy. If the European Parliament were able to promote this debate and make a proposal like this, claiming the power of fiscal policy that is an inherent prerogative of democratic legislative assemblies, the whole debate on the European resources and interventions needed to launch a major recovery plan to restart economies after the pandemic would be of a completely different nature. A targeted revision of the Treaties is a simple political choice.

To echo the appeal of a group of influential European scholars:

> The question we cannot escape today in Europe is whether we shall try to save us individually, each country for itself, or, on the contrary, we shall recognize we are all on the same boat, we are part of a Union which is not just a common market, but also a political community. Even more a community of values.
>
> The crises of the past decade should have made us aware of the centrifugal tensions that insufficient, timid and botched up responses (too little too late) have triggered in our Union. Are we going to repeat today the past failures?[25]

[24] ibid.

[25] Heinrich Best and others, 'Letter to our European friends', available at https://voiceforeurope.weebly.com/letter.html.

11

The European Rule of Law Standard, the Nordic States, and EU Law

GRAHAM BUTLER

I. INTRODUCTION: COULD IT HAPPEN HERE?

ANALYSING THE RULE of law in 2021 is a feverish topic. Historical analogies are not in short supply given the developments of the past decade, where it is apparent that the rule of law in parts of Europe has wavered. There are also fictitious equivalences that can be examined. Using their pens, popular fiction writers have long authored novels on how autocracy has corrupted developed societies. This has occurred on both sides of the Atlantic. Here in Europe, the work of George Orwell comes to mind in the form of *Nineteen Eighty-Four*.[1] Crossing the Ocean, the work of Sinclair Lewis also stands out. During the inter-war years of 1935, he published a novel entitled *It Can't Happen Here*.[2]

The central protagonist in *It Can't Happen Here* was Doremus Jessup, a journalist, who took an interest in the rise of Buzz Windrip, who electorally succeeded in becoming President of the United States. Once Windrip was in power, Jessup's worst fears about him came to pass. Several events occurred that were blatantly and evidently contrary to the rule of law – even for the time. Political opposition was suppressed, Congress was curtailed, rights of minorities withdrawn and state powers abridged. This all sounds familiar, and perhaps not too distant from the occurrences seen since the coming into office of a new administration in the United States in 2017. An imaginable scenario of 'it' occurring, in line with Lewis's novel, is ever-present, everywhere.

Importantly, the rule of law and the challenges brought to it are not something that should be of concern just to North America. The discussion around the rule of law was a topic in the 1930s in Europe too,[3] and also, regrettably, is

[1] G Orwell, *Nineteen Eighty-Four* (London, Secker & Warburg, 1949).

[2] S Lewis, *It Can't Happen Here* (New York, Doubleday, 1935).

[3] See S Zweig, *Die Welt von Gestern: Erinnerungen eines Europäers* (Stockholm, Bermann-Fischer, 1942), published during the Second World War. For a recent English reprint, see S Zweig,

presently back on the agenda as a result of the activities of some Member States of the European Union (EU). Clearly, and disappointingly, not all EU Member States are fulfilling what can now be considered, over decades of European law, a European rule of law standard, developed out of the existence and respect for the law of the EU, which permeates all EU legal texts, as well as national laws and practices.

This chapter aims to show that rule of law issues and challenges as presently seen in Europe, and as detailed in other chapters in this volume, are not merely confined to Central and East European Member States[4] but could also, at least potentially, occur in the Nordic states, given some tendencies that exist in their respective legal psyches. Of course, the sheer scale of rule of law challenges presently seen in certain parts of Central and Eastern Europe is egregious, and nothing of the sort is currently found in the Nordic states. However, the constitutional design and structure of the Nordic states, along with their wider societal discourse, it is argued, leave them open to such rule of law challenges in the future, like other Northern and Western European states, even if such degradation cannot be immediately foreseen. This chapter analyses the rule of law in a European context, and contemplates whether 'it' could happen in the Nordics. The point is far from trivial, for such analysis can evoke what type of rule of law challenges could arise in a Nordic context. The chapter argues that nothing will occur suddenly in the Nordics in this direction, but given potential deficiencies, the Nordic states are not immune from such challenges. These expressions are, in a way, similar to the concerns expressed by Mr Jessup in *The Vermont Vigilance*, a periodical featured in *It Can't Happen Here*. Arising rule of law issues, as is argued, should not just be seen as something that has the potential to occur elsewhere, but beg the reader to be conscious of rule of law challenges that can arise in a Nordic context, and what role EU law would have in such situations.

Section II discusses the rule of law in a European context, fleshing out what is meant by the European rule of law standard; section III analyses how EU Member States adhere to the rule of law. Section IV examines the rule of law in a Nordic context, elucidating some potential challenges in light of certain tendencies that can be seen. Section V details how national courts and the Court of Justice of the European Union (CJEU or 'the Court') are central actors in ensuring the rule of law in Europe, and section VI outlines how challenges to the rule of law in the Nordic states might be detected. Section VII concludes that rule of law challenges can occur anywhere – the Nordic states included – and that EU law will play a vital role in ensuring that the rule of law is maintained well into the future.

The World of Yesterday: Memoirs of a European, tr A Bell (London, Pushkin Press, 2011). Also in Danish, S Zweig, *Verden af i går: en europæers erindringer*, trs JH Monrad and J Preis (Copenhagen, Rosinante, 2013) and Swedish, S Zweig, *Världen av i går: en europés minnen*, trs H Hultenberg and A Bengtsson (Stockholm, Ersatz, 2011).

[4] See the contribution by Gábor Halmai in ch 3 of this volume.

II. THE EUROPEAN BACKDROP

The rule of law concept calls for intellectual analysis, given the theoretical concern regarding its violation, on the one hand; but it also imports material considerations for the EU and its Member States on the other hand. Over time, the rule of law has certainly seen a shift from being a mere rhetorical device, to being transformed into a concept that can be operationalised in modern Europe. Presently, the rule of law is under systematic and worrying attack.[5] All one has to do is see the assault on independent institutions such as courts and universities, platforms such as media groups, and organised demonstrations in parts of Europe to understand that the rule of law is slowly, and sometime covertly, being chipped away. In some ways, therefore, 'it', the violation and abuse of the rule of law, to use Lewis's term, has already happened in Europe. A brief look back at early to mid-twentieth-century Europe shows that rule of law challenges were rampant on a different scale than presently seen. Consequently, the violation and abuse of the rule of law is something that today should be of concern everywhere, and not just seen as something that happens elsewhere, or as something entirely confined to the past.

The heterogeneous nature of Europe as a continent has meant that its integration efforts in the late twentieth and early twenty-first century, through the EU and otherwise, have been over-reliant upon law for its constitutional underpinning[6] and its form of operation.[7] This is much more so for the Union than for the individual Member States, where the polity is bound together through law and politics for a wider variety of historical reasons. Whilst the rule of law was doubtless in mind when the EU legal order came into being, it has taken on a new life since the accession of newer Member States with recent histories of communism and considerable rule of law issues.

The rise of rule of law as a serious legal tool in the EU legal order is not fully owed to Eastern Enlargement and East European states' past however. Well-established EU Member States have had their own troubles with the rule of law. Many of these have not covered themselves in glory. As illustrated, it was the politics of Austria over 20 years ago that fuelled concerns about the rule of law in the contemporary EU.[8] Following Austrian developments, there was a schism amongst different divisions within European political groupings as to

[5] See, I Krastev, *After Europe* (Philadelphia, PA, University of Pennsylvania Press, 2017).

[6] For a comprehensive overview, see M Cappelletti, M Seccombe and JHH Weiler (eds), *Integration Through Law: Europe and the American Federal Experience* (Berlin, De Gruyter), published in numerous volumes throughout the 1980s.

[7] The seminal work being P Pescatore, *The Law of Integration: Emergence of a New Phenomenon in International Relations, Based on the Experience of the European Communities* (Leiden, AW Sijthoff, 1974).

[8] For more on this, see P Wrange and P Cramér, 'The Haider Affair, Law and European Integration' [2001] *Europarättslig Tidskrift* 28. See further W Sadurski, 'Adding Bite to a Bark: The Story of Article 7, EU Enlargement, and J Haider' (2009) 16 *Columbia Journal of European Law* 385.

choosing the right response to political changes within what was seen, in recent times before that, as an EU Member State without considerable rule of law issues. Some European political figures favoured taking action, whereas others expressed reluctance about intervening in developments that they considered to be wholly internal to Austria and not of external concern.[9] The Freedom Party of Austria (FPÖ), as it has turned out, was well before its time, given subsequent developments in the wider Europe occurring today.

It is not necessary to agree what the rule of law is when analysing it from a regional perspective. There are features of the rule of law that stretch across many different theoretical views and perspectives. Debating what the rule of law is institutes a futile exercise and endless wrangling,[10] as no approach to the rule of law can be fully neutralised of normative bias. Whilst the rule of law is extremely expansive in its potential scope,[11] it can and does have a much more concrete version for its practical application – most certainly in the EU. The main attribute is that the concept has *a* meaning in European legal cultures, whatever their history, tradition and application; and it is much more than a political idea and is, instead, a genuine legal concept that can be concretely applied.

If it cannot be agreed what the rule of law is, at least it can be agreed what the rule of law is not. It is not compatible with extra-constitutional governance arrangements, nor with authoritarianism, fascism or a regime constructed around an individual. What is clear is that arbitrary use of law for ill-gotten ends is contrary to the concept. Over time, an established array of norms has come to life in Europe, particularly in Western Europe in the latter half of the twentieth century, to which Member States subscribe by their very notion of membership of the EU, as common values in a common family. This, as will be discussed, is what may be labelled a 'European rule of law standard'. This standard is, in itself, a framework in which Member States act in all their activities, both internally and externally. It also applies to the EU within its institutional framework.[12]

The measure of rule of law is normally a comparison of a regime against another with which one is most familiar, and the latter being the norm. Such a comparison does not take account of the quality of such a normative backdrop, however. It is clear that the European rule of law standard does not conceive of the rule of law as rule *by* law. Thus, this places the European rule of law standard in opposition to other normative understandings, according to which law is

[9] For a thorough account of the time, see C Leconte, 'The Fragility of the EU as a "Community of Values": Lessons from the Haider Affair' (2005) 28 *West European Politics* 620.

[10] For one of the best popular overviews, see T Bingham, *The Rule of Law* (London, Penguin, 2010).

[11] See, BZ Tamanaha, *On the Rule of Law: History, Politics, Theory* (Cambridge, Cambridge University Press, 2004).

[12] As demonstrated in Case C-402/05 *Yassin Abdullah Kadi and Al Barakaat International Foundation v Council of the European Union and Commission of the European Communities*, ECLI:EU:C:2008:461.

used and abused by public powers,[13] which can result in the conflation of rule of law with rule by law. Adherence to the rule *of* law is a constitutional principle, and thus it is possible to see what it means from the point of view of EU law, and to prevent rule of law challenges from arising.

III. ADHERENCE TO THE RULE OF LAW IN EUROPE

Generally, it can be said with a level of assurance that the rule of law in Europe in recent years, as defined by the European rule of law standard, has deteriorated. An increasing number of Member States that were thought of as, and assumed to be, stable rule of law states have resorted to ugly inward-looking expressions, and have moved towards less open forms of government. This includes the splintering (and partial removal) of democratic, human rights and rule of law standards. For some, these concepts are inseparable in Europe.[14] With lesser standards of governance on offer in Europe, it can become more difficult for the rule of law to thrive. The difficulty this poses is that adherence to the rule of law is, by definition, mandatory within the EU. It is also self-evidently part and parcel of the state–citizen bargain in which fundamental rights are respected, as well as having a deeper meaning for the relationship between Member States and the EU.

In Europe, the rule of law is promoted by a variety of ways and means. Such manifestations do appear, on occasion, in constitutional texts. For example, in the Basic Law of Germany, there is a constitutional compulsion towards greater levels of European integration.[15] Consequently, within the constitutional framework of Germany, there is little choice but to adhere to the European rule of law standard. Much inspiration can be drawn from this idealised vision of constitutionalism, as most Member States in Europe do not have such firm constitutional commitment to Europe, or the EU's legal structure. Yet elucidation in texts alone is far from assuring the matter, as actions of Member States are not inconsequential. Member States both possess and represent the ultimate form of power over persons within their jurisdiction. For this reason, the European rule of law standard means that both internal and external oversight of such power is necessary for ensuring Member States' adherence to respect for the rule of law. Internally, there is the balance of powers between the executive, the legislature and the judiciary, as well as many other independent or quasi-independent entities. Externally, there are international agreements (treaties)

[13] J Husa, 'Nordic Law and Development – See No Evil, Hear No Evil?' (2015) 60 *Scandinavian Studies in Law* 15, 24–28.

[14] JHH Weiler, 'Epilogue: Living in a Glass House: Europe, Democracy and the Rule of Law' in C Closa and D Kochenov (eds), *Reinforcing Rule of Law Oversight in the European Union* (Cambridge, Cambridge University Press, 2016) 318.

[15] In the Preamble ('as an equal partner in a united Europe') and Art 23 ('Inspired by the determination to promote world peace as an equal partner in a united Europe …').

that states agree to abide by, as well as sophisticated integration orders through law, such as the EU legal order, that maintain sufficient checks on the conduct of internal power. The very integration of Europe involves states' undertaking international commitments, and their activity exposed to extensive critique, with monitoring from institutions beyond the states, as internal organs of any description cannot alone suffice. But both the internal and external aspects are only as good as their design, enactment, and enforcement.

Questions turn on whether the rules of the EU, and its legal order, are sufficiently well designed to withstand rule of law threats. The EU is a model case for 'divided and mediated rule',[16] for it is a powerful legal order but one that crucially rests on a framework that mandates a distinctive separation of powers between different (yet cooperative) institutions. The EU may have economic origins and not by itself have been designed to be a rule of law framework, yet it has, inadvertently, become one. Thus, the way that the EU developed has seen constitutional considerations of the rule of law being crafted around the core of the EU's internal market, and transformed from being a purely economic project into a definitive constitutional entity with the rule of law at its heart.

As a constitutional experiment, membership of the EU, both for accession and ongoing membership, is contingent upon continuous respect for the rule of law. After all, the EU is famously 'inspired by the constitutional traditions common to the Member States', which in turn 'must be ensured within the framework of the structure and objectives of the [EU]'.[17] Therefore, whilst the rule of law as a matter of EU law was initially understood as bottom-up, the rule of law can be seen as also being top-down, given its slow but explicit place within the EU Treaties. Whilst the rule of law was long textually absent from EU primary law, that did not mean that it was absent altogether. With the Treaty of Maastricht, it became a value of the EU's Common Foreign and Security Policy (CFSP)[18] – a clear *external* manifestation of the rule of law as against third parties. At present, Article 2 of the Treaty on European Union (TEU) proclaims that the rule of law is a 'value' of the EU.[19]

Long before this, however, the *Les Verts* judgment of the Court made this abundantly clear.[20] This was the espousal of what the European rule of law

[16] M Dawson, 'How Can EU Law Respond to Populism?' (2020) 40 *OJLS* 183, 194.

[17] Case C-11/70 *Internationale Handelsgesellschaft mbH v Einfuhr- und Vorratsstelle für Getreide und Futtermittel*, ECLI:EU:C:1970:114, para 4.

[18] For full constitutional analysis of the CFSP, see G Butler, *Constitutional Law of the EU's Common Foreign and Security Policy: Competence and Institutions in External Relations* (Oxford, Hart Publishing, 2019).

[19] For the historical development of the rule of law into the EU Treaties, see A Moberg, 'When the Return of the Nation-State Undermines the Rule of Law: Poland, the EU, and Article 7 TEU' in A Bakardjieva Engelbrekt et al (eds), *The European Union and the Return of the Nation State: Interdisciplinary European Studies* (New York, Springer International Publishing, 2020) 59, 64–65.

[20] *Les Verts* is so central to contemporary thinking, it applies to all fields of EU law, including 'specific' areas like the EU's CFSP. See, G Butler, 'Implementing a Complete System of Legal Remedies in EU Foreign Affairs Law' (2018) 24 *Columbia Journal of European Law* 637.

standard was to be from the perspective of EU law. The Court stated that the EU is 'based on the rule of law'; that the EU Treaties are the 'basic constitutional charter'; and that the EU has 'established a complete system of legal remedies and procedures'.[21] For some, the *Les Verts* judgment showed the Court trying to capture the German understanding of *Rechtsgemeinschaft* and *Rechtsstaat*,[22] which both translate back to 'the rule of law'. The rule of law is, in the eyes of the Court, clearly better than *no* rule of law. Therefore, it is with this insight in mind that the rule of law in the Nordic states can be analysed.

IV. THE RULE OF LAW IN THE NORDIC STATES

It is highly regrettable that challenges to the rule of law are an increasingly common feature of Europe in the 2020s – more than they were in the 1990s and 2000s. Regional variations and groupings are part-and-parcel of EU Member States' collective history. Given such developments and the closeness of the Nordic states,[23] it is necessary to examine the rule of law more carefully in the Nordics, and to assess how fit and prepared they are to fend off, pre-emptively or latterly, rule of law challenges.

The rule of law is just as much a challenge in developed, prosperous states as it is in societies with recent histories of rule of law challenges. To illustrate with the most vivid example, it is difficult to say that the United States of America, with the coming into office of a new administration in 2017, represented business as usual for American governance and leadership in the world order. Whilst there was at the time an ordinary transfer of power according to democratic procedures and the rule of law, the occasion was not without significance given the manner in which the office-holder conducted himself both prior to assuming the office and after entering into office, which concerned many as to the change of direction of the Western, democratic world.

On this basis of seeing changes to standards in ordered societies, attention turns to the Nordic states, where the rule of law is present, even if it has never been a settled concept. The Nordic states have structural similarities and comparable aspects of governance structure.[24] Both individually and collectively, they personify an understanding of the exceptionalism of the self, given their highly-developed and advanced societies. This view, however, rather regrettably leads to misplaced complacence, which might incorrectly give the impression

[21] Case C-294/83 *Parti écologiste 'Les Verts' v European Parliament*, ECLI:EU:C:1986:166, para 23.

[22] K Tuori, *European Constitutionalism* (Cambridge, Cambridge University Press, 2015) 211.

[23] Given that only three of the five Nordic states are EU Member States, in this chapter 'the Nordics' will be taken to comprise the three that are EU Member States, ie Denmark, Finland and Sweden. The two other Nordic states, Iceland and Norway, are parties to the EEA Agreement, integrating them within most aspects of the EU's internal market.

[24] This has also been positively identified elsewhere. See G Noll, 'Nostalghia: A Nordic International Law' (2016) 85 *Nordic Journal of International Law* 265.

that such uniqueness insulates them from rule of law challenges. Rather, there is a need to critically analyse the normative viewpoints that are ingrained in Nordic legal thought, since to think that the Nordic states could not suffer from rule of law challenges would be both imprudent and irrational. Ordered societies of all kinds, after all, are vulnerable entities.

There can be little doubt that at this point in time, the Nordic states represent liberal, enlightened values that incorporate the rule of law, fundamental freedoms, open markets, and the rule of law. They are not currently illiberal societies, but whilst material rule of law problems in the Nordics are few at present, they could take on the practices of illiberal entities should circumstances arise. The Nordic perspective is distinctly that the rule of law is a 'concept … [that] … starts quite pragmatically from the fact that … EU Member States are obligated to take into account the interpretations that the concept of the rule of law has received within EU law'.[25] Nordic states actively embrace the European rule of law standard, and it would be typical of them, as self-perceived ardent followers of the rule of law, and to trumpet its virtues to other EU Member States. Yet, rightly, this also works the other way around.

The Nordic states have simultaneously adopted market-based economies, well within the confines of capitalism that is compatible with a model of extensive redistribution in the name of the welfare state. Both individually and collectively, the Nordics have some of the highest living standards in the world. And whilst the standards of living do vary from one state to another, including between regions of the states, their fundamental values do not. The Nordic states are rather insular in nature, in themselves or sometimes amongst themselves, as if they formed a social cocoon within the sphere of wider European integration. As a whole, the Nordics do not take criticism of their governance models or wider societal traits very well. Moreover, they occasionally have peculiar debates and attitudes towards law beyond the state[26] – whatever its form. Sporadically, these debates tips towards asking whether external oversight should even be necessary at all.

The Nordic states could be perceived as having a lack of separation within their 'balance' of powers. In both Denmark and Sweden, national courts are deeply embedded within the fabric of the state, and it can be difficult to separate them from other branches of state. Distinct power attribution (and its separation) is fundamentally important to the rule of law, for it is 'unspoken' but nonetheless a part of the 'fundamental bargain between the individual and the state, the governed and the governor'.[27] However, in a Nordic context, the rule of

[25] J Raitio, 'The Rule of Law in Contemporary Finland: Not Just a Rhetorical Balloon' in A Bakardjieva Engelbrekt and X Groussot (eds), *The Future of Europe: Political and Legal Integration Beyond Brexit* (Oxford, Hart Publishing, 2019). 205.

[26] See, M Wind, 'The Scandinavians: The Foot-Dragging Supporters of European Law?' in J Lindholm and M Derlén (eds), *The Court of Justice of the European Union: Multidisciplinary Perspectives* (Oxford, Hart Publishing, 2018).

[27] T Bingham, 'The Rule of Law' (2007) 66 *Cambridge Law Journal* 67, 84.

law and its intersection with democracy still considers the relationship between the two concepts,[28] and does not necessarily take account of wider concerns. The rule of law and democracy should never be confused, as they are not the same. Democracy itself is not equivalent to the rule of law, nor to the separation of powers.[29] This is because democracy itself does not safeguard or guarantee against the use and abuse of state structures by means that are contrary to the rule of law. As put, 'World War II and the Nazi regime clearly demonstrated that unconstrained parliaments and majority rule are no guarantees of a democratic development'.[30]

The rule of law can come under attack in such a way that flagrant violations of it may be disguised with the language of democracy. In the Nordics, the parliament may be perceived as the ultimate form of legitimacy, and as superior to other branches of state power. This reading is manifestly misplaced, for entrusting one branch with overarching powers as against others risks a dangerous imbalance of power. This is all the more troubling when a political culture exists that demonstrates high levels of consensus, without major ideological difference between different political actors. This said, a preference for a parliament may not necessarily be a Nordic trait,[31] even if it is closely associated with the Nordic region. Minority governments, another feature of Nordic politics, remove some powers from over-ambitious executives. However, they empower legislatures. Legal positivism, prevalent in the Nordic states, is hugely problematic for the rule of law.[32] Powers granted to public authorities are thus normatively assumed to be in accordance with the rule of law. The legislatures in the Nordic states have in the past granted colossal powers to the executive, and in some cases to independent agencies, with little oversight or scrutiny once those powers have been provided for, which is a distinct rule of law challenge.

Several examples, both recent and still live issues, may be examined in relation to the Nordic states, where rule of law issues might give cause for concern in connection with the European rule of law standard. Both Denmark and Sweden have, to date, failed to join the enhanced cooperation method of participation in the European Public Prosecutor's Office (EPPO), which combats crimes linked to funds coming from the EU budget. Denmark has a particular legacy position

[28] As critiqued by J Raitio, 'Does the Concept of Rule of Law Have Any Material Content? A Nordic Point of View' (2017) 24 *Maastricht Journal of European and Comparative Law* 774, 775.

[29] That said, there is 'no automatic contradiction' between majority rule in a democracy and having a separation of powers. J Nergelius, 'North and South: Can the Nordic States and the European Continent Find Each Other in the Constitutional Area – or Are They Too Different?' in M Scheinin (ed), *The Welfare State and Constitutionalism in the Nordic Countries* (Copenhagen, Nordic Council of Ministers, 2001) 82.

[30] M Wind, 'When Parliament Comes First – The Danish Concept of Democracy Meets the European Union' (2009) 27 *Nordisk Tidsskrift for Menneskerettigheter* 272, 280.

[31] S Schaumburg-Müller, 'Parliamentary Precedence in Denmark – A Jurisprudential Assessment' (2009) 27 *Nordisk Tidsskrift for Menneskerettigheter* 170, 172.

[32] As pointed out, despite claims of 'neutrality', it is, in fact, 'highly normative': ibid 183.

regarding opt-outs,[33] which in turn prevents Denmark on legal grounds from engaging in such enhanced cooperation, unlike the vast majority of Member States. By contrast, however, Sweden's position in not joining the EPPO puts it in the company of two other illustrious EU Member States without technical opt-outs – Hungary and Poland. Whilst the latter two states may have very reasonable concerns that the EPPO might initiate actual prosecutions in their Member States, Sweden's decision not to join appears technical, and unsustainable in the longer term for its own standing on EU affairs. No other EU Member State has shared the same level of concern as Sweden, including another Nordic state, Finland, who duly joined the enhanced cooperation efforts.

Turning west, Norway previously tried to block the reappointment of a judge to the European Free Trade Association (EFTA) Court,[34] who was nominated by another EFTA state, before eventually, as a diplomatic compromise, consenting to the reappointment. Such an action by Norway, to interfere in another EFTA state's preference in the selection process for a suitably qualified judge, was completely against the norms that had been long established in both EU law and European Economic Area (EEA) law. But Norway's antics in the EFTA system did not stop there. Some years later, Norway sought to try and impose its own national retirement age for national judges on the judges of the EFTA Court, by only putting forward the reappointed a judge for the shorter term of three years, and not the usual six years as mandated under EEA law.[35] It was only after the EFTA Surveillance Authority (ESA) opened a dialogue with Norway that matters were rectified[36] and the reappointment decision regarding a shorter term of office reversed.[37] Here, it was independent institutions in the EFTA pillar of the EEA that kept the Nordic state in check.

More recently, a situation concerning the appointment of members of a newly established Court of Appeal (*Landsréttur*) in Iceland led to proceedings being

[33] To illustrate the problematic aspects of 'opt-outs', see G Butler, 'The European Defence Union and Denmark's Defence Opt-out: A Legal Appraisal' (2020) 25(1) *European Foreign Affairs Revie* 117. See further *Europæisk forsvarssamarbejde og det danske forsvarsforbehold: Udredning om udviklingen i EU og Europa på det sikkerheds- og forsvarspolitiske område og betydningen for Danmark* [*European Defence Cooperation and the Danish Defence Opt-out: Investigation on developments in the EU and Europe in the field of security and defence policy and the importance for Denmark*] (Copenhagen, Danish Institute for International Studies, 2019).

[34] For an insider account, see C Baudenbacher, *Judicial Independence: Memoirs of a European Judge* (New York, Springer, 2019) 318–20.

[35] See M Andenas and H Haukeland Frederiksen, 'EFTA-Domstolen under Press' [2017] *Europarättslig Tidskrift* 205.

[36] 'Complaint Concerning Appointment of a Judge to the EFTA Court' (EFTA Surveillance Authority, Case No 79962, Document No 830122, 6 December 2016).

[37] This was not without consequence. In the meantime, in the *Nobile* case, the EFTA Court had to rule on the legality of its composition: Case E-21/16 *Pascal Nobile v DAS Rechtsschutz-Versicherungs AG* (EFTA Court, 14 February 2017). See G Butler, 'Mind the (Homogeneity) Gap: Independence of Referring Bodies Requesting Advisory Opinions from the EFTA Court' (2020) 44(2) *Fordham International Law Journal* 307.

brought against Iceland in the European Court of Human Rights (ECtHR). In the *Ástráðsson* case, the Icelandic Government proposed a list of judges who were to be appointed to the new court, which was subsequently approved by the Icelandic Parliament. However, the composition list that had initially been drawn up by an Evaluation Committee established by law was subsequently amended by the Minister for Justice. The Supreme Court of Iceland found a violation of a national law that stated that the judges were to be approved individually by the parliament, as opposed to being appointed *en masse*. When the case came before the ECtHR, it found a violation of Article 6 of the European Convention on Human Rights.[38] This may seem trivial, but the principle was clear: the right of individuals to have an impartial and independent tribunal established by law was violated by Iceland. In light of these few but colourful examples, both above and below the surface, there are profound issues in a societal context that give rise to potentials concerns about the rule of law in Nordic societies.

The Nordic welfare states are characterised by a considerable level of intrusiveness, giving the state and its institutions enormous leverage over individuals. With a large and developed public sector, the line of command means that national governments exercise a large degree of authority over individuals, notwithstanding some national variations. This includes the centralisation of digitalised information on individuals with state actors; the use of law (or lack of it) from beyond the state by national courts and tribunals; and the ambiguous role of the monarchy in those Nordic states that have hereditary heads of state (Denmark, Norway and Sweden). Such features of constitutional design are ingrained in Nordic legal thought and practice, and stand to be used in ways that are not in conformity with the European rule of law standard. The Nordic states could, if circumstances were to change, have rule of law challenges given the framework and design of their state systems. Before matters culminate in a rule of law crisis, however, these states would likely see the erosion of certain features of their societies, or what might be labelled 'constitutional rot'.[39] Such events would not be sudden, but consistent and regular deviations from the norms of what was previously a functioning system of governance that respected checks and balances, and the need for scrutiny, would be an obvious sign of what lay ahead. To be sure, there is a broad range of decisions that the Nordic states can make to pre-emptively thwart any future rule of law challenges. But there is also the EU legal order to keep the Nordic states in check. To prevent constitutional rot, there is the European rule of law standard and the manner in which it can be relied on within EU law, with national courts and the CJEU playing a critical role.

[38] *Guðmundur Andri Ástráðsson v Iceland* App no 26374/18, Judgment of the Second Section (ECtHR, 12 March 2019). Also, Judgment of the Grand Chamber (ECtHR, 1 December 2020).

[39] With regard to the United States, see J Balkin, 'Constitutional Crisis and Constitutional Rot' (2017) 77 *Maryland Law Review* 147.

V. COURTS AND EU LAW

Keen observers of EU law will be aware that its scope and application have undergone radical transformation. All national law must be looked at through the prism of the application of EU law in all its forms. This applies to all EU Member States, no matter what perception they hold of themselves. Deficiencies in the rule of law in just a single Member State have the potential to 'disrupt the very functioning of the Union legal order',[40] wherever that occurs.

Member States of the EU, at their legal core, have the notion of judicial review as a component of the system of checks and balances. Yet it is used to varying degrees, thus giving rise to different standards of review in Member States. In all Member States, however, executive and legislative freedom is curtailed by membership of international organisations, notably (but not exclusively) the EU, thus allowing for national courts to play a stronger role when applying EU law than might otherwise have been the norm when adjudicating in the past. Power, legally and politically, is structurally fragmented in the EU for the purpose of ensuring that no single interest prevails without wider consensus. This fragmented landscape makes European interests weighing in specific rule of law concerns in individual EU Member States more difficult than might typically be envisaged. After all, 'the EU' is not a single, harmonious entity. Yet critically, the rule of law, as a legal concept in EU law, has a distinctiveness about it, in that it can be operationalised by courts of law. If the rule of law is seen as only a mere hypothetical instrument with no practical application, as demonstrated by the insufficiency of the Article 7 TEU process analysed below, then sceptics ought to examine how national courts, but more importantly the CJEU, have experimented with the rule of law through their judgments.

Principles from the Court are essential for preservation of the European rule of law standard. The safeguards come from the application of such principles. Courts of all descriptions are expected (if they are not already legally mandated) to preserve the rule of law and, thus, act as a constraint on executive and legislative power. Interpreting the law, whatever that law's source, is a court's proper role in an entity with rule of law as one of its vital components. Interpreting the rule of law, as applied to Member State actions, is a challenge for the Court too.[41] Judicial review can and is exercised for the purposes of the rule of law, but also for guaranteeing other normative qualities. In recent times, the rule of law has become an increasingly juridified concept at EU level, with judicial review slowly finding its way into ensuring the European rule of law standard in

[40] C Hillion, 'Overseeing the Rule of Law in the EU: Legal Mandate and Means' in Closa and Kochenov (eds) (n 14) 61.

[41] T Von Danwitz, 'The Rule of Law in the Recent Jurisprudence of the ECJ' in Werner Schroeder (ed), *Strengthening the Rule of Law in Europe: From a Common Concept to Mechanisms of Implementation* (Oxford, Hart Publishing, 2016) 162.

EU Member States. As a former President of the Supreme Court of Denmark has noted, '[t]he European Court of Justice is of paramount importance in ensuring a European Union based on the rule of law'.[42]

The powers of state actors are put under duress when they are undermined by other powerful entities of the state. Relying on national courts in the Nordic states may be a futile exercise. That is because decision-making by political actors (national governments and parliaments) and sometimes administrative actors, coupled with an extremely reluctant judiciary, makes reliance on legal provisions alone an insufficient response to rule of law challenges. Notably, it has even been stated that national courts, wherever their geographic location, are not fully independent actors, given that they can 'present the interest of the society, or even the state'.[43] Therefore, whilst national courts have the possibility to act as objective legal actors, their adjudication can be, by anyone's imagination, subjective. It is such a national power imbalance between the different arms of states that makes an EU Member State, such as a Nordic state, particularly susceptible to rule of law difficulties.

Member States have discretion as to how to give effect to remedies under EU law, which is an obligation they must comply with[44] within the scope of their national mechanisms.[45] This reliance upon national courts is predicated on an understanding of independent national courts, however. When Member States accede to the EU, this ensures that national courts place greater emphasis on EU legal aspects of disputes, rather than their merely being an extension of the administration of a state and national law.[46] Capturing national independent institutions is one manner in which a rule of law challenge can emerge in an EU Member State, given that without independent judiciaries of EU Member States, the rule of law would collapse in a short period of time. National courts in some EU Member States, including the Nordics, have a history of being deferential to political branches in strands of adjudication. For example, in Denmark only one act of parliament has been overturned by the courts,[47] and

[42] B Dahl, 'Keynote Address' in U Neergaard and C Jacqueson (eds), *The XXVI FIDE Congress in Copenhagen, 2014: Congress Proceedings: Speeches from the XXVI FIDE Congress*, vol 4 (Copenhagen, Djøf Publishing, 2014) 30.

[43] HP Graver, 'Judicial Independence Under Authoritarian Rule: An Institutional Approach to the Legal Tradition of the West' (2018) 10 *Hague Journal on the Rule of Law* 317, 335.

[44] Case C-222/84 *Marguerite Johnston v Chief Constable of the Royal Ulster Constabulary*, ECLI:EU:C:1986:206, paras 17–18.

[45] See Case C-432/05, *Unibet (London) Ltd and Unibet (International) Ltd v Justitiekanslern*, ECLI:EU:C:2007:163 and related case law.

[46] With regard to Sweden and a host of problems in this regard, see M Zamboni, 'The Positioning of the Supreme Courts in Sweden – A Democratic Oddity?' (2019) 15 *European Constitutional Law Review* 668, 683.

[47] The *Tvind* case. Judgment of the Supreme Court of Denmark of 19 February 1999 (295/1998). For further details, see JA Jensen, 'The 150th Anniversary of the Danish Constitution and a Landmark Decision of the Supreme Court' (1999) 5 *European Public Law* 492.

in Sweden there remains a blurring between administrative and judicial actors.[48] A complete national system of legal remedies and procedures, incorporation of EU law, independent national courts and defence of the rule of law are all necessary traits of an EU Member State clearly in line with the European rule of law standard.

National courts must have a robust set of tools at their disposal for availing themselves of EU law to ensure its application in the cases before them. One of these tools is the preliminary reference procedure, which allows the courts to engage in judicial dialogue with the CJEU to get authoritative answers to questions of EU law, necessary for its application in national settings. No superior national judicial body can interfere with this dialogue,[49] and the CJEU ought to place greater emphasis on stopping any interference that might be attempted.[50] At the Court, where there a wider degree of structural separation between internal state actors and the Court itself, there is a stronger readiness to scrutinise matters that would impinge upon the European rule of law standard. Thus, the scrutiny applied, in terms of judicial review at the Court, is far superior to that of national courts in the Nordic states.[51] This is rightly so, given that, from a rule of law perspective, much more is effectively at stake at the Court – the unity and consistence of the EU legal order – alongside the rule of law in Europe as a whole.

The way in which EU law was and is developed has been a skilful craft, and one that is taking a new harder edge as the years go by. In recent years, the Court has taken a stronger line against actions by EU Member States that violate the European rule of law standard.[52] Consequently, from a judicial perspective, the position is clear – challenges to the European rule of law standard and persistent behaviour that is contrary to the essence of the EU are not to be tolerated. As seen, rule of law challenges in other EU Member States have given rise to a litany of cases at the Court, as demonstrated below. The European Commission has stepped up, where it chooses to, litigating against Member States who have flagrantly violated the standard. The very fact that EU Member States have infringement actions brought against them by the Commission for allegedly failing to fulfil their obligations demonstrates that need for proper oversight

[48] Yet over time, the courts have increasingly become more separated. For an overview in this regard, see H Wenander, 'Full Judicial Review or Administrative Discretion? A Swedish Perspective on Deference to the Administration' in Guobin Zhu (ed), *Deference to the Administration in Judicial Review* (New York, Springer, 2019).

[49] Case C-210/06 *Cartesio Oktató és Szolgáltató bt*, ECLI:EU:C:2008:723.

[50] For the argument that the *Cartesio* doctrine could be strengthened by the Court, see G Butler and J Cotter, 'Just Say No! Appeals against Orders for a Preliminary Reference' (2020) 26(3) *European Public Law* 615.

[51] A Føllesdal and M Wind, 'Nordic Reluctance Towards Judicial Review Under Siege' (2009) 27 *Nordisk Tidsskrift for Menneskerettigheter* 131, 135.

[52] See, P Van Elsuwege and F Gremmelprez, 'Protecting the Rule of Law in the EU Legal Order: A Constitutional Role for the Court of Justice' (2020) 16 *European Constitutional Law Review* 8.

through EU institutions and an independent Court to ensure that the European rule of law standard is enforced. Such infringement procedures imply that Member States are effectively having their laws and norms audited on a rule of law basis.

The case law is becoming increasingly robust and forceful on such rule of law points. When Portuguese judges had their pay reduced,[53] this was challenged using EU law; when Poland undertook (and is still undertaking) 'reforms' to its national courts,[54] this was also challenged using EU law; when successive Spanish governments appointed their political operatives and removed previous government appointments to national tax tribunals exercising a quasi-judicial function,[55] EU law was in play; and when the French Council of State (*Conseil d'État*) failed to make a preliminary reference to the Court to resolve a matter in a case before it, France was found to have violated EU law.[56] Moreover, when a public prosecutor in Germany issued a European Arrest Warrant (EAW),[57] and the office of the prosecutor was found to have insufficient independence, EU law was also in action. Cumulatively, there is undoubted evidence of a European rule of law standard through the Court's answers to questions about the rule of law that are put to it via a variety of procedures.[58] Importantly, it is not just select Member States bearing the brunt of this adjudication; rather, the standard is applied to Member States of all kinds – irrespective of geography. Accordingly, there is no two- or multi-tier Europe when it comes to the European rule of law standard. All EU Member States are held to the same one.

That such reliance is placed upon judicial processes engaging the Court can be explained by the deficiencies contained in other mechanisms for ensuring rule of law compliance in the EU legal order. For example, the activity of EU agencies and intergovernmental methods of combatting rule of law challenges in Member States have, to date, been particularly ineffective. These methods have been extensively analysed in the literature,[59] but two methods will be briefly discussed to illustrate the wider point. First, the EU's Fundamental Rights

[53] Case C-64/16 *Associação Sindical dos Juízes Portugueses v Tribunal de Contas*, ECLI:EU:C:2018:117 ('*Association of Portuguese Judges*').

[54] Case C-192/18 *Commission v Poland*, ECLI:EU:C:2019:924 ('*Independence of Ordinary Courts*'); Case C-619/18, *Commission v Poland*, ECLI:EU:C:2019:531 ('*Independence of the Supreme Court*'); and Case C-791/19 *Commission v Poland*, pending ('*Independence of the Disciplinary Chamber of the Supreme Court*').

[55] Case C-274/14, *Proceedings brought by Banco de Santander SA*, ECLI:EU:C:2020:17. Further, see G Butler, 'Independence of Non-Judicial Bodies and Orders for a Preliminary Reference to the Court of Justice' (2020) 45(6) *EL Rev* 870.

[56] Case C-416/17 *Commission v France*, ECLI:EU:C:2018:811.

[57] Joined Cases C-508/18 and C-82/19 PPU, *Minister for Justice and Equality v OG and PI*, ECLI:EU:C:2019:456.

[58] See the contribution by Groussot and Zemskova in ch 12 of this volume.

[59] For a thorough overview, see E Wennerström, 'Can the EU Protect Its Fundamental Values?' in A Bakardjieva Engelbrekt et al (eds), *The European Union in a Changing World Order: Interdisciplinary European Studies* (New York, Springer International Publishing, 2020).

Agency (FRA), whilst important, has no role in the monitoring of Member States' actions that have rule of law implications. Its mandate, defined by Regulation, is much narrower, namely, providing 'advice and guidance',[60] 'when implementing [Union] law'.[61] Thus, the EU Agency is, in the current framework, no substitute for the role of national courts and the CJEU. Second, Article 7 TEU stands out, given that it was designed with one eye towards Eastern Enlargement and the potential rule of law challenges that might occur as a result. What is striking is that back in 2000, at the time of negotiating the new constitutional framework for the EU, candidate countries had pressed for stronger rule of law mechanisms.[62] Article 7 TEU has a strong intergovernmental logic to it, rather than being centred on the Commission.[63] The drastic nature of its consequences, namely the potential suspension of certain Member States' rights, means that it is not lightly triggered against Member States.

To date, despite particularly scandalous breaches of the rule of law in some Member States, Article 7 TEU has not been fully engaged. The failure of Article 7 TEU demonstrates that a Council-centred approach to slippages in the European rule of law standard does not,[64] and will not, work through Article 7 TEU alone. Recourse to the specific inter-state mechanism of obligations under EU law has been considered to be taken before the Court,[65] within the existing inter-state mechanism of Article 259 of the Treaty on the Functioning of the EU (TFEU).[66] Given these deficiencies, and potential over-reliance on the Court to give effect to the European rule of law standard, attention has to turn to more functional methods of detecting rule of law slippages, and what can be done to preserve the European rule of law standard beyond just turning to the Court.

[60] J Vedsted-Hansen, 'Borders and Migration Control: FRA's Research at Protection Black Spots' in R Byrne and H Entzinger (eds), *Human Rights Law and Evidence-Based Policy: The Impact of the EU Fundamental Rights Agency* (Abingdon, Routledge, 2020) 186.

[61] Council Regulation (EC) No 168/2007 of 15 February 2007 Establishing a European Union Agency for Fundamental Rights [2007] OJ L53/1, Art 2.

[62] For example, Poland. See Transmission Note: IGC 2000: Contribution from the Government of Poland (Intergovernmental Conference 2000: The Polish Position) (Conference of the Representatives of the Governments of the Member States) (CONFER/VAR 3967/00).

[63] This said, Art 7 TEU is not purely intergovernmental by any description, given it can also involve both the Commission and the Parliament.

[64] On Art 7 TEU and its problems, see I Österdahl, 'Article 7 TEU and the Rule of Law Mechanism: A Dissuasive Weapon or a Paper Tiger?' in W Heusel and J-P Rageade (eds), *The Authority of EU Law: Do We Still Believe in It?* (New York, Springer, 2019); D Kochenov, 'Article 7 TEU' in M Kellerbauer, M Klamert and J Tomkin (eds), *The EU Treaties and the Charter of Fundamental Rights: A Commentary* (Oxford, Oxford University Press, 2019).

[65] For the proposition regarding using inter-state procedure on rule of law issues in Member States, see 'Opinion of the Meijers Committee on Interstate Procedures and the Rule of Law (CM1909)' (Meijers Committee (Standing Committee of experts on international immigration, refugee and criminal law) 2019).

[66] On the means of using Art 259 TFEU as a way of bringing an inter-state dispute before the Court for alleged failures of other Member States to fulfil their obligations under EU law, see G Butler, 'The Court of Justice as an Inter-State Court' (2017) 36 *Yearbook of European Law* 179.

VI. DETECTION OF RULE OF LAW CHALLENGES

The rule of law is of fundamental importance to European societies as we know them, and, deservedly, has to be respected. The necessary respect for and adherence to the rule of law are not automatic, common public goods. Rightly, then, the rule of law must be preserved, detecting challenges to it and uncovering ways in which it can be maintained. Rule of law challenges can come slowly and softly, or swiftly and brutally. Both forms are equally dangerous. The rule of law, in the form of the European rule of law standard, needs constant efforts to preserve its effect. National executives and legislatures in EU Member States must be constrained by law against their own governing illusions. The preservation of the European rule of law standard, therefore, can be considered a normative public good, which should be actively promoted and defended from attack. The rule of law is not just about sanctioning systematic breaches, but also about taking action before rule of law concerns turn into full-blown rule of law violations.

The end of the rule of law history[67] has not been reached by any stretch of the imagination. There are major global powers that do not subscribe to any form of rule of law, as defined by a European standard. Such states, without this version of the rule of law, are nonetheless integrated into the global legal order.[68] The European rule of law standard, therefore, can be sharply contrasted with that in other regions of the world. Within Europe itself, there are only artificial differences between older EU Member States that have *had* (and continue to have) governance frameworks in place for a long time (eg the Nordic states), and newer EU Member States that have had to *find* proper governance frameworks in the recent past (eg Hungary, Poland and others). European integration has entrenched the rule of law in all EU Member States – the Nordics included. But entrenchment varies as to depth, and is by no means a one-off occurrence. Rather, the reality is that the rule of law is more deeply ingrained in some Member States, but exists only superficially in others.

Attempts by Member States to act without national or European checks and balances are inevitable, and efforts to transgress the constitutional norms have to be reprimanded in some way. It is therefore a matter of how to detect rule of law challenges. Whilst there is no optimal method, some early alarm bells can be heard from a distance away. First, when a national legal 'tradition' is invoked, this can immediately be opposed as an inadequate proposition in itself, for tradition is meant to imply reversion to a prior practice, or the prolonging

[67] F Fukuyama, *The End of History and the Last Man* (New York, NY, Free Press 1992), who argued, in effect, that liberal democracies will be the ultimate form of government prevailing around the globe. This claim has been extensively critiqued, but the premise of that argument remains, even though it has been subsequently qualified.

[68] T Ginsburg, 'Authoritarian International Law?' (2020) 114 *American Journal of International Law* 221, 222.

of a long-time state of affairs.[69] 'Tradition', in itself, is not always supportive of the European rule of law standard. Second, the invocation of 'constitutional identity'[70] within Member States should be immediately suspect, for it is typically a means to fend off any positive influences and effects from beyond the state.[71] Third, a further method of early detection is to see how Member States react to judgments of the Court that go against them, and whether such judgments are ultimately followed. There must be compliance with the Court's decisions, despite the fact that the 'pull of law in Western democracies does not rest on the gun'.[72] Fourth, and finally, alarm bells should ring if Member States fully capitulate to a majority's worst instincts that are fundamentally against the European rule of law standard. Any of these disturbing trends, if detected, would be a clear sign of declining standards in the political class and leadership.

Member States have, individually, enormous power to use the state apparatus to achieve ends of their own making – usefully or abusively. Populism is an ailment, across the Continent of Europe, to which states are susceptible. Like viral outbreaks, populism recognises no borders, cutting across intersections of political life that have little regard for the bedrock constitutional principles that underpin the legal structures of the EU and its Member States. Similarly, totalitarianism is tempting for incumbent executives, given its attraction for some of those at the helm of government. Slippage is evident, as seen from the abusive use of referendums that were legally unnecessary. For example, the 2016 referendum in the United Kingdom on membership of the Union, a referendum on the implementation of EU law in Hungary in 2016, or even, prior to that, a 2003 referendum in Sweden on the single currency[73] – all three referendums shared a similar trait, which is that none of them was legally necessary but each was politically based, with such Member States experiencing a total absence of political leadership and responsibility. These are all clear rule of law failings, and ought to be properly condemned.

To contemplate rule of law concerns in the Nordic states tells us much about the societies of the North, and how they can be expected to cope under potential

[69] Only rarely and highly exceptionally can 'tradition' be successfully invoked as a legal defence. For an example in recent times regarding rules in Switzerland around the control, acquisition and possession of firearms, see Case C-482/17 *Czech Republic v Parliament and Council*, ECLI:EU:C:2019:1035, paras 164–170.

[70] See F Fabbrini and A Sajó, 'The Dangers of Constitutional Identity' (2019) 25 *European Law Journal* 457.

[71] For a full discussion of identity in Europe more generally and in specific EU Member States, see C Calliess and G van der Schyff (eds), *Constitutional Identity in a Europe of Multilevel Constitutionalism* (Cambridge, Cambridge University Press, 2019).

[72] JHH Weiler, 'Europe in Crisis – On "Political Messianism", "Legitimacy" and the "Rule of Law"' [2012] *Singapore Journal of Legal Studies* 248, 265.

[73] J Nergelius, 'The Constitution of Sweden and European Influences: The Changing Balance Between Democratic and Judicial Power' in A Albi and S Bardutzky (eds), *National Constitutions in European and Global Governance: Democracy, Rights, the Rule of Law: National Reports* (The Hague, TMC Asser Press, 2019) 315, 326–28.

sustained challenges to the rule of law as currently seen elsewhere. No Member State is immune to rule of law challenges,[74] and efforts to promote the rule of law should not be targeted at what might now be considered the 'usual suspects'.[75] It is not as distant a topic as many would like to think. Each of the Nordic states has problematic features of its legal system that are susceptible to rule of law problems. Historically, monarchies have wronged;[76] democratic parliaments have aggrieved; national executives have wounded; and national courts have maltreated.[77] But over time, there has been a shift here towards a multi-layered framework of checks and balances to prevent the wrongs from occurring, or to minimise them before they actually occur. The rule of law cannot be enforced by Member States alone. The 'self-help mechanism', whereby Member States take retaliatory action against each other in traditional international law, has been specifically rejected in the EU as a means for Member States to act.[78] The taking of matters into individual Member States' own hands would undermine the EU if such a practice were to be tolerated, and so rightly it is not. Consequently, it has to be concluded that the combatting of rule of law issues must come externally, from the EU and its institutions.

Backsliding on the rule of law is as much an ethical problem as it is a legal or political one. It would far outstrip contemporary political debate, for it would radically alter the governance structure of any individual society. The European rule of law standard offers no easy solutions to backsliding,[79] but it cannot be excluded that indifference to political developments, and failure to detect an oncoming rule of law challenge in Nordic societies, would be the beginning of constitutional rot that would become ever-more ingrained. Not every breach

[74] For another perspective, with respect to another northern (and western) EU Member State, see P Gallagher, 'Challenges to the Rule of Law in 21st Century Ireland' in E Carolan (ed), *Judicial Power in Ireland* (Dublin, Institute of Public Administration 2018).

[75] Term borrowed from the final scene of 1942 film *Casablanca*, which, as it happens, also has a rule of law background to it, with the *Régime de Vichy* controlling the city in what is modern-day Morocco.

[76] The EU has tempered the powers of the EU's monarchies, with their powers as heads of state reduced and their divine rights slowly evaporating. See, HU Jessurun d'Oliveira, 'The EU and Its Monarchies: Influences and Frictions' (2012) 8 *European Constitutional Law Review* 63.

[77] The dualistic tendencies of the Supreme Court of Denmark, as seen in the *Dansk Industri* (*Ajos*) case. As an example, this judgment presents particularly troubling deliberations, and demonstrates a real lack of rigour by its voting members in the majority about the fundamentals of EU law. Understanding that national law must yield to other forms of law, namely EU law, has long been a feature of European integration and the European rule of law. Yet this is still, somehow, a discussion point. For the best insight, see U Neergaard and K Engsig Sørensen, 'Activist Infighting among Courts and Breakdown of Mutual Trust? The Danish Supreme Court, the CJEU, and the Ajos Case' (2017) 36 *Yearbook of European Law* 275.

[78] Joined Cases C-90/63, and C-91/63, *Commission of the European Economic Community v Grand Duchy of Luxembourg and Kingdom of Belgium*, ECLI:EU:C:1964:80. See further W Phelan, *Great Judgments of the European Court of Justice: Rethinking the Landmark Decisions of the Foundational Period* (Cambridge, Cambridge University Press 2019) 84–122.

[79] On backsliding, see L Pech and K L Scheppele, 'Illiberalism Within: Rule of Law Backsliding in the EU' (2017) 19 *Cambridge Yearbook of European Legal Studies* 3.

of the rule of law would be exceptionally objectionable, or sanctioned, or even responded to, but incremental slippage in adherence to the European rule of law standard would tear away at the very fabric of what has prevented serious deviations from the European rule of law standard since accession of the Nordic states to the EU and the latching on of the others through the EEA Agreement.

If there is no rule of law, the capacity for progress in anything else is diminished. Rule of law concerns are not just expressions in moments of madness; rather they are part-and-parcel of wider governing regimes for a prolonged period of time. Ensuring the rule of law is maintained is a struggle that never ceases. It is a concept for all times – the present included. Centralising the opposition of flagrant breaches of the rule of law within a small set of actors – activists, civil society, and intellectual debate – will never be enough to combat the force of an abusive state. Perhaps the greater risk of all is complacency, and all interested actors have a duty to perform. Worryingly, legal safeguards in certain times may not be enough.[80] Therefore, positive actions must continue to be fought for in the face of authoritarian winds, which can include free and unbridled speech, restrictions on executive power, longevity of checks on executive power and, critically, external examination through strict scrutiny by the Court, when called upon to adjudicate by national courts and the Commission.

VII. CONCLUSION: COULD IT HAPPEN HERE?

This chapter now returns to where it began, by pondering whether 'it' could happen here.[81] There ought to be no hysterical response to discussing such serious topics in our surroundings, for Europe as a whole has numerous rule of law challenges,[82] varying in their levels of seriousness. The belief that 'it' could not occur in a Nordic setting would be profoundly misgiven. No state or society is immune from such potential challenges. Warning signs must be closely intercepted and followed, as events can, and often do, go in the wrong direction. Challenges to the rule of law do not occur overnight but rather tend to be a result of several slow-moving events that build over time, to the point where opposing them becomes ever more insurmountable. The fact is that it can happen here,[83] and all relevant stakeholders involved should be prepared to act if and when that

[80] HP Graver, 'The Immoral Choice – How Judges Participate in the Transformation of Rule of Law to Rule of Evil' in EFTA Court (ed), *The EEA and the EFTA Court: Decentred Integration* (Oxford, Hart Publishing, 2014) 74.

[81] For a collection of essays considering this in an American context, see CR Sunstein (ed), *Can It Happen Here? Authoritarianism in America* (New York, NY, Dey Street Books 2018).

[82] Discussing the rule of law problems right across Europe, regardless of geography, see M Wind, *The Tribalization of Europe: A Defence of Our Liberal Values* (Cambridge, Polity Press, 2020).

[83] One notable scholar, with respect to one Member State, is already probing 'Why Did It Happen?': W Sadurski, *Poland's Constitutional Breakdown* (Oxford, Oxford University Press, 2019) 162–92.

time comes. A narrow array of views being aired in public debate opens up the potential for authoritarianism to flourish. An informed public, subject to various perspectives, and a healthy societal dialogue can pre-emptively thwart rule of law challenges. Citizen engagement has to be preserved, for when a polity has oncoming, self-inflicted dangers, an informed citizenry can do wonders for questioning state actions. Intuition should alert all to early warning signals.

This chapter has not claimed that the Nordic states are illiberal, but what it has stated is that constant vigilance and awareness are needed to fend off future rule of law challenges; and it has highlighted how EU law can be utilised as a tool to prevent onslaughts in this regard. In the United States of America, one view in recent times has been that democratic and institutional structures are so strong that this would offset any major rule of law issues that might arise.[84] As this chapter has contended, however, the contrary view is taken with respect to the Nordic states. Backsliding on the rule of law is not just something to think about as a distant issue, for, as illustrated, there are constitutional and institutional features of the Nordic states that leave them susceptible to rule of law slippages. Consequently, potential rule of law challenges can and must be assumed to have the possibility to occur anywhere, and not just in a select few Member States somewhere to the south and east in Europe. Without the rule of law within Member States, the days of their being Member States would be numbered.[85]

An ever more globalised world will involve greater legal pluralism than has ever been seen before, and it is part of the general progressive evolution of societies. The EU has had, and will continue to have, an instilling influence on the European rule of law standard as a concept that EU Member States must continuously abide by. A lively debate on the rule of law in the Nordics eventually needs to be had, when it will be realised that the time has long since passed for national institutions to learn to live with their involvement in pan-European processes, normatively and legally, in order to ensure that there are no double standards between East and West, or North and South. In 2020, Denmark, Sweden and Finland – the three Nordic EU Member States – stated they wished for stronger emphasis on 'the importance of the EU's core values of freedom, democracy and the rule of law', and furthermore stressed 'the need to strengthen the EU's ability to prevent and respond to rule of law violations'.[86] Let it be known that if those Member States themselves ever violated the European rule of law standard, they too would be on the receiving end of such action.

[84] T Cowen, 'Could Fascism Come to America?' in Sunstein (ed) (n 81) 37.

[85] For a similar view, see the speech of the former Judge of the Court of Justice of the European Union, E Levits, 'Address of the President of Latvia, Egils Levits, the 2020 Opening Sitting of the Constitutional Court of Latvia' (Constitutional Court of Latvia, 10 January 2020).

[86] Joint Press Statement of the Ministers for European Affairs of Denmark, Finland, France and Sweden, Copenhagen, 31 January 2020, Ministry of Foreign Affairs of Denmark (*Udenrigsministeriet*).

The rule of law in Europe has been an active item on the European agenda for more than a decade. These years have exposed the fragility of national legal orders, particularly for their rule of law deficiencies. In early 2020, and continuing on into 2021 through the COVID-19 pandemic, EU Member States, to varying degrees, effectively suspended normal life, with extensive curfews, closing orders, substantial data-gathering, and mass restrictions on the liberty of individuals. This has been facilitated through weak political criticism and opposition, as well as through the support of prominent media outlets, the result being mass compliance of a mostly unquestioning public. It is assumed that such restrictions will be lifted in time, but that assumption is not a given. Coercion at the instigation of the state is a slippery slope, with complicit actors engaging in simultaneous behaviour, resulting in super-majoritarian societies' being a threat to all.

In recent years, in an Aarhus bookstore called *Kristian F Møller Boghandler*, reprinted copies of Sinclair Lewis's *It Can't Happen Here* have been on sale. The very fact that the book is back in print and is being sold in the 2020s points to two important developments that should be noted. First, that no heed was paid to Jessup's critical writing about Windrip in *The Vermont Vigilance*, and the warning then is just as relevant more than 85 years after the book was first published. Second, the very fact of the reprinting of the novel in the modern era says much about the contemporary state of affairs in the world, and the rule of law challenges that all societies face. Yes, it could very well happen here, and it will be less than diligent to believe otherwise.

Part Four

Enforcing the Rule of Law in the EU: Current Mechanisms and Prospects

12

The Rise of Procedural Rule of Law in the European Union – Historical and Normative Foundations

XAVIER GROUSSOT AND ANNA ZEMSKOVA

I. INTRODUCTION

THE RULE OF law in the European Union (EU) is not only substantive and formal, it is also procedural.[1] From the early years of European integration until now – and this through the interpretative lens of either the terse Article 31 of the European Coal and Steel Community (ECSC) Treaty, or the robust Article 19 of the Treaty on European Union (TEU) – the procedural rule of law has always been thriving and jolting in the case law of both the ECSC Court and the Court of Justice of the European Union (CJEU). Yet in the last few years, the place of the procedural rule of law in the European jurisprudence has increased significantly, with the help of the newly drafted Article 19 TEU (replacing Article 220 EC, ex Article 164 EEC) and the entry into force of the EU Charter of Fundamental Rights (EUCFR) and notably its Article 47, which incorporates and codifies the general principle of effective judicial protection. Another reason for this contemporary rise of the procedural rule of law is the present 'crisis context', epitomised, for instance, by the state of economic emergency and the bailout case law of the CJEU. Claire Kilpatrick has relied on the concept of the procedural rule of law to show the malfunctioning of the EU judicial and administrative reviews of bailouts.[2] Our contribution builds on her

[1] J Waldron, 'The Rule of Law and the Importance of Procedure' (2010) 24 *Public Law and Legal Theory Research Paper Series, NYU*. For him, the rule of law at international level is under-theorised and focuses too much on formal aspects. He stresses the importance of the courts and the culture of argumentation that a legal system frames, sponsors or institutionalises.

[2] C Kilpatrick, 'On the Rule of Law and Economic Emergency: The Degradation of Basic Legal Values in Europe's Bailouts' (2015) 35 *OJLS* 325. Kilpatrick views the formal and procedural rule of law as complementary and not oppositional. Access to justice is seen as a mode of governance that allows people a voice in times of emergency. She highlights the procedural rule of law problem in the European economic crisis and the crucial role of courts in a state of emergency.

analysis, but is using a broader spectrum of investigation by not focusing merely on the situation of economic emergency and by tracing back the 'procedural rule of law culture' of the CJEU. We will therefore inquire into the historical and normative foundations of the procedural rule of law by studying the roots of *effet utile*, effectiveness and effective judicial protection in the EU legal order, and by viewing procedural effectiveness as an *idée directrice* (directing idea) of EU law. At the end of the historical circle, the ruling of the German Federal Constitutional Court in *Weiss*, of 5 May 2020, constitutes a great exemplification of the normative clash between the EU procedural rule of law applied in the context of economic emergency by the CJEU and a national judicial vision of the 'proper' standard of judicial review to be realised in such a situation.[3]

This contribution is divided into three sections. First, it maps the doctrinal debate on EU procedural law. In section II, it views the principle of effectiveness as the core 'foundational' norm of procedural rule of law.[4] Second, it analyses the various applications of the procedural rule of law as procedural effectiveness in the CJEU case law by looking at *effet utile*, national procedural autonomy and effective judicial protection. This is done by tracking the historical roots of procedural effectiveness in the case law of the ECSC Court and CJEU. Third, it uses the case law of the CJEU in the recent context of economic emergency as a test case of the application of the procedural rule of law.

II. MAPPING THE DEBATE ON EU PROCEDURAL LAW

Mapping the debate of EU procedural law is not an easy task; and to a certain extent it may appear to be a daunting exercise. In a (gigantic) nutshell, it involves looking at the role of the CJEU and national courts, how these courts interpret and set aside the law, and how these courts design and apply the general principles of EU procedural law. It is often the case that the literature looks only at one aspect of the debate. It is also often the case that the discussion focuses on the application of the general principle of effectiveness or effective judicial protection. It is further often the case that the discussion concerns the overlap between the *effet utile* and effectiveness, which are often viewed as similar concepts.[5]

A good point of departure is the general principle of effectiveness, since it is the common denominator to all the academic debates on EU procedural

[3] BVergfG, Judgment of the Second Senate of 5 May 2020, 2 BvR 859/15. ECLI:DE:BVerfG:2020:rs20200505.

[4] For a discussion on effectiveness and the rule of law in the ECSC case law, see SA Scheingold, *The Rule of Law in European Integration – The Path of the Schuman Plan* (New Orleans, LA, Quid Pro Books, 1965).

[5] See Case 30/59 *De Gezamenlijke Steenkolenmijnen in Limburg* v *High Authority* [1961] ECR 1. This is the first case making reference to *effet utile* (translated in the English version as 'effectiveness').

law.[6] It is simply impossible not to discuss effectiveness in a debate on EU proceduralism.[7] According to Lenaerts, the principle of effectiveness finds three distinct expressions in CJEU case law: a principle of effective judicial protection (eg *Unibet*);[8] a principle of full effectiveness of Union law in terms of upholding the supremacy of EU law vis-à-vis national procedural law (eg *Factortame*);[9] or a principle of effectiveness *sensu stricto* that reflects the interface between national law and EU law, establishing the principles of equivalence and effectiveness (eg *Rewe*).[10]

This particular mapping of effectiveness focuses on its analysis in relation to the legislation of Member States, but does not map the general principles in relation to EU institutional law. This position is the most common vision in the EU scholarship, which looks at effectiveness often through the prism of national procedural law and through the loaded debate on national procedural autonomy. Another important part of the debate focuses on the issue of effectiveness of judicial review of EU legislation.[11] Besides effectiveness, the two main debates often approach the thorny issue of intensity of judicial review. In this respect, the debate of effectiveness at national level often discusses the issue of primacy of EU law, whereas the debate of effectiveness at EU level often approach the theme of intensity of judicial review via federalism and the US experience.[12] This is not so strange given the dilemma of counter-majoritarian difficulty in the US federal system and the increase of democratic safeguards in the EU legislative

[6] See, for a recent study of effectiveness in EU Law, A Bouveresse and D Ritleng (eds), *L'effectivité du droit de l'Union européenne* (Brussels, Bruylant, 2018). See in particular in that volume A Bouveresse, 'L'effectivité comme argument de l'autorité de la norme', ibid 1; and O Dubos, 'L'effet utile et l'effectivité dans l'Union européenne: identification normative', ibid 49.

[7] C Kilpatrick, 'The Future of Remedies in Europe' in C Kilpatrick, T Novitz and P Skidmore (eds), *The Future of Remedies in Europe* (Oxford, Hart Publishing, 2000) 1; see also P Haapaniemi, 'Procedural Autonomy: A Misnomer?' in L Ervo, M Gräns and A Jokela (eds), *The Europeanization of Procedural Law* (Zutphen, Europa Law Publishing, 2009) 87.

[8] Case C-432/05 *Unibet*, ECLI:EU:C:2007:163.

[9] Case C-213/89 *Factortame*, ECLI:EU:C:1990:257.

[10] K Lenaerts, I Maselis and K Gutman, *EU Procedural Law* (Oxford, Oxford University Press, 2014) 110.

[11] See, eg, *Weiss* case of the German Federal Constitutional Court (n 3), 5 May 2020.

[12] O Dubos, 'The Origins of the Proceduralisation of EU Law: a Grey Area of European Federalism' (2015) 1 *Review of European Administrative Law* 7. According to Dubos, 'Although the European Union ostensibly has no competence to harmonise national procedural rules, the proceduralisation process is a long-standing reality. The phenomenon is not only a topical example of the power dynamics within the European Union but also a manifestation of the engineering behind European federalism.' See also X Groussot and S Bogojević, 'Subsidiarity as a Procedural Safeguard to Federalism' in L Azoulai (ed), *The Question of Competence in the European Union* (Oxford, Oxford University Press, 2014) 234; G Majone, 'Regulatory Legitimacy in the United States and the European Union. Procedural legitimacy' in K Nicolaidis and R Howse (eds), *The Federal Vision* (Oxford, Oxford University Press, 2001) 252, 254 and 266–67. Majone discusses procedural legitimacy and regulatory federalism as an optimal allocation of regulatory responsibilities among the different levels of government forming the federal polity.

process.[13] Both debates often compare the intensity of judicial review of the general principle of effectiveness/effective judicial protection at national and EU institutional level. The CJEU is often accused of applying, or said to apply, a double standard of judicial review.[14]

So far, there is no major difficulty in mapping the principle of effectiveness. *Effet utile* is where in fact the most slippery discussion as to the role of effectiveness lies.[15] This is so because the use of the principle of effectiveness as a tool of interpretation is often associated with the use of *effet utile* as a method of interpretation[16] by the CJEU and the national courts.[17] *Effet utile*, as a method of interpretation,[18] is not free from criticism, and is often associated with an integrative interpretation of the Treaty based on effectiveness.[19]

[13] See P Craig, 'General Principles of Law: Treaty, Historical, and Normative Foundations' in K Ziegler, P Neuvonen and V Moreno-Lax (eds), *Research Handbook on General Principles of EU Law* (Cheltenham, Edward Elgar Press, forthcoming). Craig points out the increasing role of the European Parliament in the EU legislative process.

[14] See eg Kilpatrick (n 7) 8; T Konstadinides, *The Rule of Law in the European Union: The Internal Dimension* (Oxford, Hart Publishing, 2017) 169; D Grimm, *The Constitution of European Democracy* (Oxford, Oxford University Press, 2017) 240–41; and M Bonelli, 'Effective Judicial Protection in EU Law: an Evolving Principle of a Constitutional Nature' (2020) 12(2) *Review of European Administrative Law* 62.

[15] U Sadl, 'The Role of Effet Utile in Preserving the Continuity and Authority of European Law: Evidence from the citation web of the pre-accession case law of the Court of Justice of the EU' (2015) 8(1) *European Journal of Legal Studies* 18. Sadl considers that *effet utile* is one of the most contested notions of EU law and views it interchangeably with effectiveness. See also M Ross, 'Effectiveness in the European Legal Order(s): Beyond supremacy to constitutional proportionality' (2006) 31 *EL Rev* 476. For Ross, *effet utile* constitutes a multi-contextual notion that can be used in many different legal contexts, such as for the creation of new EU principles (eg indirect effect, Member State liability and general principles); for ensuring respect for the principle of primacy; for setting aside national legislation contrary to EU law; and for enforcing the obligations resulting from the principle of loyalty.

[16] See D Grimm, *The Constitution of European Democracy* (Oxford, Oxford University Press, 2017) 91. Grimm highlights the use of *effet utile* as a methodological programme used by the CJEU and national courts. See G Fitzmaurice, 'The Law and Procedure of the International Court of Justice: Treaty Interpretation and Certain Other Treaty Points' (1951) 28 *BYBIL* 1. *Effet utile* interpretation is also used in international law and the national context (eg France). In France, it is an established interpretative principle of the civil law law of contracts (*ut res magis valeat quam pereat* – it is better for a thing to have effect than to be made void).

[17] National courts have not only the power to interpret their national legislation in light of effectiveness, but also the power to interpret EU legislation in light of, eg, EU fundamental rights and the general principle of effectiveness.

[18] See, eg, Statement of the CJEU, 8 May 2020, press release following the judgment of the German Constitutional Court of 5 May 2020. The Statement emphasises the close linkage between uniformity, *effet utile* and the national courts.

[19] N Fennelly, 'Legal Interpretation and the European Court of Justice' (1996) 20 *Fordham International Law Journal* 674. For this former Advocate General at the CJEU, a *principal* corollary of the teleological method is the doctrine of 'effectiveness', invariably called by its French name *effet utile*. For him, the Court employed this method to give priority to the proclaimed objectives of the Treaty, particularly that of European integration (ibid 678). See also H Schermers, *Judicial Protection in the EC* (Alphen aan den Rijn, Kluwer, 1976) 13. Teleological interpretation might suggest that the Court should interpret the law in the light of its own wishes and it should therefore be cautiously used. See also A Arnull, *The European Union and its Court of Justice* (Oxford, Oxford University Press, 1999) 515. Arnull argued that the purposive or teleological approach is

Yet, as we shall see, *effet utile* is much broader than an interpretation in light of *effectiveness*; it also includes other meta-interpretative[20] norms, such as unity or even solidarity.[21] Effectiveness and unity are clearly the two central norms of interpretation when it comes to *effet utile*.[22] Though they have often been used in tandem in the case law,[23] they do reflect a dissimilar normative meaning to be seriously taken into consideration when studying the semantic of the CJEU case law.

This mapping suggests that effectiveness has two main (and overlapping)[24] functions in EU law: an interpretative function as *effet utile* and a judicial review function.[25] As to the latter function, it must be divided between the judicial review of national legislation (the so-called debate on national procedural autonomy) and the judicial review of EU legislation. This contribution will now look specifically at the issues of *effet utile* interpretation, judicial review of EU legislation and judicial review of national legislation through the prism of effectiveness as the core principle of EU procedural law and as an *idée directrice* ('directing idea') of EU law.[26]

controversial. See also F Schockweiler, 'La Cour de Justice des Communautés européennes dépasse-t-elle les limites de ses attributions?' (1995) 18 *Journal des Tribunaux du Droit Européen* 73, 74. For this former judge at the CJEU, it is clear that by favouring the teleological method, the Court has chosen the interpretation best fitted to promote the attainment of the objectives pursued by the Treaty.

[20] MP Maduro, 'Interpreting European Law: Judicial Adjudication in a Context of Constitutional Pluralism' (2007) 1 *EJLS* 2, 5. The constitutional telos is not only the telos of the rule but the telos of the legal context.

[21] The Lisbon Treaty has increased the potential impact of the principle of solidarity in the Court's semantic by incorporating explicit references, notably in the opening provisions of the TEU (Arts 2 and 3 TEU). Yet the term 'solidarity' appears to have many different meanings, and this may arguably constitute a hindrance to its development. See A Biondi, E Dagylite and E Kücük (eds), *Solidarity in EU Law: Legal Principle in the Making* (Cheltenham, Edward Elgar, 2018) 13–14; P Van Cleynenbreugel, 'Typologies of Solidarity in EU Law: A Non-shifting Landscape in the Wake of Economic Crises' in Biondi et al (eds), ibid 13. See also in relation to the Covid-19 crisis, U Neergaard and S de Vries, 'Whatever is necessary … will be done – Solidarity in Europe and the Covid-19 Crisis' *EU Law Live – Weekend Edition* (April 2020).

[22] See, eg, M Lasser, 'Anticipating Three Models of Judicial Control, Debate and Legitimacy: The European Court of Justice, the Cour de cassation and the United States Supreme Court', *Jean Monnet Working Paper 1/03*. He considers that effectiveness and uniformity may be defined as meta-purposes (meta-teleological style of reasoning, meta-teleological policy arguments), ie purposes, values or policies underlying the EU and its legal structure as a whole (ibid 44). The author concluded that the ECJ's interpretative technique is therefore orientated towards developing a proper legal order, namely, one that would be sufficiently certain, uniform and effective (ibid 54).

[23] Case C-14/68 *Walt Wilhem*, ECLI:EU:C:1969:4. The two principles can work in tandem but also separetely.

[24] Case C-370/17 *Vueling*, ECLI:EU:C:2020:26, paras 82, 90–95. This point is clearly illustrated by the *Vueling* case.

[25] P Nebbia, 'The Double Life of Effectiveness' (2008) 10 *Cambridge Yearbook of Legal Studies* 287. See also Dubos (n 6) 49. Dubos distinguishes between *effet utile* as an interpretative principle and effectiveness as a rule used to frame national procedural autonomy.

[26] The phrase '*idée directrice*' is terminology taken from the research of M Hauriou, *Precis de droit administratif* (Sirey, Paris, 1933).

III. PROCEDURAL RULE OF LAW AS PROCEDURAL EFFECTIVENESS

A. *Effet Utile*, Effectiveness and Proceduralisation of EU Law

Effet utile and effectiveness are often analysed interchangeably.[27] This is arguably not the most appropriate approach for understanding the place and role of the principle of effectiveness in EU procedural law. *Effet utile* interpretation can be relied on in relationship with other meta-norms such as, for instance, the principle of 'unity' or 'uniformity' of EU law. Loic Azoulai, for example, considers that the most common justifiers in the CJEU case law are certainly to be found in the principles of uniformity of EU law and effectiveness.[28] For him, these two principles constitute instrumental explanations to justify the autonomy of EU law.[29]

It is worth noting that the narrative of unity was particularly relied on by the CJEU in its construction of the doctrine of EU fundamental rights for three decades from the 1970s to the 1990s, which resulted in the codification of the unwritten general principles into the EU Charter of Fundamental Rights.[30] Yet in recent years, the narrative of unity in the use of *effet utile* has slowly but surely faded away,[31] being replaced by a strong effectiveness narrative in the CJEU case law, which irreversibly fosters the strengthening of the procedural rule of law in the EU. We must now try to understand the reasons behind the rise and predominance of effectiveness in the *effet utile* jurisprudence of the CJEU – at the cost of the narrative of unity/uniformity.[32]

The central reason for this evolution is the entry into force of the Lisbon Treaty. It brings effectiveness and procedure to the fore with Article 19 TEU and Article 47 EUCFR. Article 19 TEU, which replaces Article 220 EC (ex article 164 EEC),[33] is not neutral like its predecessor, including an explicit reference

[27] See, eg, n 15 and also F Snyder, 'The Effectiveness of European Community Law: Institutions, Processes, Tools and Techniques' (1993) 56 *MLR* 53.

[28] A Azoulai, The Europeanization of Legal Concepts' in U Neergard and R Nielsen (eds), *European Legal Method – in a Multi-Level EU Legal Order* (Copenhagen, DJOF Publishing, 2012) 165, 182.

[29] ibid.

[30] See Sadl (n 15) 40–42. See also X Groussot, *General Principles of Community Law* (Zutphen, Europa Law Publishing, 2006). Teleological interpretation appears closely related to the gap-filling function attributed to the Court in the elaboration of individual rights as general principles, which accordingly must be compatible with the structure and objectives of the EU legal order.

[31] The semantic/rhetoric of unity is still present in the human rights case law of the CJEU. See Case C-617/10 *Åkerberg Fransson*, ECLI:EU:C:2013:280, para 29; Case C-399/11 *Melloni*, ECLI:EU:C:2013:107, para 60; and Case C-168/13 PPU *Jeremy F*, ECLI:EU:C:2013:358, para 58. See D Ritleng, 'De l'articulation des systèmes de protection des droits fondamentaux dans l'Union: les enseignements des arrêts Åkerberg Fransson et Melloni' *RTDE* 2013 (April–June) 267.

[32] A Ward, 'The Limits of the Uniform Application of Community Law and Effective Judicial Review: A Look Post-Amsterdam' in Kilpatrick et al (eds) (n 7).

[33] Such a duty was deduced from the wording of Art 220 EC (ex Art 164 EEC, now Article 19 TEU), according to which 'the Court of Justice and the CFI shall ensure that in the interpretation and application of this Treaty the law is observed'.

to the need to make available 'effective remedies'. Furthermore, the EUCFR incorporates the principle of effective judicial protection in Article 47.[34] After so many years of hiding in the CJEU case law, the principle of effectiveness finally made its appearance in the core provisions of EU law. Article 19 TEU is certainly the most important provision regarding the competence of the CJEU, whereas Article 47 EUCFR is nowadays the provision of the EUCFR most often invoked in the CJEU case law.[35] The narrative of effectiveness is now everywhere, at the expense of the principle of unity/uniformity.[36] On top of this, due to the very existence of the written EUCFR as a primary law instrument, there is no need for the CJEU to further develop a doctrine of EU fundamental rights based on *effet utile* and the principle of unity/uniformity. Also, the Lisbon Treaty (particularly Article 4 TEU) and the Preamble to the EUCFR give manifest importance to the rhetoric of diversity. In other words, the Lisbon Treaty has normalised the doctrine of constitutional pluralism and has put an end to the dominance of the principle of unity/uniformity by adopting a procedural vision of EU law founded on the principle of effectiveness.[37]

B. Judicial Review of EU Legislation, Effectiveness and Proceduralisation

The effectiveness of judicial review of EU acts has always been a contentious issue throughout the history of the EU. The problematic of judicial review was already raised in the first four cases of the ECSC Court on the so-called 'Monnet rebate' in 1954 and dealing with the judicial review of decisions of the High Authority based on Article 33 ECSC, the great grandfather of Article 263 of the Treaty on the Functioning of the European Union (TFEU).[38] At his time in history, Jean Monnet (President of the High Authority) was notoriously opposed to strongly intensive review of the decisions taken in the ECSC framework by the High Authority.[39] Yet the independent ECSC Court came to the conclusion that the decisions were invalid.[40] Jean Monnet, *bon joueur*, commented on these decisions by stating that these new judgments would certainly increase the

[34] See also Art 41 EUCFR.

[35] Seminar by Claire Kilpatrick in Lund, EU Law Discussion Group, January 2020.

[36] See eg Opinion 2/13, ECLI:EU:C:2014:2454.

[37] For the use of effectiveness in citizenship case law. S Mayr, 'Putting a Leash on the Court of Justice? Preconceptions in National Methodology v Effet Utile as a Meta-Rule' (2012/2013) 5 *EJLS* 19.

[38] The grounds of judicial review are strongly inspired by French administrative law.

[39] Jean Monnet also foresees the prospect of a supreme federal European court in Statement on 10 December 1952 (swearing of the seven judges), statement given after the speech of Judge Piloti (President of the ECSC Court). See DG Valentine, *The Court of Justice of the European Communities* (Stevens, London 1965) 4.

[40] In Case C-2/54 *High Authority v Italy*, ECLI:EU:C:1954:8.The Court relied on procedural requirement as an *ex officio* ground. See Valentine (n 39) 113–17.

'effectiveness' of the EU institutions.[41] His vision happened not to be wrong, since it appears clear that the first rulings of the ECSC Court were paradigmatic for the founding of the authority of the EU Court.[42] Interestingly, it is worth observing that in the mid-1950s, the ECSC Court relied on a very textual interpretation of the Treaty.[43] By contrast, the new Court, established by the EEC Treaty in the autumn of 1958, would take a remarkable interpretative u-turn by establishing the reign of the functionalist or *effet utile* interpretation.

It is in Case 30/59 *De Gezamenlijke Steenkolenmijnen in Limburg v High Authority*, also involving the doctrine of retained power, that the Court first explicitly relied on *effet utile* interpretation to counterbalance the national interest of Germany in providing bonuses to miners that created a competitive advantage for domestic undertakings. The Court expressly mentioned the *effet utile* of the Treaty in the French version of the text.[44] This was the official beginning of the multiform doctrine of *effet utile* – also called functional or teleological interpretation. In the 1960s, not many voices in Europe critically commented on the interpretive position of this new Court. Stuart Scheingold, a political scientist from Berkeley tutored by Ernst Haas, was the exception. His PhD thesis (originally published in 1965 by Yale University Press) – entitled *The Rule of Law in European Integration*, which remained uncited for three decades in EU law scholarship – is a true goldmine in understanding the roots and functioning of judicial review in the early years of the Court.[45]

According to Scheingold, the rejection of the bonuses in *De Gezamenlijke Steenkolenmijnen in Limburg* was mainly based on what the Court termed 'the essential ends' of the common market as defined in Article 2 ECSC: 'the most rational distribution of production at the highest level of productivity'. His research goes very deep into the Court case law pre- *Steenkolenmijnen in Limburg*, and his conclusion is that the Court is committed to a free market economy and to the general efficacy of the rationalising pressure of natural market forces.[46] In other words, the *effet utile* interpretation was present in the Court jurisprudence, but in a non-explicit form.

Scheingold's analysis does not stop here, and in his concluding chapter ('Perspectives') he enters into a discussion of whether the rule of law is compatible with the integrative process and whether judicial review can contribute to European integration. His conclusion as to the adjudicative role of the Court is

[41] EB Haas, *The Uniting of Europe – Political, Social and Economic Forces 1950–1957* (Notre Dame, Indiana, University of Notre Dame Publications, 1958, 2004 rev edn) 474.

[42] See E Stein, 'The European Coal and Steel Community: The Beginning of Its Judicial Process' (1955) *Columbia Law Review* 950, 985; and Haas (n 41) 484–85. Haas talks of a 'subservience to the Court of Justice'.

[43] Haas (n 41) 473.

[44] In the English version of the case, translated as 'effectiveness'.

[45] Scheingold (n 4).

[46] ibid 193.

quite brutal. The rules enacted by the Court provide stability and its commitment to the rule of law offers security.[47] Yet Scheingold considers that the Court must provide 'rather a wide berth to the political authorities'.[48] This constitutes for him a 'basic contradiction – an interesting sort of irony – which is a continuing threat to the Court'.[49]

Scheingold continued to study the adjudicative process in Europe in another book entitled *The Law in Political Integration* (originally published in 1971 by Harvard University),[50] where, continuing in the same direction, he argues that European regional law has allowed politics to function at the regional level in the form of greater discretion for the regional executive.[51] The study highlights that the Court of Justice has operated as a validator of decisions made by the Community executive rather than as a policy maker.[52] The famous antitrust case *Consten and Grunding* is often discussed in his book. For him, the major thrust of the decision was to validate the reasoning of the Commission.[53] Looking at recent EU law scholarship, from legal theory[54] to hard core competition law,[55] this judgment is consistently referred to and discussed as the key example for showing the wide margin of discretion granted to the EU executive and its main consequence, that is, the low intensity of judicial review exercised by the CJEU in certain fields of adjudication.[56] As a result, the executive power of the Commission in taking decisions in the field of antitrust law is often criticised, and the low intensity of judicial review undertaken by the CJEU in this procedural and technical field is often highlighted in legal doctrine.[57] This is so even after the entry into force of the Lisbon Treaty and the EUCFR.[58]

[47] ibid 202–03.

[48] ibid.

[49] ibid.

[50] SA Scheingold, *The Law in Political Integration – The Evolution and Integrative Implications of Regional Legal Processes in the European Community* (New Orleans, LA, Quid Pro Books, 2011).

[51] See ibid, Forword by Haas.

[52] Scheingold (n 50) 19 and 22–23.

[53] ibid 21. Case C-56 & 58/64, ECLI:EU:C:1966:41.

[54] See, eg, K Tuori, *European Constitutionalism* (Cambridge, Cambridge University Press, 2015) 146.

[55] See, eg, D Geradin and N Petit, 'Judicial Review in EU Competition Law: A Quantitative and Qualitative Assessment' (2010) *TILEC Discussion Paper No 2011-008*.

[56] See J Mendes, *Executive Discretion and the Limits of EU Law* (Oxford, Oxford University Press, 2019).

[57] I Forrester, 'From Regulation 17/62 to Article 52 of the Charter of Fundamental Rights' in U Bernitz, X Groussot and F Schulyok (eds), *General Principles of EU Law and European Private Law* (Alphen aan den Rijn, Kluwer, 2013). Forrester traces the different phases of procedural rules applicable to decisions by DG Competition in competition cases, and contrasts the present situation with the applicable fundamental rights standards under the ECHR (and ECtHR case law) and the Charter. He comes basically to the conclusion that the procedures are not sufficient, as competition fines have to be qualified as criminal penalties, meaning that the procedure would have to live up to the requirements under Art 6 ECHR, which they do not.

[58] HH Lidgard, 'Due Process in European Competition Procedure: A Fundamental Concept or a Mere Formality?' in P Cardonnel, A Rosas and N Wahl (eds), *Constitutionalising the EU Judicial*

In a similar vein within the field of general EU law, legal scholarship often draws a distinction, regarding the intensity of judicial review, between judicial review of EU legislative acts and judicial review of national legislation falling within the scope of EU law.[59] The judicial review of EU legislative acts is often depicted as limited and as offering a broad margin of discretion to the EU legislature.[60] Many scholars have raised this essential and constitutional dilemma of double standards of judicial review in EU law, often explaining the legal discrepancy from the CJEU side as a vital need to preserve the effectiveness or *effet utile* of the EU legal order.[61] This vital need to preserve the effectiveness of the EU adjudicative order is also very much encapsulated in the logic of the CJEU in Opinion 2/13 for rejecting accession to the European Convention on Human Rights (ECHR) and the 'full' judicial control of the European Court of Human Rights (ECtHR) over the EU's legislative acts.[62]

It is also worth mentioning that the intensity of judicial review of EU legislative acts by the CJEU has increased in recent years. Darren Harvey, in his Doctoral thesis, shows very well the evolution in the case law of the CJEU concerning serious interferences with fundamental rights of EU legislative acts.[63] This evolution leads to a stricter proportionality test and a reduction of the traditional wide margin of discretion.[64] He also shows very clearly that this shift is accompanied by an increase in 'process-oriented' review – a more procedural approach – in a number of cases outside the exceptional instances of serious interferences.[65] One of his main conclusions is that the methodology and intensity of constitutional review have shifted over the years.[66] According to Harvey, this shift in constitutional review jurisprudence has arisen in response to wider changes to the EU's legal and political order. Three elements are notably highlighted: (i) an increase in procedural obligations for the EU legislature

System (Oxford, Hart Publishing, 2012) 403, 407. For Lidgard, efficiency considerations appear as an important driving force in Regulation 1/2003, and procedural safeguards are only accepted to the extent that they do not create serious obstacles to Commission enforcement activities.

[59] A Boerger de Smedt, 'La Cour de Justice dans les négociations du Traité de Paris instituant la CECA' in Archive of European Integration, available at hhtp://aei.pitt.edu/52359. In Case C-221/88 *ECSC v Busseni*, ECLI:EU:C:1990:84, the CJEU finally recognised that Art 41 ECSC also covers matters of interpretation and not only preliminary rulings on the validity of EU legislation.

[60] See n 15. See also R Buxbaum, 'Article 177 of the Rome Treaty as Federalizing Device' (1969) 21 *Stanford Law Review* 1041. Buxbaum discusses the effectiveness of the preliminary ruling procedure, and shows the difficult and slow assimilation of EU law into the national judicial structure.

[61] See, eg, A Williams, *The Ethos of Europe. Values, Law and Justice in the EU* (Cambridge, Cambridge University Press, 2010).

[62] See X Groussot, J Hettne and GT Petursson, 'General Principles and the Many Faces of Coherence: Between Law and Ideology' in S Vogenauer and S Weatherill (eds), *General Principles of Law: European and Comparative Perspectives* (Oxford, Hart Publishing, 2017) 77.

[63] D Harvey, 'The Constitutional Court of a More Mature Legal Order: Constitutional Review by the Court of Justice of the European Union', PhD thesis, Darwin College, Cambridge University, 2019.

[64] ibid ch 8.

[65] ibid, eg, 239 and 262.

[66] ibid 265.

with the Lisbon Treaty and the Better Regulation initiative; (ii) elevation of the EUCFR to the apex of the EU constitutional order; and (iii) a change in the subject matter of litigation, with an increase in judicial review of EU legislation dealing with highly politically charged issues.[67]

There is thus undeniably a shift in the methodology of the CJEU when it comes to the judicial review of EU legislative acts. However, it is also indisputable that the CJEU in practice has only very rarely annulled EU legislative acts.[68] There is a glaring gap between (constitutional) theory and practice. The CJEU still relies heavily on the 'manifestly inappropriate test' when it comes to review of EU legislation.[69] Moreover, when the review concerns the use of EU fundamental rights, it is very often the case that the CJEU comes to the conclusion that the central core of the (fundamental) right is not affected.[70] The practice of the CJEU in the context of the economic crisis jurisprudence provides another strong argument in showing the low intensity of judicial review and even sometimes the total absence of scrutiny.[71] The paradoxical conclusion to which we are inescapably drawn is that there is a shift in the constitutional review methodology, yet the practice of the CJEU shows strong persistence in following its long-standing practice of limited (administratively inspired) judicial review.[72]

C. National Legislative Autonomy, Effectiveness and Proceduralisation

In contrast to the previous issues discussed, which find their sources in the ECSC Treaty, the judicial review of national (procedural) legislation slowly developed alongside the expansion and acceptance of Article 177 EEC (now Article 267 TFEU)[73] by the national courts after the entry into force of the Rome Treaty.[74]

[67] ibid 270.

[68] Craig (n 13). The issue of rarity is also raised by Harvey (n 63).

[69] See, eg, Case C-62/14 *Gauweiler*, ECLI:EU:C:2015:400, para 68 and Case C-72/15 *Rosneft*, ECLI:EU:C:2017:236, para 146. Accordingly, 'with regard to judicial review of compliance with the principle of proportionality, the Court has held that the European Union legislature must be allowed a broad discretion in areas which involve political, economic and social choices on its part, and in which it is called upon to undertake complex assessments. The Court has concluded that the legality of a measure adopted in those areas can be affected only if the measure is manifestly inappropriate having regard to the objective which the competent institution is seeking to pursue.'

[70] See P Craig, *EU Administrative Law* (Oxford, Oxford University Press, 2006) ch 16.

[71] See, eg, Kilpatrick (n 2). See also C Barnard, 'The Charter, The Court and the Crisis', *University of Cambridge Faculty of Law Research Paper No 18/2013*.

[72] See n 15.

[73] A Boerger de Smedt, 'Negotiating the Foundations of European Law – 1950–1957' (2012) 21 *Contemporary Legal History* 351. One of the key components of this strengthening was the preliminary ruling system under Art 177, introduced to solve the pressing problem of uniformity in the interpretation of Community law within the Member States. Art 41 ECSC already provided a similar procedure, but of much narrower scope since the Court had exclusive jurisdiction to give preliminary rulings merely on the validity of Community acts.

[74] Compare the wording of Art 41 ECSC and Art 177 EEC (now Art 267 TFEU). See JHH Weiler, 'A Quiet Revolution: The European Court of Justice and its interlocutors' (1994) 26 *Political Studies* 510, 523. See also Buxbaum (n 60).

The academic debate in this field is marked by a shift from a discussion of national procedural autonomy based on the principle of effectiveness (pre-Lisbon Treaty)[75] to discussion of effective judicial protection based on Article 47 EUCFR (post-Lisbon Treaty).[76]

In the pre-Lisbon Treaty discourse, the literature on national procedural autonomy was rich, varied and complex (as often following the ebb and flows of the Court's jurisprudence).[77] On the one hand, an important part of legal doctrine was pushing for greater harmonisation of procedural and remedial provisions in the name of the uniformity and primacy of EU law.[78] For instance, Walter van Gerven argued for the development of a new effectiveness test; a so-called 'adequate test', or the test of 'adequate (not minimum) legal protection'. He explained that the test of minimum effectiveness 'does not live up to the standard of sufficient judicial protection of Community rights' and that 'it puts national courts on the wrong footing as a matter of principle'.[79] Another part of the doctrine, on the other hand, was considering that adjudication (and its case-by-case approach) was ill-suited for the emergence of the uniformity of procedural requirements, and questioned the desirability of the very imperative of uniformity.[80]

[75] J Rideau, 'Le rôle des Etats membres dans l'application du droit communautaire', 18 *AFDI*, 1972, 864–903. The rhetoric of institutional/procedural autonomy is still persisting in the CJEU case law from 2020 (see eg *Vueling* (n 24) para 91).

[76] A Arnull, 'Remedies Before National Courts' in R Schütze and T Tridimas (eds), *Oxford Principles of European Union Law*, vol 1 (Oxford, Oxford University Press, 2018) 1011, 1039. The default position is shifting from national procedural autonomy to effective judicial protection.

[77] Compare, eg, *Rewe* (ECLI:EU:C:1976:188), *Emmot* (ECLI:EU:C:1991:333) and the procedural retreat with *Marshall II* (ECLI:C:1993:335).

[78] See also CN Kakouris, 'Do the Member States Possess Judicial Procedure "Autonomy"?' (1997) 34 *CML Rev* 1389; M Bobek, 'Why There is No Procedural Autonomy of the Member States' in HW Micklitz and B de Witte (eds), *The European Court of Justice and the Autonomy of the Member States* (Cambridge, Intersentia, 2012) 305.

[79] W van Gerven, 'Of Rights, Remedies and Procedures' (2000) 37 *CML Rev* 501, 529–30. For a discussion on adequate legal protection, see also HW Micklitz, 'The ECJ between the Individual Citizen and the Member States – A Plea for a Judge-Made European Law on Remedies' in HW Micklitz and B de Witte (eds), *The European Court of Justice and the Autonomy of the Member States* (Cambridge, Intersentia, 2012) 349, 400; and P Van Cleynenbreugel, 'Transforming Shields into Swords: the VEBIC Judgment, Adequate Judicial Protection Standards and the Emergence of Procedural Heteronomy in EU Law' (2011) 18 *Maastricht Journal of European and Comparative Law* 511, 529–30. Van Cleynenbreugel argued this on the basis that not minimum but adequate protection must be the standard to assess the sufficiency of domestic rules providing, or limiting the effect of, remedies intended to enforce the Community rights of individuals. See also N Reich, 'The Principle of Effectiveness and EU Private Law' in Bernitz, Groussot and Schulyok (eds) (n 57) 307. Reich distinguishes between three different functions and approaches of the effectiveness principle in EU law, namely, (i) the elimination rule (the traditional understanding limiting national procedural autonomy in the sense that it eliminates restrictions *to* protection but does not create remedies *for* protection), (ii) the hermeneutical use of the principle (ie use as an interpretative principle) and (iii) the remedial principle ('upgrading' of national remedies to make them sufficient for the protection of Union rights).

[80] See M Dougan, *National Remedies before the Court of Justice: Issues of Harmonisation and Differentiation* (Oxford, Hart Publishing, 2004).

The Lisbon Treaty and the entry into force of EUCFR have largely modified the debate. Arnull predicted the rise of the principle of effective judicial protection after many years of self-restraint following the *Marshall II* ruling.[81] According to him:

> The extent to which it [the Court] has been willing to interfere with national procedural autonomy has varied, however, and the case law since the early 1990s has been marked by greater restraint than that of the preceding decade or so. However, the tectonic plates of Union law may be in the process of shifting again. *The general principle of effective judicial protection seems to have established itself as hierarchically superior to that of national procedural autonomy.* Article 19(1) TEU, which partially enshrines the former principle in the Treaty, is likely to be the subject of references to the Court and perhaps even infringement actions against Member States whose remedies the Commission deems inadequate.[82]

Sacha Prechal (who is now a judge at the CJEU) discussed and suggested redefining the relationship between '*Rewe*-effectiveness' and effective judicial protection.[83] In a seminal article, she contrasts the two principles in four sets. First, she points out that the principle of effectiveness appears to be a less demanding standard of judicial review. Second, she explains that the general test of effectiveness ('practical impossibility', or the 'excessiveness' test) is formulated in a negative manner that brings, in turn, a negative obligation – whereas effective judicial protection implies both a negative and a positive obligation. Third, the principle of effectiveness is described as operating at the Member States' – not the individual's – level. Lastly, justifications applied with regard to the two principles are explained to differ. In short, effective judicial protection is a fundamental right, which, as Prechal clarifies, demands a higher intensity of scrutiny compared to *Rewe*-effectiveness. The strong impact on EU law of the principle of effective judicial protection as a fundamental right enshrined in Article 47 EUCFR is confirmed by the doctrine. Article 47 EUCFR is a crucial tool of constitutionalisation of the EU legal order, notably leading to the constitutionalisation of private law by fostering the application of the Charter in horizontal situations.[84] Moreover, the entry into force of the Charter has led to the predominance of effective

[81] A Arnull, 'The Principle of Effective Judicial Protection: An Unruly Horse' (2011) 36 *EL Rev* 51.

[82] ibid 68 (emphasis added).

[83] S Prechal, 'Redefining the Relationship between '*Rewe*-effectiveness and Effective Judicial Protection' (2011) 4 *Review of European Administrative Law* 39.

[84] C Mak, 'Rights and Remedies: Article 47 EUCFR and Effective Judicial Protection in European Private Law Matters' in H Micklitz (ed), *The Constitutionalization of European Private Law* (Oxford, Oxford University Press, 2014) 240; and A Ward, 'Remedies under the Charter in Disputes Arising in Private Law' in Bernitz, Groussot and Schulyok (eds) (n 57), where Ward points out that the Charter does not lay down any rules about the legal sanctions that should be available in cases of breach of rights contained in it. Yet she argues that the established case law by the Court on effective judicial protection (equivalent and effective protection) and Art 47 EUCFR do have significant potential for certain Charter rights to be enforceable horizontally. She also puts special emphasis on Art 47 (also in combination with Art 19(1) TEU), which, according to her, has horizontal effects by virtue of its content.

judicial protection vis-à-vis the principle of effectiveness and the rationale of national procedural autonomy. This last point is clearly confirmed by the most recent doctrinal discussion. This move towards Article 47 EUCFR suggests a more severe test of national procedural rules and reduces national procedural autonomy.[85] The rising significance of Article 47 EUCFR amounts to a lessening of the prominence of the *Rewe* principles.[86]

This evolution and rise of effective judicial protection can be explained by the codification of the principle in Article 19 TEU and Article 47 EUCFR.[87] As explained by Eliantonio and Muir, there is a need for further elaboration in the case law of the CJEU as to the relationship between Article 47 EUCFR and Article 19 TEU, 'which will need to determine the scope and "power" of Article 19 TEU next to that of Article 47 CFR'.[88] The central provision is Article 19 TEU, which the Court has considered to be applicable not only when a situation falls within the material scope of Union law, but also more largely 'in the fields covered by Union law'.[89] This recent development shows the close link between Article 2 TEU and Article 19 TEU. Article 19 TEU is akin to the key 'rule of law' provision in EU law.[90]

The text of Article 19 TEU is very rich and differs tremendously from its terse ancestors: Article 31 ECSC and Article 220 EC (ex Article 164 EEC). Whereas Article 31 ECSC and Article 220 EC merely stated that the law must be observed and applied by the CJEU, Article 19 TEU directly connects its (normative) application to the principle of loyalty (Article 4(3) TEU) and to the principle of effectiveness ('effective national remedies').[91] Article 19 TEU constitutes a paradigmatic provision of EU law that, as seen previously, not only constitutes a specific expression of the rule of law as enshrined in Article 2 TEU, but also inherently reflects and specifies in its paragraph 1 the principle of

[85] R Widdershoven, 'National Procedural Autonomy and General EU Law Limits' (2019) 12 *Review of European Administrative Law* 5.

[86] ibid.

[87] X Groussot and J Lindholm, 'General Principles: Taking Rights Seriously and Waving the Rule of Law as a Stick' in Ziegler, Neuvonen and Moreno-Lax (eds) (n 13). See also Bonelli (n 14), for whom the codification of effective judicial protection in Art 19 TEU and Art 47 of the Charter, operated by the Lisbon Treaty, has stimulated an evolution of the principle.

[88] M Eliantonio and E Muir, 'The Principle of Effectiveness: under Strain?' (2019) 12 *Review of European Administrative Law* 255.

[89] A Torres-Pérez, 'From Portugal to Poland: The Court of Justice of the European Union as Watchdog of Judicial Independence' (2020) 27 *Maastricht Journal of European and Comparative Law* 105; see also Groussot and Lindholm (n 87); and Bonelli (n 14).

[90] See Scheingold's own translation of Art 31 ECSC using 'rule of law' instead of 'law' (n 4).

[91] M Klamert, *The Principle of Loyalty in EU Law* (Oxford, Oxford University Press, 2014) 138. Klamert not only shows the close link between Art 4(3) TEU and Art 19 TEU, but also highlights the close link between loyalty and effectiveness (ibid 123). See similarly Snyder (n 27) 53. In this article, Snyder looks at the issue of effectiveness from the Commission and CJEU perspectives. When looking at the CJEU adjudicative process, he considers the two main techniques to foster effectiveness that are to be found in (i) the *effet utile* doctrine (explicit or implicit) and (ii) the gradual 'hardening of the duty of Community loyalty enshrined in Article 5 EEC (now Article 4(3) TEU) and being the cornerstone of the judicial liability system'.

loyalty enshrined in Article 4(3) TEU. Article 19(1) TEU imposes an obligation for the Member States to respect EU (rule of) law by establishing an effective (and impartial) system of remedies. The judicialisation of Article 19 TEU by the CJEU bolsters the effectiveness of EU law.[92] The reliance on Article 19 TEU also has the effect of decentralising the application of the 'rule of law' and the enforcement of EU law at the domestic level to the national courts through the preliminary ruling procedure.[93]

IV. ASYMMETRIC LEGALITY AND PROCEDURAL RULE OF LAW IN TIMES OF ECONOMIC EMERGENCY

It is in time of crisis that the procedural rule of law is kicking and shining. To a certain extent, the mantra of effectiveness fits very well the oft-relied rhetoric of 'whatever it takes' for solving a lambda crisis – be it a migrant, economic or COVID-19 crisis. In the economic emergency context of EU law, the procedural rule of law relied on by the CJEU has revealed a set of double standards of judicial review in applying the principle of effective judicial protection, leading to a situation of asymmetric legality in the Euro-Area crisis jurisprudence (section IV.A) and a broad discretion granted by the CJEU to the European Central Bank (ECB) when taking 'executive' decisions (section IV.B).

A. Asymmetric Legality and the Euro-Area Crisis

The practical application of the general principle of effective judicial protection by the CJEU is varying in the context of the jurisprudence regarding the Euro-Area crisis. However, the CJEU, as many other courts in extreme circumstances,[94] quite expectedly took recourse to a narrow,[95] light-touch,[96] quite often 'process-oriented'[97] review of crisis response measures. This limited judicial review aims to not jeopardise the use of the suggested rescue mechanisms.[98]

[92] Torres-Pérez (n 89).
[93] Groussot and Lindholm (n 87).
[94] G Vanberg and M Gulati, 'Financial Crises and Constitutional Compromise' in T Ginsburg, M Rosen and G Vanberg (eds), *Constitutions in Times of Financial Crisis, Comparative Constitutional Law and Policy* (Cambridge, Cambridge University Press, 2019) 120.
[95] See n 14.
[96] A Hinarejos, 'Gauweiler and the Outright Monetary Transactions Programme: The Mandate of the European Central Bank and the Changing Nature of Economic and Monetary Union' (2015) 11 *European Constitutional Law Review* 569.
[97] D Harvey, 'Towards Process-Oriented Proportionality Review in the European Union' (2017) 23 *European Public Law* 112. See also generally, K Lenaerts, 'The European Court of Justice and Process-oriented Review' (2012) 1 *Research Papers in Law, European Legal Studies, College of Europe* 1, 15–16.
[98] F Fabbrini, *Economic Governance in Europe: Comparative Paradoxes, Constitutional Challenges*, 1st edn, (Oxford, Oxford University Press, 2016) 98; N Alkiviadou, 'Sustainable

This mode of judicial scrutiny of the Court, through the prism of the principle of effective judicial protection, demonstrates the application of different methodologies and takes many forms. On the one hand, the principle is relied on in ambivalent cases that concern national actions originally falling outside of the scope of the application of EU law. Here the focus of the judicial review lies on national domestic measures and, technically, their potential incapacity to guarantee the rights of individuals protected by EU law (a non-scrutiny approach/methodology). On the other hand, the principle is relied on to reject the arguments alleging either the breach of effective judicial protection in relation to EU actions, or full denial of judicial scrutiny of the measures 'inspired' by EU sources. This in its turn has amounted to preservation of the EU measures at hand, safeguarding their effectiveness (a light scrutiny approach/methodology). It appears that the Court, whose jurisprudence as regards the principle of effective judicial protection is inconsistent,[99] applies a double standard of review by actively fostering judicial review of national measures connected to EU law with the help of the principle, but at the same time shielding the validity of EU measures from potential challenges,[100] not employing effective judicial protection in the context of EU actions.[101]

One of the seminal judgments that defined the further development of EU constitutional law[102] is that in *Associação Sindical dos Juízes Portugueses.*[103] Although this judgment is considered to be the flagship of protection of judicial independence[104] and a guarantee of the effective judicial protection[105] that is to be ensured in all fields covered by the Union,[106] a scope of protection that is broader than the scope of application of the Charter requiring the presence of implementation of the Union law,[107] the roots of the case lie in the budgetary austerity measures. These measures concerned temporary reduction of the amount of public sector remuneration, introduced by the Portuguese Government as one of the ways of fulfilling the conditions of the conditionality attached to the financial assistance granted within the framework of the

Enjoyment of Economic and Social Rights in Times of Crisis: Obstacles to Overcome and Bridges to Cross' (2018) 20 *European Journal of Law Reform* 22.

[99] Bonelli (n 14) 62.

[100] Kilpatrick (n 2) 418.

[101] A Arnull, 'The Principle of Effective Judicial Protection in EU law: An Unruly Horse?' (2011) 1 *EL Rev* 51.

[102] M Bonelli and M Claes, 'Judicial Serendipity: How Portuguese Judges Came to the Rescue of the Polish Judiciary: ECJ 27 February 2018, Case C-64/16, Associação Sindical dos Juízes Portugueses' (2018) 14 *European Constitutional Law Review* 622, 641–43.

[103] Case C-64/16 *Associação Sindical dos Juízes Portugueses v Tribunal de Contas*, ECLI:EU:C:2018:117.

[104] M Krajewski, 'Associação Sindical dos Juízes Portugueses: The Court of Justice and Athena's Dilemma' (2018) 3 *European Papers* 395, 402–06.

[105] V Roeben, 'Judicial Protection as the Meta-norm in the EU Judicial Architecture' (2020) 12 *Hague Journal on the Rule of Law* 39.

[106] Art 19(1) TFEU.

[107] Art 51(1) EUCFR.

European Financial Stability Mechanism (EFSM) and the European Financial Stability Facility (EFSF),[108] EU sources that the preliminary reference itself does not explicitly state.[109] It is remarkable in this respect that access to justice in the form of initiation of the proceedings at the CJEU was granted without any hindrance in *Associação Sindical dos Juízes Portugueses*. By comparison, even in the momentous *Pringle* case, the CJEU indicated that the European Stability Mechanism had been created outside the EU legal framework, meaning, consequently, that the principle of effective judicial protection could not have been invoked in those circumstances.[110] In *Associação Sindical dos Juízes Portugueses*, however, the Court focused on the vital triad of Articles 2 and 4(3) TEU and Article 19(1) TFEU, relying on and strengthening the principle of effective judicial protection that brought a clear-cut austerity case within the ambit of its jurisdiction. Due to its legacy, the subsequent *Vindel* case,[111] regarding a similar reduction of remuneration in the national civil service, resulting from national legislation, whose link to EU law was even more vaguely expressed, if at all,[112] became subject to the legal scrutiny of the Court in light of Article 21 EUCFR and Directive 2000/78. As in *Associação Sindical dos Juízes Portugueses*, the Court in *Vindel* was called upon to adjudicate on the compatibility of the national measures with Union law, without special focus on the EU sources whose implementation the anti-crisis measures technically represented, which in its turn did not create obstacles at the admissibility stage of the proceedings.

In contrast, in other preceding cases, where responses to the Eurozone crisis, potentially implying the original EU sources that lay at the basis of the adopted national legislation, were called into question, or in the cases where the applicants endeavoured to challenge the EU actions directly via annulment proceedings, the Court seemed not to apply the principle of effective judicial protection in the same way as it did in the abovementioned case law of *Associação Sindical dos Juízes Portugueses* and *Vindel*. One of the reasons for denial of jurisdiction in the context of preliminary references could potentially be poorly formulated

[108] Portugal, Memorandum of Understanding on Specific Economic Policy Conditionality of 17 May 2011, available at https://ec.europa.eu/economy_finance/eu_borrower/mou/2011-05-18-mou-portugal_en.pdf; Council Implementing Decision of 30 May 2011 on granting Union financial assistance to Portugal (2011/344/EU) [2011] OJ L159/88; Council Implementing Decision of 23 April 2014 amending Implementing Decision 2011/344/EU on granting Union financial assistance to Portugal (2014/234/EU), [2014] OJ L125/75.

[109] *Associação Sindical dos Juízes Portugueses* (n 104) para 14, 'It [the referring court] considers that those measures were adopted in the framework of EU law or, at least, are European in origin, on the ground that those requirements were imposed on the Portuguese Government by EU decisions granting, in particular, financial assistance to that Member State.'

[110] Case C-370/12 *Pringle*, EU:C:2012:756, paras 178–182; Bonelli (n 14) 62.

[111] Case C-49/18 *Carlos Escribano Vindel v Ministerio de Justicia*, ECLI:EU:C:2019:106.

[112] ibid para 15: 'The referring court is uncertain, in the first place, whether the national legislation in question, which forms part of the objective, imposed by the European Union, of reducing the public deficit, constitutes discrimination on grounds of age, prohibited by the Charter and by Directive 2000/78.'

questions from the referring courts that did not properly indicate the existing connection between EU acts and the national legislation presumably implementing them,[113] quite often for obvious reasons concerning the ambiguity of the legal parentage of economic crisis mechanisms.[114] However, the Court, which throughout its jurisprudence had taken the initiative in paraphrasing preliminary reference questions on multiple occasions,[115] did not exercise this power with regard to preliminary references challenging the anti-crisis measures, preferring to strike down the proceedings at the initial stage.

Interestingly enough, these cases do not differ that much from those that eventually became subject to the judicial scrutiny of the ECJ. For instance, in *Sindicato dos Bancários do Norte and Others*,[116] the applicants, which were the unions in the banking sector and the former employee of the nationalised public bank, sought to receive interpretation in light of the Charter[117] of the provisions of the national financial law and test the conformity of the reduction in the amount of remuneration paid to workers in public enterprises with the principles and objectives enshrined in the Treaties.[118] The textual form of the abovementioned provisions was similar to that at stake in *Associação Sindical dos Juízes Portuguese.*[119] However, the Court declared its 'manifest lack of jurisdiction', in effect refusing the applicants access to justice at the European level in the same manner as in the preliminary references concerning the austerity measures introduced in Romania,[120] a Member State, that received several rounds

[113] C Kilpatrick, 'Are the Bailouts Immune to EU Social Challenge Because They Are Not EU Law?' (2014) 10 *European Constitutional Law Review* 393, 418.

[114] The notorious trio of complexity, inaccessibility and incomprehensibility of economic responses has been highlighted by Kilpatrick in her article 'On the Rule of Law and Economic Emergency: The Degradation of Basic Legal Values in Europe's Bailouts' (n 2).

[115] K Voss, 'But That's Not What I Asked! The Reformulation of Questions Asked in Preliminary Rulings' (2016) 18 *Europarättslig Tidskrift* 942; Kilpatrick (n 2) 349.

[116] Case C-128/12 *Sindicato dos Bancários do Norte and Others v BPN – Banco Português de Negócios SA*, ECLI:EU:C:2013:149.

[117] Arts 20, 21(1) and 31(1) EUCFR; Order of the Court of Justice of 7 March 2013, ECLI:EU:C:2013:149, regarding Case C-128/12 *Sindicato dos Bancários do Norte and Others*, para 1.

[118] Order of the Court of Justice (n 117) para 15.

[119] ibid para 1.

[120] Case C-434/11 *Corpul Naţional al Poliţiştilor v Ministerul Administraţiei şi Internelor (MAI) and Others* [2011], Order of the Court of Justice of 14 December 2011, ECLI:EU:C:2011:830; Case C-134/12 *Corpul Naţional al Poliţiştilor – Biroul Executiv Central (în numele şi în interesul membrilor săi – funcţionari publici cu statut special – poliţişti din cadrul IPJ Tulcea) v Ministerul Administraţiei şi Internelor and Others* [2012], Order of the Court of Justice of 10 May 2012, ECLI:EU:C:2012:288; see a reference of the court of last instance in Case C-369/12 *Corpul Naţional al Poliţiştilor – Biroul Executiv Central, reprezentant al reclamanţilor Chiţea Constantin şi alţii v Ministerul Administraţiei şi Internelor and Others* [2012], Order of the Court of Justice of 15 November 2012, ECLI:EU:C:2012:725; Case C-462/11 *Victor Cozman v Teatrul Municipal Târgovişte* [2011], Order of the Court of Justice of 14 December 2011, ECLI:EU:C:2011:831; see, however, Case C-258/14 *Eugenia Florescu and Others v Casa Judeţeană de Pensii Sibiu and Others*, ECLI:EU:C:2017:448, where the questions regarding the jurisdiction of the Court did not arise due to the highlighted explicit link of the national law to the Memorandum of Understanding (MoU) concluded between the EC and Romania, the base of which stems from Art 143 TFEU, para 31.

of financial assistance from different actors, including the EU, on condition that structural reforms were put into practice.[121] The sensitive political issues at hand prompted the Court to stay away from adjudicating on the merits of the preliminary reference. In the event that the questions of the national court were rephrased, the Court would have to emphasise the intrinsic link of the national law to the requirements imposed by the Union actors, and if the national law were to be found incompatible with EU law, the future of the complex mechanisms, deemed to save the Eurozone from collapse, and compliance with their severe conditions would be jeopardised. The same destiny befell the preliminary reference sent by the same court in the case *Sindicato Nacional dos Profissionais de Seguros e Afins*,[122] regarding abolition of Christmas and other holiday allowances for public sector employees; the ECJ reiterated its position – expressed in the order in *Sindicato dos Bancários do Norte and Others* – and confirmed the clear lack of jurisdiction regarding the matter at stake.[123]

Apart from the jurisprudence on preliminary references, the Court did not accept the invocation of the principle of effective judicial protection in annulment actions initiated by applicants attempting to challenge EU crisis response measures. For example, in the *ADEDY* case,[124] the General Court (while stating that the contested Council Decisions regarding excessive deficit addressed to Greece were of no direct concern to the Greek trade union confederation, nor to the civil servants bringing an action on behalf of ADEDY and in their own name) concluded that effective judicial protection of the applicants was

[121] Council Decision 2009/458/EC of 6 May 2009 granting mutual assistance to Romania [2009] OJ L150/6, Council Decision 2009/459/EC of 6 May 2009 providing Community medium-term financial assistance for Romania [2009] OJ L150/8, amended by Council Decision 2010/183/EC of 16 March 2010 amending Council Decision 2009/459/EC of 6 May 2009 providing Community medium-term financial assistance for Romania [2010] OJ L83/19; First MoU between the EC and Romania of 23 June 2009, available at https://ec.europa.eu/info/sites/info/files/ecfin_publication15409_en.pdf, supplemented with 4 additional MoUs afterwards; Council Decision 2011/289/EU of 12 May 2011 granting mutual assistance to Romania [2011] OJ L132/18, Council Decision 2011/288/EU of 12 May 2011 providing precautionary EU medium-term financial assistance for Romania [2011] OJ L131/15; First MoU between the EU and Romania of 29 June 2011, available at https://ec.europa.eu/info/sites/info/files/ecfin_20110629-mou-romania_en.pdf, supplemented with two additional MoUs afterwards; Council Decision 2013/532/EU of 22 October 2013 granting mutual assistance to Romania [2013] OJ L286/4, Council Decision 2013/531/EU of 22 October 2013 providing precautionary EU medium-term financial assistance for Romania [2013] OJ L286/1; MoU between the EU and Romania of 6 November 2013, available at https://ec.europa.eu/info/sites/default/files/ecfin_20131106_mou_ecfin_en.pdf.

[122] Case C-264/12 *Sindicato Nacional dos Profissionais de Seguros e Afins v Fidelidade Mundial – Companhia de Seguros SA*, ECLI:EU:C:2014:2036.

[123] Order of the Court of Justice of 26 June 2014, ECLI:EU:C:2014:2036, regarding Case C-264/12 *Sindicato Nacional dos Profissionais de Seguros e Afins v Fidelidade Mundial – Companhia de Seguros SA*, para 22; see also Case C-665/13 *Sindicato Nacional dos Profissionais de Seguros e Afins v Via Directa – Companhia de Seguros SA* [2014], Order of the Court of Justice of 21 October 2014, ECLI:EU:C:2014:2327.

[124] Case T-541/10 *Anotati Dioikisi Enoseon Dimosion Ypallilon (ADEDY) and Others v Council of the European Union*, Order of the the General Court of Justice of 27 November 2012, ECLI:EU:T:2012:626.

not impaired and, if desired, could be fully exercised in the course of national proceedings within the route of Article 267 TFEU.[125] The appeal of the applicants to substantive examination of the questionable provisions due to their potential detrimental effect on public trust in EU bodies in light of anti-crisis measures, did not produce any effects on the reasoning of the Court.[126] The definitive denial of standing in this case prevented the Council Decisions from being subject to scrutiny, indirectly reinforcing their effectiveness and removing potential doubts of the Member States as to the legality of the EU anti-crisis measures and the necessity for their implementation.

B. Procedural Rule of Law and the Executive Discretion of the ECB

The case law on the ECB's non-conventional (or non-standard) measures is another area of application of the procedural rule of law in the context of economic emergency. One of the seminal judgments that originated in the vortex of the Euro-Area crisis in this respect is the one in the *Gauweiler* case,[127] where a decision of the ECB, announced in a press release[128] in September 2012,[129] to introduce Outright Monetary Transactions (OMTs), was challenged in the CJEU.

The peculiarity of the preliminary reference consists, most notably, in the nature of the EU act whose interpretation was sought in this case, namely, the announcement of a measure that was to be taken in the near future and that was not reflected in the adoption of any formal legal act.[130] The Court, despite the objections expressed by the governments of the Member States, the European Parliament, the European Commission and the ECB, came to the conclusion that there were no obstacles impeding the admissibility of a request for a preliminary ruling.[131] Mr Gauweiler, together with several groups of individuals, disputing the actions of the ECB on the basis of its exceeding its mandate, infringement of Article 123 TFEU and breach of the principle of democracy enshrined in the German Basic Law, demanded from the Court a *comprehensive judicial review* of the limits of the ECB's mandate.[132] The Court, however, demonstrated its

[125] ibid paras 89–97.
[126] ibid para 96.
[127] Case C-62/14 *Gauweiler and Others v Deutscher Bundestag*, ECLI:EU:C:2015:400.
[128] 'Potential judicial review of an announcement of a future policy is a rare situation', as has been highlighted by HCH Hofmann, 'Controlling the Powers of the ECB: Delegation, Discretion, Reasoning and Care. What Gauweiler, Weiss and Others Can Teach Us', *ADEMU Working Paper 2018/107*, 7.
[129] The press release featuring OMT can be found at www.ecb.europa.eu/press/pr/date/2012/html/pr120906_1.en.html.
[130] J Alberti, 'Challenging the Evolution of the EMU: The Justiciability of Soft Law Measures Enacted by the ECB against the Financial Crisis before the European Courts' (2018) 37 *Yearbook of European Law* 626, 632.
[131] *Gauweiler* (n 127) paras 18–31.
[132] ibid para 8.

more 'process-oriented' approach towards adjudication. Access to justice in the form of initiation of the proceedings before the CJEU was granted to the applicants even though the questions in the preliminary reference concerned the announcement of the measures in a press release, the ECB not yet having adopted a decision regarding OMT – as is known, the OMT programme has never been implemented in practice, at the time of the judgment representing 'regulation by information'.[133] The Court nonetheless did not consider the preliminary reference to be of a hypothetical nature, supporting its position by reference to the national (in this case German) procedural law,[134] and decided to subject the OMT to judicial scrutiny, realising the importance of direct cooperation between the courts[135] and the issue at stake, and the necessity for its resolution for the unified understanding and effectiveness of current and future EU policy instruments.

Having outlined the mandate of the ECB in the field of monetary policy, the Court carried out a procedure-focused proportionality review that indicated the willingness of the Court to review manifestations of broad discretionary powers of EU institutions, yet without attempting to scrutinise the substance of these measures that could potentially hinder the suggested measures.[136] The process-orientated judicial scrutiny of the CJEU was reflected in the textual evaluation of the objectives of the OMT provided by the ECB in its press release and their correlation with the provisions of primary legislation[137] that was underpinned by a 'proceduralised' proportionality assessment[138] of these objectives. The Court, being deferential towards measures of the ECB,[139] especially in the context of adjudication on crisis responses,[140] in its reasoning indicated that measures adopted in light of the broad discretion of an EU institution involved in 'making choices of technical nature and undertaking forecasts and complex assessments', could only be scrutinised through the prism of 'certain procedural guarantees',[141] namely, an obligation to take into consideration all the decisive factors (a variation of an impact assessment) and providing reasons for the

[133] Hofmann (n 128) 7–9.

[134] *Gauweiler* (n 127) paras 25–26.

[135] S Simon, 'Direct Cooperation Has Begun: Some Remarks on the Judgment of the ECJ on the OMT Decision of the ECB in Response to the German Federal Constitutional Court's First Request for a Preliminary Ruling' (2015) 16 *German Law Journal* 1027.

[136] Fabbrini (n 99) 98; N Alkiviadou, 'Sustainable Enjoyment of Economic and Social Rights in Times of Crisis: Obstacles to Overcome and Bridges to Cross' (2018) 20 *European Journal of Law Reform* 22.

[137] *Gauweiler* (n 127) paras 46–65.

[138] HCH Hofmann, 'Gauweiler and OMT: Lessons for EU Public Law and the European Economic and Monetary Union' (19 June 2015) 16, available at https://papers.ssrn.com/sol3/papers.cfm?abstract_id=2621933; T Tridimas and N Xanthoulis, 'A Legal Analysis of the Gauweiler Case: Between Monetary Policy and Constitutional Conflict' (2016) 23 *Maastricht Journal of European and Comparative Law* 31.

[139] Tridimas and Xanthoulis (n 138).

[140] ibid; Vanberg and Gulati (n 94) 120.

[141] *Gauweiler* (n 127) paras 68–69.

adoption of the measures at hand.[142] Such procedural thresholds were in their turn easily met by the ECB, a body with established economic expertise, in the form of stating the reasons for launching OMT in the press release and submitting supporting documents together with an analysis of the economic situation, the content of which the Court relied upon without questioning[143] and deemed to be appropriate and not going beyond what was necessary.[144] It is important to indicate, though, that such a mode of judicial review cannot be perceived as an exceptional example in light of the extraordinary economic scenarios that were encountered in the case at hand – the judgment mostly confirmed the increasing tendency towards process-based judicial review of actions of EU actors, especially in highly technical areas.[145]

Such an approach was acknowledged in subsequent judicial practice, for example in *Weiss and Others*.[146] In this judgment, delivered in 2018, the CJEU, suggesting that the lack of clear separation *between* the economic and monetary policies was intended by the authors of the Treaties,[147] outlined an even broader area of discretionary powers for the ECB and, quite expectedly, applied the same approach with regard to adjudication of the legality of the Public Sector Purchase Programme (PSPP)[148] with an eye to future economic crises.[149] It is in this procedural rule of law context, following the *Weiss* judgment of the CJEU, that the ruling in *Weiss/PSPP* of the German Federal Constitutional

[142] C Kombos, 'Constitutional Review and the Economic Crisis: In the Courts We Trust?' (2019) 25 *European Public Law* 130.

[143] *Gauweiler* (n 127) para 74; M Dawson, A Maricut-Akbik and A Bobić, 'Reconciling Independence and Accountability at the European Central Bank: The False Promise of Proceduralism' (2019) 25 *European Law Journal* 89.

[144] *Gauweiler* (n 127) para 91, 'In the third place, the ESCB weighed up the various interests in play so as to actually prevent disadvantages from arising, when the programme in question is implemented, which are manifestly disproportionate to the programme's objectives.'

[145] D Harvey, 'Towards Process-Oriented Proportionality Review in the European Union' (2017) 23 *European Public Law* 121.

[146] Case C-493/17 *Weiss and Others*, ECLI:EU:C:2018:1000.

[147] ibid para 60.

[148] Decision (EU) 2015/2464 of the European Central Bank of 16 December 2015 amending Decision (EU) 2015/774 on a secondary markets public sector asset purchase programme (ECB/2015/48) [2015] OJ L344/1; Decision (EU) 2015/2101 of the European Central Bank of 5 November 2015 amending Decision (EU) 2015/774 on a secondary markets public sector asset purchase programme (ECB/2015/33) [2015] OJ L303/106; Decision (EU) 2015/2464 of the European Central Bank of 16 December 2015 amending Decision (EU) 2015/774 on a secondary markets public sector asset purchase programme (ECB/2015/48) [2015] OJ L344/1; Decision (EU) 2016/702 of the European Central Bank of 18 April 2016 amending Decision (EU) 2015/774 on a secondary markets public sector asset purchase programme (ECB/2016/8) [2016] OJ L121/24; Decision (EU) 2017/100 of the European Central Bank of 11 January 2017 amending Decision (EU) 2015/774 on a secondary markets public sector asset purchase programme (ECB/2017/1) [2017] OJ L16/51.

[149] *Weiss* (n 146) para 67, 'if the ESCB were precluded altogether from adopting such measures … that would, in practice, prevent it from using the means made available to it by the Treaties for the purpose of achieving monetary policy objectives and might – in particular in the context of an economic crisis entailing a risk of deflation – represent an insurmountable obstacle to its accomplishing the task assigned to it by primary law'.

Court (FCC) from 5 May 2020 should be interpreted and understood.[150] The German Constitutional Court emphasised very clearly the lack of a coherent methodological approach applied by the Court.[151] For the FCC, the arguably failing methodology is exemplified by the broad margin of discretion that is combined with a limited standard of judicial review.[152] The FCC considers that this methodology fails to give sufficient effect to the principle of conferral and paves the way to a continual erosion of Member State competences.[153] For the FCC, this constitutes the limits of the 'Yes but' jurisprudence.[154] A titanic clash of norms is occurring between the deeply rooted procedural effectiveness in EU law and one of the strongest principles enshrined in the German constitutional psyche, namely, proportionality.

V. CONCLUSION

Throughout its long and rich history, European integration has demonstrated its overarching potential, aimed at fostering the European project and enhancing its effectiveness by expanding the limits of EU law and transforming the EU legal order on the basis of already existing, but sometimes 'dormant', features inherent in its design. The example of procedural rule of law in the EU is particularly telling in this respect, having been embedded in the constitutional framework of the EU and reflected in the case law of both the ECSC Court and CJEU. Procedural rule of law has proved its viability and dynamic ascent post-Lisbon Treaty with the strengthening of primary law, notably through the powerful Article 19 TEU and the introduction of the EUCFR, having Article 47, encapsulating effective judicial protection, in its arsenal, and sharpened by the extraordinary context of emergency (the Euro-Area crisis). The rise of procedural rule of law, in the long run, has been characterised by the prevalence of procedural effectiveness in the *effet utile* jurisprudence of the CJEU over the principle of unity/uniformity. The striving for effectiveness has, however, intensified the application of the double standard of judicial review applied by the CJEU with regard to national measures and EU measures. This aspect, it goes without saying, needs to be taken into consideration, especially in light of the current judicial vortex created by the decision of the FCC of 5 May 2020, following the *Weiss* case, which, interestingly enough, represents the position of the strong, creditor Member State, concerned by the mode of interpretation adopted by the CJEU and demanding reclarification of the balance of competences in the EU.

[150] See BVergfG (n 3).
[151] ibid paras 146–161.
[152] ibid, eg para 156.
[153] ibid.
[154] Grimm (n 14) 238–41. This is an expression used by Grimm in the last section of his book, where he also shows deep concern as to the double standard of judicial review used by the CJEU.

A titanic clash of norms is occurring between the deeply and historically founded doctrine of effectiveness of EU law and one of the mightiest principles enshrined in the German constitutional psyche, namely, the principle of proportionality and its robust standard of judicial review. The significance of the resolution of this conflict cannot be underestimated – it will undoubtedly define the future direction of the European project.

13

The European Commission and the EU Rule of Law Policy

ANNA PEREGO*

I. INTRODUCTION

IN RECENT YEARS, the European Union (EU), and, in particular, the European Commission, has become increasingly active in safeguarding the rule of law in its Member States. The rule of law has rapidly assumed a central importance in the EU policies, due to new challenges in Member States and their repercussions on the functioning of the Union. This chapter gives a overview of these developments, and of the instruments that the European Commission has at its disposal to safeguard the rule of law in the EU.

II. THE 'RULE OF LAW' AS A WELL-ESTABLISHED PRINCIPLE

According to the 2019 Communication on further strengthening the rule of law within the Union – State of play and possible next steps,[1] the rule of law is a well-established principle, well-defined in its core meaning, and which can be objectively assessed so that shortcomings can be identified on a sound and stable basis.

According to this Communication, and to the Commission proposal of 2018 for a Regulation on the protection of the Union's budget in case of generalised deficiencies as regards the rule of law in the Member States,[2]

* The views and opinions expressed in this chapter are those of the author and do not necessarily reflect the official position of the European Commission.

[1] Communication from the Commission on further strengthening the rule of law within the Union – State of play and possible next steps, Brussels, COM(2019) 163 final, 3 April 2019.

[2] Proposed Regulation of the European Parliament and of the Council on the protection of the Union's budget in case of generalised deficiencies as regards the rule of law in the Member States, Brussels, COM(2018) 324 final, 2 May 2018, Art 2(a). A similar, albeit slightly expanded definition appears in Art 2(a) of the final text of Regulation (EU, Euratom) 2020/2092 of the European Parliament and of the Council of 16 December 2020 on a general regime of conditionality for the protection of the Union budget, [2020] OJ L433 I/1.

> the rule of law refers to the Union value enshrined in Article 2 of the Treaty on European Union which includes the principles of legality, implying a transparent, accountable, democratic and pluralistic process for enacting laws; legal certainty; prohibition of arbitrariness of the executive powers; effective judicial protection by independent courts, including of fundamental rights; separation of powers and equality before the law.

This definition is based on the case law of the Court of Justice and the European Court of Human Rights, as well as on Council of Europe standards as summarised in the Venice Commission Rule of Law Checklist.[3]

Notably, the Court of Justice has confirmed the *principle of legality* as being a fundamental principle of the Union, by stating that 'in a community governed by the rule of law, adherence to legality must be properly ensured'.[4]

As regards the principle of *legal certainty*, the Court has emphasised that 'the effect of [Union] legislation must be clear and predictable for those who are subject to it'. The Court also stated that 'the principle of legal certainty precludes a [Union] measure from taking effect from a point in time before its publication and that it may be otherwise only exceptionally, where the purpose to be achieved so demands and where the legitimate expectations of those concerned are duly respected'.[5]

The *prohibition of arbitrariness of the executive powers* is also enshrined in the case law of the Court of Justice. The Court has stated that

> in all the legal systems of the Member States, any intervention by the public authorities in the sphere of private activities of any person, whether natural or legal, must have a legal basis and be justified on the grounds laid down by law, and, consequently, those systems provide, albeit in different forms, protection against arbitrary or disproportionate intervention. The need for such protection must be recognised as a general principle of [Union] law.[6]

The essential importance of *independent and effective judicial review, including respect for fundamental rights*, has been at the centre of the recent developments in the Court of Justice case law. According to this case law, the EU is a union based on the rule of law in which individual parties have the right to challenge before the courts the legality of any decision or other national measure relating to the application to them of an EU act.[7] The very existence of effective judicial review designed to ensure compliance with EU law is of the essence of the rule

[3] Rule of Law Checklist, adopted by the Venice Commission at its 106th Plenary Session (Venice, 11–12 March 2016), para 18.

[4] Case 294/83 *Les Verts v European Parliament*, 23 April 1986, ECLI:EU:C:1986:166, para 23.

[5] Joined Cases 212–217/80 *Amministrazione delle finanze dello Stato v Salumi*, 12 November 1981, ECLI:EU:C:1981:270, para 10.

[6] Joined Cases 46/87 & 227/88 *Hoechst v Commission*, 21 September 1989, ECLI:EU:C:1989:337, para 19.

[7] Case C-64/16 *Associação Sindical dos Juízes Portugueses*, 27 February 2018, ECLI:EU:C:2018:117, para 31; Case C-216/18 PPU, *LM*, 25 July 2018, ECLI:EU:C:2018:586, para 49.

of law.[8] The Court of Justice also established that Article 19(1) TEU requires Member States to ensure that the bodies that, as 'courts or tribunals' within the meaning of EU law, come within its judicial system in the fields covered by EU law meet the requirements of effective judicial protection.[9] This obligation concerns courts or tribunals that may rule on questions concerning the application or interpretation of EU law.[10]

In that regard, the factors to be taken into account in assessing whether a body is a 'court or tribunal' include, inter alia, whether the body is established by law, whether it is permanent, whether its jurisdiction is compulsory, whether its procedure is *inter partes*, whether it applies rules of law and whether it is independent.[11]

The Court of Justice also explicitly established that the *separation of powers* characterises the operation of the rule of law[12] and that *equal treatment* is a general principle of EU law, enshrined in Articles 20 and 21 of the Charter of Fundamental Rights of the European Union ('the Charter').[13]

As mentioned in the Venice Commission Rule of Law Checklist, the rule of law has a common core valid everywhere.[14] This does not mean, however, that its implementation has to be identical regardless of the concrete juridical, historical, political, social or geographical context. While the main components or 'ingredients' of the rule of law are constant, the specific manner in which they are realised may differ from one country to another, depending on the local context; in particular on the constitutional order and traditions of the country concerned. This context may also determine the relative weight of each of the components.[15]

III. THE IMPORTANCE OF THE RULE OF LAW

The principle of the rule of law has progressively become a dominant organisational model of modern constitutional law and international organisations

[8] Case C-619/18 *Commission v Poland*, 24 June 2019, ECLI:EU:C:2019:531, para 46; Case C-216/18 PPU, *LM*, para 49; C-64/16, *Associação Sindical dos Juízes Portugueses*, para 36; Case C-72/15, *Rosneft*, 28 March 2017, ECLI:EU:C:2017:236, para 73.

[9] Case C-64/16, *Associação Sindical dos Juízes Portugueses*, para 37; Case C-216/18 PPU, *LM*, para 52; Case C-619/18, *Commission v Poland*, para 55.

[10] Case C-64/16, *Associação Sindical dos Juízes Portugueses*, para 40; Case C-619/18, *Commission v Poland*, para 51; Order of 17 December 2018 in Case C-619/18 R *Commission v Poland*, ECLI:EU:C:2018:1021, para 55; Case C-192/18 *Commission v Poland*, para 103; Joined Cases C-585/18, C-624/18 & C-625/18 *AK and others*, ECLI:EU:C:2019:982, para 83.

[11] Case C-64/16 *Associação Sindical dos Juízes Portugueses*, para 38.

[12] Case C-477/16 PPU *Kovalkovas*, 10 November 2016, ECLI:EU:C:2016:861, para 36; Case C-452/16 PPU *Poltorak*, 10 November 2016, ECLI:EU:C:2016:858, para 35.

[13] Case C-550/07 P *Akzo Nobel Chemicals and Akcros Chemicals v Commission*, 14 September 2010, ECLI:EU:C:2010:512, para 54.

[14] See also the contribution by Iain Cameron in ch 8 of this volume.

[15] Rule of Law Checklist, adopted by the Venice Commission at its 106th Plenary Session (Venice, 11–12 March 2016), para 34.

(including the United Nations and the Council of Europe) governing the exercise of public powers.[16]

A reference to the rule of law can notably also be found in the Statute of the Council of Europe, which affirms that 'every member of the Council of Europe must accept the principles of the rule of law',[17] and in the Preamble to the European Convention on Human Rights.[18] The rule of law is a key principle in the United Nations General Assembly Resolution on the 2005 World Summit Outcome;[19] it is listed in the Constitutive Act of the African Union, among the principles according to which the African Union shall function;[20] and it is referenced in the Inter-American Democratic Charter.[21]

According to the Venice Commission Rule of Law Checklist,

> the Rule of Law is linked not only to human rights but also to democracy … Democracy relates to the involvement of the people in the decision-making process in a society; human rights seek to protect individuals from arbitrary and excessive interferences with their freedoms and liberties and to secure human dignity; the Rule of Law focuses on limiting and independently reviewing the exercise of public powers.[22]

Therefore, the rule of law fulfils a special function in the list of common values enshrined in Article 2 TEU, as it functions as an 'enabler' for other values and guarantees their protection, including democracy and respect for human rights. In fact, democracy, the rule of law and human rights form an inseparable tripod. Fundamental rights are effective only if they are justiciable. Democracy is protected if the fundamental role of the judiciary, including constitutional courts, can ensure freedom of expression, freedom of assembly, and respect for the rules governing the political and electoral process.

IV. THE PARTICULAR IMPORTANCE OF THE RULE OF LAW IN THE EUROPEAN UNION

The rule of law is one of the core values on which the EU is founded. These core values are laid down in Article 2 of the Treaty on European Union (TEU):

> The Union is founded on the values of respect for human dignity, freedom, democracy, equality, the rule of law and respect for human rights, including the rights of persons belonging to minorities. …

[16] Communication from the Commission to the European Parliament and the Council, 'A new EU Framework to strengthen the Rule of Law', COM/2014/0158 final.

[17] Statute of the Council of Europe (London, 5 May 1949), Art 3.

[18] Convention for the Protection of Human Rights and Fundamental Freedoms (Rome, 1950), Preamble.

[19] United Nations, Resolution adopted by the General Assembly on 16 September 2005, World Summit Outcome, paras 11, 21, 24, 134.

[20] Constitutive Act of the African Union 2000, Art 4(m).

[21] Inter-American Democratic Charter 2001, Arts 2–4.

[22] Rule of Law Checklist, adopted by the Venice Commission at its 106th Plenary Session (Venice, 11–12 March 2016), para 33.

In the context of the EU, the rule of law has a particular importance, as it is essential for the Union's functioning and for attaining the objectives of its policies. The rule of law is in fact an essential condition for the uniform application of Union law in all Member States; for effective civil and criminal cooperation between Member States; and more generally for mutual trust between Member States and their respective institutions. The rule of law is an essential condition for a reliable investment climate and for the functioning of the internal market in Europe. It is also one of the principles guiding the EU's external action.[23]

This special function of the rule of law for the European integration is confirmed by the references to this principle in the case law of the European Court of Justice,[24] and by its subsequent inclusion in the list of the fundamental values of the Union by Article 2 TEU.

Notably, the Court has stated that the very existence of effective judicial review designed to ensure compliance with EU law is of the essence of the rule of law,[25] and that judicial independence is essential in that regard.[26]

A. Rule of Law and the Uniform Application of EU Law

As regards the importance of the rule of law for the uniform application of EU law, the Court has consistently[27] held that judicial independence is an essential precondition for the functioning of the preliminary ruling mechanism,[28] in that, in accordance with the Court's settled case law, that mechanism may be activated only by a body responsible for applying EU law that satisfies, inter alia, that criterion of independence.[29] The preliminary reference mechanism is the keystone of the judicial system established by the Treaties to ensure consistency and uniformity in the interpretation of EU law so that the specific characteristics and the autonomy of the EU legal order are preserved.[30]

[23] Art 21 TEU.

[24] Case C-294/83 *Les Verts v Parliament*, para 23.

[25] Case C-192/18 *Commission v Poland*, ECLI:EU:C:2019:924, para 98; Case C-619/18 *Commission v Poland*, paras 46–47; Judgment in Case C-216/18 PPU *LM*, para 49; Case C-64/16 *Associação Sindical dos Juízes Portugueses*, para 36; Judgment in Case C-72/15 *Rosneft*, para 73; Joined Cases C-585/18, C-624/18 & C-625/18 *AK and others*, para 120.

[26] Case C-192/18 *Commission v Poland*, para 105; Case C-619/18 *Commission v Poland*, para 57; Case C-64/16, *Associação Sindical dos Juízes Portugueses*, para 41.

[27] Joined Cases C-558/18 & C-563/18, *Miasto Łowicz*, ECLI:EU:C:2020:234, para 59; Case C-53/03 *Syfait e.a.*, ECLI:EU:C:2005:333, paras 29–37; Case C-54/96 *Dorsch Consult*, ECLI:EU:C:1997:413, para 23.

[28] Case C-619/18 *Commission v Poland*, para 45; Case C-216/18 PPU *LM*, para 54; Case C-64/16 *Associação Sindical dos Juízes Portugueses*, para 43.

[29] Case C-64/16, *Associação Sindical dos Juízes Portugueses*, para 43; judgment in Case C-54/96, *Dorsch Consult*, paras 23, 25, 28–29, 31, 33, 35, 38.

[30] Case C-619/18 *Commission v Poland*, paras 43–44; Case C-284/16 *Achmea*, ECLI:EU:C:2018:158, para 35. It is also relevant that in *Achmea* (paras 55–59), the Court considered that the autonomy of EU law is affected by a treaty by which Member States agree to remove from the jurisdiction of their own courts, and hence from the system of judicial remedies which the second subparagraph of

B. Rule of Law and Mutual Trust

Moreover, judicial independence forms part of the premise on which the high level of trust between Member States is founded.[31] In particular, the Court clarified that the high level of trust between Member States on which the European arrest warrant mechanism is based is founded on the premise that the criminal courts of the other Member States – which, following execution of a European arrest warrant, will have to conduct the criminal procedure for the purpose of prosecution, or of enforcement of a custodial sentence or detention order, and the substantive criminal proceedings – meet the requirements of effective judicial protection, which include, in particular, the independence and impartiality of those courts.[32]

Therefore, the Court has stated that the existence of a real risk that the person in respect of whom a European arrest warrant has been issued will, if surrendered to the issuing judicial authority, suffer a breach of his fundamental right to an independent tribunal and, therefore, of the essence of his fundamental right to a fair trial, a right guaranteed by the second paragraph of Article 47 of the Charter, is capable of permitting the executing judicial authority to refrain, by way of exception, from giving effect to that European arrest warrant.[33]

C. Obligation on Member States to Ensure Judicial Independence under Article 19(1) TEU

The most important consequence of the key importance of the rule of law, and in particular judicial independence, in the EU legal system was drawn by the European Court of Justice for the first time in the judgment in *Associação Sindical dos Juízes Portugueses*. In this judgment, the Court recalled that Article 19 TEU entrusts the responsibility for ensuring judicial review in the EU legal order not only to the European Court of Justice, but also to national courts and tribunals.[34] In other words, national judges are EU judges when interpreting and applying EU law. It follows that every Member State must ensure that the bodies that, as 'courts or tribunals' within the meaning of EU law, come within its judicial system in the fields covered by that law, meet the requirements of effective judicial protection, for which judicial independence is essential.[35]

Art 19(1) TEU requires them to establish in the fields covered by EU law, disputes that may concern the application or interpretation of EU law.

[31] Judgment in Case C-216/18 PPU *LM*, para 58; Case C-619/18 *Commission v Poland*, para 43.

[32] Judgment in Case C-216/18 PPU *LM*, para 58.

[33] ibid para 59.

[34] Judgment in Case C-64/16, *Associação Sindical dos Juízes Portugueses*, para 32.

[35] ibid paras 37–38.

The Court has also underlined on a number of occasions that although the organisation of justice in the Member States falls within the competence of Member States, the fact remains that when exercising that competence, the Member States are required to comply with their obligations deriving from EU law, and in particular from the second subparagraph of Article 19(1) TEU.[36]

D. Rule of Law and Reliable Investment Climate

The importance of the rule of law for a reliable investment climate is demonstrated by the fact that the independence, quality and efficiency of justice systems, which are of the essence of the rule of law, are a well-established area of focus for the structural reforms encouraged through the European Semester, the annual cycle for aligning economic and fiscal policies in the Union.

This was once again underscored in the December 2019 Annual Sustainable Growth Strategy, which stated that

> good governance, effective institutions, independent and efficient justice systems, quality public administrations, robust anti-corruption frameworks, an efficient delivery of public procurement, effective insolvency frameworks and efficient tax systems are important determinants of a Member State's business environment …

and also clarified that '[a]ll these aspects, including those related to the rule of law, can have an impact on investment decisions and are therefore important to increase productivity and competitiveness'.[37]

E. Rule of Law and Accession to the European Union

The rule of law is also part, together with the other values of Article 2 TEU, of the conditions to access the EU according to Article 49 TEU.

Notably, the Court of Justice recently recalled that, as is apparent from Article 49 TEU, the EU is composed of states that have freely and voluntarily committed themselves to the common values referred to in Article 2 TEU, which respect those values and which undertake to promote them, EU law being based on the fundamental premiss that each Member State shares with all the other Member States, and recognises that those Member States share with it, those same values.[38]

[36] Order of the Court in Case C-791/19 R, *Commission v Poland*, ECLI:EU:C:2020:277, para 29; judgment in Case C-192/18 *Commission v Poland*, para 102; judgment in Case C-619/18 *Commission v Poland*, para 52.

[37] Communication from the Commission on the Annual Sustainable Growth Strategy 2020, Brussels, 17 December 2019, COM(2019) 650 final.

[38] Judgment in Case C-619/18 *Commission v Poland*, para 42; judgment in Case C-621/18 *Wightman and Others*, ECLI:EU:C:2018:999, para 63.

The rule of law is part of the 'Copenhagen criteria', which a candidate country must respect to be able to access the Union. These criteria were established by the Copenhagen European Council in 1993, which stated that '[m]embership requires that the candidate country has achieved stability of institutions guaranteeing democracy, the rule of law, human rights and respect for and protection of minorities'.[39]

The establishment of these criteria was rooted in the decision, taken by the same European Council, that the associated countries in Central and Eastern Europe that so desired should become members of the EU. The Council agreed that accession would take place as soon as an associated country was able to assume the obligations of membership by satisfying the economic and political conditions required.

The Copenhagen criteria are still at the basis of EU Enlargement policy. In the recent Communication on 'Enhancing the accession process – A credible EU perspective for the Western Balkans', the Commission recalled:

> A core objective of the European Union's engagement with the Western Balkans is to prepare them to meet all the requirements of membership. This includes supporting fundamental democratic, rule of law and economic reforms and alignment with core European values.[40]

V. THE ORIGINS OF THE EUROPEAN COMMISSION'S RULE OF LAW POLICY

While the rule of law has always been at the core of the European construction, a real 'rule of law policy', in an internal dimension, has developed in recent years in response to the multiplication of challenges to the rule of law in EU Member States. The European Commission has used the means available to protect European values, and has increasingly treated rule of law as a priority in its agenda.

Notably, the deterioration of the rule of law in Poland led the Commission to initiate the procedure under Article 7(1) TEU in December 2017.[41] In September 2018, the European Parliament decided to do the same for Hungary.[42] These are unprecedented steps in the history of the Union.

[39] European Council in Copenhagen, 21–22 June 1993, Conclusions of the Presidency.

[40] Communication from the Commission, 'Enhancing the accession process – A credible EU perspective for the Western Balkans', Brussels, COM(2020) 57 final, 5 February 2020.

[41] European Commission, Proposal of 20 December 2017 for a Council Decision on the determination of a clear risk of a serious breach by the Republic of Poland of the rule of law, COM/2017/0835 final – 2017/0360.

[42] European Parliament, Resolution of 12 September 2018 on a proposal calling on the Council to determine, pursuant to Article 7(1) of the Treaty on European Union, the existence of a clear risk of a serious breach by Hungary of the values on which the Union is founded (2017/2131).

A. Article 7 TEU and the Rule of Law Framework

The procedure in Article 7 TEU is an exceptional, but potentially the most far-reaching, mechanism provided by the Treaties to respond to violation of the EU fundamental values by a Member State.

The Article first appeared in the Treaty of Amsterdam,[43] and was then further modified by the Treaty of Nice[44] before assuming its current wording in the Treaty of Lisbon. The Reflection Group of 1995 that led to the Treaty of Amsterdam stated that 'during the current process of European construction, and above all in the run-up to enlargement, there is an urgent need to ensure full observance of fundamental rights, both in relations between the Union and the Member States and between States and individuals'.[45]

Article 7 can be triggered in the event of a 'clear risk of a serious breach of the [Union's] values' (Article 7(1) TEU), or in case of 'the existence of a serious and persistent breach' of the Union's values (Article 7(2) TEU). The full consequences of the procedure under Article 7 TEU are very significant – under Article 7(2) TEU a Member State's rights, including voting rights in the Council, can be suspended.

The European Commission also established, in 2014, the so-called 'Rule of Law Framework'.[46] The Framework provides a staged process of dialogue with a Member State, structured with opinions and recommendations from the Commission. The goal is to prevent the emergence of a systemic threat to the rule of law in a Member State, at which point the Article 7 TEU procedure would be required.[47] The first time the Rule of Law Framework was used – and so far the only time – came with the start of a dialogue with Poland in January 2016. While this dialogue helped in identifying problems and framing the discussion, it could not resolve the detected rule of law deficiencies.

For this reason, on 20 December 2017, the Commission considered that a clear risk of a serious breach of the rule of law in Poland existed, and adopted a reasoned proposal in accordance with Article 7(1) TEU.[48] The key consideration for the Commission to activate the Article 7(1) TEU procedure was that the cumulative effect of the different components of the reforms that limit the independence of the judiciary and infringe upon the separation of powers in Poland. The common pattern of these reforms is that the executive and

[43] Art F.1.

[44] Art 7.

[45] Reflection Group's Report, 1995, para 33, available at www.europarl.europa.eu/enlargement/cu/agreements/reflex4_en.htm?textMode=on.

[46] Communication from the Commission to the European Parliament and the Council, 'A new EU Framework to strengthen the Rule of Law', COM/2014/0158 final.

[47] E Crabit and N Bel, 'Chapter 11. The EU Rule of Law Framework' in W Schroeder (ed), *Strengthening the Rule of Law in Europe – From a Common Concept to Mechanisms of Implementation*' (Oxford, Hart Publishing, 2016).

[48] European Commission Proposal (n 41).

legislative powers can now interfere with the entire structure of the justice system.

The Commission's reasoned proposal to the Council covers a number of issues. These include: (i) the situation of the Polish Constitutional Tribunal, where concerns relate to the appointment of judges and the publication of judgments; (ii) the National Council for the Judiciary, whose judges-members are now elected by the parliament instead of by their peers as required by European standards; (iii) the retirement regime of Supreme Court judges; (iv) the new disciplinary regime for judges; (v) the Extraordinary Appeal Procedure, where the criteria remain very broad and allow for the repeal of judgments going back 20 years, creating concerns about legal certainty; (vi) those court presidents who have been arbitrarily dismissed, in particular from courts of appeal and regional courts; (vii) the retirement regime of ordinary court judges.

While three hearings on the Rule of Law in Poland took place in the General Affairs Council, at the time of drafting this chapter,[49] the Commission considers that the situation in Poland continues to deteriorate.

The European Parliament triggered the same procedure, Article 7(1) TEU, as regards Hungary on the basis of a reasoned proposal adopted in September 2018.[50] The European Parliament's reasoned proposal, based on the Sargentini Report, covered a wide range of issues: the functioning of the constitutional and electoral system; the independence of the judiciary; corruption and conflicts of interest; privacy and data protection; freedom of expression; academic freedom; freedom of religion; freedom of association; the right to equal treatment; the rights of persons belonging to minorities, including Roma and Jews; the fundamental rights of migrants, asylum seekers and refugees; and economic and social rights.

The Commission shares an important number of concerns expressed by the European Parliament in its reasoned proposal, and has provided, on different occasions, updates to the Council in this regard.

While concrete progress by the Council in these two cases of Poland and Hungary has so far been rather limited, the ongoing dialogues led to the rule of law's becoming a priority in the Council's agenda and contributed to avoiding further deteriorations.

B. Infringement Proceedings and the Case Law of the European Court of Justice

One of the most important instruments of the new EU rule of law policy is the use of value-related infringement proceedings, in particular to protect judicial

[49] May 2020.
[50] European Parliament, Resolution (n 42).

independence in EU Member States. The possibility to launch infringement proceedings to ensure judicial independence is a very important development in the EU, underlining the fundamental role of the Commission as guardian of the Treaties.

These infringement proceedings are based on the reasoning that national courts act as 'EU courts' whenever they apply EU law. Therefore, Member State must ensure that, in the fields covered by EU law, national courts meet the requirements of effective judicial protection as enshrined in Article 19 TEU and Article 47 of the Charter.

This reasoning was used for the first time by the Commission in the first infringement proceedings on judicial independence, referred to the European Court of Justice the same day as triggering the Article 7 TEU procedure for Poland.[51] This first infringement procedure concerned the retirement regime for Polish ordinary court judges. The Commission's key legal concern identified in this law relates to the discrimination on the basis of gender due to the introduction of a different retirement age for female judges (60 years) and male judges (65 years). The Commission considered that discrimination was contrary to Article 157 of the Treaty on the Functioning of the European Union (TFEU) and Directive 2006/54 on gender equality in employment.[52] The Commission also considered that the independence of Polish courts was undermined by the fact that the Minister of Justice had been given a discretionary power to prolong the mandate of judges who had reached retirement age.

A few months after the referral of this case, the European Court of Justice issued a ground-breaking judgment relating to the rule of law and judicial independence. In its judgment in *Associação Sindical dos Juízes Portugueses*[53] of February 2018, the Court of Justice underlined that the very existence of an effective judicial review by national courts, designed to ensure compliance with EU law, is part of the essence of the rule of law. The Court held that Member States are required by virtue of Article 19(1) TEU to ensure that their courts meet the requirements of effective judicial protection, and that independence is essential to ensure such protection.

This judgment confirmed the reasoning of the Commission and confirmed, for the first time, that the Commission can, in certain situations where the independence of the justice system of a Member State has come under threat, successfully bring infringement proceedings against a Member State for violating the principle of effective judicial protection and the right to an effective remedy, as guaranteed by Article 19(1) TEU and Article 47 of the Charter.

[51] Press release, European Commission, 20 December 2017, IP/17/5367, at https://ec.europa.eu/commission/presscorner/detail/en/IP_17_5367.

[52] Directive 2006/54/EC of the European Parliament and of the Council of 5 July 2006 on the implementation of the principle of equal opportunities and equal treatment of men and women in matters of employment and occupation (recast) [2006] OJ L204/23.

[53] Case C-64/16 *Associação Sindical dos Juízes Portugueses.*

The Commission subsequently used this reasoning in other infringement proceedings against Poland. One of these proceedings concerned the Polish Law on the Supreme Court, which put at risk of early retirement almost one-third of the members of the Supreme Court, including its First President. In this case, the Commission also asked the Court of Justice to impose interim measures on Poland.[54]

The Court accepted all the Commission's requests and ordered the Polish authorities in December to stop implementing this Law.[55] On 24 June 2019, the Court of Justice issued its final judgment in this case, confirming in full the position of the Commission that the Polish legislation concerning the lowering of the retirement age of Supreme Court judges was contrary to EU law regarding judicial independence.[56]

On 5 November 2019, the Court of Justice handed down the judgment in the infringement proceedings against Poland concerning the retirement regime of ordinary court judges, once more confirming in full the Commission's reasoning.[57]

In October 2019, the Commission referred to the Court of Justice a third infringement case in relation to the new disciplinary regime for judges in Poland, considering that this new regime did not provide the necessary guarantees to protect judges from political control of their judicial decisions.[58]

According to the Commission, the Polish law allowed ordinary court judges to be subjected to disciplinary investigations, procedures and sanctions on the basis of the content of their judicial decisions, including the exercise of their right under Article 267 TFEU to request preliminary rulings from the Court of Justice of the EU. Moreover, the new disciplinary regime did not guarantee the independence and impartiality of the Disciplinary Chamber of the Supreme Court, which is composed solely of judges selected by the National Council for the Judiciary, which is itself politically appointed by the Polish Parliament (*Sejm*).

Furthermore, the new disciplinary regime did not ensure that a court 'established by law' would decide in the first instance on disciplinary proceedings against ordinary court judges. Instead, it empowered the President of the Disciplinary Chamber to determine, on an ad hoc basis and with an almost unfettered discretion, the disciplinary court of first instance to hear a given case brought against an ordinary court judge.

The new regime no longer guaranteed that cases would be processed within a reasonable timeframe, allowing the Minister of Justice to keep charges pending

[54] Press release, European Commission, 24 September 2018, IP/18/5830, at https://ec.europa.eu/commission/presscorner/detail/en/IP_18_5830.

[55] Order of the Court of 17 December 2018, in Case C-619/18 R *Commission v Poland*.

[56] Case C-619/18 *Commission v Poland*.

[57] Case C-192/18 *Commission v Poland*, para 98.

[58] Press release, European Commission, IP/19/6033, at https://ec.europa.eu/commission/presscorner/detail/en/IP_19_6033.

over ordinary court judges through disciplinary officers appointed by the Minister. The new regime also affected ordinary court judges' right of defence. In short, judges would not be insulated from political control and thus judicial independence would be violated.

In January 2020, the Commission asked the Court to grant interim measures in this regard.[59] On 8 April 2020, the Court of Justice ruled that Poland must immediately suspend the application of the national provisions concerned on the powers of the Disciplinary Chamber of the Supreme Court.[60]

In this order, the Court referred to its judgment of 19 November 2019,[61] where it stated that the Polish Supreme Court must decide whether its new Disciplinary Chamber was independent on the basis in particular of a number of criteria, including the circumstances in which the members of the new National Council for the Judiciary were appointed. Based on the preliminary ruling, the Polish Supreme Court ruled that the Disciplinary Chamber did not meet the requirements of EU law on judicial independence.[62]

On 29 April 2020, the Commission launched a fourth infringement procedure on judicial independence against Poland as regards the new Polish law on the judiciary adopted in December 2019. The Commission considered that certain provisions of that legislation adversely affected judicial independence, the principle of primacy of EU law, the functioning of the preliminary ruling mechanism under Article 267 TFEU, the Charter of Fundamental Rights of the European Union, and the General Data Protection Regulation.[63]

The Commission considered that the new law broadened the notion of disciplinary offence and thereby increased the number of cases in which the content of judicial decisions could be qualified as a disciplinary offence. As a result, the disciplinary regime could be used as a system of political control of the content of judicial decisions. Second, the Commission noted that the new law granted the new Chamber of Extraordinary Control and Public Affairs of the Supreme Court the sole competence to rule on issues regarding judicial independence. This would prevent Polish courts from fulfilling their obligation to apply EU law or request preliminary rulings from the EU Court of Justice. Third, the Commission noted that the law prevented Polish courts from assessing, in the context of cases pending before them, the power to adjudicate cases by other judges. Finally, the Commission noted that the new law introduced provisions requiring judges to disclose specific information about their non-professional activities. On 30 October 2020, the Commission moved forward with the infringement procedure by sending a reasoned opinion.

[59] Press release, European Commission, MEX/20/56, at Https://ec.europa.eu/commission/presscorner/detail/en/mex_20_56.

[60] Order of the Court in Case C-791/19 R, *Commission v Poland*.

[61] Joined Cases C-585/18, C-624/18 & C-625/18, *AK and others*, ECLI:EU:C:2019:982.

[62] Judgment of the Supreme Court of Poland, 5 December 2019, File No III PO 7/18.

[63] Press release, European Commission, IP/20/772, at https://ec.europa.eu/commission/presscorner/detail/en/ip_20_772.

The developing case law on judicial independence has contributed to further clarify the content of the requirements inherent to this principle. According to this case law, the Court considers that judicial independence requires both external and internal independence, as well as the appearance of independence.

These developments built on the 2006 judgment in *Wilson*,[64] where the Court of Justice had, for the first time, systematised the requirements of judicial independence, drawing inspiration from the case law of the European Court of Human Rights.[65]

The Court of Justice has stated that the requirement of external independence presumes that the body concerned exercises its functions wholly autonomously, without being subject to any hierarchical constraint or subordinated to any other body, and without taking orders or instructions from any source whatsoever, thus being protected against external interventions or pressure liable to impair the independent judgment of its members and to influence their decisions.[66]

The requirement of internal independence, which is linked to impartiality, seeks to ensure that an equal distance is maintained from the parties to the proceedings and their respective interests with regard to the subject matter of those proceedings. That aspect requires objectivity and the absence of any interest in the outcome of the proceedings apart from the strict application of the rule of law.[67]

Moreover, guarantees of independence and impartiality are necessary to dismiss any reasonable doubt in the minds of individuals as to the imperviousness of that body to external factors, and its neutrality with respect to the interests before it.[68]

Guarantees of independence and impartiality require rules, particularly as regards the composition of the body and the appointment, length of service and the grounds for abstention, rejection and dismissal of its members,[69] remuneration[70] and the disciplinary regime.[71]

[64] Case C-506/04 *Wilson*, 19 September 2006, ECLI:EU:C:2006:587, paras 49–52.

[65] *Campbell and Fell v United Kingdom* (ECtHR, 28 June 1984) para 78; *De Cubber v Belgium* (ECtHR, 26 October 1984) para 24. See A Perego, 'La jurisprudence de la Cour de justice sur l'indépendance judiciaire' (2019) 4 *Revue de l'Union européenne* 129.

[66] Case C-619/18 *Commission v Poland*, para 72; Case C-64/16 *Associação Sindical dos Juízes Portugueses*, para 45; Case C-216/18 PPU *LM*, para 63; Case C-506/04 *Wilson*, para 51; Case C-192/18 *Commission v Poland*, para 109.

[67] Case C-619/18 *Commission v Poland*, para 73; Case C-216/18 PPU *LM*, para 65; Case C-506/04 *Wilson*, para 52; Case C-192/18 *Commission v Poland*, para 110; Joined Cases C-585/18, C-624/18 & C-625/18 *AK and others*, para 125.

[68] Case C-216/18 PPU *LM*, para 66; Case C-506/04 *Wilson*, para 53; Case C-619/18 *Commission v Poland*, paras 74, 79, 108, 111; Case C-192/18 *Commission v Poland*, paras 111 and 115; Joined Cases C-585/18, C-624/18 & C-625/18 *AK and others*, para 123.

[69] Case C-216/18 PPU *LM*, paras 64, 66; Case C-506/04 *Wilson*, para 53; Case C-619/18 *Commission v Poland*, para 74; Case C-192/18 *Commission v Poland*, para 111.

[70] Case C-64/16 *Associação Sindical dos Juízes Portugueses*, para 45; Case C-216/18 PPU *LM*, para 64.

[71] Case C-216/18 PPU *LM*, para 67; Case C-619/18 *Commission v Poland*, para 77; Case C-192/18 *Commission v Poland*, para 114.

As regards appointment, the Court held that the participation of a judicial council, in the context of a process for the appointment of judges, may, in principle, be such as to contribute to making that process more objective. However, that is only the case provided, inter alia, that that body is itself sufficiently independent of the legislature and executive, and of the authority to which it is required to deliver such an appointment proposal.[72] The Court provided elements to be taken into account to assess the independence of the council, including the way in which that body exercises its constitutional responsibilities of ensuring the independence of the courts.[73]

The Court also pointed out that the mere fact that judges are appointed by the President of the Republic does not give rise to a relationship of subordination of the former to the latter, or to doubts as to the former's impartiality, as long as, once appointed, they are free from influence or pressure when carrying out their role.[74]

However, the Court recognised that it is still necessary to ensure that the substantive conditions and detailed procedural rules governing the adoption of appointment decisions are such that they cannot give rise to reasonable doubts, in the minds of individuals, as to the imperviousness of the judges concerned to external factors, and as to their neutrality with respect to the interests before them, once appointed as judges.[75]

As regards the length of service and dismissal, the Court held that judges may remain in post, provided that they have not reached the obligatory retirement age or until the expiry of their mandate, where that mandate is for a fixed term. While it is not wholly absolute, there can be no exceptions to that principle, unless they are warranted by legitimate and compelling grounds, subject to the principle of proportionality.[76]

As regards remuneration, the Court held that receipt by judges of a level of remuneration commensurate with the importance of the functions is necessary for upholding judicial independence.[77]

As regards the disciplinary regime, the Court indicated that any dismissal procedure governing those who have the task of adjudicating in a dispute must display the necessary guarantees in order to prevent any risk of its being used as a system of political control of the content of judicial decisions. Rules that define, in particular, both conduct amounting to disciplinary offences and the penalties actually applicable, that provide for the involvement of an independent

[72] Case C-619/18 *Commission v Poland*, paras 115-116; Joined Cases C-585/18, C-624/18 & C-625/18 *AK and others*, paras 137–139.

[73] Joined Cases C-585/18, C-624/18 & C-625/18 *AK and others*, paras 142–144.

[74] ibid para 133, Requests for a preliminary ruling from the Sąd Najwyższy, para 133.

[75] ibid para 134.

[76] Case C-619/18 *Commission v Poland*, para 76; Case C-192/18 *Commission v Poland*, para 113.

[77] Case C-64/16 *Associação Sindical dos Juízes Portugueses*, para 45; Case C-216/18 PPU *LM*, para 64.

body in accordance with a procedure that fully safeguards the rights enshrined in Articles 47 and 48 of the Charter, in particular the rights of the defence, and that lay down the possibility of bringing legal proceedings challenging the disciplinary bodies' decisions, constitute a set of guarantees that are essential for safeguarding the independence of the judiciary.[78]

The Commission has also launched a series of value-related infringement proceedings against Hungary. Notably, on 7 December 2017, the Commission referred Hungary to the Court of Justice as regards the law on foreign-funded non-governmental organisations, which imposed restrictions on civil society organisations receiving funds from abroad.[79] On 18 June 2020, the Court of Justice handed down a judgment affirming that the restrictions imposed by Hungary on the financing of civil society organisations from abroad were not compatible with EU law. Those restrictions infringed the principle of free movement of capital and a number of fundamental rights.[80]

On the same day, the Commission also referred Hungary to the Court of Justice as regards its Higher Education Act, as amended on 4 April 2017, imposing restrictions on foreign universities' operation in Hungary. The Commission considered that the law disproportionally restricted EU and non-EU universities in their operations and needed to be brought back into line with EU law.[81] On 6 October 2020, the Grand Chamber confirmed that the requirements introduced in Hungary in 2017 for an international treaty with the state of origin and of genuine teaching activity in that state were not compatible with EU law and WTO law.[82]

Moreover, in July 2019, the Commission decided to refer Hungary to the Court of Justice as regards the so-called 'Stop Soros package' criminalising any assistance offered by any person, on behalf of organisations, to people wishing to apply for asylum or for a residence permit in Hungary.[83]

While infringement proceedings as regards Poland were capable of tackling a number of horizontal reforms of the justice system, infringement proceedings as regards Hungary addressed only certain specific issues. This could be partially due to the fact that a number of rule of law issues raised in the Article 7 TEU procedure against Hungary date back to a period[84] when the

[78] Order in Case C-791/19 *Commission v Poland*, ECLI:EU:C:2020:277, para 77; Case C-216/18 PPU *LM*, para 67; Case C-619/18 *Commission v Poland*, para 77; Case C-192/18 *Commission v Poland*, para 114.

[79] Press release, European Commission, IP/17/5003, at https://ec.europa.eu/commission/presscorner/detail/en/IP_17_5003.

[80] Case C-78/18 *Commission v Hungary*, ECLI:EU:C:2020:476.

[81] Press Relase, European Commission, IP/17/5004, at https://ec.europa.eu/commission/presscorner/detail/en/IP_17_5004.

[82] AG Kokott's Opinion in Case C-66/18 *Commission v Hungary*, ECLI:EU:C:2020:792172.

[83] Press Release, European Commission, IP/19/4260, at https://ec.europa.eu/commission/presscorner/detail/en/IP_19_4260.

[84] In 2010, large-scale reforms were initiated in Hungary. In April 2011, the Parliament adopted a new Constitution, introducing controversial reforms. In April 2013, the Parliament amended this

use of infringement proceedings by the Commission to tackle these issues was more limited. For instance, when concerns relating to the early retirement of judges arose in Hungary due to the constitutional reform of 2011, this was addressed by the Commission through an infringement procedure based on the anti-discrimination law rather than judicial independence.[85]

In the 2019 Communication on 'Strengthening the rule of law within the Union – A blueprint for action',[86] the Commission announced that it would further build on this case law by bringing to the Court of Justice rule of law problems affecting the application of EU law, when these problems could not be solved through the national checks and balances. It was also announced that the Commission would pursue a strategic approach to infringement proceedings related to the rule of law, requesting expedited proceedings and interim measures whenever necessary. Moreover, the Commission committed to actively promoting the standards developed in the Court of Justice case law, including by compiling the relevant findings of the Court.

Therefore, while infringement proceedings have already proved to be a very effective instrument to tackle certain rule of law issues, their potential could be further exploited in light of the developing case law of the Court of Justice.

C. EU Justice Scoreboard and European Semester

The Commission has also deployed other instruments to protect the rule of law in the Union, including measures under the European Semester, whose priorities include improving the independence, quality and efficiency of Member States' national justice systems.

The European Semester cycle starts every year in November, when the Commission presents its priorities for the next year (Communication on the Annual Growth Survey). In February, the Commission services present country-specific assessments in the Country Reports, covering all matters dealt with by the Semester. In May/June, the Commission presents its proposals for the country-specific recommendations that are addressed to Member States. These recommendations are adopted in July by the Council, after having been endorsed by the European Council.

Constitution. Certain of these concerns raised issues of compatibility with specific EU legislation: the anti-discrimination directive as regards the early retirement of judges and the data protection directive as regards the premature termination of the mandate of the data protection officer. The Commission started infringement proceedings on the early retirement of judges and on the premature termination of the mandate of the data protection authority. As a result, in both cases the Court of Justice condemned Hungary (in November 2012 and April 2014) for violating EU law (judgment in Case C-286/12 *European Commission v Hungary*, 6 November 2012, ECLI:EU:C:2012:687; judgment in Case C-288/12 *European Commission v Hungary*, 8 April 2014, ECLI:EU:C:2014:237).

[85] Judgment in Case C-288/12, *European Commission v Hungary*.

[86] Communication from the Commission, 'Strengthening the rule of law within the Union – A blueprint for action', Brussels, COM(2019) 343 final, 17 July 2019.

The EU Justice Scoreboard feeds this analysis by providing a yearly comparative overview of the independence, quality and efficiency of national justice systems. It makes it easier to identify shortcomings and best practices, and to keep track of progress made.

The 2019 EU Justice Scoreboard, for instance, presented indicators concerning judicial independence, including an overview of the authorities involved in disciplinary proceedings regarding judges[87] and of the authorities holding the main management powers over national prosecution services.[88] There is also an overview of the authorities involved in the appointment and dismissal of national prosecutors.[89]

The Semester Country Reports present country-specific assessments based on the Scoreboard data, as well as on country-specific information that allows the Commission to take into account the institutional and legal context and to provide a deeper assessment of the situation in the Member States in question. These country-specific assessments are based on bilateral dialogues with national authorities and stakeholders.

The combined outcome of these tools may lead the Commission to propose to the Council to adopt country-specific recommendations in May. In 2019, the Council adopted recommendations on the independence and efficiency of the justice system for seven Member States.

On 20 May 2020, the Commission issued its proposals for country-specific recommendations. Eight Member States[90] received a proposal relating to the rule of law.

D. The Cooperation and Verification Mechanism

A specific instrument is the Cooperation and Verification Mechanism, which was established as a mechanism for Bulgaria and Romania when they joined the Union in 2007, to assist the two Member States to address remaining shortcomings in the areas of judicial reform, the fight against corruption and, for Bulgaria, organised crime.[91] This mechanism is a transitional measure, the goal being to close it once the defined benchmarks have been satisfactorily fulfilled.

[87] Communication from the Commission, the 2019 EU Justice Scoreboard, COM(2019) 198/2, figures 52 and 53.

[88] ibid figures 55 and 56.

[89] ibid figure 57.

[90] Croatia, Italy, Cyprus, Malta, Poland, Portugal, Slovakia, Hungary: see at https://ec.europa.eu/info/publications/2020-european-semester-country-specific-recommendations-commission-recommendations_en.

[91] See at https://ec.europa.eu/info/policies/justice-and-fundamental-rights/upholding-rule-law/rule-law/assistance-bulgaria-and-romania-under-cvm/reports-progress-bulgaria-and-romania_en.

VI. A NEW PHASE

The 2019 political guidelines of President von der Leyen opened a new phase for the EU rule of law policy.[92] The guidelines announced the establishment of a comprehensive European Rule of Law Mechanism with an EU-wide scope and objective annual reporting by the European Commission. In July 2019, the Commission presented the Communication 'Strengthening the rule of law within the Union – A blueprint for action',[93] which provided concrete detail in this regard.

The establishment of the new Mechanism is based on the recognition that the EU institutions need to develop stronger awareness and understanding of developments in the individual Member States as they occur, to be able to identify risks to the rule of law, develop possible solutions and target support early on. This also aims at avoiding any misunderstanding, and at having early and transparent exchanges before an actual problem could arise.

To support this process, the Commission has prepared an annual Rule of Law Report and is further developing its EU Justice Scoreboard. The annual Report, issued for the first time on 30 September 2020, provides a synthesis of significant developments – both positive and negative – in all Member States.

The standards used for the assessment are those stemming from EU law, the case law of the Court of Justice and of the European Court of Human Rights, as well as from the Council of Europe. The scope of the monitoring will cover significant developments, both negative or positive, within four areas: justice systems, and in particular their independence, quality and efficiency; the anti-corruption framework; certain issues related to media pluralism; and other structural issues related to checks and balances. The Commission relies on a diversity of relevant sources, including contributions from Member States, stakeholders, the Fundamental Rights Agency and the Council of Europe.

The added value of the Report is to foster a genuine discussion on the situation of the rule of law in the Member States, at both EU and national level. This is why the Commission is encouraging the Council and the Parliament to follow up the Report in their discussions. The Commission also encourages the Parliament to strengthen its dialogue with national parliaments and develop inter-parliamentary cooperation on rule of law issues.

In this regard, the German Presidency has initiated, as part of the Council annual Rule of Law Dialogue, a country-specific discussion on the rule of law situation in a number of specific Member States. These discussions started in November 2020 and are planned to take place twice each year. The Commission's Rule of Law Report represents the basis for such dialogue.

[92] Ursula von der Leyen, Political Guidelines for the next European Commission 2019–2024.
[93] Communication from the Commission (n 86).

In addition to the new European Rule of Law Mechanism, the Communication 'Strengthening the rule of law within the Union – A blueprint for action' announced that the Commission will work on promoting a rule of law culture and providing an effective response when a significant problem has been identified.

As regards promotion, the Commission clearly recognised the need to strengthen the rule of law culture among the general public. It is also necessary to promote better knowledge of the requirements of EU law and European standards relating to the rule of law. The Commission has therefore committed to making full use of funding possibilities to empower stakeholders – including civil society and academia – to promote the rule of law.

As regards response, the Commission, as Guardian of the Treaties, will build on the evolving case law of the Court of Justice, and pursue a strategic approach to infringement proceedings.

VII. RULE OF LAW AND THE PROTECTION OF THE EU BUDGET

In 2018, the Commission submitted a Proposal for a Regulation on the protection of the Union budget in the event of generalised deficiencies as regards the rule of law in the Member States.[94] The objective of the new rules proposed by the Commission was to provide the Union with tools to protect its budget if deficiencies in the rule of law in a particular Member State were to affect or risk affecting the financial interests of the Union.

As recalled in recital 4 of the Proposal, the proposed Regulation was based on the understanding that

> Whenever the Member State implements the Union budget and whatever method of implementation they use, respect for the rule of law is an essential precondition to comply with the principles of sound financial management enshrined in Article 317 of the Treaty on the Functioning of the European Union.

While under the rules valid at the time Member States were already required to show that their rules and procedures for financial management of EU money were robust and that funding was sufficiently protected from abuse or fraud, there was no mechanism in place to protect EU taxpayers' money in the event of generalised deficiencies regarding the rule of law in a Member State.

In Article 3, the Proposal for a Regulation addressed generalised deficiencies as regards the rule of law in a Member State that affect or risk affecting the principle of sound financial management or the protection of the financial interests

[94] Proposal for a Regulation of the European Parliament and of the Council on the protection of the Union's budget in case of generalised deficiencies as regards the rule of law in the Member States, COM/2018/324 final – 2018/0136 (COD).

of the Union. Therefore, the proposed Regulation did not cover all generalised deficiencies as regards the rule of law, but only those that affect or could affect the Union's budget. It would allow the EU to take appropriate measures, in the event that the Union budget was affected or at risk of being affected. The list contained in Article 3(1) of the Regulation provided examples of negative effects on the Union's budget. The list in Article 3(2) provided examples of possible generalised deficiencies as regards the rule of law, which might give rise to the measures under the Regulation. However, the link between the deficiency and the negative effect on the Union's budget would have to be established for each case in which the mechanism was to be triggered.

Therefore, the proposed mechanism pursued an objective, the protection of the EU budget, different from the Article 7 TEU procedures, and from infringement proceedings.

If the Commission has reasonable grounds to believe that a generalised deficiency as regards the rule of law in a Member State affects or risks affecting the financial interests of the Union, it will start a procedure that could lead to the adoption of appropriate measures. Under the Proposal, the Union could then suspend, reduce or restrict access to EU funding proportionately to the nature, gravity and scope of the generalised deficiencies as regards the rule of law. Final beneficiaries would not be affected as, under Article 4, Member States would continue to be bound by existing obligations to implement programmes and make payments to final recipients or beneficiaries.

A provisional agreement on the Proposal was reached in November 2020 by the European Parliament and the Council of the European Union. The provisional agreement maintained the main element of the Commission's proposal while amending the voting modalities for adopting measures in Council and other aspects of the Proposal, such as the triggering criteria and the procedure for adoption. The final text of Regulation (EU, Euratom) 2020/2092 on a general regime of conditionality for the protection of the Union budget was adopted on 16 December 2020.[95]

The new conditionality regime could provide for a new important, and viable, instrument to tackle the consequences of rule of law deficiencies for the EU budget.

[95] Regulation (EU, Euratom) 2020/2092 of the European Parliament and of the Council of 16 December 2020 on a general regime of conditionality for the protection of the Union budget [2020] OJ L433 I/1.

VIII. CONCLUSIONS

European integration has always relied on the sharing of common values among its Member States. The respect for this value is the basis for the functioning of the Union and its policies.

In recent years, the Commission has developed existing instruments and announced new mechanisms to face possible rule of law crises in Member States. Certain instruments, such as the use of infringement proceedings for violation of judicial independence, have achieved important results. The triggering of the Article 7 TEU procedures has contributed to avoiding further deterioration and to bringing the rule of law to the top of the Council's agenda. The European Semester and the EU Justice Scoreboard have also contributed to the monitoring of developments in Member States.

The setting up of a new European Rule of Law Mechanism is a further keystone in the EU rule of law policy, which is capable of bringing together the Commission, the Parliament and the Council around a single Rule of Law Report. The adoption of the proposed Regulation on the protection of the Union budget in the event of generalised deficiencies as regards the rule of law in the Member States would also add a missing piece to the 'EU rule of law toolbox'.

Taken together, these measures and developments clearly show the key importance that the Commission attaches to the rule of law as a foundation stone for the future of the EU.

14

Respect for the Rule of Law: Some Thoughts on the European Parliament's Perspective

LINDA STEFANI AND MARÍA JOSÉ MARTÍNEZ IGLESIAS

I. INTRODUCTORY REMARKS

The European Parliament ('the Parliament') as we see it today is the result of a profound historical transformation, from a powerless assembly of national parliaments' delegates to the fully-fledged co-legislator of the Union. This constant transformation of its constitutional relevance within the Union is the reason for the acute institutional self-awareness and political assertiveness that characterise the vision of its own role. Our purpose in this chapter is to analyse the Parliament's conception of the rule of law and its own role in defence of the latter, as inferred from its contributions and actions. Section II sets the scene, outlining the Treaty's design for the Union's mandate on the rule of law and how the Parliament understands its place in the picture. Section III tackles the Parliament's contribution to the rule of law by tracing back its milestones, with a cursory overview of the landmark initiatives adopted by Parliament itself. By guiding through the microcosm of parliamentary works, these initiatives tell a story on the Parliament's conception of the rule of law, and they do so in the process, as well as in their content. Section IV looks closer into the nature and meaning of the Parliament's conception of the rule of law; the discussion unfolds against the backdrop of the Article 7(1) procedure pending against Hungary, at the time this chapter is being finalised in summer 2020, and the most recent procedural and factual developments. On one hand, the current affairs may be a concrete and timely occasion to grasp how these concepts operate in practice. On the other, they offer a truthful portrait of the meaning, the *modus* and the added value of the Parliament's contribution.

II. THE TREATIES' CONSTITUTIONAL FRAMEWORK

The age of a Union institution is often the age of the last Treaty reform, and the Parliament of the Treaty of Amsterdam is not the one of the Treaty of Lisbon. The Parliament's perspective on the rule of law at which this contribution looks, unfolds chronologically in the post-Lisbon period.

The Treaty on European Union (TEU) enshrines the core provisions related to respect for the rule of law under Articles 2 and 7 respectively.[1] The structure of these two provisions of primary law is profoundly intertwined: the normative core is respect for the values enshrined in Article 2, while Article 7 is the procedural mechanism conceived to protect these values.

The rule of law is included as one of the elements listed in Article 2 TEU, but very often the concept of 'the rule of law' is identified in everyday language with the ensemble of these values. There is nothing more elusive than the concept of rule of law: while in the Anglo-Saxon tradition it is close to the notion of equality before the law, and related in particular to the independence of the judiciary, in its Continental version (*état de droit*, *Rechtstaat*, *estado de derecho*, *stato di diritto*) it has more to do with the defence of fundamental rights within a democratic constitutional framework.

We will use the term in its broadest sense, as referring to the set of values protected by Article 7 TEU. This conception seems to us the most appropriate for the purposes of this contribution, to the extent we are discussing the Parliament's perspective.

This notion is coherent with the new constitutional architecture of the Lisbon Treaty. There, the mechanisms conceived in the Amsterdam Treaty have been completed with an explicit normative recognition of representative and participative democracy as the foundation of the Union (Title II TEU, 'Provisions on Democratic Principles'), with the conferral on the Charter of Fundamental Rights of the same legal value as the Treaties, and with the mandate to adhere to the European Convention on Human Rights (Article 6 TEU). That legal design translated into the Union itself the democratic values it requires from its Member States.

This constitutional framework represents the background against which the role of the Parliament in the defence of the rule of law is projected. The values in Article 2 are the fabric of the Union constitutionalism, concrete principles and rights condensing centuries of legal and political history. Their privileged

[1] For a comprehensive commentary on Art 2, see L Fumagalli, in A Tizzano (ed), *Trattati dell'Unione europea* (Milan, Giuffrè, 2014) 11, and on Art 7 see C Sanna, ibid 71. See also Art 21(2) of the European Charter of Fundamental Rights ('the Charter'); see the Preamble to both the Treaty and the Charter. See the Parliament Rules of Procedures (RoP), Rules 39, 89, 162, witnessing the importance placed by the Parliament on the rule of law and the values of Art 2, although the RoP are not norms but flexible and consensual rules for the operational functioning of the Parliament's *cuisine interne*.

positioning within the Treaties, second only to the establishment of the Union in Article 1, is in itself an eloquent indication of their importance. Their meaning for the constitutional foundations of the Union is solemnly captured in the words of the Court:

> [The Union] legal structure is based on the fundamental premiss that each Member State shares with all the other Member States, and recognises that they share with it, a set of common values on which the EU is founded, as stated in Article 2 TEU. That premiss implies and justifies the existence of mutual trust between the Member States that those values will be recognised and, therefore, that the law of the EU that implements them will be respected.[2]

The current wording of Article 2 reproduces literally Article I-2 of the Treaty establishing a Constitution for Europe, which further solemnised Article 6 TEU in the version of the Amsterdam Treaty, adding some other founding principles and values, such as human dignity.

While the values enshrined in Article 2 have informed the European project as of its inception, their transposition into norms had to await the entry into force of the Amsterdam Treaty (1999). The initial versions of the Treaties relied on a presumption of compliance on the part of Member States with the non-codified values of the Community.[3] Some described this initial conception as an asymmetric picture:[4] inasmuch as Union norms were strictly respected, the guarantee of the essential values on which those norms relied was left out of the reach of supranational institutions. The bond of mutual trust was left to the discretion of each party to the pact: each individually and autonomously responsible to abide by it, but each individually and collectively unable to enforce it on the others, oversee its implementation and sanction its infringement.

Possibly acknowledging the overly naive optimism of this architecture and in view of the envisaged enlargement, the drafters of the Amsterdam Treaty for the first time fleshed out the catalogue of values of the Union and incorporated the sanction clause. That choice was timely, as it coincided with the dramatic expansion of Union competences enacted by the Treaties of Maastricht and Amsterdam, in particular in the area of freedom, security and justice. Mutual trust underpins the whole architecture of the Union, its basic principles and instruments of integration. Particularly in the area of freedom, security and

[2] See the Opinion of the Court of Justice, 18 December 2014, 2/13, para 168, ECLI:EU:C:2014:2454. This statement was recently reiterated in the Judgment of the Court (Grand Chamber) of 6 March 2018 in Case C-284/16 *Slowakische Republik v Achmea BV*, ECLI:EU:C:2018:158. The Community was qualified as a 'community of law' already in the Judgment of the Court of Justice of 23 April 1986 in Case 294/83 *Les Verts v European Parliament*, ECLI:EU:C:1986:166, para 23.

[3] JHH Weiler, 'Deciphering the Political and Legal DNA of European Integration' in J Dickson and P Eleftheriadis (eds), *Philosophical Foundations of European Union Law* (Oxford, Oxford University Press, 2012) 137, 146.

[4] D Kochenov, 'The EU and the rule of law – naïveté or a grand design?' in M Adams, A Meuwese and E Hirsch Ballin (eds), *Constitutionalism and the Rule of Law: Bridging Idealism and Realism* (Cambridge, Cambridge University Press, 2017) 419.

justice, mutual trust between Member States is a precondition for their joint action. By weakening the principle of mutual trust, a rule of law crisis endangers the harmonious functioning of the Union. Ultimately, it is the serious risk of disturbance of European action that may justify the Union's mandate to expect a Member State to restore respect for the common constitutional standards.[5] From a functional perspective, the values codified in Article 2 are not merely abstract notions, they become concrete and tangible in the different Treaty policies, collectively making up the ability of the Union to act. Thus, the Union has a mandate to demand from Member States respect for the rule of law, in so far as on this respect depends the credibility and the harmonious functioning of its policies.

The functional importance of the rule of law is the result of the nature of European integration itself, as an essentially legal phenomenon. In order to preserve its *acquis*, and continue to exist, the Union shall protect the integrity of its legal foundations, notably the rule of law.[6] As a consequence, it is possible to attach to the values in Article 2 the expectation of a *de minimis* standard of constitutional uniformity imposed on Member States, even when they are carrying out actions falling outside the *mise en oeuvre* of Union law.[7] Indeed, values and principles at the foundations of the Union *define a sphere with which every European citizen can identify, irrespective of political or cultural differences linked to national identity*.[8]

Against this backdrop, the current mechanism codified in Article 7 acquires full meaning not only as a stand-alone endowment, but also as part of the overall Treaty architecture. The mechanism confers coherence between the internal and external dimensions of the Union, and credibility to its external action. Respect for the values is a precondition for accession to the Union under Article 49 TEU, and the Union is committed to reinforce and promote these values in its relations with third countries (Article 21(2)(b) TEU). Thus, the rule of law is a prerequisite for accession to the Union, as well as a *conditio sine qua non* of membership.[9]

[5] In this sense, the conditionality related to respect for the rule of law proposed in the context of the new Multiannual Financial Framework came as no surprise. It was adopted on 16 December 2020, Regulation (EU, Euratom) 2020/2092 of the European Parliament and of the Council on a general regime of conditionality for the protection of the Union budget, [2020] OJ L433I/1.

[6] Among many, see in this sense Editorial comments (2019), '2019 shaping up as a challenging year for the Union, not least as a community of values' (2019) 56 *CML Rev* 3.

[7] R Baratta, 'La communauté des valeurs dans l'ordre juridique de l'Union européenne' (2018) 1 *Revue des affairs europennes* 81; R Baratta, 'Rule of Law "dialogues" within the EU: a legal assessment' (2016) *Hague Journal on the Rule of Law* 357.

[8] See the Opinion of the Parliamentary Committee on Constitutional Affairs (AFCO) of 26 March 2018, addressed to the Committee on Civil Liberties, Justice and Home Affairs (LIBE) on the situation in Hungary (pursuant to the European Parliament resolution of 17 May 2017) (2017/2131(INL)).

[9] This argument finds explicit support in the Judgment of the Court of Justice of 10 December 2018 in Case C-621/18 *Wightman*, ECLI:EU:C:2018:999, para 63.

Considering at a glance the procedural design laid down in Article 7 TEU, the provision embeds a sanction mechanism in a scenario of serious and persistent infringement, or the risk thereof, of the fundamental values of the Union on the part of a Member State. For what matters here, the procedural arrangement fits the Parliament into the picture with the conferral of two types of formal competences. On one hand, under Article 7(1), the 'preventive' branch of the mechanism, the Parliament features, together with the Commission and one-third of Member States, as one of the subjects entrusted with a right to trigger the procedure, in the form of submitting a reasoned proposal to the Council. In addition, it has to grant its consent after the hearing and before the Council determines the existence of a clear risk of a serious breach. The procedural rules for both initiative and consent foresee a two-thirds majority of the votes cast, representing the majority of the component Members. On the other hand, under Article 7(2), the 'punitive' branch of the mechanism, in the determination of the existence of a serious and persistent breach of the values, the Parliament is only conferred with the responsibility to grant its consent further to the observations submitted by the Member State, with a two-thirds majority of the votes cast, representing the majority of Members.

By conferring the right of initiative on the three subjects, the Treaty seemingly opted for a mixed vision of this mechanism. In this mixed vision, the Parliament fits into the equation with the conferral of two types of formal competences.

In light of the long-standing history of these provisions, one could argue that the Union had already promoted respect for the founding values as a matter of soft power and political suasion in an era where the Treaties were silent on the rule of law.[10] Today, infringement of these values virtually leads to the most far-reaching consequences in the Union legal order – the suspension of the rights of a Member State while it remains subject to its obligations. Article 7 could lead a Member State to sink into a sort of limbo, the way out of which is offered by the triggering of Article 50 TEU.[11]

[10] P Pescatore, *Le droit de l'intégration. Émergence d'un phénomène nouveau dans les relations internationales selon l'expérience des Communautés européennes* (Leiden, AW Sijthoff, 1972; reprint Brussels, Bruylant, 2005). On the first academic literature concerning the non-written but collectively accepted condition of respect for democratic rules, see P Soldatos and G Vandersanden, 'L'admission dans la CEE – Essai d'interprétation juridique' [1968] *Cahiers droit européen* 628.

[11] Some voices in the academic literature credibly argued that Treaty drafters, even when construing the current version of this mechanism, might have imbued it with a dose of misplaced optimism about the future. Ultimately, the entire effectiveness of the design may be undermined by an alliance of convenience between one Member State and another, agreeing, or by the impasse deriving from a tacit deal between two Member States subject to the procedure, not to vote against each other. Art 7, and the constellation of initiatives revolving around the ever-richer 'rule of law toolbox' and anyhow pursuing analogous aims, has been the target of critical evaluations covering the entire spectrum of opinions: on one hand, some have argued that Art 7 lacks ambition and prospects for enforceability, and the related initiatives have been equally feeble and ineffectual; others have claimed that, given its nature as a 'nuclear' option of last resort, a dissuasive weapon 'never to be used', it lacks credibility and the prospect of efficient use.

The codification of the values and the formalisation of the procedures to ensure their respect are alone not an absolute guarantee against deterioration of the rule of law. What seems clear is that the procedure set out in Article 7 TEU entrusts the handling of democratic degradation to dialogue and political pressure. The use of this instrument is not based on a purely legal analysis that, as will be discussed later, is often impossible to carry out in an exhaustive and conclusive way; it also relies on a comprehensive political assessment of the state of health of a system and its institutions, touching upon how they operate in practice.

This dual political and legal nature of the rule of law assessment opens the door to a meaningful role for the political and pluralist institution *par excellence*, the Parliament.

Although outside the scope of our analysis, we cannot conclude this introduction without recalling that, as has become clear over the last couple of years, Article 7 TEU is not the only instrument for defending the Union's values, and in itself cannot be conceived as a panacea. The infringement procedure in the hands of the Commission is an instrument, this time of a purely legal nature, that has proved effective against specific and individualised abuses of the rights and principles codified in Article 2 TEU.[12] Its shrewd use has prompted the recognition by the Court of Justice of the direct applicability and enforceability of Article 2 TEU.

III. OVERVIEW OF SELECTED PARLIAMENT'S INITIATIVES AND THE STORY THEY TELL OF THE PARLIAMENT'S CONCEPTION OF THE RULE OF LAW

To get a sense of the Parliament's understanding of the rule of law, a useful exercise is to look at the harvest of its action, hence the initiatives it has adopted. The Parliament has been quite prolific: respect for the rule of law figured prominently in parliamentary debates in the 2014–2019 term, and at the beginning of the 2019–2024 term.[13] Most importantly, the Parliament issued a plethora of resolutions,[14] either of direct relevance for Article 7 or else pertinent for the wider constellation of initiatives revolving around the rule of law. This section

[12] See the contribution by Anna Perego in ch 13 of this volume.

[13] Among the most recent debates on the rule of law, see those on the ongoing hearings under Art 7(1) TEU regarding both Hungary and Poland, held in the plenary sitting of 15 January 2020, video recordings available at www.europarl.europa.eu/plenary/en/vod.html?mode=chapter&vodId=1579102453822 and www.europarl.europa.eu/plenary/en/vod.html?mode=chapter&vodId=1579107173968, respectively; see also, the plenary debate on the rule of law in Romania, 15 April 2019; plenary debate on the rule of law in Malta, 17 December 2019.

[14] Among those that are not specifically addressed elsewhere in this contribution, see the Parliament resolution of 13 November 2018 on the rule of law in Romania (2018/2844(RSP)) P8_TA(2018)0446; the Parliament resolution of 18 December 2019 on the rule of law in Malta following the recent revelations surrounding the murder of Daphne Caruana Galizia (2019/2954(RSP)) P9_TA(2019)0103.

addresses what could be considered the Parliament's landmark resolutions. These are not addressed for the legal solutions they craft, nor for their feasibility or desirability from a technical standpoint, but for their underlying meaning from a broader perspective. By offering an insight into the *cuisine interne* of parliamentary works, these resolutions offer a narrative of the Parliament's conception and understanding of the rule of law, and they do so both in the process, as well as in the content.

A. The EU Pact for Democracy, the Rule of Law and Fundamental Rights – The In 't Veld Report

The first high-profile initiative adopted by the Parliament was the EU Pact for Democracy, the Rule of Law and Fundamental Rights ('EU Pact for DRF').[15] In October 2016, the Parliament adopted a resolution addressing recommendations to the Commission on the establishment of a new mechanism to address rule of law backsliding across Member States. The resolution was adopted on the basis of a report drafted under the lead of the Committee on Civil Liberties, Justice and Home Affairs (LIBE), which entrusted Ms Sophie In 't Veld (NL, Renew) with the delicate role of Rapporteur. On 14 November 2018, the Parliament renewed its call, with a resolution[16] prompting the Commission to propose the adoption of an EU Pact for DRF. It has to be highlighted that, as an element of novelty, the Parliament proposed to tie the mechanism to a horizontal proposal of the Commission on the protection of the Union's financial interests in the case of generalised rule of law deficiencies.

The Pact is expressly designed, on one hand, to complete, align and integrate existing tools, filling the gaps in the regulatory framework, and, on the other, to craft a new, permanent and objective mechanism to systematically address rule of law backsliding across the Union. The Pact is in some regards inspired by the multilateral economic surveillance that materialised in the 'European Semester' mechanism. At its core, the tool aims to lay down the modality of cooperation between the Union institutions and Member States in the context of an Article 7 procedure, according to an inter-institutional agreement based on Article 295 of the Treaty on the Functioning of the European Union (TFEU). In the Parliament's design, a panel of independent experts would annually assess the state of health of key indicators across Member States. Upon consultation with that panel, the Commission would draw up an annual report including

[15] The Parliament resolution of 25 October 2016 with recommendations to the Commission on the establishment of an EU mechanism on democracy, the rule of law and fundamental rights (2015/2254(INL)), [2018] OJ C215/162. On the preparatory works for the resolution, see, among others, J Sargentini and A Dimitrovs, 'The European Parliament's Role: Towards New Copenhagen Criteria for Existing Member States?' (2016) 54 *Journal of Common Market Studies* 1085.

[16] Parliament resolution on the need for a comprehensive Democracy, Rule of Law and Fundamental Rights mechanism, 14 November 2018, P8_TA(2018)0456, (2018/2886(RSP)).

country-specific recommendations. In turn, that published report would feed into an annual inter-parliamentary debate, steered by the Parliament and framed in a multiannual structured dialogue encompassing the Parliament, the Council, the Commission and national parliaments. The mechanism aspires to rely on an evidence-based approach, and on objective benchmarks.

With this resolution, the Parliament embarked on an ambitious and quite creative exercise: some scholars may have informed its content with an active presence at the debates in the LIBE Committee, others commented on it in animated fashion, portraying it as eccentric in some respects. The solutions crafted and their political and legal feasibility may be questionable. The perplexities are well captured in the Commission's formal response to the Parliament, issued on 17 February 2017.[17] While showing sympathy and understanding for the overarching aim, notably the proposal for inter-parliamentary dialogue between the Parliament and national parliaments, the Commission expressed quite few reservations. These include the suggestions for Treaty changes, the feasibility and added value of an inter-institutional agreement in this area, and of an annual Report and a DRF policy cycle outsourced to a committee of 'experts'.

Anyhow, beyond the technical solutions proposed, and considering the EU Pact for DRF from a broader perspective, this initiative managed to tentatively develop the dimensions of inter-institutional cooperation and dialogue. The resolution speaks the language of soft measures for the promotion of a rule of law culture, rather than that of hard rules and sanctions. The overarching atmosphere informing the initiative is a consensual, inclusive and cooperative one. As part of this logic of *overture*, all the institutions and bodies concerned may adhere to the Pact, should they wish to do so. The dialogue dimension is appealing, not least for its feasibility prospects: the *mise en œuvre* of selected aspects can be independent of any inter-institutional agreement and Treaty reform. The Parliament had proved itself aware of this margin for manoeuvre, for instance by launching an informal dialogue with national parliaments.[18]

The concept of 'soft power of political suasion'[19] has been familiar in the vocabulary of the Union institutions for quite some time. Back in 2014, in the Commission Communication laying down a new framework for the rule

[17] See the Commission's follow up to the Parliament resolution on the establishment of an EU mechanism on democracy, the rule of law and fundamental rights, SP(2017)16, 17 February 2017.

[18] For a concise and complete analysis of the Pact, see O Porchia, 'Le respect de l'État de droit dans les États membres: la complémentarité des initiatives politiques et le rôle de la Cour de justice' in *Liber Amicorum per Antonio Tizzano – De la Cour CECA à la Cour de l'Union: le long parcours de la justice européenne* (Turin, Giappichelli, 2018) 769. The author notes that already on 22 June 2017, the Parliament had hosted a meeting on the role of national parliaments in the framework of the EU DRF Pact. The meeting was organised by LIBE, in the presence of the representatives of national parliaments (Documentazione per le Commissioni Riunioni interparlamentari (Dossier XVIII Legislatura), Senato, Servizio Studi-Dossier europei n 68, Camera dei deputati, Ufficio Rapporti con l'Unione europea n 87).

[19] See the fortunate periphrases of JM Barroso in full speech transcript, available at ec.europa.eu/commission/presscorner/detail/en/SPEECH_13_684.

of law,[20] in the context of the pre-Article 7 procedure, it was part of the attempt to resort to more informal tools, such as the structured dialogue with a view to eradicating a threat before the conditions to trigger Article 7 were met. Beyond this 'pre-emptive' meaning, dialogue and institutional cooperation may have a more general relevance in light of the limited margin of action allowed by the current Treaty framework. As will be discussed in more detail later, dialogue and cooperation could contribute to the improvement of the overall process, not least for the benefits in terms of the intelligibility of its procedural steps, and its increased shared ownership. In fact, besides being appealing and practically feasible, in the current Treaty framework, dialogue and inter-institutional cooperation are two of the few areas in which the Parliament could make a difference.[21]

In conclusion, the In t' Veld Report is a valuable case study of how the Parliament understood its own role and measured the scope of its powers. While part of its creative content may be questionable from a legal standpoint, from a broader perspective the Report contributes to revealing the profoundly political nature of Article 7. As will be discussed, that political nature may contribute to justifying the involvement of all political institutions at different levels. Above all, on the *modus* of this involvement, this Parliament initiative can claim to have highlighted the dimensions of cooperation and dialogue, which objectively may be improved for the sake of the overall process.

While the repeated call to forge an inter-institutional agreement remains unsurprisingly unanswered, there is an aftermath to the Parliament's initiative. The Commission paved the way for public reflection on ways to enrich and reinforce the Union 'rule of law toolbox', well captured by the Communications issued throughout 2019.[22] Whether the Parliament's calls have influenced this debate in its content, or contributed to triggering it, cannot be claimed with certainty. However, what is certain is that this public reflection is orientated towards developing the dimensions of dialogue and inter-institutional cooperation. The initiatives developed, such as the Rule of Law Review Cycle and the Annual Rule of Law Report, all speak the language of dialogue and are informed by a consensual, inclusive and cooperative atmosphere.[23] Specifically, they are

[20] See COM(2014)158, 19 March 2014.

[21] Unsurprisingly, the narrative revolving around dialogue and inter-institutional cooperation is not exempt from perplexities. These were extensively addressed in the academic literature: dialogue, which displays its benefits in the prevention of a 'pathological' situation, may simply not be an adequate response in cases where the situation is already serious. As such, dialogue could have the counterproductive effect of undermining and confusing the facts underlying a case. See L Pech and KL Schepelle, 'Illiberalism Within: Rule of Law Backsliding in the EU' (2017) 19 *Cambridge Yearbook of European Legal Studies* 3, 39.

[22] See the Commission Communications 'Strengthening the rule of law within the Union – A blueprint for action', Brussels, COM(2019) 343 final, 17 July 2019; 'Further strengthening the Rule of Law within the Union', COM(2019) 163 final, 3 April 2019.

[23] See the contribution by Anna Perego in ch 13 of this volume.

more vocal about promoting a rule of law culture through suasion, rather than sanctioning its backsliding through punitive rules. Whether one or the other dimension is more apt to achieve concrete progress remains an open question.

If the Commission has been prolific with initiatives in the field of the rule of law, the Council for its part has not been dormant either. Its initiatives too were informed by a robust component of dialogue and cooperation. Back in 2013, when the Commission launched a reflection on possible paths to safeguard the rule of law, it did so not only spontaneously but as prompted by the other institutions. In particular, the Council[24] invited the Commission to pursue, within the Treaties framework, the discussion on the prospects for a systemic approach precisely based on cooperation. Later on, the year 2014 marked the innovative Council conclusions laying the foundations for the 'Council annual rule of law dialogue'.[25] The achievement these Conclusions can boast is that they established a frame for the debate on the rule of law within the Union institutional landscape – a cooperative and inclusive one. Above all, they incorporated the dialogue on the rule of law into the ordinary activities of the Council. Practically, Member States committed themselves to setting up a dialogue to be implemented according to the principle of loyal cooperation, in all its ramifications, including with respect to the relationships between the Union's institutions (Article 13 TEU). The overarching rationale informing the dialogue is to encourage the promotion of a rule of law culture across the Union, through 'soft' tools such as sharing experience by means of exchanges of national practices. The dialogue is not conceived to address 'pathological' scenarios, nor does it construe a novel control mechanism; rather, it aims at tackling a rule of law degradation at its roots. Thus, the Council dialogue in principle operates outside the frame of Article 7 *strictu sensu*. While it does not interfere with the frame set by the Commission, it is complementary to the latter, a sort of 'propaedeutic' activity that may contribute to verifying the necessary conditions to trigger Article 7 TEU.[26] The logic of the Council, both in the content of the initiative and in the method of implementation, is complementary to that envisaged by the Commission, and it is not far apart from that of the Parliament.[27]

[24] See the Council Press Release No 10461/13 (OR. en), 3244th Council meeting Justice and Home Affairs, Luxembourg, 6 and 7 June 2013, available at www.consilium.europa.eu/ueDocs/cms_Data/docs/pressData/en/jha/137407.pdf.

[25] See Conclusions of the Council of the European Union and the member states meeting within the Council on ensuring respect for the rule of law, General Affairs Council Meeting, Brussels, 16 December 2014 (doc 17014/14). These conclusions are well analysed by O Porchia, 'Le conclusioni del Consiglio del 16 dicembre 2014 Rafforzare lo stato di diritto: un significativo risultato della Presidenza italiana', *Eurojus.it* (2015).

[26] In the opinion of the writer, the overall aim is not to construe a 'naming and shaming' procedure, although part of the academic literature may see it differently. See, for instance, C Closa, 'Reinforcing EU Monitoring of the Rule of Law' in C Closa and D Kochenov (eds), *Reinforcing Rule of Law Oversight in the European Union* (Cambridge, Cambridge University Press, 2016) 15, 32–35.

[27] As anticipated, the core of the mechanism proposed by the In 't Veld Report may be inspired in some regards by the multilateral permanent surveillance of the EU economic cycle (see Art 121 TFEU). In general, the logic of multilateral, *inter pares* or peer-to-peer review is not only familiar in the Council's work, but sponsored by the latter.

The autumn session of the Council's annual dialogue was finally evaluated at the Council meeting of 19 November 2019. Although discussions did not lead to consensus on the conclusions, the Finnish rotating Presidency determined that the conclusions published in Council Document 14173/19[28] were supported, or not objected to, by 26 delegations. In a nutshell, the 2019 conclusions advocated a yearly stocktaking exercise revolving around the state of play and key developments in the rule of law, which could draw upon the Commission's annual rule of law reports and in turn create synergies between the institutions. In the Ministers' understanding, the dialogue should be stronger, more result-orientated and better structured. In-depth discussion of rule of law issues in other Council configurations was also encouraged, as well as the continuation of the ongoing work among Member States on the concrete elaboration of a periodic peer-to-peer review mechanism on the rule of law.

Hence, all three institutions have lined up in favour of dialogue and cooperation. However, even if the institutions are looking in the same direction, they do not share one path; rather, they follow parallel ones.

B. The Resolution on Hungary – The Sargentini Report

A second landmark initiative worthy of mention is the resolution triggering for the second time in history an Article 7(1) TEU procedure, this time against Hungary. The resolution enshrines a proposal calling on the Council to determine the existence of a clear risk of a serious breach of the values on which the Union is founded. This initiative offers a truthful portrayal of the Parliament's *modus operandi* and its approach to the rule of law. The resolution was the culmination of a process involving a list of resolutions, variously addressing human rights, issued in the timeframe 2011–2017. It was triggered by a common resolution tabled on 17 May 2017 by S&D,[29] ALDE (currently, Renew), GUE and the Greens, and adopted with 393 votes in favour, 221 votes against and 64 abstentions. Since the resolution reported that the current situation in Hungary justified the triggering of an Article 7(1) procedure, the LIBE Committee was entrusted with the mandate to elaborate a report with a view to submitting to plenary a reasoned proposal inviting the Council to act. Judith Sargentini (NL, Greens) was awarded the role of Rapporteur.

[28] See the Council Note, Presidency conclusions – Evaluation of the annual rule of law dialogue, 14173/19, Brussels, 19 November 2019, available at www.consilium.europa.eu/media/41394/st14173-en19.pdf.

[29] The political groups of the European Parliament during the 2014–2019 term in decreasing order of size: EPP (Group of the European People's Party – Christian Democrats); S&D (Group of the Progressive Alliance of Socialist and Democrats in the European Parliament); ECR (European Conservatives and Reformist Group); ALDE (Group of the Alliance of Liberals and Democrats); GUE/NGL (Confederal Group of the European United Left – Nordic Green Left); Greens/EFA (Group of the Greens/European Free Alliance); EFDD (Europe of Freedom and Direct Democracy Group).

Spending a few words on the process that brought the resolution to life offers an insight into the *cuisine interne* of parliamentary work: it is a valuable exercise in understanding how the decision-making process unfolds and how consensus is built. While it is true that all parliaments differ from one another, perhaps some parliaments differ more than others. The decision-making machinery in the European Parliament is *sui generis*, and has a dynamic of its own. At the outset, internal procedures in the Parliament, and their output, are a direct consequence of the interaction of many layers and players. For instance, while the LIBE Committee could be described as 'activist' and interventionist in the rule of law domain, the plenary 'level' may offer a different picture, resulting at times in unexpected results. While the Council has the ability to look monolithic, even in circumstances where it may be torn apart internally, the Parliament does not have this ability: pluralism shapes its way of working. Since the Parliament does not follow a standard and stable majority *versus* opposition logic, its dynamic is a permanent quest for consensus, worked out through the negotiation of compromise amendments. The outcome is a political compromise, which is not always clear and straightforward.

Plurality does not concern only the bodies within the Parliament. Another quite fundamental 'layer' is represented by the individual dimension: 705 Members elected across 27 Member States,[30] all entitled to table amendments and to have their own political sensitivities and specificities. The 'individual' dimension is then combined with the dimension of national delegations: a Member may behave quite differently from his or her correspondent in national party politics, depending on the circumstances. In turn, national delegations have to liaise with the political families at European level with which they are affiliated, which in many regards are set apart from, and cannot be assimilated to, national parties. Drafting and tabling a parliamentary report is never a lonely exercise: the Rapporteur is accompanied by the Shadow Rapporteurs, representing the entire spectrum of European political parties.

Moreover, depending on the subject matter, several parliamentary committees may be entitled to leave a footprint on, or take partial ownership of, a report. Different formulas for the allocation of competences exist in the Parliament. For the Sargentini Report, four committees were responsible for issuing an opinion (Budgetary Control, Culture, Constitutional Affairs and Women's Rights). As a result of the combination of all these dimensions, of all the layers and players, the outcome is not necessarily homogeneous; rather it is colourful, and at times fragmented.

The LIBE Committee adopted its Report on 25 June 2018, and the vote in single reading in plenary took place in September 2018, pursuant to Article 354 TFEU, prescribing the majority of two-thirds of votes cast, representing the

[30] At the time of the adoption of the Sargentini Report, the Parliament comprised 751 Members elected in 28 Member States.

majority of Members. As a gesture of powerful symbolism, the vote in plenary occurred in the presence of the Hungarian Prime Minister himself,[31] after an incendiary debate. There was no unanimous consensus in the Parliament as to the appropriateness of offering a platform of such resonance to the Prime Minister.

With a closer look, the detailed outcome of the vote is quite an eloquent example of the dynamics between European political groups and national delegations within the groups. Depending on the specificities of the situation, national delegations' behaviour may depart from the political group's line. In particular, one could see how the European People's Party (EPP), the political family to which Fidesz is affiliated, was torn internally by the vote at Committee level: out of the 37 votes in favour, 8 came from the EPP, while 9 of the 19 votes against were EPP votes. The plenary adopted the resolution by 448 votes to 197, with 48 abstentions. Voting behaviour indicates a shift from the vote on the initial plenary resolution in May, when the relative majority of EPP members still supported Orbán. In September, 58 per cent of EPP members voted in favour of the Sargentini Report, 29 per cent voted against and 14 per cent of the group abstained. Ms Sargentini managed to gather quite a remarkable number of EPP votes. In the previous year's vote on the state of health of the rule of law in Hungary, these proportions were 34 per cent, 47 per cent and 20 per cent, respectively. Orbán lost some key former allies: while ÖVP abstained from the previous vote in May, Austrian Chancellor Sebastian Kurz supported the resolution, and so did influential leaders within the EPP from Germany and France, such as Manfred Weber, Joseph Daul and Daniel Caspary. Interestingly, Manfred Weber, outlining his position in the debate, nuanced the conflictual dimension of the Article 7 procedure by picturing it as a 'dialogue', maybe foretelling the prospect of a consensual conflict resolution.

Considering the resolution in its core, the Parliament reported a systemic threat against the values enshrined in Article 2. The Annex to the resolution comprises a reasoned proposal for a decision to be submitted to the Council, inviting it to assess that a clear risk of serious breach exists, and to address recommendations accordingly. In the Annex, lengthy recitals flesh out the elements underpinning the evaluation on the rule of law. Once again, the Parliament broadened the scope beyond the rule of law *strictu sensu* and touched upon all the values, and very diverse issues ranging from minority rights, to economic and social rights, the situation of migrants and freedom of expression. The focus is on what could be roughly described as factual elements and trends: the Parliament concludes in favour of a finding of rule of law backsliding in light of a comprehensive assessment. This is manifest already in the title of the resolution, which refers to the

[31] The transcript of the full speech is available at www.kormany.hu/en/the-prime-minister/the-prime-minister-s-speeches/address-by-prime-minister-viktor-orban-in-the-debate-on-the-so-called-sargentini-report; the transcript of the interventions of Members in the plenary session is available at www.europarl.europa.eu/doceo/document/CRE-8-2018-09-11-ITM-011_EN.html.

'situation' in Hungary. Thus, the content of the resolution is far from a technical exercise anchored to legal criteria. The Parliament is not assessing rule of law breaches by means of a thorough legal analysis but by addressing their political causes, and the political symptoms through which they manifest themselves.

The content analysis is particularly meaningful if compared with the correspondent Commission proposal for a Council decision related to Poland issued on 20 December 2017.[32] A comparative glance suffices to show how the perspectives of the two institutions are inherently different. The Commission's tone is carefully measured, arguments built on thorough legal analysis aimed at documenting and certifying the risk.

In this sense, the Commission response[33] to the Parliament's resolution on Hungary, issued on 11 March 2019, is eloquent. First the response underlines that the resolution contains no requests addressed to the Commission, then it lists all the actions, including prospective ones, undertaken by the Commission on the matter. These include the infringement procedures launched and the cases for which Hungary was referred to the Court of Justice. From within the 'arsenal' at its disposal, the Commission recalls the audit and investigation tools in the context of the use of EU funds. In its supervisory capacity, the Commission stresses how it was able to monitor the implementation of the measures taken in the guise of legislative amendments, *inter alia* by means of a constructive dialogue engaged in with the Hungarian authorities. Most importantly, the Commission recalls that in its function as guardian of the Treaties, in the domain of the respect of fundamental values, its intervention has been grounded on accurate and thorough legal analysis and targeted at concrete national measures.

It goes without saying that none of this could – even theoretically – feature in the exercise carried out by the Parliament with the Sargentini Report. On one hand, all the above sheds some light on what the Report is not, and cannot be; on the other hand, when it comes to what the Report 'is', in its content and process, it is the synthesis of European politics as expressed in a parliamentary assembly. That perspective is what the Parliament brought to the table and, as such, it is inherently different from that of the Commission, as well as, as will be argued, from that of the Council. The resolution should be understood through these lenses: it is the product of majoritarian decision making and consensus building in a political institution characterised by the interplay of many layers

[32] See the Commission proposal for a Council Decision on the determination of a clear risk of a serious breach by the Republic of Poland of the rule of law, COM/2017/0835 final. For the Parliament position, see the Parliament resolution of 1 March 2018 on the Commission's decision to activate Article 7(1) TEU as regards the situation in Poland, 2018/2541(RSP). See also the Parliament, LIBE Committee draft mission report following the ad hoc delegation to Poland on the situation of the rule of law, 19 November 2018.

[33] See the Commission response to text adopted in plenary, SP(2018)829, 11/03/2019, available at oeil.secure.europarl.europa.eu/oeil/popups/ficheprocedure.do?reference=2017/2131(INL)&l=en.

and players, a type of *sui generis* legislative machinery and a complex, at times fragmented, political spectrum.

IV. ON THE NATURE AND MEANING OF THE PARLIAMENT'S PERSPECTIVE

A. The Legal and Political Dimensions of the Rule of Law Assessment

Whenever an issue departs from a specific, individualised infringement, one that in principle could be addressed pursuant to Article 258 TFEU,[34] and it enters the realm of generalised and systemic breaches, there is a dual dimension to the rule of law assessment: a legal and a political one.

The legal dimension is embodied by the Commission, as Guardian of the Treaties. The Commission looks at rule of law breaches through the lenses of accurate and thorough legal analysis. To accomplish the Treaty mandate, it has at its disposal an arsenal of tools, ranging from tools of scrutiny to expedited infringement procedures.

By contrast, looking at the rule of law through the Parliament's lenses requires a shift of prism, from the legal dimension into the political one. The history of the Parliament's contributions to the rule of law, and the initiatives it has undertaken, tells a straightforward story: Parliament's conception of the rule of law is of a political nature. No one could expect anything different: politics is what the Parliament is, and what it does. The nature of the institution is political, as its way of working, both in the methodology and in the output. It stems from the mandate conferred on it by the Treaty: this trait represents at the same time its added value and potential, as well as its limitation. While the Parliament can but engage in a political exercise, this exercise potentially has very serious legal consequences, notably the most serious legal consequences foreseen in the Union legal order: it goes as far as triggering an Article 7(1) procedure, and being decisive for its conclusion with the power of consent.

Thus, assuming that the nature of the Parliament's contribution is political, it is legitimate to question whether and how this political dimension embodied

[34] In its proposal for an EU Pact for DRF, the Parliament envisioned that the Commission could decide to channel a procedure targeting a systemic infringement, in light of Art 2 TEU and Art 258 TFEU, regrouping different infringement cases. It has been noted by Porchia (n 18) that if we argue in favour of the existence of the category of systemic breaches, this does not imply that we can use this concept in a context of breach of values under Art 2 TEU to justify the launching of an infringement procedure under Art 258 TFEU. On structural or systemic infringements, see KL Scheppele, 'Enforcing the Basics Principles of EU Law through Systemic Infringement Actions' in Closa and Kochenov (eds) (n 26) 105. See also K Lenaerts et al, *EU Procedural Law* (Oxford, Oxford University Press, 2014) 167. On persistent and systemic infringement and the extension of the category to the hypothesis of breach of rule of law, L Gormley, 'Infringement proceedings' in D Kochenov and A Jakab (eds), *The Enforcement of EU law and Values* (Oxford, Oxford University Press, 2017) 65, specifically at 73.

by the Parliament has a meaning and an added value, and why this political dimension should matter in an Article 7 scenario.

At the outset, Articles 2 and 7 TEU have a robust political connotation. On one hand, the nature of the values in Article 2 is political; on the other, assuming Article 7 is construed as a procedural device to achieve the aims of Article 2, the setting of the procedure in Article 7 is political.

With its initiatives, which equate the scope of the rule of law with the ensemble of the values set out in Article 2, the Parliament has done its part to unveil the profound political nature of these values. Purely legal categories may not exhaustively capture the nature of these values, since the bond they forged among Member States is in essence political.

Even if, as discussed before, the notion of rule of law as '*garantie des garanties*' is elusive, the conception to which the Union appears to adhere has a lot to do with the framing of power, its legitimation and limitation. The framing of power, the legitimation to act only within the constraints set out by law, ensuring it is not exorbitant, absolute or arbitrary, may be a core yardstick to scrutinise the state of health of a legal system, and is a backbone of the rule of law in modern constitutionalism.

Considering the mechanism laid down in Article 7 TEU, the setting of the hearings in the Council does not imply an experts' debate, nor a thorough exchange of views at a technical level; it rather resembles a more political type of setting, especially where national Ministers question high-ranking national representatives. In turn, the limited prospect for judicial review reminds us that the outcome of the procedure entails a fundamentally political evaluation, left to the discretion of the parties to the Pact, whose motives or aims cannot be reviewed. Any Court action to the contrary would face the hurdle of overcoming the admissibility phase. In fact, while the Court retains competence to verify procedural grounds pursuant to Article 269 TFEU, in principle Article 7 TEU is shielded from judicial review on substance.[35] As long as there is no such thing as a set of parameters for reviewing acts enforceable in courts, the only tangible outcome of an Article 7(1) procedure consists of the Council recommendations. Any criticism and warnings that these recommendations may offer on the state of health of a national system, if at all capable of revitalising the rule of law, do so as a matter of political suasion, rather than legal obligation.

[35] See the Judgment of the Court (Grand Chamber) issued on 27 March 2020 in Joined Cases C-558/18 and C-563/18 *Miasto Łowicz*, ECLI:EU:C:2020:234, where both sets of preliminary questions submitted by the Polish judges, in which they essentially ask 'am I (still) independent?', were dismissed as inadmissible. The Judgment concerns the Polish law that came into effect on 14 February 2020, suspected of curtailing the independence of judges, infringing upon Union law and the separation of powers. Less recently, see the Order of the Court (Ninth Chamber) of 17 July 2014 in Case C-505/13 *Levent Redzheb Yumer*, ECLI:EU:C:2014:2129, para 22. Confronted with preliminary questions on the interpretation of Art 2 TEU, the Court found itself manifestly incompetent, on the ground that the referring decision did not offer any explanation of the relevance of that interpretation for the resolution of the main proceeding.

Especially in view of a vacuum of enforceability, the core strength of recommendations is political, rather than normative.

In any assessment of the state of health of a legal system from a rule of law perspective, one may identify two dimensions, which should be kept distinct: on one hand, there are constitutional or legal designs; on the other, the practice. As is often the case, in theory, theory and practice may be the same, but in practice, they are not.[36] A Member State may be equipped with the best-crafted and most solid constitutional framework, and have a centuries-old constitutional tradition, yet there may be a discrepancy between the legal system and reality. Legal mechanisms alone cannot guarantee that this discrepancy between legal systems and practice will not exist; nor can legal mechanisms *per se* be an absolute shield against breaches of the rule of law.

An assessment at Union level aimed at evaluating the state of health of a political system would do so by comparing Member States among themselves, aiming at relying on objective, non-discriminatory and operational benchmarks. This exercise is in itself an arduous task, and it becomes harder if those standards are aimed at setting thresholds of 'constitutional uniformity' with which Member States are supposed to comply, and eventually against which they could be sanctioned.

To begin with, there may be difficulties in the mutual understanding and definition of legal concepts, concepts whose meaning Member States may share on the substance but from which they depart in the form. Member States do not always speak the same language: this does not necessarily mean that there is no comparable level of protection. Things are just complex, and legal categories may not be enough to tell the whole story in a rule of law assessment. No system is *per se* immune from risk of deteriorations: some risks are just dormant and latent, and a strong executive with the willingness and ability to enact change may suffice for change to occur.

Much of the health and resilience of a system is entrusted to the virtuous or vicious use of the legal framework on the part of governments and their supporting majorities in national parliaments. Alone, no regulatory device could suffice to resolve underlying issues such as political fragmentation, manipulation, enduring 'pathological' phenomena or the twisted use of norms on the part of public powers. Whatever constitutional arrangement may be in place, and however effective it is, how a given institutional set-up operates ultimately depends on the underpinning political environment.

In view of all the above, it is argued that a European approach to the rule of law analysis, and a response to eventual backsliding, in order to be complete and meaningful, should go beyond technical and legal categories and be holistic and contextual. The nature and meaning of the Parliament's approach to the rule of law should be framed in this context: the Parliament's perspective

[36] B Brewster, 'Portfolio: Theory and Practice' (1882) 47 *The Yale Literary Magazine* 202.

embodies a shift from the pure legal dimension of the rule of law assessment into the political one, because rule of law breaches have political roots and manifest themselves through political symptoms. Here lies the meaning of the Parliament's contribution, and the reasons why its contribution matters.

B. The Added Value of the Parliament's Perspective

The Parliament's action and what it represents in terms of added value for the institutional framework of the Union can be better understood in the context of concrete practice. This is why this part of section IV focuses on the procedure triggered by the Parliament in relation to Hungary.

At the time this chapter was being finalised, the Council was dealing with two Article 7(1) TEU procedures. The Commission triggered the procedure against Poland on 27 February 2018, and three hearings took place between June and December 2018. Eventually, at the General Affairs Council meeting of 16 September 2019, the Commission updated ministries on the latest developments of relevance for the rule of law. For what matters here, the Parliament launched the procedure against Hungary on 12 September 2018, and the Hungarian authorities had two opportunities to explain themselves in hearings, in September and December 2019 respectively. The Finnish Presidency concluded both hearings by presenting procedural conclusions, without addressing the merits of the case. At the time of writing, in summer 2020, no further hearing had been formally scheduled.

In terms of governance, both the Treaty and the Council Rules of Procedure (RoP) are silent on how the Article 7(1) procedure should unfold.[37] Up to now, hearings had been held on the basis of the 'standard modalities' adopted by COREPER on 9 July 2019.[38] The 'standard modalities' aim at 'streamlining the process and creat[ing] a level playing field for all the Member States involved and for the three possible cases'.[39] For the hearing of the Member State, the 'standard modalities' detail the rules for the different scenarios depending on who submitted the reasoned proposal – a group of Member States, the Parliament or the Commission. They provide for a different degree of involvement of the group of Member States and the Commission, on the one hand, and the Parliament, on the other. In the first case, the modalities foresee an active role in the hearings for a representative of the group of Member States and for the Commission: they

[37] The only reference to Art 7 TEU is contained in statement (g) to Art 16 and Annex IV on the 'Absence of the possibility to participate in the vote', yet it has no relevance for the present discussion.

[38] See Council doc 10641/2/19, REV 2. According to para 25 of the standard modalities, they apply without prejudice to the application of the Council RoP.

[39] See ibid para 5.

both shall present their reasoned proposals at the first hearing. In the second case, the Parliament never takes part in the hearings. According to paragraph 11 of the 'standard modalities', at the first hearing the Presidency reports to the Council about its contacts with the Parliament on its reasoned proposal. In particular, the Council would have refused to hear Ms Judith Sargentini on the basis of legal advice issued orally by its Legal Service, and whose arguments were not disclosed.[40] Reducing the Council's approach to its core, except for respecting the Parliament's formal competences, the Council considers that once the Parliament has triggered the procedure, it should be cut off. Its involvement dies, to be revitalised only at the moment of consent.

In this 'confrontational' phase between the Union institutions and the Member State, the Parliament seized every opportunity,[41] both formal and informal, to express its perplexities as regards the procedure and how these hearings unfolded, on grounds that this *modus procedendi* curtailed its role. In particular, the Parliament regretted being deprived of any opportunity to be heard and present its reasoned proposal. Prompted by the Chair of the LIBE Committee, Mr Juan Fernando Lopez Aguilar, the Parliament Legal Service recently issued a formal legal opinion on a number of questions concerning the prerogatives of the Parliament in the procedure under Article 7(1) TEU.[42]

In that Opinion, the Legal Service acknowledged that there is no possibility under Article 7(1) TEU for the Parliament to impose its participation on the hearings. Nor can a legal obligation of the Council to involve the Parliament be inferred from the fact that the Parliament exercised a 'right of initiative' by triggering the procedure.

Assuming the Parliament cannot claim a legal right stemming from the Treaty to present its reasoned proposal before the Council, the Legal Service considers the prospect of its involvement in the hearings compatible with Article 7(1). In turn, the RoP of the Council do not provide for the possibility – nor the obligation – to invite the Parliament to the Council meetings, but they do not exclude such a possibility. If it considered this necessary in order to facilitate its task, the Council could fully invite the Parliament to present its reasoned proposal. In other words, the involvement of the Parliament is not legally imposed but it is permitted.

[40] For a critical assessment of the Council's approach, see, amongst others, D Kochenov, 'Article 7 TUE: un commentaire de la fameuse disposition "morte"' (2019) 1 *Revue des affaires européennes* 33.

[41] See the letters addressed by the President of the Parliament on 11 October 2018 and 28 November 2018 calling for the Parliament to be invited to outline its position to a full meeting of the General Affairs Council where the Art 7(1) TEU procedure would be on the agenda. Informal exchanges of views took place with the respective Presidencies and the LIBE Chair accompanied by the Rapporteur on 12 November 2018, 19 February 2019 and 4 September 2019 respectively.

[42] See Opinion of the Legal Service of the Parliament, SJ-0758/19, D(2019)42177, 20 December 2019.

In this context, two dimensions may be discerned: on one hand, the prescriptive dimension of what the Treaty norms provide, in terms of duties and rights; on the other, the dimension of what the Treaty allows. Article 7 TEU lays down a general procedural framework, without prescribing any specific model for the conduct of the procedure, leaving room for manoeuvre to the institutions in all the areas where it does not prohibit, nor impose, but allows. The Union institutions could apply the Treaty provisions in a way that would enable them to express their potential in full, a way that is respectful of both the form and the substance of the Treaty wording, and the institutional balance laid down therein. The shared objective of maximising the outcome of the procedure could be better pursued in a spirit of loyal and sincere cooperation. In European institutional history, genuine progress has sometimes come as a matter of virtuous interpretation of Treaty norms, when the institutions asked themselves what could be done to fully express the norms' potential, rather than only by formalistic compliance.[43]

This controversy between the Parliament and the Council on the conduct of the Article 7(1) procedure allows us to shed light on the meaning and added value of the Parliament's contribution to the rule of law in general.

At the outset, there are reasons of pragmatism and procedural efficiency bending in favour of the Parliament's contribution: it follows from the Court's case law that in exercising their discretion when adopting acts, the Union institutions should take into consideration 'all the relevant factors and circumstances of the situation the act was intended to regulate'.[44] Applying this jurisprudence *mutatis mutandis*, one could argue that the best and most efficient way for the Council to do so in a procedure initiated by the Parliament, is to directly involve the latter, instead of relying on informal contacts between the Council Presidency and the Parliament, as foreseen by the standard modalities. A genuine dialogue with the Parliament could have immediate and tangible beneficial effects on the procedure, and facilitate the Council's task.

In fact, in certain circumstances the Council has proved sensitive to the appropriateness of inviting other institutions. Yet it has been selective as to who these institutions should be, notably for which institutions this sensitivity should be reserved. Article 5(2) of the Council RoP, laying down general rules on meetings, provides:

> The Commission shall be invited to take part in meetings of the Council. The same applies to the European Central Bank in cases where it exercises its right of initiative. The Council may, however, decide to deliberate without the presence of the Commission or of the European Central Bank.

[43] For a recent example, see the informal or intergovernmental legal instruments conceived to overcome the financial crisis.

[44] See the Judgment of the Court in Case C-310/04 *Spain v Council*, ECLI:EU:C:2006:521, para 122; and in Case C-343/09 *Afton Chemical Limited*, ECLI:C:2010:419.

The 'Comments on the Council's Rules of Procedure', a document published by the Council General Secretariat purely for informational purposes, provides:

> Representatives of other … Union institutions or bodies are occasionally invited to attend the Council's proceedings, depending on the subject discussed and the appropriateness. A decision concerning any invitation is taken by the Council in advance, by simple majority.

This practice of ad hoc invitations of representatives of other institutions is within the remit of the Council's discretion as regards its right of self-organisation enshrined in Article 240(3) TFEU. As examples of the Council's discretion, and how it decided to use it, representatives of the Court of Justice or the Court of Auditors have been invited to attend Council meetings where issues relevant to these institutions were discussed; the same applies to the European Investment Bank (EIB). Apparently, the only institution excluded from the Council's generous hospitality is the European Parliament.

The Parliament's not being invited means that it is deprived of the possibility to have an exchange and the opportunity for confrontation with the Member State, and is equally deprived of that opportunity for dialogue with it and with the other institutions. In practice, when asked to grant its consent, the Parliament could be confronted with a blunt 'yes or no' scenario, being cut off from the process that it brought there. The insistence of the Parliament on being present and the reasons why it cares should be understood in this context.

As discussed, the hearings' setting in the Council does not imply an experts' debate at a technical level; in many regards, it is more a political type of setting. It could be argued that the Council is well placed to fill the shoes of the political institution. Yet while the Council and the Parliament may share the political nature of their perspective, the type of political perspective is in itself different, because the nature of the two institutions and their ways of working are different. On one hand, the Council is an assembly for the territorial representation of the Member States, which operates according to the logics of national executives, each of them the result of a political majority in their respective parliaments. On the other hand, the Parliament brings to the table the synthesis of European politics, built in the interplay of European political families, national parties and individual Members, in the process described in section III.B.

In this sense, the Parliament could feed the process with a complementary contribution orientated along the lines of pan-European political families and pluralism, rather than national lines. The Parliament's contribution to the deliberation could enhance the collective nature of the decision making, and the common ownership of the overall process.

Moreover, in the context of political justifications for the Union's (re)actions against rule of law regressions,[45] there are functions that the Parliament is

[45] See A Iliopoulou-Penot, 'La justification de l'intervention de l'Union pour la garantie de l'État de droit au sein des pays membres' (2019) 1 *Revue des affaires europeennes* 7.

best placed to perform. In order to strengthen the legitimacy of measures and mechanisms adopted at Union level in the political sphere, a good path is reinforcing the reasons behind them, especially vis-à-vis the public opinion.[46] The Parliament is particularly well placed to do so, because of its nature and ways of functioning. The Parliament does not speak only to the public opinion; its message is suited to reach domestic political forces on the ground.

Thus, the Parliament is a valuable platform for dialogue with the Member State concerned, eventually for sending it political messages, in particular conflictual ones. An assessment of the rule of law that aspires to be complete should encompass an understanding of the profound political roots of domestic 'pathological' phenomena, such as soft-authoritarianism shifts.[47] In this scenario, the Parliament's contribution, as a critical infrastructure for democracy, can be particularly meaningful.

In the Hungarian case, a significant field where the rule of law 'match' takes places is that of the European political family of affiliation. It is unquestioned that this is a field where the Parliament plays a meaningful role.

If, on one hand, affiliation to a European political family could shield domestic party politics (an allegation submitted by many with respect to the EPP's behaviour vis-à-vis Fidesz), on the other hand, this very affiliation may contribute to correcting domestic political degradation. Political groups have the ability to perform a crucial inclusive and unifying function.[48] For instance, some progress could come with nurturing a deeper sense of belonging to the European political family, by encouraging a trend for European groups to become more authentic and coherent political alliances.[49]

As emerged from the discussion, the Parliament's role is best understood not as stand-alone but in relation to others in the rule of law institutional landscape: this is why the discussion has touched upon how the Parliament is perceived by others, as well as how others perceive one another. Tackling the matter from the angle of institutional balance, Article 13(2) TEU provides:

> Each institution shall act within the limits of the powers conferred on it in the Treaties, and in conformity with the procedures, conditions and objectives set out in them. The institutions shall practice mutual sincere cooperation.

It stems from the case law of the Court that 'the rules regarding the manner in which the EU institutions arrive at their decisions are laid down in the

[46] See Porchia (n 18).

[47] See Kochenov (n 40).

[48] See RD Kelemen, 'The European Union's Authoritarian Equilibrium' (2020) 27 *Journal of European Public Policy* 481, DOI: 10.1080/13501763.2020.1712455.

[49] The parabola of the British Conservatives is a good example of the inclusive function that European families can perform: the time during which the Conservatives were affiliated to the EPP coincides with the development of pro-European sentiments. Conversely, the moment the Conservatives left the EPP to found their own political group coincided with the beginning of a drift towards an ever-growing Euroscepticism.

Treaties and are not at the disposal of the Member States or of the institutions themselves'.[50] In addition, the institutions should 'positively, … assume fully the political responsibilities conferred on them by the Treaties and, negatively, … refrain from "abusing" their powers, ie using them in a way that usurps the powers granted to the other institutions'.[51] Again, according to the case law of the Court, in a similar vein of sincere cooperation between the Union and the Member States under Article 4(3) TEU,[52] the principle of mutual sincere cooperation between the institutions amounts to a 'general duty …, the actual tenor of which depends in each individual case on the provisions of the Treaty or on the rules derived from its general scheme'.[53] Thus, considering the current situation, the assessment of whether or not the Council's internal 'standard modalities' respect the principle of mutual sincere cooperation must be carried out with reference to the respective rights and obligations of the institutions arising from Article 7(1) TEU. In this context, the principle of mutual sincere cooperation requires the Council to respect the Parliament's right to submit a reasoned proposal by seriously examining it, within a reasonable period of time, and by taking into account the arguments invoked by the Parliament. It does not stem from the principle of mutual sincere cooperation that the Council is obliged to involve the Parliament in the hearing of a Member State. However, there is room to argue that the meaningful involvement of the Parliament could be, on substance, a better route to attain the Treaty aims, and more respectful of the spirit of its provisions.

The Commission itself, in its 'blueprint for action' on the rule of law, acknowledged the need to inform the decision-making process in Article 7(1) and its institutional steps with clear procedural rules, and advocated *intensifying the collective nature of decision making*. In a clear *ouverture*, the Communication states that the *Parliament should be given the possibility to present its case in procedures it has initiated*,[54] and it expressly grounds this

[50] See the Judgments of the Court respectively of 28 April 2015, in Case C-28/12 *European Commission v Council of the European Union*, ECLI:EU:C:2015:282, para 42; of 23 February 1988 in Case C-68/86 *United Kingdom v Council*, EU:C:1988:85, para 38; and of 6 May 2008 in Case C-133/06 *Parliament v Council*, EU:C:2008:257, para 54.

[51] K Lenaerts and A Verhoeven, 'Institutional Balance as a Guarantee for Democracy in EU Governance' in C Joerges and R Dehousse (eds), *Good Governance in Europe's Integrated Market* (Oxford, Oxford University Press, 2002) 44. See also J-P Jacqué, 'The Principle of Institutional Balance' (2004) 41 *CML Rev* 383; P Craig, 'Institutions, Power and Institutional Balance' in P Craig and G de Búrca (eds), *The Evolution of EU Law* (Oxford, Oxford University Press, 2011) 41.

[52] See the Judgment of the Court of 30 March 1995 in Case C-65/93 *Parliament* v *Council*, EU:C:1995:91, para 23, 'However, the Court has held that inter-institutional dialogue, on which the consultation procedure in particular is based, is subject to the same mutual duties of sincere cooperation as those which govern relations between Member States and the Community institutions (see Case 204/86 *Greece v Council* [1988] ECR 5323, paragraph 16).'

[53] See the Judgment of the Court of 8 June 1971 in Case C-78/70 *Deutsche Grammophon Gesellschaft mbH v Metro-SB-Großmärkte GmbH & Co KG*, EU:C:1971:59, para 5.

[54] See the Commission Communication 'A blueprint for action' (n 22) 14.

claim on institutional balance. Some may read in the word 'its' a subtle way for the Commission to distance itself from the case and ascribe ownership only to the Parliament. Beyond any speculation on implied meanings, what matters is that the Commission is acknowledging that the Parliament could (and should) be meaningfully involved.

Considering in general the point of view of the Commission, while it shares with the Parliament the triggering of the procedure, as discussed, concerning the way to get there the two institutions are far apart. The fact that the Commission may disapprove of the *modus* of the Parliament's action does not mean, however, that it necessarily disapproves of the underlying aim or the merit of the issue. While the 'how' diverges, the 'what' and 'why' should in principle be shared. Nevertheless, whether or not the Commission empathised with the Parliament's action, ultimately it did not find grounds to trigger the procedure, nor a structured dialogue, against Hungary. This decision was not without some criticism by experts in the field. If the Commission's reticence was subject to some critiques in academic literature, the Council's behaviour with respect to Article 7 attracted many more. Some went as far as to argue that the Council 'never missed an opportunity to miss an opportunity'. Considering its overall approach, it is not far-fetched to argue that the Council has been reluctant to act.[55]

In this context, it is difficult to reconcile the approach of the Council's denying the Parliament any dialogue with the spirit and nature of the Council's initiatives in the field of the rule of law. As discussed previously, they were informed by a robust connotation in favour of dialogue and cooperation. If the Council has been an advocate of dialogue, it has, however, been quite selective regarding who shall participate in it. On the one hand, very prone and open to engage in a dialogue with Member States, possibly with the Commission, but on the other, highly sceptical towards the Parliament. From the Parliament's perspective, the rigidity of the Council's approach against dialogue is particularly surprising in view of a consistent record of Council's initiatives in theory promoting dialogue itself.

While the logic and actions of the Parliament, the Commission and the Council are inherently different, their actions should rely on the fundamental assumption that the aim – promoting and safeguarding the respect of the rule of law across the Union – is shared. The Union institutions' joint actions address a fundamental message to Member States: the message that the Union will do anything in its powers to prevent the propagation, at European level, of a vision

[55] D Kochenov and L Pech, 'Monitoring and enforcement of the rule of law in the European union: rhetoric and reality' (2015) 11 *European Constitutional Law Review* 512. See Council of the European Union, Opinion of the Legal Service of the Council 10296/14 of 27 May 2014, doc no 3, point 28. RD Kelemen, L Pech and KL Scheppele, 'Never missing an opportunity to miss an opportunity: the Council legal service opinion on the Commission's EU budget-related rule of law mechanism' *Verfassungsblog*, 12 November 2018.

of constitutionalism that cannot be reconciled with the Treaties.[56] To continue to exist, the Union is compelled to do all it can to prevent the propagation of ideas according to which the European standards of the rule of law could tolerate, under the umbrella concept of 'national differences', soft-authoritarian drifts. In this context, while the perspectives of the different Union institutions cannot be assimilated, they can be complementary and synergic. They can enrich each other, conferring more weight to the Union's action and maximising its potential for the sake of the overall process. In principle, the Union institutions voiced their favour for the complementary use of all available tools and information, not least in pursuit of procedural economy and efficiency.[57]

The narrative of inter-institutional relations, notably between the Council and the Parliament, is to some extent a conflictual narrative, with institutions perceived as behaving like 'silos'. According to this classic narrative, one always gains power at the expense of others, and progress is achieved as an outcome of inter-institutional clashes.

While there is some truth in it, this classic conflictual narrative of the relationships between the Union institutions is vitiated by some fallacies, and it may be reductive and short-sighted. The Parliament's quest to be meaningfully involved in the Article 7(1) procedure is a simple wish to have a seat at the table, to contribute to the dialogue. Arguably, this would not deprive the Council of any powers; it would remain the master of a process that it ultimately owns. Assuming the Treaty codified a mixed vision for the procedural arrangement of Article 7, the three institutions fit differently in the equation, but they are all mandated to carry out a joint action to attain a common aim, one laying at the heart of the Union legal order. In this sense, a more constructive and inclusive logic could be beneficial for the process as a whole. This reveals an underpinning question of mutual trust,[58] relevant at all levels, among institutions and Member States, a question that permeates a lot of the discourse on the European architecture, and how it functions, or malfunctions.

V. CONCLUDING REMARKS

Across the institutions, there is consensus that dialogue and cooperation are paths worth pursuing. First, in view of how the legal framework is construed,

[56] A von Bogdandy et al, 'Guest editorial: A potential constitutional moment for the European rule of law – the importance of red lines' (2018) 55 *CML Rev* 983, 'European decisions confronting the Polish Government are crucial to uphold a liberal and democratic self-understanding of European constitutionalism throughout Europe. Otherwise, the current Polish undermining of the independence of its judiciary is likely to count towards defining the European rule of law …'.

[57] See as recalled in section III.A, the Council conclusions of 16 December 2014 (para 5), where they called for respect for the functions carried out by the other institutions while preserving an institutional balance, and stressed the need to avoid futile duplications.

[58] K Lenaerts, '*La vie après l'avis*: Exploring the principle of mutual, yet not blind, trust' (2017) 55 *CML Rev* 805, esp 808.

and the limited routes for judicial review, the dimension of dialogue is one of the few fronts that can concretely be developed in the absence of Treaty reform. Article 7 cannot be conceived as a panacea, and arguably it is not realistic to assume that the Council recommendations alone can preserve the rule of law. Any criticisms and warnings that these recommendations may offer on the state of health of a national system, if at all capable of revitalising the rule of law, do so as a matter of political suasion, rather than legal obligation. Especially in view of a vacuum of enforceability, the core strength of recommendations is political rather than normative. In addition, the dimension of dialogue may be the least problematic when it comes to ensuring the delicate balance between intervention and respect for national identity and sovereignty, in turn vital to ensure mutual trust. It is by means of a dialogue that the Union institutions, and the Parliament among them, could contribute to creating a situation where *self-healing via internal processes remains possible*.[59] In the current framework, healing heavily depends on domestic processes, whether these are citizens' mobilisation, the oppositions countering drifts, or majorities willing to engage in a dialogue because driven either by a genuine will to enact political change, or by convenience, thus whatever their motives. The dialogue engaged in by the Union institutions may encourage and accompany these domestic processes. The reach and breadth of the communication is key to halt the propagation of rule of law backsliding in any Member State, as no one is immune. The Parliament is in a privileged position to make a difference by maintaining communication channels open and responsive, and it is well placed to find the register of communication most suited for public opinions and political parties.

Any rule of law assessment that aspires to capture the state of health of a legal system should go beyond thorough legal analysis and technical benchmarks and be holistic and contextual. Any European response to domestic rule of law backsliding that aspires to be comprehensive and credible should investigate the profound political roots of rule of law breaches. In this context, the Parliament's role, as a critical infrastructure of representative democracy in the Union, could be far from meaningless. Looking at the rule of law through the Parliament's lenses requires a shift of prism, from the purely legal dimension of the rule of law assessment into the political one: the Parliament is compelled to define rule of law breaches by looking at their political symptoms and causes. On the controversy revolving around the conduct of the process under Article 7(1), there is no duty of the Council to hear the Parliament, nor a right of the Parliament to impose its presence in the hearings. Yet there may be arguments advocating for the meaningful involvement of the Parliament or – in the negative – against cutting it off from the procedure it triggered. Discussing this

[59] P Sonnevend, 'Preserving the acquis of transformative constitutionalism in times of constitutional crisis: lessons from the Hungarian crisis' in A von Bogdandy et al (eds), *Transformative Constitutionalism in Latin America* (Oxford, Oxford University Press, 2017) 123.

procedural controversy allows us to offer a truthful portrayal of the meaning and added value of the Parliament's contribution to the rule of law in general.

The perspective that the Parliament represents is the synthesis of European politics expressed in a parliamentary assembly, and, as such, is unique and non-fungible. The Parliament could offer a complementary contribution to the deliberation orientated along pan-European and party-political – rather than national – lines. This political contribution could enhance the collective nature of the decision making, and its shared ownership, conferring more weight on the outcome of the process. Furthermore, the Parliament is well placed to strengthen the legitimacy of measures adopted at Union level in the political sphere vis-à-vis the public opinion, thereby increasing transparency, democratic accountability and visibility in the exercise of power.

All these ingredients could be poured in by means of a continuous dialogue to be pursued in a coherent manner in all institutional contexts and at all levels.[60] In this sense, the Parliament's meaningful involvement is to be pursued in full respect of the principles of institutional balance, and mutual, sincere and loyal cooperation.

The Union's actions in the field of the rule of law are unfolding within a context of profound crises.[61] Crises often feed growing disaffection or marginalisation of democratic infrastructures. Conversely, they amplify certain governments' stance by giving them an extraordinarily powerful pulpit, and an opportunity to consolidate powers. In terrain fertilised by crises, the consolidation of powers and soft-authoritarian drifts could fall like a downpour in the desert. The values enshrined in Article 2 TEU, as the fabric of the Union constitutionalism, are the foundations of the common European house: core democratic infrastructures, such as the Parliament, can and should do their part to ensure that these foundations are as robust and resilient as they can be.

[60] Porchia (n 18).

[61] For recent developments, see the response of the Parliament with regard to the Covid-19 outbreak, and the emergency measures adopted by Member States to address it. Specifically, see the letter sent by the President of the Parliament to the Commission President, available at drive.google.com/file/d/1QKthqwiv7mSuSoBwSnBqoRkuNuiGdpm7/view; see the Parliament resolution of 17 April 2020 on EU coordinated action to combat the COVID-19 pandemic and its consequences (2020/2616(RSP)), P9_TA-PROV(2020)0054, expressly condemning the urgency measures taken by Hungary and Poland in paras 46 and 47. See the press release already issued by LIBE on 24 March 2020, which came among the first statements issued by Union bodies, available at www.europarl.europa.eu/news/en/press-room/20200324IPR75702/ep-stands-up-for-democracy-in-hungary-during-covid-19.

15

Can We Expect Compliance with the Rule of Law without the Rule of Law?

ANDREAS MOBERG

I. INTRODUCTION

RULE OF LAW backsliding is a well-documented, ongoing process.[1] It has been defined as 'the process through which elected public authorities deliberately implement governmental blueprints which aim to systematically weaken, annihilate or capture internal checks on power with the view of dismantling the liberal democratic state and entrenching the long-term rule of the dominant party',[2] and it is particularly visible in certain states.[3] The situation is dire and most pressing. The fundamental principle of the rule of law is not fully respected in certain Member States of the European Union (EU), and it is seriously threatened in several others. Case law from the CJEU supports this view, as do the two pending cases involving Article 7 of the Treaty on European Union (TEU).[4]

* The current text reflects the law as it stood on 1 October 2020.

[1] Cf V Reding, 'The EU and the rule of law – what next?' SPEECH/13/677, 4 September 2013, available at https://ec.europa.eu/commission/presscorner/detail/en/SPEECH_13_677 (last visited 1 October 2020); L Pech and KL Scheppele, 'Illiberalism Within: Rule of Law Backsliding in the EU' in *Cambridge Yearbook of European Legal Studies* (Cambridge, Cambridge University Press, 2017) 3, 19; D Kochenov, 'Article 7: A Commentary on a Much Talked-about "Dead" Provision' *Polish Yearbook of International Law* XXXVIII (2019) DOI: 10.24425/pyil.2019.129611, 165; W Sadurski, *Poland's Constitutional Breakdown* (Oxford, Oxford University Press, 2019).

[2] Pech and Scheppele (n 1) 10.

[3] L Pech, KL Scheppele and W Sadurski, 'Before It's Too Late: Open Letter to the President of the European Commission regarding the Rule of Law Breakdown in Poland', *VerfBlog*, 28 September 2020, available at https://verfassungsblog.de/before-its-too-late/ (last visited 1 October 2020).

[4] Case C-619/18 *European Commission v Republic of Poland*, ECLI:EU:C:2019:531; Case C-192/18 *European Commission v Republic of Poland*, ECLI:EU:C:2019:924; Case C-791/19R *European Commission v Republic of Poland*, ECLI:EU:C:2020:277 (not available in English); Reasoned Proposal in Accordance with Article 7(1) of the Treaty on European Union Regarding the Rule of Law in Poland, COM(2017) 835 final, 20 December 2017.

The EU's actions to stifle this process are often described as insufficient, and there are many scholars offering suggestions on what the EU could, and should, do in relation to states that violate rule of law obligations under the Treaties.[5] However, the attempts to understand and explain the *reasons* why the EU is unable to halt the negative development, the rule of law backsliding, are relatively few. A common, although far from universal, analysis seems to be that the EU's inaction is the result of 'a lack of political will', or at least something that can easily qualify under such a heading. Most likely this is true, and it highlights that political will is the key to unlock the door. But at the same time, the answer is unsatisfactory for a number of reasons. First and foremost, it is very difficult to pinpoint what 'a lack of political will' really means, and this in turn means that it is even more difficult to come to terms with the underlying problem. Second, 'a lack of political will' says nothing about the role and inherent qualities of the legal framework as such. In fact, the analysis completely bypasses all aspects of the quality of the legal remedies. Furthermore, how can such a lack be conceived as a flaw, in particular from a democratic perspective? Is not a lack of political will also a (tacit, at least) sufficient majority, as defined by the applicable rules, in favour of the opposite position? The expression is in fact dangerously misleading in its normative allure. It would be more suitable to say that the EU's inaction is the result of 'insufficient political support for action'. Such a description acknowledges that there is support for action, but that it does not meet the requirements – set in law – for taking action. That analysis would at least connect to the question of whether or not the Treaties' requirements for political support for action are set too high?

In search of alternative explanations, one might also pose the question whether or not the lack of action is a consequence of a lack of *suitable* legal instruments? It is not easy to mend a fence without the proper tools. If you only have a wrecking ball at hand when you require a hammer, the choice not to use the wrecking ball may well be the wiser.[6] Article 7 TEU[7] is a good example of a tool that looked quite useful on the shelf but, as it turned out, was pretty useless

[5] D Kochenov and L Pech, 'Better Late than Never? On the European Commission's Rule of Law Framework and its First Activation' (2016) 54 *Journal of Common Market Studies* 1062; D Kochenov and L Pech, 'Monitoring and Enforcement of the Rule of Law in the EU: Rhetoric and Reality' (2015) 11 *European Constitutional Law Review* 512; J Müller, 'Should the EU Protect Democracy and the Rule of Law inside Member States?' (2015) 21 *European Law Journal* 141; D Kochenov and P Bárd, 'Rule of Law Crisis in the New Member States of the EU' (2018) *Reconnect Working Paper No 1*, July 2018, available at https://reconnect-europe.eu/wp-content/uploads/2018/07/RECONNECT-KochenovBard-WP_27072018b.pdf (last visited 1 October 2020).

[6] At the same time, in the cases at hand, one person's wrecking ball seems to be another person's hammer. The debate on whether or not Art 7 TEU is a 'nuclear option' has been going on for a good number of years now. D Kochenov, 'Busting the myths nuclear: A commentary on Article 7 TEU', *EUI Working Paper No LAW 2017/10* (8 May 2017), available at https://cadmus.eui.eu/bitstream/handle/1814/46345/LAW_2017_10.pdf (last visited 1 October 2020).

[7] Cf W Sadurski, 'Adding Bite to the Bark: The Story of Article 7, EU Enlargement and Jörg Haider' (2010) 16 *Columbia Journal of European Law* 385.

when taken into the field. The aim and potential effects of the article are suitable, but the process for reaching a decision is not. As we have seen, Article 7 TEU could possibly have worked in a situation with a single offender, that is, a single backsliding Member State, but with at least two backsliding rule of law offenders, the requirement for unanimity in Article 7(2) TEU makes the article practically useless. An interesting thing about Article 7 TEU is that no one really knows its full potential since it has never been fully applied. As a tool, it has been taken out of the shed and it has been taken to the fence, but it has not yet been put to the task. For all we know, it could turn out to be most perfectly suited for the task, although those who still hope so remain few and far between.[8]

The EU is struggling to secure compliance with Article 2 TEU. There are several means under the Treaties to secure compliance, but so far none of them seems to reach the desired level of effectiveness when applied to cases of rule of law backsliding. The Commission has made use of the instruments at hand, and designed new instruments to both increase the level of protection of the rule of law in the EU's Member States and deal with the situation when the Member States fail to follow the rules. In March 2014, the Commission presented its own strategy (the 'Rule of Law Framework')[9] on how to make best use of the instruments provided in the Treaties, first and foremost infringement proceedings under Article 258 of the Treaty on the Functioning of the EU (TFEU) and the mechanism in Article 7 TEU. The strategy is a three-step process focused on dialogue, aiming to find a solution to the situation without having to resort to Article 7 TEU or infringement proceedings. Following the rapid deterioration of the protection of the rule of law in several Member States, the Commission sought to revamp its strategy in April 2019, with a new Communication addressed to the European Parliament, the European Council and the Council.[10] In this Communication, the Commission presented the idea of an EU Rule of Law Toolbox.[11] The toolbox has three sections. In the first section, the Commission

[8] In previous research, I have analysed the EU Treaties in order to determine whether part of the explanation for the EU's inaction could in fact be found in the choice of how the relevant treaty provisions are constructed. I have argued that Article 7 TEU is a hybrid clause, which is based on both supranational and intergovernmental logics, a fact that renders it highly ineffective as a means to remedy the rule of law violations witnessed in a number of EU Member States. A Moberg, 'Who will be in charge of upholding the Rule of Law in the EU? An assessment of proposed changes to the EU's Rule of Law Toolbox' *Juridisk Tidskrift* 2019–20 (3) 576; A Moberg, 'When the return of the nation-state undermines the rule of law: Poland, the EU, and Article 7 TEU' in A Bakardjieva Engelbrekt, A Michalski, K Leijon and L Oxelheim (eds), *The European Union and the Return of the Nation State* (London, Palgrave MacMillan, 2020) 59.

[9] Communication from the Commission to the European Parliament and the Council, 'A new EU Framework to strengthen the Rule of Law', COM(2014) 158, 19 March 2014; cf Kochenov and Pech, 'Better Late than Never?' (n 5).

[10] Communication from the Commission to the European Parliament, the European Council and the Council, 'Further strengthening the Rule of Law within the Union. State of play and possible next steps', COM(2019) 163, 3 April 2019.

[11] ibid 3. See also Moberg, 'Who will be in charge of upholding the Rule of Law in the EU?' (n 8).

places Article 7 TEU and the Rule of Law framework. In the second section we find the infringement proceedings. Then, in a third section of the toolbox, the Commission places no fewer than 11 other mechanisms,[12] which 'have an early warning and preventive role'.[13] The Communication on the EU Rule of Law Toolbox also contains a draft for a strategy on how the Commission intends to put the tools in the toolbox to use. The strategy was presented in June 2019 in the Communication entitled 'Strengthening the rule of law within the Union. A Blueprint for action' ('the Blueprint', or 'the Blueprint for action').[14]

The question of the effectiveness of EU action is ultimately a question of what competence the Member States have conferred on the EU,[15] and the way the exercise of the said competence is regulated in the Treaties. Within the scope of those competences, the EU institutions need to find ways to make the Member States comply with their obligations under the Treaties. Any attempt to evaluate the effectiveness of EU action to ensure the respect of the rule of law must contain an appraisal of the suitability of the available instruments, and those instruments are both enabled and limited by the principle of conferral.

Scholars, primarily from the disciplines of international law and international relations, for many decades have sought to describe, analyse and understand why states comply with obligations under international treaties.[16] Understanding how to best ensure compliance is an important aspect of policy design. There simply is little to gain from proposing policy and regulation that is unlikely to influence and affect the actions of the subjects. Raustiala and Slaughter proclaim that '[e]xplanations of why and when states comply with international law … provide critical policy guidance for the design of new institutions and agreements'.[17]

[12] These are the European semester, the annual EU Justice Scoreboard, the Cooperation and Verification Mechanism, the Commission's Structural Reform Support Service, the European Structural and Investment Funds, Funds supporting Justice and Security policies, a new mechanism to protect the Union's budget when generalised deficiencies regarding the rule of law in Member States affect or risk affecting that budget (this was, and still is, a proposal not yet implemented), the European Anti-Fraud Office (OLAF), the European Public Prosecutor's Office (EPPO), the EU Accession process and EU Neighbourhood policy. COM(2019) 163 (n 10) 4–6.

[13] ibid 4.

[14] Communication from the Commission to the European Parliament, the European Council, the Council, the European Economic and Social Committee and the Committee of the Regions, 'Strengthening the rule of law within the Union. A Blueprint for action', COM(2019) 343, 17 July 2019.

[15] Art 5(2) TEU.

[16] K Raustiala and A Slaughter, 'International Law, International Relations and Compliance' in W Carlsnaes, T Risse and BA Simmons (eds), *Handbook of International Relations* (Thousand Oaks, CA, Sage Publications, 2002) 538, 542ff; C Lutmar and CL Carneiro, *Compliance in International Relations, Oxford Research Encyclopedia of Politics* (Oxford, Oxford University Press, 2016), online publication June 2018 available at https://edisciplinas.usp.br/pluginfile.php/4424948/mod_resource/content/1/Lutmar%20and%20Carneiro%202018.pdf (last visited 1 October 2020).

[17] Raustiala and Slaughter (n 16) 538.

This makes compliance theory a useful instrument when gauging the Blueprint's potential for success. Therefore, this chapter deals with the following question: Based on what we know from previous research on compliance, can the Commission's Blueprint be successful?

II. HOW TO ANALYSE THE BLUEPRINT

Theories on why states comply with rules are not born in a vacuum. They are developed based on references to events that occur, in relation to other theories. Often, theories develop in response to an already existing theory, seeking to improve the explanatory value of the previous theory. The distinction can be subtle, and it can be strong, but it is important to acknowledge that different theories on compliance are parts of a general discussion on why states comply with rules.[18]

The ensuing analysis will identify what theories on compliance are present in the Blueprint, and whether or not there are inherent theoretical inconsistencies. Based on two opposing approaches to compliance, an analytical framework is designed. The aim is to analyse the measures presented in the Blueprint in order, first, to categorise these measures and, second, to determine whether or not the measures suffer from inherent theoretical inconsistencies.

A. Classification of Instruments and Measures

The compliance theories chosen for the analysis conducted in this chapter are 'enforcement theory', on the one hand, and 'managerial theory', on the other. The main reason for choosing these two theories is because the 'two schools present contending claims about the sources of non-compliance and the most effective means for addressing this problem, thus creating strong counter-expectations'.[19]

i. The Enforcement Approach to Compliance

The enforcement approach to compliance stems from the realist argument that state behaviour is directed by cost–benefit analysis. The main tenet is that enforcement, which in the broadest sense means negative consequences, is required to make states comply with international rules. It is the threat of

[18] The definition of compliance I use is the same as the one used by Raustiala and Slaughter (ibid 539): 'We define compliance as a state of conformity or identity between an actor's behaviour and a specified rule.'

[19] J Tallberg, 'Paths to Compliance: Enforcement, Management, and the European Union' (2002) 56 *International Organization* 609, 611.

negative consequences that is important, and the actual punishment is only necessary to make the threat plausible.[20]

Enforcement theory builds on political economy theory, which uses game theory to argue that a punishment strategy is necessary in order to deter individual states from defecting from collective cooperation, when the incentives to defect mean that they gain a short-term advantage compared to following the rules. For the deterrence to work, the punishment must hurt the state to the extent that the potential gains of a violation of the rule are outweighed. It is not a question of fair and just punishment that applies in the same way to all states. It is a simple question of deterrence, on an individual basis.[21]

One basic assumption is that states act rationally, and that they will choose to comply with the rules as long as they know that the cost of defection is higher than the gains. Thus, enforcement theorists will emphasise the importance of monitoring state behaviour and the administration of sanctions in the wake of transgression, or as Tallberg puts it, '[c]ompliance problems are therefore best remedied by increasing the likelihood and costs of detection through monitoring and the threat of sanctions'.[22]

Downs et al highlight that the severity of the sanction increases with the depth of cooperation. They define 'a treaty's depth of cooperation as the extent to which it requires states to depart from what they would have done in its absence'.[23] The depth of cooperation is important for enforcement theory, as it can explain why more advanced collaboration situations require more severe sanctions to ensure compliance.

Measures and instruments that build on the enforcement approach are characterised by increased enforcement, increased punishment, enhanced monitoring of Member State behaviour, and increased reporting and inspection.

ii. Managerial Theory

Managerial theory, or the management approach to compliance, is a reaction to the main tenet of the enforcement school; that compliance in essence is a rational choice on behalf of the state. Instead, according to management theory, non-compliance is best explained by the occurrence of one or more of the following three circumstances: '(1) ambiguity and indeterminacy of treaty language, (2) limitations on the capacities of parties to carry out their undertakings, and (3) the temporal dimension of the social and economic changes contemplated by regulatory treaties'.[24]

[20] GD Downs, 'Enforcement and the Evolution of Cooperation' (1998) 19 *Michigan Journal of International Law* 319, 320f.

[21] GD Downs, DM Rocke and P Barsoom, 'Is the good news about compliance good news about cooperation?' (1996) 50 *International Organization* 379, 386.

[22] Tallberg (n 19) 611.

[23] Downs et al (n 21) 383.

[24] A Chayes and AH Chayes, 'On Compliance' (1993) 47 *International Organization* 175, 188.

So, basically, Chayes and Chayes refute the enforcement school's claim that states choose to neglect their treaty obligations. In fact, enforcement and retaliation do not necessarily enlist compliance, and they also risk destroying cooperation. Non-compliance is seen as a problem for cooperation (to be resolved), instead of as something to be punished. The blame for non-compliance is externalised rather than accepted, meaning that the reasons for non-compliance cannot be understood simply by analysing the intentions of the non-conforming state; or as Downs et al put it, 'on those rare occasions when compliance problems do occur they should not be viewed as violations or self-interested attempts at exploitation, but as isolated administrative breakdowns'.[25]

The managerial school works with a background assumption that states very rarely break their commitments. This is obviously very difficult to test empirically, but as Chayes and Chayes point out, the opposite has not been proved either.[26] Instead, they use this assumption as an underlying hypothesis, inspired by Henkin's quite famous quote, 'it is probably the case that *almost all nations observe almost all principles of international law and almost all of their obligations almost all of the time*'.[27] Even though Henkin's book maybe is not so much a theory on compliance as it is an argument that compliance is common, Chayes and Chayes argue that the assumption as such is a useful starting point when seeking new methods to improve compliance.[28]

Based on analysis of a selection of treaties,[29] Chayes and Chayes find that ambiguity and indeterminacy of treaty language are significant explanations for non-compliance. The way rules in treaties are written often leaves a 'considerable range' within which different acceptable textual interpretations of the text may fit. The indeterminacy of the exact range creates friction between the parties to the agreement, and the general lack of authoritative dispute settlement in the international legal system amplifies this situation.[30]

As regards the parties' limitations in capacity, also described as their *capability*, Chayes and Chayes have found that states sometimes over-commit when it comes to accepting obligations. It may also be the case that internal circumstances change, and that the capability drops. Non-compliance due to a lack

[25] Downs et al (n 21) 380.

[26] Chayes and Chayes (n 24) 177.

[27] L Henkin, *How Nations Behave*, 2nd edn (Columbia, NY, Columbia University Press, 1979) 47 (original emphasis).

[28] To be fair, Chayes and Chayes acknowledge that Henkin's statement cannot be seen as a result of research: 'The observation is frequently repeated without anyone, so far as we know, supplying any empirical evidence to support it.' Chayes and Chayes (n 24) 177.

[29] Downs et al rightly point out the selection bias in the empirical data on which Chayes and Chayes base their theorising (the endogeneity problem). Downs et al (n 21) 382.

[30] It should also be noted that the very same circumstances may actually be what makes the treaty function in the first place. Ambiguity and indeterminacy must not be normatively fixed as either 'good' or 'bad'. They are best viewed as an indication that law is a socially constructed phenomenon, and its meaning is determined by the relative power of the actors involved.

of capability is most often caused by a 'severe dearth of the requisite scientific, technical, bureaucratic, and financial wherewithal to build effective domestic enforcement systems'.[31]

Finally, the temporal dimension. This basically means that there will be a time lag before the states can be expected to comply with the obligations. The amount of time varies with how much adaptation the new regime requires, and different states will have different capacity to adapt.[32]

Since non-compliance is seen as an effect rather than a choice, and as 'deviant rather than an expected behaviour',[33] it can be lowered to an acceptable degree through management. As Chayes and Chayes conclude,

> the improvement of dispute resolution procedures goes to the problem of ambiguity; technical and financial assistance may help cure the capacity deficit; and transparency will make it likelier that, over time, national policy decisions are brought increasingly into line with agreed international standards.[34]

Measures and instruments that build on the management approach are characterised by enhanced cooperation between the EU institutions and the Member States, increased transparency, measures that help build capacity, education and awareness-raising initiatives, and enhanced dialogue.

iii. Enforcement and Management in the EU

Enforcement theory and management theory may seem irreconcilable, at least in their underlying assumptions. Tallberg has sought to demonstrate that the two schools are not irreconcilable. In fact, in the EU, they even strengthen each other.[35]

Tallberg sees a 'strategic combination' in how the components of the EU's compliance system are put to use on two levels – the centralised system (managed by the EU's supranational institutions) and the decentralised system (individuals securing rights in national courts).[36]

Tallberg makes a convincing argument that the EU regime bolsters a high level of compliance, due to the mix of coercion (threatened as well as realised) and management. He also identifies sources for non-compliance in the EU and concludes that there are two main reasons. The first one chimes well with enforcement theory: the states choose not to conform with EU harmonisation measures, because of national preferences. The second reason is a typical managerial theory reason: non-compliance caused by legislative and administrative capacity limitations.[37]

[31] Chayes and Chayes (n 24) 194.
[32] ibid 194f.
[33] ibid 204.
[34] ibid.
[35] Tallberg (n 19) 614.
[36] ibid.
[37] ibid 623.

Although Tallberg does not consider the antithetical positioning of the enforcement approach and the management approach as a problem for compliance in a regime such as the EU, he does not pose the question whether an enforcement approach would have been more suitable where a management approach was adopted, and vice versa. Neither does he refute that the theoretical underpinnings – the underlying assumptions about why states comply with norms – are wrong. In fact, he claims that both theses are right, and that '[c]ompliance systems that offer both forms of instruments tend to be particularly effective in securing rule conformance, whereas systems that only rely on one of the strategies often suffer in identifiable ways'.[38]

B. Tracing Inherent Theoretical Inconsistencies

When analysing the potential of a strategy such as the Blueprint, in light of compliance theory, the aim does not have to be to identify which specific theory it seems to resemble the most. This is especially so, since the strategy is a compilation of several different parts into a whole. It is also reasonable to assume that the Blueprint was not written with a single particular theory of compliance in mind. Instead, it makes good sense to expect that the measures described in the Blueprint are compatible with several theories. When that is the case, the next step is to determine whether such an eclectic approach should be considered a strength or a weakness.

Since any given theory requires the presence of a chain of specific features, a kind of path dependency if you will, it is important to take account of all the component aspects of a theory when analysing. Whether the Blueprint consists of measures that are compatible with, or that draw on, several different theories or not, is not as interesting to know as whether the various components actually build on different – incompatible – theoretical assumptions.

A single measure that incorporates the logic of enforcement as well as that of management is unlikely to be effective. Article 7 TEU combines a managerial dialogue-based deliberative approach with very far-reaching sanctions. Inherent theory inconsistency, although not only compliance theory-related, is a plausible explanation for the failure of Article 7 TEU to force Poland and Hungary to comply with the rule of law standards expressed in Article 2 TEU.[39]

III. THE COMMISSION'S BLUEPRINT – AN OVERVIEW

As mentioned in the introduction to this chapter, the Blueprint builds on a Communication from the Commission issued in April 2019.[40] The two

[38] ibid 610.
[39] Moberg, 'When the return of the nation-state undermines the rule of law' (n 8).
[40] COM(2019) 163 (n 10).

Communications may well be seen as two parts of a whole, as the April Communication initiated a debate on how to strengthen the rule of law in the EU. The Commission received more than 60 written contributions 'from national, EU and international institutional actors, as well as from civil society and academia',[41] and the Commission states that it has benefitted from these interventions. Although there is no reason to doubt that the input received has been fruitful, it is at the same time reasonable to assume that many different approaches and perspectives have influenced those working on the final text of the Blueprint. This strengthens the assumption that the Commission has not worked with a particular compliance theory in mind when developing the Blueprint.

The Rule of Law Toolbox has three sections: 'Article 7 and the Rule of Law Framework'; 'Infringement proceedings' and 'Other mechanisms and frameworks'. The first two are basically self-explanatory, and focus heavily on responses to threats to the rule of law. The third section includes a variety of 'early-warning' mechanisms, such as various coordinating mechanisms on fiscal and administrative policies – first and foremost the European Semester, but also the annual EU Justice Scoreboard. The April Communication is primarily a stock-taking exercise, and it assesses experiences so far. It finds that the EU needs to improve its reactions to rule of law issues. The conclusion is that EU intervention must come in different forms, ranging from informal dialogue all the way to Article 7 TEU, and it must be better coordinated amongst the EU institutions.

The Blueprint for Action follows up on the April Communication, and it structures the EU's various tools to strengthen the rule of law around three so-called pillars: *Promotion*, *Prevention* and *Response*.

The work on *promotion* aims at building knowledge about the importance of the rule of law. Academia and educational systems are specifically mentioned as important actors in this endeavour. The EU's role as regards these measures is to act as support to the Member States rather than as the actual agent, as most of the promotion will rely on the individual Member States. The Commission claims that knowledge building is 'the best guarantee for the respect of our common values'.[42] The initiative engages civil society, media and the education systems. There is also a commitment to make the Commission's own work more transparent.[43] In the event that this turns out to include the Commission's assessments on the state of rule of law protection in various Member States, this may turn out to be a significant innovation.

[41] COM(2019) 343 (n 14) 2.
[42] ibid 5.
[43] ibid 6, 'In order to make the rule of law more visible, the Commission intends to develop a dedicated communication strategy on rule of law, including to make related information accessible in all official languages and to clearly explain its significance for the Union as a whole and for individual citizens and businesses.'

When it comes to *prevention*, the Commission highlights the importance of cooperation both between the EU institutions and between the Member States and the EU, mainly on information sharing about potential threats to the rule of law. At the same time, it is clear that the Commission's idea of what the EU is doing, and can do, as regards prevention, is very much centred around the Commission itself.[44] The most interesting part of the *prevention* work is the new Rule of Law Review Cycle, proposed by the Commission. It is quite an ambitious and elaborate mechanism, including an annual Rule of Law report as well as both an inter-institutional dialogue on the rule of law and a network of national contact points in the Member States for dialogue on rule of law issues.[45] Cooperation and dialogue between both institutions and Member States is envisaged as the way forward under the *prevention* pillar, although the Commission clearly states that regarding the supervision of rule of law in the Member States, the Commission regards itself as *primus inter pares* because of its role as the guardian of the Treaties, which requires it to 'maintain its autonomy in terms of both the content and the timing of its own assessments'.[46]

Turning to the final section of the Blueprint for Action, the *response*, it is important to note that an EU *response* should, it is hoped, in the view of the Commission, never be necessary. The whole point of the *promotion* and *prevention* pillars is that the *response* will become redundant – at least on the EU level. However, the Commission clearly acknowledges that there is need for a strategy for response as well, and interestingly enough the Commission does not present Article 7 TEU first. Instead, the judicial arena – the Court of Justice – gets the limelight.[47] This is a shift in focus, compared with the April Communication on the Rule of Law Toolbox, and since the Commission emphasises the importance of swift action from the EU institutions, this may indicate that the Commission in the future will turn towards the supranational judicial arena first, rather than to the predominantly intergovernmental arena where Article 7 TEU operates, when reacting to threats to the rule of law.

This does not mean that the Commission is ready to abandon Article 7 TEU. While calling for more collaboration between the institutions, the Commission proposes several improvements to the procedure. Its main point is a proposition to further juridify the procedure, by creating clear procedural rules for the decision-making process.[48] More procedural rules, and more transparency,

[44] ibid 9, 'Nonetheless, the EU has a legitimate role to play in supporting national authorities and ensuring that negative developments are addressed at an early stage. The role of the EU institutions should be to facilitate cooperation and dialogue in order to prevent problems from reaching the point where a formal response is required under the Rule of Law Framework, by infringement procedures or by actions under Article 7 of the Treaty on European Union.'

[45] ibid 11.

[46] ibid 12.

[47] ibid 13.

[48] On the pros and cons of a more juridified Art 7 TEU procedure, see Moberg, 'When the return of the nation-state undermines the rule of law' (n 8).

is typically not what the intergovernmental decision-making process thrives under, so it is highly unlikely that we will see these procedural changes to how Article 7 TEU operates materialise, at least not without changes to the Treaty itself. It is also hard to see that the Council would concur in this analysis of how to improve Article 7 TEU.

IV. ANALYSIS OF THE BLUEPRINT

The analysis carried out in this chapter is done on several levels but primarily directed at the separate individual measures proposed in the Blueprint. First of all, each individual measure described in the Blueprint is characterised as belonging to either the enforcement approach or the management approach. Second, each individual measure is checked for inherent theoretical coherency. The assumption is that measures will not be successful as long as they are based on antithetical theories on compliance. Third, the Blueprint as a coherent strategy is characterised according to the two categories. There are no hypotheses concerning what theory the Commission leans towards. On the contrary, it is assumed that the strategy is formed without a conscious decision between enforcement or management – or indeed, following Tallberg, a combination of the two.[49] The fact that the Commission openly called for input from stakeholders all over Europe,[50] and specifically mentioned that the contributions were beneficial for the development of the Blueprint,[51] is taken as an indication that the approach is eclectic rather than tied to, or even inspired by, a specific school of compliance theory.[52]

A. Characterising the Individual Measures

The measures mentioned in the strategy will be analysed individually, and each pillar will be dealt with in separate sections. The key features of the management approach are *enhanced cooperation* between the EU institutions and the Member States, *increased transparency*, measures that help *build capacity*, *education and awareness-raising initiatives*, and *enhanced dialogue*. The key features of the enforcement approach are *increased enforcement*, *increased punishment*, *enhanced monitoring* of Member State behaviour, and *increased reporting* and *inspection*.

[49] Tallberg (n 19).
[50] COM(2019) 163 (n 10) 3.
[51] COM(2019) 343 (n 14) 2.
[52] The contributions are available online, and a summary of them can be found here in European Commission, Strengthening the Rule of Law in the Union. Stakeholder contributions, July 2019, available at https://ec.europa.eu/info/sites/info/files/ruleoflaw_summary_150719_v3.pdf.

i. Promotion

The headline in the Blueprint reads 'Promotion: Building knowledge and a common rule of law culture'.[53] The caption highlights education from a long-term perspective, and the aim is to change societal values on a deeper societal level. The measures proposed under the promotion pillar are mainly compatible with the management school. They focus to a large degree on education and raising awareness of the principle of rule of law. The overall idea is to 'embed the rule of law in national and European political discourse'.[54] The measures proposed under the promotion pillar therefore seek to fill the knowledge gaps, among both professionals and the general public.[55] The Blueprint highlights six items to focus on in the work to promote the rule of law in the Union.

a. Civil Society, Media, Academia and Member States' Education Systems

All of these actors can play a part, according to the Commission, by 'ensuring a place for the rule of law in public debate and educational curricula'.[56] There are ideas about reoccurring events,[57] and most measures mentioned are clearly about education and raising awareness,[58] which are typical features of the managerial school. However, there is also a bit of monitoring, present under this heading, which is a key feature of the enforcement approach:

> The Commission will also continue to pay … special attention to attempts to pressurize civil society and independent media and further support their work.[59]

The mix is not to be understood as inherent theoretical inconsistency, however, as it concerns separate initiatives.

b. Transparency and Access to Information

> In order to make the rule of law more visible, the Commission intends to develop a dedicated communication strategy on rule of law, including to make related information accessible in all official languages and to clearly explain its significance for the Union as a whole and for individual citizens and businesses.[60]

Transparency and the sharing of information are typical managerial school measures.

[53] COM(2019) 343 (n 14) 5.
[54] ibid.
[55] ibid, 'These gaps need to be filled with proactive actions to promote the rule of law within the EU, both at professional level and in the general public at large.'
[56] ibid 6.
[57] ibid, 'The Commission will follow up on the idea of a yearly event on rule of law for dialogue with, and between, civil society organisations and policy-makers at EU level.'
[58] ibid, 'EU-funded research on the rule of law should continue to be encouraged, and the results of ongoing projects duly disseminated.'
[59] ibid.
[60] ibid.

c. European Networks

> Within the judiciary, networks such as the European Network of the Presidents of Supreme Courts of the EU, the Association of the Councils of State and Supreme Administrative Jurisdictions of the EU, the European Network of Councils for the Judiciary, and the European Training Network for Judges should be supported to further promote the rule of law.[61]
>
> Commission support to all these networks should prioritise projects promoting the rule of law, with a particular focus on Member States facing rule of law challenges.[62]

The building of transnational networks is a typical management approach.

d. National Parliaments

> The European Parliament, the Conference of Parliamentary Committees for Union Affairs of Parliaments of the EU and the Conference of Speakers of the EU Parliaments could prioritise inter-parliamentary dialogue on rule of law issues, for example through an annual event. This could also be made a theme in national parliamentary debates on EU issues. The Commission stands ready to contribute to stimulating such dialogue.[63]

Although the Commission clearly cannot instruct either the European Parliament, or the national parliaments of the Member States on what action to take, it offers to contribute to developing dialogue and cooperation between these actors. Building and managing such networks is a typical feature of a management approach to compliance.

e. Council of Europe

> In full respect of the institutional and political responsibilities of both institutions, the Commission intends to build on this cooperation and increase EU participation in the Council of Europe bodies, making cooperation at service level stronger and more systematic.[64]
>
> An important additional step is for the EU to have observer status in the Council of Europe group of states against corruption (GRECO). In agreement with the Council, the Commission has taken the necessary steps to request observer status, which was granted in July 2019. The EU provides significant funding for the Council of Europe's activities.[65]

[61] ibid.
[62] ibid.
[63] ibid 7.
[64] ibid.
[65] ibid.

Cooperation with the Member States, as well as the other states that are members of the Council of Europe, and in particular with the Venice Commission, is also a clear example of the management approach. However, in relation to the Council of Europe, the Commission further mentions the ongoing process of accession to the European Convention on Human Rights, which when finalised will constitute a clear example of an enforcement measure, due to the jurisdiction of the European Court of Human Rights. Courts are also important in the management school, however, as they clarify unclear or ambiguous obligations.

f. Other International Institutions

> The Commission will also make cooperation with other international institutions working on rule of law issues deeper with stronger and more systematic cooperation at service level. This includes the Organisation for Security and Cooperation in Europe (OSCE), which works on the rule of law as part of its work on democratisation, and the Organisation for Economic Cooperation and Development (OECD), where cooperation could explore the socio-economic benefits of the rule of law.[66]
>
> The Commission intends to build on the willingness of all these actors to engage in promoting the rule of law.[67]

The Commission also states its intention to reinforce the cooperation with other international actors, and specifically mentions the OSCE and the OECD. Increased international cooperation is a management school approach.

ii. Prevention

> The role of the EU institutions should be to facilitate cooperation and dialogue in order to prevent problems from reaching the point where a formal response is required under the Rule of Law Framework, by infringement procedures or by actions under Article 7 of the Treaty on European Union.[68]
>
> For the EU to play fully its role in this respect, EU institutions need to develop a stronger awareness and understanding of developments in the individual Member States, through dedicated monitoring, to be able to identify risks to the rule of law, develop possible solutions, and target support early on.[69]

These extracts are from the first paragraph describing the prevention pillar. The first is a good example of the management approach, emphasising cooperation and dialogue with the aim of preventing non-compliance. This goes hand in hand with the message formulated in the caption ‘Prevention: Cooperation

[66] ibid 8.
[67] ibid.
[68] ibid 9.
[69] ibid.

and support to strengthen the rule of law at national level'.[70] The second extract, however, shows that the facilitation of cooperation also comes with a monitoring function, which is a clear example of an enforcement approach. This is not the way that Chayes and Chayes perceives of 'management' but rather, as will be discussed further in section V, an example of what Tallberg refers to as a mix of coercion and management.[71]

In order to deepen its monitoring of rule of law events in the Member States, the Commission launches the 'Rule of Law Review Cycle'. This will collect information on the state of rule of law protection in all of the Member States, from a great number of sources – governmental, intergovernmental and non-governmental:

> The specific forms such an enhanced monitoring could take will have to be developed, including in cooperation with national authorities and the other EU institutions, and should involve a process of continuous information gathering and dialogue with national authorities and stakeholders.[72]

The monitoring will also entail enhanced cooperation between the Commission and the Member States:

> The Commission will invite all Member States to engage further in a mutual exchange of information and a dialogue on rule of law related topics such as judicial reform, the fight against corruption, and the law-making process, or on measures supporting civil society and independent media as actors of the rule of law.[73]

The cooperation will take the form of a transgovernmental mechanism, where national contact points will be set up.[74] Creating this type of transgovernmental mechanism, in lieu of the already existing structures, is a management approach to compliance, sometimes referred to as a fire-alarm approach.[75]

Also included in the Review Cycle is the annual Rule of Law Report. This is presented as an attempt to increase transparency, quite clearly in line with the management approach, but possibly also a common feature in enforcement measures (in order to increase legitimacy and, in the long run, effectiveness). Monitoring is a necessary component of enforcement:

> In order to ensure the necessary transparency and awareness, and to keep the rule of law on the political agenda of the EU, the Commission intends to publish an annual Rule of Law Report summarising the situation in the Member States.[76]

[70] ibid.
[71] Tallberg (n 19) 623.
[72] COM(2019) 343 (n 14) 10.
[73] ibid.
[74] ibid, 'a network of national contact points in Member States should be set up for dialogue on rule of law issues'.
[75] M Hobolth and D Sindbjerg Martinsen, 'Transgovernmental networks in the European Union: improving compliance effectively?' (2013) 20 *Journal of European Public Policy* 1406.
[76] COM(2019) 343 (n 14) 11.

The Commission published the first annual Rule of Law Report on 30 September 2020.[77]

Finally, the Commission also envisages that the Rule of Law Report may improve cooperation between the EU institutions, and suggests that the annual Rule of Law Report 'could form the basis of debates in the European parliament and the Council'.[78] Although cooperation between the EU institutions should not be taken as the same thing as cooperation between the EU and the Member States, as regards the management approach to compliance, such cooperation is still likely to strengthen the EU side in its dialogue with the Member States.

iii. Response

The Commission's ambition is that the work under the promotion and prevention pillars will halt the rule of law backsliding and, consequently, the measures in the response pillar need not be used.[79] This approach is clearly signalled in the heading of the section describing the response pillar: 'Response: Enforcement at EU level when national mechanisms falter'.[80]

> Nevertheless, when national rule of law safeguards do not seem capable of addressing threats to the rule of law in a Member State, it is a common responsibility of the EU institutions and the Member States to take action to remedy the situation.[81]

It is obvious that the response pillar is thought of as a 'plan B', which will be reverted to when rule of law infringements occur. In the light of compliance theory, the response pillar is mainly geared towards the enforcement approach, which is highlighted both in the heading and in the second paragraph, where the Commission emphasises the importance of the CJEU:

> These decisions have added an important dimension to the rule of law processes under way at EU level, and play an important part in resolving these issues.[82]

However, the measures included in the response pillar also include aspects that emphasise dialogue, such as parts of the Article 7 TEU mechanism, and even larger parts of the Rule of Law Framework.

a. Article 258 TFEU

In the description of the response pillar, the Commission speaks about what the Court has done, and potentially could do in the future. Preliminary references are

[77] Communication from the Commission to the European Parliament, the Council, the European Economic and Social Committee and the Committee of the Regions, 2020 Rule of Law Report, 'The rule of law situation in the European Union', COM(2020) 580, 30 September 2020.

[78] COM(2019) 343 (n 14) 12.

[79] ibid 13, '[t]he aim is that the need for response at EU level would be significantly reduced'.

[80] ibid.

[81] ibid.

[82] ibid.

mentioned as an important way to clarify the requirements stemming from the obligation to respect the principle of the rule of law. Clarification of the requirements is a management approach to increase compliance. The Commission is, for obvious reasons, not able to initiate references for preliminary rulings, but as a general rule the Commission submits observations in all references, which means that it has a chance to affect the development of the principle of the rule of law as such. Preliminary references are very interesting from the perspective of compliance theory, as the instrument is a good example of a management approach, while a Court typically would be associated with enforcement (although, as previously mentioned, the specific role of clarifying the rules is mentioned by Chayes and Chayes as important in managerial theory).

Regarding the infringement proceedings, the 'Commission will pursue a strategic approach to infringement proceedings related to the rule of law, requesting expedited proceedings and interim measures whenever necessary'.[83] The ultimate sanction at the end of the infringement proceedings is a fine. This may not seem very discouraging as an enforcement measure, but many cases equal many fines, and many cases equal a lot of resources tied up in court proceedings, so one should not too easily dismiss the use of the infringement procedure as an enforcement measure.

b. Article 7 TEU

Only one paragraph in the Blueprint is devoted to the Article 7 TEU mechanism. The first sentence signals that the Commission is looking to make the procedure more effective:

> On Article 7 TEU, the institutions should work together to intensify the collective nature of decision-making between them.[84]

It is not clear what that 'collective nature of decision-making' means, but it is clear from the text that the Commission feels that the mechanism needs to be improved and that the institutions need to do what they can, that is, that which does not require the support of (all of) the Member States. The Commission does not propose any changes to how the Commission has made use of the mechanism as such. Instead, focus lies on the Council's procedure:

> It would be particularly beneficial for the Council to reflect on whether the discussions in the General Affairs Council could be improved through their preparation at technical level in a Council working group. It could also be helpful to improve the decision-making process in terms of the institutional steps, with clear procedural rules.[85]

It is not as straightforward as one might think to characterise Article 7 TEU either as a tool from the enforcement school, or as one from the management

[83] ibid 14.
[84] ibid.
[85] ibid.

school. In fact, it has clear-cut elements from both. There are sanctions, potentially more severe than most in the Treaty, but these are under the lock and key of unanimity. Judging by the only two cases ever to be brought under the Article 7 procedure, the unanimity requirement has meant that the deliberations could go on forever. This may not in itself turn an enforcement measure into a management measure, but the context also highlights that the mechanism is pretty useless as an enforcement mechanism in a situation where one state declares that it would veto certain decisions.

Improvement of the procedure could be interpreted as a management-inspired approach, as it seeks to clear up potential uncertainties and ambiguities in the Treaty. However, since the focus is on improving the enforcement procedure, a better interpretation is that the proposed measures are in fact examples of influence of the enforcement approach on compliance. At the end of the day, though, the Council's procedure is not something the Commission can alter unilaterally. As regards the Rule of Law Framework, the situation is slightly different.

c. 2014 Rule of Law Framework

The Commission acknowledges the need for dialogue with the Member State concerned, and that this dialogue need be kept confidential. The Framework is based on dialogue and compromise, and it is the most management-orientated measure within the response pillar:

> The main objective should always be to find solutions as early as possible. However, when this does not succeed, ensuring that the European Parliament and the Council are fully updated and can express informed views before a critical stage is reached can help find a settlement. This will be coherent with a more collective approach to the rule of law among the institutions.[86]

The Rule of Law Framework is a set of procedural rules for the Commission, written by the Commission itself. However, the Commission seeks to improve cooperation among the institutions in this measure as well. This reinforces the character of the Rule of Law Framework as a measure from the management school.

d. Rule of Law Conditionality

> This protective approach for the functioning of the EU is also the basis of the Regulation proposed by the Commission in 2018 to ensure the protection of the EU budget in case of generalised deficiencies as regards the rule of law in Member States.[87] Such an approach could be needed in EU policies other than the protection of EU financial interests in order to avoid or remedy specific risks to the

[86] ibid 14.

[87] Proposal for a Regulation of the European Parliament and of the Council on the protection of the Union's budget in case of generalised deficiencies as regards the rule of law in the Member States, COM(2018) 324, 2 May 2018. (The footnote reference in the extract is in the original source.)

> implementation of EU law or policies. The Commission will explore the need for further measures to address the possible impact of persistent rule of law problems on other EU policies.[88]

Finally, the Commission finishes the section on the response pillar with a call[89] to the European Parliament and the Council to adopt a regulation proposed by the Commission, which would enable the EU to suspend funds in a case 'where a generalised deficiency as regards the rule of law in a Member State affects or risks affecting the principles of sound financial management or the protection of the financial interests of the Union'.[90] The proposal is interesting, but it is still – closing in on two years now – being negotiated. The European Parliament adopted its position at the first reading in April 2019,[91] and the proposal has since been awaiting the Council's position after its first reading. Concerns have been raised regarding its suitability, in particular concerning legal certainty – what is a 'generalised deficiency'? – and furthermore, as is often the problem with sanctions, concerning the potential negative effects for individuals in the sanctioned state.[92] As this measure is not yet available, it does not – as such – form part of the current strategy that is the Blueprint. However, in the first ever Rule of Law Report, the Commission expressed the hope that the European Council conclusions from the meeting held 17–21 July 2020[93] were the signal needed to push the EU legislator to adopt the proposal.[94]

B. Characterising the Blueprint as a Coherent Strategy

The promotion and prevention pillars primarily contain measures taken from the managerial recipe book, while those in the response pillar, at least at first

[88] COM(2019) 343 (n 14) 15.

[89] ibid 16, 'The Commission calls on … [t]he European Parliament and the Council to adopt rapidly the Regulation on the protection of the Union's budget in case of generalised deficiencies as regards the rule of law in the Member States.'

[90] Art 3 in Proposal 2018/0136 (COD), COM(2018) 324 (n 87) 8.

[91] European Parliament legislative resolution of 4 April 2019 on the proposal for a regulation of the European Parliament and of the Council on the protection of the Union's budget in case of generalised deficiencies as regards the rule of law in the Member States (COM(2018)0324 – C8-0178/2018–2018/0136(COD)), P8_TA(2019)0349, 4 April 2019.

[92] A von Bogdandy and J Łacny, 'Suspension of EU funds for breaching the rule of law – a dose of tough love needed?' (2020) 7 *European Policy Analysis*, SIEPS, available at https://www.sieps.se/publikationer/2020/suspension-of-eu-funds/ (last visited 1 October 2020).

[93] 'The Union's financial interests shall be protected in accordance with the general principles embedded in the Union Treaties, in particular the values of Article 2 TEU. The European Council underlines the importance of the protection of the Union's financial interests. The European Council underlines the importance of the respect of the rule of law.' Special meeting of the European Council (17, 18, 19, 20 and 21 July 2020) – Conclusions, EUCO 10/20, 21 July 2020, 7 and (identically) 15.

[94] COM(2020) 580 (n 77) 26, 'The commitment of the European Council should accelerate the adoption of the Commission's proposal to protect the EU budget in case of breaches of the rule of law in a Member State under discussion in the European Parliament and the Council.'

glance, would seem to be enforcement measures. Managerialists would most likely point to the potentially detrimental effects of enforcement, while the enforcement camp could argue that resources spent on education and enhancing cooperation are wasted resources.

It would seem that the general theoretic frame of the Blueprint is informed more by the managerial school than by the enforcement school:

> The primary responsibility to ensure respect for the rule of law at national level lies with the Member States. The national judiciary, together with other national checks and balances such as constitutional courts and ombudspersons, are the first key lines of defence against attacks to the rule of law from any branch of the state. Nonetheless, the EU has a legitimate role to play in supporting national authorities and ensuring that negative developments are addressed at an early stage. The role of the EU institutions should be to facilitate cooperation and dialogue in order to prevent problems from reaching the point where a formal response is required under the Rule of Law Framework, by infringement procedures or by actions under Article 7 of the Treaty on European Union.[95]

However, there is always the looming threat of enforcement. Perhaps this is enough to qualify all measures as enforcement measures of varying degree? This is, however, not how the theoretical lens applied in this chapter works. There is nothing to be gained from approaching the task of categorisation as either management or enforcement, as a contest between the two camps. The idea is to use these perspectives in order to analyse whether or not the Blueprint stands a chance of being successful.

V. DISCUSSION OF RESULTS

The Blueprint is primarily about enhancing Member State compliance with the rule of law, by strengthening the protection of the rule of law in the individual Member States, thereby indirectly assuring that violations will not occur. Such an approach is a long-term investment. The reason why the Blueprint seeks to enhance the Member States' capacity to strengthen the rule of law is best thought of as a result of a conscientious choice, much in line with the management approach to compliance, even though the text itself contains no such references. The lack of references is not at all surprising, but one consequence is that it is not possible to attribute the traces of the management approach to a strategic decision. The all-out-enforcement approach would be not to present a Blueprint at all, but to devote all resources to monitoring behaviour and bringing those who do not comply with the (extremely) indeterminate rule in Article 2 TEU to Court.

[95] COM(2019) 343 (n 14) 9.

However, the publishing of the Blueprint must also be seen in the context of the ongoing rule of law backsliding, that is, as a response to non-compliance with the foundational principle in Article 2 TEU. It is clear that the Blueprint comprises measures that are based on either managerial theory or enforcement theory – or both. When based on both, such as, for example, the response pillar measure Article 7 TEU, it would seem that the specific measure's effectiveness drops. There is, however, no conclusive evidence as to the causality between these observations.

Tallberg claims that a mix of management and enforcement measures has been very successful for ensuring Member State compliance with EU regulations, at least on the systemic level. Tallberg argues that the reason why the EU system is 'more effective in inducing compliance than interstate systems, where enforcement and management functions are executed by the signatories themselves',[96] is because of the strategic combination of a *centralised level* – the supranational institutions – and a *decentralised level* – 'individuals securing their rights in national courts'[97] – which Tallberg refers to as the 'fire alarm'.[98] Tallberg's conclusions are drawn from a study on compliance across the board, and it is based on a large number of infringement proceedings. It is interesting to consider the mix of measures suggested in the Blueprint in the light of Tallberg's findings, but it is submitted here that his findings cannot be used, at least not without reservation, as support for the choice to mix approaches in the specific context of rule of law protection/compliance with the rule of law. The reason is because of Tallberg's reliance on the decentralised level, which in extension means that his theorising *requires* the rule of law. In the current climate of rule of law backsliding, one of the most serious infringements has been the Polish Government's deconstruction of the judiciary, including the attempts to prevent national courts from referring preliminary references.[99] It is important to emphasise that the type of violations that the Blueprint aims to counter is especially difficult to handle from within the Member State, simply because the violations in themselves are attacks on the system.

But, most importantly, a very basic assumption of the management approach to compliance is that the state in question willingly accepts the obligation. Education, dialogue and cooperation are practically ineffective when the obligated state is unwilling to accept the obligation. Basically, this means that all the measures in the Blueprint that are based on the management approach will be close to useless when trying to halt rule of law backsliding in a Member State that openly disagrees with the interpretation of the obligation and perseveres with open non-compliance. In such a situation, the managerial school fails to explain

[96] Tallberg (n 19) 611.
[97] ibid 614.
[98] ibid 620. Tallberg's use of the fire-alarm metaphor is not the same as the fire-alarm metaphor used by Hobolthand and Sindbjerg Martinsen (n 75), noted in section IV.A.ii.
[99] Case C-619/18 *European Commission v Republic of Poland*, ECLI:EU:C:2019:531.

non-compliance, and simply has no remedy.[100] Enhanced cooperation between the EU institutions and the Member States will not resolve such a deadlock. Nor will increased transparency or measures that help build capacity. Education and awareness-raising initiatives will not work, and neither will enhanced dialogue. At that stage, it is the enforcement measures presented mainly in the response pillar that stand a chance, and among those three, only the infringement procedure has been seen to gain some traction so far. The proposed regulation on rule of law conditionality may, if adopted, also be of use.

VI. CONCLUSION

Can we expect compliance with the rule of law without the rule of law? The irony makes the question rhetorical, at best, but there is in fact more to it than one may find at first glance.

In this chapter, the Commission's Communication 'Strengthening the rule of law within the Union. A Blueprint for action'[101] has been analysed through the lens of compliance theory. The analysis has shown that the 'Blueprint', as a compliance strategy, is a compilation of management theory and enforcement theory. As these approaches to compliance are thought of as antithetical, the general assumption is that a strategy based on both approaches may not be optimal. There are prominent examples of the opposite as well, such as the EU system, which mixes both approaches in its compliance framework and, as Tallberg has shown, is more effective at ensuring compliance than other international regimes.

Following Tallberg, since the Blueprint is a mix of approaches, it should be a better strategy compared to one that followed the management or the enforcement approach respectively. However, Tallberg's analysis is based on a slightly different situation compared to one where the judicial systems in the Member States are flawed, and where Member States of the EU are not considered as democratic states.[102] Therefore, it could be argued that the strategy is not optimal when applied in such circumstances.

[100] Cf Chayes and Chayes's summary of the remedies offered by the management approach, 'the improvement of dispute resolution procedures goes to the problem of ambiguity; technical and financial assistance may help cure the capacity deficit; and transparency will make it likelier that, over time, national policy decisions are brought increasingly into line with agreed international standards'. Chayes and Chayes (n 24) 204.

[101] COM(2019) 343 (n 14).

[102] In 'Nations in Transit 2020', Freedom House ranks Poland as a 'semi-consolidated democracy' and Hungary as a 'transitional/hybrid regime', as opposed to the category called 'consolidated democracies'. Freedom House, 'Nations in Transit 2020', available at https://freedomhouse.org/sites/default/files/2020-04/05062020_FH_NIT2020_vfinal.pdf (last visited 1 October 2020).

Although the analysis conducted here has shown that the Commission is unlikely to have considered compliance theory when drawing up the strategy, it is quite clear that the strategy is deeply rooted in the management approach. It is also clear that the Commission's version of management leans heavily on the ever-present possibility of enforcement – should the management measures not suffice – which makes the Commission's management approach different when compared to the orthodox management approach.

However, although the Blueprint may turn out to be an effective strategy to halt rule of law backsliding at an early stage, and possibly even more effective at preventing it from ever happening, there is little in the strategy that can be used to make states who voluntarily shirk the obligation respect the rule of law. In such a situation, it is no longer reasonable to speak about 'rule of law backsliding'; rather, we need to refer to 'rule of law rejection'. Then, the only viable option in the Blueprint is the infringement procedure.[103]

Looking ahead, it will be interesting to follow the Rule of Law Review Cycle. This type of monitoring, if connected to transparent and legitimate consequences, is very likely to have an effect. Even more interesting is the progress of the proposed Regulation on the protection of the Union's budget in case of generalised deficiencies as regards the rule of law in the Member States. Putting a price on rule of law rejection may be the only way to stop it.

[103] Cf KL Scheppele, 'Enforcing the Basic Principles of EU Law through Systemic Infringement Actions' in C Closa and D Kochenov (eds), *Reinforcing the Rule of Law Oversight in the European Union* (Cambridge, Cambridge University Press, 2016) 105; Pech and Scheppele (n 1) 38ff.

Index

www.ingramcontent.com/pod-product-compliance
Ingram Content Group UK Ltd.
Pitfield, Milton Keynes, MK11 3LW, UK
UKHW020906190926
475560UK00010B/304